THE CRITICAL HERITAGE SERIES

GENERAL EDITOR: B. C. SOUTHAM, M.A., B.LITT. (OXON.)

Formerly Department of English, Westfield College, University of London

---

Volumes in the series include

JANE AUSTEN	B. C. Southam
BROWNING	Boyd Litzinger, *St. Bonaventure University* and Donald Smalley, *University of Illinois*
BYRON	Andrew Rutherford, *University of Aberdeen*
COLERIDGE	J. R. de J. Jackson, *Victoria College, Toronto*
DICKENS	Philip Collins, *University of Leicester*
HENRY FIELDING	Ronald Paulson, *The Johns Hopkins University, Baltimore* and Thomas Lockwood, *University of Washington*
THOMAS HARDY	R. G. Cox, *University of Manchester*
HENRY JAMES	Roger Gard, *Queen Mary College, London*
ſAMES JOYCE (2 vols)	Robert H. Deming, *University of Miami*
D. H. LAWRENCE	R. P. Draper, *University of Leicester*
MILTON	John T. Shawcross, *University of Wisconsin*
SCOTT	John O. Hayden, *University of California, Davis*
SWIFT	Kathleen Williams, *Rice University, Houston*
SWINBURNE	Clyde K. Hyder
TENNYSON	J. D. Jump, *University of Manchester*
THACKERAY	Geoffrey Tillotson and Donald Hawes, *Birkbeck College, London*
TROLLOPE	Donald Smalley, *University of Illinois*

COLERIDGE

THE CRITICAL HERITAGE

Edited by

J. R. de J. JACKSON
Associate Professor of English
University of Toronto

LONDON: ROUTLEDGE & KEGAN PAUL

Published 1970
in Great Britain
by Routledge & Kegan Paul Limited
© J. R. de J. Jackson 1970
No part of this book may be reproduced
in any form without written permission from
the publisher, except for the quotation
of brief passages in criticism

ISBN 0 7100 6594 9

Printed in Great Britain by
C. Tinling & Co. Ltd, Prescot

General Editor's Preface

The reception given to a writer by his contemporaries and near-contemporaries is evidence of considerable value to the student of literature. On one side we learn a great deal about the state of criticism at large and in particular about the development of critical attitudes towards a single writer; at the same time, through private comments in letters, journals or marginalia, we gain an insight upon the tastes and literary thought of individual readers of the period. Evidence of this kind helps us to understand the writer's historical situation, the nature of his immediate reading-public, and his response to these pressures.

The separate volumes in the *Critical Heritage Series* present a record of this early criticism. Clearly for many of the highly-productive and lengthily-reviewed nineteenth- and twentieth-century writers, there exists an enormous body of material; and in these cases the volume editors have made a selection of the most important views, significant for their intrinsic critical worth or for their representative quality—perhaps even registering incomprehension!

For earlier writers, notably pre-eighteenth century, the materials are much scarcer and the historical period has been extended, sometimes far beyond the writer's lifetime, in order to show the inception and growth of critical views which were initially slow to appear.

In each volume the documents are headed by an Introduction, discussing the material assembled and relating the early stages of the author's reception to what we have come to identify as the critical tradition. The volumes will make available much material which would otherwise be difficult of access and it is hoped that the modern reader will be thereby helped towards an informed understanding of the ways in which literature has been read and judged.

B.C.S.

Contents

ACKNOWLEDGMENTS   *page* xii

NOTE ON THE TEXT   xiii

INTRODUCTION   I

The Fall of Robespierre (1794)

1   'D.M.' in *Analytical Review* 1794   21
2   Review in *Critical Review* 1794   22
3   Notice in *British Critic* 1795   23

A Moral and Political Lecture (1795)

4   Review in *Critical Review* 1795   24

Conciones ad Populum (1795)

5   Review in *Analytical Review* 1796   25
6   Notice in *Monthly Review* 1796   27
7   Review in *Critical Review* 1796   27
8   Review in *British Critic* 1796   28

The Plot Discovered (1795)

9   Review in *Analytical Review* 1796   29
10   Review in *British Critic* 1796   29

The *Watchman* (1796)

11   Letter in *Bristol Gazette* 1796   30

Poems on Various Subjects (1796)

12   Notice in *British Critic* 1796   32
13   Review in *Analytical Review* 1796   32
14   Review in *Critical Review* 1796   34
15   JOHN AIKIN in *Monthly Review* 1796   36
16   Notice in *Monthly Mirror* 1796   38

Ode on the Departing Year (1796)

17   ALEXANDER HAMILTON in *Monthly Review* 1797   39
18   Notice in *Monthly Mirror* 1797   40
19   Review in *Critical Review* 1797   41

CONTENTS

Poems second edition (1797)

20	Review in *Critical Review* 1798	42

Fears in Solitude (1798)

21	'D.M.S.' in *Analytical Review* 1798	44
22	C. L. MOODY in *Monthly Review* 1799	45
23	Review in *British Critic* 1799	48
24	Review in *Critical Review* 1799	49

Lyrical Ballads (1798)

25	Review in *Analytical Review* 1798	51
26	ROBERT SOUTHEY in *Critical Review* 1798	53
27	CHARLES BURNEY in *Monthly Review* 1799	55
28	Review in *British Critic* 1799	57
29	Notice in *Anti-Jacobin* 1800	59
30	Private opinions by LAMB, SOUTHEY, FRANCIS JEFFREY, SARA COLERIDGE	60

Wallenstein (1800)

31	JOHN FERRIAR in *Monthly Review* 1800	62
32	Review in *Critical Review* 1800	64
33	Review in *British Critic* 1801	65

Poems third edition (1803)

34	Review in *Annual Review* 1803	67
35	Notice in *Poetical Register* 1806	69

General Estimates (1809–10)

36(a)	Lampoon in *Satirist* 1809	70
36(b)	Article in *Edinburgh Annual Register for 1808* 1810	72

The Friend (1809–10)

37	Serial letter in *Monthly Mirror* 1810	73
38	JOHN FOSTER in *Eclectic Review* 1811	92

Remorse the performance (1813)

39	Review in *Morning Chronicle* 1813	111
40	Review in *Morning Post* 1813	117
41	Review in *The Times* 1813	118
42	THOMAS BARNES in *Examiner* 1813	122
43	Review in *Satirist* 1813	125
44	Review in *Theatrical Inquisitor* 1813	131

45	Review in *European Magazine* 1813	134
46	Review in *Literary Panorama* 1813	135
47	Review in *Universal Magazine* 1813	136
48	Review in *La Belle Assemblée* 1813	137
49	Private opinions by ROBINSON, MICHAEL KELLY, SOUTHEY	138

Remorse the publication (1813)

50	'H.' in *Theatrical Inquisitor* 1813	140
51	Review in *Christian Observer* 1813	145
52	Review in *Critical Review* 1813	153
53	FRANCIS HODGSON in *Monthly Review* 1813	155
54	Review in *British Review* 1813	166
55	J. T. COLERIDGE in *Quarterly Review* 1814	

General Estimates (1814-15)

		175
56	THOMAS BARNES in *Champion* 1814	189
57	Coleridge as poet and dramatist in *Pamphleteer* 1815	194

Christabel; Kubla Khan, a Vision; The Pains of Sleep (1816)

58	Review in *Critical Review* 1816	199
59	WILLIAM HAZLITT in *Examiner* 1816	205
60	JOSIAH CONDER in *Eclectic Review* 1816	209
61	Review in *Literary Panorama* 1816	213
62	Review in *Anti-Jacobin* 1816	217
63	WILLIAM ROBERTS in *British Review* 1816	221
64	THOMAS MOORE in *Edinburgh Review* 1816	226
65	G. F. MATHEW in *European Review* 1816	236
66	Review in *Monthly Review* 1817	244

The Statesman's Manual (1816)

67	WILLIAM HAZLITT in *Examiner* 1816	248
68	WILLIAM HAZLITT in *Examiner* 1816	253
69	WILLIAM HAZLITT in *Edinburgh Review* 1816	262
70	Notice in *Monthly Magazine* 1817	278
71	HENRY CRABB ROBINSON in *Critical Review* 1817	278

'Blessed Are Ye That Sow Beside All Waters!' A Lay Sermon (1817)

72	Review in *Monthly Magazine* 1817	285
73	Review in *Monthly Repository* 1817	286
74	HENRY CRABB ROBINSON in *Critical Review* 1817	289

Biographia Literaria (1817)

75	WILLIAM HAZLITT in *Edinburgh Review* 1817	295

CONTENTS

76	Review in *New Monthly Magazine* 1817	322
77	Review in *Monthly Magazine* 1817	323
78	'CHRISTOPHER NORTH' in *Blackwood's Edinburgh Magazine* 1817	325
79	'J.S.' in *Blackwood's Edinburgh Magazine* 1817	351
80	Review in *British Critic* 1817	355
81	Notice in *New Annual Register* 1817	376
82	Review in *Monthly Review* 1819	376

Sybilline Leaves (1817)

83	Review in *Literary Gazette* 1817	388
84	Notice in *Monthly Magazine* 1817	392
85	Review in *Edinburgh Magazine* 1817	392
86	Review in *Monthly Review* 1819	399

Zapolya (1817)

87	Review in *Edinburgh Magazine* 1817	413
88	Notice in *Monthly Magazine* 1818	419
89	Notice in *New Monthly Magazine* 1818	420
90	Review in *Theatrical Inquisitor* 1818	420
91	Private opinions by ROBINSON, SARA COLERIDGE, SARA HUTCHINSON, DOROTHY WORDSWORTH, LAMB 1816-17	424

The *Friend* (1818)

92	Review in *European Magazine* 1819	425
93	'R.' in *Edinburgh Review* 1821	
	General Estimates (1818-23)	427
94	Article in *Monthly Magazine* 1818	433
95	J. G. LOCKHART in *Blackwood's Edinburgh Magazine* 1819	436
96	Contemporary theatre in *London Magazine* 1820	452
97	'The Mohock Magazine' in *London Magazine* 1820	454
98	H. N. COLERIDGE in *Etonian* 1821	461
99	LEIGH HUNT in *Examiner* 1821	471
100	'R.' in *Literary Speculum* 1822	480
101	JOHN WILSON in *Blackwood's Edinburgh Magazine* 1823	484

Aids to Reflection (1825)

102	Notice in *British Review* 1825	485

103 Review in *British Critic* 1826   486

The Poetical Works (1828)

104 Review in *London Weekly Review* 1828   514
105 Review in *Literary Gazette* 1828   521

The Poetical Works second edition (1829)

106 JOHN BOWRING in *Westminster Review* 1830   525
107 Article in *Athenaeum* 1830   556

On the Constitution of Church and State (1830)

108 Review in *Eclectic Review* 1831   562

Aids to Reflection second edition (1832)

109 J. H. HERAUD in *Fraser's Magazine* 1832
     General Estimate (1833)   585
110 WILLIAM MAGINN in *Fraser's Magazine* 1833   606

The Poetical Works third edition (1834)

111 Review in *Literary Gazette* 1834   609
112 Review in *Gentleman's Magazine* 1834   611
113 Review in *Literary Gazette* 1834   614
114 H. N. COLERIDGE in *Quarterly Review* 1834   620

SELECT BIBLIOGRAPHY   652

INDEX   653

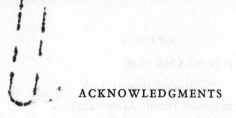

ACKNOWLEDGMENTS

My obligations to previous studies of Coleridge's reputation will be obvious throughout this volume. Laurence Wynn's unpublished Ph.D. dissertation ('The Reputation of Samuel Taylor Coleridge Among His Contemporaries in England', Princeton 1951), deserves particular mention for having provided a very helpful starting point. I am grateful to the following institutions for answering letters of inquiry or furnishing photographic copies of scarce reviews: the Library, Queen's University, Belfast; Yale University Library; the British Museum Newspaper Library, Colindale. The North Library of the British Museum, where most of the work was done, was a haven of efficiency and co-operation. Professor George Whalley and Eric Rothstein kindly solved puzzles which had baffled me; my wife's help has made the drudgery of proof-reading a pleasure.

The following publishers have permitted the reprinting of copyright materials: the Clarendon Press, Oxford (*The Collected Letters of Samuel Taylor Coleridge*, ed. Earl Leslie Griggs, Oxford 1956; *The Letters of William and Dorothy Wordsworth: The Middle Years*, ed. Ernest de Selincourt, Oxford, 1937); Columbia University Press (*New Letters of Robert Southey*, ed. Kenneth Curry, New York and London 1965); J. M. Dent & Sons Ltd. (*The Complete Works of William Hazlitt*, ed. P. P. Howe, London and Toronto 1900-34; Henry Crabb Robinson *On Books and Their Writers*, ed. Edith J. Morley, London 1938; *The Letters of Charles and Mary Lamb*, ed. E. V. Lucas, London 1935); and the Nonesuch Press (*Minnow Among Tritons*, ed. Stephen Potter, London 1934).

Certain alterations have been made in the materials presented in this volume. Obvious printers' errors have been silently corrected; lengthy quotations which were merely repetitive have been omitted, but the omissions are indicated; decorative capital letters at the opening of reviews, long 's's', titles and abbreviations have been made to conform with modern usage. Page references in the reviews have been deleted and redundant punctuation has been pruned. The spelling of Shakespeare's name has been made uniform. Original footnotes are indicated by a star (*) or a dagger(†); square brackets within quotations indicate the reviewer's insertions—elsewhere they draw attention to editorial corrections.

The following forms of reference have been used:

BL: Samuel Taylor Coleridge, *Biographia Literaria,* ed. J. Shawcross (London 1907), 2 vols.

CL: The Collected Letters of Samuel Taylor Coleridge, ed. Earl Leslie Griggs (Oxford 1956-), 4 vols.

Howe: *The Complete Works of William Hazlitt,* ed. P. P. Howe (London and Toronto 1930-4), 21 vols.

Hayden: John O. Hayden, *The Romantic Reviewers 1802-1824* (London 1969).

Nangle: Benjamin Christie Nangle, *The Monthly Review Second Series 1790-1815* (Oxford 1955).

PW: The Complete Poetical Works of Samuel Taylor Coleridge, ed. Ernest Hartley Coleridge (Oxford 1912), 2 vols.

Wellesley Index: The Wellesley Index to Victorian Periodicals, 1824-1900, ed. Walter E. Houghton (London and Toronto 1966-), 1 vol.

Introduction

Reviewers are remembered for their mistakes. When they recognize genius we imagine that it must have been self-evident; when they do not we suppose them to have been wilfully obtuse. One has only to add our common assumption that what we regard as great literature must be great in some absolute sense, to see why they occupy such a humble place in literary history.

The relationship of a writer to his reviewers is generally discussed from the writer's point of view. Looked at from the point of view of the reviewer, however, it takes on a different aspect. The reviewer's job, after all, is to read what is published, the bad as well as the good, and to select for his contemporaries the few works which he thinks they will enjoy. If he is high-minded he will also feel it his duty to draw to their attention works which they may not like at first but which he believes are nevertheless of merit. He is forced by the conditions of his profession to read rapidly and widely and to expose his reactions immediately in print. The more original and demanding a work is, the harder it is for him to respond to it adequately.

The reviews of a previous age provide us with an excellent introduction to the intellectual climate and literary taste which prevailed during it, but they also remind us that recognizing talent has always been a chancy business. The Romantic period is one of the most interesting, because it was during it that the review as we now know it came into being. Within a span of about twenty years reviews developed from little more than descriptive notices into elaborate analyses which would do credit to any modern journal. The men who wrote them were often authors of distinction in their own right, and most of them were intelligent, well-read, and fair-minded.

Coleridge's career coincides with this phase in the emergence of the review, and looked at retrospectively it seems to be ideally calculated as a sort of reviewer's obstacle course. It contains all the pitfalls which beset the critic. As a poet he was innovative and eccentric; he published his verse in such a way as to conceal the chronology of his development; his prose was unrelentingly obscure in its expression and quixotically organized; and his political commitments and public personality both tended to divert attention from the works themselves. In the face of such handicaps it is remarkable that his contemporaries were able to make as much of him as they did. Where they fall short it is usually easy to see why.

The present collection is drawn entirely from reviews or general estimates of Coleridge which were written during his lifetime. At his death and in the years that followed there was a great wave of writing about him, much of it very good indeed; but these posthumous assessments lack the immediacy of reviews and belong to another chapter in the history of his reputation.

II

Coleridge first attracted the attention of the reviewers as a political controversialist. The publication in 1794 of a play called *The Fall of Robespierre*, which he and Robert Southey had written in collaboration, had suggested where his sympathies lay and had prompted questions about the propriety of dramatizing events that were so recent. But it was the series of lectures which he gave in Bristol in the spring of 1795, attacking the policies of the government, which identified him as a radical in the public mind.

Political feelings were running high at the time, and his bold decision to expound the iniquities of the slave trade in a city where handsome profits were being made by it accounts for the vehemence of his opponents. He described it in a letter to his friend George Dyer:

. . . the opposition of the Aristocrats is so furious and determined, that I begin to fear that the Good I do is not proportionate to the Evil I occasion—Mobs and Press gangs have leagued in horrible Conspiracy against me—The Democrats are as sturdy in the support of me—but their number is comparatively small—Two or three uncouth and unbrained Automata have threatened my Life—and in the last Lecture the Genus infimum were scarcely restrained from attacking the house in which the 'damn'd Jacobine was jawing away'.

(CL, i, 152)

In the same letter he explained that charges of treason had obliged him to publish the first of the lectures unrevised.

The reactions of the reviewers to *A Moral and Political Lecture*, *Conciones ad Populum*, and *The Plot Discovered*, all of which appeared before the end of the year, depended, as one would expect, upon their various political sympathies. While the *Critical Review* (No. 4) spoke of his sentiments as 'manly and generous', the *British Critic* (No. 10) complained of 'the petulance and irritability of youth, assertion without proof, and the absurdest deductions from the most false and unreasonable premises'. Most of the reviewers referred to the quality of Coleridge's diction, calling it passionate and imaginative if they approved of what he was saying, and intemperate and overblown if they did not. These early publications were important factors in the development of Coleridge's reputation, however, because they identified him with a particular political faction, and because the identification lingered on long after his views had changed.

The response to his *Poems on Various Subjects* (1796), by contrast, was tentative. Read in isolation from other reviews of the period it seems complimentary enough,—but the standard policy seems to have been to praise when in doubt, and to do so condescendingly. Coleridge anticipated one of the criticisms that was to be made when he sent a copy of the book to his friend John Thelwall: 'You will find much to blame in them—much effeminacy of sentiment, much faulty glitter of expression' (*CL*, i, 205). By and large the reviewers agreed, adding that his metres were not always harmonious; but they found much to admire—lively imagination, tenderness and sublimity of sentiment, and a ready command of poetic language. The *Monthly Review* (No. 15) singled out 'Religious Musings', on which Coleridge had told Thelwall that he built all his 'poetic pretensions', and described it as being 'on the top of the scale of sublimity'.

Coleridge's comment on his critics seems a trifle ungrateful: 'The *Monthly* has *cataracted* panegyric on me—the *Critical cascaded* it—& the *Analytical dribbled* it with civility: as to the British Critic, they *durst not* condemn and they would not praise—so contented themselves with "commending me, as a *Poet* ["]—and allowed me "tenderness of sentiment & elegance of diction" ' (*CL*, i, 227). But his good-humoured indifference to their opinions probably rose as much from his feeling that reviews did not matter very much and from his confidence that he had better poetry in him as from dissatisfaction with their superficiality.

His next publications, the one-shilling pamphlet of his *Ode on the Departing Year* (1796) and the second edition of his *Poems* (1797), were less widely noticed. The reviewers of the 'Ode' agreed that its language was extravagant or affected, but differed as to whether or

3

not his experiment with the form was successful. Writing to his publisher, Joseph Cottle, Coleridge refers to the poem 'which some people think superior to the "Bard" of Gray, and which others think a rant of turgid obscurity . . .' (*CL*, i, 309).

Fears in Solitude (1798) linked his poetical reputation to his political views even more firmly. In addition to the title poem the volume includes 'France, an Ode', and 'Frost at Midnight'. Although these have since come to be thought of as among his more successful poems, the reviewers did not sense any marked improvement. They concentrated on the sentiments which he expressed and praised or condemned them according to their own political bias. While the *Analytical Review* (No. 21) refers to him as a person of the 'purest patriotism', the *British Critic* (No. 23) laments 'his absurd and preposterous prejudices against his country'. As to the literary merits of the poems, the critics merely single out beauties and blemishes without committing themselves to anything amounting to analysis. All of them treat Coleridge as a poet of promise, while continuing to mention the unevenness of his work.

The reception of *Lyrical Ballads*, which Coleridge and Wordsworth published anonymously in 1798, is much more interesting. The anonymity of the volume prevented the reviewers from talking about Coleridge's politics; 'The Rime of the Ancient Mariner', which opened the collection, presented them with a marked departure from the sort of verse they were used to; and the short 'Advertisement' provided them with a poetical manifesto of sorts.

Coleridge's other contributions were 'The Nightingale', 'The Dungeon', and 'The Foster-Mother's Tale'. These were received with varying degrees of polite approval. 'The Ancient Mariner', however, was uniformly abused. The *Analytical Review* (No. 25) described the poem as having 'more of the extravagance of a mad german poet, than of the simplicity of our ancient ballad writers'. Southey, writing anonymously in the *Critical Review* (No. 26), remarked that 'Many of the stanzas are laboriously beautiful, but in connection they are absurd or unintelligible', and concluded that it was 'a Dutch attempt at German sublimity'. The *Monthly Review* (No. 27) was even blunter, calling it 'the strangest story of a cock and a bull that we ever saw on paper', but added that it contained 'poetical touches of an exquisite kind'. Indeed, while the reviewers agreed that 'The Ancient Mariner' was a failure, they spoke respectfully of its unknown author.

Before condemning them for failing to rise to the occasion, it is only fair to mention that when 'The Ancient Mariner' first appeared its diction was more archaic than it is in the familiar version, and it lacked the explanatory gloss. Further, Wordsworth, who had had a hand in the planning of the poem, seems on the whole to have agreed with the reviewers' strictures. Very few readers recognized the merits of the work immediately (No. 30).

With *Lyrical Ballads* we come to the end of the first phase of Coleridge's career. His visit to Germany in 1798-1799 bore fruit in his translation of Schiller's *Wallenstein*, but he found translating to be so uncongenial that when the *Monthly Review* (No. 31) ventured to call him 'by far the most rational partizan of the German theatre whose labours have come under our notice', he objected. The reviews of *Wallenstein* provide further evidence of the respect being accorded to Coleridge's poetical skills, but they continue to comment upon his lapses from decorum.

III

Looking back over his literary life in 1817, Coleridge complained that, having been properly criticized for faults when he was publishing poetry, he had been harried unremittingly by the critics for faults which he did not have, during a period of seventeen years when he was not publishing poetry. He overstated the case a little, but he was essentially right.

With the exception of the second edition of *Lyrical Ballads* (1800) and the third edition of his *Poems* (1803) there is a hiatus in Coleridge's career until 1813. He continued to write, but what he wrote was published in newspapers or annual anthologies. Even his own periodical, the *Friend* (1809-10), was not the sort of work which the reviews normally discussed. Having achieved something of a name for his political verse and his 'Conversation Poems', he suddenly stopped furnishing the reviewers with subject matter. Had he vanished from the literary stage completely he would probably have been left in peace; in fact, however, although the medium of his publications changed, his presence continued to be felt in London. He was active as a political journalist, first for the *Morning Post* and later for the *Courier*; in 1809 he began to give public lectures and continued to do so at irregular intervals until 1819; his fame as a talker began to spread beyond his circle of close friends. In addition, his former associates, Southey and Wordsworth, were writing a great deal, and it was only natural for reviewers referring to the characteristics of the Lake poets to toss Coleridge's name in with those of his friends.

Lord Byron's inclusion of Coleridge in *English Bards and Scotch Reviewers* (1809) would have surprised no one.

> Shall gentle COLERIDGE pass unnoticed here,
> To turgid ode and tumid stanza dear?
> Though themes of innocence amuse him best,
> Yet still Obscurity's a welcome guest.
> If Inspiration should her aid refuse
> To him who takes a Pixy for a muse,
> Yet none in lofty numbers can surpass
> The bard who soars to elegize an ass:
> So well the subject suits his noble mind,
> He brays, the Laureate of the long-eared kind.

Had anyone made the objection that the verse which Byron was mocking belonged to the previous decade, he would have been perfectly justified in retorting that no matter when it was written Coleridge's reputation was based on it.

A similar line is taken in a lampoon published in the *Satirist* (No. 36a) in 1809, and the publication of two parts of 'The Three Graves' in the *Friend* was greeted by a long and archly ironical critique in the *Monthly Mirror* (No. 37) in 1810. In the same year the *Edinburgh Annual Register for 1808* (No. 36b) reproached Coleridge for his silence, complaining that 'He has only produced in a complete state one or two small pieces, and every thing else, begun on a larger scale, has been flung aside and left unfinished'. Even his lectures were not immune to the cheerful satire of the time. Leigh Hunt's description of them in 'The Feast of the Poets' touches on the discrepancy between the public Coleridge and the private one.

> And Coleridge, they say, is excessively weak;
> Indeed he has fits of the painfullest kind:
> He stares at himself and his friends, till he's blind;
> Then describes his own legs, and claps each a long stilt on;
> And this he calls *lect'ring* on 'Shakspeare and Milton'.

During these years appreciative comments were rare. One of the few was a long, detailed, and enthusiastic review of *The Friend*, which appeared in the *Eclectic Review* (No. 38). Although Coleridge is reported to have written to the editor about it, his letter has not been found.[1] The review deserves a careful reading as the first description of

Coleridge's thought and prose style, and for its anticipations of later apologists. The author, said to be John Foster, begins by noticing the difference between the qualities of Coleridge's mind and those required for the successful production of a weekly journal. He admits the obscurity of Coleridge's style and the difficulty of his ideas without losing patience with either, and he concludes that they must have been partly responsible for the failure of *The Friend* to become popular. The essay closes with a plea to Coleridge to benefit the public with 'successive volumes of essays' and the advice that he submit to 'a resolute restriction on that mighty profusion and excursiveness of thought, in which he is tempted to suspend the pursuit and retard the attainment of the one distinct object which should be clearly kept in view . . .'. More than ten years were to pass before Coleridge was to be served as well by a reviewer.

His lectures on Shakespeare, his long silence as a poet, and the depressingly low state of the drama, combined to make the presentation of his tragedy, *Remorse*, on 25 January 1813, an event of unusual interest to the literary world. The play was well received on the first night, ran for twenty nights—at the time a long run—, was published at the end of the month, and went through three editions before the year was out. In terms of profit and public recognition it was Coleridge's most successful literary enterprise. In a letter to his friend Thomas Poole he mentions the profit: 'I shall get more than all my literary Labors put together, nay thrice as much, subtracting my heavy Losses in the Watchman & the Friend—400£: including the Copy-right' (*CL*, iii, 437). He was immediately caught up in a flurry of social engagements.

According to his own account the play succeeded 'in spite of bad Scenes, execrable Acting, & Newspaper Calumny' (*CL*, iii, 436). It is, of course, impossible to assess the quality of the performance now, but the reviews were not as bad as Coleridge thought. The *Morning Chronicle* (No. 39) praised the psychological refinement of the characterization, the variety and elegance of the diction, and even ventured to compare Coleridge with Shakespeare. The *Satirist* (No. 43) was so unkind as to suggest that Coleridge must have written the review himself. The short notice in the *Morning Post* (No. 40) was wholly favourable, although the longer review which was promised for the next issue failed to materialize. *The Times* (No. 41), however, was very cool and contemptuous and devoted most of the little praise it permitted itself to the efforts of the actors. Coleridge was vexed by this review, as much because it contained references to his sentimental and German manner as because it was unfavourable. He vented his indignation in a letter to Southey:

> ... that was one *big Lie* which the Public cried out against—they were force[d] to affect admiration of the Tragedy—but yet abuse me they must—& so comes the old infamous Crambe bis millies cocta of the 'sentimentalities, puerilities, whinings, and meannesses (both of style & thought)' in my former Writings— but without (which is worth notice both in these Gentlemen, & in all our former Zoili), without one single Quotation or Reference in proof or exempli- fication. ... This Slang has gone on for 14 or 15 years, against us—& really deserves to be exposed. (*CL*, iii, 433)

These remarks anticipate Coleridge's later fulminations in *Biographia Literaria*.

Reviews of the published version of *Remorse* considered its merits as a dramatic poem—a genre that was enjoying a temporary vogue while the theatre was weak. The reviewers all found beautiful poetry in the play, and most of them felt that it was more suitable for reading than for acting (it is worth remembering that a number of Romantic critics said the same of Shakespeare's plays). Only the *British Review* (No. 54) was so tactless as to assert that *Remorse* owed its success to the stage performance. The comparison with Shakespeare was taken up by the *Monthly Review* (No. 53), but the prevailing opinion was that the play contained too much description, too much reflective soliloquy, too little action, and too involved and improbable a plot. The most elaborate discussion, a long essay in the *Quarterly Review* (No. 55), expressed surprise that *Remorse* had been well received in performance and prophesied accurately that it was unlikely to hold the stage.

IV

The years 1816 to 1817 mark a change in the public reception of Coleridge's work. After a long interval of silence, broken towards the end by the publication of *Remorse*, he suddenly produced half a dozen books in quick succession. In the summer of 1816, *Christabel, Kubla Khan, a Vision; The Pains of Sleep* appeared and rapidly went through three editions. It was followed in December by *The Statesman's Manual* and in April 1817 by his second *Lay Sermon*. *Biographia Literaria*,

Sibylline Leaves, and *Zapolya* were published before the end of the year. The immediate reaction to this spate of activity was breathtakingly hostile. It had an adverse effect on sales at a time when Coleridge was desperately poor, and it included attacks on his personal integrity at the very moment when he was beginning to emerge from the depths of his opium addiction in the kindly and well-regulated household of the Gillmans in Highgate. A number of these reviews would deserve a place in any collection of notorious literary attacks. They are notorious partly because critics have disagreed with them since, but mainly because they are splendid examples of invective. The authors of these criticisms were all highly qualified and intelligent men; looked at dispassionately, after a century and a half, they do not even seem to have been particularly ill-natured. Nevertheless, the treatment of Coleridge's writing during this period is one of the sorriest performances in the history of reviewing. A word of explanation seems to be in order.

As Coleridge himself had already become aware, there had been a change in the manners of reviewing; attacks on Wordsworth and Southey had alerted him to it as early as 1808. There had been an appreciable difference between the tone of the reviews which greeted *Remorse* and those which his own poems had received in the 1790's. The foundation of the *Edinburgh Review*, the *Quarterly Review*, and later of *Blackwood's Edinburgh Magazine*, ushered in an era of literary partisanship and provocation. Hazlitt, who was particularly active as a reviewer, looked back nostalgically to a time when critics 'were somewhat precise and prudish, gentle almost to a fault, full of candour and modesty, "And of their port as meek as is a maid" '. 'There was', he said, 'none of that Drawcansir work going on then that there is now; no scalping of authors, no hacking and hewing of their lives and opinions . . .' (Howe, viii. 216). It was Coleridge's misfortune to present the bulk of his writing to the public at the very time when the cut and thrust of reviewing was at its height.

Apart from this change in the conduct of the reviews, there were reasons why Coleridge was particularly vulnerable. The new journals were identified with political parties; Coleridge, having been a radical and having since become conservative, was distrusted by both sides and caught in the cross-fire between them. He was known to favour German philosophy at a time when Scottish philosophy was in fashion. Associated with the Lake poets' earliest experiments, he had been named as a poet of mawkish sentimentality, and he was about to offer new poems which seemed obscure and pretentiously Gothic. Further, he was well-known and was therefore fair game for abuse.

Christabel was published as a four-and-sixpenny pamphlet in a brown paper cover. Of the three poems which it contained, two were unfinished, and one of these, 'Kubla Khan', was offered as a psychological curiosity which had been composed in a dream. Taken by itself the volume seems modest enough. As various reviewers were to remark, however, 'Christabel' had been preceded by the 'puff direct', Byron having referred to it in his preface to *The Siege of Corinth* as 'That wild and singularly original and beautiful poem'. It had been read to or by many literary men during the sixteen years which intervened between its composition and its publication and had even been parodied in the *European Magazine* the year before.[2] Like its author, the poem already had a reputation.

Coleridge could hardly have asked for a more sympathetic review than the first one, which appeared in the *Critical Review* (No. 58); the gist of it was that the collection contained great beauty amid imperfections. It refers to 'Christabel', which it discusses in some detail, as 'this very graceful and fanciful poem, which we may say, without fear of contradiction, is enriched with more beautiful passages than have ever been before included in so small a compass'. It mentions 'Kubla Khan' and 'The Pains of Sleep' briefly but respectfully.

The next review established the tone for those that followed. In the *Examiner* (No. 59) Hazlitt set out to mock the volume. 'Christabel', like 'The Three Graves', is an easy poem to make fun of if one has a mind to, and Hazlitt assumes an air of playful condescension and regret. He makes a few perceptive observations about 'Christabel', admits its beauties, and quotes twenty-eight lines approvingly. Even his comment that ' "Kubla Khan", we think, only shews that Mr. Coleridge can write better nonsense verses than any man in England', which is sometimes quoted disapprovingly out of context, is qualified by the assertion that 'It is not a poem but a musical composition', and the conclusion that 'We could repeat these lines to ourselves not the less often for not knowing the meaning of them'.

Thomas Moore's critique in the *Edinburgh Review* (No. 64) moves from condescension to high-spirited ridicule. He is by turns indignant and droll, and his trial of 'Christabel' by the standards of 'common sense' makes entertaining reading. His attack is framed by an opening salvo at the Lake poets and a closing broadside at Coleridge's political change of heart. Within this framework he gleefully abuses 'Christabel' and concludes that with the exception of six lines ('even these are not very brilliant') 'there is literally not one couplet in the publication . . . which would be reckoned poetry, or even sense, were it found in the corner of a newspaper or upon the window of an inn'. Such reviews tend to be self-defeating in the long run, but the combined effect of Moore's anonymous disapproval, the more restrained disappointment of other reviews, and the silence of the influential *Quarterly Review*, seems to have been to damage sales and to make it difficult for Coleridge to find publishers for his other works.

The reviews of *The Statesman's Manual* and the second *Lay Sermon* are less interesting to the modern reader because the works themselves are relatively unfamiliar. Nevertheless, the reception of these two essays into theological politics was to have a lasting effect on his reputation.

William Hazlitt played a disproportionately large part in the hostilities. He reviewed *The Statesman's Manual* anonymously three times, once before it was published (on the basis of a prospectus) and twice after (Nos. 67, 68 and 69). His unparalleled ferocity as a reviewer is such a diverting spectacle as to make one want to go back to the works he is deriding. Yet for all the scorn and contempt he expresses, it is plain, particularly in the light of his later essays on Coleridge, that it was Coleridge's falling away from the man whom he had once admired that has roused him. It is Coleridge the political turncoat, Coleridge the dabbler in incomprehensible German metaphysics, Coleridge the intolerant condemner of men and beliefs which he had formerly supported, that rankles. Hazlitt writes with such spirit and clarity, and his target was so open to raillery on the grounds of being obscure and paradoxical, that the formidable reviewer seems to have much the best of the encounter. As Crabb Robinson mildly pointed out, 'The author's great mistake has been, we apprehend, the supposing that the higher classes, "men of *clerkly* acquirements", would be willing to acquiesce in that kind of abstraction which has been produced by a school of metaphysics, foreign equally to our language and philosophy' (No. 71).

It was at this point that Coleridge joined battle with his tormentors. We do not yet know very much about the order in which the various parts of *Biographia Literaria* were written, but we do know that, although the book makes remarks about the specific inadequacies of Coleridge's own reviewers in 1816, it had contained a lengthy discussion of the shortcomings of contemporary reviewing as early as 1815. Three conclusions follow from this fact. The first is that Coleridge's complaints are not just those of an author who had himself been badly mauled. The second is that although we know this, with the advantage of hindsight, Coleridge's reviewers did not. And the third follows from the preceding two: a book meant as a serious commentary on the methods of reviewing was mistaken for a wholly personal riposte.

The publication of *Biographia Literaria* was a heavensent opportunity for the very reviewers whose influence it was supposed to undermine, and they took full advantage of it. Coleridge had singled out the *Edinburgh Review* and its editor, Jeffrey, for criticism. The answer was a masterful and scathing round of abuse from Hazlitt, accompanied by a lofty refutation of Coleridge's personal charges by Jeffrey himself in a long footnote (No. 75). Accusations of lack of organization, unintelligibility, disingenuousness and downright silliness are combined with remarks about the Lake poets and dishonest politics. The review concludes with the statement: 'Till he can do something better, we would rather hear no more of him'.

Worse was to come. The next major review, by 'Christopher North' in *Blackwood's Edinburgh Magazine* (No. 78), made Hazlitt's seem moderate and reasonable by comparison. To the charges of wilful obscurity, inconsistency, and political hypocrisy, are added attacks on Coleridge's conceit, spitefulness and domestic irregularities. The air throughout is that of a stern judge condemning a malefactor in highly personal terms. Coleridge was dissuaded with some difficulty from bringing an action for libel (*CL*, iv, 884-5).

The remaining reviews were much less extravagant in their disapproval, and some admitted that the autobiographical sections of the book were entertaining, but all agreed that a prominent writer had made a sorry spectacle of himself.

Considering the sharpness of the reception of *Biographia Literaria*, one would have expected that the publication of *Sibylline Leaves* about a month later would have given rise to another chorus of disapproval. In fact, the volume was not widely reviewed; and while a number of the old objections to Coleridge's sentimentalities, Germanic wildness, obscurities, and political change of heart were repeated, the comments were fairly gentle and in some instances positively favourable.

Sibylline Leaves is a collection of almost all the poetry on which Coleridge's reputation now rests. Omitted are 'Christabel', 'Kubla Kahn', and 'The Pains of Sleep', which, as we have seen, had been published separately the year before. The only new contributions of any importance were the explanatory gloss to 'The Rime of the Ancient Mariner' and 'Dejection: an Ode'. But even if most of the poems were familiar, the book offered the reviewers a chance to write retrospectively about Coleridge. Their failure to do so can be most plausibly explained by their feeling that *Sibylline Leaves* was merely another edition of his verse, and by their already being taken up with the problem of coping with the *Biographia*—which must have been a difficult book to review, even with prejudice.

The *British Critic* (No. 80) mentioned *Sibylline Leaves* briefly in the course of its review of *Biographia Literaria*. The *Edinburgh Review* and *Blackwood's* ignored it. The *Monthly Magazine* (No. 84) dismissed it in a short notice with the remark, 'Alas, poor Yorick!' Both the *Edinburgh Magazine* (No. 85) and the *Monthly Review* (No. 86) discussed if favourably, and in terms which remind one of the milder reviews ot Coleridge's youth.

The *Edinburgh Magazine* mixes praise and blame fairly evenly. It picks 'The Ancient Mariner' as the most characteristic of Coleridge's poems (and this was one of the earliest public indications of its eventual prominence), and while it enumerates the defects of his style admits that his poetry has 'other qualities . . . which entitle it to a place among the finest productions of modern times'. The review refers to the variety of the poems in *Sibylline Leaves*, but argues that 'the prevailing characteristic of the compositions of this author is a certain wildness and irregularity'.

The *Monthly Review's* offering is more instructive. Its opinions about the relative merits of the poems are conventional, and its claim that 'Love' was the best of them was to be echoed in the 1820's. But it raises the question as to why Coleridge had failed to become a popular author and charges him with having had a corrupting effect on the taste of his contemporaries. These remarks go a long way towards explaining why Coleridge had been receiving such a bad press. The *Monthly Review* observes that the scattered way in which his work had been published showed little business sense, and complained that, unlike other poets of the age, he had written no long poems.[3] It added that through his literary lectures and his own poems he had been 'gothicizing' his contemporaries and contributing to the decline of the reputation of the Augustan poets. It is unlikely that Coleridge could have had such an influence by himself, but he may have seemed to epitomize those who were turning away from Pope and Dryden. If so, it is easy to see why the rather old-fashioned literary tastes of the Edinburgh reviewers were offended.

Coleridge's last major publication in 1817 was *Zapolya*. Its failure to reach the stage of Covent Garden for which it was intended probably accounts for its having aroused so much less interest than *Remorse*. The reviewers disagreed over whether it was a good play or a bad play and over whether it was a good poem or a bad poem, but do not seem to have cared much one way or the other.

V

There was, inevitably one feels, a reaction against the severity of the reviews which Coleridge had received in 1816 and 1817. The aftermath was quiet but steadily favourable. In 1819 a long and perceptive reappraisal of his poetry was published in *Blackwood's* by J. G. Lockhart (No. 95). A survey of Coleridge's life and works appeared in the *Examiner* (No. 99) in 1821; and a long letter which appeared in the *Edinburgh Magazine* (No. 93) in the same year belatedly drew attention to the qualities of the *Friend* (1818). Not very much was written about Coleridge between 1818 and 1825, when his next major publication, *Aids to Reflection*, came out, but with the exception of a waspish essay in the *Monthly Magazine* (No. 94) it tended to be complimentary.

Lockhart's essay (No. 95) deserves to be read carefully. It is a discussion of Coleridge's characteristics as a poet, and the views which it expresses were accepted until well into our own century. He stresses Coleridge's originality and oddness, arguing that these characteristics have stood between him and the public. He devotes considerable space to outlining the structure and meaning of 'The Rime of the Ancient Mariner' and 'Christabel' which, with 'Love', he classes as Coleridge's best poems. He describes Coleridge as 'the prince of superstitious poets' and 'a most inimitable master of the language of poetry'. It was for music and mystery that the next two generations were to value him.

It is tempting to accept Lockhart's essay as the amends due to an author who had been unfairly injured by other reviewers. But as the *London Magazine* was quick to point out, it was in *Blackwood's* itself that the fiercest attack on Coleridge's personal and literary character had appeared in 1817. A letter protesting against the review of *Biographia Literaria* had been printed in *Blackwood's* in 1819, as had a parody of 'Christabel' and a hoax letter which purported to come from Coleridge. All of these *jeux d'esprit* had been written by the editorial staff of *Blackwood's*, of which Lockhart was himself a prominent member. As if this were not enough, *Blackwood's* was trying, through the good offices of Lockhart, to persuade Coleridge to become a contributor. These circumstances in no way invalidate Lockhart's essay—his praise of Coleridge's poems seems to have been perfectly genuine—, but they do reveal something of the frolicsome way in which the great reviews of the age were conducted.

By 1825 Coleridge's reputation as a poet was well established. He had become increasingly well known as a thinker and a number of his young disciples had become sufficiently prominent themselves to begin to write reviews of his work of the partisan kind which had previously been denied him. The suggestion that he had plagiarized from the Germans was made in a lighthearted context in *Blackwood's* (No. 101), but it was not until after Coleridge's death that De Quincey's articles on this topic began to require refutation. *Aids to Reflection* was not well received at first, but it must have seemed a very specialized book. The *British Review* (No. 102) opened its notice with the statement: 'We can recollect no instance, in modern times, of literary talent so entirely wasted . . .'. The *British Critic* (No. 103) gave it a long and circumstantial consideration and ended by disapproving of Coleridge's unorthodox religious views. But *Aids to Reflection*, like *On the Constitution of Church and State* (1830) which also attracted little attention at first, gradually won adherents for reasons that were not primarily literary.

Three editions of Coleridge's *Poetical Works*, in 1828, 1829, and 1834, reflect the improvement in his reputation. Some fine reviews were written of these. One, in the *Westminster Review* (No. 106) in 1830, claimed him as a Utilitarian—a curious foreshadowing of John Stuart Mill's later essay on Coleridge and Bentham. The poems which continued to be praised were 'The Ancient Mariner', 'Christabel' and, above all, 'Love'. A month after Coleridge's death in 1834, Henry Nelson Coleridge's great essay appeared in the *Quarterly Review* (No. 114). It had been written before Coleridge died and it is obvious that H. N. Coleridge had benefited from his close association with his uncle. For the first time serious consideration was given to poems which Coleridge had written after 1800, and to 'Dejection: an Ode' in particular, and the necessary connection between his metaphysical pursuits and his poems was emphasized.

VI

The war with France may have had something to do with Coleridge's failure to make any immediate impression abroad.[4] The outbreak of hostilities made it difficult for Continental writers to keep in touch with their contemporaries in Britain, and forced them to rely on the opinions of the new reviews without having a lively sense of the social context in which they were being written. A Londoner might be expected to sense the biases of the *Edinburgh Review* and the *Quarterly Review* and to allow for them; the foreign interpreter of English literature was obliged to accept them at face value. As the lull which followed the defeat of Napoleon happened to coincide with the worst phase of Coleridge's reputation, it is not surprising that little notice was taken of him either in Europe or in the United States until the 1820's.

In Germany, from which Coleridge had himself drawn so much inspiration, he was known as a missionary for Schiller's plays but for little else. An early review of his poetry which appeared in the Stuttgart *Morgenblatt für gebildete Stände* in 1811 was merely an adaptation of the essay in the *Edinburgh Annual Register* (No. 36(b)).[5] F. J. Jacobsen's influential account of the state of English poetry, published in 1820, paid more attention to the work of Moore, Campbell and Wilson; most of the nine pages he allowed Coleridge were taken up with a reprinting of 'Love'.[6] In 1832, Wolff's lectures on contemporary European literature reflected the improvement in Coleridge's English reputation, provided a translation of 'Love', but had nothing original to say.[7] German readers had to wait until 1836 for F. Freilingrath's translation of 'The Ancient Mariner'.

In France, where Coleridge was later to have an influence on the Symbolist poets, his initial reception was even sketchier. Apart from comments derived from English reviewers, the earliest essay of substance seems to have been Amédée Pichot's in 1825.[8] It presented Coleridge as a man of indolent genius and of improvised fragments, referred to his exploitation of dreams, and singled out 'Love', 'The Ancient Mariner' and *Remorse* for special praise. This essay and the 1829 Paris edition of *The Poetical Works of Coleridge, Shelley and Keats* anticipate the direction which French appreciation of Coleridge was to take.

Although Coleridge's name is used freely enough in American periodicals of the time, they contain surprisingly little direct comment on his writings. One comes upon announcements of his forthcoming lectures in London, sedulously copied from English journals, but nothing that could be called a review. In 1819, for instance, R. H. Dana, Sr., invoked his authority while talking about Hazlitt. 'Mr. Coleridge's criticism', he said, 'has more good taste and philosophy in it, than any that has been written upon Mr. Wordsworth, or any other man in modern times.⁹' But when *Biographia Literaria* was published in New York in 1817, it had been allowed to pass almost unnoticed by the reviews of New York, Boston, and Philadelphia. Like the reviewers on the Continent, and with rather less excuse, American reviewers accepted the fashionable British opinion that Byron, Campbell, Wordsworth and Scott were the authors who mattered.

Towards the end of his life Coleridge's prose began to be championed by the Transcendentalists. The publication of *Aids to Reflection* in Vermont in 1829, with a long prefatory essay by James Marsh, opened the way for serious discussion. By 1835 two major essays had appeared in the *North American Review*.[10]

VII

When trying to assess the quality of previous critics it is tempting to suppose that whenever they disagree with us they must be wrong. We are sometimes a little precipitate in assuming the mantle of posterity. It is more satisfying to look into differences between their approach to a writer's work and our own. Coleridge's reviewers singled out 'The Ancient Mariner' and 'Christabel' as being especially remarkable, but it took them almost twenty years to come round to this view. 'Kubla Khan' was liked, but was not thought to be much more than the curiosity which Coleridge himself had called it. In the twentieth century his 'Conversation poems' and 'Dejection: an Ode' have begun to receive more attention, and the later poems too are beginning to be talked about. Where the Romantic reviewers differ most sharply from modern critics is in their complete failure to think of interpreting poems like 'The Ancient Mariner' allegorically. There is no evidence to suggest that Coleridge minded.

Coleridge's present eminence as a critic might also have surprised his contemporaries, but at the time they would no more have thought of a man's critical writing as being part of his creative work than we would think of a writer's scientific treatises as being relevant to our assessment of his novels. Until one began to think in terms of a history of criticism it would have been difficult to see Coleridge's place in it.

His philosophical writings, and his theology and politics, were not received very sympathetically, and none of them has become a classic. Much of what he was trying to say had specific relevance to his own times, and it is easy to see that the reviewers who disapproved of what he was saying were in a far better position to have an opinion than anyone can be today. What they had at their fingertips takes years of study to acquire now. This is one of the reasons why we cannot afford to ignore the early reviews. They bring Coleridge into sharp focus against the contemporaries whom he resembled in so many respects, and by allowing us to distinguish between him and them they help us to define the sort of writer he really was.

NOTES

1. Henry Crabb Robinson, *On Books and Their Writers*, ed. Edith J. Morley (London 1938), i, 55.
2. *The European Magazine*, lxvii (April 1815), 345-6.
3. For the background of this complaint, see Donald M. Foerster, 'Critical Approval of Epic Poetry in the Age of Wordsworth', *Publications of the Modern Language Association*, lxx (1955), 682-705. Useful descriptions of the prevailing tastes and intellectual climate are to be found in John Clive, *Scotch Reviewers: the Edinburgh Review 1802-1815* (London and Cambridge, Mass. 1957), Upali Amarasinghe, *Dryden and Pope in the Early Nineteenth Century: A Study of Changing Literary Taste, 1800-1830* (Cambridge 1962), and William S. Ward, 'Some Aspects of the Conservative Attitude Toward Poetry in English Criticism, 1798-1820', *Publications of the Modern Language Association*, lx (1945), 386-98.
4. The lack of adequate censuses of foreign periodicals has obliged me to rely on the following sources for bibliographical information: Luise Sigmann, *Die englische Literatur von 1800-1850 im Urteil der zeitgenössischen deutschen Kritik* (Heidelberg 1918); Laurence Marsden Price, *English Literature in Germany* (Berkeley and Los Angeles 1953); Eric Partridge, *The French Romantics' Knowledge of English Literature (1820-1848)* (Paris 1924); *Literary History of the United States: Bibliography* (New York and London 1964), 35-9.
5. Number 147; quoted in Sigmann, 28.
6. Friedrich Johann Jacobsen, *Briefe an eine deutsche Edelfrau über die neuesten englischen Dichter* (Altona 1820), 220-8.
7. O. L. B. Wolff, *Die schöne Litteratur in der neuesten Zeit* (Leipzig 1832), 337-44.
8. Amédée Pichot, *Voyage historique et littéraire en Angleterre et en Écosse* (Paris 1825), 395-421.

9. *The North American Review*, viii (March 1819), 320.

10. One on his poetry by R. C. Waterston in the *North American Review*, xxxix (October 1834), 437-58, the other a general account by G. B. Cheever in the *North American Review*, xl (April 1835), 299-351.

THE FALL OF ROBESPIERRE

1794

1. 'D. M.', *Analytical Review*

November 1794, 480-481

Although Robert Southey was co-author to the extent of contributing two of the three acts, Coleridge, who was looking after the details of publication in Cambridge, decided to let his own name stand alone on the title-page. For his explanation to Southey that two names would have seemed pretentious and that his own would sell more copies, see *CL*, i, 106.

Though, for reasons which we have of late had repeated occasions to specify, and which are indeed sufficiently obvious, we cannot approve of the practice of exhibiting recent political events in a dramatic form, we must do the author of this piece the justice to say, that he has been tolerably successful in his attempt to imitate the impassioned language of the french orators. Whether he have succeeded equally in his developement of the characters of the chief actors of this great political theatre, it may not, perhaps, at present be easy to determine. The plot of the piece being nothing more than a simple representation of a recent fact, needs not be decyphered. The concluding lines, spoken by Barrere, may serve as a specimen of the author's talent for dramatic declamation.
[quotes ll. 192-213 (Southey's) (*PW*, ii, 516-17)]

2. From an unsigned review, *Critical Review*

November 1794, xii, 260-2

The fall of Robespierre was an event of the greatest importance to the affairs of France, and is a very proper subject for the tragic muse. It may, however, be thought by some to be too recent an event to admit of that contrivance which is essentially necessary in unravelling the plot of the drama. Indeed, we have been informed, that the work before us was the production of a few hours exercise, and must, therefore, not be supposed to smell very strongly of the lamp. Several parts too being necessarily made up of such reports of the French convention, as have already been collected through the medium of newspapers, may be expected to have little of the charms of novelty.

By these free remarks, we mean not to under-rate Mr. Coleridge's historic drama. It affords ample testimony, that the writer is a genuine votary of the Muse, and several parts of it will afford much pleasure to those who can relish the beauties of poetry. Indeed a writer who could produce so much beauty in so little time, must possess powers that are capable of raising him to a distinguished place among the English poets. ...

At the end of this work, Mr. Coleridge has subjoined, proposals for publishing by subscription, Imitations from the modern Latin Poets, with a critical and biographical Essay on the Restoration of Literature: a work in which we most heartily wish him success. The present is a very agreeable specimen of Mr. Coleridge's poetical talents, and as the writers, from whose works he proposes to frame imitations are but little known to English readers, though many of them possess much merit, he will render, we doubt not, an acceptable service to the public.

3. Unsigned notice, *British Critic*

May 1795, v, 539-40

Mr. Coleridge has aimed at giving a dramatic air to a detail of Conventional speeches, which they were scarcely capable of receiving. The sentiments, however, in many instances are naturally, though boldly conceived, and expressed in language, which gives us reason to think the Author might, after some probation, become no unsuccessful wooer of the tragic muse.

A MORAL AND POLITICAL LECTURE

1795

4. From an unsigned review, *Critical Review*

March 1795, xiii, 455

This little composition is the production of a young man who possesses a poetical imagination. It is spirited, and often brilliant; and the sentiments manly and generous. Though, with one or two exceptions, we admire the style of this little work, we think it rather defective in point of precision; and, instead of saying we have shown the necessity of forming some fixed and determinate principles of action, he should have said, we have represented certain characters. We also think our young political lecturer leaves his auditors abruptly, and that he has not stated, in a form sufficiently scientific and determinate, those principles to which, as he expresses it, he now proceeds as the most *important point*. We confess we were looking for something further, and little thought that we were actually come to the *Finis*. One or two more lectures might give a fulness to the whole, and be very useful. There is, however, much more than sixpenny-worth of good sense in this Lecture. . . .

CONCIONES AD POPULUM
1795

5. Unsigned review, *Analytical Review*
January 1796, xiii, 90-1

These addresses were delivered to a popular assembly in the month of february last. They are eloquent harangues on interesting political topics: the first, on the general subject of liberty; the second, on the nature and consequences of the present war. The orator asserts the rights of free citizens with confidence; but it is not the confidence of an unprincipled demagogue, who, like Robespierre, 'despotises in all the pomp of patriotism, and masquerades on the bloody stage of revolution, a Caligula with the cap of liberty on his head'. The ends which he pursues are reformation; but the instruments, which he wishes to employ, are only those of truth and reason. In order to render men susceptible of their rights, his plan is, to teach them their duties: and he would prepare them to maintain the one, and practise the other, by instilling into their minds the principles of religion. The philanthropic spirit, and the superiour talents of this writer, will be seen in the following description of that small but glorious band, whom he distinguishes by the title of 'thinking and dispassionate patriots'.

These are the men who have encouraged the sympathetic passions till they have become irresistible habits, and made their duty a necessary part of their self interest, by the long continued cultivation of that moral taste which derives our most exquisite pleasures from the contemplation of possible perfection, and proportionate pain from the perception of existing *depravation*. Accustomed to regard all the affairs of man as a process, they never hurry and they never pause. Theirs is not that twilight of political knowledge which gives us just light enough to place one foot before the other; as they advance the scene still opens upon them, and they press right onward with a vast and various landscape of existence around them. Calmness and energy mark all their actions. Convinced that vice originates not in the man, but in the surrounding circum-

25

stances; not in the heart, but in the understanding; he is hopeless concerning no one—to correct a vice or generate a virtuous conduct he pollutes not his hands with the scourge of coercion; but by endeavouring to alter the circumstances would remove, or by strengthening the intellect, disarms, the temptation. The unhappy children of vice and folly, whose tempers are adverse to their own happiness as well as to the happiness of others, will at times awaken a natural pang; but he looks forward with gladdened heart to that glorious period when justice shall have established the universal fraternity of love. These soul-ennobling views bestow the virtues which they anticipate. He whose mind is habitually imprest with them soars above the present state of humanity, and may be justly said to dwell in the presence of the Most High.

> would the forms
> Of servile custom cramp the patriot's power?
> Would sordid policies, the barbarous growth
> Of ignorance and rapine, bow him down
> To tame pursuits, to indolence and fear?
> Lo! he appeals to nature, to the winds
> And rolling waves, the sun's unwearied course,
> The elements and seasons—all declare
> For what the Eternal Maker has ordain'd
> The powers of man: we feel within ourselves
> His energy divine: he tells the heart
> He meant, he made us to behold and love
> What he beholds and loves, the general orb
> Of Life and Being—to be great like him,
> Beneficent and active.
>
> AKENSIDE

While we see much to admire in these addresses, we are sorry sometimes to remark a degree of vehemence in language, rather adapted to irritate than enlighten.

6. Unsigned notice, *Monthly Review*

January 1796, xix, 80-1

This is followed by a brief notice of *The Plot Discovered*, with the comment 'Ditto repeated'.

This animated author tells us, in his preface, that these two discourses were delivered in February 1795, and were followed by six others, in defence of natural and revealed religion. They are replete with violent antiministerial declamation, but not vulgar. His fearless idea is, that 'truth should be spoken at all times, but more especially at those times when to speak truth is dangerous'. The author dates from 'Clevedon, Nov. 16, 1795'.

7. Unsigned review, *Critical Review*

February 1796, xvi, 216

Of the former of these we have had occasion to speak before, and we spoke in terms of approbation.

In the second address our orator gives an affecting and animated description of the crimes and distresses of the present war. We lay before our readers the closing paragraph—

Such in addition to the evils attending all wars, are the peculiar horrors of the present. Our national faith hath been impaired; our social confidence hath been weakened, or made unsafe; our liberties have suffered a perilous breach, and even now are being (still more perilously) undermined; the dearth, which would otherwise have been scarcely visible, hath enlarged its terrible features into the threatening face of Famine; and finally, of *us* will justice require a dreadful account of whatever guilt France has perpetrated, of whatever miseries

France has endured. Are we men? Freemen? rational men? And shall we carry on this wild and priestly war against reason, against freedom, against human nature? If there be one among you, who departs from me without feeling it his immediate duty to petition or remonstrate against the continuance of it, I envy that man neither his head nor his heart.

Mr. Coleridge possesses ingenuity and good sense. We would advise him to study correctness, and to guard against the swell in composition.

8. Unsigned review, *British Critic*

June 1796, vii, 682-3

The two following addresses, Mr. C. says, were delivered in the month of February 1795, and were followed by six others in defence of natural and revealed religion. Where, or to whom they were delivered, does not appear. These addresses are by the same author, whose address to the people on a supposed plot, we noticed last month. They contain similar sentiments and are expressed with similar consistency and similar elegance. His tender and compassionate anxiety for the welfare of mankind, he dwells upon through many pages, and with that spirit of patriotism, which has frequently actuated the writers of his party, attempts to ascribe the murders of Robespierre, and all the horrors acted in France, to the obstinate hostility of this country. When shall we cease to see this nonsense repeated, which the best informed even of our French enemies have again and again contradicted?

THE PLOT DISCOVERED

1795

9. Unsigned review, *Analytical Review*

January 1796, xiii, 92

This piece is written in the same free spirit, and in the same bold and animated language, with the preceding article [*Conciones ad Populum*]. The author comments upon the several clauses of the late bill; but his observations, now that the bills are passed into laws, it would be of little avail to repeat. *Actum est!*

10. Unsigned review, *British Critic*

May 1796, vii, 562

We abhor, not only as critics, but as men of morals, the custom which has of late prevailed among certain individuals, of taking a detached sentence from a speech or publication, and commenting upon it, without any consideration of the context. Mr. Coleridge, whom we have commended as a poet, has done this with respect to an expression of the Bishop of Rochester, which, when explained, was found not only to be harmless, but truly constitutional. The violence of this pamphlet supersedes all criticism; it breathes all the petulance and irritability of youth, assertion without proof, and the absurdest deductions from the most false and unreasonable premises.

THE WATCHMAN

1796

11. Letter, *Bristol Gazette*

24 March 1796

This pseudonymous letter, placed as a paid advertisement, was republished by Coleridge in a later number of the *Watchman* (2 April 1796, 157-8).

Messrs. Printers.

The *Watchman* having within these few weeks attracted the Notice of the Citizens of Bristol, through the Channel of your Paper I presume to make a few Comments on the Execution of that Work. In the first Number we observe the *Debut* of this Publication upon the political Theatre made with 'professions of Meekness'. The Author's bias being towards principles not men, will lead him to write in the 'Spirit of Meekness'. The first effects of this Spirit, are, an abuse of every existing Review, implicating them with party and calumniating opinions—fully convinced of the little prejudice he possesses, he becomes Reviewer, declaring that he will execute the Trust 'without Compliment or Resentment'. The first specimen of his Critical Abilities is exhibited on the brilliant Pamphlet of *Mr. Burke*—His 'Spirit of Meekness' is evident when he says 'when men of low and creeping faculties wish to depreciate Works of Genius, it is their fashion to sneer at them as meer Declamation;—this mode has been practised by some low minded Sophisters with respect to the Work in Question', and passing immediately from these characters to himself and his opinions of Mr. Burke, he becomes the herald of his own fame; and with his 'ere I begin the task of blame' adds to the many Trophies he already enjoys in his own ideas. In a few Numbers we shall it is probable, see his

'Exegi monumentum aere perennius'—announced.

30

In the Court and Hand-bill news, he wished to have displayed his wit; but, as he soars above vulgar prejudices the Humour is hid from the profane Eye.

Odi profanum vulgus.[1]

His 'Spirit of Meekness' is visible in the Note under the Poem—had it been a Verse of the *Æneid* of *Virgil*, or the *Iliad* of *Homer*, less pomp could not have been used. I leave the Public to judge of the 'Meekness of Spirit', so evident in this. Inconsistency in the character of this Philosopher, seems a prominent feature. Thus . . . does he say 'how vile must that system be, which can reckon by anticipation among its certain enemies the Metaphysician, who employs the strength and subtlety of his Reason to investigate by what causes being acted upon, the human mind acts most worthily'. The *Enquiry concerning Political Justice* by Mr. *Godwin*, except by the prejudiced, will be allowed to be a deep Metaphysical Work though abstruse, yet to those who are earnest enquirers after Truth sufficiently clear in its deductions from every argument. It is a Work, which, if many of the ideas are not new has concentered the whole mass of argument in a manner unequalled in the English Language—Therefore, do we class it among those productions who seek by their discussions to meliorate the condition of Man. In page 73, we find a chapter entitled 'Modern Patriotism' 'sententious and prejudiced';[1]—in this Mr. *Godwin's* Enquiry is considered as vicious, and improper in its tendency. The Philosopher has mentioned the Arguments of Mr. *Goodwin* without giving the Reasons of or the Deductions drawn from them by that acute writer; should he find himself competent let him take up the Gauntlet and defend in a regular train of Argument supported by Reason, the system which he conceives to be injured by the Work. But the Difference would be too great—the one a cool Reasoner supporting his Doctrine with propriety, and waiting for the human mind to be more enlightened to prepare it for his theory, the other an Enthusiast supporting his Arguments by lofty Metaphors and high-toned Declamation.

Wishing that the *Watchman* in future, may be conducted with less prejudice and greater liberality,

I remain, yours &c.

Caius Gracchus

[1] 'Exegi monumentum . . .' 'I have raised a monument more enduring than brass' (Horace, *Odes*, iii, 30, 1). 'Odi . . .' 'I hate the uninitiated many' (Horace, *Odes*, iii, 1, 1).

POEMS ON VARIOUS SUBJECTS

1796

12. Unsigned notice, *British Critic*

May 1796, vii, 549-50

This collection is marked by tenderness of sentiment, and elegance of expression, neither however sufficiently chastened by experience of mankind, or habitude of writing. The following will be no unacceptable specimen of its merit.

[quotes 'The Sigh'. (*PW*, i, 62-3)]

13. Unsigned review, *Analytical Review*

June 1796, xiii, 610-12

Coleridge's account, in *Biographia Literaria*, of the reception of his first volume of poems, seems to refer particularly to this review (*BL*, i, 2).

From the proofs which Mr. C. has already given of considerable talents for eloquence, in his *Conciones ad Populum*, it was to be expected, that he would be qualified to exercise with success the kindred art of poetry: and the perusal of this small volume will justify the expectation.

Though several of the pieces are strongly expressive of an ardent love of liberty, the general character of the publication is by no means political. The poems, which are, for the most part, short, are written on a variety of subjects, and with very different degrees of merit: some of them appear to have been elaborated with great pains; others to have been the negligent productions of a momentary impulse. The numbers are not always harmonious; and the language, through a redundancy of metaphor, and the frequent use of compound epithets, sometimes becomes turgid: but every where the writer discovers a lively imagination, and a ready command of poetical language. The general character of the composition is rather that of splendour than of simplicity; and the reader is left more strongly impressed with an idea of the strength of the writer's genius, than of the correctness of his taste. As a pleasing example of Mr. C.'s inventive powers, we shall quote two or three stanzas from a piece which he entitles, 'Songs of the Pixies', who in the superstition of Devonshire are a race of invisible beings, harmless, and friendly to man.

[quotes ll. 47-88 (*PW*, i, 42-4)]

In a monody on the death of Chatterton, the disappointed hopes of that unfortunate youth are strongly represented in the following allegorical picture.

[quotes twelve lines which were omitted from the second edition (1797), but restored in *The Poetical Works* (1828) (see variant readings, *PW*, i, 128)]

To a collection of small pieces the author has chosen to give the name of Effusions: some of these are political, others descriptive, and others sentimental.

A very small number of these effusions are devoted to love: we are much pleased with the plaintive tenderness of the following.

[quotes 'The Sigh' (*PW*, i, 62-3)]

Poetical epistles form one division of this volume: but we do not think the author very successful in this class of poetry. The last piece is a pretty long poem, in blank verse, chiefly valuable for the importance of the sentiments which it contains, and the ardour with which they are expressed: it is entitled, 'Religious Musings'.

For two or three pieces in this volume, Mr. C. acknowledges his obligation to his friends.

14. Unsigned review, *Critical Review*

June 1796, xvii, 209-12

Of Mr. Coleridge we have already had occasion to speak as a poet. He certainly possesses a fine invention, and a lively imagination; and his poems glow with that ardor of passion, that enthusiastic love of liberty, which give energy to poetic composition, and force the reader into immediate admiration. They consist of sonnets, which, however, Mr. Coleridge chooses to call Effusions, a Monody on the Death of Chatterton, a few other copies of verses on various occasions, Epistles, and, what the author entitles 'Religious Musings'.

The Effusions are in general very beautiful. The following will please every lover of poetry, and we give them as a specimen of the rest:

[quotes 'Effusion 9, to Fayette' and 'Effusion 17, to Genevieve' (*PW*, i, 82 and 19-20)]

The following pretty copy of verses we cannot deny ourselves the pleasure of transcribing:

[quotes 'Effusion 27' ('The Rose', *PW*, i, 45-6)]

Mr. Coleridge tells us that he was indebted for three of the Effusions to Mr. Charles Lamb, of the India House,—these are very beautiful. For the rough sketch of another pretty sonnet, Mr. Coleridge is indebted to Mr. Favel.[1] The first half of the fifteenth was written by Mr. Southey, the ingenious author of Joan of Arc. The production of a young lady, addressed to the author of a volume of poems published anonymously at Bristol, possesses great harmony and good sense.[2]

Notwithstanding the commendations to which these poems are entitled, they are accompanied with some blemishes. The Monody

---

[1] Favell, who had been at school with Coleridge, was one of the supporters of the plan to found a Pantisocracy in Pennsylvania.

[2] The 'young lady' was Coleridge's wife: she later declared that she had only contributed to writing 'The Silver Thimble' (*PW*, i, 104n).

addressed to Chatterton possesses many excellent passages: but that irregular species of versification in which it is written, is not, in our judgment, consistent with the laws of poetry. The production of the young lady, whose ear, however, seems admirably tuned to harmony, is objectionable on the same ground: this blemish we before noted in 'The Poetical Sketches' of the ingenious miss Cristall.[1]

We must also observe that we frequently meet, in these poems, with expressions which, however pleasing in Spenser and Shakespeare, accord not with the present state of the English language. The versification is not always sufficiently polished, and, by not having the pause and accent in the proper place, grates upon a correct ear. The liberty too taken by Mr. Coleridge of coining words, and the impetuosity of a most powerful imagination, hurry him sometimes into what his readers will call bombast. For example:

> yea, and there
> Unshuddered, unaghasted, he shall view
> Ev'n the Seven Spirits, who in the latter day
> Will shower hot pestilence on the sons of men.

The superior excellence which characterises Mr. Coleridge's poems, compels us to wish that they possessed that uniform correctness of versification which frequently accompanies productions of far inferior merit; but Mr. Coleridge's blemishes are such as are incident to young men of luxuriant imaginations, which time and experience will, we doubt not, enable him to correct. His beauties are those of a very superior genius:—a richer line than the last of the three following we scarcely ever remember reading:

> O! aged women, ye who weekly catch
> The morsel tossed by law-forc'd charity,
> And die so slowly, that none call it murder.

Mr. Coleridge makes the following judicious apology for what some readers may choose to call the querulous egotism that is wont to accompany the sonnet:

[quotes the first three paragraphs of the preface (*PW*, ii, 1135-36)]

---

[1] *The Poetical Sketches* of Ann Batten Cristall had appeared in 1795.

15. John Aikin, *Monthly Review*

June 1796, xx, 194-5

This unsigned review is attributed to John Aikin (1747-1822), physician and literary editor of the *Monthly Magazine* (Nangle, 104).

Two authorial footnotes have been omitted.

The promise of poetical talents, which this writer gave to the world in the lines inserted in the poem of his friend Mr. Southey, entitled *Joan of Arc*, is here brought to the proof by a small volume of his own composition; and we doubt not that he will be thought to have made good the expectations which he had raised by that specimen. It might thence be inferred, that the bent of his powers lay towards those loftier displays of the art which consist in boldness and novelty of conception, strength of figure, and sublimity of sentiment; and notwithstanding the admixture of subjects in this collection, apparently more calculated for the gentler graces of poetry, the leading character of his genius is still equally discernible. Not that we mean to represent him as unqualified for producing pictures of beauty and elegance, or for depicting the soft and tender emotions; of both which there are such striking examples in his works, that the sweet and the pathetic may be reckoned peculiarly congenial to his nature: but even in these the manner of an original thinker is predominant; and as he has not borrowed the ideas, so he has not fashioned himself to the polish and correctness of modern verse. Such a writer may occasionally fall under the censure of criticism: but he will always be, what so few proportionally are, an interesting object to the genuine lover of poetry. On this account we shall devote somewhat more space to the present publication, than its bulk alone would seem to demand.

The first piece is a 'Monody on the Death of Chatterton'; a subject to which the author was naturally led from proximity of birth-place, and also, as we are sorry to find, from a melancholy resemblance in disappointed hope. It is in a wild irregular strain, suited to the theme, with some very moving and some very fanciful touches. We could with pleasure transcribe a few passages, but we rather leave it to entertain the reader as *a whole*. It concludes with an allusion to a project of which we have already heard, as emanating from the fervid minds of this poet and two or three congenial friends, to realize a golden age in some imaginary *'undivided* dale of freedom': but which, on sober reflection, we do not wonder to find him call

> vain Phantasies! the fleeting brood
> Of Woe self-solac'd in her dreamy mood![1]

The next piece of moderate length is entitled 'Songs of the Pixies'; which are, it seems, in the rustic superstition of Devonshire, a kind of fairies, harmless or friendly to man. Ariel, Oberon, and the Sylphs, have contributed to form the pleasing imagery of which the two following stanzas will give a specimen:

[quotes from the poem]

Other short pieces, of which one of the most pleasing consists of 'Lines to a beautiful Spring in a Village', lead the way to a principal division of the volume, styled 'Effusions'. These are short poems, many of them regular sonnets, others in a different form, but generally like them turning on a single thought, the topics of which are various; some breathing the high notes of freedom or fancy, some the softer strains of love and pity. A few of these, and of no inferior merit, are written by a friend, and distinguished by his signature. We shall copy, however, one of the author's own:

[quotes 'Effusion 26, on a Kiss' (*PW*, i, 63-4)]

A few 'poetical Epistles' come next: but their merit is not, we think, appropriate to epistolary writing, for which our author's style is little adapted. The most considerable of them, addressed to his 'Sara', is rather an ode, filled with picturesque imagery; of which the following stanzas compose a very striking sea-piece:

[quotes ll. 36-60 of 'Lines written at Shurton Bars' (*PW*, i, 98)]

The longest piece in the volume, entitled 'Religious Musings, a desultory Poem written on Christmas Eve', is reserved for the conclusion; and properly so, since its subject, and the manner of treating it, place it on the top of the scale of sublimity. It is, indeed, that in which we chiefly recognize the writer of the Maid's Vision in *Joan of Arc*;

---

[1] A reference to the Pantisocracy.

possessing the same characteristic excellencies and defects. Often obscure, uncouth, and verging to extravagance, but generally striking and impressive to a supreme degree, it exhibits that ungoverned career of fancy and feeling which equally belongs to the poet and the enthusiast. The book of Revelations may be a dangerous fount of prophecy, but it is no mean Helicon of poetic inspiration. Who will deny genius to such conceptions as the following?

[quotes ll. 276-322 (*PW*, i, 119-21)]

Let not our readers suppose that we have beggared this volume by our extracts. The lover of poetry may be assured that much remains to repay his purchase; and we presume that he will not be less satisfied with his bargain, if, while it contributes to his own pleasure, it tends to disperse the clouds which have darkened the prospects of a man of distinguished worth as well as of uncommon abilities.

16. Unsigned notice, *Monthly Mirror*

June 1796, ii, 97

Mr. Coleridge is a poet of the first class, as not only the present volume, but also some fine philosophical verses in Mr. Southey's admirable poem of Joan of Arc amply testify. It is not to be disguised, however, that he is one of those young men, who, seduced into a blind and intemperate admiration of theoretic politics, forget the necessary discrimination between liberty and licentiousness. We mean not by this to meddle with political opinions; Mr. Coleridge may have better reasons for his compliment to Lord Stanhope than we are aware of.[1]

---

[1] The volume was dedicated to Lord Stanhope (1753-1816), a radical peer who had been persecuted for his sympathies with the French Revolution.

ODE ON THE DEPARTING YEAR

1796

17. Alexander Hamilton, *Monthly Review*

March 1797, xxii, 342-3

This unsigned review is attributed to Hamilton (1762-1824), a Sanscrit scholar and until 1790 an officer in the army of the East India Company (Nangle, 104).

The higher species of ode is the *genuine* offspring of enthusiasm. The *imitated* enthusiasm of a cold and artificial imagination will never reach its tones of fancy and feeling; and all the mechanical tricks of abrupt transition, audacious metaphor, unusual phraseology, &c. produce nothing better than turgid obscurity and formal irregularity. It would be easy to produce examples, and from high authority too, of miserable waste of effort in attempts of this kind; which, indeed, are so commonly unsuccessful, that a reader of taste is very apt to turn over, in a miscellaneous collection, every piece which he sees marked with *strophe* and *antistrophe*.

The writer before us, however, will not be thought, by any one who is acquainted with his former compositions, defective in that first essential of sublime poetry, *ardent conception*; and the present effusion, faulty as it may be from extravagance in some parts, and from haste in others, will never be read without the emotions which true genius alone can call forth. For the hurry with which it was written, the author has, indeed, a better apology than is generally urged. The *departing year* would not stop for him; and when he first thought of addressing it, he could not stay to polish and revise his lines till the new year and new events had obliterated its traces. With respect to the strain of sentiment, we doubt not that Mr. C. has poured out the deliberate feelings of his soul, and would reject with scorn the excuse of precipitation. If general philanthropy has made him look with detestation on the schemes of policy in which his country is unfortunately engaged, and the warmth of an ingenuous mind has dictated adequate expressions, he certainly would not acknowledge the apparent want of patriotism to be his fault; and he has taken care to assure us in sober prose, that, 'although he prophesies curses, he fervently prays for blessings'.

As a specimen of the poem, we shall copy the first two strophes; and we shall be deceived if they do not excite a desire in the real lovers of poetry to peruse the whole:

[quotes ll. 1-37 (*PW*, i, 160-1; the variant reading)]

Some striking lines to a young man of fortune, who had abandoned himself to indolent melancholy, close this short publication.[1]

18. Unsigned notice, *Monthly Mirror*

April 1797, iii, 221

This ode, notwithstanding it is affected in some parts, and unintelligible in others, breathes the genuine spirit of poesy. The sentiments of Mr. Coleridge, with regard to public affairs, are already well known. He takes occasion to reprobate and lament the political events of the last year, and to augur very fatal consequences therefrom in the present. Such, however, as may disapprove of his sentiments, will receive considerable delight from his poetry, which is of the first order of merit.

---

[1] 'Addressed to a Young Man of Fortune' (*PW*, i, 157-8).

19. Unsigned review, *Critical Review*

July 1797, xx, 343-4

Mr. Coleridge, to whose former productions we have given impartial commendation, now attempts the flight of the Theban eagle, the great Pindar: but we are sorry to say that he too frequently mistakes bombast and obscurity, for sublimity. The poem certainly possesses some nervous lines; but in general we dare not applaud. We are displeased at finding such a number of affected phrases as a *bowed mind—skirts* of the departing year, which is rather a vulgar figure, notwithstanding the '*blanket*' of Shakespeare may be brought forward to keep him in countenance.

Foeman—lidless—recenter—bedim—strangeyed destruction—marge—warfield—frost-winds—uncoffin'd—cum multis aliis, are affectations. The fault of our lyric poets is to support trifling ideas with a pomposity of thought, and shunning that simplicity which should for ever accompany the lyric Muse. Pegasus is a fiery steed; and when spurred, as he seems to have been on the present occasion, he is apt to fling his rider in the dirt:—*sat verbum*. The above strictures are by no means meant to discourage, but to *reform*. Poetical Enthusiasm should take Reason for her companion. We shall present our readers with an extract from the Ode, to prove that our animadversions are not dictated by the spirit of severity:

[quotes ll. 1-0 (*PW*, i, 160-1)]

POEMS

Second Edition 1797

20. Unsigned review, *Critical Review*

July 1798, xxiii, 266-8

As no author can justly be offended at liberal criticism, Mr. Coleridge 'returns his acknowledgments to the different reviewers for the assistance which they have afforded him in detecting his poetic deficiencies'. Upon a revisal of his productions, he has omitted some with which he was less pleased, and has substituted new pieces for the discarded poems.

The dedication is one of the novelties of this edition. It is written in blank verse; and, while it does credit to the author, it also impresses a favourable idea of the brother to whom he offers the produce of his talents. The following passage is a part of it.

[quotes ll. 48-61 of 'To the Rev. George Coleridge' (*PW*, i, 175)]

The 'Ode on the Departing Year' (1796) was first published separately; and, when we reviewed it, we condemned the affectation and pomposity of the writer: but the piece, though it has since been altered, is still liable, in some degree, to the same imputations.

From the new sonnets we select that which is addressed to the river Otter, as it will gratify those who love to refer to the scenes of early enjoyment.

[quotes 'Sonnet: To the River Otter' (*PW*, i, 48)]

The 'Reflections on having left a Place of Retirement' evince a feeling heart. The comparison between the weeping eyes of a humane friend and the unmoved face of another equally benevolent, and the contrast between the latter and those who merely affect sympathy, are well drawn.

[quotes ll. 49-59 (*PW*, i, 107)]

In the invitation to Mr. Lloyd, many of the lines are stiff and affected; and a passage near the close of the piece may be misconstrued. When the poet says, 'she, whom I love, shall love thee', will not some readers be reminded of Cato's offer of his wife to his friend, even though such a thought could not enter into the head of the writer?

The lines 'On the Christening of a Friend's Child' are trifling; and some of the expressions and rhymes are ludicrous, though not intended to be so.

[the concluding remarks, devoted to the contributions of Charles Lloyd and Charles Lamb, are omitted]

FEARS IN SOLITUDE

1798

21. 'D. M. S.,' *Analytical Review*

December 1798, xxviii, 590-2

We took occasion to remark the very unequal merit of Mr. Coleridge's poetry in a former volume, (vol. xxiii, p. 610). The specimen at present before us partakes of this general character: perhaps we must impute it to his *fears*, that Mr. C. is unusually sparing of imagery; it should, however, be added, that what imagery he has given us is unusually free from extravagance. Our author attributes the approach of those evil days, which, at the time this poem was written, seemed to threaten us with immediate and terrible confusion, to the strong and retributive justice of all-avenging Providence for our sins and wickedness.

[quotes ll. 41-63 of 'Fears in Solitude' (*PW*, i, 258)]

Mr. C., in common with many others of the purest patriotism, has been slandered with the appellation of an enemy to his country. The following passage, we presume, will be sufficient to wipe away the injurious stigma, and show that an adherence to the measures of administration is not the necessary consequence of an ardent love for the constitution.

[quotes ll. 129-53 of 'Fears in Solitude' (*PW*, i, 260-1)]

'France, an Ode'; and 'Frost at Midnight': in the former of these odes, the poet reconciles to the strictest consistency, his former attachment to french politics, with his present abhorrence of them. He yet remains the ardent worshipper of liberty; it is France—the apostate France, who impiously profanes her holy altars, and deluges them with blood. The few lines, written at a midnight hour in winter—the inmates of his cottage all at rest—do great honour to the poet's feelings,

44

as the husband of an affectionate wife, and as the father of a cradled infant. May he long enjoy the life and the felicity of them both!

22. C. L. Moody, *Monthly Review*

May 1799, xxix, 43-7

This unsigned review is attributed to Moody (1753-1815), a clergyman (Nangle, 104).

Had poetry always been guided by reason and consecrated to morality, it would have escaped the contemptuous reproach with which it has been loaded both by antient and modern philosophers. Had this divine art been appropriated with due effect to divine subjects, wisdom could not have withholden her admiration. It is matter of serious regret, therefore, that its professors seem to have been solicitous rather to please by the coruscations of a wild frenzy, than by a mild and steady ray, reflected from the lamp of truth. Poets have been called *maniacs*; and their writings frequently too well justify the application of this degrading epithet. Too long has the modern copied the antient poet, in decorating folly with the elegant attractions of verse. It is time to enthrone reason on the summit of Parnassus; and to make poetry the strengthener as well as the enlivener of the intellect;—the energetic instructor as well as the enchanting amuser of mankind.

Mr. Coleridge seems solicitous to consecrate his lyre to truth, virtue, and humanity. He makes no use of an exploded though elegant mythology, nor does he seek fame by singing of what is called Glory. War he reprobates, and vice he deplores. Of his country he speaks with a patriotic enthusiasm, and he exhorts to virtue with a Christian's ardor. He tells, as he says,

> Most bitter truth without bitterness;

and though, as we learn from his own confession, he has been deemed the enemy of his country, yet, if we may judge from these specimens, no one can be more desirous of promoting all that is important to its security and felicity.

He begins, in the first poem, 'Fears in Solitude', with describing his rural retreat, suited by its stillness and beauty to the contemplative state of his mind: but scarcely has he indulged himself with the view of the pleasures which it yields, than his heart is painfully affected by a recollection of the horrid changes which the march of armies, and the conflicts of war, would introduce on 'his silent hills'. His fears realize an invasion to his imagination; and were the horrors of war brought into our island, he owns that it would be no more than our crimes deserve:

[quotes ll. 41-129 of 'Fears in Solitude' (*PW*, i, 258-60)]

There is so much truth, with so much serious, pointed, and suitable exhortation, in these lines, that we feel it a duty, more for the sake of the public than of the author, to solicit their perusal.

Mr. C.'s invocation to the Great Ruler of Empires to spare this guilty country, and his address to his countrymen to return to virtue and to unite in repelling an impious invading foe, are equally excellent. His description of the French is such as must animate Britons, were the enemy to attempt an invasion of us, to unite as one man in accomplishing what the poet requires:

[quotes ll. 140-53 of 'Fears in Solitude' (*PW*, i, 260-1)]

From bodings of misery to his country, he returns to the brighter prospects of hope. While, with the spirit of the Christian muse, he indulges,

> Love and the thoughts that yearn for human kind

he expresses a peculiar attachment to his native soil;

> There lives nor form nor feeling in my soul
> Unborrow'd from my country! O divine
> And beauteous island, thou hast been my sole
> And most magnificent temple, in the which
> I walk with awe, and sing my stately songs,
> Loving the God that made me!

In the Ode entitled 'France', the author, like a true Arcadian shepherd, adores

> The spirit of divinest liberty;

and he in course professes how much he wished, at the commencement of the revolution [*without bloodshed*] that France might break her fetters

and obtain freedom;—how he hung his head and wept at our interference;—and how, amid all the horrors and atrocities attending the
revolution, he cherished the hope that these black clouds, which darkened the horizon of French liberty, would disperse, and that France
would be happy in herself and just to surrounding states. These hopes
he now considers as vain. He invokes Freedom 'to forgive these idle
dreams', and particularly reprobates France for her conduct to
Switzerland.

> O France! that mockest heav'n, adult'rous, blind,
> And patriot only in pernicious toils!
> Are these thy boasts, champion of human kind:
> To mix with kings in the low lust of sway,
> Yell in the hunt, and share the murd'rous prey:
> T' insult the shrine of liberty with spoils
> From freemen torn; to tempt and to betray!

A beautiful address to Liberty constitutes the last stanza.

'Frost at Midnight' is a pleasing picture of virtue and content in a
cottage. The author's cradled babe seems to have inspired him, and
here he dedicates his infant to solitude and religious contemplation.

Much as we admire the poetic spirit of this bard, we are forced to
censure some of his lines as very prosaic. In his choice of words, also,
he is not always sufficiently nice. The last line

> As thou would'st fly for very eagerness,

is extremely flat, and gives the idea of an exhausted muse. Small
poems, like those before us, should be highly finished. Neither
coarseness nor negligence should be seen in cabinet pictures.

23. Unsigned review, *British Critic*

June 1799, xiii, 662-3

We by no means deny this writer the praise of sensibility and poetic taste, and, on this account, we the more seriously lament his absurd and preposterous prejudices against his country, and give a decided preference to the last of these compositions, as having no tincture of party. We would seriously ask Mr. Coleridge where it is that Englishmen have been so 'tyrannous' as to justify the exclamation,

> From east to west
> A groan of accusation pierces heaven,
> The wretched plead against us, multitudes,
> Countless and vehement, &c. &c.

Again he calls his countrymen,

> A selfish, lewd, effeminated race,
> Contemptuous of all honourable rule;
> Yet bartering freedom, and the poor man's life,
> For gold, as at a market.

A little further on;

> We have loved
> To swell the war-whoop, passionate for war.

Now all this we deny, and consider it as the hasty emotion of a young man, who writes without experience and knowledge of facts. All these bitter things he has told, he says, without bitterness—credat Judæus. In his Ode to France, he tells his readers, somewhat inaccurately, that when France 'said she would be free',

> *Bear witness for me*, how I hoped and feared,
> With what a joy my lofty gratulation,
> Unawed I sung *amid a slavish band*.

It is not apparent who is to bear witness for the poet, and we are sorry that one who sings so well should be obliged *to sing amid a slavish band*. We should like to know *where this slavish band* existed. There

48

are none of that description in this country. The Poem called 'Frost at Midnight', not being defaced by any of these absurdities, is entitled to much praise. A few affectations of phraseology, are atoned for by much expressive tenderness, and will be avoided by the author's more mature judgment.

24. Unsigned review, *Critical Review*

August 1799, xxvi, 472–5

A poem by Mr. Coleridge must attract the attention of all who are capable of understanding the beauties of poetry. The present publication has all the characteristic excellencies of his former ones. The opinions expressed are not indeed the same: without being a ministerialist, Mr. Coleridge has become an alarmist. He pictures the horrors of invasion, and joins the war-whoop against what he calls

> an impious foe,
> Impious and false, a light yet cruel race,
> That laugh away all virtue, mingling mirth
> With deeds of murder.

The ode entitled 'France' is in the same strain; and it has even been copied into a miscellaneous volume under the title of 'The Recantation'.

But those who conceive that Mr. Coleridge has, in these poems, recanted his former principles, should consider the general tenor of them. The following passage surely is not written in conformity with the fashionable opinions of the day.

[quotes ll. 43-129 of 'Fears in Solitude' (*PW*, i, 258-61)]

The conclusion of the ode is very ridiculous.

> Yes! while I stood and gaz'd, my temples bare,
> And shot my being thro' earth, sea, and air,
> Possessing all things with intensest love,
> O Liberty, my spirit felt thee there!

What does Mr. Coleridge mean by liberty in this passage? or what connexion has it with the subject of civil freedom?

The concluding poem is very beautiful; but the lines respecting the film occupy too great a part of it. The first poem strikes us as the best; the passage we have quoted from it is admirable; and we could have given many of equal beauty.

LYRICAL BALLADS

1798

Published anonymously. Most of the poems in the collection were by Wordsworth; Coleridge's contributions to the first edition were 'The Rime of the Ancient Mariner', 'The Nightingale', 'The Dungeon', and 'The Foster-Mother's Tale'.

---

25. From an unsigned review, *Analytical Review*

December 1798, xxviii, 583-5

'It is the honourable characteristic of poetry', says the author of these ballads, in the advertisement which is prefixed to them, 'that its materials, are to be found in every subject which can interest the human mind. The evidence of this fact is to be sought, not in the writings of critics, but in those of poets themselves'.

'The majority of the following poems are to be considered as experiments. They were written chiefly with a view to ascertain how far the language of conversation in the middle and lower classes of society is adapted to the purposes of poetic pleasure. Readers accustomed to the gaudiness and inane phraseology of many modern writers, if they persist in reading this book to its conclusion, will perhaps frequently have to struggle with feelings of strangeness and awkwardness: they will look round for poetry, and will be induced to enquire by what species of courtesy these attempts can be permitted to assume that title. It is desirable that such readers, for their own sakes, should not suffer the solitary word poetry, a word of very disputed meaning, to stand in the way of their gratification; but that, while they are perusing this book, they should ask themselves if it contains a natural delineation of human passions, human characters, and human incidents; and if the answer be favorable to the author's wishes, that they should consent to be pleased in spite of that most dreadful enemy to our pleasures, our own pre-established codes of decision'.

There is something sensible in these remarks, and they certainly serve as a very pertinent introduction to the studied simplicity, which pervades many of the poems. The 'Rime of the ancyent Marinere', a ballad in seven parts, is written professedly in imitation of the style as well as of the spirit of the ancient poets. We are not pleased with it; in our opinion it has more of the extravagance of a mad german poet, than of the simplicity of our ancient ballad writers.

Some of our young rhymesters and blank-verse-men, highly delighted with the delicacy of their own moral feelings, affect to look down on every thing human with an eye of pity. To them the face of nature is eternally shaded with a funereal gloom, and they are never happy but when their affections, to use the words of Sterne, are fixed upon some melancholy cypress. We are happy to conjecture, from some passages in these poems, that the author of them classes not with these sable songsters; in his ode to the nightingale he says,

[quotes ll. 7-23 of 'The Nightingale' (*PW*, i, 264-5)]

Among the poems which particularly pleased us from their character either of simplicity or tenderness, or both, are, that from which we have made the preceding extract, 'The Thorn', 'The Mad Mother', 'The Idiot Boy', and that with which we shall present our readers, the tale of 'Goody Blake and Harry Gill'. . . .

26. Robert Southey, *Critical Review*

October 1798, xxiv, 197-204

This unsigned review has been attributed to Robert Southey
(Jack Simmons, *Southey*, London 1945, 78). Southey (1774-1843)
was Coleridge's brother-in-law, and was aware of the identities
of the authors.
The review from which the following extracts are taken, begins
by referring to the claim of the 'advertisement' to *Lyrical Ballads*
that the majority of the poems in the collection are to be regarded
as experiments, and goes on to heap scorn on Wordsworth's
'The Idiot Boy' and 'The Thorn'.

In a very different style of poetry, is the 'Rime of the Ancyent Marinere'; a ballad (says the advertisement) 'professedly written in imitation of the *style*, as well as of the spirit of the elder poets'. We are tolerably conversant with the early English poets; and can discover no resemblance whatever, except in antiquated spelling and a few obsolete
words. This piece appears to us perfectly original in style as well as in
story. Many of the stanzas are laboriously beautiful; but in connection
they are absurd or unintelligible. Our readers may exercise their
ingenuity in attempting to unriddle what follows.

[quotes ll. 309-30 (*PW*, i, 199)]

We do not sufficiently understand the story to analyse it. It is a
Dutch attempt at German sublimity. Genius has here been employed
in producing a poem of little merit.

With pleasure we turn to the serious pieces, the better part of the
volume. 'The Foster-Mother's Tale' is in the best style of dramatic
narrative. 'The Dungeon', and the 'Lines upon the Yew-tree Seat', are
beautiful.

[praises 'The Tale of the Female Vagrant' and 'Lines Written near
Tintern Abbey', but is displeased with 'most of the ballads']

The 'experiment', we think, has failed, not because the language of conversation is little adapted to 'the purposes of poetic pleasure', but because it has been tried upon uninteresting subjects. Yet every piece discovers genius; and, ill as the author has frequently employed his talents, they certainly rank him with the best of living poets.

27. Charles Burney, *Monthly Review*

June 1799, xxix, 202-10

This unsigned review has been attributed to Charles Burney, (Aubrey Hawkins, 'Some Writers on *The Monthly Review*', *The Review of English Studies*, vii, 1931, 180). Burney (1726-1814), the music historian, had been a friend of Johnson's.

The author of these ingenious compositions presents the major part of them to the public as *experiments*; since they were written, as he informs us in the *advertisement* prefixed, 'chiefly with a view to ascertain how far the language of conversation in the middle and lower classes of society is adapted to the purposes of poetic pleasure'.

Though we have been extremely entertained with the fancy, the facility, and (in general) the sentiments, of these pieces, we cannot regard them as *poetry*, of a class to be cultivated at the expence of a higher species of versification, unknown in our language at the time when our elder writers, whom this author condescends to imitate, wrote their ballads. Would it not be degrading poetry, as well as the English language, to go back to the barbarous and uncouth numbers of Chaucer? Suppose, instead of modernizing the old bard, that the sweet and polished measures, on lofty subjects, of Dryden, Pope, and Gray, were to be transmuted into the dialect and versification of the XIVth century? Should we be gainers by the retrogradation? *Rust* is a necessary quality to a counterfeit old medal: but, to give artificial rust to modern poetry, in order to render it similar to that of three or four hundred years ago, can have no better title to merit and admiration than may be claimed by any ingenious forgery. None but savages have submitted to eat acorns after corn was found. We will allow that the author before us has the art of cooking his acorns well, and that he makes a very palatable dish of them for *jours maigres*: but, for festivals and *gala* days,

Multos castra juvant, & lituo tubae
Permistus sonitus.[1]

[1] 'Many delight in the camp, in the sounds of trumpets mixed with the clarion . . .' (Horace, *Odes*, i, 23-4).

55

We have had pleasure in reading the *reliques of antient poetry*, because it was antient; and because we were surprised to find so many beautiful thoughts in the rude numbers of barbarous times. These reasons will not apply to *imitations* of antique versification. We will not, however, dispute any longer about names; the author shall style his rustic delineations of low-life, 'poetry', if he pleases, on the same principle on which Butler is called a poet, and Teniers a painter: but are the doggrel verses of the one equal to the sublime numbers of a Milton, or are the Dutch boors of the other to be compared with the angels of Raphael or Guido? When we confess that our author has had the art of pleasing and interesting in no common way by his natural delineation of human passions, human characters, and human incidents, we must add that these effects were not produced by the *poetry*—we have been as much affected by pictures of misery and unmerited distress, in *prose*. The elevation of soul, when it is lifted into the higher regions of imagination, affords us a delight of a different kind from the sensation which is produced by the detail of common incidents. For this fact, we have better authority than is to be found in the writings of most critics: we have it in a poet himself, whose award was never (till now) disputed:

> The poet's eye, in a fine frenzy rolling,
> Doth glance from heaven to earth, from earth to heav'n;
> And, as imagination bodies forth
> The forms of things unknown, the poet's pen
> Turns them to shape, and gives to aiery nothing
> A local habitation and a name.
>
> SHAKESPEARE

Having said thus much on the *genus*, we now come more particularly to the *species*.

The author's first piece, the 'Rime of the ancyent Marinere', in imitation of the *style* as well as of the spirit of the elder poets, is the strangest story of a cock and a bull that we ever saw on paper: yet, though it seems a rhapsody of unintelligible wildness and incoherence, (of which we do not perceive the drift, unless the joke lies in depriving the wedding guest of his share of the feast) there are in it poetical touches of an exquisite kind.

'The Dramatic Fragment', if it intends anything, seems meant to throw disgrace on the savage liberty preached by some modern *philosophes*. . . . [1]

[1] 'The Foster-Mother's Tale'.

... 'The Nightingale' sings a strain of true and beautiful poetry; Miltonic, yet original; reflective, and interesting, in an uncommon degree.

[quotes the poem (*PW*, i, 264-7)]

... 'The Dungeon'. Here candour and tenderness for criminals seem pushed to excess. Have not jails been built on the humane Mr. Howard's plan, which have almost ruined some counties, and which look more like palaces than habitations for the perpetrators of crimes?[1] Yet, have fewer crimes been committed in consequence of the erection of those magnificent structures, at an expence which would have maintained many in innocence and comfort out of a jail, if they have been driven to theft by want? ...

So much genius and originality are discovered in this publication, that we wish to see another from the same hand, written on more elevated subjects and in a more cheerful disposition.

28. From an unsigned review, *British Critic*

October 1799, xiv, 364-5

This is the only review of *Lyrical Ballads* in which Coleridge is named as author.

... The Poem of 'The ancyent Marinere', with which the collection opens, has many excellencies, and many faults; the beginning and the end are striking and well-conducted; but the intermediate part is too long, and has, in some places, a kind of confusion of images, which

---

[1] John Howard (?1726-1790), philanthropist and prison reformer.

loses all effect, from not being quite intelligible. The author, who is confidently said to be Mr. Coleridge, is not correctly versed in the old language, which he undertakes to employ. 'Noises of a *swound*', and 'broad as a *weft*', are both nonsensical; but the ancient style is so well imitated, while the antiquated words are so very few, that the latter might with advantage be entirely removed without any detriment to the effect of the Poem. The opening of the Poem is admirably calculated to arrest the reader's attention, by the well-imagined idea of the Wedding Guest, who is held to hear the tale, in spite of his efforts to escape. The beginning of the second canto, or fit, has much merit, if we except the very unwarrantable comparison of the Sun to that which no man can conceive: 'like God's own head', a simile which makes a reader shudder; not with poetic feeling, but with religious disapprobation. The following passage is eminently good.

[quotes ll. 103-22 (*PW*, i, 190-1)]

The conclusion, as we remarked before, is very good, particularly the idea that the Marinere has periodical fits of agony, which oblige him to relate his marvellous adventure; and this,

> I pass, like night, from land to land,
> I have strange power of speech;
> The moment that his face I see,
> I know the man that must hear me;
> To him my tale I teach.

Whether the remaining poems of the volume are by Mr. Coleridge, we have not been informed; but they seem to proceed from the same mind; and in the Advertisement, the writer speaks of himself as of a single person accountable for the whole. It is therefore reasonable to conclude, that this is the fact. They all have merit, and many among them a very high rank of merit, which our feelings respecting some parts of the supposed author's character do not authorize or incline us to deny. The Poem on the Nightingale, which is there styled 'a conversational Poem', is very good; but we do not perceive it to be more conversational than Cowper's 'Task', which is the best poem in that style that our language possesses. . . .

The purchasers of this little volume will find that, after all we have said, there are poems, and passages of poems, which we have been obliged to pass over, that well deserve attention and commendation; nor does there appear any offensive mixture of enmity to present institutions, except in one or two instances, which are so unobtrusive as hardly to deserve notice.

29. Unsigned notice, *Anti-Jacobin*

April 1800, v, 334

334 is a misprint for 434.

This is a volume of a very different description from the above.[1] It has genius, taste, elegance, wit, and imagery of the most beautiful kind. 'The ancyent Marinere' is an admirable 'imitation, of the style as well as of the spirit of the elder poets'. 'The foster Mothers Tale' is pathetic, and pleasing in the extreme—'Simon Lee the old Huntsman'—'The idiot Boy', and the Tale of 'Goody Blake, and Harry Gill' are all beautiful in their kind; indeed the whole volume convinces us that the author possesses a mind at once classic and accomplished, and we, with pleasure, recommend it to the notice of our readers as a production of no ordinary merit.

---

[1] The preceding review ridicules R. J. Thorne's *Lodon and Miranda* (1799).

30. Private opinions

Charles Lamb (1775-1834), essayist and intimate of the Coleridge circle—extract from a letter written to Robert Southey, 8 November 1798: 'If you wrote that review in "Crit. Rev." [No. 26], I am sorry you are so sparing of praise to the "Ancient Marinere";—so far from calling it, as you do, with some wit, but more severity, "A Dutch Attempt," &c., I call it a right English attempt, and a successful one, to dethrone German sublimity. You have selected a passage fertile in unmeaning miracles, but have passed by fifty passages as miraculous as the miracles they celebrate. I never felt so deeply the pathetic as in that part,

> A spring of love gush'd from my heart,
> And I bless'd them unaware—

It stung me into high pleasure through sufferings' (*The Letters of Charles and Mary Lamb*, ed. E. V. Lucas, London 1935, i, 136).

Robert Southey (see No. 26)—extract from a letter written on 17 December 1798: 'The *Lyrical Ballads* are by Coleridge and Wordsworth. The Night[ing]ale, the Dungeon, the Foster Mothers Tale, and the long ballad of the Old Mariner are all that were written by Coleridge. The ballad I think nonsense, the nightingale tolerable'. (*New Letters of Robert Southey*, ed. Kenneth Curry, New York and London 1965, i, 176-7).

Francis Jeffrey (1773-1850), later to become the hostile editor of the *Edinburgh Review* (see No. 76)—extract from a letter written on 21 March 1799: '. . . I have been enchanted with a little volume of poems, lately published, called *Lyrical Ballads*, and without any author's name. In the "Rime of the Ancient Marinere", with which it begins, there is more true poetical horror and more new images than in all the German ballads and tragedies, that have been holding our hair on end for these last three years. I take this to be some of Coleridge's doings, though I am no infallible discoverer of styles' (*Memorials of the Life and Writings of the Rev. Robert Morehead, D.D.*, ed. Charles Morehead, Edinburgh 1875, 102).

Sara Coleridge (1770-1845), Coleridge's wife—extract from a letter written in March, 1799: 'The Lyrical Ballads are laughed at and disliked by all with very few excepted' (*Minnow among Tritons*, ed. Stephen Potter, London 1934, 4).

WALLENSTEIN

1800

As this was the first English translation of Schiller's *Die Piccolomini* and *Wallensteins Tod*, the reviewers naturally devoted more of their space to the quality of the plays than to the merits of the translation.

---

31. John Ferriar, *Monthly Review*

October 1800, xxxiii, 127-31

This unsigned review is attributed to Ferriar (1761-1815), a physician and versifier (Nangle, 199).

The story of the aspiring Duke of Friedland, whose family name was Walstein, or Wallenstein, and who was the fortunate opponent of Gustavus Adolphus, has long been familiar to men of historical knowledge. Lately, it has been introduced to general readers, in a Concise View of the Thirty-years'-war, published by Schiller. In Germany, the plot will naturally be interesting, as the poet has adhered pretty closely to the facts: but in this country it is not calculated to excite much attention, especially under the disadvantage of the languid translation through which it is offered to our view.

Mr. Coleridge, indeed, has spoken very modestly respecting the merits of his version, which he professes to have rendered as literal as the idioms of the two languages would permit. Perhaps, however, a judicious alteration of Schiller's work would have been more acceptable to readers of good taste. The division of the action into two plays renders the plot insufferably tedious; and, even with the engrafted love-intrigue, the interest flattens extremely before the catastrophe. To compensate for this defect, however, the pieces are more regular than many other productions of the German theatre; and they are at least free from absurdity. Wallenstein's belief in astrology forms a part of both tragedies: but this error was almost universal in that age.

It is remarked by Mr. Coleridge, that these plays may be said to bear the same relation to the *Robbers* and the *Cabal and Love* of Schiller, with that which the historical plays of Shakespeare bear to his *Lear* and *Othello*. Yet, in the most meagre of Shakespeare's *Histories*, we occasionally meet with passages of uncommon beauty, which imprint themselves indelibly on our minds; and we have not observed any sentiments or expressions of this kind in the tragedies before us.

That we may do justice to the translator, we shall extract part of two scenes, which he has pointed out as singularly deserving of praise. First, from the first drama:

[quotes ll. 80-160 of Act I, Scene iv, 'The Piccolomini' (*PW*, ii, 613-15)]

The other passages are taken from the last act of the second play, immediately before the murder of Wallenstein:

[quotes ll. 21-68 of Act V, Scene i, 'The Death of Wallenstein' (*PW*, ii, 794-6)]

We own that the comparison of the crescent to a sickle does not convey a very delightful idea to our mind: nor do the expressions in the remainder of the sentence assimilate with this metaphor.[1]

We have allowed an unusual length to this article, because we think that Mr. Coleridge is by far the most rational partizan of the German theatre whose labours have come under our notice; and because we are glad to see any thing void of absurdity and extravagance from an author whose bold genius has so completely defied all rules.

[1] The image complained of is a rendering of Schiller's '*die Mondessichel*'. Coleridge's admiration of the passage in a learned footnote may have provoked the reviewer.

32. From an unsigned review, *Critical Review*

October 1800, xxx, 175–85

The name of Schiller will no doubt awaken the attention of the admirers of impassioned writing; and many sublime effusions from Mr. Coleridge's own pen must prepare our readers to expect from his competency an interesting translation of these announced dramas of the German Shakespeare. On a perusal of the first of them, our feelings, however, sanctioned the prediction of Mr. Coleridge, as thus expressed in his preface to *The Death of Wallenstein*.

The admirers of Schiller, who have abstracted their idea of that author from the Robbers, and the Cabal and Love, plays in which the main interest is produced by the excitement of curiosity, and in which the curiosity is excited by terrible and extraordinary incident, will not have perused without some portion of disappointment the dramas which it has been my employment to translate. . . .

From an attentive examination of these dramas with the original, we have no hesitation in affirming that Mr. Coleridge's translation happily unites, for the most part, the qualities of fidelity and elegance. In many pages, however, he exhibits a surprising debility, becomes extremely prosaic, and degenerates into the most culpable carelessness. Amidst a variety of faulty passages, we will content ourselves with selecting the following.

> *This walk which you have ta'en me* thro' the camp
> Strikes my hopes prostrate.

> What! and not warn him *either what bad hands*
> His lot has plac'd him in?

> *They know about* the emperor's requisitions,
> And are tumultuous.

> How intend you
> *To manage with the generals* at the banquet?

Mr. Coleridge is the founder of a distinct school in poetry. He is deservedly regarded with much deference by many of his disciples: but the elevation he has attained on the Aönian mount imposes on him an obligation to study the art of correctness:

64

Decipit exemplar vitiis imitabile:[1]

and it were well if Mr. Coleridge would teach his pupils, both by
precept and example, the art of blotting—would instruct them that
hasty effusions require the file, that carelessness is not ease, and that
obscurity in no instance constitutes the true sublime.

33. From an unsigned review, *British Critic*

November 1801, xviii, 542-5

'May the wretch', said Horace, 'who shall murder his aged father, eat
garlic for his punishment!'—'May the critic,' we may justly exclaim,
'for his highest offences, be doomed to review a German historical
play!' This penance we have, though 'with difficulty and labour
hard', at length performed; the story of Wallenstein, though dramatized
into a large octavo volume, may, as to its leading circumstances, be
related in few words.

[a summary of the plot follows]

For the tediousness of most of the scenes and speeches in the dramas,
the translator, Mr. Coleridge, makes the best apology in his power,
comparing them to Shakespeare's three historical plays of Henry the
Sixth. But, not to mention that a very small part of those plays is supposed, by the best critics, to have been the work of Shakespeare, is not
this comparison to the *worst* of our bard's historical dramas, somewhat
like that of the actor, who assured himself of success, 'because he was
taller than Garrick, and had a better voice than Mossop'?[2] Yet the three
parts of Henry the Sixth are full of bustle and incident; so that they
form, in that respect, a perfect contrast to the two dramas of Wallenstein. We admit, however, the merit of those passages which are

---

[1] 'A pattern with imitable faults can lead one astray' (Horace, *Epistles*, i, 19, 17).
[2] The point being that Garrick was short and that Henry Mossop (1729?-
1774?) had a poor voice.

pointed out by the translator, and could cite some others which exhibit proofs of genius. The best scene, or at least the most dramatic and interesting, is, in our opinion, the first in the fifth act of the second play; but it is too long to transcribe here. We will, as a specimen, extract another favourite passage with the translator, the description given of Thekla, of the astrological tower, in the first drama.

[quotes ll. 82-138 of Act II, Scene iv, 'The Piccolomini' (*PW*, ii, 647-9)]

Not having the original with which to compare it, we cannot give any opinion respecting the fidelity of the translation: as an English composition, it does not want spirit and energy; but is frequently faulty in rhythm, and devoid of harmony and elegance.

POEMS

Third Edition 1803

---

34. Unsigned review, *Annual Review*

1803, ii, 556

The character of Mr. Coleridge, as a poet, is so well known, and his merit so fully acknowledged, that nothing more can be expected of us on announcing the third edition of his poems, than a few remarks suggested by comparison with the last. The diminished bulk of the volume, caused by the omission of the works of Messrs. Lloyd and Lamb, instantly excited our warmest approbation, particularly as we were inclined to consider it as an evidence of the ripened taste and improved discernment of our author. In his own productions we remarked a few highly judicious alterations, with some others which we could not equally approve—on the whole we must suggest, that he has still to learn 'the art to blot'. He omits scarce any thing, and so far from sinking, his juvenile productions appear to rise in his esteem; several of these, which in the last edition were thrown into a supplement, with a kind of confession of their inferiority, now boldly thrust themselves into the body of the volume, without apology and without abbreviation.

The pieces now first offered to the public are few and short, but such as afford examples of the best and worst manner of this striking and peculiar writer. Novel and picturesque personification, sometimes almost expanding into allegory, forms perhaps the most prominent and most beautiful feature of the highly figurative style of Mr. Coleridge, but never did he display this characteristic with more exquisite grace than in the following lines:

> Ah, fair delights! that o'er my soul
> On Mem'ry's wing, like shadows, fly!

67

Ah, flowers! which Joy from Eden stole
While Innocence stood smiling by!
'Absence, a Farewell Ode'

The political sentiment of the following sonnet is now obsolete, but the animated simile by which it is ushered in, is worthy of a longer date.

As when far off the warbled strains are heard
That soar on Morning's wing the vales among,
Within his cage th' imprison'd matin bird
Swells the full chorus with a generous song:
He bathes no pinion in the dewy light,
No father's joy, no lover's bliss he shares,
Yet still the rising radiance cheers his sight—
His fellows' freedom soothes the captive's cares!
Thou, Fayette! who didst wake with startling voice
Life's better sun from that long wintry night,
Thus in thy country's triumphs shalt rejoice
And mock with raptures high the dungeon's might:
For lo! the morning struggles into day,
And slavery's spectres shriek and vanish from the ray!

Some other political sonnets, which are far from possessing equal poetical merit, and are disgraced by much coarse vehemence of thought and expression, surely ought not now to have been brought forward for the first time.

In the complaint of Ninathoma, and another metrical imitation of Ossian, we cannot discern the slightest trace of Mr. Coleridge's hand, though we clearly recognise that of a correct and cultivated poet; these proofs of versatility of talent are pleasing, and show that it is perfectly at the option of this favoured genius, to dance along the fairy paths of elegance, or soar into the loftiest regions of sublimity.

Among the poets of the present day Mr. Coleridge holds a distinguished place. For energy of thought, splendour of diction, and
command of language, he is not often equalled. His versification also
is both polished and animated. In the present edition of his works some
pieces which were admitted into the former are excluded, and their
place is filled by some of his early productions. The poems of Lloyd
and Lamb are now left out.

36(a). From an unsigned lampoon, 'The Bards of the Lake', *Satirist*

December, 1809, v, 550-2

... another bard started from his seat, and with a violent bound dashed into the middle of the circle. He seemed to labour with all the inspiration of poetry, and to be agitated by some mighty thoughts. For some time he spoke not; and meanwhile my friend took occasion to inform me, that this bard had published some odes which were supposed to be very fine, but they were too sublime for vulgar comprehension. He had also written an elegy to an ass, which was more level to its subject, but it was on the ode he prided himself. He had formerly, he said, been of Cambridge, but enlisted as a private of dragoons: he had often been known to harangue his comrades on themes of liberty, and had endeavoured to inspire them with the free spirit of the citizens of the ancient republics, to which he was enthusiastically devoted. His learning, which was various and classical, had astonished his officers, and on his real circumstances and quality being in consequence discovered, he had quitted the service. He still however, dreams of nothing but liberty, continued my friend, and talks of nothing but freedom. Not long ago, he read lectures on poetry at a fashionable institution, but, whether—At that instant the bard, without announcing his subject, which, however, it was afterwards agreed to entitle 'The Breeches', burst forth with the utmost vehemence into the following short ode.

BREECHES
AN ODE

On some high mountain's rugged top sublime,
   Where mortal tyrant never trod,
Through all the rounds of time,
   Free as the unpolluted clod

Fain would I sit *bare breech'd!* most fitly so,
That the free wind might blow.

It's welcome rude, changing the native hue
Of those unclothed parts from red to blue,
    And every rainbow tint and dye,
    Making sweet variety.
I love such honest freedom, better far
Than the false sunshine of the court, or smile
    Of fickle beauty earn'd by slavish suit,
    Keeping the free thought mute,
In bondage vile
As slaves of Turkey are.

    Breeches are masks, which none would wear,
    If all were honest, all were fair!
    Naked truth needs no disguise,
    Falsehood then in breeches lies,
Therefore I love them not;
But him most honest hold, who's most a *sans culotte*.

    When thus bare-breech'd on high,
Upon the mountain's top 'mid purer air,
    Thinking sublimer thoughts I lie,
Ask you, what I do there?
Why, I would say, and I would sing
    Whate'er to sing or say I list,
    Till that 'the winds in wonder whist'
Listen'd to my minstrelsing.
    And when ended was my strain,—
    I'd walk down again![1]

I was no less delighted with this inimitable production itself than
with the effect it seemed to have on those to whom it was immediately
addressed. The countenances of the female part of the groupe were lit
up with a wonderful expression of intelligence and animation: and so
powerfully did it seem to work on the minstrel brotherhood, that from
some preparatory motions, I began to suspect that a general denudation
was about to take place; but this inclination was repressed by the
ladies. It was some time before the violent sensations excited by the
Breeches Ode had subsided, so that I had sufficient time to complete
my copy of this also, before another bard arose.

[1] This ode bears some resemblance to a satirical sonnet which Coleridge had
contributed to the *Monthly Magazine* in November over the pseudonym
Nehemiah Higginbottom (*PW*, i, 211).

36(b). From an unsigned article, *Edinburgh Annual Register for 1808*

1810, i, Part 2, 427-8

We are, in some degree, uncertain whether we ought to view Coleridge as subject to our critical jurisdiction, at least under this department. He seems to have totally abandoned poetry for the mists of political metaphysics—mists which, we fear, the copious eloquence showered from his cloudy tabernacle will rather increase than dispel. With extensive learning, an unbounded vigour of imagination, and the most ready command of expression both in verse and prose—advantages which none of his predecessors enjoy in a greater, if any possess them in an equal degree; this author has been uniformly deficient in the perseverance and the sound sense which were necessary to turn his exquisite talents to their proper use. He has only produced in a complete state one or two small pieces, and every thing else, begun on a larger scale, has been flung aside and left unfinished. This is not all: although commanding the most beautiful poetical language, he has every now and then thought fit to exchange it for the gratuitous pleasure of introducing whole stanzas of quaint and vulgar doggrel. These are the passages which render learning useless, and eloquence absurd; which make fools laugh, and malignant critics 'dance and leap', but which excite, in readers of taste, grief and astonishment, as evidence of talents misapplied, and genius furnishing arms against itself to low-minded envy. To Mr. Coleridge we owe some fragments of the most sublime blank verse, and some lyric passages of a soft and tender nature, we believe unequalled. The verses addressed to 'The Memory of a Deceased Friend', and those called 'An Introduction to the Tale of the Dark Ladie', are sufficient proofs of our assertion. But these are short or unfinished performances, and others which we could quote from the same author are of a nature so wild, so unrestrained by any rules either in the conception or in the composition; forming such a mixture of the terrible with the disgusting, of the tender with the ludicrous, and of moral feeling with metaphysical sophistry, that we can hardly suppose the author who threw forth such crude effusions is serious in obtaining a rank among the poets of his country, nor do we feel at liberty to press upon him a seat of honour, which, from his conduct, he would seem to hold in no esteem.

THE FRIEND

1809-10

37. Serial Letter, *Monthly Mirror*

June-September 1810, viii, 26-31, 98-105, 186

This unsigned serial letter was entitled 'Commentary on Coleridge's Three Graves'. Only the third and fourth parts of the poem appeared in *The Friend*.

Mr. Editor,
There is now in course of publication, by Mr. Coleridge, a periodical paper, called *The Friend*; and oh! Mr. Editor, there is in that *Friend* a poem called 'The Three Graves', a piece of such exquisite simplicity, that I have never once ceased to admire it, from the twenty-first day of September, 1809, the day of its publication, till now, the seventeenth day of April, 1810, '*dinners and suppers and sleeping hours excluded*'. My sole ambition in this world is to elucidate its beauties. I would sooner be the author of it, as Scaliger says of an ode in Horace, than be King of Arragon; but as that I cannot be, the next desire of my soul is to be its commentator; commentator, I do not mean, to render it intelligible, for it is already so *to the meanest capacity*; but commentator, to enlarge upon its beauties, to expatiate on its charms, to '*grow wanton in its praise*'. Mr. Coleridge introduces his poem thus:

As I wish to commence the important subject of the *principles* of political justice with a separate number of the *Friend*, and shall at the same time comply with the wishes communicated to me by one of my *female* readers, who writes as the representative of many others, I shall conclude this number with the following fragment, or the third and fourth parts of a tale consisting of six.

Let us pause here for a moment, and reflect how great an obligation we owe to this 'lady'. '*Name! name!*' we cry out with the House of Commons. 'The representative of many others!' Do Mr. Coleridge's female readers then form themselves into a body, and elect a representative? Had he any female readers till he wrote 'The Three Graves'? But why do I ask these questions? Have we not the blessed assurance that 'The Three Graves' consists of *six parts*, which, as my little boy, who has just wiped his slate, correctly observes, is exactly two parts to each grave? And do we 'not live in hope' of seeing the four parts, which are yet unpublished? As Lady Anne says, 'all men I hope live so'. Mr. Coleridge goes on to promise us:

The *two last* parts may be given hereafter, if the present shall appear to have afforded pleasure, and to have answered the purpose of a relief and amusement to my readers.

I will do my best to make it appear that it has afforded the greatest amusement, and the most agreeable relief from the pages of *The Friend*. 'For this relief much thanks'.

The story, as it is contained in the first and second parts is as follows: Edward, a young farmer, meets, at the house of Ellen, her bosom friend, Mary, and commences an acquaintance which ended in a mutual attachment. With her consent, and by the advice of their common friend, Ellen, he announces his hopes and intentions to Mary's mother, a widow-*woman*, [not a man] bordering on her fortieth year, and from constant health, the possession of a competent property, and from having had no other children but Mary and another daughter (the father died in their infancy), retaining, for the greater part, her personal attractions and comeliness of appearance; but a woman of low education and violent temper. The answer, which she at once returned to Edward's application was remarkable—'Well, Edward! you are a handsome young fellow: and you shall have my daughter.' From this time all their wooing passed under the mother's eyes; and, in fine, she became herself enamoured of her future son-in-law, and practised every art, both of endearment and of calumny, to transfer his affections from her daughter to herself. (The outlines of the tale are positive facts, and of no very distant date, though the author has purposely altered the names, and the scene of action, as well as invented the characters of the parties, and the detail of the incidents.) Edward, however, though perplexed by her strange detractions from her daughter's good qualities, yet, in the innocence of his own heart, still mistaking [mistook] her increasing fondness for motherly affection; she, at length, overcome by her miserable passion, after much abuse of Mary's temper, and moral tendencies, exclaimed with violent emotion: 'Oh Edward! indeed, indeed, she is not fit for you; she has not a heart to love you as you deserve. It is I that love you! Marry me, Edward! and I will settle all my property on you'. The lover's eyes were now opened; and thus taken by surprise, whether from the effect of the horror which he felt, acting as it were hysterically on his nervous system, or that at the first moment he lost the sense of the guilt of the proposal in the feeling of its strangeness and absurdity, he flung her from him, and burst into a fit of laughter. Irritated by this almost to frenzy, the woman fell on her knees, and in a loud voice, that approached to a scream, she prayed for a curse both on him and on her own child. Mary happened to be in the room directly above them, heard Edward's laugh, and her mother's blasphemous prayer, and fainted away. He hearing the fall, ran up stairs, and taking her in his arms, carried her off to Ellen's home; and, after some fruitless attempts on her part, towards a reconciliation with her mother, she was married to him. And here the third part of the tale begins. . . .

The tale is supposed to be narrated by an old sexton, in a country church-yard, to a traveller, whose *curiosity* had been awakened by the appearance of *three graves, close by each other, to two only of which there were grave-stones.* [Enough to waken the curiosity of the most indifferent!] On the first of these was the name and dates as usual: on the second no name, but only a date, and the words, 'the mercy of God is infinite'.

The language was *intended* to be dramatic, that is, *suited to the narrator*, and the metre to correspond to the homeliness of the diction; and for this reason I here present it not as the fragment of a *poem*, but of a tale in the common ballad metre.

And how, Mr. Editor, do your readers think this tale begins? Why, *secundum artem*, by marking the time of the year. The language is to be *dramatic*, which means, as Mr. Coleridge rightly informs us, *suited to the narrator*: and who is the narrator? a sexton: and by whom does a sexton date and swear? why, by his parson. What then can be so natural as for our sexton to commence his tale thus?

> The grapes upon the vicar's wall
>   Were ripe as they could be;
> And yellow leaves in sun and wind,
>   Were falling from the tree.
> On the hedge-elms, in the narrow lane,
>   Still swang the spikes of corn.

This is as much as to say it was autumn; but can anything be more beautiful than the idea of the parson's grapes being

> Ripe as they could be?

I think, indeed, this line would have been more 'dramatic, that is, suited to the narrator', if it had run,

> Were ripe as *ripe* could be.

But nothing is wanting to the perfection of the line,

And yellow leaves in sun and wind,

for it at once shews us, that it is the united influence of the sun and the wind, which forces the leaves to fall from trees, a circumstance, of which many persons may not have been before aware. The sun renders the leaves brittle, and the wind breaks them from the tree. I say nothing about the idea of the 'spikes of corn still swinging upon the hedge-elms of a narrow lane', for that I do not think equally beautiful.

And now, the sexton having fixed the time of year, breaks out, in the most artless manner,

> Dear Lord! it seems but yesterday;

and then presuming it probable that the traveller would ask him, what 'seemed but yesterday', good-naturedly adds,

> Young Edward's marriage-morn.

The sexton now descends to particulars:

> Up through that wood, behind the church,
> There leads from Edward's door
> A mossy track, all over bough'd,
> For half a mile or more.

I should have preferred '*to* Edward's door', considering the situation of the speaker; but that is of little consequence.

> And from their house-door by that track
> The bride and bridegroom went:

Really, this should have been '*came*': the sexton and the traveller are in the church-yard, and would never talk there of *going thither*, but of *coming hither*. My great impartiality as a commentator, induces me to give up my author's incorrectness in these slight particulars: he can well afford the tax.

> Sweet Mary, though she was not gay,
> Seem'd cheerful and content.
> But when they to the church-yard`came,
> I've heard poor Mary say,
> As soon as she stepp'd into the sun,
> Her heart—it died away.

The sun in general revives and invigorates the heart; but upon Mary's it had quite the contrary effect. The infant simplicity of the last line of this stanza is to be felt, not described.

> And when the vicar join'd their hands,
> Her limbs did creep and freeze;
> But when he pray'd, she thought she saw
> Her mother on her knees.

This is exquisitely natural: the vicar in his surplice doubtless very much resembled Mary's mother in her night-gown.

> And o'er the church-path they return'd—
> I saw poor Mary's back;
> Just as she stepp'd beneath the boughs,
> Into the mossy track.

This is a very important circumstance; and the sexton is properly accurate as to the *locus in quo* he 'saw poor Mary's *back*'. This abundantly proves that Mary did not keep her face towards the church, all the way she returned home. The sexton goes on to shew that although Mary might have been so agitated as not to know whether she stood on her head or her heels, she in point of fact did stand as other people usually do.

> Her *feet* upon the mossy track,
> The married maiden set:
> That moment I have heard her say,
> She wish'd she could forget.

Would she then have preferred to have stood upon her head? I profess myself unable to divine why she should wish to forget the particular moment, when she put her feet upon the mossy track, that led from the church just as she had been married: but perhaps this obscurity heightens the interest and beauty of the tale.

> The shade o'erflush'd her limbs with heat,
> Then came a chill-like death:
> And when the merry bells rang out,
> They seem'd to stop her breath.

As the sun had the effect of saddening the heart of Mary, so the shade had that of 'flushing her limbs with heat'; but the church-bells used her worst of all, for they literally 'stopped her breath', a phrase, by which I presume the poet to mean, in the usual simplicity of his heart, that Mary could not put in a word for the noise, which the church-bells made. The phrase is sufficiently familiar, and is used as an oath by Lord Foppington, who often exclaims, '*Stap* my breath'.

> Beneath the foulest mother's curse,
>   No child could ever thrive:
> A mother is a mother still;
>   The holiest thing alive.

This stanza is eminently calculated to feed the amiable superstitions of the vulgar: how true is it that the 'foulest mother' is the 'holiest thing'.

> So five months pass'd: the mother still
>   Would never heal the strife;
> But Edward was a loving man,
>   And Mary a fond wife.
> 'My sister may not visit us;
>   My mother says her nay:
> O Edward! you are all to me;
>   I wish for your sake I could be
> More lifesome and more gay.
> I'm dull and sad! indeed, indeed
>   I know I have no reason!
> Perhaps I am not well in health,
>   And 'tis a gloomy season'.

How unaffected is all this! how natural the language! Those, whose taste is vitiated by refinement, would call the language vulgar, and the versification prosaic. But far from the volumes of Wordsworth and Coleridge be such readers! I should prefer to read

> More lifesome *like* and gay.

The lines,

> I'm dull and sad! indeed, indeed
>   I know I have no reason!

in which again I should like to read 'indeed *and* indeed', do not mean that Mary knew she had lost her reason, but that she knew she had no cause to be dull and sad.

> 'Twas a drizzly time—no ice, no snow!
>   And on the few fine days,
> She stirr'd not out, lest she might meet
>   Her mother in the ways.

> But Ellen, spite of miry ways,
>   And weather dank and dreary,
> Trudg'd ev'ry day to Edward's house,
>   And made them all more cheery.
> O! Ellen was a faithful friend,
>   More dear than any sister!
> As cheerful too, as singing lark;
> And she ne'er left them till 'twas dark,
>   And then they always miss'd her.

The poet's description of the weather here is natural in the highest degree: I wish he had called it *muggy*, among the rest of his happy epithets. The picturesqueness of the word '*trudg'd*', in this passage, defies praise. The word '*cheery*' is equally choice with the word '*lifesome*', in the former passage.

> And now Ash Wednesday came—that day
>   But few to church repair:
> For on that day, you know, we read
>   The commination-prayer.
> Our late old vicar, a kind man,
>   Once, sir, he said to me,
> He wish'd that service was clean out
>   Of our good liturgy.
> The mother walk'd into the church,
>   To Ellen's seat she went:
> Tho' Ellen always kept her church,
>   All church-days during Lent;
> And gentle Ellen welcom'd her,
>   With courteous looks and mild:
> Thought she, 'what if her heart should melt,
>   And all be reconcil'd!'
> The day was scarcely like a day,
>   The clouds were black outright,
> And many a night with half a moon,
>   I've seen the church more light.

I have little to say upon all this gossip of the season; but he is evidently begetting an awful attention to what is to follow.

> The wind was wild; against the glass,
>   The rain did beat and bicker;
> The church-tower singing over head—
>   You could not hear the vicar.

How charming is this last line! it is the very climax of terror. The sexton must have thought this a fortunate circumstance, however, considering his opinions of the commination-prayer. If the vicar was not heard to pray, however, the steeple was heard to sing; and, although *the vicar's* commination-prayer was not heard, there was a commination-prayer in the church, which was 'audible', as the next stanza will inform us:

> And then and there the mother knelt,
>   And audibly she cried—
> 'O may a clinging curse consume
>   This woman by my side!
> O hear me, hear me, Lord in Heaven,
>   Although thou take my life.
> O curse this woman, at whose house
>   Young Edward woo'd his wife.
> By night and day, in bed and bower,
>   O let her cursèd be!'
> So having pray'd steady and slow,
>   She rose up from her knee;
> And left the church, nor e'er again
>   The church-door enter'd she.

The sexton's 'then and there', has all the beautiful accuracy of a law-pleading; but the poet has yet to explain why the mother's commination-prayer was 'audible', while the vicar's was not.

> I saw poor Ellen kneeling still,
>   So pale! I guess'd not why:
> When she stood up, there plainly was
>   A trouble in her eye.
> And when the prayers were done, we all
>   Came round and ask'd her why:
> Giddy she seem'd, and sure there was
>   A trouble in her eye,
> But ere she from the church-door stepp'd,
>   She smil'd and told us why:
> 'It was a wicked woman's curse',
>   Quoth she, 'and what care I?'

The first beauty to be remarked in this passage is the simplicity of the rhymes, or rather rhyme, for there is only one, throughout the whole twelve lines, viz. *why* and *eye*, or once *I*. This circumstance, and the repetition of the whole line,

A trouble in her eye,

give the story an infantine air of narration, which marks it for truth itself. My old impartiality induces me to say that the beauty of this exquisite passage is disfigured by a reversal of my author's error of *went* for *came*; for in the sixth line, we have *came*, where it ought to have been *went*.

> She smil'd, and smil'd, and pass'd it off,
>   Ere from the door she stepp'd—
> But all agree it would have been
>   Much better had she wept.
> And if her heart was not at ease,
>   This was her constant cry—
> 'It was a wicked woman's curse,
>   God's good! and what care I?'
> There was a hurry in her looks,
>   Her struggles she redoubled:
> 'It was a wicked woman's curse,
>   And why should I be troubled?'

Nothing can be more natural than the supposition of this first stanza, that the whole parish met, and resolved that it would have been better, if Ellen had wept, instead of laughed. What a beautiful union of ideas does the following line present!

> God's good! and what care I?

The 'what care I?' is infinitely preferable to the 'why should I be troubled?' of the last line, and I wish it had been repeated once more. There cannot be many more just pictures of human nature than that of a sensible and virtuous young woman of the nineteenth century, 'troubled', 'ill at ease', 'hurried', and 'struggling', under 'the curse of a wicked woman'.

> These tears will come! I dandled her,
>   When 'twas the merest fairy!
> Good creature! and she hid it all—
>   She told it not to Mary.
> But Mary heard the tale—her arms
>   Round Ellen's neck she threw:
> 'O Ellen, Ellen! she curs'd me,
>   And now she has curs'd you!'

This first stanza evinces the poet's usual felicity of rhyme: it is extremely beautiful; but I should prefer to read:

> This tear will come—'tis no use talking—
> Indeed I could not stop it;
> I dandled her in these old arms,
> O! bless it for a poppet.

The agony of the two *sisters accursed*, is painted to the life in the second stanza. Partridge, in *Tom Jones*, would see no merit in it; for, if he had been cursed, he would have done and said just the same. So should we all; and therein consists the beauty of the stanza.

> I saw young Edward by himself
> Stalk fast adown the lea;
> He snatch'd a stick from ev'ry fence,
> A twig from ev'ry tree.
> He snapt them still with hand or knee,
> And then away they flew!
> As if with his uneasy limbs
> He knew not what to do!

A tasteless lawyer, unable to relish the beauty of this picture of Edward's agitation, observed to me that his snatching a stick from every fence, and a twig from every tree, was most assuredly trespass, and that, according to the opinion of Lawyer Scout, in *Joseph Andrews*, the taking of a single twig was larceny, and punishable by imprisonment in Bridewell, and *that* 'with great lenity too, for if it had been called a young tree, the delinquent would have been hanged'. How exquisite is the idea of Edward's employing himself in snapping these sticks and twigs with his hand or knee. I would rather read:

> And then away *them threw*.

The broken sticks could not fly away of themselves.

> You see, good sir! that single hill?
> This farm lies underneath:
> He heard it there—he heard it all,
> And only gnash'd his teeth.

The house in which Edward heard of Ellen's curse, the *locus in quo*, is here well particularized: it was very important to know it. This last line must be taken *cum grano*. Edward broke sticks and twigs, as well as gnashed teeth.

> Now Ellen was a darling love,
>   In all his joys and cares;
> And Ellen's name and Mary's name,
> Fast linked they both together came,
>   Whene'er he said his prayers.
> And in the moment of his prayers,
>   He lov'd them both alike:
> Yea, both sweet names with one sweet joy,
>   Upon his heart did strike.

I have not much to say for this passage, which I think rather a falling off: it rises, however, in the last two lines, where there is a most beautiful antithesis; the phrase, '*sweet joy*', is felicitous in the extreme.

> He reach'd his home, and by his looks
>   They saw his inward strife;
> And they clung round him with their arms,
>   Both Ellen and his wife.
> And Mary could not check her tears,
>   So on his breast she bow'd;
> Then phrenzy melted into grief,
>   And Edward wept aloud.
> Dear Ellen did not weep at all,
>   But closelier she did cling;
> And turn'd her face, and look'd as if
>   She saw some frightful thing!

We have now a natural picture of the effect of this curse upon three persons, and the variety of the poet's pencil is truly admirable: 'grief', 'frenzy', and 'terror', were never betrayed upon so worthy an occasion before. The third part of the tale ends here; and leaves the reader in obscurity, what 'frightful thing' it was that Ellen 'looked as if she saw'. Happy poet! who has such absolute power over both the pathetic and the sublime!

The fourth part of the tale opens with a very enlightened general remark, which, although like Moses Primrose's[1] 'thunder and lightening coat', it does not fit very well, is 'much too good to be thrown away'.

> To see a man tread over graves,
>   I hold it no good mark:
> 'Tis wicked in the sun and moon,
>   And bad luck in the dark.

[1] See *The Vicar of Wakefield*.

This just assertion can allude only to graves in a *churchyard*; for it is generally impossible to get up to your pew-door, without 'treading over the graves' within the *church-walls*: this is neither 'wicked', nor 'bad luck'.

> You see that grave? The Lord he gives,
>> The Lord he takes away!
> O, sir! the child of my old age
>> Lies there as cold as clay.

This is exquisitely beautiful, and shews the piety and reading of the sexton, although, to allude to *The Vicar of Wakefield* again, it has no more to do with the tale in narration, than the cosmogony man's account of the creation of the world had with the subject of Dr. Primrose's conversation. The manner of it is not the worse for being borrowed from Dennis Brulgruddery's speech to Peregrine, in Colman's *John Bull*, when his wife is quitting the scene: 'You see that woman? she's my wife, poor soul: she has but one fault, but that's a wapper'. The words 'as cold as clay', serve the same turn to Mr. Coleridge's verse, as the saint does to Master Stephen's 'posey to his ring', in *Every Man in his Humour*:

> The deeper the sweeter,
> I'll be judg'd by St. Peter!

'*Edward Knowell*. How by St. Peter? I do not conceive that.
'*Stephen*. Marry, St. Peter, to take up the metre.'

> Except that grave, you scarce see one
>> That was not dug by me:
> I'd rather dance upon them all,
>> Than tread upon these three!

Now, we are coming to the point. But was the sexton's child's grave one of *the three*? We shall have deaths enough at the end of the tale to fill '*three* graves' without the child. The sexton talks rather flippantly about *dancing*, considering the age at which we now find him declaring himself:

> 'Aye, sexton! 'tis a touching tale':
>> You, sir, are but a lad:
> This month, I'm in my *seventieth* year,
>> And still it makes me sad.
> And Mary's sister told it me,

> For three good hours and more,
> Though I had heard it, in the main,
> From Edward's self before.

The traveller is now impatient that the sexton should continue his narrative, and artfully reminds him that his tale is a '*touching*' one; but the sexton is still garrulous, and, in the last highly poetic four lines, gives up his authorities for the story:

> Well, it pass'd off—the gentle Ellen
> Did well-nigh dote on Mary;
> And she went oft'ner than before,
> And Mary lov'd her more and more;
> She manag'd all the dairy.

Not to dwell upon the beautiful simplicity of the phrases, 'pass'd off' and 'well-nigh', can any thing be more natural than the abrupt, but important transition of this last line, 'though I am satisfied', as the *Spectator* says of a similar passage in the ballad of *Chevy-Chase*, 'your little buffoon readers will not be able to take the beauty of it'. The circumstance of Ellen's 'managing all the *dairy*', affords not only a rivet to *Mary's* friendship, but a clinch or rhyme to her name.

> To market she on market-days,
> To church on Sundays came:
> All seem'd the same—all seem'd so, sir;
> But all was not the same.

The poet is here as beautiful in his accuracy as he is elsewhere sublime in his '*brave disorder*'. Ellen never went to church on market-day, nor to market on Sunday: she was still collected enough not to deviate into this mistake. By the conclusion of this stanza, it should seem, as Moore's Almanack says, '*something great is hatching*'.

> Had Ellen lost her mirth? O no!
> But she was seldom cheerful;
> And Edward *look'd as if he thought*
> That Ellen's mirth was fearful.

'*Cautious*, that's his character', as *Puff* says in *The Critic*,[1]

> When by herself, she to herself
> Must sing some merry rhyme—

[1] Sheridan's play.

She could not now be glad for hours,
Yet silent all the time.

Few women can! But, jesting apart, how delicately is this beautiful idea expressed! The commencement of the stanza is almost equal to that infantine ballad, beginning:

As I walk'd by myself, I talk'd to myself,
And I said to myself, says I.

And when she sooth'd her friend, thro' all
Her soothing words, 'twas plain
She had a sore grief of her own,
A haunting in her brain.

Sternhold and Hopkins could not have outdone this:[1]

And oft she said, 'I'm not grown thin!'
And then her wrist she spann'd;
And once, when Mary was downcast,
She took her by the *hand*,
And gaz'd upon her, and at first
She gently press'd her *hand*;
Then harder, till her grasp at length,
Did gripe like a convulsion:
'Alas', said she, 'we ne'er can be
Made happy by compulsion'.

What an exquisite touch of madness does the first two of these lines contain! The next four are such perfect natural prose, that Mr. Coleridge has even forgotten to give them a rhyme. The inspirations of nature led him into the fault, if it can be imputed to a poet as a fault, that he is too natural. Happy poet whose only fault consists in this! 'And once, when Mary was downcast, she took her by the hand, and gazed upon her; and at first she gently pressed her hand, then harder', &c. Am I sure that Mr. Coleridge's analysis of the first and second parts of his story is not poetry, *as well as this*? The last of the lines just quoted breathes all the soul of the sublime Falstaff: 'By compulsion? No; were we at the strappado, or all the racks in the world, we could not be happy by compulsion. Happy by compulsion! if happiness were as plenty as blackberries, no man could be happy by compulsion'. Thomas Little has the same idea as Mr. Coleridge, only infinitely worse expressed:

[1] Thomas Sternhold (d. 1549) and John Hopkins (d. 1570) were noted for their incompetent versification of the psalms.

> Bliss itself is not worth having,
> If we're by compulsion blest.[1]

> And once her both arms suddenly
> Round Mary's neck she flung:
> And her heart panted, and she felt
> The words upon her tongue.
> She felt them coming, but no power
> Had she the words to smother;
> And with a kind of shriek she cried,
> 'O Christ! you're like your mother!'

The sexton refines here a little too much, perhaps, for one in his situation; but the sensation of *feeling words upon the tongue*, is true to nature. The phrase, her *both arms*, is much superior to her *two arms*. The exclamation, 'O Christ!' must be read with proper reverence; and not by one of 'your little buffoon readers'. The important cry, 'you're like your mother', well follows up the 'kind of shriek' after which it is uttered, and well atones for the suspense in which the sexton keeps us—'Parturient montes', but nothing 'ridiculus nascetur'.

> So gentle Ellen, now no more,
> Could make this sad house cheery;
> And Mary's melancholy ways,
> Drove Edward wild and weary.
> Ling'ring he rais'd his latch at eve,
> Tho' tir'd in heart and limb:
> He lov'd no other place, and yet
> Home was no home to him.

This first stanza is exquisite; and the idea of *driving* a man *weary*, is quite original: the second stanza is far inferior. But ample amends are made in what follows:

> One ev'ning he took up a book,
> And nothing in it read;
> Then flung it down, and groaning cried,
> 'O heav'n! that I were dead!'
> Mary look'd up into his face,
> And nothing to him said;
> She try'd to smile, and on his arm
> Mournfully lean'd her head!
> And he burst into tears, and fell
> Upon his knees in prayer;

[1] A reference to Thomas Moore's pseudonymous *Poetical Works* (1801).

Her heart is broke—O God! my grief—
It is too great to bear!'

Nothing can equal the beauty of the second line in both the first and the second of these stanzas. Edward 'took up a book, and nothing in it read'; but Mary was even with him, for she 'look'd up into his face, and nothing to him said'.—The seriousness of manner, in the whole ballad, well warrants the scriptural imitation with which this passage concludes.

'The short dialogue between Duncan and Banquo', says Sir Joshua Reynolds, 'whilst they are approaching the gates of Macbeth's castle, has always appeared to me a striking instance of what in painting is termed *repose*. Their conversation very naturally turns upon the beauty of its situation, and the pleasantness of the air; and Banquo, observing the martlet's nests in every quarter of the cornice, remarks that "where those birds most breed and haunt, the air is delicate". The subject of this quiet and easy conversation gives that *repose* so necessary to the mind after the tumultuous bustle of the preceding scene, and perfectly contrasts the scene of horror that immediately succeeds'.[1] Just so, or with much more beauty, does our sexton now descant upon the weather, and well contrasts the horror of Edward's past exclamation, by observing upon those times, when 'the hot days come, one knows not how':

'Twas such a foggy time, as makes
Old sextons, sir, like me,
Rest on their spades to cough; the spring
Was late, uncommonly.
And then the hot days, all at once
They came, one knew not how:
You look'd about for shade, when scarce
A leaf was on a bough.

The word 'uncommonly' here, is uncommonly beautiful; but I think it would be more natural like, if it had been pronounced as a rhyme to *my* and not to *me*. The sexton should have been made to say, 'the spring was uncommon*ly* late, sure'.

It happen'd then, ('twas in the bower,
A furlong up the wood—
Perhaps you know the place, and yet
I scarce know how you should).

[1] 'Discourse viii'.

Easy and familiar! 'The Blue Boar—but perhaps you may frequent it, Ma'am', as Zekiel Homespun says to Miss Caroline Dormer.[1]

> No path leads thither: 'tis not nigh
>   To any pasture plot;
> But, cluster'd near the chatt'ring brook,
>   Some hollies mark the spot.
> Those hollies, of themselves a shape,
>   As of an arbour took,
> A close round arbour, and it stands
>   Not three strides from the brook.

Accurate as a direction-post! Having painted the scenery, now for the *dramatis personæ*!

> Within this arbour, which was still
>   With scarlet berries hung,
> Were these three friends, one Sunday morn,
>   Just as the first bell rung.
> 'Tis sweet to hear a brook; 'tis sweet
>   To hear a Sabbath bell!
> 'Tis sweet to hear them both at once
>   Deep in a wooden dell.

I much admire the antithesis of '*three* friends', and '*one* Sunday'; but the second stanza is not so beautiful: the sexton should not have praised his own music. But I adore the particularity of the first two of the following lines:

> His limbs along the moss, his head
>   Upon a mossy heap,
> With shut-up senses, Edward lay:
> That brook ev'n on a working-day,
>   Might chatter one to sleep.
> And he had pass'd a restless night,
>   And was not well in health!
> The women sat down by his side,
>   And talk'd as 'twere by stealth.

All this is beautiful and familiar. It being Sunday, Edward's 'senses' were like his shop, 'shut up'. The line,

> And was not well in health,

could not be improved; but I do wish that 'working-day' had been 'worky-day': however, any thing is better than 'week-day', the phrase,

[1] Characters in George Colman the younger's *The Heir-at-Law* (1797).

which any inferior poet would have used. But my readers must be impatient to know what was the important conversation which 'the women' (familiar!) thought it absolutely necessary to snatch from Edward's repose.

> 'The sun peeps through the close thick leaves,
>   See, dearest Ellen, see,
> 'Tis *in* the leaves! a little seen,
>   No bigger than your ee'.

I cannot refrain from interrupting this charming philosophy. The infantine simplicity of that word *ee* is worth a million of money. I wish the poet had thought of *wee*, as a rhyme for it. However, he does call the sun,

> 'A *tiny* sun, and it has got
>   A perfect glory too:
> Ten thousand threads and hairs of light,
> Make up a glory gay and bright,
>   Round that small orb so *blue*'.

Blue! but this point will be argued. Let me forbear!

> And then they argued of those rays,
>   What colour they might be:
> Says this, 'they're mostly green'; says that,
>   'They're amber-like to me'.

Then, who said they were *blue*? It is strange that both of them should have forgotten *yellow* and *red*; but the phrase, 'amber-like', disarms all criticism by its simple beauty. *Peace* to the sexton, for recollecting such amiable and philosophical gossip!

> So they sat chatting, while bad thoughts
>   Were troubling Edward's rest;
> But soon they heard his hard quick pants,
>   And the *thumping* in his breast.

This *beats* the word *bating* in the Irish song:

> Says he, 'at my *heart* I've a *bating*',
> Says I, 'then take one at your *back*'.

> 'A mother too!' these self-same words
>   Did Edward mutter plain;
> His face was drawn back on itself,
>   With horror and huge pain.

Such critics as Polonius would say here, '*huge* pain! that's a vile phrase'. It is, in my mind, a noble and daring originality.

> Both groan'd at once, for both knew well
> What thoughts were in his mind:
> When he wak'd up, and star'd like one
> That hath been just struck blind.

Did the sexton ever see such a one? and is it not a *bull* to say that a *blind* man *stares*? I choose to read, *meo periculo*,

> That hath been just *stuck pig*.

Here is sense and propriety. To *stare like a stuck-pig* is familiar and natural, and is of a piece with the sexton's former similies, *as cheerful as a lark, as cold as clay*, &c. The second line of the stanza may rhyme with *pig* in this manner:

> With what his head was big.

To proceed:

> He sat upright; and ere the dream
> Had had time to depart,
> 'O God, forgive me!' he exclaim'd,
> 'I have torn out her heart!'

Whose heart? But *obscurity* is a very great part of Mr. Coleridge's *sublime*. The phrase, *torn out her heart*, is beautiful and new.

> Then Ellen shriek'd and forthwith burst
> Into ungentle laughter:
> And Mary shiver'd where she sat,
> And never she smil'd after.

Here ends the fourth part of the tale of the 'Three Graves'.

> And word spake never more,

as the far inferior ballad of 'William and Margaret' concludes.[1] Mr. Coleridge now sits down to enjoy the praises of his readers, and commences the next number of his *Friend*:

It is gratifying to me to find from my correspondents, that the homeliness of the language and metre, in the fragment of *The Three Graves*, has not prevented the philosophical interest of the tale from being felt. In that rude ballad, I attempted to exemplify the effect, which one painful idea vividly impressed on

---

[1] By David Mallet (1705?-1765).

the mind, under unusual circumstances, might have in producing an alienation of the understanding; and in the parts hitherto published, I have endeavoured to trace the progress to madness, step by step. But though the main incidents are facts, the detail of the circumstances is of my own invention; that is, not what I knew, but what I conceived likely to have been the case, or at least equivalent to it.

Modest, unassuming poet! '*Homeliness* of the language!' yes, because it comes *home* to the heart. *Home is home, let it be never so homely*, as the sexton would say. '*Rude* ballad!' They are *rude*, who call it so. The 'interest' of the tale is '*philosophical*' indeed! Does it not tell every envious old woman that her curses may be effective on weak minds? Does it not teach the young to encourage and foster their gloomy impressions, and to believe that the curses of the wicked are of more avail than the blessings of the virtuous? In short, does not the tale tend to encourage superstition and witchcraft, to discountenance the exertions of cheerful industry, and to discredit the happiness of a clear conscience?

38. John Foster, *Eclectic Review*

October 1811, vii, 912-31

This unsigned review has been attributed to John Foster (J. E. Ryland ed., *Critical Essays Contributed to the Eclectic Review by J. Foster*, London 1856, ii, 1-24). Foster (1770-1843), a Baptist minister, was a regular contributor.

It was with no small pleasure we saw any thing announced of the nature of a proof or pledge that the author of this paper was in good faith employing himself, or about to employ himself, in the intellectual public service. His contributions to that service have, hitherto, borne but a small proportion to the reputation he has long enjoyed of being qualified for it in an extraordinary degree. This reputation is less founded on a small volume of juvenile poems, and some occasional essays in periodical publications, than on the estimate formed and avowed by all the intelligent persons that have ever had the gratification of falling into his society.

After his return, several years since, from a residence of considerable duration in the South East of Europe, in the highest maturity of a mind, which had, previously to that residence, been enriched with large acquisitions of the most diversified literature and scientific knowledge, and by various views of society both in England and on the continent; his friends promised themselves, that the action of so much genius, so long a time, on such ample materials, would at length result in some production, or train of productions, that should pay off some portion of the debt, due to the literary republic, from one of the most opulent of its citizens. A rather long period, however, had elapsed, and several projects had been reported in the usual vehicles of literary intelligence, before this paper was undertaken. An idea of the mental habits and acquirements brought to its execution, will be conveyed by an extract from the prospectus, which was written in the form of a letter to a friend.

It is not unknown to you that I have employed almost the whole of my life in acquiring, or endeavouring to acquire, useful knowledge, by study, reflection, observation, and by cultivating the society of my superiors in intellect, both at home and in foreign countries. You know too, that, at different periods of my life, I have not only planned, but collected the materials for many works on various and important subjects; so many indeed, that the number of my unrealized schemes, and the mass of my miscellaneous fragments, have often furnished my friends with a subject of raillery, and sometimes of regret and reproof. Waiving the mention of all private and accidental hindrances, I am inclined to believe that this want of perseverance has been produced in the main by an over-activity of thought, modified by a constitutional indolence, which made it more pleasant to me to continue acquiring, than to reduce what I had acquired to a regular form. Add too, that almost daily throwing off my notices or reflections in desultory fragments, I was still tempted onwards by an increasing sense of the imperfections of my knowledge, and by the conviction that, in order fully to comprehend and develope any one subject, it was necessary that I should make myself master of some other, which again as regularly involved a third, and so on, with an ever-widening horizon. Yet one habit, formed during long absences from those with whom I could converse with full sympathy, has been of advantage to me—that of daily writing down in my memorandum or common-place books, both incidents and observations; whatever had occurred to me from without, and all the flux and reflux of my mind within itself. The number of these notices, and their tendency, miscellaneous as they were, to one common end (*'quid sumus, et quid futuri gignimur'*, *what we are, and what we are to become; and thus from the end of our being to deduce its proper objects*) first encouraged me to undertake the Weekly Essay of which you will consider this letter as the prospectus.

Being printed on stamped paper, these essays were conveyed by the post, free of expence, to any part of the country. In the mode of publication, therefore, and what may be called the exterior character of the project *The Friend* was an imitation of those sets of essays which, from the *Tatler* down to the *Rambler*, and several much later works, had first supplied entertainment and instruction in small successive portions, during several months or years, and then taken their rank among books of permanent popularity. Mr. Coleridge has correctly distinguished, in a brief and general manner, the objects to which these works were mainly directed, and rendered a tribute of animated applause to their writers; at the same time bespeaking the candour of his readers to a series of essays, which should attempt to instruct after a very different method. It was avowed, that they would aim much more at the developement of general principles; it would be inferred, of course, that they would be of a much more abstract and metaphysical character. Mr. C. fairly warned those whom he invited to become his readers, that, though he should hope not unfrequently to interest the affections, and captivate the imagination, yet a large proportion of the essays were intended to be of a nature, which might require a somewhat resolute exercise of intellect.—It was not proposed to terminate the series at any assigned point; it might be expected to proceed as long as the writer's industry and resources should command the public approbation. With one or two considerable interruptions, it reached as far as twenty-eight numbers, and there ended so abruptly that a memoir of Sir Alexander Ball was left unfinished. At several points in the progress of the work, the writer confessed that the public patronage was not such as to make it probable he could carry it forward to any great length: but no explanation was given of the suddenness of its discontinuance.

Perhaps it may be questioned, now after a portion of the intended work has been given, whether the project did not involve some degree of miscalculation. Even the consideration of a rather excessive price was likely to affect the success of a work which, though coming with some of the exterior marks of a newspaper, was yet to derive nearly as little aid from the stimulant facts and questions of the day, as if it had been a commentary on Aristotle or Plato. A still more unfavourable augury might, perhaps, have been drawn from the character of Mr. Coleridge's composition, as taken in connection with the haste inseparable from a weekly publication. The cast of his diction is so unusual, his trains of thought so habitually forsake the ordinary tracts, and therefore the whole composition is so liable to appear strange and obscure, that it was evident the most elaborate care, and a repeated revisal, would be indispensable in order to render so original a mode of writing sufficiently perspicuous to be in any degree popular. And it is equally evident that the necessity of finishing a sheet within each week, against a particular day and hour, must be totally incompatible with such patient and matured workmanship. A considerable portion of the short allotment of time might, in spite of every better resolution, be beguiled away in comparative indolence; or it might be consumed by casual and unforeseen avocations; or rendered fruitless by those lapses into languor and melancholy, to which genius, especially of the refined and poetic order, is extremely subject; or even wasted in the ineffectual endeavour to fix exclusively on some one of many equally eligible subjects. It was to be foreseen that the natural consequences would be, sometimes such a degree of haste as to leave no possibility of disposing the subject in the simplest clearest order, and giving the desirable compression, and lucidness, and general finishing to the composition; sometimes, from despair of doing this, a recourse to shifts and expedients to make up the number, in a slighter way than had been intended, and perhaps promised; and often a painful feeling of working at an ungracious task, especially if, in addition, the public approbation should be found to be less liberally awarded than had been expected. Such compulsory dispatch would have been a far less inconvenience in the conducting of a paper intended merely for amusement, or for the lightest kind of instruction, or as a weekly commentary on the contemporary measures and men—a department in which the facility and attractiveness of the topics, and the voracity of the public, exempt the writer from any severity of intellectual toil, or solicitude for literary perfection: but it was almost necessarily fatal in a work to be often occupied with deep disquisitions, and under the added disadvantage that the author had been previously much less accustomed to write than to think. When, besides, the work aspired to a very high rank in our permanent literature, there was perhaps an obvious impolicy in subjecting it to such circumstances of publication, as should preclude the minute improvements of even a tenth revision. It should seem probable, on the whole, that a mode better adapted to the effective exertion of Mr. Coleridge's great talents might have been devised, in the form of a periodical publication to appear in larger portions, at much longer intervals.

Some of the consequences thus to be anticipated from the plan of the undertaking, are actually perceptible in the course of the work. The writer manifests great indecision as to the choice and succession of his subjects. After he appears to have determined on those to be treated in the immediately ensuing numbers, those numbers, when they come, may be employed on totally different subjects—introduced by accidental suggestion—or from their being such as would be more easily worked, in the brief allowance of time, into the required length and breadth of composition. Questions avowedly intended to be argued very early, as involving great fundamental principles, are deferred till the reader forgets what the author has said of their importance. Various subjects are adverted to, here and there in the course of the work, as to be hereafter investigated, and are never mentioned again. In some instances, the number to which the commencement or the conclusion of an important inquiry has stood over, will be found made up perhaps, for the greater part, of letters, or short fragments, with translations from a minor Italian poet. Several of the numbers, towards the latter end of the series, are employed on the character of the late Sir Alexander Ball, which, however meritorious, was not probably, in the opinion of the majority of the readers, of sufficient celebrity to claim so considerable a space in an expensive work; especially while several most interesting points of inquiry, of which they had been led to expect an early investigation were still, and indefinitely deferred. It is fair, however, to quote the author's apology or vindication, in which, toward the conclusion of the series, he attributes to his readers, the procrastination or relinquishment of the refined disquisitions, which he should himself have been happy to prosecute.

The remainder of my work, therefore, hitherto, has been devoted to the purpose of averting this mistake (that which had imputed to him a co-incidence of opinion with the 'French physiocratic philosophers') as far as I have not been compelled by the general taste of my readers to interrupt the systematic progress of the plan, by essays of a lighter kind, or which at least required a less effort of attention. In truth, since my twelfth number, I have not had courage to renew any subject which *did* require attention. The way to be admired, is to tell the reader what he knew before, but clothed in a statelier phraseology, and embodied in apt and lively illustrations. To attempt to make a man wiser, is of necessity to remind him of his ignorance: and, in the majority of instances, the pain actually felt is so much greater than the pleasure anticipated, that it is natural that men should attempt to shelter themselves from it by contempt or neglect. For a living writer is yet sub judice; and if we cannot follow his conceptions or enter into his feelings, it is more consoling to our pride, as well as more agreeable to our indolence, to consider him as lost beneath, rather than as soaring out of our sight above us. Itaque id agitur, ut ignorantia etiam ab ignominiâ liberetur. Happy is that man, who can truly say, with Giordano Bruno, and whose circumstances at the same time permit him to *act* on the sublime feeling—

> Procedat nudus, quem non ornant nubila,
> Sol! Non conveniunt Quadrupedum phaleræ
> Humano dorso! *Porro Veri species*
> *Quæsita, inventa, at patefacta, me efferat!*
> *Etsi nullus intelligat,*
> *Si cum naturâ et sub lumine,*
> *Id vere plusquam satis est.*

It may easily be believed that Mr. C. had cause to complain of the impatience of some of his readers, under those demands of a strong mental exertion which some of his essays have made on them; but the degree of this required exertion is greatly under-rated, we think, in the following observations in the same number.

Themes like these, not even the genius of a Plato or a Bacon could render intelligible without demanding from the reader, *thought* sometimes, and *attention* generally. By *thought* I here mean the voluntary production in our own minds of those states of consciousness, to which, as to his fundamental facts, the writer has referred us: while *attention* has for its object, the order and connection of thoughts and images, each of which is in itself already and familiarly known. Thus the elements of geometry require attention only; but the analysis of our primary faculties, and the investigation of all the absolute grounds of religion and morals, are impossible without energies of thought in addition to the effort of attention. The Friend never attempted to disguise from his readers, that both attention and thought were efforts, and the latter a most difficult and laborious effort; nor from himself that to require it often, or for any continuance of time, was incompatible with the nature of a periodical publication, even were it less incongruous than it unfortunately is, with the present habits and pursuits of Englishmen. Accordingly, after a careful re-perusal of the preceding numbers, I can discover but *four* passages which supposed in the reader any energy of thought and voluntary abstraction. But attention I confess two thirds of the work hitherto have required. On whatever subject the mind feels a lively interest, attention, though always an effort, becomes a delightful effort; and I should be quite at ease, could I secure for the whole work, as much of it as a party of earnest whist-players often expend in a single evening, or a lady in the making up of a fashionable dress. But where no interest previously exists, attention, (as every schoolmaster knows) can be procured only by terror: which is the true reason why the majority of mankind learn nothing systematically, but as schoolboys or apprentices.

Not to dwell on the arbitrary and rather tenebrious distinction between thought and attention (which might be given as a fair specimen of the extent of the demand made on the reader's mind in a multitude of passages) we cannot help saying, that this is a somewhat too reserved acknowledgment—that the 'Friend' has produced a volume, of which a considerable portion is hard to be understood, and some passages of which it may be doubted whether any one reader, after his very best efforts, has felt sure that he did so understand as to be able to put the meaning into other equivalent words of his own. We cannot but think that, in some still later re-perusal, the author himself will have perceived that not a few of his conceptions, taken as detached individual thoughts, are enounced with an obscurity of a somewhat different kind from that which may seem inevitably incident, in some degree, to the expression of thoughts of extreme abstraction. And sometimes the conjunctive principle among several thoughts that come in immediate succession is so unobvious, that the reader must repeatedly peruse, must analyze, we might almost say must excruciate, a considerable portion of the composition, before he can feel any confidence that he is master of the connexion; and at last he is so little sure of having a real hold of the whole combination, that he would not trust himself to state that particular part of the 'Friend's' opinions and sentiments to an intelligent inquirer. When he could perhaps give, in a very general form, the apparent result of a series of thoughts, he would be afraid to attempt assigning the steps by which his author had arrived at it.

There can be no doubt that, by such patient labour as the adopted mode of publication entirely forbade, the writer could have given, if we may so express it, more roundness and prominence to the logical fibres of his composition, and a more unequivocal substance to some of its more attenuated components; in short left nothing obscure but what was invincibly and necessarily so, from the profound abstraction and exquisite refinement of thought, in which Mr. C. would have extremely few equals in whatever age he had lived.

Our contracted limits will not allow more than a very brief notice of the several subjects on which the author's intellect and imagination have thrown their light and colours, in a more fixed or in a momentary manner, in the course of this desultory performance. It would be fully as interesting, though a more difficult task, to discriminate some of the qualities which distinguish his manner of thinking and writing: and we shall make a short attempt at this, though with no small degree of diffidence in our ability to render the more subtle characteristics palpable in description. Some of them are almost as undefinable, as the varied modifications of the air by which very susceptible organs can perceive the different state of that element as subsisting in one district and in another; almost as undefinable, as the tinge by which the light of the rising and setting sun in spring or autumn, is recognized as of a quite different character from its morning and evening radiance in the other seasons.

And while we are making this reference to the elements and phenomena of nature, we will confess that this author, beyond any other (Mr. Wordsworth is next), gives us the impression, or call it the fancy, of a mind constructed to bear a certain indescribable analogy to nature —that is to the physical world, with its wide extent, its elements, its mysterious laws, its animated forms, and its variety and vicissitude of appearances. His mind lives almost habitually in a state of profound sympathy with nature, maintained through the medium of a refined illusion of genius, which informs all nature with a kind of soul and sentiment, that bring all its forms and entities, animate and inanimate, visible and invisible, into a mystical communion with his feelings. This sympathy is, or involves, an exceedingly different feeling from that with which a strictly philosophic mind perceives and admires in nature the more definable attributes of variety, order, beauty, and grandeur. These are acknowledged with a vivid perception; but, in our author's powerful imagination, they become a kind of moral attributes of a half-intelligential principle, which dimly, but with mysterious attraction, discloses itself from within all matter and form. This sympathy has retained him much more effectually in what may be called the school of nature, than is usual to men of genius who enter so much into artificial society, and so extensively study the works of men. And the influences of this school have given that form to his habits of thinking which bears so many marks of analogy to the state of surrounding physical nature. To illustrate this we may observe, that he perpetually falls on analogies between moral truth and facts in nature: in his figurative language he draws his similes and metaphors from the scenes of nature in preference to the departments of art—though these latter are also very much at his command: his ideas have much of the unlimited variety of nature; they have much also of its irregularity, being but little constrained into formal artificial method: there is in his train of thinking a great deal of what may be called colour and efflorescence, and but little of absolutely plain bare intellectual material: like nature, as to her productions, he seems as willing to bestow labour and completeness on little thoughts as on great ones; we may add, he does not shew any concern about mixing the little and great together—sublime and remote ideas, and humble and familiar ones, being readily admitted, if they happen to come in immediate succession.

The above description of our author's sympathy with nature, and his mystical perception of something like soul and sentiment residing in all material elements and forms, will not be misunderstood to impute to him any thing like a serious adoption of the atheistical principle of Spinoza, or of the Stoic or Platonic dogmas about the Soul of the World. This converse with all surrounding existence is, in the perfect consciousness of our author's mind, no more than the emancipation of that mind itself; imparting, in its meditative enthusiasm, a character of imaginary moral being and deep significance to all objects, but leaving his understanding in the full and solemn belief of a Supreme Intelligence, perfectly distinct from the whole universe. But there is strong reason to suspect, that certain of his poetical contemporaries renounce the idea of such a Divine Intelligence, in their fancy of the all-pervading, inexplicable something, which privileged and profoundly thoughtful spirits may perceive, and without illusion, in the light of the sun, in clouds, in silent groves, and in the sound of winds and mountain torrents.

But we ought to have remarked, first, on some of the more easily definable of the distinguishing properties of the 'Friend's' intellectual and literary character. Among the foremost may be mentioned the independence and the wide reach with which he thinks. He has given attendance in all the schools of moral and metaphysical philosophy, ancient and modern, but evidently has attended there rather to debate the matter with the professors, than with submissive homage to receive their dictates. He would have been a most factious and troublesome pupil in the academy of Pythagoras. He regards all subjects and doctrines as within the rightful sphere of free examination: and the work affords evidence, that a very large number of them have actually been examined by him with extraordinary severity. Yet this freedom of thinking, supported as it is by the conscious possession of great power and exceedingly ample and diversified knowledge, does not degenerate into arrogance; a high and sincere respect being uniformly shewn for the great intellectual aristocracy of both the past and present times, but especially of the past. Of the eminent writers of our own country, he evinces a higher veneration for those of the seventeenth, than those of the subsequent century, and of the present time; and professes to have been of late years more familiar with them, and to have involuntarily acquired some degree of conformity to their manner of thinking and to their style.

Another instantly apparent distinction of our author's manner of thinking, is its extreme abstractedness. Considering that many of his subjects are not of that class which, by the necessity of their nature, *can* be discussed in no other than a metaphysical manner, he has avoided, in a wonderful and unequalled degree, all the superficial and obvious forms of thought which they might suggest. He always carries on his investigation at a depth, and sometimes a most profound depth, below the uppermost and most accessible stratum; and is philosophically mining among its most recondite principles of the subject, while ordinary intellectual and literary workmen, many of them barely informed of the very existence of this Spirit of the Deep, are pleasing themselves and those they draw around them, with forming to pretty shapes, or commodious uses, the materials of the surface. It may be added, with some little departure from the consistency of the metaphor, that if he endeavours to make his voice heard from this region beneath, it is apt to be listened to as a sound of dubious import, like that which fails to bring articulate words from the remote recess of a cavern, or the bottom of the deep shaft of a mine. However familiar the truths and facts to which his mind is directed, it constantly, and as if involuntarily strikes, if we may so speak, into the invisible and the unknown of the subject: he is seeking the most retired and abstracted form in which any being can be acknowledged and realized as having an existence, or any truth can be put in a proposition. He turns all things into their ghosts, and summons us to walk with him in this region of shades—this strange world of disembodied truths and entities.

He repeatedly avows, that it is less his object to teach truth in its most special and practical form, and in its detailed application, than to bring up into view and certainty a number of grand general principles, to become the lights of judgement, on an endless variety of particular subjects. At least this was the proposed object of the earlier part, the first twenty or thirty numbers, of the intended series. These principles were to be brought into clearness and authority, partly by statement and argument in an abstract form, and partly by shewing them advantageously in operation, as applied to the trial and decision of several interesting questions. But the abstruseness often unavoidable in the pure intellectual enunciation of a principle, prevails also in an uncommon degree, in the present work, through the practical illustrations—even when the matter of those illustrations consists of very familiar facts. The ideas employed to explain the mode of the relation between the facts and the principle, are sometimes of such extreme tenuity as to make a reader who is anxious to comprehend, but unaccustomed to abstraction, feel as if he were deficient by nearly one whole faculty, some power of intellectual sight or tact with which he perceives the author to be endowed—for there is something that every where compels him to give the author credit for thinking with great acuteness, even when he is labouring in vain to refine his own conceptions into any state that can place him in real communication with the author's mind. The surpassing subtlety of that mind is constantly describing the most unobvious relations, and detecting the most veiled aspects of things, and pervading their substance in quest of whatever is most latent in their nature. This extreme subtlety is the cause of more than one kind of difficulty to the reader. Its *necessary* consequence is that refinement of observation on which we have so prolixly remarked; but it has another consequence, the less or greater degree of which depended on the author's choice. He has suffered it continually to retard him in, or divert him from, the straight forward line of thought to his object. He enters on a train of argumentative observations to determine a given question. He advances one acute thought, and another, and another: but by this time he perceives among these which we may call the primary thoughts, so many secondaries—so many bearings, distinctions, and analogies—so many ideas starting sideways from the main line of thought—so many pointings towards subjects infinitely remote—that, in the attempt to seize and fix in words these secondary thoughts, he will often suspend for a good while the progress toward the intended point. Thus each thought that was to have been only *one* thought, and to have transmitted the reader's mind immediately forward to the next in order and in advance, becomes an exceedingly complex combination of thoughts, almost a dissertation in miniature: and thus our journey to the assigned point (if indeed we are carried so far, which is not always the case) becomes nothing less than a visit of curious inspection to every garden, manufactory, museum, and antiquity, situated near the road, throughout its whole length. Hence too it often happens, that the transitions are not a little perplexing. The transition directly from one primary thought, as we venture to call it, in the train to the next, might be very easy: we might see most perfectly how, in natural logic, the one was connected with the other, or led to it: but when we have to pass to this next principal thought in the train, from some divergent and remote accessory of the former principal idea, we feel that we have lost the due bearing of the preceding part of the train, by being brought in such an indirect way to the resumption of it.

The same kind of observation is applicable to the comparisons and metaphors with which our author illustrates and adorns his speculations. In this component of good writing, we believe he has no superior in this or any other age. His figures are original, and various, and often *complexly* apposite, to a degree of which we do not at present recollect any example. They are taken indifferently from any part of a prodigious sphere of knowledge, and presented with every possible advantage of rich and definite expression. In the choice of them he very justly scorns, what has been noticed as a leading point of contradistinction of the French orators and poets from ours, the fastidiousness which declines similies taken from things of so humble a quality as to give to the figure a character of meanness. While he can easily reach, if he pleases, as far into remoteness and magnificence as the aphelion of a comet, for an object of illustrative comparison, he is not afraid to turn to literary account in the next paragraph, even a thing of so little dignity as those fastenings of garments called *hooks and eyes*. But the fault we venture to charge is, analogously to what we have said of the more austerely intellectual parts of the composition, the frequent extension of a figure into a multiformity which beguiles both the author and the reader from the direct and pressing pursuit of the main object. When the object is grave and important truth, the beauties of imagery, when introduced with a copiousness greatly beyond the strictest necessities of explanation, should be so managed as to be like flowery borders of a road: the way may have on each side every variety of beauty, every charm of shape, and hue and scent, to regale the traveller: but, it should still be absolutely a *road*—going right on—with defined and near limits—and not widening out into a spacious and intricate wilderness of these beauties, where the man that was to travel is seduced to wander. When an apt figure occurs to our author, his imagination (which has received with wonderful accuracy, and retained with wonderful fidelity, *all* the ascertainable points of appearance and quality of almost all objects) instantaneously expands and finishes this figure, within his own mind, into a complete object or scene, with all its absolute and relative distinctions and circumstances; and his intellectual subtlety suddenly perceives, besides its principal and most obvious analogy with the abstract truth he is stating, various other more refined and minute analogies and appositenesses, which are more gratifying to his own mind than the leading analogy, partly from the consideration that only a very acute perception would have discerned them, and partly because a double intellectual luckiness is more unusual than a single one. Now, we have mentioned the *complexity* of appositeness, the several-fold relation between the figure and the truth to which it is brought as correspondent, as one of the *excellencies*, of our author's figures: and we have done so, because none but a writer of great genius will very frequently fall on such figures—and because a very specific rather than a merely general relation, an interior and essential rather than a superficial and circumstantial analogy, between the subject and the corresponding figure, *is* a great excellence as exhibiting the laws of reason prevalent through the operations of imagination; and it would often be found that the specific and pointed appropriateness of the comparison consists in its containing a double analogy. But when a subtle intelligence, perceiving something much beyond this duplicity of relation, introduces a number of perhaps real and exquisite, but extremely recondite correspondences, the reader, though pleased with the sagacious perception, so long as not confused by the complexity, is, at the same time, certainly diverted from the leading purpose of the discourse.

It is not alone in the detection of refined analogies that our author too much amplifies his figurative illustrations. He does it sometimes in the way of merely perfecting, for the sake of its own completeness, the representation of the thing which furnishes the figure, which is often done equally with philosophical accuracy and poetic beauty. But thus extended into particularity, the illustration exhibits a number of colours, and combinations, and branchings of imagery, neither needful nor useful to the main intellectual purpose. Our author is therefore sometimes like a man, who, in a work that requires the use of wood, but requires it only in the plain bare form of straight-shaped poles and stakes, should insist that it shall be *living* wood, retaining all its twigs leaves and blossoms. Or, if we might compare the series of ideas in a composition to a military line, we should say that many of our author's images, and of even his more abstracted conceptions, are super-numerarily attended by so many related, but secondary and subordinate ideas, that the array of thought bears some resemblance to what that military line would be, if many of the men, veritable and brave soldiers all the while, stood in the ranks surrounded with their wives and children.

Of the properties which we have attempted, we sincerely acknow-ledge very inadequately, to discriminate and describe as characteristic of our author's mode of writing, the result is—that readers of ordinary, though tolerably cultivated faculties, feel a certain deficiency of the effective force which they believe such an extraordinary course of thinking ought to have on their minds. They feel, decisively, that they are under the tuition of a most uncommonly powerful and far-seeing spirit, that penetrates into the essences of things, and can also strongly define their forms and even their shadows—and that is quite in earnest to communicate, while they are equally in earnest to obtain, the most important principles which such a mind has deduced from a severe examination of a vast variety of facts and books. And yet there is some kind of haze in the medium through which this spirit transmits its light, or there is some vexatious dimness in the mental faculty of seeing: so that looking back from the end of an essay, or of the volume, they really do not feel themselves in possession of any thing like the full value of as much ingenious, and sagacious, and richly illustrated thinking as ever, probably, was contained in the same proportion of writing.

We would not set down much of the difficulty of comprehending, so much complained of, to the *language*, so far as it is distinguishable from the thought; with the exception of here and there a scholastic phrase, and a certain degree of peculiarity in the use of one or two terms—especially *reason*, which he uses in a sense in which he endeavours to explain and prove, that all men are in equally full possession of the faculty which it denominates. Excepting so far as a slight tinge of antiqueness indicates the influence of our older writers, especially Milton and Bacon, on the complexion of our author's language, it is of a construction original in the greatest possible degree. That it could not well be otherwise may easily be supposed, when, premising, as we have done, the originality of the author's manner of thinking, we observe that the diction is in a most extraordinary degree conformed to the thought. It lies, if we may so speak, close to the mental surface, with all its irregularities, throughout. It is therefore perpetually varying, in perfect flexibility and obsequiousness to the ideas; and, without any rhetorical regulation of its changes, or apparent design, or consciousness in the writer, is in succession popular and scientific, familiar and magnificent, secular and theological, plain and poetical. It has none of the phrases or combinations of oratorical common-place: it has no settled and favourite appropriations of certain adjectives to certain substantives: its manner of expressing an idea once, gives the reader no guess how the same idea will be expressed when it comes modified by a different combination. The writer considers the whole congregation of words, constituting our language, as something so perfectly and independently his own, that he may make any kind of use of any part of it that his thinking requires. Almost every page therefore, presents unusual combinations of words, that appear not so much made *for* the thought as made *by* it, and often give, if we may so express it, the very colour, as well as the substantial form, of the idea. There is no settled construction or cadence of the sentences; no two, perhaps, of about the same length being constructed in the same manner. From the complexity and extended combination of the thought, they are generally long, which the author something less than half-apologizes for, and therefore something more than half defends. We will quote what he says on this point.

Doubtless, too, I have in some measure injured my style, in respect to its facility and popularity, from having almost confined my reading, of late years, to the works of the ancients and those of the elder writers in the modern languages. We insensibly admire what we habitually imitate; and an aversion to the epigrammatic unconnected periods of the fashionable *Anglo-Gallican* taste, has too often made me willing to forget, that the stately march and difficult evolutions, which characterize the eloquence of Hooker, Bacon, Milton, and Jeremy Taylor, are, notwithstanding their intrinsic excellence, still less suited to a periodical essay. This fault I am now endeavouring to correct, though I can never so far sacrifice my judgement to the desire of being immediately popular, as to cast my sentences in the French moulds, or affect a style which an ancient critic would have deemed purposely invented for persons troubled with asthma to read, and for those to comprehend who labour under the more pitiable asthma of a short-witted intellect. It cannot but be injurious to the human mind never to be called into effort; and the habit of receiving pleasure without any exercise of thought, by the mere excitement of curiosity and sensibility, may be justly ranked among the worst effects of novel-reading. It is true, that these short and unconnected sentences are easily and instantly understood: but it is equally true, that, wanting all the cement of thought as well as of style, all the connections, and (if you will forgive so trivial a metaphor) all the *hooks-and-eyes* of the memory, they are as easily forgotten; or rather, it is scarcely possible they should be remembered. Nor is it less true that those who confine their reading to such books, dwarf their own faculties, and finally reduce their understandings to a deplorable imbecility.

He might, in contradiction to the vulgar notion that long sentences *necessarily* shew the author guilty of what is termed diffuseness, have added, that length of sentences furnishes a capital mean of being concise; that, in fact, whoever is determined on the greatest possible parsimony of words, *must* write in long sentences, if there is any thing like combination in his thoughts. For, in a long sentence, several indispensable conditionalities, collateral notices, and qualifying or connecting circumstances, may be expressed by short members of the sentence, which must else be put in so many separate sentences; thus making two pages of short sentences to express, and in a much less connected manner what one well-constructed long sentence would have expressed in half a page:—and yet an unthinking reader might very possibly cite these two pages as a specimen of concise writing, and such a half page as a sample of diffuseness.

We had intended to make a few remarks on the several essays in this volume, considered as to their subjects; and on the most prominent of the principles endeavoured to be illustrated and established. But we have dwelt so long on the more general qualities of its intellectual and literary character, that our readers will very willingly excuse us from prolonging a course of observations, in which we have by no means succeeded to our wish in the attempt to convey a general idea of the most extraordinary production that has, at any time, come under our official notice. We confess, too, that we should feel no small degree of diffidence in undertaking any thing like an analysis of disquisitions so abstruse, so little reduced to the formal arrangement of system, so interrupted and unfinished, and so often diverging to a great distance from the leading direction.

The subjects largely discussed are few. Among them are, the duty and laws of communicating truth, including the liberty of the press; the theories of the several most celebrated political philosophers, or schools of philosophers; errors of party spirit; vulgar errors respecting taxation; the law of nations; Paley's doctrine of general consequences as the foundation of the criterion of morality; sketches of Sir Alexander

Ball; the proper discipline for rising, in point of intellectual freedom and vigour, above the general state of the age; and several other topics of less comprehensive denomination. But no adequate guess can be made, from these denominations, at the variety and latitude of the inquiries and observations. There is not a great deal expressly on the subject of religion; the intended statement of the author's general views of it having been delayed till the work prematurely closed; but there are many occasional references in a spirit of great seriousness. He asserts the radical depravity, to a very great extent, of human nature, though in forms of language most widely different, to be sure, from that of orthodox sermons and bodies of divinity. As the basis, however, of some of his principles of moral philosophy, he claims a certain profound and half mystical reverence for the mental and moral essence and organization of man, which we find it somewhat difficult to render. He is a most zealous assertor of free-agency. In one place the word Methodism is used exactly in the way in which it is employed by those whom the author knows to be fools, profligates, or bigots. He is perfectly apprized, how much of intelligent belief and ardent piety is comprehended within the tenets and the state of the affections, to which this term of opprobrium is generally applied; and we were astonished therefore to see him so far consenting to adopt what he knew to be the lingo of irreligion.

A portion of his political reasonings and reflections, is retrospective to the times of the French revolution; and distinguishes and censures, with very great judgment and eloquence, the respective errors of our aristocratic and democratic parties at that time. Some interesting references are made to the author's own views, and hopes, and projects at that period. As those views and projects had nothing to do with revolutions in England, we wish that some passages expressed in the tone of self-exculpation had been spared. It was no great harm, if a young man of speculative and ardent genius saw nothing in the political state of any country in Christendom to prevent him wishing, that a new constitution of society could be tried somewhere in the wildernesses of America. In his professing to have very long since renounced the visionary ideas and wishes which, under various modifications of the notion and the love of liberty, elated so many superior minds in that eventful season, we were anxious to see him preserve the dignity of keeping completely clear of the opposite extreme of approving all things as they are—to see him preserve, in short, the lofty spirit in which he wrote, many years since, his sublime 'Ode to France'.

And there is in the work less to displease on that head, than in many instances of the 'impetuous recoil' of men of talents from the principles of violent democracy. But we confess we have perceived a more favourable aspect than we should deem compatible with the spirit of a perfect moralist, philanthropist, and patriot, towards the present state of political institutions and practices. We should think that at least these are not times to extenuate the evil of enormous taxation; to make light of the suggestion of the superior benefit of employing a given number of men rather in making canals and building bridges than in destructive military expeditions; to celebrate the happiness of having the much greater part of a thousand millions of a national debt, and the attendant benefit of a paper-currency; or to join in reprobating any party who are zealous for a reform of the legislature and political corruptions.—There is, however, in the work, much acute speculation on political systems that has no direct reference to the practical politics of the day. It should be observed too, that, beyond all other political speculators, our author mingles important moral and philosophical principles with his reasonings.

The most of what may be called entertainment, may perhaps be found in a number of letters written from Germany by a young Englishman, who passed among his college companions by the name of Satyrane, and whom, if there were not so much said or implied in his praise, accompanied too by some slight expression as if he were not now surviving, we should mightily suspect to be no other than the author himself.

A whole number (the 13th) is occupied with the story of a tragical event that happened at Nuremberg, a little before Mr. C. first saw that place. The principal personages were a baker's orphan and outcast daughter, and a washerwoman. He is very particular in asserting the truth of the account; but if he had not, we should have believed it nevertheless; for the plain reason, that we think it surpasses the powers of fiction, the powers of invention of even Mr. C. No abstract can be given to make it at all intelligible; but it is so strange, so horrible, and so sublime, that we should think meanly of the feelings of any person, who, after reading it, would not turn with indifference from the comparative insipidity of any thing to be found in tragedy or romance.

We ought to have given a few extracts from the work; but we did not know where to select them, amidst such a wilderness of uncommon ideas. Many other passages may be more interesting than the following representation of one of Luther's skirmishes with Satan, in the Warteburg, a castle near Eisenach, in which he was confined many months, by a friendly and provident force, and where our author was shewn the black mark on the wall, produced, as every visitant is told, by the intrepid reformer's throwing his ink-stand at the enemy.

[quotes the passage]

We cannot conclude without expressing an earnest wish, that this original thinker and eloquent writer may be persuaded to put the literary public speedily in possession, by successive volumes of essays, of an ample portion of those refined speculations, the argument and the strongest illustrations of which he is well known to have in an almost complete state in his mind—and many of which will never be in any other mind, otherwise than as communicated from him. The chief alteration desirable, for his readers' sake, to be made in his mode of writing, is a resolute restriction on that mighty profusion and excursiveness of thought, in which he is tempted to suspend the pursuit and retard the attainment of the one distinct object which should be clearly kept in view; and, added to this, a more patient and prolonged effort to reduce the abstruser part of his ideas, as much as their subtle quality will possibly admit, to a substantial and definable form.

given by *Teresa* to the pretensions of *Don Alvar* alienates the friendship of his brother from him, and resentment for slighted love, aided by a secret consciousness of his brother's superior virtues and amiable qualities, at length so inflames the mind of *Ordonio*, naturally proud, gloomy, and revengeful, that he resolves upon the destruction of his rival. For this purpose he employs *Isidore*, a Moresco chieftain, but pretended Christian, who with two others, watching the expected return of *Don Alvar* from abroad, attack him in a solitary place by the sea-side, but are disarmed by him, and compelled to a parley. *Ordonio* had not revealed to *Isidore* the secret that it was his brother's life which was to be sacrificed to his jealousy, but misleads him by a feigned story of a stranger, whose betrothed mistress he had first dishonoured, and then married, and whose revenge could only be appeased by blood. In the contest between them, however, both *Isidore* and *Don Alvar* discover that it is his brother who has attempted his life, and that that brother has dishonoured his mistress. Heart-struck at the news, he throws away his sword, and offers his breast to the assassin, who touched with pity spares his life, on condition that he absents himself from Spain for a certain period, and swears to observe an inviolable secrecy. Accordingly, *Don Alvar*, with his faithful servant, *Zulimez*, departs, and after fighting for three years under Prince Maurice in the wars of the Low Countries, returns to his native land, his mind still torn with anguish at the remembrance of disappointed love, and of a brother's wrongs. At this point of time, the play opens. *Don Alvar*, with the aid of his companion, and disguised in a Moorish dress, proposes to see *Teresa*, and learn from her the truth of the story he had heard from *Isidore*. For, armed with proof, as that story was, faint as his hopes were, yet his despair had never been able to banish from his mind the image of *Teresa*, her gentle virtues, her former love—'the garden and first play-time of their youth'. She, in the mean time, doubting the death of *Don Alvar*, who is said to have perished in a storm, within sight of shore, and confirmed in her dislike to the person and manners of *Don Ordonio*, in opposition to the entreaties of her guardian, the father of *Alvar* and of *Ordonio*, remains faithful to her first vows. An interview, which soon after takes place, between *Teresa* and her lover, when he mysteriously relates his own story, but without disclosing his person, confirms her in her fears and resolutions. *Isidore* having fallen into the hands of the Inquisition, *Alhadra*, his wife, applies to *Ordonio* to protect her husband. This renews the intercourse between them, and *Ordonio* once more consults with *Isidore* on the subject of his love, who recommends him to a neighbouring wizard. The magician, whom *Ordonio* seeks in the wild and rocky dell where he conceals himself, proves to be *Alvar* in disguise. He tries indirectly to probe the conscience of his brother, and first learns from him the fidelity of *Teresa*, and the cruel artifice which had been practised to impose upon his credulity. He at length consents to assist *Ordonio* in a project to persuade *Teresa* of the death of *Alvar*, by invoking his spirit, and by giving her pretended preternatural proofs of the fate of her lover. This scene takes place with much pomp and ceremony; and the invocation, addressed by the supposed sorcerer to the spirit of *Alvar*, is replete with poetry and pathos. *Donna Teresa* retires from this scene, shocked at its impiety; and the ceremony is suddenly interrupted by the entrance of the Inquisitors, who have been informed of the unhallowed proceeding. *Ordonio* contrives to justify himself to the chief Inquisitor, by pretending that his real object was to obtain a more pregnant proof against the sorcerer, and the latter is consigned, under the care of *Ordonio*, to a dungeon in the castle. *Ordonio*'s suspicions having fixed upon *Isidore*, as connected with *Alvar*, whom he does not yet know, but of whose designs he is apprehensive, he finds out his Moorish accomplice in his retreat in the Alpuxarras, and at once rids himself of his fears, and satisfies his revenge by treacherously taking his life. Meanwhile *Teresa*, struck with a fancied resemblance in the supposed sorcerer to her lover, and feeling for the honour of his situation, visits the cell of *Alvar*, who discovers himself to her. Just at the moment of this affecting recognition, *Ordonio* enters with a poisoned goblet, which he presents to his brother, *Teresa* having retired out of sight. A scene of high-wrought interest now follows between the two brothers: *Ordonio*, alarmed and stung to madness by *Alvar*'s keen reproaches, attempts to kill him, but is prevented by *Teresa*, who rushes in between them, and discovers that it is his brother. *Ordonio*, filled with remorse and shame, feeling himself unworthy to live, tries to fall on his own sword. But while *Alvar* and *Teresa* are endeavouring to reconcile him to life, the doors of the dungeon burst open, and *Alhadra*, with a band of Morescoes rushing in, revenges the death of her husband, by that of his murderer. The Moors hastily retire at the approach of *Lord Valdez* and his followers, and *Don Alvar* is restored to his *Teresa*, amidst the tears and blessings of his father, who is yet ignorant of the death and the crimes of *Ordonio*.

The story of this play, of which our readers will be able to form a tolerably correct idea from the foregoing outline, affords an admirable opportunity for the display of those powers of natural description and sentiment, which Mr. Coleridge is so well known to possess. The author's name stands high for the reputation of genius, and he has very successfully employed that genius in the production of a dramatic work, which is fraught with beauty and interest. In the progress of the fable, the wild and romantic scenery of Spain, the manners and super-stitions of the age, are described with a grace of poetic fancy, which, while it brings the objects before us by a magic charm, forwards the developement of the plot, and gives a peculiar interest to the characters and sentiments of the persons represented. The wild harp of poetry mingles with, and softens the sterner voice of the tragic muse. In the judicious appropriation, as well as in the richness and beauty of his decorations, we have no hesitation in saying that Mr. Coleridge has highly succeeded. His images are not less striking from their originality, and a peculiar felicity of expression, than from their intrinsic merit. Among many other passages we might notice the description of *Alvar*'s love for music when a child, the sorcerer's invocation, and the song in the third act; and the beautiful and impassioned apostrophe on life, near the conclusion of the play. The conduct of the story does not involve any violent transitions, or gross improbabilities. In executing this part of his task, the author discovers equal judgment and skill. The interest is kept alive by a succession of situations and events, which call forth the finest sensibilities of the human breast, without shocking the imagination by an accumulation of hopeless and unmerited suffer-ing. The artful management by which, in the distribution of poetical justice, the punishment of guilt is effected by the guilty, or devolves on a fierce and uncontroulable spirit of revenge, in the person of *Alhadra*, so as to leave no stain on the more perfect and interesting characters of the play, deserves the highest praise. In the conception and delinea-tion of character, Mr. Coleridge has shewn a powerful imagination, as well as deep reflection on the general principles which regulate and modify our stronger passions. The characters of *Alhadra*, *Isidore*, and *Ordonio* are the most marked and prominent. The last of these appears the most studied, the most complex and refined, and is, we should suspect, the author's favourite. Besides the obvious features, and stronger workings of the passions in this character, there are many traits of a more subtle nature which, we trust, will not escape the nice observation of an enlightened audience, though they may be regarded as too meta-physical for tragedy. The character of *Ordonio*, as Mr. Coleridge has described it, is that of a man of originally strong understanding, and morbid feelings; whose reason points out to him a high and severe standard of unattainable perfection, while his temperament urges him on to a violation of all the ordinary distinctions of right and wrong; whose pride finds consolation for its vices in its contempt for the dull virtues, or perhaps hypocritical pretences of the generality of men: whose conscience seeks a balm for its wounds in theoretical speculations on human depravity, and whose moody and preposterous self love, by an habitual sophistry, exaggerates the slightest affront, or even a suspicion of possible injury, into solid reasons for the last acts of hatred and revenge. A lie is with him a sufficient provocation of a murder, and the destruction of his supposed enemy, from which he shrinks as an assassination, is instantly converted into an act of heroism by the attempt of his antagonist to defend himself. Thus he says to *Alvar*, whom he suspects of deceiving him: 'I thank thee for that lie, it has restored me! Villain, now I am thy master, and thou shalt die!' And again to *Isidore*, when he reluctantly draws his sword in the cavern scene—'now this is excellent, and warms the blood. My heart was drawing back with weak and womanish scruples. Now my vengeance beckons me onward with a warrior's mien, and claims that life my pity robbed her of. Now I will kill thee, thankless slave, and count it among my comfortable thoughts hereafter'. There are many instances of the same kind, by which the Author has carried on what may be called the underplot of the character, and which shew the hand of a master. We have insisted the longer on this excellence, because of its rarity, for, except Shakespeare, who is every where full of these double readings and running accompaniments to the ruling passion, there is scarcely any other dramatic writer who has so much as attempted to describe the involuntary, habitual reaction of the passions, and understanding on each other: We say, the involuntary, or unconscious reaction which takes place, for as to the known, conscious opposition and struggle for mastery between reason and passion, duty and inclination, there is no want of rhetorical declamation, of profound calculations, and able casuistry on the subject in the generality of dramatic writers, ancient or modern, foreign or domestic. The gradation of confidence in villainy, corresponding with the rank and power of the guilty, is very pointedly marked in the character of *Isidore*, the accomplice of *Ordonio*. There is a selfish, calculating cunning, a servile meanness, a cowardly superstitious hesitating scrupulousness in his conduct, corresponding with his subordination in crime, and which the stronger will and self-originating passions of his employer almost

E

totally subdue in him. The two principal female characters, *Alhadra* and *Teresa*, have a very beautiful effect, as contrasted with each other. The former of these is a Moorish woman, of high spirit, and dauntless activity, ever mindful of her wrongs, full of fears, and ready for revenge. Her natural temperament, the spirit of her religion, the persecution she has suffered, her husband's death, combine in working her up to a pitch of heroic energy and frenzied passion, which is finely relieved by the tender sensibility, the meek piety, and resigned fortitude of the orphan ward of the *Marquis Valdez*. The scene in the beginning of the first act, in which *Teresa* is introduced defending her *widowed* attachment to her first love, is full of a dignified sorrow, mingled with an artless simplicity of nature, which has been seldom equalled. In some parts of this character, however, there is something of a German cast, of that sentimental whine and affectation of fine feeling, of which we have had a full quantity at secondhand, and in translations. There are also some occasional words and phrases, which are too often repeated, and which savour too much of a particular style, to be perfectly to our taste. *Sed ubi plurima nitent*, &c. The language is in general rich, bold, elegant, natural,—and the verse unites to the studied harmony of metrical composition, a variety of cadence, an ease and flexibility, by which it can be adapted, without effort, to the characteristic expression and sudden transitions of impassioned declamation.

It has been observed, that dramatic writers may be divided into two classes, that Shakespeare alone gives the substance of tragedy, and expresses the very soul of the passions, while all other writers convey only a general description or shadowy outline of them—that his is the real text of nature, and the rest but paraphrases and commentaries on it, rhetorical, poetical, and sentimental. If Mr. Coleridge has not been able to break the spell, and to penetrate the inmost circle of the heart, he has approached nearer than almost any other writer, and has produced a very beautiful representation of human nature, which will vie with the best and most popular of our sentimental dramas.

Too much praise cannot be bestowed on the exertions of the actors. Mr. Elliston's representation of *Don Alvar* preserved a tone of solemn and impressive dignity, suited to the elevation of the character. Mr. Rae, by the force of his action, and by the striking changes both of his voice and countenance, pourtrayed, with admirable effect, the conflict of passions in the bosom of *Ordonio*. The management of the scenery, decorations, &c. gave every possible assistance to the success of the play. The *coup-d'œil* of the invocation scene was one of the most novel and picturesque we remember to have witnessed. The play might, perhaps, be reduced to a more convenient length by omitting some of the scenes in the third act, after the entrance of the Inquisitors, which retard the progress of the story, without heightening the interest or developing the characters. The remonstrances between *Valdez* and *Teresa*, on the subject of her love, become tedious from repetition; and the contrast between the pictures of the brothers is too evidently copied from the well-known passage in Shakespeare. We are decidedly of opinion, that the entrance of the Moors, and their assassination of *Ordonio*, ought to precede the final reconciliation between him and his brother. 'The quality of mercy' ought not to be 'strained',—especially on the stage. The duty of forgiveness, however amiable in itself, is not a dramatic virtue; and a tragic writer ought rather to effect his purpose by appealing to the passions of his audience, than to their goodness. The play was received throughout with marks of the deepest attention, and reiterated bursts of applause, and announced for a second representation amidst the acclamations of the audience.

40. Unsigned review, *Morning Post*

25 January 1813

The review opens with a summary of the plot.

Such is a hasty sketch of the story. Of the manner in which it has been dramatized, we have not time at present to say little more, than that it appeared to merit the extraordinary applause with which it was received. The language is equally poetic and impassioned, the incidents are sufficient to keep the attention alive during the whole of the representation, and some of the situations are strikingly calculated for dramatic effect. The characters of the two brothers are admirably drawn and finely contrasted. That of *Teresa* does not rise to much above mediocrity; but the conception of the part of the Moorish woman is as full of poetic imagination as it is bold and masterly; and the opening scenes in particular are truly sublime and interesting.

The moral is perfect, and strict poetical justice is done on the guilty alone. The style is throughout poetical and classical, and far above the common level. It abounds with fine touches of nature, and the tender feelings are almost incessantly appealed to. Many of the passages were received with loud, general, and prolonged applause; while not one instance occurred of meanness or vulgarity, or affectation, to excite the disapprobation of the audience. The Tragedy was indeed heard from beginning to end with the most marked distinction, and announced for repetition amid shouts from every corner of the Theatre. But all particular criticism, both of the Piece and of the Actors, we must defer till our next Paper; the more willingly, because we consider a first night's representation as little more than a mere regular and formal rehearsal.

Some music introduced in the Spell (3d act) is very beautiful, and an invocation to the spirits of the dead, finely composed by Kelly,[1] was exquisitely sung by Mrs. Bland. The Epilogue is lively, and makes several happy hits at some of the reigning follies of the day. The house was crowded in all parts at a very early hour.

41. Unsigned review, *The Times*

25 January 1813

So much of the general attention has been in later years turned upon Spain, that it might not seem unnatural to expect deeper results than those connected with mere passing curiosity. There was even in the nature of the crisis what might well have awakened the higher and more secluded feelings. War is the scene for the fiercer qualities of

---

[1] Michael Kelly (1764?-1826), singer and composer.

man: but there is nothing single in the human heart; and those qualities, repulsive as they are, are surrounded with a crowd of others full of nobleness and generosity, partially shaded, perhaps, by the alliance: like Milton's fallen spirits, their brightness dimmed by their following 'that leading spirit of ill', but exhibiting traces of grandeur, haughty bearing, and faded beauty, that compel the wonder of less towering and perturbed natures. The Spanish war, offering to us the perpetual spectacle of heroic resolution struggling against arrogant strength, individual bravery and disunited counsel proudly waving the sword in the eyes of the most powerful, connected, and disciplined mass of force that the modern world had seen, was still 'more germane' to the impressions which generous spirits love; and we should not have been surprised to see the most distinguished geniuses of the age engrossed by the contest, and, in the language of Philosophy and the Muse, bequeathing to the ages to come the high lessons of wisdom for which that contest had been ordained. Yet upon this striking subject, our poets and philosophers have been eminently silent; and, with the exception of a few poems of moderate merit, we are scarcely able to recollect any thing by which English genius will have paid its contribution to the cause of patriotism and honour. A drama has at length been produced by Mr. Coleridge, a writer already known to the public; and we were inclined to hope, that the stigma of indolence and apathy was about to be taken away, by a man, presumed to be at least not cold to the pressure of the higher powers, in other countries than Spain. This drama was presented for the first time on Saturday, and called, or in the more scrupulous phrase of the author, 'is to be called *Remorse*'. The plot was singularly involved and laboured....

[a summary of the plot follows]

The first impression which we have to notice, is, that the Author, if his object had been to asperse the Spanish character, could not have constructed his machinery with more obvious designs; and for the sympathies which that recovered and purified name excites, has only offered us the painful memory of that time, when, by the vices of the Government, and the habits of a half-barbarous and irritated people, it was synonimous with persecution. But scarcely forgiving him for this infidelity to the reason and feeling of our day, we pass to those features in which the public opinion may more pointedly coincide with that which we are forced to express. Mr. Coleridge is a poet, and it would be next to impossible that a work of his could be utterly destitute of poetic value; but he is one of a school whose conceptions scorn the bounds of humbler taste, and his 'vaulting ambition hath o'erleapt them all'. There are, however, intermingled with those fierce ventures, occasional passages of true poetic cadence. The speech of the Moresco woman, describing her imprisonment, is a strong and deep picture of feelings that could scarcely be coloured too strongly. Her story of her husband's murder is finely told; her eager listening, her hearing his last groan from the bottom of the chasm, her finding his sword, and her solemn determination to have blood for blood, did honour to the capacity that conceived and expressed them: and in defiance of the foolish blasphemy, in which she is made to talk about 'plucking the dead out of Heaven' and other exploded plagiarisms from the German school, the whole dialogue of the part received great applause. The actress who performed it deserves a higher mention than we now have time to give to her. Mrs. Glover, as a comic actress, exhibits decided talents; but we have long been of opinion, that her strength lies in a superior department, and that as a tragedian, she has but little to fear from any competition. On Saturday, she exhibited some of the most subduing and striking powers of the art, and if the play is to live, she has a most important share in the merit of keeping it in existence. We speak with restraint and unwillingly of the defects of a work which must have cost its author so much labour. We are peculiarly reluctant to touch the anxieties of a man who has already exhibited talent, and whose various acquirements and manly application of them deserve the favour of those who value literature. But to conceal the truth is only to do final injury: and it must be acknowledged that this drama has sins, nay, a multitude, almost beyond the covering of charity. Its first fault, and the most easily avoided, is its unwieldy length: it was almost five hours long. Its next, is its passion for laying hold of every thing that could allow an apology for a description. Murderers stop short with the dagger in their hands, to talk of 'roses on mountain sides': fathers start back from their children to moralise: and a lover, in the outrage of disappointed love, lingers to tell at what hour of the day he parted from his mistress, how she smiled, and how the sun smiled, how its light fell upon the vallies, and the sheep, and the vineyards, and the lady, and *how red her tears were* in 'the slant beam'. This may be poetical, but it has no connexion with the plain, rapid, and living truth of the Drama. There is an essential difference in those two branches of the art. With the mere poet, time is as nothing, he may wonder and rest, and indulge his eye—like a pilgrim offer his hymn at every shrine, by the way—and then resume his sandals and his staff, and pace onward to the altar of his patron. To the dramatist, time is as every thing. He has not a moment to waste, he carries an important mission, life and death are hanging on his steps, and he must speed forward without venturing to turn his eye from that spot in the horizon, which at every moment enlarges as he speeds, and where his coming is to agitate or appease so many hearts. We are slow to speak of faults as applied to this writer: but he has not yet learned this value of time. His plot is intolerably curved and circuitous, indistinct beyond all power of pleasurable apprehension, and broken beyond all reach of continued interest. The author has not brought to his task, the one greater quality which is above all, and atones for all—a vigorous and combing mind, that muscular grasp of understanding, capable by its force of compressing the weak and the scattered, into a firm and vigorous solidity. The dramatist must be this, or he is nothing. His office has its difficulty. It can be no common or inferior intelligence, that can thus combine in the next degree to creation, embody its loose and fluctuating materials into substantial shapeliness, and breathe 'the breath of life into his nostrils', and bid it come forth active and animated, clothed with beauty, and instinct with soul. We must conclude our observations here. The performers exerted themselves with great zeal. Rae, who had a most laborious part, displayed unusual spirit, and was loudly cheered. Elliston, Miss Smith, De Camp, were equally favoured. The prologue was, we hope, by some 'd—d good-natured friend', who had an interest in injuring the play: it was abominable. The epilogue seemed to come from the same hand, and had precisely the same merits.[1] It seemed to be composed for the express purpose of trying how many pure stupidities might be comprised in fifty lines, and how far Miss Smith's popularity might be proof against her performance. This specimen of her recitation was singularly lachrymose and lamentable. The applause was violent at the fall of the curtain.

[1] Charles Lamb furnished the prologue and Coleridge himself the epilogue (see P*W*, ii, 816n.).

42. Thomas Barnes, *Examiner*

31 January 1813, 73-4

This unsigned review has been attributed to Thomas Barnes (Edmund Blunden, *Leigh Hunt's 'Examiner' Examined*, London 1928, 36). Barnes (1785-1841) was editor of *The Times* from 1817 and a member of Leigh Hunt's literary circle.

Dunces have so long kept exclusive possession of the stage, and by a sort of intelligent consciousness rather inconsistent with their general want of apprehension, are so unanimous in their praise and support of each other, that we almost despaired to see a man of genius step forward to dispute their (from its long existence) almost sacred title. It is one of the pains as well as pleasures of genius—by which term we mean powerful intellect combined with strong-feeling—to be tenderly delicate and exquisitely alive to ridicule and censure: though eagerly fond of praise, it shuns the bustle of public competition, and wishes rather to appeal to a few similarly constructed minds. As that timidity is founded on pride, not on modesty, it is easily convertible into a less amiable feeling: though every sneer tortures the very heart's core, self-approbation presents a haughty convincing firmness against every attack, and as the bashfulness of an aukward school-boy speedily degenerates into hard-faced impudence, so the shrinking man of genius, by a short process, becomes an insolent, overweening being, despising the opinions of all men out of his own partial circle, and looking upon all the rest of mankind as 'mere dung o' the soil'. We have thrown out these preliminary remarks, to explain at once the general absence of men of genius from the stage, and the few exceptions. Mr. Coleridge, whose poetic talents are undisputed, though they are deformed by sentimentalities, and whines, and infant lispings, has, it appears, hardened by the public ordeal which he has for some years undergone, manfully disregarded the pelting scorn of many a critic, and ventures now to lay his claims before a mixed multitude. Instead of the heart-expressed approbation of refined and feeling taste, he

122

courts the applause of unsmirched artificers, young unintellectual citizens, and of those negatives of feeling and of thought, who, by a term more opprobrious than any which satire ever invented, call themselves people of fashion. His appeal has been crowned, as the French say, with complete success, and we will now examine a little how far it deserved it.

According to the most approved plan of criticism, it is necessary, we believe, to give first an account of the plot: though, as Burke somewhere says, 'nothing is more dull in telling than the plot of a play', that however is not our fault: so, begging pardon of our Readers if we make them yawn, we proceed to the story:

[a brief summary of the plot follows]

Such is the story, which we dismiss with little care, as in most dramas, and especially in this, it is a thing of minor importance: a very poor story, well-conducted, may excite the highest interest, and here Mr. Coleridge has excelled. The fable is managed and developed with a rapidity which never languishes, an intelligibility which a child might follow, and a surprize which would keep awake the most careless attention. The skill indeed with which the situations are disposed, so as to create effect, would have done honour to a veteran dramatist; for this we suppose Mr. Coleridge is indebted to his acquaintance with the German drama, which, in the hands of Schiller at least, redeems all its faults by its excellence, and among its other striking beauties, abounds in the picturesque. We never saw more interest excited in a theatre than was expressed at the sorcery-scene in the third act. The altar flaming in the distance, the solemn invocation, the pealing music of the mystic song, altogether produced a combination so awful, as nearly to overpower reality, and make one half believe the enchantment which delighted our senses.

The characters most laboured by the author are *Ordonio* and *Alhadra*. The first is a philosophic misanthrope, a *Hamlet* corrupted by bad passions—a man of distempered feelings and perverted intellect; who reasons not to subdue, but to excuse his bad appetites; who satisfies his conscience that assassination is a mere bagatelle—nay more, that it is praiseworthy, because man is an air-bladder, a bubble, and because the death of a man gives occasion for the birth of 10,000 worms, who of course having equal capacity of happiness, are equally happy with the displaced gentleman. This last reasoning might appear conclusive to a jury of worms, but we think no beings else, not even twelve metaphysicians, could be found who would acquit *Ordonio*. We do not object to it as immoral, but as silly, and not consistent with the powerful intellect ascribed to this bad man. The character of *Alhadra* deserves unmixed praise; it is an impressive, high-wrought picture of a strongly-feeling, noble-spirited woman, whom tenderness supplies with energy, and whose daring springs from the gentlest affections—maternal and conjugal love. Such a woman, if her lot had been happy, would have been an example of virtues but misery converts her into a revengeful murderer. Both these characters are developed with a force of thinking, and a power of poetry, which have been long strangers to the stage, and the return of which we hail as the omen of better days. Indeed, in none of his works has Mr. C. exhibited so much of his sentimental and descriptive power, so little deformed with his peculiar affectations. His images have his usual truth and originality without their usual meanness: his tenderness is as exquisite as in his best pieces, and does not degenerate into his usual whining. There are many passages to which we could refer as instances of his poetical excellence: the invocation of *Alvar*, in the 3d act, is indeed a strain of a higher mood: so is *Alhadra's* description of her feelings, when she rushed to the cavern where her husband was murdered, yet feared to speak lest no voice should answer. Nor were we less pleased with *Teresa's* delineation of the two brothers, though it brought to our minds *Hamlet's* contrasted pictures of his father and his uncle.

The piece does not owe much to its acting. Mrs. Glover, indeed, surprised us: with a face comic in every feature, with a person which engages no interest, with a voice whose every tone is unpleasing, she contrived to present to us one of the most impressive portraitures of strong passion that we ever recollect to have seen:

> Before such merit all objections fly,
> Pritchard's genteel, and Garrick's six feet high.[1]

Mr. Rae, in the last scene, shewed that his face was capable of expressing the most complex workings of the soul. Mr. Elliston was animated, and that is all. Of Miss Smith we would rather say nothing.

---

[1] Hannah Pritchard (1711-1768), a fine actress whose pretensions to gentility were a source of merriment.

43. Unsigned review, *Satirist*

February 1813, xii, 187-92

On Saturday the 23d, while the new comedy[1] was acting at Covent Garden, the visitors to Drury Lane were treated with the extraordinary production of a *new tragedy* called *Remorse*, and written by Mr. Coleridge.

As we like to have people's *own* account of matters, we have extracted the following *modest* sketch of the plot from the newspapers, to which it was kindly furnished by the person most likely to understand what the said plot really was.

[a plot summary and list of the cast follows]

There are peculiar circumstances in the case of Mr. Coleridge, which induce us not to animadvert, with the severity it merits, on the littleness of self panegyric; and the small reliance which must be placed by a poet, on the validity of his claims to public favour, who dare not trust his fame to unbiassed criticism; but practises the delusion of passing sentence upon himself, in every channel (and they are very numerous) to which he has access. This is a meanness unworthy a bard of Mr. Coleridge's acknowledged abilities, and deserving of more pointed reprehension than we shall now bestow.

Such of the critics in diurnal and hebdomadal publications, as have delivered their opinions, out of the sphere of the author and his friends, have, with all that capacity of mind and acuteness of intellect which enables them at once to grasp and comprehend a composition so elevated in the literary scale as tragedy, with equal facility, to their understanding of a pantomime, or a farce, have upon the whole been less favourable to the pretensions of *Remorse*, than the immediate friends of the author, though, in most instances, their flimsy censures have been as devoid of good foundation, as the sweeping encomia of the latter have been notoriously ridiculous, offensive, and absurd. Endeavouring to divest ourselves of the feelings of disgust, created on the one side by fulsome flattery, and the prejudices excited on the other by unmerited rebuke, we shall proceed, as impartially as possible, to

[1] R. F. Jameson's *The Students of Salamanca*.

consider this play as it appears on the stage; reserving our comments upon those points which are more peculiarly fitted for the study and analysis of the closet, till such time as we shall have the opportunity of perusing it in print.

The tragedy of *Remorse* is by no means a dramatic felicity. The author belongs to a school of sentimental whiners—or affectors of babyish simplicity—of amateurs of pretty touches of nature—of descriptive bardlings—the whole scope and tendency of whose writings are as dissimilar as can be conceived to whatever has been or can be effective upon the stage. We are ready to acknowledge that Mr. Coleridge is one of the least tainted of this flock; and has given proofs of talents and judgment very superior to most of the fraternity. But still there was sufficient of the leaven of the 'Naturals' about him, to cause us not to be very sanguine in our expectations upon the present occasion.

The radical defect of the play is *description*—It is all description and no action. An impatient lover stops to *describe* moonlight, and silvan scenery, and the looks of his mistress, and his own dreams—a murderer replaces the ready dagger under his cloak, to *describe* his feelings and his sights, and his past actions, and his present apprehensions—a despairing damsel rushing out to 'seek the *grave*', retards her immediate journey to *describe* moral combinations, and descant an ethical truism, with all the acumen of a learned divine or logical professor—each person has to perform such a task of description as is suited to their various capacities; and there is no relief to the tedium of didactic poetry, in heavy dialogue, altogether incompatible with stage effect, or dramatic excellence. Take the best of these *Laments*—the story told by *Alhadra* of her pangs, when some half dozen years ago she fell under the fangs of the Inquisition, and was imprisoned in a dark cell with her infant, it affords only an example to be shunned, of fine writing thrown away upon an unworthy subject. The force and violence of the feelings are not natural, to the mere recollection and relation of the distant misery, and, if without blasphemy, we might mention Shakespeare and Coleridge together, we would refer for a contrast to the scene in *Macbeth*, where Macduff is informed of the desolation of his house. This is the agony of humanity, that the colouring of the author—this the action of life, that the description of the poet.

Another main objection to this play is its want of general probability, and the numerous partial aberrations with which it abounds. These arise principally out of the mis-shapen nature of the characters, which are drawn with a profound disregard of truth or consistency. Nothing, for instance, can be more difficult for the mind to yield to, as the obstinate refusal of a ruffian, who out of gratitude had undertaken and attempted a murder, to enter upon a harmless stratagem which was to effect that which the designed assassination had failed to accomplish. This is to swallow a camel, and strain at a gnat, with a vengeance, and no alteration in the relative circumstances of the parties warrants so gross a departure from all that is likely or natural. Again, what can bend our reason to endure the exploit of a virtuous lady, Teresa, who only knowing the disguised Alvar as a dreamer and a sorcerer, and strongly suspecting him as the murderer of her lamented lover, yet undertakes to visit him in his lonely dungeon, and thence to liberate him. When she comes thither, indeed her conduct is perfectly of a piece with her errand; for she very humanely falls upon the fancied assassin's neck, and charitably and with Christian-like piety forgives him. The dream of Isidore about the cavern, and the whole of the scene in which he is slain, are peculiarly reprehensible for dereliction from the common workings of nature, and the difference in the actions of the parties from what they should have been, had the writer inquired what men in such situations would do, rather than what would be most convenient for him to portray.

But we shall dwell no longer on these points—the entire contrivance of the play is bad—the plot is not adapted to be the vehicle for the finer effusions of the tragic muse. None of the persons employed excite any considerable degree of interest; for they are all (with one exception, *Alhadra*) artificial pictures, and not men and women acting under the impulses by which mankind are governed. The subject indeed seems better suited for the ground-work of a comedy, than a tragedy—convert, or rather soften down, the atrocity of *Ordonio* into a crime of a dye less deep, and 'do no murder' on Isidore, and there is not an event in the play which might not be turned advantageously to excellent comic effect.

We have already noticed, that the characters are inconsistent, and unnatural—the observation applies with peculiar force to those of Ordonio, Isidore, Teresa, and Alhadra. The first is a very laboured subject, and laboured to little effect. The following is the author's *own* manifesto in the *Morning Chronicle*, in which his *own* critique on his *own* tragedy (*perhaps though a friend*) appeared on Monday the 25th:

The character of *Ordonio*, as Mr. Coleridge has described it, is that of a man of originally strong understanding, and morbid feelings; whose reason points out to him a high and severe standard of unattainable perfection, while his temperament urges him on to a violation of all the ordinary distinctions of right and wrong; whose pride finds consolation for its vices in its contempt for the dull virtues, or perhaps hypocritical pretences of the generality of men: whose conscience seeks a balm for its wounds in theoretical speculations on human depravity, and whose moody and preposterous self-love, by an habitual sophistry, exaggerates the slightest affront, or even a suspicion of possible injury, into solid reasons for the last acts of hatred and revenge.

This is altogether an imaginary man, for, we will venture to pronounce, that a mind of this description never had existence. But what shall we say when we find this picture compared to Shakespeare's men, and that this unblushing critic awards Mr. Coleridge a seat on the same bench with the immortal Avon Swan, to whom we are told (see same Newspaper) '*he has approached nearer than almost any other writer*'!! We started when we read this paragraph—it really exceedeth even modern puffing!!! Isidore is a delineation of similar inconsonancy. He, as already noticed, undertakes and attempts a murder, but boggles at a stratagem—he consents to the commission of the most horrible and atrocious of all crimes, but starts with dread, and spurns with mouthfuls of honour, the proposition to take part in an insignificant and almost guiltless delusion. Teresa is intended for a model of purity, discretion, and dignified sense, mingled with natural simplicity; but the part is feebly drawn, totally destitute of interest, and replete with absurdities. She is by turns strong-minded and weak, sensible and foolish, observant of strict decorum and improperly unreserved, as it suits the author to have her. She is the creature of his brain, and not the creature of nature, impelled to action by the circumstances amid which she is placed. She does this, and abstains from that, not as reason or passion would prompt, but as Mr. Coleridge dictates, and there appears to be no sound or rational ground for the most of her resolves. She determines to fly from her guardian's protection, and find a grave because a farce of necromancy has been got up, yet before she goes, she thinks it right to set the supposed necromancer at liberty. In fine, she is inconsistent in every thing; interesting in nothing. Alhadra is a bold and original conception, but equally removed from nature. Her blood-thirsty fierceness and maternal fondness are incompatible—an animal of the brute creation may combine such extremes, but they never yet met in a being at all influenced by the light of understanding. The puling sentimentalities and Germanized pathetic affectations which disfigure all the other characters, absolutely distort that of Alhadra. From her mouth, and from the mouth of Isidore, they flow with a peculiarly ill-effect, and are as unnatural as it would be for a Lioness to whistle, or a Wolf to sing. The abundant overload of *sensibilities*, which are lavished upon every scene, adds another to the list of the defects which prevent this tragedy from '*breaking the spell of Shakespeare*'.

Having said so much of this play as it is impressed on our minds from witnessing its representation, we shall not venture to offer a very minute criticism upon its language and style, of which we hold ourselves incompetent to form a correct judgment till we have perused the work. In so far, however, as we are enabled to form an opinion, it appears to us that the versification is smooth, diversified, and poetical— the language generally correct and harmonious—some of the images happily chosen—and most of the descriptions highly beautiful. At sublimity there is no aim; or, at least, if there be, it is imperceptible to the audience. The tender seems to have been the prominent object of the author's endeavour; but he has mixed too little of action in his fable to admit of its attainment in any eminent degree. The essence of dramatic skill in reaching the heart, is to *show something* to the spectator; upon which, the sentiment delivered by the poet (having thus first laid a solid foundation for effect in the mind of his audience) adorned with all the energy of poetical feeling, and the felicity of admirable language, readily wins its way to the breast, and awakens those emotions which it is his desire to implant; but it is rarely that mere description, however excellent, and especially upon the stage, can succeed in kindling sentiments of pity, love, fear, or rousing any of the passions congenial with tragedy. There are, nevertheless, numerous sweet and captivating passages in this production—passages of uncommon grace, and singular beauty, both in thought and expression; though we could not observe much of originality in any of the images employed. From this, however, we ought to except the expression of Teresa, who talks of Alvar and herself as resembling

> Twins of the same parents born.

We never heard of Twins *not* of the same parents born!

The denouëment is poetically just, and the guilty alone suffer; but, at the same time, it possesses the distressing quality of not satisfying the mind. The death of Ordonio is too abrupt, and the manner of it excessively aukward. His remorse is not perfected; and yet it gives that shade to his character, that we are loath to see him murdered in the very budding of his apparently only real feeling of repentance. The morality of the piece is unexceptionable.

With respect to the performers; after commending them for their unlimited exertions, we must qualify our applause with very many *buts*.

Miss Smith's part is not at all suited to her, and she made nothing of it, except when she gave way to the loftier bursts of passion; which were unfortunately unsuitable to the character of Teresa. Pope has also an insignificant and unfitting part, to which he could add no interest. Ordonio was well performed by Mr. Rae, who was particularly effective in the last scene. We never saw him to greater advantage; and if he could only let his arms swing with freedom and ease, his acting would be more correspondent in excellence with his conception of the character. Alvar was represented by Elliston, who really appears so much in earnest with his part, that, we are sorry to say, it is most miserably performed. Some of the short passages he gave with the utmost success; but he ought never to have to repeat any thing in tragedy longer than a line and a half. He is the most unlimited murderer of long sentences that we ever heard upon the stage; and has no idea of delivering three consecutive lines without half-a-dozen of unnecessary and destructive pauses. He speaks by measure, and not by the sense of his author—a most vile mode of meting out a tragic effusion! Of the performance of Mrs. Glover we cannot say too much in praise—she displayed powers of the highest class; and, though her vehemency was, on some occasions, uncalled for, it yet inherited spirit and excellence, so pre-eminent as scarcely to permit us to wish she were more adherent to pure propriety.

The Prologue seems to have been culled from scraps of rejected Addresses, as it is a bungling collection of patched phrases in praise of the new theatre—the sooner it is omitted the better. The Epilogue is from the pen of Mr. James Smith, and not possessed of any brilliancy. —We should have expected a more profitable composition at his hands.[1] It is spoken by Miss Smith, as if to show how many of that lady's deficiencies can be exposed in one night. She is considerably unfit for the delivery of any thing pretending to be humorous.

---

[1] An ironical allusion. James Smith (1775–1839) was best known for his witty contributions to *Rejected Addresses* (1812).

44. Unsigned review, *Theatrical Inquisitor*

February 1813, iv, 57-64

A Tragedy from the pen of Coleridge may justly be regarded as a dramatic curiosity: but that he should be the author of a successful tragedy is a decisive proof of the vitiated taste, or immoveable good nature of a British audience. Mr. Coleridge combines in a pre-eminent degree the various peculiarities and absurdities of the school of poetry, that his exertions first contributed to establish; his images are in general unnatural and incongruous; his diction uncouth, pedantic, and obscure: he mistakes abruptness for force, and supposes himself to be original when he is only absurd. That he should exhibit occasional glimpses of poetical excellence, was necessary to the favourable reception of his writings, even among a limited circle of admirers. If they fatigue and disgust the reader notwithstanding the occasional pathos and sublimity that pervade the general confusion or obscurity of composition, what would have been their fate had they exhibited in addition to their absurdities, the heavy uniformity of unvaried but eccentric dullness?

[summarizes the plot]

It is impossible not to be struck, on the first examination, with the utter improbability of the circumstance on which the plot is made to depend. Alvar returns after the lapse of a few short years in no other disguise than a Moorish habit, and provokes and defies the scrutiny of a woman, on whose mind the remembrance of his lineaments is indelibly impressed; who sees his image in the air; and who examines the countenance of the pretended Moor with all the minuteness of a professed physiognomist. To render the absurdity more obtrusive, the author has put into the mouth of Teresa, a series of rapturous expressions, on the resemblance between the expression of the stranger's countenance and that of her adored and lamented Alvar. Had the influence of climate and fatigue been such as to change so effectually the features of his countenance, the 'beloved' and well-known voice that she hears in the winds, and on the aërial sound of which she dwells with raptures, would have awoke her senses to all the extacies of reality. Nor should it be forgotten that, by common dramatists, the air, the

131

gait, and the manners of a personage, are supposed to lead to a suspicion of his identity.

The same blindness that thus precludes the suspicion of Teresa, is attributed, for the better carrying on of the plot, to the brother, the father, and the servants. They do not even discover a resemblance between the form or voice of the Moor, and that of their lamented relative or master. A prayer that calls forth all the powers of the human voice, is repeated by Alvar without awakening their remembrance. Not even Isidore recognizes the voice that had subdued him to Remorse, or the countenance of which he had borne the portrait.

The incantation scene, on which the business of the piece so materially depends, exhibits a singular combination of profaneness and absurdity. To address the throne of heaven in solemn mockery; to assume the language of devotion, while his thoughts are intent on artifice; to fall in prostrate adoration before his maker while he is exulting in the anticipated triumph, of successful artifice, was reserved for the dramatic hero of Mr. Coleridge. He addresses the host of heaven, while falsehood mingled with impiety trembles on his lips, and calls upon God to become the partner and the witness of his deception.

The character of Ordonio is feebly drawn, and the passion that gives a name to the piece obscurely and imperfectly developed. The supposed brother is, in the first three acts, a mere ranter, full of sound and fury. Rage and unsubdued malignity are the most prominent features of his character, and though he raves and murders, he is not afflicted with any compunctious visitings of conscience. Even up to the close of the fifth act, he perseveres in his intention of poisoning the supposed magician. After an indulgence of many years in the malignant and revengeful passions, he is transformed into a penitent by the magic of a speech, and terminates a life of villainy in the anguish of remorse.

The only character indeed that delights the spectator, or does credit to the talents of the author, is the wife of Isidore; and even she excites our interest by the story of her wrongs, rather than by any peculiar traits of original character. To her description indeed of her sufferings in the prison of the Inquisition the endurance of the piece was exclusively owing; and Mr. Coleridge may learn from this unexpected triumph of forcible description, unclouded by the mist of pedantic and obsolete phraseology, and undebased by paltry affectation and laborious prettiness, over the feelings of the public, how much may be obtained by consulting the established models of natural taste, and forsaking the irregularites of a poetical sect, for the honourable and pleasing path of legitimate simplicity.

With the preceding and a few other exceptions, the language of the piece is destitute of that ease and fluency that constitute the principal charm in the best dramas of Shakespeare, and indispensably necessary to the interest of the dialogue. The business of the piece is, on numerous occasions, interrupted, to give the author an opportunity of displaying his talents for *fine writing*; there is a continual attempt at force, which often degenerates into abruptness, and no opportunity is lost of stringing metaphors and balancing antitheses. The *dramatis personœ*, might be mistaken in some of the in-door scenes, for a set of poetesses and poets assembled together for the purpose of recitation. The adjuration of Alvar in the incantation scene, is a vain and unsuccessful imitation of Milton; having as little resemblance to genuine poetry as to the common and intelligible language of social intercourse. One of his illustrations is too remarkable to be omitted. Ordonio comparing his own powers of combat with Alvar's, exclaims:

> When one hard body meets another, the least must crack.

Had not this production aspersed the dignity of tragedy, but appeared under the form of *spectacle* or a *melo-drame*, it might have been regarded, by the impartial critic, as somewhat superior in its construction to many of its predecessors. The incantation scene would have been sufficiently effective in a piece of three acts, and an equestrian combat between the dependants of Valdez, and the partizans of Isidore, would have preceded the dropping of the curtain with no contemptible *eclat*. But as it is, Mr. Coleridge is neither so entertaining as Reynolds, nor so correct or poetical as many unfortunate bards, who attempted to attain the honours of tragic excellence, long before the Committee of Drury undertook the superintendance of the drama.[1]

The prologue and epilogue were among the most stupid productions of the modern muse; the former was, in all probability a Rejected Address; for it contained many eulogiums on the beauty and magnificence of the 'dome' of Drury; talked of the waves being not quite dry, and expressed the happiness of the bard at being the first whose muse had soared within its limits. More stupid than the doggerel of Twiss, and more affected than the pretty verses of Miles Peter Andrews, **the**

---

[1] Frederic Reynolds (1764-1841), playwright.

epilogue proclaimed its author and the writer of the prologue, to be *par nobile fratrum; in rival dullness both pre-eminent*.[1]

Mr. Rae unites to a good figure and an expressive countenance, much vigor of intellectual conception, and considerable power and distinctness of elocution. But his attitudes have too much of the popular strut, and his breast always 'heaves high in martial swell'; the actor conceals the hero. His chief defect, however, is a certain effeminacy of tone in the vehement efforts of his voice, that does away with the impression of manly energy or convulsive passions; in one or two of the scenes it was difficult to distinguish, merely by the tone, between his speeches and those of Mrs. Glover. We have many hopes of seeing this gentleman attain the highest honours of his profession; his progress was marked and his eminence predicted by our lamented friend Mr. Cumberland;[2] and where so much private virtue is united with professional talent, who can refrain from feeling more than a critical interest in his success?

45. From an unsigned review, *European Magazine*

February 1813, lxiii, 137-8

[The review begins with a summary of the plot.]

The language of this play is poetic and impassioned; the incidents are sufficient to keep the attention alive during the representation; and some of the situations are strikingly calculated for dramatic effect. The characters of the two brothers are well drawn and finely contrasted. That of *Teresa* does not rise much above mediocrity; but the concep-

[1] Horace Twiss (1787-1849), wit, politician and dramatist, had supplied the farewell address recited by his aunt, Mrs. Siddons, on 29 June 1812. Miles Peter Andrews (d. 1814), M.P. and author of comedies, was famed for his prologues and epilogues.

[2] Richard Cumberland (1732-1811), playwright.

tion of the part of the Moorish woman is full of poetic imagination; and the opening scenes in particular are sublime and interesting. The moral is perfect, and strict poetical justice is done on the guilty. The style is, throughout, poetical and classical, and far above the common level. It abounds with fine touches of nature, and the tender feelings are almost incessantly appealed to. Many of the passages were received with loud, general, and prolonged applause. The tragedy was, indeed, heard from beginning to end with the most marked distinction, and announced for repetition amid shouts from every corner of the theatre.

Its principal faults were, too great length; and an exuberance of passages merely descriptive.

Much praise is due to the performers, who played with great spirit and effect.

46. From an unsigned review, *Literary Panorama*

February 1813, xiii, 78-9

Mr. Coleridge has long been honourably known to the public as a poet whose pen propagated neither immorality nor prophaneness. His muse was rather sentimental than prompt to

> Catch the manners living as they rise.

He has now favoured this theatre with a tragedy, in which these parts of his poetical character are conspicuous. Genius he certainly possesses; the graces of diction, and brilliant passages in this tragedy distinguish it among the efforts of modern times; and once more correct language and classical graces adorn the stage.

But, if criticism observe that Mr. C. has drawn rather from the stores of his own mind, than from the workings of nature at large, from the ordinary passions of men, we know not what defence he could make to the charge. It is thought, however, that he has endeavoured to pourtray nature; that he has watched himself with a jealousy which marks his own opinion of his mental bias; and therefore in deference to the real merits of the piece and the intentional correctness of its author, we shall treat his attempt with kindness, and his errors with lenity.

This tragedy is called the *Remorse*, and the following is a compendium of its incidents.

[a brief plot summary follows]

The moral of this piece, inculcates the principle that though perfidy and cruelty combined with talent, may be for a while triumphant, yet that vengeance eventually and certainly befalls their enormities. Objections may be raised to the inadequacy of the causes assigned for the deep villainy of Ordonio; and the interposed contrivances towards the end of the piece, by their number rather bewilder the mind of the spectator. This is the contrary extreme from suffering him to discern in the first act who is to be successful, and by what means. Teresa, the heroine, is well drawn. And on the whole, the piece, which was extremely well received, is honourable to the genius of its author, and reputable to the discernment of the managers of the new theatre.

47. From an unsigned review, *Universal Magazine*

February 1813, xix, 144-6

[after a lengthy plot summary the review concludes as follows; cf. No. 45]

Strict poetical justice is done on the guilty alone. The style is throughout poetical and classical, and far above the common level. It abounds with fine touches of nature, and the tender feelings are almost incessantly appealed to. Many of the passages were received with loud, general, and prolonged applause; while not one instance occurred of meanness or vulgarity, or affectation, to excite the disapprobation of the audience. The tragedy was indeed heard from beginning to end with the most marked distinction, and announced for repetition amid shouts from every corner of the theatre.

48. From an unsigned review, *La Belle Assemblée*

February 1813, vii, 81-5

[the review opens with a list of the cast]

This Tragedy does great credit to the genius of Mr. Coleridge; it is a pledge of greater excellence to be expected hereafter, and holds out a promise that the Muse of Tragedy has not quite deserted the English stage. The merit of *Remorse* consists in its proper union of the leading requisites of the Tragic Drama, combined by nature and reason, invigorated by passion, and embellished by the graces of poetry. The great defect of our modern Tragedies is, that they are either a sour and morose compendium of ethics in the mouths of particular characters, or that they substitute declamation and rhetorical flourishes for natural passion, and scenery and pomp for action. But this objection does not extend to Mr. Coleridge's present Drama. The action is simple, single, varied in its progress, and occasionally diverged from the regularity of narrative, by an ingenious and natural complication of events. The characters though in some degree too picturesque and fanciful, are upon the whole natural agents, and have that kind of novelty which shews the invention of the author, without subjecting him to much sacrifice of probability to produce them. The dialogue is in the true dramatic spirit: it never flags, nor declines into the supineness and stagnation of narrative.

The poetry is rather vigorous than elegant; and it has more of the nerve of a didactic poem, than of the fancy and melody of the drama. It has not the pastoral sweetness of the *Honeymoon*, nor the natural dignity of *Douglas*.[1] It is something too much upon the level of familiar life.

The Tragedy was admirably represented, and received with general approbation. We trust that it will satisfy every expectation of its excellent author.

We deem it our duty to make the following extracts from this Tragedy, as a specimen of Mr. Coleridge's talents:

[quotes Act IV, Scene i (*PW*, ii, 858-64) and ll. 106-264 of Act V, Scene i (*PW*, ii, 874-80)]

[1] John Tobin's *Honey Moon* (1805) and John Home's *Douglas* (1756).

137

49. Private opinions

Henry Crabb Robinson (1775-1867), journalist, barrister and diarist, and one of Coleridge's friends—extract from his diary, 23 January 1813: 'Evening at Drury Lane, the first performance of Coleridge's tragedy, *Remorse*. . . . My interest for the play was greater than in the play, and my anxiety for its success took from me the feeling as a mere spectator I should have had. I have no hesitation, however, in saying that its poetical is far greater than its dramatic merit; that it owes its success rather to its faults than its beauties, and that it will have for its less meritorious qualities applause which is really due for its excellencies . . . . Coleridge's great fault is that he indulges before the public in those metaphysical and philosophical speculations which are becoming only in solitude and with select minds' (*On Books and Their Writers*, ed. Edith J. Morley, London 1938, i, 117).

Michael Kelly (c. 1764-1826), singer and composer who provided the music for *Remorse*: 'There were some musical situations in the play which I had to compose. The poetry of the incantation was highly animating; it was sung by Mrs. Bland, with all the refreshing purity of her unsophisticated style, and with that chaste expression and tenderness of feeling which speak at once as it were to the heart. The chorus of the boatmen chaunting on the water under the convent walls, and the distant peal of the organ, accompanying the monks while singing within the convent chapel, seemed to overcome and soothe the audience; a thrilling sensation appeared to pervade the great mass of congregated humanity, and, during its performance, it was listened to, with undivided attention, as if the minds and hearts of all were rivetted and enthralled by the combination presented to their notice; and at the conclusion the applause was loud and protracted' (*Reminiscences of Michael Kelly*, ed. Theodore Hook, London 1826, ii, 309).

Robert Southey—extract from a letter written 27 January 1813: 'I never doubted that Coleridge's play would meet with a triumphant reception. Be it known and remembered hereafter, that this self-same play, having had no other alterations made in it now than C. was willing to have made in it then, was rejected in 1797 by Sheridan and Kemble. Had these sapient caterers for the public brought it forward at that time, it is by no means improbable that the author might have produced a play as good every season: with my knowledge of Coleridge's habits I verily believe he would' (*The Life & Correspondence of the Late Robert Southey*, ed. C. C. Southey, London 1850, iv, 12-13n.).

REMORSE

the publication, 1813

50. 'H.' in *Theatrical Inquisitor*

March 1813, iv, 111-16

The first production of the *Modern Shakespeare*, for such is the title by which his judicious friends have chosen to distinguish the author of a tragedy in which the diction is laboriously effeminate, the various compartments of the dialogue dove-tailed into each other with scrupulous exactness, and one eternal effort to astonish and delight, destroys the charm of the successful passages, and aggravates the disappointment and disgust of the reader at occasional examples of bathos or insipidity. We willingly confess indeed that we have *read* Mr. Coleridge's tragedy with considerable pleasure; as one of the best productions of a vicious and pedantic school, exhibiting frequent examples of original genius surmounting the fetters of prejudice and false taste by which it was encumbered; and as containing many insulated passages of considerable pathos and beauty, notwithstanding their faults of tumor and affectation, it possesses unusual and unexpected merit; but that it has any pretensions to superior excellencies as a drama; that it displays an intuitive knowledge of the human character; a magic power of exciting and developing the complicated passions of the soul; or that practiced skill in the business of the drama, which atones by the irresistable interest of incident and situation for the absence of more important qualities, we firmly deny. The perusal and reperusal of the tragedy, has more and more impressed us with a conviction that Mr. Coleridge may have been born a didactic or descriptive poet, but that to an intimate knowledge of the human heart, or a minute acquaintance with the character and operation of the human passions, he has no legitimate pretensions.

But the managers and performers declare it to be a *fine tragedy*; Elliston is in raptures, and Tom Dibdin in the exercise of his professional duty is speechless with extacy. Arnold the Monarch and the Magnus Apollo of regenerated Drury; Johnstonian Raymond too; the immortal author of that elegant and classical production the life of Dermody; whose looks are full of wisdom, and whose very gestures indicate philosophy; and Thomas Dibdin, the determined enemy of puns and quibbles, who shrinks with horror from the jingling of unmeaning rhymes, and the great object of whose literary cultivation, are elegance and simplicity of style, and chastity of diction, all declare, that, since the time of Shakespeare, so wonderful a production has not appeared to improve the taste and awake the feelings of a British public.[1] But we all know that managers and actors are the most friendly, obliging, good-tempered set of fellows on the face of the earth, and it is not impossible that, on this occasion, their judgment may have been guided by their wishes.

With respect to the characters, we have already observed that Ordonio has been drawn without any determinate outline in the mind of the author, of the portrait that he was about to sketch: that Remorse is only the secondary impulse by which he is guided, and that even when that sentiment is called into action, it is imperfectly developed. A weekly critic has drawn an ingenious and fanciful portrait of a man whom he presents to his readers as the Ordonio of Mr. Coleridge, but it has no resemblance to its avowed original.[2] When Ordonio presents the goblet to Alvar, he displays neither the magnanimity of desperate courage, nor the sensibility of Remorse. Selfish and relentless lust (for it would be profanation to the name of *love*, to apply it to the passion of Ordonio) awakens his rage and suspicion at the opening of the scene, and, as the business proceeds, his soul is exclusively possessed by rancorous and pitifully [?blind] revenge.

It has been observed that nothing can be more absurd than that Isidore, who, in the warmth of his former gratitude, had consented to assassinate the rival of his preserver, should afterwards refuse to aid in his pretended incantations; and though the objection appears less striking when we reflect that, subsequent to the attempt at assassination, Isidore had discovered the relation of Alvar to Ordonio, it cannot be entirely evaded. Were Mr. Coleridge, however, to omit the exclama-

[1] Thomas Dibdin, Robert Elliston, J. G. Raymond and Samuel J. Arnold were all connected in one way or another with the management of the Theatre Royal, Drury Lane.

[2] This reference and the one in the following paragraph seem to be to the review in the *Examiner* (No. 42).

tion, '*I'll perish first*', and thus to leave the audience in doubt of Isidore's final determination, should he fail in another expedient satisfactory to his master; this character, whatever may be its other claim to critical praise, would possess at least merit of consistency.

But the great fault of the piece is its exuberant volubility of soliloquy and dialogue. Instead of proceeding through their parts with the forcible, but expressive rapidity of actual passion, the dramatis personæ indulge in their most agitated moments, and on the very brink of anxious expectation or precipitate revenge, in long and flowery descriptions of the scenery that surrounds them, in narratives of dreams, and fancies, and sweet remembrancies; in rhetorical raptures, and splendid amplifications of imagery. The following speech of Teresa, which exhibits some pretension to poetical power, far exceeds the proper limits of dramatic expansion, and betrays the usual faults of its author's school of poetry, tumor and affectation, fanciful allusion, and laborious conceit.

> There are woes
> Ill bartered for the GARISHNESS of joy!
> If it be wretched with an untired eye
> To watch those skiey tints, and this green ocean;
> Or in the sultry hour beneath some rock,
> My hair dishevell'd by the pleasant sea breeze,
> To shape sweet visions, and live o'er again
> All past hours of delight! If it be wretched
> To watch some bark, and fancy Alvar there;
> To go through each minutest circumstance
> Of the blest meeting; and to frame adventures
> Most terrible and strange, and hear him tell them;
> (As once I knew a crazy Moorish maid,
> Who drest her in her buried lover's cloaths,
> And o'er the smooth spring in the mountain cleft,
> Hung with her lute, and play'd the self same tune
> He used to play, and listened to the shadow
> Herself had made)—if this be wretchedness,
> And if indeed it be a wretched thing
> To trick out mine own death-bed, and imagine
> That I had died, died just ere his return! &c. &c.

After this model it is obvious that any one of the performers may occupy the scene for any required length of time, with good set speeches, signifying nothing. To the introduction of rhetorical flourishes, and abortive attempts at tenderness of sentiment, Mr.

Coleridge has sacrificed much of the dramatic interest of which the fable was susceptable.

On the absurd profaneness of the invocation we expressed ourselves with considerable warmth in our strictures of last month, but as some of our readers might conclude from the silence of the daily and weekly critics, that we had censured a violation of propriety and common sense that did not exist, we shall quote the passage to which our strictures refer. Let the reader call to his remembrance, that the person who utters the following invocation is himself the Alvar whose spirit he supplicates; that while he addresses the throne of heaven, he is the principal actor in a scene of deception and unreal mockery, and calls the almighty to witness the truth of his pretended powers; and then decide on the piety of the author, and the discrimination of a British audience.

> Soul of Alvar!
> Hear our soft suit, and HEED my milder spell:
> So may the Gates of Paradise, unbarr'd,
> CEASE thy swift toils! Since haply thou art one
> Of that innumerable company
> Who in broad circle, lovelier than the rainbow,
> Girdle this ROUND earth in a DIZZY motion,
> With noise too vast and constant to be heard:
> Fitliest unheard! &c. &c.

Were another *Scriblerus* to arise, and elucidate the art of sinking by recent examples, he could not find a more useful auxiliary than Mr. Coleridge. Behold the proofs.

> How sad she look'd and pale! but not like guilt—
> And her calm tones, sweet as a song of mercy.
> IF THE BAD SPIRIT RETAIN'D HIS ANGEL'S VOICE,
> HELL SCARCE were HELL, And why not innocent,
> Who meant to murder me might well cheat her?
> But ere she married him he'd stained her honor;
> Ah! there I'M HAMPER'D ! ! !

Again,

> In the assassin's heart, they MADE THEIR TERMS.

Females recording in the anguish of excruciating remembrance, the pangs and arrows of former years, do not as in the subjoined passage,

143

recal the words for the purpose of shewing their metaphorical ingenuity.

> The very wish, too, languished,
> With the fond hope that nursed it.
> The sick babe drooped at the bosom of its famished mother.

Mr. Coleridge sometimes disgusts, by affected homeliness, and sometimes confounds by the absolute absence of meaning. He speaks of a person being *waned* to melancholy, of a *scathing* curse, and the *airs* of love.

The author of a New Art of Prosody, must in common gratitude inscribe his treatise to Mr. Coleridge, e.g.

> We loiter yet awhile to enjoy the SEA breeze,
> 'And she spoke to me with her INNOCENT face,
> That voice that INNOCENT FACE,
> My life wearied me, and but for the imperative voice'.

In the first of these examples, as well as in the following, and many other instances, he compels the reader by the adjustment of the pause to lay the prosodial emphasis on an unemphatic adjective, and on the unaccented syllable of a trisyllable.

> Here where her LAST kiss when with SUPPRESSED feelings &c.

The preface to the tragedy of *Remorse* is without exception the most slovenly and incoherent performance that ever appeared from the pen of a gentleman pretending to critical talent, and accustomed to composition. If Mr. Coleridge's threatened Essay on the Theatres have any resemblance to this specimen of his prose, woe be to the purchaser of the copy right!

Of all the females who could have been selected to fill the part of Teresa, Miss Smith was in all probability the worst calculated for the task. It is impossible for this lady to assume the appearance, of loveliness, or of interesting sensibility. It is in the expression of the less amiable passions, of the more violent emotions of hatred jealousy, and revenge: in the representation, of woe worn misanthropy, or comfortless despair that she excells herself and electrifies the audience. In such parts as Cora and Teresa, she bears on her features the character of distressed *old maidism*; the most unfortunate expression of which the countenance of a female is susceptible.

will deny, that a great majority of the pieces most commonly represented on our stage either directly inculcate, or at least have a tendency
to encourage, sentiments not only below the religious standard but in
direct opposition to the feelings of every true Christian; and that, to
be in the habit of attending the exhibition of pieces of this character,
implies, according to all fair and candid construction, an approbation
of the sentiments they enforce. While, on these grounds, we adhere
firmly to the puritanical tenet of the unlawfulness of stage amusements,
we do not feel ourselves disposed to involve, in the same condemnation,
the practice of reading plays, provided that it is not suffered to encroach
upon the time which should be allotted to more useful occupations,
and that it extends to such plays only as are not licentious in their
tendency. The worldliness of their sentiments is not, in our judgment,
a sufficient cause for prohibiting them to the Christian reader. In this,
as well as in every other species of reading, let him be on his guard
against the seductive influence of false principle; but if, from the fear
of this, he is to banish the drama from his library, then, to be consistent,
he must store his shelves with books of divinity only, and abandon the
ornaments of polite literature and the advantages of science to those
who are the least likely to apply them to any useful or pious purpose.

We are happy to be able, conscientiously, to hold the opinion here
expressed; for deeply indeed should we regret the necessity of urging a
doctrine which should tear us from Shakespeare and Corneille, and
which, admitting us only to the scriptural pieces of Racine, should
interdict the *Phèdre* or the *Andromaque*. By a man of cultivated mind,
such offerings at the shrine of duty are, of all others, made with the
most reluctance. He must always feel a deeper pang at the renunciation
of intellectual than of sensual pleasure, for the latter species of sacrifice
is attended with a consciousness of elevation, while the former has a
tendency to degrade him in his own estimate. Happily, religion exacts
ignorance of nothing that is really worth knowing. She concedes the
fruit of the tree of knowledge, as well as that of the tree of life.

In the class of plays which we would not prohibit to our readers,
we assign a high place to the subject of this Review. Its appearance
must be considered as an important occurrence in the annals of the
English drama; for we do not hesitate to characterise it as one of the
best tragedies which has been produced on our stage since the time of
Otway. Unlike the ordinary dramas of the day, it relies not for its main
attraction upon the illusions of scenery, the decorations of dress, or
any dexterity of what is called stage effect, by which, whatever is

wanting to the mind or to the ear, is compensated to the eye of the spectator. It is the production of a mind relying on its unassisted powers, and well able to rely on them; and will, perhaps, be read with even greater pleasure than it produces in the exhibition. With numerous blemishes, and glaring inequalities, it abounds in just and original sentiment, in powerful description, in strong conceptions of character, and fervid effusions of passion. Rivalling some of the best of the German plays in their philosophical spirit and passionate energy, it has no resemblance to them in their affectation of strained and extravagant sentiment, and still less in their *sublime* inversions and suspensions of the ordinary rules of morality. It is, indeed, a work of highly moral, and, we may almost say, of religious tendency. Its general design is to exhibit the moral dangers of pride; the proneness of the descent from imaginary perfection to the lowest depths of depravity; the miseries attendant upon conscious guilt; the consolations and the rewards of virtue. It has, besides, the rare recommendation of being totally free from every stain of indelicacy, and the praise, among all other plays, peculiar (we believe) to this, of enforcing the Christian duty of the forgiveness of injuries. On this last ground it is not easy to applaud Mr. Coleridge too highly. We hail with delight every attempt to infuse genuine principle into a class of composition which, of all others perhaps the most effective in the formation of character, has hitherto been exclusively employed either in cherishing the bad passions, or, at best, in inculcating the heathen virtues. What Christian has not lamented that the fascinations of the stage, the mingled attractions of shew, and song, and dance, of graceful gesture and impressive intonation, should be so inseparably in league with a pernicious or defective moral, lending their whole influence in opposition to that sacred cause which they might be applied with irresistible effect to promote. It may, indeed, be said, that if their object were reversed, they would lose their power; that their force is principally derived from their co-operation with the passions which they foment; and that a play which should inculcate Christian sentiments would never become popular. This proposition is true, we apprehend, only to a certain extent. That such a play would be the less popular for its Christianity, must, we fear, be admitted; but that it might, notwithstanding this disrecommendation, become a favourite piece with the public, is sufficiently proved by the instances of *Esther* and *Athalie*.[1] As to these pieces, however, it must be confessed, that they have been in a great

[1] Racine's plays.

measure supported by the novelty of their pretensions; and that besides they have a character of excellence too high for any but the most exalted genius to attain: that it does not follow, therefore, because these plays have succeeded, that similar success would be often experienced by other compositions formed on the same model. Accordingly, it is not exactly on this model that we would wish plays to be formed. In the *Esther* and *Athalie*, not only the sentiments are pious, but the action and characters are entirely scriptural. Pieces constructed on this plan, having little relation to the feelings or events with which men are actually conversant, can never excite a deep interest of the dramatic kind. They will be considered merely as poetical compositions, and, as such, can never keep possession of the stage, unless they possess in this character a merit so transcendent as to atone for every other defect. We would not impose so hopeless a task on the dramatist. We permit him to pourtray the scenes of ordinary life, and to 'catch the living manners as they rise'; but in availing himself of this his proper province, to establish his dominion over the passions, let him, at the same time, endeavour to controul and purify them, by the inculcation of a genuine and Christian morality. We are convinced that no play, clearly entitled in other respects to the favour of the public, would be endangered in its success by an adherence to this principle; and we think the opinion confirmed by the example of *Remorse*. This play, we understand, has been received with an unanimity and warmth of applause due to its extraordinary merit, and apparently unchecked by the unusual purity and elevation of its moral tone.

[a detailed summary of the plot follows]

Of this plot, the faults are too obvious to require much comment. Sufficiently long and complicated to form the basis of a novel in four volumes, in its dramatic form it imposes an unseasonable task both on the comprehension and memory of the spectator. The effort of attention which it requires, to keep in steady view the connection of its different parts, is painful, and far exceeds that gentle stimulation of the faculties to which those whose ambition is to amuse should cautiously confine their efforts. There is something unskilful, too, in the adoption of so intricate a fable. It is in barren subjects that the hand of the master is most visible, and the dazzling fabrics of genius are generally constructed of few and simple materials.

It may also be fairly objected to this story, that the interest excited by the brothers, though different in kind, is too equal in degree, and that it is impossible to pronounce either of them the hero of the piece. In a review of Scott's *Lady of the Lake*, the want of a principal character is treated by eminent critics as a dubious fault, and the example of Milton is cited in its defence. Whatever may be the case in epic composition, it is an unequivocal defect in the drama. We cannot but think, indeed, that, in any species of writing, the interest that is divided is weakened; but in a play this is more peculiarly the case than in an epic poem, because in the former, the action is condensed into narrower limits of time and place, and the incidents are fewer. Unity of effect is therefore one of its most important objects; and it can as little bear a double hero as an episode.

We are afraid, too, that the sorcery and conjuration, on which the intrigue of this piece so much depends, will be denounced by the severe censor as below the tragic dignity. It is true that the magic is represented as deceptive merely; but it is exactly for this reason that we consider it as a paltry agent. Were we introduced to a real magician, the scene is laid in times remote enough perhaps to countenance the fiction. We do not revolt at the witches in *Macbeth*; but had Shakespeare thought proper to represent them as designing women successfully practising on the credulity of the usurper, the tragic terror of the piece had been in a great measure lost, and its whole effect deteriorated.

But the most serious charge which we have to make against the conduct of this play is, that much of its action is but feebly connected with the catastrophe. It is a dramatic rule, not founded in the pedantry of system, but in an obvious principle of good taste, that the several incidents of the plot should all co-operate towards the final result. This connection may be more or less immediate, but it is clear that the more immediate it is, the more spirited and forcible will be the general effect. In this respect, the present play appears to us to be lamentably defective. From the appearance of Alvar on the stage, till the catastrophe takes place in the death of his brother, and his own re-union with Teresa, there is not one incident in which he is an actor (his very appearance not excepted) which has any direct and immediate effect in the production of that catastrophe. His return and disguise effect nothing, until Isidore points him out to Ordonio. His resolution to awaken his brother's penitence, and the scheme which he devises for that purpose, the invocation, and the picture, no further affect the final result than that they tend, in coincidence with other circumstances, to persuade Ordonio that he is betrayed, and in that view, lead him to assassinate Isidore, which, by exciting the widow's vengeance, occasions the death of Ordonio himself. How remote and feeble a concatenation of incident is this! It serves fully to explain why the readers and spectators of *Remorse*, impressed in every scene with occasional beauties of the highest order, are yet, as we have been informed, afflicted occasionally with a sensation approaching to ennui, and often yawn in the very act of admiration.

After thus cursorily stating some of our objections to the plot and action of this play, we hasten to justify the encomiums which we nevertheless have thought fit to bestow on it, by extracting some of the passages which have pleased us most.

Much of the first scene in which Teresa is introduced appears to us to be written with extraordinary energy.

[quotes ll. 1-104, Act I, Scene ii (*PW*, ii, 823-6)]

We have already noticed the inequalities of composition with which this work abounds. The preceding extract exemplifies the remark. The lines marked in Italics are not only prosaic, but they are vulgar, both in the conception and the expression.[1] Yet it will be allowed, that in parts of this scene there is merit to which no parallel could easily be found in any other modern drama.

The next passage we shall copy is part of the first Scene of the second Act, in which Ordonio unsuccessfully proposes to Isidore the scheme of personating a wizard. Irritated by his refusal, the former taunts him with his past guilt and the inconsistency of his present scruples. To this Isidore replies,

[quotes ll. 73-123 (*PW*, ii, 837-8)]

Nothing can be more finely conceived than this narrative. Its thrilling pathos belongs to the first class of tragic composition, and will even call to remembrance the manner of Schiller without sustaining any injury by the association.

We now introduce our readers to the scene of the invocation—the excellence of which, though in a very different style, is not inferior to that of the last extract.

[quotes ll. 36-114, Act III, Scene i (*PW*, ii, 848-50)]

The address to the spirit of Alvar is remarkable for the lofty flow of its versification, and for its highly poetical conceptions. We think there is here a visible imitation of the style of Milton; and we can

[1] Ll. 85-8 are italicized.

bestow no higher praise, than to say we think the attempt not unsuccessful. The grandeur and variety of the images, and the skill with which they are selected, remind us of some of the finest passages in the *Paradise Lost*. In this respect, nothing can be more happy than the introduction of the *Lapland wizard's skiff*. This wild and romantic appendage to the scene of terror is conceived in the true spirit of that great model, whom the author seems to have had in view.

The concluding speech of the preceding extract is characterised by remarkable energy. This, indeed, is one of the most distinguished qualities of Mr. Coleridge's style. The following passage also very forcibly expresses the stubborn pride, and self-defensive ferocity, of a bold bad man supposing himself beset by his enemies!

[quotes ll. 168-82, Act III, Scene ii (*PW*, ii, 857-8)]

The cavern scene, in which the murder of Isidore is perpetrated, is finely terrific, and contains some very powerful description; but from this we can afford to make no extract. We hasten to the quotation of a few lines, of which the sentiment is so peculiarly touching, that in our sympathy we almost forget to admire the soft elegance with which it is conveyed.

In the beginning of the last act we have Alvar alone in his dungeon.

[quotes ll. 1-30, Act V, Scene i (*PW*, ii, 871-2)]

We have now cited several of the passages with which we were most gratified on our perusal of this work. In order to give the reader a just notion of its merits, we ought next, perhaps, to lay before him some of those specimens of mean and flat composition by which its general character is depreciated. We think it sufficient, however, for the purpose, to remark, that they are faults principally arising from a careless remission of effort. Immediately on the close, and sometimes in the midst of a fine passage, the author's genius suddenly relaxes. His wing is unsteady, and after soaring to the skies, he is too often seen to grovel on the earth. Greater vigilance would certainly prevent these discreditable descents. Occasionally, however, his errors seem to be deliberate, and are owing not to want of care, but to perversion of taste; as, for instance, in the following perspicuous statement.

> In the Future,
> As in the optician's glassy cylinder,
> The indistinguishable blots and colours
> Of the dim Past, collect and shape themselves,

Upstarting in their own completed image,
To scare or to reward.

> Act ii, Sc. 2

Or in this ingenious exposition of the effects of solitary confinement:

Each pore and natural outlet shrivelled up,
By ignorance and parching poverty,
His energies roll back upon his heart,
And stagnate and corrupt, till, chang'd to poison,
They break out on him like a loathsome plague spot.
                                        . . . So he lies
Circled with evil till his very soul
Unmoulds its essence, hopelessly deform'd
By sights of evermore deformity.

> Act v, Sc. 1

In the Preface, we are informed that this tragedy was written so long ago as in the year 1797; that the person, at whose request it was undertaken, not only failed to patronise it, but, without the consent of the author, suffered it to pass into private circulation; making it, at the same time, the theme of his ridicule, and even mis-quoting the play and misrepresenting the author, to give his satire the keener edge; that he constantly neglected every request to return the manuscript; and that the result of this injurious treatment was the suppression of the piece during the long period that has since elapsed.

This liberal patron is understood to be a gentleman distinguished for his own theatrical productions, and to whom, whatever other demerits are assignable, we have not been used to hear the praise of good-nature or of good taste denied.[1] In this instance, he appears to have been lamentably deficient in both these qualities, as well as in others much more important; and the public will not easily forgive a line of conduct, to which they probably owe not only the long suppression of Mr. Coleridge's dramatic efforts, but the publication of many of his rhapsodies and sonnets.

[1] R. B. Sheridan.

52. Unsigned review, *Critical Review*

April 1813, iii, 402–5

The representation of a new tragedy, written by an author of established poetical fame, is, alas! so great a novelty in our theatrical annals, that it was hailed by the few surviving amateurs of the drama as the commencement of a new æra in dramatic history. Remembering the failure of *De Montfort*,[1] we were not quite so sanguine in our prognostications as some of those 'whose wish', we fear, 'was father to their thought'; and, on the contrary, had our opinion been asked after the second performance of the piece (which we witnessed in person) we should probably have predicted a less degree of success than that which it has actually since experienced. To say the truth, then, it is our firm persuasion that no important revolution can be effected in the present degraded state of the stage, so long as the monopoly of the theatres continues. Whenever a new theatre shall be established, of the old moderate dimensions, and devoted exclusively to the representation of such works as do honour to the national taste and genius, abandoning to the present magnificent houses those departments for which they are alone calculated, of broad farce and splendid spectacle, then, and not till then, we may hope to see a new æra of the drama which shall rival that of Elizabeth in warmth and vigour, without sacrificing the more correct attainments of a refined and critical age of poetry.

From this Utopia, we must now turn to the tragedy of Mr. Coleridge; and, while we admit with pleasure that this work would have appeared to much greater advantage under circumstances such as we have been imagining than it has done, exhibited on the immense canvas, and with the gorgeous and overpowering frame of the new Drury Lane stage, we cannot, however, ascribe to it so much intrinsic merit as would entitle it to a very high rank among the productions of true dramatic genius. It announces, indeed, a poetical mind, such as its author is known already, upon other evidence, undoubtedly to possess; and we think it gives sufficient assurance that, with proper encouragement of his dramatic talent, his second, or third, or fourth essay in the art might have raised him far above his present level. With

[1] Joanna Baillie's *De Montfort*, first performed in 1800.

153

such an opinion, we can hardly repress our indignation at the treatment which this play experienced in a quarter from which, of all others, it might have been expected that that proper encouragement should have proceeded. The public is already pretty generally acquainted with the circumstances under which its representation was kept back ever since the year 1797, when it was first offered to, and received by, the then manager: and all, who feel the least interest in the success and advancement of the dramatic art, have participated in our sentiments while they reflected that the time so unworthily lost to the author, might (with different treatment) have been employed by him in attaining an eminence at once honourable to himself and to his country. We are however glad that these circumstances are now publicly known. They may operate as an useful example to the future conductors of our stage—and we are convinced (however remote we may be from the realization of our Utopian visions in other respects) that a much more liberal, a more considerate, and a more humane spirit has prevailed since the period of those unfeeling and detrimental abuses.

It appears unnecessary to give any analysis of the fable of this tragedy, with which very few of our readers can now be supposed to be unacquainted. Our principal objection to it is its great moral improbability; a defect which, whenever it occurs, cannot fail to involve in it the absence of all strong dramatic interest. The disguise of Don Alvar has scarcely an adequate motive even in his misapprehension respecting the fidelity of his mistress; since that misapprehension is made (in his imagination), to amount even to certainty, and to leave little, if any, room for doubt and trial. But, after this misapprehension is removed, the continuance of the disguise is altogether inexplicable by any of the motives that influence ordinary humanity; and the exposure both of his own happiness and that of an innocent, afflicted, and beloved woman to the most imminent hazard for the romantic object of awakening remorse in the mind of his brother, may perhaps find some parallel in the extravagant and unnatural sentiment of a German theatre, but certainly none in the heart or head of any truly affectionate or reasonable being. After so serious a shock to the very foundation of the structure, no excellence of parts could in our apprehension have saved the vessel from a total wreck. But we can with difficulty find any such excellence as to warrant us in entertaining a very strong wish that it were possible to preserve it. The character of Ordonio is, we think, well sketched; but it is imperfectly finished. That of Naomi is less original, but is painted with some strength of colouring. The rest of the dramatis personæ have little variety or discrimination to recommend them. Of the machinery, the scene of the murder of Isidore in the cavern, is gloomy and terrible, but nothing can be conceived more outré and ill-placed, nothing less calculated to produce any effect in point of interest or pathos, than the clumsy and unnecessary contrivance of the mock incantation. It tends to no end or purpose whatever; and Macbeth's three Witches have just as much to do with the progress and denouement of the plot, as this silly and puerile piece of spectacle. The author was aware of the nakedness of the plot he had chosen, but knew not how to remedy the radical evil.

After this, it is evident that in our opinion the whole reputation of the piece must hereafter rest upon its merits in respect of poetical sentiment and expression; and (in this point of view only) we think it will always maintain a respectable station on the shelves of a dramatic library, long after it shall have ceased to figure on the boards of a theatre.

[quotes ll. 18-50, Act I, Scene ii (*PW*, ii, 824-5)]

This is extremely tender, and beautifully reminds us of the similar picture drawn by Miss Baillie, in her exquisite little opera of *The Beacon*.[1] The following 'Prison Thoughts' of Don Alvar will more forcibly call to our recollection the peculiar and distinguishing traits of Mr. Coleridge's own poetical character.

[quotes ll. 1-30, Act V, Scene i (*PW*, ii, 873-4)]

53. Francis Hodgson, *Monthly Review*

May 1813, lxxi, 82-93

This unsigned review has been attributed to Hodgson (1781-1852), clergyman, reviewer, and for a time editor of the *Monthly Review* (Nangle, 104).

Good tragedies have seemed, for some years past, to be a species of composition almost extinct in England. It might be interesting to investigate the causes of this strange decay of one branch of national

[1] Published in her *A Series of Plays*, Volume iii, 1812.

genius, and to ascertain whether they are to be found in the size and pantomimic splendor of our theatres; whether the taste of the public, which demands that size and splendor, be not, in fact, too frivolous for so high and grave a kind of entertainment; or whether our dramatic authors themselves have not unaccountably failed in ambition to reach the highest point of their art, as if some penal law depressed their efforts and forbade them to rise above a certain station. These questions, however, we must at present decline to discuss; and confining ourselves principally to the play before us, which has more than common claims to our attention, we shall endeavour to appreciate its merits, and also to throw some light on the obstacles which have prevented this, and (by implication) other dramas of the day from attaining a greater degree of excellence. First, then, let us offer a tolerably full analysis of the story of *Remorse*, which will include some remarks on the conduct of that story; and examine the delineation and contrast of the characters, interspersing our observations with a few passages, which may give the reader an adequate idea of the dialogue.

The scene of this drama is in Spain, and the time is the reign of Philip the Second, just at the close of the civil wars against the Moors, and during the heat of the persecution which raged against them; shortly after the edict which forbad the wearing of Moresco apparel, under pain of death. The Marquis Valdez, a noble Spaniard, has two sons, Alvar and Ordonio. He is also guardian to the orphan Donna Teresa, who is alike the object of Alvar's and Ordonio's passion. So far we are reminded of the plot of *The Orphan*:[1] but the resemblance here ceases. Alvar, indeed, is the favoured brother, but the atrocious character of Ordonio is borrowed from some other source. He hires assassins to remove his rival: but the principal of them, Isidore, 'a Moresco chieftain, ostensibly a Christian', relents, on being informed by Alvar that he is Ordonio's brother. Alvar leaves the country, but at the opening of the play he has returned to Spain; having just landed on the coast of Granada, where he intends to assume the disguise of a Moor. The years, too, which have elapsed during his exile, and his youth at the time of its commencement—his long imprisonment (which followed on his being wounded and taken in a battle for 'the better cause' in the Belgic states)—and the scar of his wound—all conspire to complete his disguise. He adds:

——— Besides, they think me dead:

[1] Thomas Otway's play.

> And what the mind believes impossible,
> The bodily sense is slow to recognize.*

He determines to seek an interview with Ordonio's wife, as, he was informed by the assassin, Teresa had already become; yet he retains some doubt of the tale, and a sort of general persuasion of the fidelity of his betrothed mistress. He is also resolved to awaken the conscience of his guilty brother; Isidore having betrayed that he was employed by Ordonio.

We are made acquainted with the chief of these circumstances in the first scene between Alvar and Zulimez, his faithful attendant. The full disclosure of such important events to that attendant, by his master, is opportunely delayed till their arrival in Spain; and thus the audience is made acquainted with them inartificially enough. A scene between Valdez and Teresa follows, in which the father unsuccessfully pleads the cause of his son Ordonio; the fact being that Teresa is not married to him, and is entirely averse from his addresses. Monviedro, a Dominican and Inquisitor, now enters, with Alhadra the wife of Isidore, who has appealed to Ordonio for testimony of his 'soundness in the Catholic faith', he having been accused of a relapse into Mohammedanism. On Ordonio's entrance, a scene ensues, which excites strong symptoms of 'Remorse'in the guilty brother, and increases Teresa's aversion for him. When the men have retired, she lingers with Alhadra on the beach, where the whole of the scene has hitherto passed; and while the latter is expressing her fears for her husband, they are interrupted by Alvar in his Moorish dress. After some agitation on his part, he converses with them, and, under the fiction of a dream, relates or rather shadows out the principal circumstances of his attachment to Teresa, and of the attempt to assassinate him. Teresa, of course, is greatly interested by this conversation; and she leaves Alvar more inclined than ever to believe in her fidelity.

Act ii introduces Ordonio and Isidore, near the house of the latter, in a wild and mountainous country. The patron again wishes to employ his dependant in his intrigues; and his desire now is that Isidore should disguise himself as a magician, and endeavour by some pretended act of sorcery to convince Teresa of the death of Alvar. For the furtherance of this design, he tells him to make use of the portrait of Teresa, which she had given to Alvar at their parting (overseen by Ordonio) and which, according to Ordonio's orders,

---

* Was this philosophical piece of poetry suggested by the doubts of the Apostle Thomas?

Isidore had taken from Alvar when his life was spared—an event of which Ordonio is still uninformed. Isidore refuses compliance with this new deceit; urging that, at the time of the assassination, Ordonio had told him he was beloved by Teresa, and that he was ignorant of her attachment to Alvar—nay ignorant who Alvar really was. A quarrel ensues, in the course of which Ordonio learns that his brother (before his supposed death) was informed that he was the planner of the assassination. This circumstance produces a design of bitter revenge against Isidore: but it is now proposed that the Moorish stranger (the unknown Alvar) about whose character much of mystery has appeared, shall be employed in this stratagem on Teresa. An interview between the two brothers therefore takes place, at a cottage in the mountains, in which the elder has been concealed. After some delay, and several home-thrusts directed by Alvar against the conscience of Ordonio, the former learns the delightful secret that Teresa is not the wife of his brother, and is overjoyed to receive her portrait (which he had been obliged to surrender in order to save his life) for the purpose of the intended deception: but neither the plot, nor its object on Alvar's part, namely, the wish to rouse the conscience of his brother, can excuse such cold-blooded delay in the lover's recognition of his mistress; and besides, there is something so strange, and at the same time so ludicrous, in this incident of *mock-magic*, on which the whole piece turns, that we cannot but consider it as a capital and insurmountable defect in the story.

Act iii opens in the castle of Lord Valdez, with the solemn mummery of soft music and invisible choristers, an altar, and incense suddenly taking fire on it, &c. &c. In the midst of the farce, instead of the picture of Teresa (whose aversion to the 'unholy rite' saves her the pain of being present) is exhibited an illuminated representation of the scene of Alvar's supposed assassination. This, it seems, Alvar had executed (for, *opportunely*, he is a limner) during his banishment; and the conscience of the villain is aroused by this exhibition (which we do not despair of seeing hereafter at the Royal Academy) as keenly as that of the king by the play in *Hamlet*. The Inquisitor and his attendants, however, break in on the scene of sorcery, and hurry off Alvar to the dungeon under the castle. A scene succeeds between Valdez, Teresa, and Ordonio, which calls forth still more eloquently the compunction of the guilty brother.

The IVth act introduces Isidore waiting for Ordonio in a cavern among the rocks; where, after some dark and pregnant interchange of words, in which Ordonio bodies forth their own situation under a feigned tale (reminding us of Alvar's pretended dream before*) the wily villain assaults his agent, and attempts to destroy him. Isidore, although summoned by a most '*moving* letter' to the interview, yet entertained some suspicions of Ordonio, and came ready armed: but he is disarmed in their rencontre, and flies from his superior into the inner part of the cavern. Hither Ordonio pursues him, but presently returns, alone: exclaiming,

> I have hurl'd him down the chasm! Treason for treason.

At first thought, and still more at first sight, this incident commits some sin against poetical justice, and consequently we are beginning to recoil from it: but on a moment's consideration, we acquiesce in it, as the probable though shocking result of the situation of the desperate Ordonio.

Teresa now appears at the gate of the dungeon in which Alvar is confined. Valdez enters, and again vainly endeavours to reconcile her to the love of Ordonio. Meanwhile, a peasant brings him an alarming but unintelligible letter from his son, and he hastens to unravel it. The scene changes to the 'mountains by moonlight', and Alhadra appears in her Moorish dress. She is shortly joined by a band of her countrymen, who are all eager to revenge the death of Isidore, which Alhadra in burning grief communicates to them. She had followed her husband to the cavern, and, looking down the chasm in its last recess, had seen his blood on the jutting rocks. They rush off, impatient for revenge. The whole of this scene strikes us as natural and spirited.

Act v discloses the interior of the dungeon, and Alvar soliloquizing on his sad estate. Teresa enters; a most beautiful scene follows; and their recognition is gradually and tenderly completed. Ordonio now appears, with a poisoned goblet in his hand: a very impressive dialogue takes place between the brothers; and Ordonio at last, in an agony of horror, discovers his much-injured Alvar. Just as his shame, grief, pride, and 'Remorse', are mingling together into one wild distraction, Alhadra and her devoted Moors burst into the prison, and Ordonio dies by the hand of the wife of Isidore. The rest may be imagined; Alvar and Teresa bend over the body of their 'guilty brother'.

---

* We have throughout the play too much dreaming, and allusion to dreams; and we are almost tempted to imagine that on some of these occasions the author's will was suspended (as is the case in dreams) and that he was mechanically forced to dwell on such airy subjects by some involuntary impulse.

We have thus analyzed the story of the play; and in so doing we have anticipated some of our intended remarks on the more striking scenes, as well as offered the observations which we promised on the conduct of the plot. It remains for us to call the attention of the reader, and to recall that of the spectator, to the more prominent beauties of the tragedy; and to point out the contrast of character in the *Dramatis Personæ*. Descriptions, of a high and unusual merit, occur in every act. The detached passages, in which some common thought (or rather some thought which we fancy is common, from its acknowledged force and general intelligibility) is clothed in its own language, we mean in the very best and most poetical, are also numerous:

> Remorse is as the heart in which it grows:
> If that be gentle, it drops balmy dews
> Of true Repentance; but if proud and gloomy,
> It is a poison-tree, that, pierced to the inmost,
> Weeps only tears of poison!

This is well: but much that follows is better. Of Shakespeare we are frequently reminded; not by any paltry plagiarism, but by bold and *original imitation*, if we may be allowed the expression. For instance,

> My long captivity
> Left me no choice: The very *Wish* too languish'd
> With the fond *Hope* that nurs'd it; the sick babe
> Droop'd at the bosom of its famish'd mother.

> Thy *wish* was father, Harry! to that *thought*.
> Harry the Fourth.

Both, perhaps, are conceits: but the copy is superior to the original. Then, as a description:

> *Alvar*. As we passed by, I bade thee mark the base,
> Of yonder cliff—
> *Zulimez*.   That rocky seat you mean,
> Shaped by the billows?—
> *Alvar*.   There Teresa met me,
> The morning of the day of my departure.
> We were alone: the purple hue of dawn
> Fell from the kindling east aslant upon us,
> And, blending with the blushes on her cheek,
> Suffus'd the tear-drops there with rosy light.
> There seem'd a glory round us, and Teresa
> The angel of the vision!—
>   —Hadst thou seen

How in each motion her most innocent soul
Beam'd forth and brighten'd, thou thyself would'st tell me,
Guilt is a thing impossible in her,
She must be innocent!

The touching fancies of Teresa, in her description to Valdez of the employment of her lone hours, occupied as they are in sanguine dreams of the safety of his son,* display a very powerful range over the wildest and least frequented lands of poesy, in the mind of the writer: but these we must omit. Alhadra's description of her miseries in prison, when first she fell under the censure of the Inquisition, is equally forcible in a different manner:

> *Teresa.* What might your crime be?
> *Alhad.*   I was a Moresco!
> They cast me, then a young and nursing mother,
> Into a dungeon of their prison house,
> Where was no bed, no fire, no ray of light,
> No touch, no sound of comfort! The black air,
> It was a toil to breathe it! when the door,
> Slow opening at the appointed hour, disclosed
> One human countenance, the lamp's red flame
> Cower'd as it enter'd, and at once sunk down.
> Oh miserable! by that lamp to see
> My infant quarrelling with the coarse hard bread
> Brought daily: for the little wretch was sickly—
> My rage had dried away its natural food.
> In darkness I remain'd—the dull bell counting,
> Which haply told me, that the all-cheering sun
> Was rising on our garden. When I dozed,
> My infant's moanings mingled with my slumbers
> And waked me.—If you were a mother, lady,
> I should scarce dare to tell you, that its noises

* Surely Miss Baillie must have seen (or must have dreamt of) this trait in the character of Teresa. Her own 'Aurora' is not a more ardent picture of Hope; and, in a passage which follows, we fancy that we trace some resemblance to 'Orra'.[1] Is not this '*superstitious fear?*'

> ——Still a tale of spirits works upon her—
> She is a lone enthusiast, sensitive,
> Shivers, and cannot keep the tears in her eye:—
> And such do love the marvellous too well
> Not to believe it.

[1] Aurora is the heroine of *The Beacon*, and Orra the heroine of *Orra* (1812).

And peevish cries so fretted on my brain,
That I have struck the innocent babe in anger.

We omit much that follows, of very curious observation on character, and of truly pathetic poetry. If a due occasion arise for the introduction of such a thought as the following, who will reject it?

TIME, as he courses onwards, still unrolls
The volume of concealment. In the FUTURE,
As in the optician's glassy cyclinder,
The indistinguishable blots and colors
Of the dim PAST collect and shape themselves,
Upstarting in their own completed image,
To scare or to reward.

Should we have doubted for a moment of the genuineness of the subjoined passage, had we found it even in a *doubtful* work of Shakespeare?

Valdez.   My Alvar lov'd sad music from a child.
Once he was lost: and after weary search
We found him in an open place in the wood,
To which spot he had followed a blind boy,
Who breath'd into a pipe of sycamore
Some strangely moving notes: and these, he said,
Were taught him in a dream. Him we first saw
Stretch'd on the broad top of a sunny heath-bank:
And lower down poor Alvar, fast asleep,
His head upon the blind boy's dog. It pleas'd me
To mark how he had fasten'd round the pipe
A silver toy his grandam had late given him.
Methinks I see him now as he then look'd—
Even so!—He had outgrown his infant dress.
Yet still he wore it.
      Alv.   My tears must not flow!
I must not clasp his knees, and cry, My Father!

Some of the morbid and atheistical reflections of Ordonio are strongly expressed:

[quotes ll. 94-115, Act III, Scene ii (*PW*, ii, 855)]

The directions to the actors in this passage, and in many others, are too German and too minute: but, says the author, in the preface,* 'from

* We cannot avoid remarking the inaccurate composition of this preface, particularly in the first page.

the necessity of hastening the publication I was obliged to send the manuscript intended for the stage, which is the sole cause of the number of directions printed in Italics'. His gratitude to the performers is surely overcharged.

Isidore's description of the chasm, down which he is afterward hurled, in the fourth act, is poetical, if not dramatic. Whatever these expressions may be, they are living and energetic:

> My body bending forward, yea, o'erbalanced
> Almost beyond recoil, on the dim brink
> Of a huge chasm I stept. The shadowy moonshine,
> Filling the void, so counterfeited substance,
> That my foot hung aslant adown the edge.

Teresa's contrast of Alvar and Ordonio, when she is resisting their father's sollicitation for the latter, is a passage which may modestly be compared with the comparison of Hamlet's father and uncle:

[quotes ll. 49-73, Act IV, Scene ii (*PW*, ii, 866)]

Her exclamation of melancholy joy, when reflecting on her past days of love, is not inferior:

[quotes ll. 98-115, Act IV, Scene ii (*PW*, ii, 867)]

Alvar's reflections on the ill-judging conduct of men towards their erring brethren, and his eulogy on the reforming powers of Nature,

> (With other ministrations, thou, Oh, Nature!
> Healest thy wand'ring and distemper'd child,)

may perhaps remind our readers of the German sentimentality which was so fashionable a few years since; and which, among other *sublime* effusions, produced—'Oh holy Nature! thou dost never plead in vain!'—but such ebullitions of sentiment ought to be and are less offensive now; and perhaps the recoil of opinion, by which we have been led to despise and laugh at every thing sentimental, requires check rather than encouragement at present. When Ordonio offers the poisoned cup to Alvar, the remark of the latter, by which he conveys or rather hints his suspicions that the cup *is* poisoned, appears to us to be conceived and expressed in the last corruption of taste:

> *Alvar.* Yon insect on the wall,
> Which moves, this way and that, its hundred limbs,
> Were it a toy of mere mechanic craft,

It were an infinitely curious thing!
But it has life, Ordonio! life, enjoyment!
And by the power of its miraculous will
Wields all the complex movements of its frame
Unerringly to pleasurable Ends!
Saw I that insect on this goblet's brim
I would remove it with an anxious pity!
   Ordonio. What meanest thou?
   Alv. There's poison in the wine.

Alvar's reproof, however, to his half-reasoning and wholly abandoned brother, is most eloquent and instructive:

What then art thou? For shame, put up thy sword!
What boots a weapon in a wither'd arm?
I fix mine eye upon thee, and thou tremblest!
I speak, and fear and wonder crush thy rage,
And turn it to a motionless distraction!
Thou blind self worshipper! thy pride, thy cunning,
Thy faith in universal villany,
Thy shallow sophisms, thy pretended scorn
For all thy human brethren—out upon them!
What have they done for thee? have they given thee peace?
Cur'd thee of starting in thy sleep? or made
The darkness pleasant when thou wak'st at midnight?
Art happy when alone? Can'st walk by thyself
With even step and quiet cheerfulness?
Yet, yet thou may'st be sav'd——
   Ord. (*vacantly repeating the words.*)   Sav'd? sav'd?
   Alv.   One pang!
Could I call up one pang of true Remorse!

We conclude our extracts with the last speech of Alhadra:

I thank thee, Heaven! thou hast ordain'd it wisely,
That still extremes bring their own cure. That point
In misery, which makes the oppressed Man
Regardless of his own life, makes him too
Lord of the Oppressor's—Knew I an hundred men
Despairing, but not palsied by despair,
This arm should shake the Kingdoms of the World;
The deep foundations of iniquity
Should sink away, earth groaning from beneath them;
The strong-holds of the cruel men should fall,
Their Temples and their mountainous Towers should fall;

Till Desolation seem'd a beautiful thing,
And all that were and had the Spirit of Life,
Sang a new song to her who had gone forth,
Conquering and still to conquer.

Our readers, we think, will now be ready to join with us in our approbation of the vigorous and animated versification of this drama. It is indeed occasionally irregular and inharmonious, but scarcely ever psiritless. The characters demand a more unqualified panegyric. Alvar (with the above-mentioned drawback of his unnatural conduct as a lover) is an admirable draught of the gentle, ardent, and generous cavalier. Isidore is human nature itself, exposed to dangerous temptation, and displayed in some of its most striking varieties of weakness and strength, of good and bad. Alhadra is Moorish nature. Teresa, as the author confesses, is imperfectly developed, but still is interesting from her fidelity, and excites no common sympathy from that sanguine disposition which is so congenial to the kinder part of our species. Valdez is little or nothing; and Ordonio, on whom the author has expended his utmost strength, is far from being adequately successful. With the exception, almost with the sole exception, of the passages to which we have referred, there is something broad, coarse, and rudely marked in the features of his 'Remorse'. He seems mad with anticipated detection too soon: yet he is the *sketch* of no vulgar imagination.

In a word, we think that Mr. Coleridge has only to put some rein on his fancy, to prune some of the exuberant branches of his taste (if we may venture to offer critical advice in a mixed metaphor), and to lean, in future, to an imitation of the pathos and the melody of Otway rather than of the nerve and roughness of the elder play-wrights, in order to become a dramatic ornament of his age and nation.

54. Unsigned review, *British Review*

May 1813, iv, 361-70

In the most exposed and perilous station among the ranks of literature stands the dramatist. But in the proportion in which his danger from inherent disqualifications is increased, the field of fortuitous success is widened. We are all sensible of the lucky force of stage effect, and the artificial aids of scenic representation.

Had the writer of *Remorse* composed his tragedy merely to be read, we hesitate not to pronounce that he would completely have failed in his object: but genius has more resources than one, and the dramatist who has both the eye and the ear to appeal to, where his claims are feeble with the one, knows how to make his court to the other.

We can easily imagine the triumphant feelings of the author when the plaudits overwhelmed the dismal note of disapprobation in the eventful moment that was to decide his doom; and very far is it from our wish or intention to alloy the thrillings of his self congratulations. We have, however, a duty to the public to perform, in taking a strict and impartial view of the merits of the piece under consideration; and this is the more imperative, as we are sure that none of our readers, after having seen it performed, have made it the lucubration of their closets, or can charge their memories with any very accurate account of it, however great their resignation and devotion may have been at the time of the exhibition. We are desirous of shewing them, by the short notices we shall offer, how much both in quality and quantity may have escaped their penetration, and how many have been the aberrations to which, as true penitents at the shrine of offended authorship, they will have to confess themselves guilty if ever they should be called to account.

Mr. Coleridge informs us in his preface, that his tragedy was written in the summer and autumn of the year 1797; why it has not been brought forward till now is a matter of no importance, but we question if it is a property that was, or ever will be, the better for keeping. At the present moment, however, any thing relating to the Peninsula is an object of interest; together with our victorious dispatches we have Spanish buttons, chocolate, mantles, fans, feathers, and bolderos; was

166

it then to be supposed that the zeal of managers, shouldering each other in the eager discharge of a new office, should forget to provide us with a Spanish play? Undoubtedly not. Circulars, we conclude, were distributed with diplomatic diligence by the secretaries of the green room, to all the tributary drudges of the drama wheresoever dispersed. It is not unlikely that these poor souls, rendered desperate by the fate of their 'Rejected Addresses', had flung away their slighted quills, and turned out their lean Pegasuses to grass, and their vagrant Muses into the streets. What was to be done?—the theatre had been burnt, and all the rubbish in and about it had been either consumed, or stolen, or lost.[1]

Whether the tragedy of *Remorse* had been taken away from the theatre before the conflagration, or dug out like a precious monument from the ruins of Herculaneum, it is not of much importance to determine; it was found that its scene was laid in Spain; there were Dons and Donnas for the chief agents; and this was exactly what the managers wanted. The time of the story is the reign of Philip II at the close of the civil wars against the Moors, and during the heat of the persecution in which an edict had been promulgated, forbidding the wearing of Moresco apparel under pain of death. The Marquis Valdez, who seems to have been a respectable old lord with an excess of credulity, which is of great service, as will presently appear, to the plot, has two sons, the elder Don Alvar, and the younger Don Ordonio, and a beautiful and amiable ward called Donna Teresa. A tender attachment takes place between Don Alvar and Donna Teresa, and nothing seems to counteract their mutual wishes. Some delay, however, is interposed by the departure of the young lord from his native country, for the purpose as it should seem of travelling; though this, like many other incidents, is left to be supplied by the good-natured reader or spectator. The younger son, Don Ordonio, who seems to enjoy the larger share of his father's affection, is secretly his brother's rival, and as he flatters himself that he has only to remove Don Alvar out of the way to ensure his own success with Donna Teresa, he engages a certain Morescan, by name Isidore, to murder his brother whilst on his travels; and it is upon a firm conviction of his death, that he is pressing his suit for the hand of the fair Donna Teresa, when Don Alvar returns to his native shore with a faithful attendant, whose name is Zulimez. The Morescan, who had been suborned to murder Don Alvar, had spared his life on the condition that he would bind himself by oath to a 'year of absence and of secrecy'.

[1] The Theatre Royal, Drury Lane, burned down in 1809.

Zulimez is of opinion, that his master might have returned before with great propriety, as the oath was not binding, and seems a convert to the poet's doctrine, that it is

> He who enjoins the oath that breaks it,
> Not he that for convenience takes it.

The fratricide is not wanting in an excuse for his brother's absence, and the old marquis is put off with a story which he readily believes—that his son had been attacked on his homeward-bound voyage by an Algerine, and that his

> brave Ordonio
> Saw both the pirate and the prize go down.

Thus satisfied of the death of his eldest son, the credulous old man uses all his influence with his ward to persuade her to accept the hand of Ordonio. Nothing, however, can shake her constant affection; she raises some queries upon the voucher; and when she is told that her union with Ordonio will make

> her aged father
> Sink to the grave in joy,

she replies with frankness and firmness,

> I have no power to love him.
> His proud forbidding eye, and his dark brow,
> Chill me like dew damps of the unwholesome night:
> My love, a timorous and tender flower,
> Closes beneath his touch.

Such being the state of affairs at the beginning of the first act, our readers may pretty well guess at the development of the piece. Do they imagine that Teresa's constancy is rewarded by the hand of her unfortunate lover—that Ordonio pays the price of his infamy by some unlucky end—do they guess this is the case?—because if they do they are right. And yet we will not say that they will not be disappointed. The catastrophe of this play is like a distant mark on a wearisome road, constantly in sight, but constantly inaccessible. The play has a sort of secondary story in the fortunes of Isidore and his wife Alhadra, which, however, is totally destitute of any attractions or interest of its own.

We have already heard of the expedition on which Isidore had set out at the request of one brother to murder the other, and of his shrinking from the horrid act when just on the point of executing it. Isidore, it seems, had professed himself a Christian, but in some points having fallen short of satisfying the scruples or the cupidity of Monviedro, an inquisitor, he is of course consigned to a dungeon, a circumstance which very naturally inflames the irritable and revengeful disposition of his wife Alhadra. Whilst she is brooding over her vegeance, her husband is released through the interest of Ordonio, and is invited to another little piece of secret service, which however he at first refuses upon very creditable grounds. He accounts for his conduct in the following terms:

> Why, why, my lord,
> You know you told me that the lady loved you,
> Had loved you with *incautious* tenderness;—
> That if the young man, her betrothed husband,
> Returned, yourself, and she, and the honour of both
> Must perish.

This is doing evil that good may come of it with a vengeance. The upshot of the conversation is that they both agree to turn conjurors, for, says Ordonio,

> We would wind up her (Teresa's) fancy
> With a strange music that she knows not of—
> With fumes of frankincense, and mummery;
> Then leave, as one sure token of his death,
> That portrait, which from off the dead man's neck,
> I bade thee take, the trophy of thy conquest.

At last, Isidore, reflecting upon some strange things he had heard drop from Alvar (who was wandering about disguised as a Moor, and thus kept himself unknown to every one but the faithful Zulimez), whilst questioned on the sea-shore by an inquisitor; and that he had called himself

> He that can bring the dead to life again;

and thinking the assertion, upon consideration of the person addressed, to be very tolerable evidence of the truth of what was professed, intimates that this wizard would be a desirable agent in the business. Ordonio is of the same opinion, and immediately sets off for the supposed conjuror's abode; and here he gets a promise, after a great deal of mysterious emotion, hints, and gestures, that every thing should be done according to his proposed plan, which was no other than by some very unintelligible means to play off certain illusions upon the fancy of Teresa which might satisfy her beyond all doubt of the death of Don Alvar. To forward this curious contrivance, he leaves with Alvar the miniature of which he had been robbed in his travels. When the time comes, the conjuror fairly outwits his employers, for, instead of this miniature, he commands the spirits to represent the picture of his intended assassination. At the moment while the minds of Teresa, Valdez, and Ordonio are filled with astonishment and horror, a band of inquisitors appear, and march off the sorcerer without further ceremony, whilst Ordonio, having great reason to be displeased at what had been done, exclaims,

> Why haste you not? Off with him to the dungeon!

Ordonio very naturally begins to distrust Isidore, and invites him to a cavern under some pretence with intent to kill him. They meet accordingly, and a strange dialogue takes place. Ordonio, who seems to have no small difficulty in working up his mind to the execution of his bloody purpose, entertains his companion, who, from some ominous dream of the preceding night, appears to be full of frightful apprehension, with a long rambling story which affords very strong hints of what was intended; so strong, indeed, that Isidore draws upon the Don by way of anticipation, and a fight and a scuffle ensue, which end in the precipitation of the ill-fated Moor down a horrid chasm at one end of the cavern. And thus Isidore is disposed of, and makes way by this abrupt disappearance for the more convenient dispatch of the business that remained.

Alhadra, who had watched her husband into the cavern, and had also seen Ordonio enter the same frightful place, and after a while come out of it flinging his torch towards the moon with a sort of wild sportiveness in his manner, soon makes a discovery which decides her conduct. She summons a faithful band of Moorish followers, of whom Isidore had been the chieftain, to whom she describes the murder of her husband by Ordonio, and engages them to revenge their leader. In the mean time Teresa had visited the dungeon where Don Alvar was confined by the inquisitors, and a complete development had taken place, with all the joy and tenderness, tears and caresses, which belong to these tumultuous moments. In the midst of these endearments the ruthless Ordonio, fresh from the murder of Isidore, bursts into the dungeon with a dose of poison which he had prepared for the supposed wizard, whom he was determined to rid himself of, as his communications with Isidore seemed to have made him too well acquainted with

Ordonio's crimes. Here Alvar discovers himself to his brother, who is too far gone in the horrors of guilt and remorse to receive comfort from the assurances of forgiveness on the part of Alvar and Teresa. While things are in this state between these parties, in comes the infuriated Alhadra and her Morescan band of followers. After some efforts on the part of Teresa to incline the heart of the injured wife to pity, the voice of Valdez is heard crying rescue! rescue! as he runs towards the prison. At that instant Ordonio is stabbed by Alhadra, who is carried off by the Moors, and in a moment after Valdez enters, who of course is made acquainted with the whole truth, and receives his son Alvar into his embrace in an ecstacy of parental joy: we have only to suppose the nuptials of Don Alvar and his beloved Teresa, to make the happiness of the survivors of the house of Valdez complete.

We may add ourselves, also, to the number of the persons made happy by arriving at this consummation; for we cannot help reckoning the task of reading to the end the tragedy of *Remorse*, with the attention requisite to form a judgment of its merits, among the wearisome labours to which a Reviewer submits in the discharge of his duty. What has made the reading of this play more than ordinarily troublesome, has been the unhappy confusion of the plot. By a singular inversion in the process of this piece, what is called the denouement takes place in the first act, and all which happens between that and the concluding scene are so many inexplicable incidents, impelling the reader's mind in a direction retrograde to the development of the story. The surrounding mist grows thicker and heavier as we draw towards the catastrophe, till at length all necessary parties are brought together by a coincidence, the cause of which is to us an impenetrable secret, in a dungeon of the inquisition; and here, where no sunshine ever found an entrance, the author on a sudden lets in a flood of light; and amidst poison, blood, daggers, tears, caresses, sorrow, joy, reconciliation, and remorse, a thorough explanation of every thing takes place, and complete justice is done, for the first time, perhaps, within the walls of the holy brotherhood. But if we have used the word 'mystery' we would not be understood to advert to any mystery in the story. We have nothing to complain of in this respect. We are let at once into the whole story; and every thing is done that the most tender regard to our feelings could suggest, for preventing all surprise upon us, and to spare us the distress of eager expectation, anxious suspense, or alarming conjecture. The mystery is, how the fact and the truth could, amidst the flimsy disguises in which the incidents of the play are wrapped up, escape the immediate detection of all the parties concerned. But the duration of the piece was necessary to be provided for; and it was expedient to guard against an anticipation of the catastrophe, on which account it was clearly incumbent on the author to give to each of his characters that degree of stupidity which might be proof against the most palpable hints, and able to withstand the plainest inferences from facts and appearances.

We cannot help feeling the propriety of the author's gratitude, as expressed in the preface, to the several actors and actresses whose shoulders sustained the burthen of the performance. To the one, Mr. Coleridge gives his thanks for his full conception of the character of Isidore; to another, for his accurate representation of the partial yet honourable father; to a third, for his energy in the character of Alvar; to another, for her acceptance of a character not fully developed, and quite inadequate to her extraordinary powers, meaning, we presume, that of Donna Teresa. As we think the play extremely defective in character, the performers were doubtless well entitled to the author's gratitude, if by the transfusion of their own energies into their several parts they could inform them with a spirit not their own. Isidore being a character of which the author speaks of the actor's full conception is probably his favourite. For our own part we are totally unable to say whether he was, upon the whole, wicked or virtuous, brave or timorous, a Christian or a Mahommedan: he consented out of gratitude to slay the brother of his benefactor, though compassion afterwards arrested his hand; and he seems to excuse the bloody undertaking on this truly equitable ground, viz. that he considered that the young lady had loved Ordonio with an *incautious* tenderness, and that it was necessary to prevent the return of her betrothed husband by killing him, in order to save the guilty couple from being lost, together with their honour. We must therefore join in respect for that acting which could animate this insipid sentimental assassin into the semblance of a consistent villain, a decided hypocrite, or a generous friend.

We agree also with Mr. Coleridge in the deserts of that actor who performed the part of Alvar, if, indeed, he '*gave* to that character', as Mr. Coleridge expresses it, 'beauties and striking points which not only delighted but surprised him'. We agree with him in this surprise, because we really find nothing in Alvar very striking or pointed. He seems to have been a very gentle, forgiving, well-meaning, moral Spaniard; and very strenuously in love; but not a little degraded by being made to play off the tricks of a conjuror. The fidelity of Zulimez, and the revengefulness of Alhadra, we will say nothing about. If neither the one nor the other of these qualities is exhibited in its peculiar colours, it is enough that the one is called faithful, and the other confesses herself to be revengeful: as we have the facts upon such good authority, what need was there of a circumstantial and circuitous proof by any dramatic process of exposition?

Without doubt the character of Ordonio exhibits the most vigorous strokes of Mr. Coleridge's pencil; but even here there is a want of that distinguishing force of conception which is capable of bringing out a character surrounded as it were with its own moral atmosphere, and saved from being merely one of a class by certain special and peculiar characteristics. Don Ordonio is desperately in love, and stops at nothing, not even the murder of his brother, to obtain possession of the object of his passion. In him is proposed to be exemplified the full operation of the remorse that follows inexpiable crimes; and it must be admitted, that the remembrance of his villainy does not seem to sit quite easy upon him, especially when something like an exposure threatens him while in the presence of his father, Teresa, or the inquisitor. But his remorse does not interfere with his desires, or his vivacity in the prosecution of them; nor does it stay his hand from murdering his old friend Isidore, and attempting the life of the supposed wizard in the dungeon. That the design of the piece, however, may be sufficiently present to the reader's mind, care is taken to place the word 'Remorse' before the eye in capitals in the sixteenth page; and in the sixty-seventh page the word is many times rung in our ears for the same purpose.

Mr. Coleridge, though entitled undoubtedly to the praise of genius for many truly poetical and brilliant passages in this piece, sinks very much in a comparison with Miss Joanna Baillie, as a delineator of the passions. Conscious, perhaps, of this inferiority, he seems to have had recourse to a sort of wildness in his fable as a substitute for the moral vigour of his pencil; and has brought before us a sort of conjuring scene, very unfitted to the grave and lofty genius of tragedy. It is to be recollected that Miss Baillie, with astonishing art, framed her story in entire subservience to the passion she was pourtraying, shewing it to us in its specific operation, and developing its progress from its earliest stages through all its struggles, and gradual confirmation, to its last overbearing and fatal results. We have already declared our opinion, that, as far as this play can be admitted in proof, Mr. Coleridge possesses not the power of fixing the mind of the reader with a deep interest on the dreadful phenomena of a single passion.

Nor can we conclude our observations without adding one which it really distresses us to make, as it touches most sensibly a poet's feeling: we cannot help giving it as our opinion, that the play of *Remorse* exhibits a palpable want of taste. The thoughts are sometimes laboured into false refinement, and the descriptions are often overstrained. The poet evidently lends himself too much to his imagination, and is but too apt to forget that there ought to be a sort of sobriety in the enthusiasm of genius that keeps it within the limits of nature and just sentiment.

After delivering ourselves with so much freedom of censure, it is but justice to Mr. Coleridge to allow, that however we may think he has failed in this attempt, the attempt, executed as it is, indicates a powerful and creative mind; and induces us to hope that his muse will vindicate in some future production her tragic ascendancy. There are many passages which we think are written in a false taste, but there are others of great sublimity, and which display a truly poetical compass of thought and diction. We cannot refuse ourselves the pleasure of extracting the first part of the scene between Donna Teresa and her father Don Valdez, where the old man is endeavouring to convince her of Alvar's death, and to persuade her to give her hand to Ordonio his brother.

[quotes ll. 1-51, Act I, Scene ii (*PW*, ii, 823-5)]

We shall conclude these hasty observations on the play of *Remorse*, with declaring our general opinion to be as follows: that the production is not upon the whole calculated to satisfy good taste, either on the stage or in the closet; that it is unequal to the author's general, high, and deserved reputation; and as it contains some beauties which few could equal, so its faults are in general such as too nearly approach the sublime for many to be capable of committing.

55. J. T. Coleridge, *Quarterly Review*

April 1814, xi, 177-90

This unsigned review is attributed to J. T. Coleridge (Walter Graham, *Tory Criticism in the Quarterly Review*, New York 1921, 26). Coleridge (1790-1876) was a nephew; in 1834 he was briefly editor of the *Quarterly Review*.

When a system of opinions, either new, or apparently so, is formally laid before the world, no judgment can be formed respecting its merits, till the whole has been attentively considered: but when philosophical opinions come to us cursorily scattered through volumes of miscellaneous poetry, it can scarcely be expected that their merits will be so fairly tried. The premises being sometimes not at all, and, perhaps, never formally laid down, the conclusion appears to rest on little authority; in this page the reader is startled with one peculiar idea, in the next with another, and between both, perhaps, traces no connection. Thus he proceeds nearly through the book, still ignorant of its characteristic feature; his vanity is mortified, and forgetting that his ignorance should in justice prevent his forming any judgment, he suffers it to be the very groundwork of his condemnation. Or if towards the conclusion, he should have acquired a knowledge of the general theory, the previous disgust is in most instances so strong, that he feels no inclination with the new light he has acquired, to reperuse the volume.

That Mr. Coleridge and his poetical friends (or, to use a colloquial title, the Lake Poets) have suffered in the judgment of the world from this circumstance, we cannot but believe; and we lament that no one of them should have stated briefly and plainly to the public the nature of their poetical theory. We lament this the more, because, though it will be found, perhaps, erroneous in parts, on the whole we think it contains truth enough for all the purposes of poetry, and in its effects must be beneficial to all the noble and gentle affections of the heart. Without undertaking to supply the deficiency, we will yet venture a few remarks, which may help us in forming our judgment on the work before us.

To a profound admiration of Shakespeare, Milton, and our earlier poets, the authors of the system, on which we are remarking, appear to have united much of metaphysical habit, and metaphysical learning. This admiration was not of the kind which displays itself in the conventional language of criticism; it was real, practical and from the heart; it led to ceaseless study, to imitation of its objects. Analysing by metaphysical aids the principles on which these great men exercised such imperial sway over the human heart, they found that it was not so much by operating on the reason as on the imagination of the reader. We mean that it was not so much by argument, or description, which the reason acknowledged to be true, as by touching some chord of association in the mind, which woke the imagination and set it instantly on a creation of its own. An example or two will make this clear. In the parting speech of Polonius to Laertes we admire consummate prudence and beautiful expression, and there the labour and the enjoyment of the mind ceases; but when Gertrude says of the frantic Hamlet:

> Anon as patient as the female dove,
> When that her golden couplets are disclosed,
> His silence will set drooping.

Beautiful as the description is, the mind does not rest there; a thousand ideas of a gentle, placid, and affectionate nature rise within us in a train, which we seem ourselves to have created and arrayed. Once more—in the following passage from Milton every reader of taste will admit that he is very differently affected by different parts of it, and that the difference solely results from the exercise of the imagination in some lines, and its repose in others.

> Bring the rathe primrose that *forsaken* dies,
> The tufted crow-toe and pale jessamine,
> The white pink, and the pansy freck'd with jet,
> The glowing violet,
> The musk rose, and the well-attir'd woodbine,
> *With cowslips wan that hang the pensive head,*
> *And every flower that sad embroidery wears.*

It was evident in fact, that the latter process must be far more delightful to the mind than the former; as in the one case, however we may be instructed and improved, we are still conscious of our inferiority;

we stand as pupils before our master, and advance not a single step beyond the limit, which he marks for us. But in the other, it is our master, indeed, who presents us with the key of Paradise, but we ourselves open the gate, all our wanderings are unconstrained, and we find beauties, and trace likenesses with all the delight of original composition. It is true, that a closer analysis would shew that in this apparent freedom we are in fact following a prescribed direction: but the restraint which is neither seen, nor felt, is in fact no restraint.

In so far then as metaphysical inquiry led them to this conclusion, it did them good service; and no one who has read Mr. Alison's beautiful Essays on Taste, will doubt for an instant that they had arrived at the true theory of poetic delight.[1] Beyond this point metaphysics (prompting, indeed, at times peculiar beauties) were on the whole dangerous companions; and from the habits of making every mental emotion the subject of analysis have resulted, we think, most of the defects which continue to impede their progress to popular favour.

It is observed of Marivaux, by one of his countrymen, that, 'Il ne donne pas le résultat de son observation, mais l'acte même de l'observation'. The remark will apply to our Poets; minute in their analyses and analysing the minutest emotions; preferring, indeed, from the greater skill required in the task, to trace to their causes the slight and transient, rather than the strong and permanent feelings of the mind, they have too often become not so much the painters of nature as the commentators upon her.

By this method they have sacrificed the chance of general popularity for the devoted admiration of a few; and it may be said that the alternative was entirely at their option. But still we think the choice a faulty one; the majority of mankind are little conversant in metaphysical pursuits; whereas it should be at least a principal object of poetry to please generally, and it is one of the highest boasts of genius that its strains, like the liturgy of our church, are not too high for the low and simple, nor yet too low for the wise and learned.

But this is not all; for it may be reasonably doubted, whether, from the continual habit of studying these slighter emotions, certain results, having a tendency to erroneous conclusions in philosophy, do not of necessity follow. For first it seems likely that the heart itself would become more susceptible of emotion from slight causes than those of the generality of men; as it is certain that the mind of the artist, or the

[1] Archibald Alison's *Essays on the Nature and Principles of Taste* (Edinburgh 1790).

connoisseur, will receive the most exquisite delight from parts of a production, which leave the common observer in a state of indifference. Now though it may be desirable that a picture should contain some of these latent beauties, yet it is evident that the artist who built his fame entirely upon them, must resign his claims to genius for the reputation of mere science, and can never aspire to the praise of being a perfect painter.

Again, such a study long continued can scarcely fail of attaching a greater degree of importance to the emotions so raised, than they merit. Whatever we dwell upon with intenseness and ardour invariably swells in our conception to a false magnitude; indeed this is implied by the very eagerness of our pursuit; and if this be true with the weed, the shell, or the butterfly, it is evident how much more strongly it will apply, where the study (as must be the case with all studies conversant about the operations of the soul) unites much of real dignity and importance as the basis on which to build the exaggerations of partial fondness. The native of a flat country gradually swells his mole-hills to mountains; no wonder then, if by constantly beholding, and deeply feeling the grandeur and beauty of their own lakes, Mr. Coleridge and his friends have learned to invest every part with a false appearance of greatness; if, in their eyes, every stream swells to a river, every lake to an ocean, and every headland, that breaks or ornaments their prospect, assumes the awful form of a giant promontory. But what is still worse, the habitual examination of their own feelings tends to produce in them a variation from nature almost amounting to distortion. The slight and subtle workings of the heart must be left to play unobserved, and without fear of observation, if they are intended to play freely and naturally; to be overlooked is to be absolutely restrained. The man who is for ever examining his feet, as he walks, will probably soon move in a stiff and constrained pace; and if we are constantly on the watch to discover the nature, order, and cause of our slightest emotions, it can scarcely be expected that they will operate in their free course or natural direction.

Now if we are justified in any of these suppositions, we cannot wonder that to a large portion of mankind the views of nature exhibited by the Lake Poets, and their own feelings with the excitement of them, should often appear strained, and even fictitious. The majority of their readers have passed glow-worms and bird's-nests, celandines and daisies, without any emotion lively enough to be remembered; and they are surprised, unfairly perhaps, but not unnaturally, that so much sensation should be attributed to so trifling a cause. They lose their fellowship of feeling with the poet, and are therefore at the best but uninterested by the poem.

Another source of peculiarities in the poets under consideration is the particular warmth and energy of their feeling in the contemplation of rural scenery. They are not the tasteful admirers of nature, nor the philosophic calculators on the extent of her riches, and the wisdom of her plans; they are her humble worshippers. In her silent solitudes, on the bosom of her lakes, in the dim twilight of her forests, they are surrendered up passively to the scenery around them, they seem to feel a power, an influence invisible and indescribable, which at once burthens and delights, exalts and purifies the soul. All the features and appearances of nature in their poetical creed possess a sentient and intellectual being, and exert an influence for good upon the hearts of her worshippers. Nothing can be more poetical than this feeling, but it is the misfortune of this school that their very excellences are carried to an excess. Hence they constantly attribute not merely physical, but moral animation to nature. Ocean has an heart, and as might be expected in consequence, all the passions of love, pride, joy, &c.; the moon is at one time merciful, at another cruel, at one time loves, at another hates; and the waves, the stars, the clouds, the music of the sky are all friends to the mariner. These are to be carefully distinguished from the common-places of poetry; to say that a river kisses its banks, or that the sea embraces an island are but metaphors borrowed from physical appearances, and bear a broad difference from passages in which an inanimate being performs an external action in obedience to some internal feeling.

To an extension or rather a modification of this last mentioned principle may perhaps be attributed the beautiful tenet so strongly inculcated by them of the celestial purity of infancy. 'Heaven lies about us in our infancy', says Mr. Wordsworth, in a passage which strikingly exemplifies the power of imaginative poetry; and Mr. Wilson, on seeing an infant asleep, exclaims:

> Thou smil'st as if thy thoughts were soaring
> To heaven, and heaven's God adoring.
> And who can tell what visions high
> May bless an infant's sleeping eye![1]

---

[1] Ll. 65-8 of 'To a Sleeping Child' by John Wilson (see *Poetical Works*, Edinburgh and London 1865, 224).

The tenet itself is strictly imaginative; its truth, as matter of philosophy, may well be doubted; certainly in the extent in which they take it, it does not rest on Scripture foundation, and may seem to be contradicted by the experience of every mother, who, in the wayward fretfulness of her infant, finds constant exercise for that unweariable love which, seemingly on this very account, the Eternal Wisdom has so wonderfully implanted in her breast. Still, however, we hold that in poetry that may be allowed to be true which accords with general feeling.

There are yet a few points of no common importance to be noticed, in which we scruple not to rank the Lake Poets above all that have gone before them. In their writings the gentle and domestic virtues of an affectionate heart are uniformly exalted above the splendid and dangerous heroism which has been too generally the theme of other poets. In their writings women are drawn, as they deserve to be, lofty yet meek; patient and cheerful; dutiful, affectionate, brave, faithful, and pious; the pillars that adorn and support the temple of this life's happiness.

> Playful and artless, on the summer wave
> Sporting with buoyant wing, the fairy scene
> With fairest grace adorning, but in woe,
> In poverty, in soul-subduing toils,
> In patient tending on the sick man's bed,
> In ministerings of love, in bitterest pangs
> Faithful and firm; in scenes where sterner hearts
> Have cracked, still cheerful and still kind.

Lastly, love is purified from the grossness of passion: it is idle to say, that this is an unattainable exaltation; all models should be perfect, though man remains imperfect, that in striving to reach what is impossible we may attain to what is uncommon. Love, with the Lake Poets, becomes what he should be, a devout spirit, purifying the soul, and worshipping God most in his most beauteous or his most noble work.

It would not impair the authority of the preceding remarks were we to admit that they do not apply with precisely the same force to the writings of all the Lake Poets. It appears to us that chance or a congenial mode of thinking has brought into intimate connection minds of very distinct powers and peculiarities. Thus a school of poetry has arisen of which all the members agree in some points, but differ in others; and even where they agree in kind they sometimes differ in degree. In examining their writings, therefore, we are to expect a general resemblance in all, which yet shall be neither so strong nor universal as to obliterate a peculiar character in each. Mr. Southey, for instance, appears to us more active, and playful, than those with whom his name is here associated: metaphysical enough to gratify the vanity, without fatiguing the attention, of the common reader; rather sweetly developing the virtues of the heart, than curiously untwisting the subtleties of the mind; diffusing over his whole picture a colouring more grateful and soothing, but less contrasted with strong light and shade; more delightful and amiable, more curious and excursive, but, on the whole, perhaps possessing less of that touching and irresistible power which incidentally redeems the wilder eccentricities of his friends.

We now turn to the poem which has given rise to the preceding remarks, in which we think the defects and the beauties which have been noticed as characteristics of the school will be found to be strongly exemplified.

The Marquis Valdez, a nobleman residing on the sea coast of Grenada, has two sons, Alvar and Ordonio, of whom the first being betrothed to Teresa, an orphan ward of his father, departs on his travels. At their parting Teresa had bound round his neck her own portrait, with a solemn promise from him

> That, save his own, no eye should e'er behold it
> Till his return.

Ordonio, who had conceived a passion for Teresa, had been an unperceived witness of this interview, and when, at the expiration of three years, Alvar's return was expected, he sends three Morescoes to waylay and assassinate him. To Isidore, one of the three, whose life he had spared in battle, he states that the man they are to murder is betrothed to a lady whose affections were placed on himself, and whose honour had been surrendered to his passion; he informs him also of the picture and particularly insists on that as the assurance of his death. Alvar meets the assassins, and fights so bravely as to compel them to a parley; he offers Isidore his purse, which is rejected, he then exclaims,

> I have a brother, and a promised wife,
> Who make life dear to me; and if I fall
> That brother will roam earth and hell for vengeance.

There was a likeness in his face to yours.
I ask'd his brother's name; he said Ordonio,
Son of Lord Valdez! I had well nigh fainted.
At length I said, (if that indeed I said it,
And that no spirit made my tongue its organ,)
That woman is dishonoured by that brother,
And he the man who sent us to destroy you.
He drove a thrust at me in rage. I told him
He wore her portrait round his neck. He looked,
Aye, just as you look now, only less ghastly!
At length, recovering from his trance, he threw
His sword away, and bade us take his life—
It was not worth his keeping.

The discovery overcomes the spirit of Alvar; he surrenders the
pledge, which had lost its value, and promises absence and secrecy.
Meantime his fate is variously reported, and Ordonio, assured of his
death by the picture, roams the seas in a pretended search of him,
and returns with an account of his having been lost in a storm. He
then professes his love for Teresa, who still cherishes a romantic hope
of Alvar's safety, and feels the strongest aversion to Ordonio. Some time
elapses, during which Alvar serves under 'the heroic Maurice' in Bel-
gium, and is taken prisoner. Upon his release, he determines to return
home, still feeding a visionary hope that Teresa may be innocent, and
determining, at all events, to awaken *remorse* in the breast of his
brother. At this point the drama opens. Alvar lands in Grenada disguised as a Morescoe chief, and meets Teresa on the sea shore; he
converses with her without disclosing himself, believing her innocent,
yet convinced that she is married to Ordonio. At this interview was
present Alhadra, the wife of Isidore, who had come to solicit Ordonio
to rescue her husband from the Inquisition by attesting his Christianity;
Ordonio consents, and Isidore is released. He is then desired by his
benefactor to assist him in convincing Teresa of Alvar's death. He is to
act the part of a wizard, and, at the end of a solemn scene of enchantment, to produce the picture as the last thing which Alvar grasped in
death. Isidore declines the task, and recommends the stranger, who has
already acquired the reputation of a sorcerer in the neighbourhood.
Ordonio visits Alvar, who agrees to perform the part, and, in receiving
instructions, becomes fully assured of Teresa's innocence, and that she
is still unmarried. The scene commences with mysterious music and
invocation to the spirit of the departed, but, at the conclusion, instead

of the portrait, is presented the picture of the assassination of Alvar. Ordonio has just time to exclaim,

> the traitor Isidore!

when the familiars of the Inquisition rush in. Valdez and Ordonio are freed, but Alvar is committed to a dungeon as a dealer in magic. Ordonio now determines on the death of Isidore and the stranger. He lures the former to a cavern and kills him. He returns to execute his revenge on the stranger, who had just been visited and recognized by Teresa. An animated scene ensues, in which Alvar discovers himself, and rouses in Ordonio the strongest feelings of remorse. In the midst of his agonies Alhadra enters with a band of Morescoes to avenge the death of her husband, and, after some parley, on an alarm of 'Rescue and Valdez', stabs Ordonio. She has just time to retire, when Valdez appears at the head of the armed peasantry, and the play concludes.

There is enough of incident and interest; events follow each other in rapid succession, and though there is room for sentiment, it is not made to supply the place of incident, or to bear the burthen of the play. Neither is there any deficiency of marked and accurately drawn character. Isidore is invested with the virtues and vices, which are so often found allied in the same mind, when oppression compels to habitual deceit, when the moral principles are unsettled; consenting at one time to be an assassin through gratitude, yet at another refusing to lend himself to a comparatively innocent artifice, when he had found himself once deceived by his benefactor. Alhadra too possesses some decisive features, exhibiting, as women often must in a state of semi-barbarism, and under the pressure of adversity, many of the virtues, many of the faults, and none of the graces of the female character; faithful to her husband, watchful over her children, but implacable to her enemies. Her character gives us an opportunity of citing a remarkable instance of the strong powers which Mr. Coleridge possesses in depicting the mind under feelings of the most acute agony. She is describing her state of mind on discovering the murder of her husband:

> I stood listening,
> Impatient for the footsteps of my husband!
> *Naomi.*—Thou calledst him?—
> *Alhadra.*—I crept into the cavern;
> 'Twas dark and very silent. (*wildly*) What saidst thou?
> No, no, I did not dare call Isidore,
> *Lest I should hear no answer.* A brief while

> Belike, I lost all thought and memory
> Of that for which I came! After that pause,
> O heaven! I heard a groan, and followed it;
> And yet another groan, which guided me
> Into a strange recess—and there was light,
> A hideous light—his torch lay on the ground;
> Its flame burnt dimly o'er a chasm's brink.
> I spake, and whilst I spake, a feeble groan
> Came from that chasm! It was his last! his death-groan.
>   *Naomi.*—Comfort her, Allah!
>   *Alhadra.*—I stood in unimaginable trance
> And agony that cannot be remembered,
> *Listening with horrid hope to hear a groan!*
> But I had heard his last—my husband's death-groan.

Ordonio however is evidently the poet's favourite, and we think he has reason to be proud of him. It is difficult to select any one passage, which will give a full idea of the various yet not inconsistent peculiarities of his character; they are collected only (and this we think a merit) from a perusal of the whole poem. In the following extract however, where he is preparing himself for the murder of Isidore, he draws the prominent features of his character, omitting at the same time the brightest traits of it. The scene is in the cavern.

[quotes ll. 98-138, Act IV, Scene i (*PW*, ii, 862-3)]

To this heartless suspicion and contempt of all men, he unites a certain degree of generosity and honour; and when he finds Isidore armed and prepared to meet him, he joyfully exclaims:

> Now this is excellent, and warms the blood!
> My heart was drawing back; drawing me back
> With weak and womanish scruples. Now my vengeance
> Beckons me onwards with a warrior's mien,
> And claims that life, my pity robb'd her of.—
> Now will I kill thee, thankless slave, and count it
> Among my comfortable thoughts hereafter.

He strikes us as bearing in many points a strong resemblance to the murderer of the lamented Perceval;[1] in his moral madness framing a new code of action, in which he is self-constituted judge and executioner, and by which the most dreadful acts of vengeance stand justified of guilt; feeling indeed at times the tortures of unperverted conscience

---

[1] John Bellingham, who in 1812 had assassinated the Prime Minister, Spencer Perceval.

yet neither terrified nor subdued and angry, at the weaknesses of a nature, which he deems unworthy of him.

We have endeavoured to give our readers some idea of Ordonio; but we pass over the remainder of the characters, because they are either slightly drawn, or are in themselves rather interesting and amiable, than strongly marked or original. But we do not consider this as a defect in the composition of the play. No scene, to be natural, should be exclusively filled with prominent characters; indeed these are qualities which may be said to exist only by comparison, and certainly cannot have their due effect, unless they are relieved by contrast.

To the merits of incident and character, we have to add the charm of a rich and glowing poetry. Indeed in all that Mr. Coleridge writes are to be observed a loftiness and purity of sentiment, a picturesque conception of imagery, and a luxuriance of fancy, which make us regret that he has so much abused his endowments. The following description is highly poetical:

> The morning of the day of our departure
> We were alone: the purple hue of dawn
> Fell from the kindling east aslant upon us,
> And blending with the blushes on her cheek,
> Suffus'd the tear-drops there with rosy light;
> *There seem'd a glory round us, and Teresa*
> *The angel of the vision.*

There is something of uncommon richness and wildness of fancy in the following speech of Teresa:

> There are woes
> Ill barter'd for the garishness of joy.
> If it be wretched with an untir'd eye,
> To watch those skiey tints, and this green ocean;
> Or in the sultry hour, beneath some rock,
> My hair dishevelled by the pleasant sea-breeze,
> To shape sweet visions, and live o'er again
> All past hours of delight. If it be wretched
> To watch some bark, and fancy Alvar there,
> To go through each minutest circumstance
> Of the blest meeting, and to frame adventures
> Most terrible and strange, and hear *him* tell them;
> And if indeed it be a wretched thing
> To trick out mine own death-bed, and imagine
> That I had died, died just ere his return!

Then see him listening to my constancy,
Or hover round, as he at midnight oft
Sits on my grave, and gazes at the moon;
Or haply in some more fantastic mood,
To be in Paradise, and with choice flowers
Build up a bower, where he and I might dwell,
And there to wait his coming! O my sire,
If this be wretchedness, what were it, think you,
If in a most assured reality
He should return, and see a brother's infant
Smile at him from my arms!

Highly, however, as we think of the merits of the *Remorse*, we confess we are rather surprised that it should ever have been popular on the stage. The plot has radical errors, and is full of improbabilities. It is improbable, that Teresa should not recognise Alvar; it is improbable, that neither Ordonio nor Isidore should discover him; it is improbable, that Alhadra should have been able to collect her band of Morescoes in so short a time; it is improbable, that she should have penetrated, undiscovered, with them, to the dungeon in the castle; it is still more improbable, that she should escape with them, unmolested, when Valdez and his peasantry must have been in the very entrance. There is also a considerable awkwardness in the conduct of the plot; between the closing of each act and the opening of the following one, more of the action is carried on, than it is possible by any stretch of imagination to suppose natural. We do not, however, build upon those errors our opinion, that the play is not likely to keep possession of the stage. We know, that in the illusion of splendid scenery, and the bustle of representation, greater defects than these may well be overlooked; but we think that the great merits of the *Remorse* are precisely those which in representation would be neglected, or ill understood by the majority of spectators. The character of Ordonio is the masterly conception of an original mind, but to be duly appreciated it must be not merely seen, but studied: it is strongly marked with the metaphysical habits of the author; and the parts must be compared with each other, and with the whole, before we can enter into the poet's own ideas of Ordonio.

Again, the poetry, beautiful as it is, and strongly as it appeals in many parts to the heart, is yet too frequently of a lofty and imaginative character, far removed from the ready apprehension of common minds. We consider the invocation to be appropriate and happy: and aided by music, scenery, and the solemn feelings that naturally arise on such occasions, we can conceive that the whole effect must have been awful and imposing; but how few of the audience would comprehend at a single hearing poetry so full of mysterious and learned allusion, as the following!

> With no irreverent voice, or uncouth charm
> I call up the departed. Soul of Alvar,
> Hear our soft suit——
>   Since haply thou art one
> Of that innumerable company,
> Who in broad circle, lovelier than the rainbow,
> Girdle this round earth in a dizzy motion,
> With noise too vast and constant to be heard:
> Fitliest unheard! For oh ye numberless
> And rapid travellers, what ear unstunn'd,
> What sense unmaddened might bear up against
> The rushing of your congregated wings! [*Music.*
> Even now your living wheel turns o'er my head.
> Ye, as ye pass, toss high the desert sands
> That roar, and whiten, like a burst of waters,
> A sweet appearance, but a dread illusion
> To the parch'd caravan, that roams by night.
> And ye build up on the becalmed waves
> That whirling pillar, which from earth to heaven
> Stands vast and moves in blackness, &c.

Throughout the play, the reader who is at all conversant with Shakespeare, will perceive the author's ardent admiration of the father of the English drama. Mr. Coleridge is, however, no servile copyist; in general his imitation is of that judicious kind which is felt every where, and seen no where, a likeness of the whole, rather than a copy of any part; in some instances, however, by boldly venturing to try his strength with his great master, he forces us to a comparison of particular passages which is not favourable to him. The imitation, for example, of Hamlet's picture of his father and uncle, though not without some beautiful lines, appears to be the effort of an injudicious and mistaken ambition. Should we even allow, that in any instance of this sort Mr. Coleridge had equalled the parallel passage in Shakespeare, this would not in any way affect our judgment of the merits of the two poets. It is one thing to invent, another to imitate; it is one thing as by inspiration to throw out a bright passage, which shall become a text in the mouths of all men for ever, and another to study that passage, to enlarge its beauties, to supply its defects, to prune its luxuriancies, and thus at length produce a faultless copy of an imperfect original. Mr. Coleridge is not often guilty of this fault; he has in general rather given us the character, than the features of Shakespeare. For these and many other excellences, which our limits prevent us from noticing, we will venture to recommend the *Remorse* to our readers. We are confident of its success in the closet, we wish we could be as sanguine of our own, when we exhort Mr. Coleridge to a better application of the talents, which Providence has imparted to him. He has been long before the public, and has acquired a reputation for ability proportioned rather to what he is supposed capable of performing, than to any thing which he has accomplished. In truth, if life be dissipated in alternations of desultory application, and nervous indolence, if scheme be added to scheme, and plan to plan, all to be deserted, when the labour of execution begins, the greatest talents will soon become enervated, and unequal to tasks of comparative facility. We are no advocates for book-making, but where the best part of a life, and endowments of no ordinary class have been devoted to the acquiring and digesting of information on important subjects, it is neither accordant with the duty of a citizen to his country, nor the gratitude of a creature to his maker, to suffer the fruits of his labour to perish. We remember the saying of the pious Hooker, 'that he did not beg a long life of God for any other reason but to live to finish his three remaining books of Polity'. In this prayer we believe that personal views of fame had little or no concern; but it is not forbidden us to indulge a reasonable desire of a glorious name in the aftertime.

56. Thomas Barnes, 'Mr. Coleridge', *Champion*

26 March 1814, 102-3

This article, written under the pseudonym 'Strada', is attributed to Thomas Barnes (Derek Hudson, *Thomas Barnes of 'The Times'*, Cambridge 1943, 171). It is the sixth in a series of 'Portraits of the Authors'.

'For long and early habits of exerting my intellect in metrical composition, have not so enslaved me, but that for some years I have felt, and deeply felt, that the Poet's high functions were not my proper assignment.'

The Friend: by Mr. Coleridge, No. 1

After such a declaration, voluntarily made, it may seem uncandid to bring the poems of this gentleman to the ordeal of criticism: but the self-denying deprecations of authors, and especially of such delicately-coy authors as Mr. Coleridge, must never be interpreted in their literal meaning. That this passage was never intended to be construed into common terms, is evident from the contents of the volume of which it is one of the earliest paragraphs. In that work he is perpetually coming before the reader, displaying the pretensions, and exercising the functions of a poet, for which he had affectedly pronounced himself unfit. His depreciation, therefore, of his own poetical powers, must be considered as one of those amiable, but rather fantastic artifices, with which an enchanting singer sometimes prefaces her song, at once to excite interest, and to subdue by astonishment.

If it really be his opinion, that he is merely an intruder into the haunts of the Muses, and, what is worse, a shameless intruder, because perfectly conscious of his rudeness—in this case he must be numbered among those numerous blunderers, who totally mistake their real powers, and, abandoning their strongest holds, fly for refuge to their weakest and least sheltered places. It is, indeed, very difficult to ascertain exactly what we should understand from the quoted sentence. It is very possible, that, measuring himself by some highly exalted standard, he may feel that he does not belong to the same class as Shakespeare or Milton: it is possible that, comparing his own elaborate efforts with the facile majesty of his friend Wordsworth, he may for the time experience a humiliating consciousness of his inferiority: but to suppose that the man whose every metaphor and illustration is a poetic image, whose metaphysics are led through the flowers of fancy, instead of the intricacies of reason, and whose diction aims at all the gorgeous array and musical pomp of the most stately verse—that such a man should believe himself utterly incapable of poetry, is a paradox only to be allowed by those who will believe, that the mind can be so thoroug[h]ly purged of self love, as to hold it impossible to attain any eminence in the pursuit to which it dedicates all its affections, and all its energies.

But whatever may be the real opinion of Mr. Coleridge, I must for myself declare, that though I hold in high admiration his extensive knowledge, his profound thinking, and the comprehensive range of his intellect, yet I conceive he has shewn little claim to the gratitude of his contemporaries or of posterity, except by his poems. His prose essays are so full of morbid vanity, of independent boldness in the thinking, and the most shrinking horror lest his thoughts should offend the established orders, of grand views of general truth, and the most pusillanimous meanness in the application of it, that the mind, though interested with such striking peculiarities, turns with strong dislike from a picture, made up of such harsh and unharmonizing contrasts. His poems are very different: they have indeed enough of vanity, and enough of affectation, but who cares for such errors when listening to the enchantments of a rich and graceful imagination; or of a metrical music, which reminds one sometimes of the softness of the flute, sometimes of the full swelling tones of the organ? His mind has evidently been from the earliest youth, devoted to those peculiar studies which form the poet, while the intensity of his feeling, and the depth of his understanding, seem to mark him out as fitted to fill one of the highest seats of that Parnassus which he pretends to desert. There can be no doubt, that, if he would seriously apply his powers to a great poem, he would rise to an immeasurable height above his friend Southey, in all whose works, there is scarcely one paragraph which indicates deep feeling, and not one which is distinguished for profound reflection. In some of the few poems which he has published, Mr. Coleridge has drawn such tenderly-pleasing scenes of domestic love, as might have refreshed even the bowers of Paradise: in others, there is an indignant strain of moral remonstrance against tyranny and vice, which might appal the heart, though cased in a hundred folds of the dullest apathy.

Yet these are powers which Mr. Coleridge holds worthless: the praise of a poet, which satisfied the ambition of Homer or Milton is beneath his views: he must forsooth become a metaphysician, and shew how easy it is for the clearest sighted man to become blind, when he goes into an atmosphere to which his organs of vision are not accustomed. It appears, that having occasion to go into Germany, he there became enamoured, as he ought to have been, of Schiller, and Goethe, and Wieland, and even of Klopstock: and one fine specimen he has given us both of his fondness and of his taste, in his noble translation of Schiller's noble play,* on the fortunes and death of Wallenstein. But this was not enough: like Dr. Faustus, his great prototype in curiosity and audacity of research, he looked about for fresh objects for the exercise of his intellect, and most unluckily was, all at once, spell-bound, by the incomprehensible grandeur of the philosophy of Kant. From that time he has never been disenchanted: he has ever since affected to refine wisdom into obscurity, and to struggle with subjects which he scarcely has skill enough to touch. This does not arise from want of mental power, but of science: he has the strength of a giant, but he has not any knowledge of the weapons with which he is foolish enough to choose to combat. Hence proceeds the great confusion in his ideas, and consequently in his language; nor is he unaware of this defect; but he ascribes it to any cause rather than the right one. He insinuates that the expressions of deep feeling must ever be obscure to general readers. Now this seems to me a misapprehension: he confounds that which is obscure with that which is not obvious; and yet, no two things can be more separate in their nature. A profound remark may be entirely new, and yet every mind shall at once understand it and allow its propriety: an obscure idea is one of which the mind cannot comprehend the form, nor, with all its exertions, recognize the naturalness. Had Mr. Coleridge, at the time when he offered such an excuse for his want of perspicuity, thought a little about his old favourites, Bacon and Milton, and Jeremy Taylor, he would at once have seen the fallacy of his position. These men all thought deeply and felt keenly, yet their ideas are as clear as those of the shallowest writers: their page is sometimes encumbered with the gorgeousness of their diction, or the exuberance of their images, but their meaning is always accessible to the commonest apprehension: and, if Mr. Coleridge would imitate those great

* The title of the play, or plays, is *The Piccolomini*: the translation is scarce, but well worthy any search which may be made after it.

masters, and treat only of such subjects as he understands, he would not only be as intelligible as they are, but almost as eloquent. He has, indeed, many points of resemblance with those heroes of our literature: great sensibility, a mind stored with images, and a manly spirit of enterprize which leads him to dive into the abysses of his subject, instead of playing on its surface. His great defect, which will ever keep him at immense distance from their sphere, is his want of accurate erudition. I know (for it is impossible for a reader of Mr. Coleridge not to know) that his knowledge is various and extensive: he is considerably versed in languages, and well read in all the best authors: yet there is scarcely one subject (except poetical criticism) among the many on which in his last publication, he ventures to dogmatize, of which he has more than the merest elementary knowledge. He pretends to expose the vulgar errors respecting taxation, and yet has recourse to the vulgar expedient of begging all the principles on which he builds the refutation of them. He objects, properly enough, to Paley's doctrine of General Consequences,[1] and, after a great deal of blundering, mixed, however, with much truth, comes as well as I can understand him, precisely to the same conclusion. He ridicules, very skilfully, the philosophy of the Œconomists, who talk of the state, and of society, as if it were a mystical something, and not merely an aggregate of particular individuals: yet in the same* essay, he expends many pages to prove that the happiness of states is governed by rules separate from those of ordinary life, and that their morality stands on another basis. The source of all these contradictions, is vanity, which leads him to go out of his sphere to play the fool, when, within it, he might shine with the lustre of a first-rate genius. He is like Hobbes, or Berkely, the first of whom, tried to injure his own well-earned fame, by translating Homer; and the latter, came off with disgrace and sore defeat, for presuming to contend with Newton, on a subject of which he knew not the first principles. Let him cease to waste his powers on such topics, and write more sonnets and more tragedies: if he must be metaphysical, let it be in verse and not in prose: and, if his next tragedy shall contain as much fanciful description, and impassioned sentiment as his *Remorse*, he will easily be forgiven, though the hero of it should be Kant himself, and should talk nothing but Kantism, from the first act to the last.

* The whole of these remarks on Mr. Coleridge's prose, refers to a work called the *Friend*.

[1] William Paley (1753–1805), whose arguments in the *Evidences of Christianity* (1794) Coleridge opposed.

I cannot conclude this article without alluding to the very unjustifiable severity with which this gentleman has been treated for certain
changes in his opinions. It seems that Mr. Coleridge, at forty, is not
the same ignorant indiscriminating enthusiast which he was at twenty:
he has grown wiser and recanted his errors: and for this reason he is
to be assailed as an apostate and a hypocrite. The cruelty of such invective is only equalled by its absurdity: for its principle is this: all wisdom
is intuitive, and he only is an honest man whose understanding is as
stagnant and as dull as the waters of Lethe. True it is, that the elements
of morality are not only unalterable, but are intelligible even to a child.
'Murder is execrable, and tyranny only fit for dæmons'. These are
principles which the boy of sixteen understands as well as the grey-
beard of sixty: but does he equally understand the right mode of
applying these rules to every particular case? Would he be equally
fit to sit as a Judge, or to organize a Reformation? When the French
Revolution broke out, Mr. Coleridge, like every youth of ardent
temperament, was, as he ought to have been, enchanted at the promise
then given, that liberty was to be erected on the ruins of a corrupt and
intolerable tyranny. That promise was made by men of high character:
philosophers, who had devoted all their studies to the improvement
of their country, and whose motives were scarcely impeached by their
bitterest enemies. No wonder that the young became enthusiastic,
when even the old and the wise were seduced by such appearances.
The French philosophers, however, did not keep their promise because
they could not: they destroyed abuses, but they had not the skill to
substitute any systems in their room: admirable theorists, they were
mere children in practice: so they stood still or vaccilated, and wasted
the hopes of the impatient nation, till their formidable rivals, who had
learned from those very men to prate of philosophy, but who owned
no influence but self-interest, marched irresistibly to power over the
dead bodies of their poor honest-hearted tutors. Then followed all
those evils which will be a standing illustration of the dangers of
revolution till the end of the world. Now, let me ask any man, who
takes a survey of all these circumstances, whether he cannot easily
forgive the writer who having been carried to a blind excess of admiration at the outset of these events, should at last never be able to allude
to them without shrinking and dismay. But it seems that Mr. Coleridge
has rendered the motive of his conversion questionable: he has consented to wear a badge, to receive a pension from the Government.
I do not know whether this be the case: if it is, I am sorry for it: for,

While Mr. Lamb sought only to drink pleasure from the humble urn of serene enjoyment, his friend was carrying the light of his genius into the most abstruse investigations, covering a thousand visionary schemes of freedom with its dazzling lustre, and uniting the apparently opposite qualities of ardent thirst for knowledge, with the dreaminess of poetical contemplation. He is alike skilled in throwing a thousand natural charms round the commonest objects, and of exciting by lovely description the purest sensations of delight, and of casting a deadly glare over the awful recesses of the heart, and laying bare its most terrible workings. In the deepest of his metaphysical speculations, every word is a poetical image. The most thorny paths of controversy are thick strewn with the freshest garlands when he enters them. If we are entangled in an intricate maze, its construction is of gold, and every turn opens some bewildering prospect, dim and indistinct from the delicate filminess of the tints by which it is shaded. He illumines whatever he touches. In the most gloomy desert which he traverses, there arise beneath his feet plots of ever-living verdure. In spell poetry he is far more potent than any writer of the present age, his enchant-ments are more marvellous and deeper woven, his fictions wilder, and his mysteries more heart-touching and appalling. In his 'Ancient Mariner', the solemn helplessness of the narrator, condemned to live amidst supernatural horrors, is awfully expressed by the lines, 'a thousand thousand slimy things liv'd on and so did I'. How the image of strange loneliness strikes upon the heart, when he with the fatal ship and her ghastly crew burst into the sea, 'where God himself' scarcely seemed to be present! And with how pure a thrill of delight are we refreshed, in the midst of this terrible witchery, when the poor creature, whom superior power has enchanted, sees the water-snakes sporting in the sun, which at happier seasons would have filled him with disgust, bursts into a blessing of these 'happy living things', and a 'gush of love' comes from a spirit haunted with unutterable terrors. One other peculiar faculty of our author is displayed in his charming delineations of love which, without partaking in the feebleness of Mr. Southey's pictures of infantine affection, throw over the most voluptuous images an air of purity, which at once softens and encreases their loveliness. They combine something of that extasy of tenderness which Milton has revealed among the bowers of Paradise, with that holy attachment which stirs the bosoms of his angels, and delights the seclusions of his heaven.

The Tragedy of *Remorse* is the most popular of all the works of Mr.

Coleridge, though by no means the fairest production of his genius. The theatre presents so near a path to fame, that it is not surprising that, seduced by its tumultuous applause, a superior writer should quit for a while the secluded walks of purer inspiration in which he delights to wander. But, although this work does not possess that still and deep charm, which its author has thrown around the holy retirements of his fancy, although its coloring has less of chasteness and more of brilliancy, it exhibits a rich vein of thought in a glowing luxuriance of diction, which the most unpoetical are compelled to admire. Its misfortune, indeed, is that it attempts too much, though even in failure the author has shewn himself acquainted with the great source of dramatic interest, in the various modifications through which it excites our sympathies. We have already had occasion to observe that the nature of Man is formed to derive gratification from all that calls forth his faculties—all that stirs and animates his soul—all that awakes into a more powerful throb the various pulses of existence. Thus the delight which he derives from the view of a tragedy, arises from a variety of causes, all of which stimulate and excite the feelings; and not from any single emotion, as some have endeavoured to maintain. Man appears on the stage elevated above the common level of his species, and the pleasure we derive from the spectacle is in proportion to the height to which he is exalted, and the ease and rapidity with which our hearts pursue him in his aspiring and stormy career. It is not that we are gratified by the mere prospect of misery, for that is in many cases disgusting. It is not that we are interested in the events represented, from a belief that they are actually passing, because no such belief ever existed. Above all, it is not that we are delighted in proportion as the representation is brought home to common nature—to the actual state of man—and to the display of his ordinary emotions. It is that we are elevated above the common occurrences of life, and the vexatious harassings of vulgar anxiety, that we are filled with noble images and lofty thoughts, and that we are animated by a mixed admiration of the poet, of the actor, and of the overpowering emotions which they combine to delineate. We do not indeed stop to analyse: we are carried along by a torrent of mingled sensation which assists in spiritualizing our nature, and lifting it above its weakness. Those who have seen Mrs. Siddons[1] embody the noblest delineations of genius, have enjoyed all this mysterious rapture in its highest perfection: they saw a human being convulsed with superhuman agony, alternately

[1] Sarah Siddons (1755-1831), the leading tragic actress of the period.

pourtraying each of the sterner and more terrific passions, and at last bursting forth superior to them all; they mingled with their admiration of her, a yet loftier delight in the powers of the writer who had raised the storm in which she rode triumphant; and they sometimes were carried beyond both into a mysterious joy in the passions themselves, thus mingled with all that is stormy in imagination, and heroic in virtue. When the mind paused from the sensation which its momentary illusion had occasioned, the remembrance of that illusion heightened its admiration of the powers by which it had been excited. Thus all our delight may be resolved into the exaltation of our spirit, and its excursions beyond itself—into our pride in the strength of human emotion and of human talent—and the interest produced by the variations of the former, and the correspondent flashes of the latter. Now there are two modes by which the poet may indulge our propensities to love and wonder, at the passions and the faculties of our nature. He may exalt his characters above the world, by giving them supernatural energy of thought and boundless depth of passion, and surrounding them with the glories of imagination, and the playful coruscations of fancy, or he may encircle them merely with the stateliness of kings and heroes, the pomp of sentiment and diction, and the gorgeous pall of misery. Shakespeare has done the former, the classical school of dramatists the latter; and Mr. Coleridge, without towering nearly so high as either in their peculiar walk, has imitated both the models to which we have referred. Like the first, he made his personages talk like poets, and like the last, he has made them think and act as heroes and kings. He imitates the wild originality of Shakespeare in the regular and pompous iambics of Addison. With the strictest mechanism of plot, he has united the breathing witchery of natural enchantment. His Ordonio thinks like one of Shakespeare's loftiest characters; but then he must tell all he thinks in the set speeches of Racine. He is a metaphysical villain, who justifies to himself the vileness of his actions by the subtleties of his perverted reason; but unlike those strange and mysterious, yet perfectly human, beings which we meet with in our great poet, he does not display the secrets of his wonderful frame by transient flashes, unconscious bursts, and sudden resolves, but in long-set dissertations, in which he finishes off his own portrait with the most careful exactness. At the same time, they are unquestionably grand, and interspersed with dreadful pictures of agony and passion, and lovely images of pity and of peace. In a word, as the essence of tragedy is to elevate the soul either by the intellectual strength or the gorgeous

CHRISTABEL; KUBLA KHAN, A VISION; THE PAINS OF SLEEP

1816

---

58. Unsigned review, *Critical Review*

May 1816, iii, 504–10

There is no quality of the mind more despicable than that love of censure and ridicule which has its origin in our own weakness, and which hunts for faults or singularities, not for the purpose of amending them, but for the sake of gratifying an imaginary superiority: those who thus flatter their vanity by reducing genius to the degraded level of their own understandings, who 'damn the worth they cannot imitate', may find in the fragment before us some food to satisfy their diseased appetite; while those on the other hand who are hopeful yet humble, emulous yet not envious, who triumph in every fresh display of talent and genius as a fresh incentive to exertion, will read with generous enthusiasm the pages upon our table. If we had no other reason for so thinking, than the rapid sale of this poem,[1] we should judge that the latter are a very numerous class: to the former Ben Jonson alludes in his *Discoveries* where he says that 'Critics are a sort of Tinkers, who ordinarily make more faults than they mend'. As it is a maxim of the criminal law of England, that it is better to find one man innocent than to convict ten men as guilty, so it ought to be a maxim of the critical law of literature, that it is more advantageous to point out one beauty than to discover ten deformities.

We apprehend that the most fastidious would find much more to praise than to blame in this newly published effort; but reading it in the wholesome spirit to which we have above referred, the defects will appear to bear a most insignificant proportion to the perfections: we could, it is true, point out expressions that might have been better

---

[1] It went through three editions in 1816.

turned, and lines that perhaps might have been better omitted; but deviations are not necessarily defects, and peculiarities may either be those of excellence or of error.

'Christabel' is a romantic fragment; the first part, as the author informs us, having been written in 1797, and the second in 1800, during which interval Mr. Coleridge visited Germany, still retaining the fabric of the complete story in his mind 'with the wholeness no less than with the liveliness of a vision', and as the vivid impression continues to the present day, he undertakes 'to embody in verse the three parts yet to come, in the course of the present year'. We sincerely hope that this promise will be realized, but we fear that the task will be at least wearisome to a man of the listless habits of Mr. Coleridge. For ourselves we confess, that when we read the story in M.S. two or three years ago, it appeared to be one of those dreamlike productions whose charm partly consisted in the undefined obscurity of the conclusion—what that conclusion may be, no person who reads the commencement will be at all able to anticipate. The reader, before he opens the poem, must be prepared to allow for the superstitions of necromancy and sorcery, and to expect something of the glorious and unbounded range which the belief in those mysteries permits; the absurd trammels of mere physical possibility are here thrown aside, like the absurd swaddling clothes of infants, which formerly obstructed the growth of the fair symmetry of nature.

The lady Christabel, in consequence of ill-boding dreams, repairs at midnight in April to the forest, a furlong from the castle of Sir Leoline, her father, and while in the fearlessness of innocence she is engaged in prayer 'for the weal of her lover that's far away', she hears behind the old oak, at the foot of which she is kneeling, a low moan.

> The night is chill—the forest bare;
> Is it the wind that moaneth bleak?
> There is not wind enough in the air,
> To move away the ringlet curl
> From the lovely lady's cheek—
> There is not wind enough to twirl
> The one red leaf, the last of its clan,
> That dances as often as dance it can,
> Hanging so light and hanging so high
> On the topmost twig that looks up at the sky.

It was impossible to select two circumstances that more perfectly shewed the dead calmness of the night. Christabel stealing to the other side of the tree, beholds a lovely lady in distress, who informs her that her name is Geraldine, that she had been conveyed to the forest by five warriors, and that she had lain there devoid of sense, till awakened by the distant sound of a castle bell. Christabel thus takes compassion on the unhappy lady.

> Sir Leoline is weak in health,
> And may not awakened be;
> So to my room we'll creep in stealth
> And you to-night must sleep with me.
> They cross'd the moat and Christabel
> Took the key that fitted well;
> A little door she opened straight,
> All in the middle of the gate;
> The gate was iron'd within and without,
> Where an army in battle array had march'd out.

What a beautiful picture is here afforded of these two delicate and lovely females passing the iron'd gate, contrasted with an army in battle array, that had shortly before marched through it. Geraldine faints at the gate, but is revived by her companion, who afterwards requires her to join in praise to the Virgin who had rescued her in the forest.

> Alas, alas! said Geraldine,
> I cannot pray for weariness.

The truth is that she is one of those evil ministers, who are fancifully supposed for a time to obtain power over the innocent. The manner in which the reader is prepared for this disclosure is gradual and beautiful, though it fails at first to alarm the unsuspicious Christabel. The first indication we have above given—the next is an involuntary and angry moan made by an old faithful mastiff that lay asleep in one of the baillies of the castle: a third is thus conveyed:

> They pass'd the hall, that echoes still,
> Pass as lightly as you will,
> The brands were flat, the brands were dying,
> Amid their own white ashes lying;
> But when the lady pass'd there came
> A tongue of light a fit of flame;
> And Christabel saw the lady's eye,
> But nothing else she saw thereby.

The distinguishing of Geraldine's bright eye reflecting back the flame, is a most effective finish. When they reach the chamber of Christabel, the weary Geraldine again sinks to the floor, and is again recovered. Her evil designs are soon afterwards fully disclosed when she appears to be contending for masterdom with the unseen spirit of the dead mother of Christabel.

Geraldine requested Christabel to unrobe, while she pretended to employ herself in prayer; the daughter of Sir Leoline complied, 'and lay down in her loveliness'.

> But through her brain of weal and woe
> So many thoughts moved to and fro,
> That vain it were her lids to close;
> So half way from the bed she rose,
> And on her elbow did recline
> To look at lady Geraldine—
> Beneath the lamp the lady bow'd,
> And slowly roll'd her eyes around;
> Then drawing in her breath aloud,
> Like one that shuddered she unbound
> The cincture from beneath her breast:
> Her silken robe and inner vest
> Dropt to her feet, and full in view,
> Behold! her bosom and half her side—
> A sight to dream of not to tell
> And she is to sleep with Christabel.

By a poetical and most judicious abruption the poet leaves it to the imagination of the reader to figure what terrible and disgusting sight presented itself to Christabel. Geraldine then pressed Christabel to her bosom, where worked a spell that restrained the utterance of what she had just beheld. After a night of fearful visions, Christabel awakes, and finding the lady Geraldine sleeping in renovated beauty at her side, she imagines she had but dreamt what had given her such alarm. She introduces Geraldine to her father, Sir Leoline, who learns that she was the daughter of Sir Roland de Vaux of Tryermaine, and then follow these lines, finer than any in the language upon the same subject, with which we are acquainted, more especially the noble image at the end.

> Alas they had been friends in youth;
> But whispering tongues can poison truth;
> And constancy lives in realms above;
> And life is thorny, and youth is vain;

And to be wroth with one we love
Doth work like madness in the brain.
And thus it chanc'd, as I divine
With Roland and Sir Leoline.
Each spake words of high disdain
And insult to his heart's best brother;
They parted—ne'er to meet again!
But never either found another
To free the hollow heart from paining—
They stood aloof the scars remaining,
Like cliffs which had been rent asunder;
A dreary sea now flows between
But neither heat, nor frost, nor thunder
Shall wholly do away, I ween,
The marks of that which once hath been.

Pity for Geraldine supersedes all other considerations, and Sir Leoline swears to revenge her wrongs: he summons his Bard, Bracy, whom he commands to repair to the castle of Lord Roland, to inform him of the safety of his daughter, but Bracy alleges as a reason for postponement, a dream he had had, that he had seen the gentle dove of Christabel struggling with a green serpent round its neck in the forest, and as he fancied that some 'thing unblest' lingered there, he had vowed to expel it by music. While the bard was relating his dream, Geraldine turned towards her victim;

And the lady's eyes they shrunk in her head,
Each shrunk up to a serpent's eye,
And with somewhat of malice and more of dread
At Christabel she look'd askance
          *   *   *
The maid alas! her thoughts are gone,
She nothing sees—no sight but one!
The maid devoid of guile and sin,
I know not how in fearful wise
So deeply had she drunken in
That look, those shrunken serpent eyes,
That all her features were resign'd
To this sole image in her mind:
And passively did imitate
That look, of dull and treacherous hate.
And thus she stood in dizzy trance
Still picturing that look askance,
With forc'd unconscious sympathy

Full before her father's view—
As far as such a look could be
In eyes so innocent and blue.

When she awoke from this trance, she entreated her father to send Geraldine away, but the powerful spell prevented her from assigning any reason, and Sir Leoline who had marked this 'look of dull and treacherous hate', which was the mere reflection of Geraldine's countenance on the pure mirror of his daughter's face, is instantly struck with the conviction that Christabel is the serpent of whom Bracy had dreamt, and Geraldine the innocent and trembling dove; for to Sir Leoline she appeared all beauty and simplicity. The fragment concludes with these lines:

His heart was cleft with pain and rage,
His cheeks they quiver'd, his eyes were wild,
Dishonoured thus in his old age,
Dishonoured by his only child,
And all his hospitality
To the insulted daughter of his friend
By more than woman's jealousy,
Brought thus to a disgraceful end—
He roll'd his eye with stern regard
Upon the gentle minstrel bard,
And said in tones abrupt, austere—
Why Bracy! dost thou loiter here?
I bade thee hence! The bard obey'd
And turning from his own sweet maid
The aged knight, Sir Leoline,
Led forth the lady Geraldine.

We lament that our limits will not allow us to give more of this very graceful and fanciful poem, which we may say, without fear of contradiction, is enriched with more beautiful passages than have ever been before included in so small a compass. Nothing can be better contrasted than Christabel and Geraldine—both exquisite, but both different—the first all innocence, mildness, and grace; the last all dignity, grandeur, and majesty: the one with all those innate virtues, that working internally, mould the external shape to corresponding perfectness—the other possessing merely the charm of superficial excellence: the one the gentle soul-delighting Una—the other the seeming fair, but infamous Duessa.

Of the rich and luxuriant imagery with which this poem abounds, our imperfect sketch will afford but a faint idea, and we have been compelled to omit many descriptive passages of the first order. For these we must refer to the original, assured that, after reading our extracts, none will throw it aside because they meet with a passage or two in the threshold not exactly according with their pre-conceived notions of excellence.

'Kubla Khan, a Vision', is one of those pieces that can only speak for itself, but from 'The Pains of Sleep' we cannot refrain from giving the following dreadful and powerful picture of a horrid dream.

[quotes ll. 14-32 of 'The Pains of Sleep' (*PW*, i, 389-90)]

59. William Hazlitt, *Examiner*

2 June 1816, 348-9

This unsigned review is attributed to William Hazlitt (Howe, xix, 338). Hazlitt (1778-1830), himself one of the major writers of the period, knew Coleridge personally. His early admiration was replaced by a bitterly expressed hostility towards what seemed to him to be a change in Coleridge's political outlook. The best account of the relationship is to be found in Herschel Baker's *William Hazlitt*, Cambridge, Mass. 1962, 356-64.

The fault of Mr. Coleridge is, that he comes to no conclusion. He is a man of that universality of genius, that his mind hangs suspended between poetry and prose, truth and falsehood, and an infinity of other things, and from an excess of capacity, he does little or nothing. Here are two unfinished poems, and a fragment. 'Christabel', which has been much read and admired in manuscript, is now for the first

time confided to the public. 'The Vision of Kubla Khan' still remains
a profound secret; for only a few lines of it ever were written.
The poem of 'Christabel' sets out in the following manner.

> 'Tis the middle of night by the castle clock,
> And the owls have awaken'd the crowing cock;
> Tu—whit! Tu——whoo!
> And hark, again! the crowing cock,
> How drowsily it crew.
> Sir Leoline, the Baron rich,
> Hath a toothless mastiff bitch;
> From her kennel beneath the rock
> She makes answer to the clock,
> Four for the quarters and twelve for the hour;
> Ever and aye, moonshine or shower,
> Sixteen short howls, not over loud;
> Some say, she sees my lady's shroud.

We wonder that Mr. Murray,[1] who has an eye for things, should
suffer this 'mastiff bitch' to come into his shop. Is she a sort of Cerberus
to fright away the critics? But—gentlemen, she is toothless.

There is a dishonesty as well as affectation in all this. The secret of
this pretended contempt for the opinion of the public, is that it is a
sorry subterfuge for our self-love. The poet, uncertain of the approbation of his readers, thinks he shews his superiority to it by shocking
their feelings at the outset, as a clown, who is at a loss how to behave
himself, begins by affronting the company. This is what is called
throwing a crust to the critics. If the beauties of 'Christabel' should not be
sufficiently admired, Mr. Coleridge may lay it all to two lines which
he had too much manliness to omit in complaisance to the bad taste
of his contemporaries.

We the rather wonder at this bold proceeding in the author, as his
courage has cooled in the course of the publication, and he has omitted,
from mere delicacy, a line which is absolutely necessary to the understanding the whole story. The Lady Christabel, wandering in the
forest by moonlight, meets a lady in apparently great distress, to whom
she offers her assistance and protection, and takes her home with her
to her own chamber. This woman,

> beautiful to see,
> Like a lady of a far countree,

---

[1] John Murray (1778-1843), the publisher.

is a witch. Who she is else, what her business is with Christabel, upon what motives, to what end her sorceries are to work, does not appear at present; but this much we know [——] that she is a witch, and that Christabel's dread of her arises from her discovering this circumstance, which is told in a single line, which line, from an exquisite refinement in efficiency, is here omitted. When the unknown lady gets to Christabel's chamber, and is going to undress, it is said:

> Then drawing in her breath aloud
> Like one that shuddered, she unbound
> The cincture from beneath her breast:
> Her silken robe and inner vest
> Dropt to her feet, and full in view
> *Behold! her bosom and half her side—*
> A sight to dream of, not to tell!
> And she is to sleep by Christabel!

The manuscript runs thus, or nearly thus:

> Behold her bosom and half her side—
> *Hideous, deformed, and pale of hue.*

This line is necessary to make common sense of the first and second part. 'It is the keystone that makes up the arch'. For that reason Mr. Coleridge left it out. Now this is a greater physiological curiosity than even the fragment of 'Kubla Khan'.

In parts of 'Christabel' there is a great deal of beauty, both of thought, imagery, and versification; but the effect of the general story is dim, obscure, and visionary. It is more like a dream than a reality. The mind, in reading it, is spell-bound. The sorceress seems to act without power—Christabel to yield without resistance. The faculties are thrown into a state of metaphysical suspense and theoretical imbecility. The poet, like the witch in Spenser, is evidently

> Busied about some wicked gin.

But we do not foresee what he will make of it. There is something disgusting at the bottom of his subject, which is but ill glossed over by a veil of Della Cruscan sentiment and fine writing—like moon-beams playing on a charnel-house, or flowers strewed on a dead body. Mr. Coleridge's style is essentially superficial, pretty, ornamental, and he has forced it into the service of a story which is petrific. In the midst of moon-light, and fluttering ringlets, and flitting clouds, and enchanted echoes, and airy abstractions of all sorts, there is one genuine burst of humanity, worthy of the author, when no dream oppresses him, no spell binds him. We give the passage entire:

> But when he heard the lady's tale,
> And when she told her father's name,
> Why waxed Sir Leoline so pale,
> Murmuring o'er the name again,
> Lord Roland de Vaux of Tryermaine?
> Alas! they had been friends in youth;
> But whispering tongues can poison truth;
> And constancy lives in realms above;
> And life is thorny, and youth is vain;
> And to be wroth with one we love,
> Doth work like madness in the brain.
> And thus it chanced, as I divine,
> With Roland and Sir Leoline.
> Each spake words of high disdain,
> And insult to his heart's best brother:
> They parted—ne'er to meet again!
> But never either found another
> To free the hollow heart from paining—
> They stood aloof, the scars remaining
> Like cliffs which had been rent asunder;
> A dreary sea now flows between,
> But neither heat nor frost nor thunder,
> Shall wholly do away, I ween,
> The marks of that which once hath been.
> Sir Leoline a moment's space
> Stood gazing in the damsel's face;
> And the youthful Lord of Tryermaine
> Came back upon his heart again.

Why does not Mr. Coleridge always write in this manner, that we might always read him? The description of the Dream of Bracy the bard, is also very beautiful and full of power.

The conclusion of the second part of 'Christabel', about 'the little limber elf', is to us absolutely incomprehensible. 'Kubla Khan', we think, only shews that Mr. Coleridge can write better *nonsense* verses than any man in England. It is not a poem, but a musical composition.

> A damsel with a dulcimer
> In a vision once I saw:

It was an Abyssinian maid,
And on her dulcimer she play'd,
Singing of Mount Abora.

We could repeat these lines to ourselves not the less often for not knowing the meaning of them.

60. Josiah Conder, *Eclectic Review*

June 1816, v, 565-72

This unsigned review is attributed to Conder (1789-1855), author, bookseller, and proprietor of the *Eclectic Review* (Hayden, 49).

We had frequently heard of Mr. Coleridge's manuscript of 'Christabel', as a singularly wild and romantic poem, the perusal of which had obviously suggested the idea of certain popular metrical romances of specious originality. Our curiosity to see this long-hoarded treasure, was proportioned to the pre-eminent abilities of which its Author is known by his friends, we cannot say to have the command, but to sustain the responsibility. A note in *The Siege of Corinth*, has recently attracted more general attention towards it; and at length, after sixteen years of concealment, it comes forth, a fragment still.[1] Two Cantos only out of five, are contained in the present publication: the remaining three exist only in the teeming chaos of the Author's brain. His poetic powers have, it seems, been, 'till very lately, in a state of suspended animation'. We should rejoice indeed to find, that the spell which has so long locked up Mr. Coleridge's powers, not only is dissolved, but has left them unimpaired, in all the freshness of youth, as, according to romantic fable, the enchanted virgin wakes from her age-long slumber, untouched by time. Mr. Coleridge *trusts* that he 'shall be able to embody in verse the three parts yet to come, in the course of the present year!' We shall be glad to find that this trust is better founded than were the hopes which his friends so long indulged in vain.

In the mean time, we cannot conceal that the effect of the present publication upon readers in general, will be that of disappointment. It may be compared to a mutilated statue, the beauty of which can only be appreciated by those who have knowledge or imagination sufficient

[1] Byron's praise had been quoted in the advertisements.

to complete the idea of the whole composition. The reader is obliged to guess at the half-developed meaning of the mysterious incidents, and is at last, at the end of the second canto, left in the dark, in the most abrupt and unceremonious manner imaginable. Yet we are much mistaken if this fragment, such as it is, will not be found to take faster hold of the mind than many a poem six cantos long. Its merit, in point of originality, will be lost on most readers, in consequence of the prior appearance of so great a quantity of verse in the same style and measure. But the kind of interest which the tale is calculated to awaken, is quite different from that of the description of poems alluded to. Horror is the prevailing sentiment excited by 'Christabel': not that mixture of terror and disgust with which we listen to details of crime and bloodshed, but the purely imaginative feeling, the breathless thrill of indefinite emotion of which we are conscious when in the supposed presence of an unknown being, or acted upon by some influence mysteriously transcending the notice of the senses—that passion which Collins has so beautifully apostrophized under the name of Fear, in the Ode beginning

> Thou to whom the world unknown
> With all its shadowy shapes is shewn;
> Who seest appall'd the unreal scene,
> When Fancy lifts the veil between.[1]

'Christabel' opens with the following lines:

[quotes ll. 1-70 (*PW*, i, 215-18)]

The lady, if lady she be, describes herself as a hapless virgin ruthlessly seized by five warriors the yestermorn, and left by them underneath the oak till their return.

She appeals successfully to the compassion of the unsuspecting Christabel, who proffers to conduct her to her father's castle, and, as all the household are at rest, to share her couch with her. Two incidents, which were sufficient to awaken the suspicion of a less ingenuous and inexperienced person, occur, in reaching the hall. The lady sank at the threshold of the gate, and Christabel was obliged to lift her over; and when urged to join in praising the virgin for her safety,

> Alas! Alas! said Geraldine,
> I cannot speak for weariness.

[1] 'Ode to Fear' (1746).

The old mastiff that lay asleep in the cold moon-shine, made an angry moan as they crossed the court.

> They pass'd the hall, that echoes still,
> Pass as lightly as you will!
> The brands were flat, the brands were dying,
> Amid their own white ashes lying;
> But when the lady pass'd, there came
> A tongue of light, a fit of flame;
> And Christabel saw the lady's eye,
> And nothing else she saw thereby!
> Save the boss of the shield of Sir Leoline tall,
> Which hung in a murky old nitch in the wall.

They pass the Baron's room in breathless silence, and at length reach Christabel's chamber.

> The moon shines dim in the open air,
> And not a moonbeam enters here.
> But they without its light can see
> The chamber carv'd so curiously,
> Carv'd with figures strange and sweet,
> All made out of the carver's brain,
> For a lady's chamber meet;
> The lamp with twofold silver chain
> Is fasten'd to an angel's feet.

Christabel, at the lady's request, did first her 'gentle limbs undress, and lay down in her loveliness'. But, unable to compose herself to slumber, she is rude enough to raise herself on her elbow, to look at the lady Geraldine.

[quotes ll. 245-78 (*PW*, i, 224-5)]

Christabel lies for one hour in fearful trance, imprisoned in the embrace of this 'lady': a gentle sleep then falls upon her, during which her face regains its smile.

> No doubt, she hath a vision sweet,
> What if her guardian spirit 'twere,
> What if she knew her mother near!
> But this she knows, in joys and woes,
> That saints will aid, if men will call,
> For the blue sky bends over all!

With these lines the first part of the Poem concludes.

In the second, we are made imperfectly acquainted with the effect of the hideous spell worked by this false Geraldine. It appears to consist in the strange and terrible power of so working on the sympathy, as to make its victim passively conform itself to the impression made on the external senses, and by this means the framer of the spell is represented as exchanging both feeling and expression with the unhappy subject of her perfidious and refined sorcery. If this be the invention of the Poet's brain, and it partakes of his wildly metaphysical cast of thought, it must be conceded that he deserves a patent for its ingenuity. One cannot conceive of a more terrible engine of supernatural malice. But are not the spells of vicious example in real life almost a counterpart to this fiction?

Sir Leoline is fascinated by the false loveliness of Geraldine. Christabel shudders at the sight, but has no power to disclose what she has seen. The bard Bracy informs the Baron of a dream, in which he saw a dove within the coil of a bright green snake. Sir Leoline misapplies the dream to Geraldine, and vows to crush the snake. The scene which ensues, is finely conceived.

[quotes ll. 572-620 (*PW*, i, 233-4)]

Here we may close our account of this singular production. The Conclusion to Part the Second, is, we suppose, an enigma. It is certainly unintelligible as it stands. We suspect that Mr. Coleridge's poetical powers began to yield to their sixteen years' nap just at this moment, and that he dreamed the few last lines.

As to 'Kubla Khan', and the 'Pains of Sleep', we can only regret the publication of them, as affording a proof that the Author over-rates the importance of his name. With regard to the former, which is professedly published as a psychological curiosity, it having been composed during sleep, there appears to us nothing in the quality of the lines to render this circumstance extraordinary. We could have informed Mr. Coleridge of a reverend friend of ours, who actually wrote down two sermons on a passage in the Apocalypse, from the recollection of the spontaneous exercise of his faculties in sleep. To persons who are in the habit of poetical composition, a similar phenomenon would not be a stranger occurrence, than the spirited dialogues in prose which take place in the dreams of persons of duller invention than our poet, and which not unfrequently leave behind a very vivid impression.

We closed the present publication with sentiments of melancholy and regret, not unmixed with pity. In what an humbling attitude does such a man as Coleridge present himself to the public, in laying before them these specimens of the rich promise of excellence, with which sixteen years ago he raised the expectations of his friends—pledges of future greatness which after sixteen years he has failed to redeem! He is now once more loudly called upon to break off his desultory and luxurious habits, and to brace his mind to intellectual exertion. Samson could never have despaired of recovering his strength, till the baldness of age should fall upon him. We cherish a hope that the principle of strength, though dormant, is still unimpaired in our poet's mind, and that he will yet awake in his strength.

61. Unsigned review, *Literary Panorama*

July 1816, iv, 561-5

The first of these Poems, or rather—the fragment of a poem which stands first in this collection, has had honourable testimony borne to its merits by Lord Byron, who lately acknowledged its beauties, in a note to his *Siege of Corinth*. The Author states the first part of 'Christabel' to have been written in 1797, at Stowey, in the county of Somerset, and the second in 1800, at Keswick, in Cumberland. Since the latter date, he says his poetic powers have been, till very lately, in a state of suspended animation, and he assigns his indolence as the cause of that long trance or syncope, which all who know his abilities will regret. Mr. Coleridge, however, raises hopes that he may so far rouse himself as to conclude the story of 'Christabel' in the course of the present year; but we fear it is from some lurking distrust of his best resolutions, that he has been tempted to mar the strong interest which his wild romantic tale would otherwise have excited, by thus communicating it in piecemeal. In such a case we are effectually prevented from giving our readers any idea of the main incidents of the poem:

> Daughter, the Spanish Fleet thou can'st not see
> Because it is not yet in sight—

To extract parts from such a *morçeau* is to reduce what remains to a mere nothing; yet to content ourselves with general observations on its style and character, is impossible.

The opening is in the very spirit of 'Betty Foy'.

> 'Tis the middle of night by the castle clock,
> And the owls have awakened the crowing cock,
> Tu——whit!——Tu——whoo!
> And hark, again! the crowing cock
> How drowsily it crew.

But the poet soon quits insignificant objects—and the reader enters the regions of romance, and of romance described in the vivid colouring, and with the energetic pencil of our early writers, whose witching strain could arrest alike the attention of the mail-clad warrior, the blushing maid, the thoughtful scholar, and the unlettered vassal. The 'lovely Lady Christabel' disturbed by bad dreams rises from her couch at midnight, and goes into an adjoining wood to pray for her absent lover:

> The night is chilly, but not dark,
> The thin gray cloud is spread on high,
> It covers but not hides the sky.
> The moon is behind and at the full,
> And yet she looks both small and dull.
> The night is chill, the cloud is gray,
> Tis a month before the month of May,
> And spring comes slowly up this way.

The lady advances to the foot of an aged oak, covered with moss and misseltoe, and prays in silence; when lo! a groan from the other side of the tree makes her 'leap up suddenly'.

> The night is chill; the forest bare;
> Is it the wind that moaneth bleak?
> There is not wind enough in the air
> To move away the ringlet curl
> From the lovely lady's cheek—
> There is not wind enough to twirl
> The one red leaf, the last of its clan,
> That dances as often as dance it can
> Hanging so light, and hanging so high,
> On the top-most twig that looks up to the sky.

The groan proves to have come from a distressed damsel in silken robe, and with jewelled hair, who states herself to have been left in the forest by five warriors who had carried her by force from her father's house. Christabel takes her home very hospitably: and invites her to share her bed, maugre the inauspicious sight of the stranger's *stumbling over the threshold*, which, as every body knows, was formerly protected by *holy* spell in order to preserve the habitation from the entrance of witches, or evil spirits. Having crossed the court in safety, Christabel proposes an acknowledgement of praise to the Virgin, for her protection; but Geraldine, the stranger lady, pleads her extreme weariness as an excuse for not joining in the pious office, and they pass on, to the great displeasure of a certain mastiff-bitch, who had never before been known to

utter yell
Beneath the eye of Christabel.

The accumulation of ominous signs is well described, and the mysterious lady begins to excite a most powerful interest 'ere the first part closes.

The second opens with the introduction of Geraldine to Sir Leoline, the father of Christabel.

[quotes ll. 404-26 (*PW*, i, 228-9)]

It would be injustice to the author to break the powerful spell in which he holds his readers, by any imperfect description of the thraldom of Christabel to the mysterious Geraldine. Never was the withering glance of an evil eye better described. The poet's mind has combined the wilder graces of fiction, with the most vigorous and speaking descriptions.

'Kubla Khan' is merely a few stanzas which owe their origin to a circumstance by no means uncommon to persons of a poetical imagination. Our author falling asleep, under the influence of an anodyne draught, over *Purchas his Pilgrimage* was sensible of composing from two to three hundred lines of poetry—'if that indeed', says he, 'can be called composition, in which all the images rose up before him as *things*, with a parallel production of the correspondent expressions, without any sensation, or consciousness of effort'.—On awaking he began to write down these effusions; but being called off, and detained above an hour, he found to his great mortification on his return, that his visions of the night had melted into thin air, and left only a vague recollection of their general form and tendency. It is well known that a ruling passion will predominate even in sleep. The Alderman 'eats in dreams the custards of the day', and the scholar, 'chewing the cud of sweet and bitter fancy', ruminates on an intellectual banquet. Tartini, the celebrated musician, dreamed that the devil took his violin from him, and played in strains so delightful that he awoke in utter despair of rivalling so skilful a performer; he however wrote down what he remembered, or something like it, and the piece is known by the name of the Devil's Concerto. But Tartini always declared it to be utterly unworthy of comparison with the production of his sleeping moments. It should however be recollected, that in sleep the judgment is the first faculty of the mind which ceases to act, therefore, the opinion of the sleeper respecting his performance is not to be trusted, even in his waking moments. Still if Mr. Coleridge's two hundred lines were all of equal merit with the following which he has preserved, we are ready to admit that he has reason to be grieved at their loss.

> Then all the charm
> Is broken—all that phantom—world so fair
> Vanishes, and a thousand circlets spread,
> And each mis-shape the other—Stay awhile
> Poor youth! who scarcely dar'st lift up thine eyes—
> The stream will soon renew its smoothness—soon
> The visions will return! and lo he stays
> And soon the fragments dim of lovely forms
> Come trembling back, unite, and now once more
> The pool becomes a mirror.

'The Pains of Sleep' shews the vividness of the author's conceptions, mingled with that peculiarity of thought and diction which the mountain scenery of our lakes seems to inspire in all who court its influence. That Mr. Coleridge possesses strong powers of thought, with a command of original and striking images, united to those softer touches of nature which speak at once to the heart, our readers have not now to learn.

62. Unsigned review, *Anti-Jacobin*

July 1816, i, 632–6

These verses have been ushered into the world by a new species of *puff direct*; under the auspices of Lord Byron, who, as the newspapers informed the public, had read them in manuscript, and, in a letter to the author, had called 'Christabel', it seems, a 'singularly wild and beautiful Poem'. The artifice has succeeded so far as to force it into a second edition! for what woman of fashion would not purchase a book recommended by Lord Byron? For our part, we confess, that the perusal of it has excited in our minds, nothing but astonishment and disgust; we have discovered in it, wildness enough to confound common-sense, but, not having the acuteness of the noble bard, the *beauty* of the composition has wholly eluded our observation.

As any attempt to characterize such versification would be vain, the only mode by which any thing like an adequate idea of its *wildness* and its *beauty* can be conveyed, is by laying a specimen of the composition before our readers. And that we may not be suspected of unfair dealing towards the poet, we shall extract the very first lines.

> 'Tis the middle of the night by the castle clock,
> And the owls have waken'd the crowing cock;
> Tu—whit!——Tu—whoo!
> And hark, again! the crowing cock,
> How drowsily it crew.
>
> Sir Leoline, the Baron rich,
> Hath a toothless mastiff bitch;
> From her kennel beneath the rock,
> She makes answer to the clock,
> Four for the quarters, and twelve for the hour;
> Ever and aye, moonshine or shower,
> Sixteen short howls, not overloud;
> Some says she sees my lady's shroud.

Whoever has taste enough to relish this introduction, may peruse the tale, or vision, or reverie, or whatever it may be called; when he will learn, how my Lady Christabel, the daughter of this 'Baron rich', had strayed out, one chilly, but not dark, night, into a neighbouring wood,

> The night is chill, the cloud is grey,
> 'Tis a month before the month of May,
> And the spring comes slowly up this way—

in order to pray for her absent lover. The only reason assigned for the strange preference given to the wood over her own chamber, as the scene of her evening orisons, is, that she had had some strange dreams the night before.

> Dreams, that made her moan and *leap*,
> As on her bed she lay in sleep.

Behind an oak tree, Christabel discovers

> A damsel bright,
> Drest in a silken robe of white;
> Her neck, her feet, her arms were bare,
> And the jewels disordered in her hair.
> I guess, 'twas frightful there to see
> A lady so richly clad as she—
> Beautiful exceedingly!

Frightful, indeed, to see a handsome girl, half naked, exposed to the chill damps of an April night! The lady tells Christabel that her name is Geraldine, that her father is Lord Roland de Vaux, of Tryermaine, that she had been forced from home by five Knights, who were strangers to her, but who had left her in the wood, and promised to return. Christabel, moved by this tale of distress, conducts the lady to her father's castle. The Baron and his family had all retired to rest, it seems, while Miss Christabel had been employed in saying her prayers in the wood. But she had taken the prudent precaution to put the key in her pocket.

> and Christabel
> Took the key that fitted well;
> A little door she opened strait,
> All in the middle of the gate;
> The gate that was ironed within and without,
> Where an army in battle-array had marched out.

The lady was extremely fatigued, and requested to go to bed without delay; which request appears to have produced a very extraordinary effect on the mastiff-bitch, who was introduced to our notice, at the opening of the poem.

> Outside her kennel, the mastiff old
> Lay fast asleep, in moonshine cold.
> The mastiff old did not awake,
> Yet she an angry moan did make!
> And what can ail the mastiff bitch?
> Never till now she utter'd yell
> Beneath the eye of Christabel.
> Perhaps it is the owlet's scritch;
> For what can ail the mastiff bitch?

They reached, however, fair Christabel's chamber in safety; when Christabel trimmed her lamp—and gave her guest some wine.

> Again the wild-flower wine she drank:
> Her fair large eyes gave glitter bright,
> And from the floor whereon she sank
> The lofty lady stood upright!
> She was most beautiful to see,
> Like a lady of far countree. ! ! ! ! ! !¹

Geraldine requests Christabel to get into bed before her, which she does; but, not being inclined to sleep, she rose in her bed, and laying her cheek on her hand, looked through the curtains at her destined bed-fellow; when,

> full in view,
> Behold! her bosom and half her side—
> A sight to dream of, not to tell!
> And she's to sleep by Christabel.

She got into bed, took Christabel in her arms, and said,

> In the touch of this bosom there worketh a spell
> Which is Lord of thy utterance, Christabel!

We suppose, it is meant, by this, to inform us that Christabel is bewitched!

In the morning Christabel introduced her guest to her father, who was infinitely pleased with her, and resolved to espouse her cause, and, like a *preux chevalier*, to avenge the insult that had been offered her. While, she appeared all beauty to Sir Leoline, she appeared all deformity to Christabel.

> A snake's small eye blinks dull and shy,
> And the lady's eyes they shrunk in her head,

¹ Reviewer's exclamation.

> Each shrunk up to a serpent's eye,
>   And with somewhat of malice, and more of dread,
> At Christabel she look'd askance!—
>   One moment—and the sight was fled!
> But Christabel in dizzy trance,
> Stumbling on the unsteady ground—
> Shuddered aloud, with a hissing sound.

When Christabel recovered from the kind of trance into which she had been thrown, she earnestly besought her father to send the woman away; but being, by the spell it is supposed, prevented from stating her reasons for such request, her father expressed his displeasure, paid greater attention to Geraldine, and dispatched a messenger to her father, to inform him where his daughter had taken shelter—and thus ends 'this singularly wild and beautiful poem'—that is, all of it that is, at present, printed. But, in his preface, the author threatens us with *three more parts*. It is to be hoped, however, that he will think better of it, and not attempt to put his threats in execution. Had we not known Mr. Coleridge to be a man of genius and of talents, we should really, from the present production, have been tempted to pronounce him wholly destitute of both. In truth, a more senseless, absurd, and stupid, composition, has scarcely, of late years, issued from the press. Yet is it not, we are surprised to learn, a *hasty* composition; the first part of it having been written nineteen years, and the second, eight years, ago! That a man, at a time when he had not his sober senses about him, might commit such balderdash to paper, is conceivable; but that, after it had been thrown by for so many years, he should calmly look over it, and deliberately resolve to give it to the public, is scarcely credible! Mr. Coleridge might have spared himself the trouble of anticipating the charge 'of plagiarism or of servile imitation' —it is a perfectly original composition, and the like of it is not to be found in the English language. The metre of this poem, the author gravely tells the public, 'is not, properly speaking, irregular, though it may seem so for its being founded on a new *principle*, namely, that of counting in each line the accents, not the syllables'. If we were called upon seriously to investigate this new principle, we could soon show the folly of it—but really, gravely to discuss so wretched a performance is beneath the dignity of criticism.

The *et cætera* in the title-page[1] applies to two short poems, one called 'Kubla Khan', a fragment, composed, as it were, in his sleep, and put

---

[1] The reviewer is using the second edition.

upon paper as soon as he awoke; and 'The Pains of Sleep', descriptive
of a restless night, and unpleasant dreams. These have none of the
wildness or deformity, of 'Christabel'; and though they are not marked
by any striking beauties, they are not wholly discreditable to the author's
talents.

63. William Roberts, *British Review*

August 1816, viii, 64-81

Unsigned review attributed to Roberts (1767-1849), barrister
and editor of the *British Review* (Arthur Roberts, *The Life,
Letters, and Opinions of William Roberts*, London 1850, 56-7).
R. C. Maturin's *Bertram, or the Castle of St. Aldobrand* was
included in the review—a fact worth noting if only because of
Coleridge's harsh discussion of the play (later incorporated into
Biographia Literaria), which appeared in the *Courier* of 29 August,
and 7, 9, 10 and 11 September 1816.

'That wild and singularly original and beautiful poem' as Lord Byron
calls the production which stands first at the head of this article, in
terms sufficiently uncouth, but of a convenient length and authori-
tativeness for the bookseller's purpose in his announcement of the
work, was read by us before we saw the advertisement, and therefore
without that prejudice against it which the above applauding sentence
would certainly have produced in us.

That the poem of 'Christabel' is wild and singular cannot be denied,
and if this be not eulogy sufficient, let it be allowed to be original; for
there is a land of dreams with which poets hold an unrestricted
commerce, and where they may load their imaginations with whatever
strange products they find in the country; and if we are content with
the raw material, there is no end to the varieties of chaotic originalities
which may be brought away from this fantastic region. But it is the
poet's province, not to bring these anomalous existences to our view in

the state in which he has picked them up, but so shaped, applied, worked up, and compounded, as almost to look like natives of our own minds, and easily to mix with the train of our own conceptions. It is not every strange phantasy, or rambling incoherency of the brain, produced perhaps amidst the vapours of indigestion, that is susceptible of poetic effect, nor can every night mare be turned into a muse; there must be something to connect these visionary forms with the realities of existence, to gain them a momentary credence by the aid of harmonizing occurrences, to mix them up with the interest of some great event, or to borrow for them a colour of probability from the surrounding scene. It is only under the shelter of these proprieties and correspondencies that witchcraft has a fair and legitimate introduction into poetical composition. A witch is no heroine, nor can we read a tale of magic for its own sake. Poetry itself must show some modesty, nor be quite unforbearing in its exactions. What we allow it the use of as an accessory it must not convert into a principal, and what is granted to it as a part of its proper machinery it must not impose upon us as the main or only subject of interest. But Mr. Coleridge is one of those poets who if we give him an inch will be sure to take an ell: if we consent to swallow an elf or fairy, we are soon expected not to strain at a witch; and if we open our throats to this imposition upon our goodnature, we must gulp down broomstick and all.

We really must make a stand somewhere for the rights of common sense; and large as is the allowance which we feel disposed to give to the privileges and immunities of the poet, we must, at the hazard of being considered as profane, require him to be intelligible; and as a necessary step towards his becoming so, to understand himself, and be privy to the purposes of his own mind: for if he is not in his own secret, it is scarcely probable that he can become his own interpreter.

It was in vain that, after reading the poem of 'Christabel', we resorted to the preface to consult the poet himself about his own meaning. He tells us only that which, however important, doubtless, in itself, throws very little light upon the mysteries of the poem, viz. that great part of the poem was written in the year 1797, at Stowey, in the county of Somerset: the second part, after his return from Germany, in the year 1800, at Keswick, in Cumberland. 'Since the latter date my poetic powers', says the author, 'have been till very lately in a state of suspended animation'. Now we cannot but suspect that there is a little anachronism in this statement, and that in truth it was during this suspense of the *author's poetical* powers, that this 'wild and singularly original and beautiful poem' of 'Christabel' was conceived and partly executed.

——Nondum facies viventis in illa,
Jam morientis erat.

Nor can we perceive any symptoms of recovery from this state of 'suspended animation' in what has been lately added as the completion of the poem; we shall watch, however, like one of the agents of the Humane Society, for the signs of returning life, and consider the rescue of such a muse as that of Mr. Coleridge from suffocation by submersion as some gain to the cause of true poetry.

In the preceding paragraph of the preface Mr. Coleridge discovers no small anxiety to obviate the suspicion of having borrowed any part of this poem from any of 'our celebrated poets', and this accounts for his particularity with respect to the chronology of the performance, which, short as it is, appears at each stage of it to have occasioned so much mental exhaustion as to demand long restorative intermissions. We never suspected Mr. Coleridge of plagiarism, and think he betrays an unreasonable mistrust of the credit which the critics will give him for originality. Our own opinion most decidedly is that he is honestly entitled to all the eccentricities of this poem; and that in asserting his exclusive property in them he has done great negative justice to the rest of the literary world. Lord Byron seems as anxious to remove from himself the imputation of having borrowed from the author of 'Christabel'. With this question we shall not trouble ourselves: where two are afflicted with an epidemic it is of little importance which caught it of the other, so long as *we* can escape the contagion.

The epidemic among modern poets is the disease of affectation, which is for ever carrying them into quaint, absurd, and outrageous extremes. *One* is determined to say nothing in a natural way, *another* is for saying every thing with infantine simplicity, while a *third* is persuaded that there is but one language for the drawing room, the Royal Exchange, the talk of the table, and the temple of the Muses. One consequence of this fatal propensity to affectation among our poets is a terrible sameness or mannerism in each of those who have been encouraged to write much; and the worst of it is that each of these luminaries, while he moves in his own orbit in perpetual parellel-ism with himself, has a crowd of little moons attending him, that multiply the malignant influence, and propagate the deceptious glare. But the most insufferable of all the different forms which modern affectation in composition has assumed is the cant and gibberish of the German school, which has filled all the provinces, as well of imagination as of science, with profound nonsense, unintelligible refinement, metaphysical morals, and mental distortion. Its perfection and its boast is, to be fairly franchised from all the rules and restraints of common sense and common nature; and if domestic events and social manners are the theme, all the natural affections, ties, charities, and emotions of the heart, are displaced by a monstrous progeny of vice and sentiment, an assemblage of ludicrous horrors, or a rabble of undisciplined feelings. We shall hail the day, as a day of happy auspices for the moral muse, when our present fanatic race of poets shall have exhausted all their 'monstrous shapes and sorceries', and the abused understandings of our countrymen shall break these unhappy spells, forsake the society of demons, and be divorced from deformity. To us especially whose duty condemns us to the horrible drudgery of reading whatever men of a certain reputation may choose to write, it will be a great refreshment, if it be only for the novelty of the scene, to find ourselves once more, if not at the fount of Helicon, or on the summit of Parnassus, yet at least in a region where fog and gloom are not perpetual, and poetry is so far mindful of its origin and ancient character as to proceed in the path of intelligibility, and to propose to itself some meaning and purpose, if not some moral end.

And now for this 'wild and singularly original and beautiful poem' of 'Christabel'. Could Lord Byron, the author of this pithy sentence, shew us wherein consists its singular beauty? This is the only specimen we have yet seen of his Lordship's critical powers; but from the experience we have had of his Lordship's taste in these matters, we do not think he could give a better account of the principles of his admiration, or dilate with better success on the meaning of his sententious eulogium, than the bookseller who has borrowed its magical influence in all his advertisements of this poem.

We learn two things, and two things only, with certainty from this 'wild and singularly original and beautiful poem': that Sir Leoline was 'rich', and that he 'had a toothless mastiff bitch'; and if any one should be so unpoetical as to ask in plain terms what these two circumstances have to do with the business, story, or catastrophe of the poem, we must frankly confess that, wise as we are, we cannot tell; nor do we know to whom to refer him for information, unless it be to Lord Byron. The last person he should apply to in this distressing difficulty is the writer himself, who, if he has written with the true inspiration of a poet of the present day, would laugh at the ignorance of those who would expect him to understand himself, and tell them that by the laws and usages of modern poetry it was for the reader and the old toothless bitch to make out the meaning as they could between them.

From the moment we leave the picturesque old lady (for we cannot but suspect the bitch to be a witch in that form) all is impenetrable to us, except the exact information which the poet gives us that 'the night was chilly but not dark', and the strong suspicion we are led to entertain from its being 'the month before the month of May', that it could not be, after all, any other than that month which a plain man would call April. As our readers may by this time have some curiosity to see a little of this 'wild and singularly original and beautiful poem', the old toothless bitch shall turn out for his entertainment; and he shall go with Christabel into the wood and attend her there until she meets with the Lady Geraldine.

[quotes ll. 1-68 (*PW*, i, 215-18)]

Now this strange lady, who is to be sure some preternatural personage, comes home with Christabel, and passes the night with her. What the result of this adventure was is so very darkly intimated, that it would be hazardous to frame a conjecture. That all was not as it should be, that some mysterious spells were wrought both upon Christabel and Sir Leoline, producing strange external and internal transformations, is evident; but what is meant to be understood to have been actually done, to what purpose, how produced, or with what consequences to the parties, we know as little as Mr. Coleridge himself. We should not be much surprised if the object of the poet was to make fools of the public, having observed Lord Byron to have succeeded so well in this art; and if it was really published on the *first* of 'the month before the month of May', we cannot altogether disapprove of the pleasantry.

Come we now from the castle of Sir Leoline to the castle of St. Aldobrand; passing over the two other poems which are bound together with 'Christabel', called 'The Fragment of Kubla Khan', and 'The Pains of Sleep'; in which, however, there are some playful thoughts and fanciful imagery, which we would gladly have extracted, if our room would have allowed it. The change is so far an advantage to us, that we are no longer under a necessity to grope in the dark for a meaning. . . .

We take our leave of 'Christabel' and *Bertram*, but not without adverting, as in justice we ought, to the great disparity between these productions in the merits of the compositions. The poem which has been denominated 'wild and singularly original and beautiful' is, in our judgment, a weak and singularly nonsensical and affected performance; but the play of *Bertram* is a production of undoubted genius. . . .

64. Thomas Moore, *Edinburgh Review*

September 1816, xxvii, 58-67

This unsigned review is attributed to Thomas Moore (Elisabeth Schneider, 'The Unknown Reviewer of *Christabel*', *The Publications of the Modern Language Association*, lxx [1955], 417-32). Moore (1779-1852), Irish poet and songwriter, was a close friend of Byron's and eventually his biographer.

The advertisement by which this work was announced to the publick, carried in its front a recommendation from Lord Byron, who, it seems, has somewhere praised 'Christabel', as 'a wild and singularly original and beautiful poem'. Great as the noble bard's merits undoubtedly are in poetry, some of his latest *publications* dispose us to distrust his authority, where the question is what ought to meet the public eye; and the works before us afford an additional proof, that his judgment on such matters is not absolutely to be relied on. Moreover, we are a little inclined to doubt the value of the praise which one poet lends another. It seems now-a-days to be the practice of that once irritable race to laud each other without bounds; and one can hardly avoid suspecting, that what is thus lavishly advanced may be laid out with a view to being repaid with interest. Mr. Coleridge, however, must be judged by his own merits.

It is remarked, by the writers upon the Bathos, that the true *profound* is surely known by one quality—its being wholly bottomless; insomuch, that when you think you have attained its utmost depth in the work of some of its great masters, another, or peradventure the same, astonishes you, immediately after, by a plunge so much more vigorous, as to outdo all his former outdoings. So it seems to be with the new school, or, as they may be termed, the wild or lawless poets. After we had been admiring their extravagance for many years, and marvelling at the ease and rapidity with which one exceeded another in the unmeaning or infantine, until not an idea was left in the rhyme—or in the insane, until we had reached something that seemed the untamed effusion of an author whose thoughts were rather more free than his actions—forth steps Mr. Coleridge, like a giant refreshed with sleep, and as if to redeem his character after so long a silence (his poetic powers having been, he says, from 1808 till very lately, in a state of suspended animation) and breaks out in these precise words:

> 'Tis the middle of night by the castle clock,
> And the owls have awaken'd the crowing cock;
> Tu—whit!——Tu—whoo!
> And hark, again! the crowing cock,
> How drowsily it crew.
>
> Sir Leoline, the Baron rich,
> Hath a toothless mastiff bitch;
> From her kennel beneath the rock
> She makes answer to the clock,
> Four for the quarters, and twelve for the hour;
> Ever and aye, moonshine or shower,
> Sixteen short howls, not over loud;
> Some say she sees my lady's shroud.
> Is the night chilly and dark?
> The night is chilly, but not dark.

It is probable that Lord Byron may have had this passage in his eye, when he called the poem 'wild' and 'original'; but how he discovered it to be 'beautiful', is not quite so easy for us to imagine.

Much of the art of the wild writers consists in sudden transitions—opening eagerly upon some topic, and then flying from it immediately. This indeed is known to the medical men, who not unfrequently have the care of them, as an unerring symptom. Accordingly, here we take leave of the Mastiff Bitch, and lose sight of her entirely, upon the entrance of another personage of a higher degree,

> The lovely Lady Christabel,
> Whom her father loves so well—

And who, it seems, has been rambling about all night, having, the night before, had dreams about her lover, which 'made her moan and *leap*'. While kneeling, in the course of her rambles, at an old oak, she hears a noise on the other side of the stump, and going round, finds, to her great surprize, another fair damsel in white silk, but with her dress and hair in some disorder; at the mention of whom, the poet takes fright, not, as might be imagined, because of her disorder, but on account of her beauty and her fair attire:

> I guess, 'twas frightful there to see
> A lady so richly clad as she—
> Beautiful exceedingly!

Christabel naturally asks who she is, and is answered, at some length, that her name is Geraldine; that she was, on the morning before, seized by five warriors, who tied her on a white horse, and drove her on, they themselves following, also on white horses; and that they had rode all night. Her narrative now gets to be a little contradictory, which gives rise to unpleasant suspicions. She protests vehemently, and with oaths, that she has no idea who the men were; only that one of them, the tallest of the five, took her and placed her under the tree, and that they all went away, she knew not whither; but how long she had remained there she cannot tell:

> Nor do I know how long it is,
> For I have lain in fits, I *wis*;

although she had previously kept a pretty exact account of the time. The two ladies then go home together, after this satisfactory explanation, which appears to have conveyed to the intelligent mind of Lady C. every requisite information. They arrive at the castle, and pass the night in the same bed-room; not to disturb Sir Leoline, who, it seems, was poorly at the time, and, of course, must have been called up to speak to the chambermaids, and have the sheets aired, if Lady G. had had a room to herself. They do not get to their bed, however, in the poem, quite so easily as we have carried them. They first cross the moat, and Lady C. 'took the key that fitted well', and opened a little door, 'all in the middle of the gate'. Lady G. then sinks down 'belike through pain'; but it should seem more probably from laziness; for her fair companion having lifted her up, and carried her a little way, she then walks on 'as she were not in pain'. Then they cross the court—

but we must give this in the poet's words, for he seems so pleased with them, that he inserts them twice over in the space of ten lines.

> So free from danger, free from fear,
> They crossed the court—right glad they were.

Lady C. is desirous of a little conversation on the way, but Lady G. will not indulge her Ladyship, saying, she is too much tired to speak. We now meet our old friend, the mastiff bitch, who is much too important a person to be slightly passed by:

> Outside her kennel, the mastiff old
> Lay fast asleep, in moonshine cold.
> The mastiff old did not awake,
> Yet she an angry moan did make!
> And what can ail the mastiff bitch?
> Never till now she uttered yell
> Beneath the eye of Christabel.
> Perhaps it is the owlet's scritch:
> For what can ail the mastiff bitch?

Whatever it may be that ails the bitch, the ladies pass forward, and take off their shoes, and tread softly all the way up stairs, as Christabel observes that her father is a bad sleeper. At last, however, they do arrive at the bed-room, and comfort themselves with a dram of some home-made liquor, which proves to be very old; for it was made by Lady C.'s mother; and when her new friend asks if she thinks the old lady will take her part, she answers, that this is out of the question, in as much as she happened to die in childbed of her. The mention of the old lady, however, gives occasion to the following pathetic couplet. Christabel says,

> O mother dear, that thou wert here!
> I would, said Geraldine, she were!

A very mysterious conversation next takes place between Lady Geraldine and the old gentlewoman's ghost, which proving extremely fatiguing to her, she again has recourse to the bottle—and with excellent effect, as appears by these lines.

> Again the wild-flower wine she drank;
> Her fair large eyes 'gan glitter bright,
> And from the floor whereon she sank,
> The lofty Lady stood upright:
> She was most beautiful to see,
> Like a Lady of a far countrée.

From which, we may gather among other points, the exceeding great beauty of all women who live in a distant place, no matter where. The effects of the cordial speedily begin to appear; as no one, we imagine, will doubt, that to its influence must be ascribed the following speech:

> And thus the lofty lady spake—
> All they, who live in the upper sky,
> Do love you, holy Christabel!
> And you love them—and for their sake
> And for the good which me befel,
> Even I in my degree will try,
> Fair maiden, to requite you well.

Before going to bed, Lady G. kneels to pray, and desires her friend to undress, and lie down; which she does 'in her loveliness'; but being curious, she leans 'on her elbow', and looks towards the fair devotee— where she sees something which the poet does not think fit to tell us very explicitly.

> Her silken robe, and inner vest,
> Dropt to her feet, and full in view,
> Behold! her bosom and half her side—
> A sight to dream of, not to tell!
> And she is to sleep by Christabel.

She soon rises, however, from her knees; and as it was not a double-bedded room, she turns in to Lady Christabel, taking only 'two paces and a stride'. She then clasps her tight in her arms, and mutters a very dark spell, which we apprehend the poet manufactured by shaking words together at random; for it is impossible to fancy that he can annex any meaning whatever to it. This is the end of it.

> But vainly thou warrest,
> For this is alone in
> Thy power to declare,
> That in the dim forest
> Thou heard'st a low moaning,
> And found'st a bright lady, surpassingly fair:
> And didst bring her home with thee in love and in charity,
> To shield her and shelter her from the damp air.

The consequence of this incantation is, that Lady Christabel has a strange dream—and when she awakes, her first exclamation is, 'Sure I have sinn'd'—'Now heaven be praised if all be well!' Being still perplexed with the remembrance of her 'too lively' dream—she then dresses herself, and modestly prays to be forgiven for 'her sins unknown'. The two companions now go to the Baron's parlour, and Geraldine tells her story to him. This, however, the poet judiciously leaves out, and only signifies that the Baron recognized in her the daughter of his old friend Sir Roland, with whom he had had a deadly quarrel. Now, however, he despatches his tame poet, or laureate, called Bard Bracy, to invite him and his family over, promising to forgive every thing, and even make an apology for what had passed. To understand what follows, we own, surpasses our comprehension. Mr. Bracy, the poet, recounts a strange dream he has just had, of a dove being almost strangled by a snake; whereupon the Lady Geraldine falls a hissing, and her eyes grow small, like a serpent's,—or at least so they seem to her friend; who begs her father to 'send away that woman'. Upon this the Baron falls into a passion, as if he had discovered that his daughter had been seduced; at least, we can understand him in no other sense, though no hint of such a kind is given; but, on the contrary, she is painted to the last moment as full of innocence and purity. Nevertheless,

> His heart was cleft with pain and rage,
> His cheeks they quiver'd, his eyes were wild,
> Dishonour'd thus in his old age;
> Dishonour'd by his only child;
> And all his hospitality
> To th' insulted daughter of his friend
> By more than woman's jealousy,
> Brought thus to a disgraceful end—

Nothing further is said to explain the mystery; but there follows incontinently, what is termed '*The conclusion of Part the Second*'. And as we are pretty confident that Mr. Coleridge holds this passage in the highest estimation; that he prizes it more than any other part of 'that wild, and singularly original and beautiful poem Christabel', excepting always the two passages touching the 'toothless mastiff Bitch'; we shall extract it for the amazement of our readers—premising our own frank avowal that we are wholly unable to divine the meaning of any portion of it.

> A little child, a limber elf,
> Singing, dancing to itself,

A fairy thing with red round cheeks,
That always finds and never seeks;
Makes such a vision to the sight
As fills a father's eyes with light;
And pleasures flow in so thick and fast
Upon his heart, that he at last
Must needs express his love's excess
With words of unmeant bitterness.
Perhaps 'tis pretty to force together
Thoughts so all unlike each other;
To mutter and mock a broken charm,
To dally with wrong that does no harm.
Perhaps 'tis tender too, and pretty,
At each wild word to feel within
A sweet recoil of love and pity.
And what if in a world of sin
(O sorrow and shame should this be true!)
Such giddiness of heart and brain
Comes seldom save from rage and pain,
So talks as it's most used to do.

Here endeth the Second Part, and, in truth, the 'singular' poem itself; for the author has not yet written, or, as he phrases it, 'embodied in verse', the 'three parts yet to come'; though he trusts he shall be able to do so 'in the course of the present year'.

One word as to the metre of 'Christabel', or, as Mr. Coleridge terms it, '*the* Christabel'—happily enough; for indeed we doubt it the peculiar force of the definite article was ever more strongly exemplified. He says, that though the reader may fancy there prevails a great *irregularity* in the metre, some lines being of four, others of twelve syllables, yet in reality it is quite regular; only that it is 'founded on a new principle, namely, that of counting in each line the accents, not the syllables'. We say nothing of the monstrous assurance of any man coming forward coolly at this time of day, and telling the readers of English poetry, whose ear has been tuned to the lays of Spenser, Milton, Dryden, and Pope, that he makes his metre 'on a new principle'! but we utterly deny the truth of the assertion, and defy him to show us *any* principle upon which his lines can be conceived to tally. We give two or three specimens, to confound at once this miserable piece of coxcombry and shuffling. Let our 'wild, and singularly original and beautiful' author, show us how these lines agree either in number of accents or of feet.

Ah wel-a-day!—
For this is alone in—
And didst bring her home with thee in love and in charity—
I pray you drink this cordial wine—
Sir Leoline—
And found a bright lady surpassingly fair—
Tu—whit!——Tu—whoo!

'Kubla Khan' is given to the public, it seems, 'at the request of a poet of great and deserved celebrity'; but whether Lord Byron the praiser of 'the Christabel', or the Laureate, the praiser of Princes,[1] we are not informed. As far as Mr. Coleridge's 'own opinions are concerned', it is published, 'not upon the ground of any *poetic* merits', but 'as a Psychological Curiosity'! In these opinions of the candid author, we entirely concur; but for this reason we hardly think it was necessary to give the minute detail which the Preface contains, of the circumstances attending its composition. Had the question regarded *Paradise Lost*, or Dryden's 'Ode', we could not have had a more particular account of the circumstances in which it was composed. It was in the year 1797, and in the summer season. Mr. Coleridge was in bad health; the particular disease is not given; but the careful reader will form his own conjectures. He had retired very prudently to a lonely farm-house; and whoever would see the place which gave birth to the 'psychological curiosity', may find his way thither without a guide; for it is situated on the confines of Somerset and Devonshire, and on the Exmoor part of the boundary; and it is, moreover, between Porlock and Linton. In that farm-house, he had a slight indisposition, and had taken an anodyne, which threw him into a deep sleep in his chair (whether after dinner or not he omits to state), 'at the moment that he was reading a sentence in Purchas's Pilgrims', relative to a palace of Kubla Khan. The effects of the anodyne, and the sentence together, were prodigious: they produced the 'curiosity' now before us; for, during his three-hours sleep, Mr. Coleridge 'has the most vivid confidence that he could not have composed less than from two to three hundred lines'. On awaking, he 'instantly and eagerly' wrote down the verses here published; when he was (he says, '*unfortunately*') called out by a 'person on business from Porlock, and detained by him above an hour'; and when he returned, the vision was gone. The lines here given smell strongly, it must be owned, of the anodyne; and, but that an

---

[1] A hit at Southey's changed politics.

under dose of a sedative produces contrary effects, we should inevitably have been lulled by them into forgetfulness of all things. Perhaps a dozen more such lines as the following would reduce the most irritable of critics to a state of inaction.

> A damsel with a dulcimer
> In a vision once I saw:
> It was an Abyssinian maid
> And on her dulcimer she play'd,
> Singing of Mount Abora.
> Could I revive within me
> Her symphony and song,
> To such a deep delight 'twould win me
> That with music loud and long,
> I would build that dome in air,
> That sunny dome! those caves of ice!
> And all who heard should see them there,
> And all should cry, Beware! Beware!
> His flashing eyes, his floating hair!
> Weave a circle round him thrice,
> And close your eyes with holy dread:
> For he on honey-dew hath fed, &c. &c.

There is a good deal more altogether as exquisite—and in particular a fine description of a wood, 'ancient as the hills'; and 'folding sunny spots of *greenery*'! But we suppose this specimen will be sufficient.

Persons in this poet's unhappy condition, generally feel the want of sleep as the worst of their evils; but there are instances, too, in the history of the disease, of sleep being attended with new agony, as if the waking thoughts, how wild and turbulent soever, had still been under some slight restraint, which sleep instantly removed. Mr. Coleridge appears to have experienced this symptom, if we may judge from the title of his third poem, 'The Pains of Sleep'; and, in truth, from its composition—which is mere raving, without any thing more affecting than a number of incoherent words, expressive of extravagance and incongruity. We need give no specimen of it.

Upon the whole, we look upon this publication as one of the most notable pieces of impertinence of which the press has lately been guilty; and one of the boldest experiments that has yet been made on the patience or understanding of the public. It is impossible, however, to dismiss it, without a remark or two. The other productions of the Lake School have generally exhibited talents thrown away upon subjects so mean, that no power of genius could ennoble them; or perverted and rendered useless by a false theory of poetical composition. But even in the worst of them, if we except the *White Doe* of Mr. Wordsworth and some of the laureate odes, there were always some gleams of feeling or of fancy. But the thing now before us, is utterly destitute of value. It exhibits from beginning to end not a ray of genius; and we defy any man to point out a passage of poetical merit in any of the three pieces which it contains, except, perhaps, the following lines, and even these are not very brilliant; nor is the leading thought original:

> Alas! they had been friends in youth;
> But whispering tongues can poison truth;
> And constancy lives in realms above;
> And life is thorny; and youth is vain;
> And to be wroth with one we love,
> Doth work like madness in the brain.

With this one exception, there is literally not one couplet in the publication before us which would be reckoned poetry, or even sense, were it found in the corner of a newspaper or upon the window of an inn. Must we then be doomed to hear such a mixture of raving and driv'ling, extolled as the work of a '*wild and original*' genius, simply because Mr. Coleridge has now and then written fine verses, and a brother poet chooses, in his milder mood, to laud him from courtesy or from interest? And are such panegyrics to be echoed by the mean tools of a political faction, because they relate to one whose daily prose is understood to be dedicated to the support of all that courtiers think should be supported?[1] If it be true that the author has thus earned the patronage of those liberal dispensers of bounty, we can have no objection that they should give him proper proofs of their gratitude; but we cannot help wishing, for his sake, as well as our own, that they would pay in solid pudding instead of empty praise; and adhere, at least in this instance, to the good old system of rewarding their champions with places and pensions, instead of puffing their bad

[1] This charge of political sycophancy was playfully objected to by Leigh Hunt ('Mr. Coleridge and the Edinburgh Reviewers', the *Examiner*, 24 November 1816, 743-4), who pointed out that at the time when 'Christabel' had been written, Coleridge was on the other side of the political fence. Cf. Hazlitt's similar treatment of Southey as a political turncoat ('The Courier and Wat Tyler', the *Examiner*, 30 March 1817, 194-7).

poetry, and endeavouring to cram their nonsense down the throats of all the loyal and well affected.

65. G. F. Mathew, *European Magazine*

November 1816, lxx, 434-7

This review, initialed 'G.F.M.', is attributed to Keats's friend George Felton Mathew (c. 1795-c. 1850) (Hayden, 57).

Mr. Coleridge's last publication, containing the fragment of 'Christabel', &c., &c. has already passed into a second edition; it has been read, it has been talked of, and it is at least not blighted by the cold overhanging atmosphere of neglect, however harshly it may have been visited by the rude breezes of disapprobation, trampled upon by the cold-blooded critic by profession and ill-spoken of in many a motley circle.

Every poet is not a Homer; nor, it may be retorted, is every critic an Aristotle; nor indeed, is it at all times that every reader is capable of encountering either the one or the other.

Surely however some merit, some considerable merit, ought not to be denied the individual who possesses the ability to sustain us throughout those hours of indolence and weariness which we all so frequently experience—in that midway of imagination which, though it be below the mountain heights of reason, is nevertheless above the depths of sensuality and corruption: and however numerous at the present day this class of authors may be, there are few, the beauty of whose descriptions, the delicacy of whose characters, the simplicity of whose sentiments, and the morality of whose pages, may be placed in competition with these qualities in Coleridge.

In days of Gothic severity, when the convent and the castle were the temples of Virtue and of Beauty; when virgins were more loved, because they were more retired; when they were more sought after, because they were more backward to be found: when the simplicity of their lives and their ignorance of the world, were equalled only by the purity of their manners and the sincerity of their hearts, the mild, the tender-hearted, the virtuous, the amiable Christabel 'shone upon the dark earth'.

Motherless from her birth, whether she possessed so much of the spirit of her deceased parent as to be formed in character and in shape after so excellent a model, or who she had for her companion and her patron, is not upon record; this however appears: she is charitable, religious, beautiful, and tender; and Mr. Coleridge has, with the taste and delicacy of an able artist, pourtrayed his heroine in the sweetest and most interesting colours.

It has been said of poetry, as of music and of painting, that dark shades and discordant passages seem absolutely necessary to the exposition of the bright and the harmonious. But it may also be contended that, for the setting forth of beauty, however necessary may be the introduction of deformity; however suitable to the exaltation of what is good may be the combination of that which is bad; however Virtue may appear more amiable in distress, and Vice more contemptible in power: it does not follow that, because a poet is harmonious he should be discordant; or, because he is manly, that he should be also puerile, in other words, discordant in the language of that whose essence is harmonious, and puerile in the conception of that whose character is heroism. Such weaknesses of style, and such puerilities of thought, are not under these pretensions to be reconciled either to our approbation or endurance; but who will condemn the lily because it has not the colour of tulip, or discard the unassuming primrose because it bears not upon its stem the glory of the sunflower.

This Poem, as we have before observed, is not heroic, neither is there any thing of Dryden or of Goldsmith in it's composition: little also (though what it does contain includes the *worst* parts of both) either of Scott or Southey. It is, as Lord Byron says of it, *'wildly original'*: his lordship might have added, in some places, 'incoherently unintelligible'; it is not, therefore, to be judged of by comparison, but by those effects which it produces upon the hearts and imaginations of its readers. Its greatest peculiarity exists in the contrariety of its combinations, it's descriptions, it's incidents, are almost all of them made more imposing by the power of contrasted circumstances:

> Perhaps 'tis pretty to force together
> Thoughts so all unlike each other

And:

> At each wild word to feel within
> A sweet recoil of love and pity!

We ourselves know several ladies who, in the act of caressing their children, make use of the most singular and *outré* expressions: this is eminently characteristic of the peculiarities of 'Christabel', and Coleridge has not forgotten it:

> A little child, a limber elf,
> Singing, dancing, to itself,
> A fairy thing with red round cheeks
> That always finds, and never seeks,
> Makes such a vision to the sight
> As fills a father's eyes with light:
> And pleasures flow in so thick and fast
> Upon his heart, that he at last
> Must needs express his love's excess
> With words of unmeant bitterness.

Christabel having been disturbed during the previous night by dreams of terror and ill-forboding visions of her lover, in the depth of melancholy wanders into the forest alone and late: and here the feminine beauty and helplessness of Christabel, together with her sincerity and pious spirit, are *admirably contrasted* with the depression which her unfortunate dreams had occasioned, and the wintry desolation and the gloomy silence of the surrounding scene:

> It was a lovely sight to see
> The lady Christabel, when she
> Was kneeling at the old oak tree.
>   Amid the jagged shadows
>   Of mossy leafless boughs,
>   Kneeling in the moonlight,
>   To make her gentle vows;
> Her slender palms together prest,
> Heaving sometimes on her breast;
> Her face resign'd to bliss or bale—
> Her face, Oh call it fair, not pale,
> And both blue eyes more bright than clear,
> Each about to have a tear.

But the terrors of Christabel become more lively at the melancholy and plaintive sounds which proceed from the other side of the oak:

> It moan'd as near as near could be,
> But what it is, she cannot tell.

* * * *

> She folded her arms beneath her cloak,
> And stole to the other side of the oak.
>   What sees she there ?

She discovers a strange and beautiful lady, elegantly attired, but in a most pitiable situation, having been ruthlessly seized by two unknown warriors, conveyed from her father's hall, and left alone, and without assistance, in this wild and desolate spot.

The name of this lady is Geraldine, the daughter of Baron Roland de Vaux, formerly the friend of Christabel's father; but, in consequence of a violent dispute which had arisen between them, former friendship only served to heighten their present animosity.

Bold and beautiful is the image by which Coleridge illustrates this circumstance, and we shall transcribe the passage which contains it:

> Alas! they had been friends in youth:
> But whisp'ring tongues can poison truth;
> And constancy lives in realms above;
> And life is thorny; and youth is vain;
> And to be wroth with one we love,
> Doth work like madness in the brain.
> And thus it chanced, as I divine,
> With Roland and Sir Leoline.
> Each spake words of high disdain
> And insult to his heart's best brother:
> They parted—ne'er to meet again!
> But never either found another
> To free the hollow heart from paining—
> They stood aloof, the scars remaining,
> *Like cliffs which had been rent asunder;*
> *A dreary sea now flows between;*
> *But neither heat, nor frost, nor thunder,*
> *Shall wholly do away, I ween,*
> *The marks of that which once hath been.*

But, to return to our story: Christabel speaks words of comfort to her distress, with the assurances of the service of Sir Leoline in her behalf; she must however be contented with the shelter and protection of the castle for the night; and the domestics having all retired to rest, she must sleep with Christabel:

> So up they rose, and forth they pass'd.
> With *hurrying steps*, yet *nothing fast:*

Rather, by the way, an Irish mode of proceeding.

> They cross'd the moat, and Christabel
> Took the key that fitted well;
> A little door she opened straight,
> All in the middle of the gate;
> *The gate that was iron'd within and without,*
> *Where an army in battle array had march'd out.*

This poem, however romantic, is entirely domestic, and we cannot but esteem the poet who delights to remember, and to dwell upon such delicate and interesting incidents as these:

> O softly tread! said Christabel,
> My father seldom sleepeth well.
> Sweet Christabel her feet she bares,
> And they are creeping up the stairs;
> Now in glimmer, and now in gloom,
> And now they pass the Baron's room
> As still as death, with stifled breath!

The following description of the bed-chamber, however minute, is not the tedious account of an upholsterer:

> The moon shines dim in the open air,
> And not a moonbeam enters here.
> But they without its light can see
> The chamber carv'd so curiously,
> Carv'd with figures strange and sweet,
> All made out of the carver's brain;
> For a lady's chamber meet:
> The lamp with twofold silver chain
> Is fasten'd to an angel's feet.

Christabel lost her mother the hour that she was born; but from her father and from her friends, as well as also from the domestics, she must have continually heard those little tales which Memory, in love and admiration of her qualities, took pleasure in repeating. Christabel loved her mother, and she would dwell upon the remembrance of many instances of her domestic providence with peculiar fondness; she does not forget, therefore, what to her was an additional recommendation of it, when offering the wild flower wine to the weary lady, who had sunk down upon the floor through weakness, to inform her that her mother made it:

O weary lady, Geraldine,
I pray you drink this cordial wine!
It is a wine of virtuous powers;
My mother made it of wild flowers.

It has been observed, that 'Christabel is not so censurable in itself, as it is in consideration of the source from which it sprang'. We must honestly confess we do not understand this: it is assuredly the legitimate offspring of Coleridge's imagination; its relationship to his other compositions is strongly marked in all the more important features of it: it is, indeed, the twin-sister of his *Remorse*. Besides, supposing it to be of quite a different character and complexion: is Hogarth's 'Sigismunda'[1] more censurable on its author's account comparatively, than upon it's own intrinsically? If it had been equal to his works of humour in execution, however different in character, it had called forth equal approbation from the connoisseur; nay, would not the painter have attained to higher glory because of the versatility of his genius? And shall it be considered unlawful for Coleridge to pay his addresses to more than one muse? or for the children of his imagination to be not only sons, but daughters? and shall the offspring of that muse, whose coral mansion is the human heart, wherein she sings so wildly and so sweetly, be condemned because it is not so sublime, or because it is not so terrific as it might have been?

The Lady Geraldine is a very mysterious character, and there seems to be something preternatural both in her power and her appearance. The poet describes her as having a withered side—a mark of shame upon her—of fearful shuddering effect to the beholder; but from whom the touch of which takes away the power of expressing the abhorrence which it excites. All this Christabel sees and experiences on the fearful night of her charity to the bewildered lady, when she divides with her the pillow of her repose: at this sight the terrors of Christabel are excited; by this spell the tongue of Christabel is enchained. The fine eye of this strange lady also now and then assumes to the shuddering observation of Christabel, the size, the colour, the treacherous and malignant spirit of the serpent's orb of vision. These circumstances affect the imagination not more on their own account, than in dependence upon the style in which they are narrated, and upon the gentle spirit by which their horrors are experienced. These preternatural peculiarities the sequel of the poem must elucidate; till its appearance, we must look upon them as strong figures, indicative of the quality

[1] Historical painting, now in the Tate Gallery.

of the lady's disposition, or of the result of her introduction at the castle: we may imagine that she affects the happiness of Christabel, by an unfortunate attachment to her lover; or, by alienating from his own sweet maid the affection of her father; or, by introducing a chain of unhappy circumstances in the re-union of the two long-sundered friends.

These appearances, which disturb the peace of Christabel so evidently, are not visible to Sir Leoline, and the portion of the poem which is now before the public is concluded by the catastrophe which this occasions.

The morning after the silent introduction of Lady Geraldine at the castle, Christabel presents her to Sir Leoline: he receives her with a courteous surprise, learns the circumstances of her distress, remembers his former friendship with Sir Roland, is anxious for a reconciliation, is warm and knightly in his professions to the lady, and all this in the presence of his daughter: before whom, in the mean time, passes in the person of this creature, a repetition of these frightful and abhorred appearances. Affected thus in spirit, but without the power of expressing herself any further in explanation to Sir Leoline, she says:

> By my mother's soul I do entreat
> That you this woman send away!

Highly offensive is this apparent jealousy, on the part of Christabel, to Sir Leoline, at that instant warmly attached to the interests of the fair stranger—the child of his early friend—beautiful in person—honourable in birth—grateful, timid, and lowly in demeanor. Highly offensive, therefore, to Sir Leoline was this apparently ungenerous breach of hospitality on the part of Christabel; hospitality which he was then violently expressing; but which, to make the mortification more exquisite, it should be remembered Christabel herself had been the first tenderly to practice.

Again he caresses the lady Geraldine; who, in consequence of the conduct of Christabel, seemed for her sake to be embarrassed and distressed. Angrily he dismisses the bard Bracy from his presence, who had been relating a vision of parallel mystery with all that Christabel had suffered; and, leading forth the lady, he leaves his daughter alone to the melancholy wandering of her thoughts, and the acute vibration of her feelings.

Among the descriptions which, as they have not immediately fallen into our relation of the tale we have hitherto omitted, we cannot deny ourselves the pleasure of transcribing the following:

The night is chill, the forest bare;
Is it the wind that moaneth bleak?
There is not wind enough in the air
To move away the ringlet curl
From the lovely lady's cheek—
There is not wind enough to twirl
The one red leaf, the last of its clan,
That dances as often as dance it can,
Hanging so light, and hanging so high,
On the topmost twig that looks up at the sky.

The larger and more imposing appearances of nature are generally made use of in description; but although the '*one red leaf* on the topmost twig', be minute on the one hand, it is on the other too new, too natural, and too obvious not to be considerably effective; and this one passage may atone for many of the inconsistencies of 'Christabel'. We shall close our quotations from the poem by this pathetic appeal to Sir Leoline, in behalf of his daughter:

Why is thy cheek so wan and wild,
Sir Leoline? Thy only child
Lies at thy feet, thy joy, thy pride,
So fair, so innocent, so mild;
The same for whom thy Lady died!
O by the pangs of thy dear mother
Think thou no evil of thy child!
For her, and thee, and for no other,
She pray'd the moment ere she died:
Pray'd that the babe for whom she died,
Might prove her dear lord's joy and pride.
That prayer her deadly pangs beguil'd,
Sir Leoline!
And would'st thou wrong thy only child,
Her child and thine?

In fine, 'Christabel' is a composition which may be read often, and in every instance with increase of pleasure; it is neither calculated to relax the morals nor to degenerate the feelings; the ideas and incidents are for the most part natural and affecting; the language and versification, sweet, simple, and appropriate. In our opinion, it carries with it the peculiarity of Sterne's writings, it is hard of imitation; the attempt published in the *Poetic Mirror* is a burlesque, without similar combination of circumstances, and without a suitable application of style: we here allude to the 'Isabell', of that volume;[1] the 'Cherub' is more successful, shining forth with beautiful conceptions, though in point of style too tame, too diffuse.

There are hours when the mind is so fitted for the reception of such a work as 'Christabel', that, could the pictures, the images, the incidents, containing all the spirit and all the novelty of this specimen, be so extensively diversified, were it continued to the completion of four and twenty cantos:

> Itself should save, above the critic's breath,
> Its leaves from mould, ring and its fame from death!

66. Unsigned Review, *Monthly Review*

January 1817, lxxxii, 22-5

In a very circumstantial though short preface, Mr. Coleridge informs us that 'Christabel' was written long ago; that consequently all marks of plagiarism which may be discovered in it are only chance-coincidences; and also that the metre of 'Christabel', though irregular, still has a 'method in its madness', and 'counts the accents, not the syllables, in each line'. This variation from every former rule of versification is called 'a new principle'; and the reader is to be reasoned into a belief that a line of ten syllables is no longer than one of five, if there be no more *emphatic* syllables (for this is all that the author means by accent) in the one than in the other.

We have long since condemned in Mr. Scott and in Miss Holford,[2] and in fifty other males and females, the practice of arbitrary pronunciation, assumed as a principle for regulating the length or rhythm of a verse; and we hereby declare to all whom it may concern, that they are guilty of neither more nor less than bombastic *prose*, and not even conscious of *bombastic* verse, who rest their hopes on the acquiescence of their readers in their own 'arbitrary pronunciation'. Let those readers

---

[1] Published anonymously in 1816 by James Hogg (1770–1835).
[2] Margaret Holford (1778–1852), whose *Margaret of Anjou* appeared in 1816.

only weigh and measure a few of Mr. Coleridge's lines in this poem of 'Christabel', which unfortunately was so long delayed in its publication, and which really did *not* pilfer any thing from previous poems. Let them form their opinion; and then let them say whether Mr. Coleridge originally conceived, or surreptitiously obtained, such superb ideas!

> 'Tis the middle of night by the castle clock!
> And the owls have awaken'd the crowing cock;
> Tu—whit!——Tu—whoo!
> And hark, again! the crowing cock,
> How drowsily it crew.

Are we to be told that this is *nature?* '*Avec permission, Monsieur*', &c. &c. (as Voltaire said in Dr. Moore's *Travels*), we do not allow the plea.[1] When Virgil describes the dead hour of night; when Homer in a still bolder manner strikes out the scene before us; when Shakespeare, boldest, truest and yet gentlest of all, presents the same picture to our eyes; they all fill their canvas with living objects, and with actual sounds: but they are all equally above that imitative harmony, that affected adaptation of sound to sense, which nothing but German music and German poetry could ever have attempted. They would have started with horror and astonishment from such an effort, in any language, as that which Mr. Coleridge is constantly making; namely, to dignify meanness of conception, to versify the flattest prose, and to teach the human ear a new and discordant system of harmony.

We shall give the public one opportunity of judging of this extravagant but not ingenious production:

> Yea, she doth smile, and she doth weep,
> Like a youthful hermitess,
> Beauteous in a wilderness,
> Who, praying always, prays in sleep.
> And, if she move unquietly,
> Perchance, 'tis but the blood so free,
> Comes back and tingles in her feet.
> No doubt, she hath a vision sweet.
> What if her guardian spirit 'twere?
> What if she knew her mother near?
> But this she knows, in joys and woes,
> That saints will aid if men will call:
> For the blue sky bends over all!

[1] John Moore, *A View of Society and Manners* (1779).

This precious production is not finished, but we are to have more and more of it in future! It would be truly astonishing that such rude unfashioned stuff should be tolerated, and still more that it should be praised by men of genius (witness Lord Byron and some others), were we not convinced that every principle of correct writing, as far as poetry is concerned, has been long *given up;* and that the observance, rather than the breach, of such rules is considered as an incontrovertible proof of rank stupidity. It is grand, in a word, it is sublime, to be lawless; and whoever writes the wildest nonsense in the quickest and newest manner is the popular poet of the day! Whether this sentence be considered as a positive truth, or as a splenetic effusion, by the different parties who *now* divide the literary world, we think that the time is fast approaching when all minds will be agreed on it; and when any versifier, who widely differs from the established standard of our nobler authors, will be directly remanded into that Limbo of vanity from which he most certainly emerged.

The fragment of 'Kubla Khan' is declared to have been composed in a dream, and is published as the author wrote it. Allowing every possible accuracy to the statement of Mr. Coleridge, we would yet ask him whether this extraordinary fragment was not rather the effect of rapid and instant composition after he was awake, than of memory immediately recording that which he dreamt when asleep? By what process of consciousness could he distinguish between such composition and such reminiscence? Impressed as his mind was with his interesting dream, and habituated as he is (notwithstanding his accidental cessation from versifying) to the momentary production of verse, will he venture to assert that he did not *compose*, and that he did *remember*, the lines before us? Were they dreamt, or were they spontaneously poured forth instantly after the dream,

> Without stop or stay,
> Down the rocky way
> That leads, &c. &c.?

His 'psychological curiosity', as he terms it, depends in no slight degree on the establishment of the previous fact which we have mentioned: but the poem itself is below criticism. We would dismiss it with some portentous words of Sir Kenelm Digby, in his observations on Browne's *Religio Medici:* 'I have much ado to believe what he speaketh confidently; that he is more beholding to Morpheus for learned and rational as well as pleasing dreams, than to Mercury for smart and facetious conceptions'.

'The Pains of Sleep', a little poem at the end of the pamphlet, has some better verses in it than its predecessors. Without in the least approving the spirit, we admire the simplicity of the following lines:

[quotes ll. 1-32 (*PW*, i, 389-90)]

We close the slight publication before us with unmingled regret. The author of *Remorse* may perhaps be able to explain our feeling better than ourselves: but that so much superior genius should be corrupted and debased by so much execrable taste must be a subject of sincere lamentation to every lover of the arts, and to every friend of poetry.

THE STATESMAN'S MANUAL

1816

67. William Hazlitt, *Examiner*

8 September 1816, 571-3

This unsigned review, attributed to William Hazlitt (Howe, vii, 380), seems to have been based on a prospectus and appeared before *The Statesman's Manual* was published.

> Function
> Is smother'd in surmise, and nothing is
> But what is not.

> Or in Franciscan think to pass disguis'd.

This Lay-Sermon puts us in mind of Mahomet's coffin, which was suspended between heaven and earth, or of the flying island at Laputa, which hovered over the head of Gulliver. Or it is like the descent of the Cloven Tongues. The ingenious author, in a preface which is a master-piece in its kind, having neither beginning, middle, nor end, apologizes for having published a work, not a line of which is written, or ever likely to be written. He has, it seems, resorted to this expedient as the only way of appearing before the public in a manner worthy of himself and his genius, and descants on the several advantages he promises himself from this original mode of composition: that as long as he does not put pen to paper, the first sentence cannot contradict the second; that neither his reasonings nor his conclusions can be liable to objection, *in the abstract;* that omne ignotum pro magnifico est,[1] is an axiom laid down by some of the best and wisest men of antiquity; that hitherto his performance, in the opinion of his readers, has fallen short of the vastness of his designs, but that no one can find fault with what he does not write; that while he merely haunts the public imagination with obscure noises, or by announcing his spiritual appearance for the next week, and does not venture out *in propria*

[1] 'As unknown things are always magnified' (Tacitus, *Agricola*, 30).

248

persona with his shroud and surplice on, the Cock-lane Ghost of mid-day, he may escape in a whole skin without being handled by the mob, or uncased by the critics; and he considers it the safest way to keep up the importance of his oracular communications, by letting them remain a profound secret both to himself and the world.

In this instance, we think the writer's modesty has led him into a degree of unnecessary precaution. We see no sort of difference between his published and his unpublished compositions. It is just as impossible to get at the meaning of the one as the other. No man ever yet gave Mr. Coleridge 'a penny for his thoughts'. His are all maiden ideas; immaculate conceptions. He is the 'Secret Tattle' of the press. Each several work exists only in the imagination of the author, and is quite inaccessible to the understandings of his readers—'Yet virgin of Proserpina from Jove'. We can give just as good a guess at the design of this Lay-Sermon, which is not published, as of the *Friend*, the Preliminary Articles in the *Courier*,[1] the *Watchman*, the *Conciones ad Populum*, or any of the other courtly or popular publications of the same author. Let the experiment be tried, and if, on committing the manuscript to the press, the author is caught in the fact of a single intelligible passage, we will be answerable for Mr. Coleridge's loss of character. But we know the force of his genius too well. What is his *Friend* itself but an enormous Title-page; the longest and most tiresome Prospectus that ever was written; an endless Preface to an imaginary work; a Table of Contents that fills the whole volume; a huge bill of fare of all possible subjects, with not an idea to be had for love or money? One number consists of a grave-faced promise to perform something impossible in the next; and the next is taken up with a long-faced apology for not having done it. Through the whole of this work, Mr. Coleridge appears in the character of the Unborn Doctor; the very Barmecide of knowledge; the Prince of preparatory authors!

He never is—but always to be *wise*.

He is the Dog in the Manger of literature, an intellectual Mar-Plot, who will neither let any body else come to a conclusion, nor come to one himself.* This gentleman belongs to the class of Eclectic philoso-

---

[1] The newspaper to which Coleridge had been contributing.

* This work is so obscure, that it has been supposed to be written in cypher and that it is necessary to read it upwards and downwards, or backwards and forwards, as it happens, to make head or tail of it. The effect is monstrously like the qualms produced by the heaving of a ship becalmed at sea; the motion is so tedious, improgressive, and sickening.

phers; but whereas they professed to examine different systems, in order to select what was good in each; our perverse critic ransacks all past or present theories, to pick out their absurdities, and to abuse whatever is good in them. He takes his notions of religion from 'the sublime piety' of Jordano Bruno, and considers a belief in a God as a very subordinate question to the worship of the Three Persons of the Trinity. The thirty-nine articles and St. Athanasius's creed are, upon the same principle, much more fundamental parts of the Christian religion than the miracles or gospel of Christ. He makes the essence of devotion to consist in Atheism, the perfection of morality in a total disregard of consequences. He refers the great excellence of the British Constitution to the prerogative of the Crown, and conceives that the old French Constitution must have been admirably defended by the States-General from the abuses of arbitrary power. He highly approves of *ex-officio* informations and special juries, as the great bulwarks of the liberty of the press; taxes he holds to be a providential relief to the distresses of the people, and war to be a state of greater security than peace. He defines Jacobinism to be an abstract attachment to liberty, truth, and justice; and finding that this principle has been abused or carried to excess, he argues that Anti-Jacobinism, or the abstract principles of despotism, superstition, and oppression, are the safe, sure, and undeniable remedy for the former, and the only means of restoring liberty, truth, and justice in the world. Again, he places the seat of truth in *the heart*, of virtue in the *head*; damns a tragedy as shocking that draws tears from the audience, and pronounces a comedy to be inimitable, if no body laughs at it; labours to unsettle the plainest things by far-fetched sophistry, and makes up for the want of proof in matters of fact by the mechanical operations of the spirit. He judges of men as he does of things. He would persuade you that Sir Isaac Newton was a money-scrivener, Voltaire dull, Bonaparte a poor creature, and the late Mr. Howard a misanthrope; while he pays a willing homage to the Illustrious Obscure, of whom he always carries a list in his pocket. His creed is formed not from a distrust and disavowal of the exploded errors of other systems, but from a determined rejection of their acknowledged excellences. It is a transposition of reason and common sense. He adopts all the vulnerable points of belief as the triumphs of his fastidious philosophy, and holds a general retainer for the defence of all contradictions in terms and impossibilities in practice. He is at cross-purposes with himself as well as others, and discards his own caprices if ever he suspects there is the least ground for them. Doubt succeeds to doubt, cloud rolls over cloud, one paradox is driven out by another still greater, in endless succession. He is equally averse to the prejudices of the vulgar, the paradoxes of the learned, or the habitual convictions of his own mind. He moves in an unaccountable diagonal between truth and falsehood, sense and nonsense, sophistry and common-place, and only assents to any opinion when he knows that all the reasons are against it. A matter of fact is abhorrent to his nature: the very *air* of truth repels him. He is only saved from the extremities of absurdity by combining them all in his own person. Two things are indispensable to him—to set out from no premises, and to arrive at no conclusion. The consciousness of a single certainty would be an insupportable weight upon his mind. He slides out of a logical deduction by the help of metaphysics; and if the labyrinths of metaphysics did not afford him 'ample scope and verge enough', he would resort to necromancy and the cabbala. He only tolerates the science of astronomy for the sake of its connection with the dreams of judicial astrology, and escapes from the *Principia* of Newton to the jargon of Lily and Ashmole. All his notions are floating and unfixed, like what is feigned of the first forms of things flying about in search of bodies to attach themselves to; but *his* ideas seek to avoid all contact with solid substances. Innumerable evanescent thoughts dance before him, and dazzle his sight, like insects in the evening sun. Truth is to him a ceaseless round of contradictions: he lives in the belief of a perpetual lie, and in affecting to think what he pretends to say. His mind is in a constant estate of flux and reflux: he is like the Sea-horse in the Ocean; he is the Man in the Moon, the Wandering Jew. The reason of all this is, that Mr. Coleridge has great powers of thought and fancy, without will or sense. He is without a strong feeling of the existence of any thing out of himself; and he has neither purposes nor passions of his own to make him wish it to be. Mr. Shandy would have settled the question at once: 'You have little or no nose, Sir'. All that he does or thinks is involuntary; even his perversity and self-will are so. They are nothing but a necessity of yielding to the slightest motive. Everlasting inconsequentiality marks all that he does. All his impulses are loose, airy, devious, casual. The strongest of his purposes is lighter than the gossamer, 'that wantons in the idle summer-air': the brightest of his schemes a bubble blown by an infant's breath, that rises, glitters, bursts in the same instant:

> Or like the Borealis race,
> That's gone ere you can mark their place:

> Or like the snow falls in the river,
> A moment white, then gone for ever.

His mind has infinite activity, which only leads him into numberless, chimeras; and infinite resources, which not being under the guidance of his will, only distract and perplex him. His genius has angels' wings; but neither hands nor feet. He soars up to heaven, circles the empyrean, or dives to the centre of the earth, but he neither lays his hands upon the treasures of the one, nor can find a resting place for his feet in the other. He is no sooner borne to the utmost point of his ambition, than he is hurried away from it again by the same fantastic impulse or his own specific levity. He has all the faculties of the human mind but one, and yet without that one, the rest only impede and interfere with one another—'Like to a man on double business bound who both neglects'. He would have done better if he had known less. His imagination thus becomes metaphysical, his metaphysics fantastical, his wit heavy, his arguments light, his poetry prose, his prose poetry, his politics turned, but not to account. He belongs to all parties and is of service to none. He gives up his independence of mind, and yet does not acquire independence of fortune. He offends others without satisfying himself, and equally by his servility and singularity, shocks the prejudices of all about him. If he had had but common moral principle, that is, sincerity, he would have been a great man; nor hardly, as it is, appears to us:

> Less than arch-angel ruined, and the excess
> Of glory obscur'd.

We lose our patience when we think of the powers that he has wasted and compare them and their success with those for instance of such a fellow as the ———, all whose ideas, notions, apprehensions, comprehensions, feelings, virtues, genius, skill, are comprised in the two words which *Peachum* describes as necessary qualifications in his gang, 'To stand himself and bid others stand'!

When his six Irish friends, the six Irish gentlemen, Mr. Makins, Mr. Dunkely, Mr. Monaghan, Mr. Gollogher, Mr. Gallaspy, and Mr. O'Keeffe, after an absence of several years, discovered their old acquaintance John Buncle, sitting in a mixed company at Harrowgate Wells, they exclaimed with one accord—'There he is—making love to the finest woman in the universe!'[1] So we may say at a venture of Mr. Coleridge—'There he is, at this instant (no matter where)

[1] An episode in Thomas Amory's *The Life of John Buncle* (1756, 1766).

talking away among his gossips, as if he were at the Court of Semir-
amis, with the Sophi or Prestor John'. The place can never reach the
height of his argument. He should live in a world of enchantment,
that things might answer to his descriptions. His talk would suit the
miracle of the Conversion of Constantine, or Raphael's Assembly of
the Just. It is not short of that. His face would cut no figure there, but
his tongue would wag to some purpose. He is fit to take up the deep
pauses of conversation between Cardinals and Angels—his cue would
not be wanting in presence of the beatific vision. Let him talk on for
ever in this world and the next; and both worlds will be the better for
it. But let him not write or pretend to write, nonsense. Nobody is the
better for it. It was a fine thought in Mr. Wordsworth to represent
Cervantes at the day of judgment and conflagration of the world
carrying off the romance of Don Quixote under his arm. We hope that
Mr. Coleridge, on the same occasion, will leave the *Friend* to take its
chance and his *Lay Sermon* to get up into the Limbo of Vanity, how
it can.

68. William Hazlitt, *Examiner*

29 December 1816, 824-7

This unsigned review is attributed to William Hazlitt (Howe, vii,
381).

We have already given some account of this Sermon. We have only
to proceed to specimens in illustration of what we have said.

It sets out with the following sentence:

If our whole knowledge and information concerning the Bible had been confined to the one fact of its immediate derivation from God, we should still
presume that it contained rules and assistances for all conditions of men under
all circumstances; and therefore for communities no less than for individuals.

Now this is well said; 'and 'tis a kind of good deed to say well'. But why did not Mr. Coleridge keep on in the same strain to the end of the chapter, instead of himself disturbing the harmony and unanimity which he here very properly supposes to exist on this subject, or questioning the motives of its existence by such passages as the following:

Thank heaven! notwithstanding the attempts of Mr. Thomas Paine and his compeers, it is not so bad with us. *Open infidelity* has ceased to be a means even of gratifying vanity; for the leaders of the gang themselves turned apostates to Satan, as soon as the number of their proselytes became *so large*, that Atheism ceased to give distinction. Nay, it became a mark of original thinking to defend the Belief and the Ten Commandments; so the *strong* minds veered round, and religion came again into fashion.

Now we confess we do not find in this statement much to thank heaven for; if religion has only come into fashion again with the strong minds—(it will hardly be denied that Mr. Coleridge is one of the number)—as a better mode of gratifying their vanity than 'open infidelity'. Be this as it may, Mr. Coleridge has here given a true and masterly delineation of that large class of Proselytes or their teachers, who believe any thing or nothing, just as their vanity prompts them. All that we have said of modern apostates is poor and feeble to it. There is however one error in his statement, inasmuch as Mr. Thomas Paine never openly professed Atheism, whatever some of his compeers might do.

It is a pity that with all that fund of 'rules and assistances' which the Bible contains for our instruction and reproof, and which the author in this work proposes to recommend as the Statesman's Manual, or the best Guide to Political Skill and Foresight, in times like these, he has not brought forward a single illustration of his doctrine, nor referred to a single example in the Jewish history that bears at all, in the circumstances, or the inference, on our own, but one, and that one he has purposely omitted. Is this to be credited? Not without quoting the passage.

But do you require some one or more particular passage from the Bible that may at once illustrate and exemplify its application to the changes and fortunes of empires? Of the numerous chapters that relate to the Jewish tribes, their enemies and allies, before and after their division into two kingdoms, it would be more difficult to state a single one, from which some guiding light might *not* be struck. [Oh, very well, we shall have a few of them. The passage goes on.]

254

And in nothing is Scriptural history more strongly contrasted with the histories of highest note in the present age, than in its freedom from the hollowness of abstractions. [Mr. Coleridge's admiration of the inspired writers seems to be very much mixed with a dislike of Hume and Gibbon.] While the latter present a shadow-fight of Things and Quantities, the former gives us the history of Men, and balances the important influence of individual minds with the previous state of national morals and manners, in which, as constituting a specific susceptibility, it presents to us the true cause, both of the influence itself, and of the Weal or Woe that were its consequents. *How should it be otherwise?* The histories and political economy of the present and preceding century partake in the general contagion of its mechanic philosophy ['still harping on my daughter'], and are the *product* of an unenlivened generalizing understanding. In the Scriptures they are the living *educts* of the Imagination; of that reconciling and mediatory power, which incorporating the reason in Images of the Sense, and organizing (as it were) the flux of the Senses by the permanence and self-circling energies of the Reason, gives birth to a system of symbols, harmonious in themselves, and consubstantial with the truths, of which they are the *conductors*. These are the Wheels which Ezekiel beheld when the hand of the Lord was upon him, and he saw visions of God as he sat among the captives by the river of Chebar. *Whither soever the Spirit was to go, the wheels went, and thither was their spirit to go; for the spirit of the living creature was in the wheels also.* The truths and the symbols that represent them move in conjunction, and form the living chariot that bears up (for us) the throne of the Divine Humanity. *Hence by a derivative, indeed, but not a divided influence, and though in a secondary, yet in more than a metaphorical sense, the Sacred Book is worthily* entitled the Word of God.

So that after all the Bible is not the immediate word of God, except according to the German philosophy, and *in something between a literal and metaphorical sense.* Of all the cants that ever were canting in this canting world, this is the worst! The author goes on to add, that 'it is among the miseries of the present age that it recognises no medium between *literal* and *metaphorical*', and laments that 'the mechanical understanding, in the blindness of its self-complacency, confounds Symbols with Allegories'. This is certainly a sad mistake, which he labours very learnedly to set right, 'in a diagonal sidelong movement between truth and falsehood'. We assure the reader that the passages which we have given above are given in the order in which they are strung together in the Sermon; and so he goes on for several pages, concluding his career where the Allies have concluded theirs, with the doctrine of Divine Right; which he does not however establish quite so successfully with the pen, as they have done with the sword. 'Herein' (says this profound writer) 'the Bible differs from all the books of Greek philosophy, and in a two-fold manner. It doth not affirm a Divine Nature only, but a God; and not a God only, but the living God. *Hence in the Scriptures alone is the* Jus Divinum *or direct Relation of the State and its Magistracy to the Supreme Being, taught as a vital and indispensable part of* all moral and all political wisdom, *even as the Jewish alone was a true theocracy!'*

Now it does appear to us, that as the reason why the *Jus Divinum* was taught in the Jewish state was, that that alone was a true theocracy, this is so far from proving this doctrine to be a *part of all moral and all political wisdom*, that it proves just the contrary. This may perhaps be owing to our mechanical understanding. Wherever Mr. C. will shew us the theocracy, we will grant him the *Jus Divinum*. Where God really pulls down and sets up kings, the people need not do it. Under the true Jewish theocracy, the priests and prophets cashiered kings; but our lay-preacher will hardly take this office upon himself as a part of the *Jus Divinum*, without having any thing better to shew for it than his profound moral and political wisdom. Mr. Southey hints at something of the kind in verse, and we are not sure that Mr. Coleridge does not hint at it in prose. For after his tremendous career and interminable circumnavigation through the heaven of heavens, after being rapt in the wheels of Ezekiel, and sitting with the captives by the river of Chebar, he lights once more on English ground, and you think you have him.

But I refer to the demand. Were it my object to touch on the present state of public affairs in this kingdom, or on the prospective measures in agitation respecting our Sister Island, I would direct your most serious meditations to the latter period of the reign of Solomon, and the revolutions in the reign of Rehoboam his son. *But I tread on glowing embers.* I will turn to a subject on which all men of reflection are at length in agreement—the causes of the Revolution and fearful chast'sement of France.

Here Mr. Coleridge is off again on the wings of fear as he was before on those of fancy. This trifling can only be compared to that of the impertinent barber of Bagdad, who being sent for to shave the prince, spent the whole morning in preparing his razors, took the height of the sun with an astrolabe, sung the song of Zimri, and danced the dance of Zamtout, and concluded by declining to perform the operation at all, because the day was unfavourable to its success. As we are not so squeamish as Mr. Coleridge, and do not agree with him and all other men of reflection on the subject of the French Revolution, we shall turn back to the latter end of the reign of Solomon, and that of his successor Rehoboam, to find out the parallel to the present reign and regency which so particularly strikes and startles Mr. Coleridge. Here it is for the edification of the curious, from the First Book of Kings:

And the time that Solomon reigned over all Israel was forty years. And Solomon slept with his fathers, and was buried in the city of David his father: and Rehoboam his son reigned in his stead. And Rehoboam went to Shechem: *for all Israel were come to Shechem to make him king.*★ And Jeroboam and all the congregation of Israel came and spake unto Rehoboam, saying, Thy father (Solomon) made our yoke grievous; now, therefore, make thou the grievous service of thy father, and his heavy yoke which he put upon us, lighter, *and we will serve thee.* And he said unto them, Depart yet for three days, then come again to me. And the people departed. And King Rehoboam consulted with the old men that stood before Solomon his father while he yet lived, and said, How do ye advise, that I may answer this people? And they spake unto him, saying, *If thou wilt be a servant unto this people* this day, and wilt serve them, and answer them, and speak good words unto them, *then* they will be thy servants for ever. But he forsook the counsel of the old men, which they had given him, *and consulted with the young men that were grown up with him, and which stood before him:* And he said unto them, What counsel give ye, that we may answer this people, who have spoken to me, saying, Make the yoke which thy father did put upon us lighter? And the young men that were grown up with him spake unto him, saying, Thus shalt thou speak unto this people that spake unto thee, saying, Thy father made our yoke heavy, but make thou it lighter unto us; thus shalt thou say unto them, *My little finger shall be thicker than my father's loins. And now, whereas my father did lade you with a heavy yoke, I will add to your yoke: my father hath chastised you with whips: but I will chastise you with scorpions.* So Jeroboam and all the people came to Rehoboam the third day, as the king had appointed, saying, come to me again the third day. And the king *answered the people roughly,* and forsook the old men's counsel that they gave him: And spake to them after the counsel of the young men, saying, *My father made your yoke heavy, and I will add to your yoke; my father also chastised you with whips, but I will chastise you with scorpions.* Wherefore the king hearkened not unto the people; *for the cause was from the Lord,* that he might perform his saying which

★ Does this verse come under Mr. C.'s version of *Jus Divinum?* Hypocrisy does not relate to the degree of success with which a man imposes on himself, but to the motives which make him attempt it. The greatest hypocrites are those who can impose most successfully on themselves; that is, conceal from their own minds their sinister motives for judging, or suppress their real, *under*-opinions. We think it a piece of hypocrisy for a man to insinuate, after reading this part of the Bible, that that Manual of the Statesman is favourable to the doctrine of Divine right.

the Lord spake by Ahijah, the Shilonite, unto Jeroboam the son of Nebat. [We here see pretty plainly how the principle of 'a true theocracy' qualified the doctrine of *Jus Divinum* among the Jews; but let us mark the sequel.] *So when all Israel saw that the King harkened not unto them, the people answered the king, saying, What portion have we in David: neither have we inheritance in the son of Jesse: to your tents, O Israel: now see to thine own house David. So Israel departed unto their tents.* Then king Rehoboam sent Adoram, who was over the tribute; and all Israel stoned him with stones that he died; therefore king Rehoboam made speed to get him up to his chariot to flee to Jerusalem. So Israel rebelled against the house of David unto this day. And it came to pass when all Israel heard that Jeroboam was come again, that they sent and called him unto the congregation and made him king over all Israel.

Here is the doctrine and practice of divine right with a vengeance. We do not wonder Mr. Coleridge was shy of instances from his *Statesman's Manual*, if the rest are like this. He does not say (neither shall we, for we are not salamanders any more than he, *to tread on glowing embers*) whether he approves of the conduct of all Israel in this case, or of the *grand, magnificent, and gracious* answer of the son of Solomon; but this we will say, that his bringing or alluding to a passage like this immediately after his *innuendo* (addressed to the higher classes) that the doctrine of divine right is contained *par excellence* in the Scriptures alone, is, we should suppose, an instance of a power of voluntary self-delusion, and of a delight in exercising it on the most ticklish topics, greater than ever was or ever will be possessed by any other individual that ever did or ever will live upon the face of the earth. 'Imposture, organized into a comprehensive and self-consistent whole, forms a world of its own, in which inversion becomes the order of nature'. Compared with such powers of inconceivable mental refinement, hypocrisy is a great baby, a shallow dolt, a gross dunce, a clumsy devil!

Among other passages unrivalled in style and matter by any other author, take the following:

When I named this Essay a Sermon, I sought to prepare the inquirers after it for the absence of all the usual softenings *suggested by worldly prudence*, of all compromise between truth and courtesy. But not even as a Sermon would I have addressed the present Discourse to a promiscuous audience: and for this reason I likewise announced it in the title-page, as exclusively *ad clerum;* i.e. (in the old and wide sense of the word*) to men of *clerkly* acquirements, of whatever profession. [All that we know is, that there is no such title-page to our

* That is, in a sense not used and without any intelligible meaning.

copy.] I would that the greater part of our publications could be thus *directed*, each to its appropriate class of readers. But this cannot be! For among other odd burs and kecksies, the misgrowth of our luxuriant activity, we have a READING PUBLIC, as strange *a phrase*, methinks, as ever forced a splenetic smile on the staid countenance of meditation; and yet *no fiction!* For our readers have, in good truth, multiplied exceedingly, and have waxed proud. It would require the *intrepid accuracy* of a Colquhoun—[Intrepid and accurate applied to a Colquhoun! It seems that whenever an objection in matter of fact occurs to our author's mind, he instinctively applies the flattering unction of words to smooth it over to his conscience, as you apply a salve to a sore]—to venture at the precise number of that vast company only, whose heads and hearts are dieted at the two public *ordinaries* of literature, the circulating libraries and the periodical press. But what is the result? Does the *inward man* thrive on this regimen? Alas! if the average health of the consumers may be judged of by the articles of largest consumption—[Is not this a side-blow at the *Times* and *Courier?*]—if the secretions may be conjectured from the ingredients of the dishes that are found best suited to their palates; from all that I have seen, either of the banquets or the guests, I shall utter my *profaccia*—['Oh thou particular fellow!'] —with a desponding sigh. From a popular philosophy, and philosophic populace, good sense deliver us!

Why so, any more than from a popular religion or a religious populace, on Mr. Coleridge's own principle, 'Reason and religion are their own evidence'? We should suspect that our unread author, the Secret Tattle of the Press, is thus fastidious, because he keeps an ordinary himself which is not frequented. He professes to be select: but we all know the secret of 'seminaries for a limited number of pupils'. Mr. Coleridge addresses his lay-sermon to 'the higher classes', in his printed title-page: in that which is not printed he has announced it to be *directed ad clerum*, which might imply the clergy, but no: he issues another EXTENT for the benefit of the Reading Public, and says he means by the annunciation *ad clerum*, all persons of clerkly acquirements, that is, who can read and write. What wretched stuff is all this! We well remember a friend of his and ours saying, many years ago, on seeing a little shabby volume of Thomson's *Seasons* lying in the window of a solitary ale-house, at the top of a rock hanging over the Bristol Channel, '*That is true fame!*' If he were to write fifty Lay-Sermons, he could not answer the inference from this one sentence, which is, that there are books that make their way wherever there are readers and that there ought every where to be readers for such books!

To the words READING PUBLIC, in the above passage, is the following note, which in wit and humour does not fall short of Mr. Southey's Tract on the Madras System[1]:

Some participle passive in the diminutive form, *eruditorum natio* for instance, might seem at first sight a fuller and more exact designation: but the superior force and humor of the former become evident whenever the phrase occurs, as a step or stair in the climax of irony.... Among the Revolutions worthy of notice, the change in the introductory sentences and prefatory matter in serious books is not the least striking. The same gross flattery, which disgusts us in the dedications to individuals, in the elder writers, is now transferred to the nation at large, or the READING PUBLIC; while the Jeremiads of our old moralists, and their angry denunciations against the ignorance, immorality, and irreligion of the *people* appear (*mutatis mutandis*, and with an appeal to the worst passions, envy, discontent, scorn, vindictiveness,* &c.) in the shape of bitter libels on Ministers, Parliament, the Clergy; in short, on the State and Church, and all persons employed in them. Likewise, I would point out to the reader's attention the marvellous predominance at present of the words, Idea and Demonstration. Every talker now-a-days has an *Idea;* aye, and he will demonstrate it too! A few days ago, I heard one of the READING PUBLIC, a thinking and independent smuggler, euphonise the latter word with much significance, in a tirade against the planners of the late African Expedition: '*As to Algiers, any man that has half an Idea in his skull must know, that it has been long ago dey-monstered, I should say, dey monstrified*', &c. But the phrase, which occasioned this note, brings to my mind the mistake of a lethargic Dutch traveller, who, returning highly gratified from a showman's caravan, which he had been tempted to enter by the words LEARNED PIG, gilt on the pannels, met another caravan of a similar shape, with the READING FLY on it, in letters of the same size and splendour. 'Why, dis is voonders above voonders', exclaims the Dutchman, takes his seat as first comer, and soon fatigued by waiting, and by the very hush and intensity of his expectation, gives way to his constitutional somnolence, from which he is roused by the supposed showman at Hounslow, with a '*In what name, Sir, was your place taken? are you booked all the way for Reading?*' Now a Reading Public is (to my mind) more marvellous still, and in the third tier of 'Voonders above voonders'.

A public that could read such stuff as this with any patience would indeed be so. We do not understand how, with this systematic antipathy to the Reading Public, it is consistent in Mr. Coleridge to declare of 'Dr. Bell's original and unsophisticated plan', that he 'himself regards it as an especial gift of Providence to the human race, as an incomparable machine, a vast moral steam-engine'. Learning is an old university mistress, that he is not willing to part with, except for the

[1] *The Origin, Nature, and Object, of the New System of Education* (1812).

* If these are the worst passions, there is plenty of them in this Lay-Sermon.

use of the Church of England; and he is sadly afraid she should be debauched by the 'liberal ideas' of Joseph Lancaster![1] As to his aversion to the prostitution of the word *Idea* to common uses and in common minds, it is no wonder, from the very exalted *idea* which he has given us of this term.

'What other measures I had in contemplation it has been my endeavour to explain elsewhere. . . . O what treasures of practical wisdom would be once more brought into open day by the solution of this problem', to wit, 'a thorough re-casting of the moulds in which the minds of our gentry, the characters of our future land-owners, magistrates, and senators, are to receive their shape and fashion. Suffice it for the present to hint the master-thought. *The first man, on whom the light of an* IDEA *dawned, did in that same moment receive the spirit and the credentials of a Lawgiver:* and as long as man shall exist, so long will the possession of that antecedent knowledge which exists only in the power of an *idea*, be the one lawful qualification for all dominion in the world of the senses'. Now we do think this a shorter cut towards the undermining of the rotten boroughs, and ousting the present Ministry, than any we have yet heard of. One of the most extraordinary ideas in this work is where the Author proves the doctrine of free will from the existence of property; and again, where he recommends the study of the Scriptures, from the example of Heraclitus and Horace. To conclude this most inconclusive piece of work, which sums up the distant hopes and doubtful expectations of the writer's mind, in the following rare rhapsody.

Oh what a mine of undiscovered treasures, what a new world of power and truth would the Bible promise to our future meditation, if *in some gracious moment one solitary text of all its inspired contents* should but dawn upon us in the pure untroubled brightness of an IDEA, that most glorious birth of the godlike within us, which even as the light, its material symbol, reflects itself from a thousand surfaces, and flies homeward to its parent mind, enriched with a thousand forms, itself above form, and still remaining in its own simplicity and identity! O for a flash of that same light, in which the first position of geometric science that ever loosed itself from the generalizations of a groping and insecure experience, did for the first time reveal itself to a human intellect in all its evidence and in all its fruitfulness, Transparence without Vacuum, and Plenitude without Opacity! O! that a single gleam of our own inward experience would make comprehensible to us the rapturous EUREKA, and the grateful

---

[1] Coleridge's support of Andrew Bell's educational theory and opposition to Joseph Lancaster's had been expressed publicly as early as 1808.

hecatomb of the philosopher of Samos! or that vision which, from the contemplation of an arithmetical harmony, rose to the eye of Kepler, presenting the planetary world, and all their orbits in the divine order of their ranks and distances; or which, in the falling of an apple, revealed to the ethereal intuition of our own Newton the constructive principle of the material universe. The promises which I have ventured to hold forth concerning the hidden treasures of the Law and the Prophets will neither be condemned as paradox, or as exaggeration, by the mind that has learnt to understand the possibility that the reduction of the sands of the sea to number should be found a less stupendous problem by Archimedes than the simple conception of the Parmenidean ONE. What, however, is achievable by the human understanding without this light may be comprised in the epithet κενοσπουδοι; and *a melancholy comment on that phrase would the history of the human Cabinets and Legislatures for the last thirty years furnish!* The excellent Barrow, the last of the disciples of Plato and Archimedes among our modern mathematicians, shall give the description and state the value; and, in his words, I shall conclude:

'*Aliud agere, to be impertinently busy, doing that which conduceth to no good purpose, is, in some respect, worse than to do nothing. Of such industry we may understand that of the Preacher, "The labour of the foolish wearieth every one of them".*'

A better conclusion could not be found for this Lay-Sermon: for greater nonsense the author could not write, even though he were inspired expressly for the purpose.

69. William Hazlitt, *Edinburgh Review*

December 1816, xxvii, 444-59

Unsigned review attributed to William Hazlitt (Howe, ix, 424).

'The privilege' (says a certain author) 'of talking, and even publishing nonsense, is necessary in a free state; but the more sparingly we make use of it, the better'. Mr. Coleridge has here availed himself of this privilege—but not sparingly. On the contrary, he has given full scope to his genius, and laid himself out in absurdity. In this his first Lay-sermon (for two others are to follow at graceful distances) we meet with an abundance of 'fancies and good-nights', odd ends of verse, and sayings of philosophers; with the ricketty contents of his commonplace book, piled up and balancing one another in helpless confusion; but with not one word to the purpose, or on the subject. An attentive perusal of this Discourse is like watching the sails of a windmill: his thoughts and theories rise and disappear in the same manner. Clouds do not shift their places more rapidly, dreams do not drive one another out more unaccountably, than Mr. Coleridge's reasonings try in vain to 'chase his fancy's rolling speed'. His intended conclusions have always the start of his premises—and they keep it: while he himself plods anxiously between the two, something like a man travelling a long, tiresome road, between two stage coaches, the one of which is gone out of sight before, and the other never comes up with him; for Mr. Coleridge himself takes care of this; and if he finds himself in danger of being overtaken, and carried to his journey's end in a common vehicle, he immediately steps aside into some friendly covert, with the Metaphysical Muse, to prevent so unwelcome a catastrophe. In his weary quest of truth, he reminds us of the mendicant pilgrims that travellers meet in the Desert, with their faces always turned towards Mecca, but who contrive never to reach the shrine of the Prophet: and he treats his opinions, and his reasons for them, as lawyers do their clients, and will never suffer them to come together lest they should join issue, and so put an end to his business. It is impossible, in short, we find, to describe this strange rhapsody, without falling a little into the style of it; and, to do it complete justice, we must use its very words. '*Implicitè*, it is without the COPULA—it wants the possibility—of every position, to which there exists any correspondence in reality'.

Our Lay-preacher, in order to qualify himself for the office of a guide to the blind, has not, of course, once thought of looking about for matters of fact, but very wisely draws a metaphysical bandage over his eyes, sits quietly down where he was, takes his nap, and talks in his sleep—but we really cannot say very wisely. He winks and mutters all unintelligible, and all impertinent things. Instead of inquiring into the distresses of the manufacturing or agricultural districts, he ascends to the orbits of the fixed stars, or else enters into the statistics of the garden plot under his window, and, like Falstaff, 'babbles of green fields': instead of the balance of the three estates, King, Lords and

Commons, he gives us a theory of the balance of the powers of the human mind, the Will, the Reason, and—the Understanding: instead of referring to the tythes or taxes, he quotes the Talmud; and illustrates the whole question of peace and war, by observing, that 'the ideal republic of Plato' was, if he judges rightly, to 'the history of the town of "Man-Soul" what Plato was to John Bunyan': a most safe and politic conclusion!

Mr. Coleridge is not one of those whom he calls 'alarmists by trade', but rather, we imagine, what Spenser calls 'a gentle Husher, Vanity by name'. If he does not excite apprehension, by pointing out danger and difficulties where they do not exist, neither does he inspire confidence, by pointing out the means to prevent them where they do. We never indeed saw a work that could do less good or less harm; for it relates to no one object, that any one person can have in view. It tends to produce a complete *interregnum* of all opinions; an *abeyance* of the understanding; a suspension both of theory and practice; and is indeed a collection of doubts and moot-points—all hindrances and no helps. An uncharitable critic might insinuate, that there was more quackery than folly in all this; and it is certain, that our learned author talks as magnificently of his *nostrums*, as any advertizing imposter of them all—and professes to be in possession of all sorts of morals, religions, and political panaceas, which he keeps to himself, and expects you to pay for the secret. He is always promising great things, in short, and performs nothing. The vagaries, whimsies, and pregnant throes of Joanna Southcote,[1] were sober and rational, compared with Mr. Coleridge's qualms and crude conceptions, and promised deliverance in this Lay-Sermon. The true secret of all this, we suspect, is, that our author has not made up his own mind on any of the subjects of which he professes to treat and on which he warns his readers against coming to any conclusion, without his especial assistance; by means of which, they may at last attain to 'that imperative and oracular form of the understanding', of which he speaks as 'the form of reason itself in all things purely rational and moral'. In this state of voluntary self-delusion, into which he has thrown himself, he mistakes hallucinations for truths, though he still has his misgivings, and dares not communicate them to others, except in distant hints, lest the spell should be broken, and the vision disappear. Plain sense and plain speaking would put an end to those 'thick-coming fancies', that lull him to repose. It is in this

[1] Joanna Southcote (1750-1814), religious enthusiast, who at an advanced age mistakenly supposed that she was about to give birth to a 'Shiloh'.

sort of waking dream, this giddy maze of opinions, started, and left, and resumed—this momentary pursuit of truths, as if they were butter-flies—that Mr. Coleridge's pleasure, and, we believe, his chief faculty, lies. He has a thousand shadowy thoughts that rise before him, and hold each a glass, in which they point to others yet more dim and distant. He has a thousand self-created fancies that glitter and burst like bubbles. In the world of shadows, in the succession of bubbles, there is no prefer-ence but of the most shadowy, no attachment but to the shortest-lived. Mr. Coleridge accordingly has no principle but that of being governed entirely by his own caprice, indolence, or vanity; no opinion that any body else holds, or even he himself, for two moments together. His fancy is stronger than his reason; his apprehension greater than his comprehension. He perceives every thing, but the relations of things to one another. His ideas are as finely shaded as the rainbow of the moon upon the clouds, as evanescent, and as soon dissolved. The subtlety of his tact, the quickness and airiness of his invention, make him perceive every possible shade and view of a subject in its turn; but this readiness of lending his imagination to every thing, prevents him from weighing the force of any one, or retaining the most impor-tant in mind. It destroys the balance and *momentum* of his feelings; makes him unable to follow up a principle into its consequences, or maintain a truth in spite of opposition: it takes away all *will* to adhere to what is right, and reject what is wrong; and, with the will, the power to do it, at the expense of any thing difficult in thought, or irksome in feeling. The consequence is, that the general character of Mr. Coler-idge's intellect, is a restless and yet listless dissipation, that yields to every impulse, and is stopped by every obstacle; an indifference to the greatest trifles, or the most important truths; or rather, a preference of the vapid to the solid, of the possible to the actual, of the impossible to both; of theory to practice, of contradiction to reason, and of absur-dity to common sense. Perhaps it is well that he is so impracticable as he is: for whenever, by any accident, he comes to practice, he is dangerous in the extreme. Though his opinions are neutralized in the extreme levity of his understanding, we are sometimes tempted to suspect that they may be subjected to a more ignoble bias; for though he does not ply his oars very strenuously in following the tide of corruption, or set up his sails to catch the tainted breeze of popularity, he suffers his boat to drift along with the stream. We do not pretend to understand the philosophical principles of that anomalous produc-tion, *The Friend*; but we remember that the practical measures which he there attempted to defend, were the expedition to Copenhagen, the expedition to Walcheren, and the assassination of Buonaparte, which, at the time Mr. Coleridge was getting that work into circulation, was a common topic of conversation, and a sort of *forlorn hope* in certain circles. A man who exercises an unlimited philosophical scepticism on questions of abstract right or wrong, may be of service to the progress of truth; but a writer, who exercises this privilege, with a regular leaning to the side of power, is a very questionable sort of person. There is not much of this kind in the present Essay. It has no leaning any way. All the sentiments advanced in it are like the swan's down feather:

> That stands upon the swell at full of tide,
> And neither way inclines.

We have here given a pretty strong opinion on the merits of this performance: and we proceed to make it good by extracts from the work itself; and it is just as well to begin with the beginning.

If our whole knowledge and information concerning the Bible had been confined to the one fact, of its immediate derivation from God, we should still presume that it contained rules and assistances for all conditions of men, under all circumstances; and therefore for communities no less than for individuals. The contents of every work must correspond to the character and designs of the work-master; and the inference in the present case is too obvious to be overlooked, too plain to be resisted. It requires, indeed, all the might of superstitition, to conceal from a man of common understanding, the further truth, that the interment of such a treasure, in a dead language, must needs be contrary to the intentions of the gracious Donor. Apostasy itself dared not question the *premise;* and, that the practical *consequence* did not follow, is conceivable only under a complete *system* of delusion, which, from the cradle to the death-bed, ceases to to overawe the will by obscure fears, while it preoccupies the senses by vivid imagery and ritual pantomime. But to such a scheme, all forms of sophistry are native. The very excellence of the Giver has been made a reason for withholding the gift; nay, the transcendent value of the gift itself assigned as the motive of its detention. We may be shocked at the presumption, but need not be surprised at the fact, that a jealous priesthood should have ventured to represent the applicability of the Bible to all the wants and occasions of men, as a wax-like pliability to all their fancies and prepossessions. Faithful guardians of Holy Writ! &c.

And after a great deal to the same effect, he proceeds:

The humblest and least educated of our countrymen must have wilfully neglected the inestimable privileges secured to all alike, if he has not himself found, if he has not from his own personal experience discovered, the sufficiency of the Scriptures in all knowledge requisite for a right performance of his duty as a man and a Christian. Of the labouring classes, who in all countries form the great majority of the inhabitants, more than this is not demanded, more than this is not perhaps generally desirable.... They are not sought for in public counsel, nor need they be found where politic sentences are spoken. It is enough if every one is wise in the working of his own craft: so best will they maintain the state of the world.

Now, if this is all that is necessary or desirable for the people to know, we can see little difference between the doctrine of the Lay Sermon, and 'that complete system of papal imposture, which inters the Scriptures in a dead language, and commands its vassals to take for granted what it forbids them to ascertain'. If a candidate is to start for infallibility, we, for our parts, shall give our casting vote for the successor of St. Peter, rather than for Mr. Coleridge. The Bible, we believe, when rightly understood, contains no set of rules for making the labouring classes mere 'workers in brass or in stone', 'hewers of wood or drawers of water', each wise in his own craft. Yet it is by confining their inquiries and their knowledge to such vocations, and excluding them from any share in politics, philosophy, and theology, 'that the state of the world is best upheld'. Such is the exposition of our Lay-Divine. Such is his application of it. Why then does he blame the Catholics for acting on this principle, for deducing the *practical consequence* from the acknowledged *premise*? Great as is our contempt for the delusions of the Romish Church, it would have been still greater, if they had opened the sacred volume to the poor and illiterate; had told them that it contained the most useful knowledge for all conditions and for all circumstances of life, public and private; and had then instantly shut the book in their faces, saying, it was enough for them to be wise in their own calling, and to leave the study and interpretation of the Scriptures to their betters, to Mr. Coleridge and his imaginary audience. The Catholic Church might have an excuse for what it did in the supposed difficulty of understanding the Scriptures, their doubts and ambiguities, and 'wax-like pliability to all occasions and humours'. But Mr. Coleridge has no excuse; for he says, they are plain to all capacities, high and low together. 'The road of salvation', he says, 'is for us a high road, and the wayfarer, though simple, need not err therein'. And he accordingly proceeds to draw up a provisional bill of indictment, and to utter his doubtful denunciations against us as a nation, for the supposed neglect of the inestimable privileges, *secured alike to all*, and for the lights held out to all for 'maintaining the state' of their country in the precepts and examples of Holy Writ; when, all of a sudden, his eye encountering that brilliant auditory which his pen had conjured up, the Preacher finds out, that the only use of the study of the Scriptures for the rest of the people, is to learn that they have no occasion to study them at all, 'so best shall they maintain the state of the world'. If Mr. Coleridge has no meaning in what he writes, he had better not write at all: if he has any meaning, he contradicts himself. The truth is, however, as it appears to us, that the whole of this Sermon is written to sanction the principle of Catholic dictation, and to reprobate that diffusion of free inquiry—that difference of private, and ascendancy of public opinion, which has been the necessary consequence, and the great benefit of the Reformation. That Mr. Coleridge himself is as squeamish in guarding *his* Statesman's Manual from profanation as any Popish priest can be in keeping the Scriptures from the knowledge of the Laity, will be seen from the following delicate *morceau*. . . .

When I named this Essay a Sermon, I sought to prepare the inquirers after it *for the absence of all the usual softenings suggested by worldly prudence, of all compromise between truth and courtesy.* But not even as a Sermon would I have addressed the present Discourse *to a promiscuous audience;* and for this reason I likewise announced it in the title-page, as exclusively *ad clerum, i.e.* (in the old and wide sense of the word) to men of *clerkly* acquirements, of whatever profession. I would that the greater part of our publications could be thus *directed,* each to its appropriate class of readers.* But this cannot be! For among other odd burrs and kecksies, the misgrowth of our luxuriant activity, we have now a READING PUBLIC—as strange a phrase, methinks, as ever forced a splenetic smile on the staid countenance of Meditation; and yet no fiction! For our readers have, in good truth, multiplied exceedingly, and have waxed proud. It would require the intrepid accuracy of a Colquhoun to venture at the precise number of that vast company only, whose heads and hearts are dieted at the two public *ordinaries* of Literature, the circulating libraries and the periodical press. But what is the result? Does the inward man thrive on this regimen? Alas! if the average health of the consumers may be judged of by the articles of largest consumption; if the secretions may be conjectured from the ingredients of the dishes that are found best suited to their palates; from all that I have seen, either of the banquet or the guests, I shall utter my *Profaccia* with a desponding sigh. From a popular philosphy and a philosophic populace, good sense deliver us!

If it were possible to be serious after a passage like this, we might

* Do not publications generally find their way there, without a *direction?*   R.[1]
[1] The initial probably indicates an editorial insertion.

ask, what is to hinder a convert of 'the church of superstition' from exclaiming in like manner, 'From a popular theology, and a theological populace, Good Lord deliver us!' Mr. Coleridge does not say—will he say—that as many sects and differences of opinion in religion have not risen up, in consequence of the Reformation, as in philosophy or politics, from 'the misgrowth of our luxuriant activity'? Can any one express a greater disgust (approaching to *nausea*) at every sect and separation from the Church of England, which he sometimes, by an hyperbole of affectation, affects to call the Catholic Church? There is something, then, worse than 'luxuriant activity'—the palsy of death; something worse than occasional error—systematic imposture; something worse than the collision of differing opinions—the suppression of all freedom of thought and independent love of truth, under the torpid sway of an insolent and selfish domination, which makes use of truth and falsehood equally as tools of its own aggrandisement and the debasement of its vassals, and always must do so, without the exercise of public opinion, and freedom of conscience, as its control and counter-check. For what have we been labouring for the last three hundred years? Would Mr. Coleridge, with impious hand, turn the world 'twice ten degrees askance', and carry us back to the dark ages? Would he punish the *reading public* for their bad taste in reading periodical publications which he does not like, by suppressing the freedom of the press altogether, or destroying the art of printing? He does not know what he means himself. Perhaps we can tell him. He, or at least those whom he writes to please, and who look 'with jealous leer malign' at modern advantages and modern pretensions, would give us back all the abuses of former times, without any of their advantages; and impose upon us, by force or fraud, a complete system of superstition without faith, of despotism without loyalty, of error without enthusiasm, and all the evils, without any of the blessings, of ignorance. The senseless jargon which Mr. Coleridge has let fall on this subject, is the more extraordinary, inasmuch as he declares, in an early part of his Sermon, that 'Religion and Reason are their own evidence'; a position which appears to us 'fraught with *potential infidelity*' quite as much as Unitarianism, or the detestable plan for teaching reading and writing, and a knowledge of the Scriptures, without the creed or the catechism of the Church of England. The passage in which this sweeping clause is introduced *en passant*, is worth quoting, both as it is very nonsensical in itself, and as it is one of the least nonsensical in the present pamphlet.

In the infancy of the world, signs and wonders were requisite, in order to startle and break down that superstition, idolatrous in itself, and the source of all other idolatry, which tempts the natural man to seek the true cause and origin of public calamities in outward circumstances, persons and incidents: in agents, therefore, that were themselves but surges of the same tide, passive conductors of the one invisible influence, under which the total host of billows, in the whole line of successive impulse, swell and roll shoreward; there finally, each in its turn, to strike, roar, and be dissipated.

But with each miracle worked there was a truth revealed, which thenceforward was to act as its substitute: And if we think the Bible less applicable to us on account of the miracles, we degrade ourselves into mere slaves of sense and fancy; which are, indeed, the appointed medium between earth and heaven, but for that very cause stand in a desirable relation to spiritual truth then only, when, as a mere and passive medium, they yield a free passage to its light. It was only to overthrow the usurpation exercised in and through the senses, that the senses were miraculously appealed to. Reason and Religion are their own evidence. The natural sun is, in this respect, a symbol of the spiritual. Ere he is fully arisen, and while his glories are still under veil, he calls up the breeze to chase away the usurping vapours of the night-season, and thus converts the air itself into the minister of its own purification: not surely in proof or elucidation of the light from heaven, but to prevent its interception.

Here is a very pretty Della Cruscan image: and we really think it a pity, that Mr. Coleridge ever quitted that school of poetry to grapple with the simplicity of nature, or to lose himself in the depths of philosophy. His illustration is pretty, but false. He treats the miracles recorded in the Scriptures, with more than heretical boldness, as mere appeals to 'sense and fancy', or to 'the natural man', to counteract the impressions of sense and fancy. But, for the light of Heaven to have been like the light of day in this respect, the Sun ought to have called up other vapours opposite, as mirrors or pageants to reflect its light, dimmed by the intermediate vapours, instead of chasing the last away. We criticize the simile, because we are sure higher authority will object to the doctrine. We might challenge Mr. Coleridge to point out a single writer, Catholic, Protestant or Sectarian, whose principles are not regarded as *potential infidelity* by the rest, that does not consider the miraculous attestation of certain revealed doctrines as proofs of their truth, independently of their internal evidence. They are a distinct and additional authority. Reason and Religion are no more the same in this respect, than ocular demonstration and oral testimony are the same. Neither are they opposed to one another, any more. We believe in credible witnesses. We believe in the word of God, when we have reason to suppose, that we hear his voice in the thunder of his power: but we cannot, consistently with the principles of reason or of sound faith, suppose him to utter what is contrary to reason, though it may be different from it. Revelation utters a voice in the silence of reason, but does not contradict it: it throws a light on objects too distant for the unassisted eye to behold. But it does not pervert our natural organs of vision, with respect to objects within their reach. Reason and religion are therefore consistent, but not the same, nor equally self-evident. All this, we think, is clear and plain. But Mr. Coleridge likes to darken and perplex every question of which he treats. So, in the passage above quoted, he affirms that Religion is its own evidence, to confound one class of readers; and he afterwards asserts that Reason is founded on faith, to astonish another. He proceeds indeed by the *differential method* in all questions; and his chief care, in which he is tolerably successful, is *not* to agree with any set of men or opinions. We pass over his Jeremiad on the French Revolution, his discovery that the state of public opinion has a considerable influence on the state of public affairs, particularly in turbulent times, his apology for imitating St. Paul by quoting Shakespeare, and many others: for if we were to collect all the riches of absurdity in this Discourse, we should never have done. But there is one passage, upon which he has plainly taken so much pains, that we *must* give it.

A calm and detailed examination of the facts, justifies me to my own mind, in hazarding the bold assertion, that the fearful blunders of the late dread Revolution, and all the calamitous mistakes of its opponents, from its commencement even to the era of loftier principles and wiser measures (an era, that began with, and ought to be named from, the war of the Spanish and Portuguese insurgents), every failure, with all its gloomy results, may be unanswerably deduced, from the neglect of some maxim or other that had been established by clear reasoning and plain facts, in the writings of Thucydides, Tacitus, Machiavel, Bacon, or Harrington. These are red-letter names, even in the almanacks of wordly wisdom: and yet I dare challenge all the critical benches of infidelity, to point out any one important truth, any one efficient practical direction or warning, which did not preexist, and for the most part in a sounder, more intelligible, and more comprehensive form IN THE BIBLE.

In addition to this, the Hebrew legislator, and the other inspired poets, prophets, historians and moralists, of the Jewish church, have two immense advantages in their favour. First, their particular rules and prescripts flow directly and visibly from universal principles, as from a fountain: they flow from principles and ideas that are not so properly said to be confirmed by reason, as to be reason itself! Principles, in act and procession, disjoined from which, and from the emotions that inevitably accompany the actual intuition of their truth, the widest maxims of prudence are like arms without hearts, muscles without nerves. Secondly, from the very nature of these principles, as taught in the Bible, they are understood, in exact proportion as they are believed and felt. The regulator is never separated from the main spring. For the words of the Apostle are literally and philosophically true: *We* (that is the human race) *live by faith.* Whatever we do or know, that in kind is different from the brute creation, has its origin in a determination of the reason to have faith and trust in itself. This, its first act of faith, is scarcely less than identical with its own being. *Implicitè*, it is the copula—it contains the *possibility*—of every position, to which there exists any correspondence in reality. It is itself, therefore, the realizing principle, the spiritual substratum of the whole complex body of truths. This primal act of faith is enunciated in the word, God: a faith not derived from experience, but its ground and source; and without which, the fleeting *chaos of facts* would no more form experience, than the dust of the grave can of itself make a living man. The imperative and oracular form of the inspired Scripture, is *the form of reason itself,* in all things purely rational and moral.

If it be the word of Divine Wisdom, we might anticipate, that it would in all things be distinguished from other books, as the Supreme Reason, whose knowledge is creative, and antecedent to the things known, is distinguished from the understanding, or creaturely mind of the individual, the acts of which are posterior to the things it records and arranges. Man alone was created in the image of God: a position groundless and inexplicable, if *the reason* in man do not differ from *the understanding.* For this the inferior animals (many at least) possess *in degree:* and assuredly the divine image or idea is not a thing of degrees, &c. &c. &c.

There is one short passage, just afterwards, in which the author makes an easy transition from cant to calumny: and, with equal credit and safety to himself, insults and traduces the dead. 'One confirmation of the latter assertion you may find in the history of our country, written by the same Scotch Philosopher, who devoted his life to the undermining of the Christian Religion; and *expended his last breath in a blasphemous regret, that he had not survived it!'* This last assertion is a gratuitous poetical fabrication, as mean as it is malignant. With respect to Mr. Hume's History, here spoken of with ignorant petulance, it is beyond dispute the most judicious, profound, and acute of all historical compositions, though the friends of liberty may admit, with the advocate of servility, that it has its defects; and the scepticism into which its ingenious and most amiable author was betrayed in matters of religion, must always be lamented by the lovers of genius and virtue. The venom of the sting meant to be inflicted on the memory of 'the Scotch Philosopher', seems to have returned to the writer's own bosom, and to have exhausted itself in the following bloated passage.

At the annunciation of PRINCIPLES, of IDEAS, the soul of man awakes, and starts up, as an exile in a far distant land at the unexpected sounds of his native language, when, after long years of absence, and almost of oblivion, he is suddenly addressed in his own mother tongue. He weeps for joy, and embraces the speaker as his brother. *How else can we explain the fact so honourable to Great Britain,* that the poorest amongst us will contend with as much enthusiasm as the richest for the rights of property?* These rights are the spheres and necessary conditions of free agency. But free agency contains the idea of the free will; and in this he intuitively knows the sublimity, and the infinite hopes, fears, and capabilities of his own (English) nature. On what other ground but the *cognateness of ideas* and principles to man as man, does the nameless soldier rush to the combat in defence of the liberties or *the honour* of his country? Even men, wofully neglectful of the principles of religion, will shed their blood for its truth.

How does this passage agree with Mr. C.'s general contempt of mankind, and that especial aversion to 'Mob-Sycophancy' which has marked him from the cradle, and which formerly led him to give up the periodical paper of the *Watchman*, and to break off in the middle of his *Conciones ad Populum?* A few plain instincts, and a little common sense, are all that the most popular of our popular writers attribute to the people, or rely on for their success in addressing them. But Mr. Coleridge, the mob-hating Mr. Coleridge, here supposes them intuitively to perceive the cabalistical visions of German metaphysics; and compliments the poorest peasant, and the nameless soldier, not only on the cognateness of their ideas and principles to man as man, but on their immediate and joyous excitation at the mere annunciation of such delightful things as '*Principles* and *Ideas*'. Our mystic, in a Note, finds a confirmation of this cognateness of the most important truths to the vulgarest of the people, in 'an anecdote told with much humour in one of Goldsmith's Essays'. Poor Goldy! How he would have stared at this transcendental inference from his humorous anecdote! He would have felt as awkwardly as Gulliver did, when the monkey at the palace of Brobdignag took him an airing on the tiles, and almost broke his neck by the honour. Mr. Coleridge's patronage is of the same un-wieldy kind. The Preacher next gives him authorities for reading the Scriptures. They are—Heraclitus and Horace. In earnest? In good sooth, and in sad and sober earnest.

* Why to Great Britain alone? R.

Or would you wish for authorities?—for great examples?—You may find them in the writings of Thuanus, of Lord Clarendon, of Sir Thomas More, of Raleigh; and in the life and letters of the heroic Gustavus Adolphus. But these, though eminent statesmen, were Christians, and might lie under the thraldom of habit and prejudice. I will refer you then to authorities of two great men, both Pagans; but removed from each other by many centuries, and not more distant in their ages than in their characters and situations. The first shall be that of Heraclitus, the sad and recluse philosopher. Πολυμαθιη νοον οὐ διδασκει· Σιβυλλα δε μαινομένῳ στόματι αγελαστα και ακαλλωπιστα και αμυριστα φθεγγομενη, χιλιων ετων ἐξικνεῖται ιῃ φωνῃ δια τον θεον.* Shall we hesitate to apply to the prophets of God, what could be affirmed of the Sibylls by a philosopher whom Socrates, the prince of philosophers, venerated for the profundity of his wisdom?

For the other, I will refer you to the darling of the polished court of Augustus, to the man whose works have been in all ages deemed the models of good sense, and are still the pocket-companions of those who pride themselves on uniting the scholar with the gentleman. This accomplished man of the world has given an account of the subjects of conversation between the illustrious statesmen who governed, and the brightest luminaries who then adorned, the empire of the civilized world—

> Sermo oritur non de villis domibusve alienis
> Nec, male, nec ne lepus saltet. Sed quod magis ad nos
> Pertinet, et nescire malum est, agitamus: utrumne
> Divitiis homines, an sint virtute beati?
> Et quod sit natura boni? summumque quid eius?

It is not easy to conceive any thing better than this; only the next passage beats it hollow, and is itself surpassed by the one after it, 'as Alps o'er Alps arise'.

So far Mr. Coleridge has indulged himself in 'a preparatory heat' and said nothing about the Bible. But now he girds himself up for his main purpose, places himself at the helm, and undertakes to conduct the statesman to his desired haven in Scripture prophecy and history.

But do you require some one or more particular passage from the Bible, that may at once illustrate and exemplify its applicability to the changes and fortunes of empires? Of the numerous chapters that relate to the Jewish tribes, their enemies and allies, before and after their division into two kingdoms, it would be more difficult to state a single one, from which some guiding light might *not* be struck.

* 'Multiscience (or a variety and quantity of acquired knowledge) does not teach intelligence. But the Sibyll with wild enthusiastic mouth shrilling forth unmirthful, inornate, and unperfumed truths, reaches to a thousand years with her voice through the power of God.'

Does Mr. Coleridge then condescend to oblige us with any one? Nothing can be farther from his thoughts. He is here off again at a tangent, and does not return to the subject for the next seven pages. When he does—it is in the following explicit manner.

But I refer to the demand. *Were it my object to touch on the present state of public affairs in this kingdom, or on the prospective measures in agitation respecting our sister island, I would direct your most serious meditations to the latter period of the reign of Solomon, and to the revolutions in the reign of Rehoboam, his successor. But I should tread on glowing embers: I will turn to the causes of the revolution, and fearful chastisement of France.*

Let the reader turn to the first book of Kings, in which the parallel passage to our own history at the present crisis stands, according to our author, so alarmingly conspicuous; and he will not be surprised that Mr. Coleridge found himself 'treading on glowing embers'. The insidious loyalty or covert Jacobinism of this same parallel, which he declines drawing on account of its extreme applicability, is indeed beyond our comprehension, and not a less 'curious specimen of psychology', than the one immediately preceding it, in which he proves the doctrine of *divine right* to be revealed in an especial manner in the Hebrew Scriptures.

We should proceed to notice that part of the Sermon, where the orator rails at the public praises of Dr. Bell, and abuses Joseph Lancaster, *con amore*. Nothing more flat and vapid, in wit or argument, was ever put before the public, which he treats with such contempt. Of the wit, take the following choice sample.

But the phrase of the READING PUBLIC, which occasioned this note, brings to my mind the mistake of a lethargic Dutch traveller, who returning highly gratified from a showman's caravan, which he had been tempted to enter by the words, THE LEARNED PIG, gilt on the pannels, met another caravan of a similar shape, with THE READING FLY on it, in letters of the same size and splendour. 'Why, dis is voonders above voonders!' exclaims the Dutchman; takes his seat as first comer; and, soon fatigued by waiting, and by the very hush and intensity of his expectation, gives way to his constitutional somnolence, from which he is roused by the supposed showman at Hounslow, with a—'*In what name, Sir! was your place taken? Are you booked all the way for Reading?*'—Now a Reading Public is (to my mind) more marvellous still, and in the third tier of 'voonders above voonders!'

Mr. Coleridge's wit and sentimentality do not seem to have settled accounts together; for in the very next page after this 'third tier of wonders', he says:

And here my apprehensions point to two opposite errors. The first consists in a disposition to think, that as the peace of nations has been disturbed by the diffusion of a false light, it may be re-established by excluding the people from all knowledge and all prospect of amelioration. O! never, never! Reflection and stirrings of mind, with all their restlessness, and all the errors that result from their imperfection, from the *Too much*, because *Too little*, are come into the world. The powers that awaken and foster the spirit of curiosity, are to be found in every village: Books are in every hovel: The infant's cries are hushed with *picture*-books: and the Cottager's child sheds his first bitter tears over pages, which render it impossible for the man to be treated or governed as a child. Here, as in so many other cases, the inconveniences that have arisen from a thing's having become too general, are best removed by making it universal.

And yet, with Mr. Coleridge, a reading public is 'voonders above voonders'—a strange phrase, and yet no fiction! The public is become a reading public, down to the cottager's child; and he thanks God for it—for that great moral steam-engine, Dr. Bell's original and unsophisticated plan, which he considers as an especial gift of Providence to the human race—thus about to be converted into one great reading public; and yet he utters his *Profaccia* upon it with a desponding sigh; and proposes, as a remedy, to put this spirit which has gone forth, under the tutelage of churchwardens, to cant against 'liberal ideas', and 'the jargon of this enlightened age'; in other words, to turn this vast machine against itself, and make it a go-cart of corruption, servility, superstition and tyranny. Mr. Coleridge's first horror is, that there should be a reading public: his next hope is to prevent them from reaping an atom of benefit from 'reflection and stirrings of mind, with all their restlessness'.

The conclusion of this discourse is even more rhapsodical than the former part of it; and we give the pulpit or rostrum from which Mr. Coleridge is supposed to deliver it, 'high enthroned above all height', the decided preference over that throne of dulness and of nonsense which Pope did erst erect for the doubtful merits of Colley and Sir Richard.

The notes are better, and but a little better than the text. We might select, as specimens of laborious foolery, the passage in which the writer defends *second sight*, to prove that he has unjustly been accused of visionary paradox, or hints that a disbelief in ghosts and witches is no great sign of the wisdom of the age, or that in which he gives us to understand that Sir Isaac Newton was a great astrologer, or Mr. Locke no conjurer. But we prefer (for our limits are straitened) the author's description of a green field, which he prefaces by observing, that 'the book of Nature has been the music of gentle and pious minds in all ages; and that it is the poetry of all human nature to read it likewise in a figurative sense, and to find therein correspondences and symbols of a spiritual nature'.

MR. COLERIDGE'S DESCRIPTION OF A GREEN FIELD.

I have at this moment before me, in the flowery meadow on which my eye is now reposing, one of Nature's most soothing chapters, in which there is no lamenting word, no one character of guilt or anguish. For never can I look and meditate on the vegetable creation, without a feeling similar to that with which we gaze at a beautiful infant that has fed itself asleep at its mother's bosom, and smiles in its strange dream of obscure yet happy sensations. The same tender and genial pleasure takes possession of me, and this pleasure is checked and drawn inward by the like aching melancholy, by the same whispered remonstrance, and made restless by a similar impulse of aspiration. It seems as if the soul said to herself—'From this state' [from that of a flowery meadow] 'hast *thou* fallen! Such shouldst thou still become, thyself all permeable to a holier power! Thyself at once hidden and glorified by its own transparency, as the accidental and dividuous in this quiet and harmonious object is subjected to the life and light of nature which shines in it, even as the transmitted power, love and wisdom, of God over all fills, and shines through, Nature! But what the plant *is*, by an act not its own, and unconsciously—*that* must thou *make* thyself to *become!* must by prayer, and by a watchful and unresisting spirit, *join* at least with the preventive and assisting grace to *make* thyself, in that light of conscience which inflameth not, and with that knowledge which puffeth not up'.

This will do. It is well observed by Hobbes, that 'it is by means of words only that a man becometh excellently wise or excellently foolish'.

70. Unsigned notice, *Monthly Magazine*

January 1817, xlii, 545

In Theology, this month has not been so prolific as the last; its principal curiosity, if it can be classed properly under the head, is the *Lay Sermon* of Mr. Coleridge, addressed to the higher classes. Should the latter ever be induced to honour it with more attention than sermons in general obtain from them, it is to be feared they will split upon another rock—that of never being able to understand it. Mr. Coleridge ought, by this time, to know that the high, as well as low, mob comprehend only what is exceedingly clear. It seems he is about to address other sermons to the middle and lower ranks; but, if not more *translucent*, as he would say himself, the whole of these edifying compositions may as well be transmitted to the capitol of the Tower, and there be preserved to puzzle posterity, like the Sybil's leaves.

71. Henry Crabb Robinson, *Critical Review*

January 1817, v, 42-8

This unsigned review is attributed to Robinson (E. J. Morley ed., *On Books and Their Writers*, London 1938, i, 202).

It is very true, as Johnson said in his formal way, 'Every writer writes not for every reader'. Unfortunately, too many readers presume that they are written for in every book they take in hand, and too many writers aspire to the rare glory of addressing, with effect, readers of every description. Hence, on the part of the public, a great deal of incompetent and presumptuous criticism; and on the part of authors, a great deal of ambitious and unsuccessful composition. The department of literature, in which this vice is most apparent, is that which in Germany is called philosophy, and by us, metaphysicks; and, for a very obvious reason, that this *prima scientia* appertains to the people in its results, and to the few in its scientific study. In our country the well known division of doctrines and modes of instruction into the exoteric and esoteric has been nearly lost. Mr. Locke's philosophy is essentially popular, professing, as it does, to bring down the most interesting and importing subjects to the level of ordinary minds, and with ordinary labour; all his followers of the French and English schools have proceeded on the same plan; and the *Scotch* philosophers, though the tendency of their system is to revive, in some points, the scholastic doctrines, have not dared to dispossess the larger public of their jurisdiction in the decision of the great questions which have ever been, and ever will be, in dispute among philosophers of all classes. In the mean while, scholastic subtleties have been revived with great ardour in Germany: and metaphysics now form, among that very studious people, an object of study requiring its distinct language and its laborious discipline. The metaphysicians there write for each other; and all their eminent writers, adopting a scholastic language, disclaim popularity. They no more expect their personal friends and acquaintances to read their works, than in this country a professor of oriental languages would. It is only in Germany that such a body of scholastic metaphysicians could well have sprung up, for it is only in Germany that readers sufficiently numerous could be found to repay even the expense of publication; and though an ignoble impediment, it will for a long time be found, we expect, an effectual one against the introduction of similar works in this country. Readers must be first formed by writers, but without an immediate expectation of readers there will be no publishers. These remarks have been forced from us by a perusal of this pamphlet, which will assuredly be but little read, and by its readers be but little enjoyed or understood; not without some blame to the author, we conceive, but, for the greater part, from the general cause we have already indicated. Mr. Coleridge has formed his taste and opinions in the German schools, he himself possessing congenial talent with those of the distinguished men who have given the law to the public mind there. We have found, on a comparison of his writings with those of his continental contemporaries, coincidencies which cannot always be accidental, at the same time we owe it to him to acknowledge that, in those writings, there is a felicity of statement and illustration, which are a sure proof that he is by no means a general borrower or translator; however, it is not very important to ascertain how much of Mr. Coleridge's philosophy is derived from sources within or out of himself, it is certain that that philosophy is directly hostile to all the systems current in this country; and, therefore, in presenting it to a public so little congenial with himself he has insuperable difficulties to encounter. What he has to say cannot be rendered intelligible in merely popular language; and if he uses only the language of the schools, nobody *will* understand it. Under such circumstances the temptation is scarcely to be resisted, of endeavouring to blend in one mass heterogeneous materials, and adorn the abstractions of a scholastic system by a popular rhetorick. This has been attempted in the present work. The failure was inevitable, if by success the author contemplated either the recommendation of his philosophy to the serious, by shewing the pious tendency of his metaphysics; or the enforcement of religion to the thinking, by an original and striking exhibition of its principle. At the same time it abounds in eloquent and impressive passages, which the indulgent reader will be gratified by, who is content to take what he finds excellent, and pass over what he may besides meet with that appears obscure or extravagant.

The author's great mistake has been, we apprehend, the supposing that the higher classes, 'men of *clerkly* acquirements', would be willing to acquiesce in that kind of abstraction which has been produced by a school of metaphysics, foreign equally to our language and philosophy. Which of our writers on the great question concerning the freedom of the will has yet distinguished between a mathematical, a logical, and an absolute necessity? How many professed metaphysicians have we who retain the word idea in its primitive sense, and are, therefore, able to follow Mr. C. in what he terms the master-thought. 'The first man on whom the light of an IDEA dawned, did in that same moment receive the spirit and the credentials of a law-giver'?

The object of the discourse is to point out the great excellence of the Bible as a source of political instruction, and as its miraculous character is its great peculiarity, our author thus points out the effect of miracles on an earlier stage of society.

In the infancy of the world, signs and wonders were requisite in order to startle and break down that superstition, idolatrous in itself and the source of all other idolatry, which tempts the natural man to seek the true cause and origin of public calamities in outward circumstances, persons and incidents: in agents therefore that were themselves but surges of the same tide, passive conductors of the one invisible influence, under which the total host of billows, in the whole line of successive impulse, swell and roll shoreward; there finally, each in its turn, to strike, roar, and be dissipated.

And he then proceeds to shew that the rules and precepts with which the Old Testament abounds, flow from universal principles. We were in want of illustrations in order to follow Mr. C. in this part of his discourse, as in that in which he contrasts the Bible histories with those of profane writers.

The histories and political economy of the present and preceding century partake in the general contagion of its mechanic philosophy, and are the *product* of an unenlivened generalizing understanding. In the Scriptures they are the living *educts* of the imagination; of that reconciling and mediatory power, which incorporating the reason in images of the sense, and organizing (as it were) the flux of the senses by the permanence and self-circling energies of the reason, gives birth to a system of symbols, harmonious in themselves, and consubstantial with the truths, of which they are the *conductors*. These are the wheels which Ezekiel beheld, when the hand of the Lord was upon him, and he saw visions of God as he sate among the captives by the river of Chebar. *Withersoever the spirit was to go, the wheels went, and thither was their spirit to go: for the spirit of the living creature was in the wheels also.*

We extract this passage as a beautiful description of the imagination, at the same time confessing that we do not comprehend its bearing on the subject. More intelligible is Mr. C.'s enforcement of the familiar argument, that morality requires a deeper source than mere expediency; and very clear are also his scornful deridings of the present generation, for its presumptuous claim to the character of an enlightened and liberal age. It is, however, a satisfaction to us to find that, with a strong bias on Mr. C.'s mind against the favourite pursuits of the day, he has yet spoken strongly in favour of the improved education of the lower classes. He eulogises Dr. Bell though he characterises the liberal system recommended under the captivating title of *Schools for all*, as 'a plan of poisoning the children of the poor with a sort of *potential* infidelity, under the liberal idea of teaching those points only of religious faith in which all denominations agree'. It is assuredly a triumph to the great cause of reform, and the improvement of mankind that there is no longer a *hostile* conflict concerning the end, but an *amicable* contest concerning the means.

Mr. Coleridge enters at large, though in a desultory way, into the practical questions arising out of the intellectual wants of the age; and urges, in the same breath, the devout study of the Bible as the sole source of divine truth, and the laborious study of the ancient philosophers as the records of human wisdom.

These topics are, however, treated in a much more satisfactory manner in the appendix of notes. Until we can obtain a systematic view of the author's philosophy, we must be content with these fragments which are rendered very stimulant by the impassioned and florid style in which they are written. The motto in the title page sufficiently indicates the author's suspicion of the opinion which may probably be entertained of them.

We can afford space only for a few extracts, and we must leave the consideration of them to our readers' taste. The literary merits of a book are a fair subject for periodical criticism, but not schemes of philosophy which characterise nations and ages.

All men who have anxiously attended to the operations of their own minds, must have frequently felt a difficulty in reconciling, as it were, the incompatible demands of their several faculties. All objects, whether of sense or of moral observation, address themselves to men as what are to be coolly thought upon and, if possible, comprehended and understood. At the same time a large proportion of these same objects are to be felt, and to be loved or hated: they connect themselves with moral and laudable, or illaudable affections. Now the powers or tendencies of the mind are unequally distributed: and some men are naturally prone to feeling or religion, and others to thought which delights, in discussion and inquiry. It is well known what serious hostilities flow from these opposite tendencies of character; how the one class are apt to despise; and the others, to hate those who respectively believe too much or too little: yet it is certain that wisdom and virtue lie only in that wise medium, that central combination of thought and sentiment which excludes nothing, and embraces the most essential qualities of our nature; and that great evils spring from the exclusive exercise of any one power. These truths we think require to be more generally felt and understood by all parties, and with that view we extract some parts of our author's interesting third note on this subject.

There exists in the human being, at least in man fully developed, no mean symbol of Tri-unity, in Reason, Religion, and the Will. For each of the three, though a distinct agency, implies and demands the other two, and loses its own nature at the moment that from distinction it passes into division or separation.

The comprehension, impartiality, and far-sightedness of Reason, (the Legislative of our nature), taken singly and exclusively, becomes mere visionariness in *intellect*, and indolence or hard-heartedness in *morals*. It is the science of cosmopolitism without country, of philanthropy without neighbourliness or consanguinity, in short, of all the impostures of that philosophy of the French revolution, which would sacrifice each to the shadowy idol of ALL.

From all this it follows, that Reason as the science of All as the Whole, must be interpenetrated by a Power, that represents the concentration of All in Each—a Power that acts by a contraction of universal truths into individual duties, as the only form in which those truths can attain life and reality. Now this is Religion, which is the Executive of our nature, and on this account the name of highest dignity, and the symbol of sovereignty.

Yet this again—yet even Religion itself, if ever in its too exclusive devotion to the *specific* and *individual* it neglects to interpose the contemplation of the *universal*, changes its being into Superstition, and becoming more and more earthly and servile, as more and more estranged from the one, in all, goes wandering at length with its pack of amulets, bead-rolls, periapts, fetisches, and the like pedlary, on pilgrimages to Loretto, Mecca, or the temple of Jaggernaut, arm in arm with sensuality on one side and self-torture on the other, followed by a motley group of friars, pardoners, faquirs, gamesters, flagellants, mountebanks, and harlots.

But neither can reason or religion exist or co-exist as reason and religion, except as far as they are actuated by the WILL (the platonic $\Theta\upsilon\mu\dot{o}\varsigma$,) which is the sustaining, coercive, and ministerial power, the functions of which in the individual correspond to the officers of war and police in the ideal Republic of Plato. In its state of immanence (or indwelling) in reason and religion, the WILL appears indifferently, as wisdom or as love: two names of the same power, the former more intelligential, the latter more spiritual; the former more frequent in the Old, the latter in the New Testament. But in its utmost abstraction and consequent state of reprobation, the Will becomes satanic pride and rebellious self-idolatry in the relations of the spirit to itself, and remorseless despotism relatively to others; the more hopeless as the more obdurate by its subjugation of sensual impulses, by its superiority to toil and pain and pleasure; in short, by the fearful resolve to find in itself alone the one absolute motive of action, under which all other motives from within and from without must be either subordinated or crushed.

This is the character which Milton has so philosophically as well as sublimely embodied in the Satan of his Paradise Lost. Alas! too often has it been embodied in *real* life. Too often has it given a dark and savage grandeur to the historic page! And wherever it has appeared, under whatever circumstances of time and country, the same ingredients have gone to its composition, and it has been identified by the same attributes. Hope in which there is no Chearfulness; Stedfastness within and immovable Resolve, with outward Restlessness and whirling Activity; Violence with Guile; Temerity with Cunning; and, as the result of all, Interminableness of Object with perfect Indifference of Means:

these are the qualities that have constituted the COMMANDING GENIUS! these are the Marks that have characterized the Masters of Mischief, the Liberticides, and mighty Hunters of Mankind, from NIMROD to NAPOLEON!

We regret that we cannot extend our extracts or observations. We regret particularly that the author should not be furnished with the means of doing justice to himself by the publication of a connected and systematic work. For our own part, we are not offended, though we do not approve of the scornful bitterness with which the latitudinarians in religion are noticed; nor are we scandalized by the imputation cast on Mr. Locke's philosophy, as tending so directly to the encouragement of infidelity. It is well known that this was the reproach of that great man's contemporaries; and that his philosophy has been most implicitly relied on by the French and Franco-English philosophers. The sincerity of his own faith, the excellence of his personal character, and the practical worth of his political writings, will be ever acknowledged, whatever be the duration of his system. That system prevails in this country almost universally: whether the schools of other nations have any thing substantially better, is at least worth inquiring into. We shall rejoice when any work of competent skill appears, which may unfold to us the vaunted mysteries of the German school. Till then we must be content with the scanty fragments which can be afforded by the few English disciples of that school; among whom Mr. C. certainly holds the first place for the splendour of his talents, however unsatisfactorily it may be thought those talents have yet been exerted in either of the walks of lyric poetry and metaphysical speculation.

'BLESSED ARE YE THAT SOW BESIDE ALL WATERS!' A Lay Sermon

1817

72. Unsigned review, *Monthly Magazine*

May 1817, xliii, 354

Mr. S. T. Coleridge has stolen another march upon the public, in the shape of a second *Lay Sermon*. Of its contents we need not say much, as all who have read or heard of the first of these absurd rhapsodies may well suppose that the *new* principles adopted by this *reverend* seceder from just opinions are followed up with all the argumentative ability he possesses. To reason with a person of this cast would be as hopeless an undertaking as to reason with the inmates of Bedlam—where the error is in the heart, no illumination will reach the understanding. Mr. Coleridge, adopting a scriptural expression, says, *'Blessed are ye that sow beside all waters'*; this is his text—at least his *motto*—no reference to which is made, that we can perceive, throughout his discourse. Now this, we think, is a clear proof that the lay-preacher is not quite an adept in the selection of texts; and, as we are not uncharitably disposed towards him, we recommend the following as the subject of his *third* sermon: 'Wisdom resteth in the heart of him that hath understanding: *but that which is in the midst of fools is made known'*.—Prov. chap. xiv. verse 33.

73. Unsigned review, *Monthly Repository*

May 1817, xii, 299-301

The 'wandering bards', 'Coleridge, Southey and Co.' whom in 1798 the *Anti-Jacobin* represented as moving 'in sweet accord of harmony and love' and tuning all their 'mystic harps to praise Lepaux', the French Theo-philanthropist, are still consentaneous in their movements but their harps are tuned to another theme, the demerits of the Unitarians. These hard-headed Christians have little liking for fiction in the articles of their faith, and none for 'mystic' rant, and hence they are singled out by the Lake poets for reprobation. It may be an amusing speculation whether the praise or the censure of these mystics will be accounted honourable half a century hence.

Mr. Coleridge laments, with his Holiness of Rome, that 'we hear much in the present day of the *plainness* and *simplicity* of the Christian religion', and that hence the necessity of believing *in* Christ is transformed 'into a recommendation to believe him'. This is we allow a hopeful beginning of the removal of Christian *plainness* and *simplicity*. The Lay-Preacher proceeds: 'The advocates of the latter scheme grew out of a sect that were called Socinians, but having succeeded in disbelieving far beyond the last footmarks of the Socini, have chosen to designate themselves by the name of Unitarians'. Is this writer, who lays claim to 'all knowledge and all mysteries', really ignorant of the history of the sect which he denounces? Did he read none of their books and learn nothing of their early advocates *when he was amongst them? During the time he officiated as an Unitarian teacher at Shrewsbury and elsewhere*, did he never look into the Fratres Poloni or any other of their standard volumes? But perhaps he has not only, like the Poet Laureate, 'outgrown his opinions', but also, like Mr. Pitt, whom he and the Laureate cannot now be ashamed to resemble, lost the faculty of memory with regard to all past connections that do not flatter his present humour. Let us then remind this 'some time' Unitarian preacher, that the term *Unitarian* is not of modern invention, nor a name of choice; that it is as old as the Reformation; that *Socinian* was always the epithet of an adversary; and that fair and honourable foes have for

286

two centuries and a half spoken of such as believed in and worshipped One God in One Person as Unitarians. It is of no consequence therefore whether the word be etymologically correct; custom has assigned it a definite sense; it serves truly to designate the worshipper of One Divine Person in contradistinction from the Trinitarian who worships Three Divine Persons; and in this signification it will continue to be used when it shall have been forgotten that Mr. Coleridge was a Unitarian preacher, and the inquiry shall have ceased what arguments have transformed him into a Trinitarian layman.

'This is a word', says Mr. Coleridge, referring to the name of *Unitarian*, 'which in its proper sense can belong only to their antagonists: for Unity or Union and indistinguishable *Unicity* or Oneness, are incompatible terms; while in the exclusive sense in which they mean the name to be understood, it is a presumptuous boast and an uncharitable calumny'. The Trinitarians will not thank the Lay-Preacher for this gloss: according to this exposition of terms, the Polytheist who believes in a number of Divine Persons united in one common nature is a proper Unitarian; and again, the orthodox believer in the Trinity is not a believer in the *Oneness* of God, though he may hold the Unity of the Deity, or the composition of parts in a whole. Such a comment as this was well preceded by a complaint of the Christian religion being erroneously supposed to be *plain* and *simple*.

'Their true designation', adds the Lay-Preacher of the Unitarians, amongst whom he is no longer numbered, 'which simply expresses a fact admitted on all sides, would be that of *Psilanthropists*, or assertors of the *mere* humanity of Christ'. Many a man has wished to christen the Unitarians anew; the name that our quondam preacher proposes is amongst the oddest that ingenuity or envy or bigotry has suggested, *Psilanthropists*, that is, if it may be Englished, *Mere-Humanists*. Passing by the *humour* of this nickname, we may remark it as rather singular that Mr. Coleridge should denominate a sect not from what they believe but from a part of that which they do not believe, and in his new *cognomen* should overlook wholly that which they believe and carry into practice with regard to the great object of worship and which is in truth their only distinction. All Christians believe in the humanity of Christ; and no Christians that we are acquainted with profess to believe in the *mere humanity* of Christ. How would Mr. Coleridge have named the Apostle Peter, who preached 'Jesus of Nazareth—*a man*— *approved of God, by miracles*, wonders and signs, *which* GOD DID *by him!*' Yet the inventor of the memorable term *Psilanthropists* charges those that take the antient and universal name of *Unitarians*, in the sense of the believers in and worshippers of One God in One Person, with 'a presumptuous boast and an uncharitable calumny'.

'Wissowatius' and the Fratres Poloni are allowed to have been 'undeniably men of learning'; but this candour to divines that have long been dead costs nothing, and it serves for a cover to the insinuation that since their time there have been no 'learned Socinian divines'. How base is the spirit of party! What stuff will not bigotry feed upon! Mr. Coleridge has withdrawn his stock of learning from the Unitarian church and he affects to pity its intellectual poverty. Without him, however, the Unitarians have sufficient learning and vigour of mind to detect sophistry, to unmasque misrepresentation, to expose absurdity, though hidden in the trappings of mystic phrases, and to trace up the *odium theologicum* to its source in a disordered head or (in language which Mr. Coleridge may understand) an unregenerate heart.

The only other point on which we shall remark is the *creed* which the Lay-Preacher has *fabricated* for the Unitarians and which shews his deplorable ignorance of the people whom he sets himself at once to reprove and instruct. His creed contains six articles, of which only three are Unitarian! The Unitarians believe, says their former friend, 1. In One God—True. 2. In the necessity of human actions and in all remorse for sins being precluded by Christianity—Not true. On this philosophical question there is as much diversity of opinion amongst the Unitarians as amongst other Christians. 3. In the Gospels and in the resurrection of Jesus Christ—True, and in the Epistles also, and in the *'inspiration'* of all these books as far as inspiration was necessary to constitute them an authentic revelation of the will of God. 4. In the resurrection of the body—Not true. They differ widely as to what constitutes 'the whole man', but they all agree in condemning the substitution of the *modern* notion of the resurrection of the *body* for the scriptural doctrine of the resurrection of the *man*. 5. In the final happiness of the righteous and the corrective punishment of the wicked—Can this latter article of faith outrage the feelings of one who like our author professes a benign and bland philosophy? 6. In a redemption, but (as they hold that there is no *moral* difference in the actions and characters of men, and that men are not *responsible* beings, and as they merge all the attributes of Deity in Power, Intelligence and Benevolence, making nothing of the Holiness of God and representing His anger as a mere metaphor addressed to a barbarous people) not by the cross of Christ—Not true. The premises, including all the Unitarians, are absolutely false; the conclusion is false applied to any Unitarians. It is the peculiar doctrine of Unitarianism, because it is the peculiar doctrine of the New Testament, that Christ is *the way, the truth and the life*, that he is *the Saviour of the world*, and that the *cross* was the instrument and is the symbol of salvation.

'These', says Mr. Coleridge, with great faith in his reader, 'are all the positives of the modern Socinian creed', and half of these are his own dreams. We might enlarge the number of Unitarian 'positives', but the Lay-Preacher has succeeded so ill in creed-making that we are not tempted to follow his example. In this apocryphal creed appear two marked features of the author's mind; first, an incapacity of conceiving that a body of Christians should not be disciplined under the faith of a leader but should each think and judge for himself; and secondly, a secret persuasion that a creed like an ingot is valuable according to its bulk, so that the Apostles' Creed would be greatly improved if it could be extended to the length of the Athanasian, and on the same principle the Lord's Prayer, which is a creed in another form, would be indefinitely more excellent if it were spread out into the size of the Book of Common Prayer.

74. Henry Crabb Robinson, *Critical Review*

June 1817, v, 581-6

This unsigned review is attributed to Henry Crabb Robinson (*On Books and Their Writers*, i, 207).

Mr. Coleridge's second lay sermon answers its title much better than the first. A discourse which professes expressly either to proceed from one of the people, or to be addressed to certain classes of the people, ought to be popular in its style and tendency; and Mr. C. has perhaps in this respect succeeded quite as well as could be expected from him: indeed he has had the strongest inducement in a polemical spirit, which has thrown unusual animation over a discussion in which religion and political economy are singularly blended together. We do not mean to reproach the author with such a treatment of his subject. His theme was the distresses and discontents of the times. These may certainly be considered religiously—that is, they may be contemplated under the impressions which religion imparts, either as themselves entering into the scheme of divine providence in their origin, or as calling for the exercise of religious duties in their consequences; and at the same time, as far as it is of importance to understand their immediate causes and probable effects, it is not incongruous to introduce considerations of merely human prudence and experimental science.

The sermon opens with vehement declamations, enriched with the emphatic phraseology and solemn denunciations of the Hebrew prophets, against the factious demagogues, 'deceivers of the people', 'the vile', who 'will talk villany'—in a word, that whole class of politicians who, either from weakness of judgment, or perversity of will, misrepresent the causes of the present discontents, and in their expositions of those causes, are eager to irritate, instead of appeasing, the public mind. We should have been better pleased with Mr. Coleridge's exertions, if he could have corrected this error, without at the same time imbibing its spirit; and while he reproached his adversaries with narrow views, had been careful to guard against recrimination.

That the peace, which was so ardently desired by all benevolent men, was the immediate occasion of so much national distress, is a fact equally undeniable and humiliating, as an evidence of the shortsightedness even of the wise; and though the opponents of the war of 1793 may, if the triumph in their own sagacity delights them, urge with truth, that without that war the subsequent reverse could not have occurred; yet it is certain that the prophetic spirit was given to them as little as to their adversaries. The whole series of wonderful events during the last twenty-eight years were without a parallel in history, and each successive revolution, from the first abolition of monarchy in France in 1793, to the final restoration of the Bourbons in 1815 (if the word *final* may yet be safely employed) utterly unforeseen; and this conviction ought to assuage the heat of political contests. Our author having before pointed out the temporary prosperity produced by the war, thus remarks on the mischief attending the imputing false causes for the acknowledged distresses of the times.

That the depression began *with* the Peace would have been of itself a sufficient proof with the Many, that it arose *from* the Peace. But this opinion suited ill with the purposes of sedition. The truth, that could not be precluded, must be removed; and *'when the needy speaketh aright'* the more urgent occasion is there for the *'wicked device'* and the *'lying words'*. Where distress is felt, tales of wrong and oppression are readily believed, to the sufferer's own disquiet. Rage and Revenge make the cheek pale and the hand tremble, worse than even want itself: and the cup of sorrow overflows by being held unsteadily. On the other hand nothing calms the mind in the hour of bitterness so efficaciously as the conviction that it was not within the means of those above us, or around us, to have prevented it. An influence, mightier than fascination, dwells in the stern eye of Necessity, when it is fixed steadily on a man: for together with the *power* of resistance it takes away its agitations likewise. This is one mercy that always accompanies the visitations of the Almighty when they are received *as* such. If therefore the sufferings of the lower classes are to supply air and fuel to their passions, and are to be perverted into instruments of mischief, they must be attributed to causes that can be represented as removeable; either to individuals who had been previously rendered unpopular, or to whole classes of men, according as the immediate object of their seducers may require.

Having treated of the immediate occasions of the existing distress, Mr. C. resolves the 'true seat and sources' of it into the 'overbalance of the commercial spirit, in consequence of the absence or weakness of the counter-weights'. Among these counter-weights, he mentions the 'ancient feeling of rank and ancestry', which he opposes as a counterpoise 'to the grosser superstition for wealth'. He next adverts to the neglect of austerer studies—in other words, ancient metaphysics: with this subject he connects the influence of religion, and introduces some observations on the union of philosophy and religion, which we anticipate will not be relished by either the pious or the speculative, though Mr. C. has done his utmost to flatter the orthodox, by inserting a very bitter and scornful note against Unitarianism. But, notwithstanding Mr. Coleridge's extreme contempt for the rational Christians, he seems to consider religion alone, unallied to philosophy, as an inefficient protection against the wordly spirit.

My argument is confined to the question, whether Religion in its present state and under the present conceptions of its demands and purposes does, even among the most religious, exert any efficient force of controul over the commercial spirit, the excess of which we have attributed not to the extent and magnitude of the commerce itself, but to the absence or imperfection of its appointed checks and counteragents. Now as the system of the Friends in its first intention is of all others the most hostile to worldly-mindedness on the one hand; and as, on the other, the adherents of this system both in confession and *practice* confine Christianity to feelings and motives; they may be selected as representatives of the strict, but unstudied and uninquiring, Religionists of every denomination. Their characteristic propensities will supply, therefore, no unfair test for the degree of resistance, which our present Christianity is capable of opposing to the cupidity of a trading people. That species of Christianity I mean, which, as far as knowledge and the faculties of thought are concerned—which, as far as the growth and grandeur of the *intellectual* man is in question—is to be learnt extempore! A Christianity poured in on the Catechumen all and all at once, as from a shower-bath: and which, whatever it may be in the heart, yet for the understanding and reason is from boyhood onward a thing past and perfected! If the almost universal opinion be tolerably correct, the question is answered. But I by no means *appropriate* the remark to the wealthy Quakers, or even apply it to them in any particular or eminent sense, when I say, that often as the motley reflexes of my experience move in long procession of manifold groups before me, the distinguished and world-honored company of Christian Mammonists appear to the eye of my imagination as a drove of camels heavily laden, yet all at full speed, and each in the confident expectation of passing through the EYE OF THE NEEDLE, without stop or halt, both beast and baggage. . . . The Religion here spoken of, having long since parted company with that inquisitive and bookish Theology which tends to defraud the student of his wordly wisdom, inasmuch as it diverts his mind from the accumulation of wealth by pre-occupying his thoughts in the acquisition of knowledge. For the Religion of best repute among us holds all the truths of Scripture and all the doctrines of Christianity so very transcendent, or so very easy, as to make study and research either vain or needless. It professes, therefore, to hunger and thirst after Righteousness alone, and the rewards of the Righteous; and thus habitually *taken for granted* all truths of spiritual import leaves the understanding vacant and at leisure for a thorough insight into present and temporal interests: which, doubtless, is the true reason why its followers are in general such shrewd, knowing, wary, well-informed, thrifty and thriving men of business. But this is likewise the reason, why it neither does or can check or circumscribe the Spirit of Barter.

It would not be fair to our author, were we thus to point out his skill and alacrity in exposing what he deems the erroneous systems, if we were not to state the system or sect to which he professes to belong. The objects of his admiration, then, are the divines of the seventeenth century.

It is well known, and has been observed of old, that Poetry tends to render its devotees careless of money and outward appearances, while Philosophy inspires a contempt of both as objects of Desire and Admiration. But Religion is the Poetry and Philosophy of all mankind; unites in itself whatever is most excellent in either, and while it at one and the same time calls into action and supplies with the noblest materials both the imaginative and the intellective faculties, superadds the interests of the most substantial and home-felt reality to both, to the poetic vision and the philosophic idea. But in order to produce a similar effect it must act in a similar way; it must reign in the thoughts of a man and in the powers akin to thought, as well as exercise an admitted influence over his hopes and fears, and through these on his deliberate and individual acts.

Now as my first presumptive proof of a difference (I might almost have said, of a contrast) between the religious character of the period since the Revolution, and that of the period from the accession of Edward the Sixth to the abdication of the second James, I refer to the Sermons and to the theological Works generally, of the latter period. It is my full conviction, that in any half dozen Sermons of Dr. Donne, or Jeremy Taylor, there are more thoughts, more facts and images, more excitements to inquiry and intellectual effort, than are presented to the congregations of the present day in as many churches or meetings during twice as many months. Yet both these were the most popular preachers of their times, were heard with enthusiasm by crowded and promiscuous audiences, and the effect produced by their eloquence was held in reverential and affectionate remembrance by many attendants on their ministry, who, like the pious Isaac Walton, were not themselves men of learning or education.

Mr. C. next discusses the nature of the commercial spirit, and with great earnestness and effect comments on the evils produced by the gambling habits fostered by commerce, and the calamitous consequences of commercial failures.

We shall perhaps be told too, that the very Evils of this System, even the periodical *crash* itself, are to be regarded but as so much superfluous steam ejected by the escape pipes and safety valves of a self-regulating machine: and lastly, that in a free and trading country *all things find their level.* . . . But Persons are not *Things*—but Man does not find his level. Neither in body nor in soul does the Man find his level! After a hard and calamitous season, during which the thousand wheels of some vast manufactory had remained silent as a frozen water-fall, be it that plenty has returned and that trade has once more become brisk and stirring: go, ask the overseer, and question the parish doctor, whether the workman's health and temperance with the staid and respectful manners best taught by the inward dignity of conscious self-support, have found *their* level again! Alas! I have more than once seen a group of children in Dorsetshire, during the heat of the dog-days, each with its little shoulders up to its ears, and its chest pinched inward, the very habit and *fixtures*, a ist were, that had been impressed on their frames by the former ill-fed, ill-clothed, and unfuelled winters. But as with the body, so or still worse with the mind. Nor is the effect confined to the labouring classes, whom by an ominous but too appropriate a change in our phraseology we are now accustomed to call the Laboring Poor. I cannot persuade myself, that the frequency of Failures with all the disgraceful secrets of Fraud and Folly, of unprincipled Vanity in expending and desperate Speculation in retrieving, can be familiarized to the thoughts and experience of Men, as matters of daily occurrence, without serious injury to the Moral Sense: more especially in times when Bankruptcies spread, like a fever, at once contagious and epidemic; swift too as the travel of a Earthquake, that with one and the same chain of Shocks opens the ruinous chasm in cities that have an ocean between them!

The introduction of commercial principles into the management of land, is eloquently and justly inveighed against; and certainly a more deplorable evil could not well be conceived, than the principle of considering the labour of the peasantry as a marketable commodity; like any merchant's wares, to be the subject of profit, without any reference to the welfare of the labourer himself.

We have no room for further extracts. Our readers will have observed that our author has discussed certain topics with an impartiality that is a pledge for the integrity and purity of his principles; though on matters of party politics and polemical divinity, he has betrayed an intemperance of feeling and expression, which the more immediate objects of his attack will perhaps be the most ready to overlook and excuse,

BIOGRAPHIA LITERARIA

1817

75. William Hazlitt, *Edinburgh Review*

August 1817, xxviii, 488-515

An unsigned review attributed to Hazlitt (Howe, xvi, 425).
The long footnote, signed 'F.J.', is by the editor of the *Edinburgh
Review*, Francis Jeffrey.

There are some things readable in these volumes; and if the learned
author could only have been persuaded to make them a little more
conformable to their title, we have no doubt that they would have
been the most popular of all his productions. Unfortunately, however,
this work is not so properly an account of his Life and Opinions, as an
Apology for them. 'It will be found', says our Auto-Biographer, 'that
the least of what I have written concerns myself personally'. What
then, it may be asked, is the work taken up with? With the announcement of an explanation of the author's Political and Philosophical
creed, to be contained in another work—with a prefatory introduction
of 200 pages to an Essay on the difference between Fancy and Imagination, which was intended to form part of this, but has been suppressed,
at the request of a judicious friend, as unintelligible—with a catalogue
of Mr. Southey's domestic virtues, and author-like qualifications—a
candid defence of the *Lyrical Ballads*—a critique on Mr. Wordsworth's
poetry—quotations from the *Friend*—and attacks on the *Edinburgh
Review*. There are, in fact, only two or three passages in the work which
relate to the details of the author's life, such as the account of his school-
education, and of his setting up the *Watchman* newspaper. We shall
make sure of the first of these curious documents, before we completely
lose ourselves in the multiplicity of his speculative opinions.

At school, I enjoyed the inestimable advantage of a very sensible, though at
the same time, a very severe master, the Rev. James Bowyer, many years Head
Master of the Grammar-School, Christ's Hospital. He early moulded my taste

to the preference of Demosthenes to Cicero, of Homer and Theocritus to Virgil, and again, of Virgil to Ovid. He habituated me to compare Lucretius (in such extracts as I then read), Terence, and, above all, the chaster poems of Catullus, not only with the Roman poets of the so called silver and brazen ages, but with even those of the Augustan era; and, on grounds of plain sense, and universal logic, to see and assert the superiority of the former, in the truth and nativeness both of their thoughts and diction. At the same time that we were studying the Greek tragic poets, he made us read Shakespeare and Milton as lessons: and they were the lessons, too, which required most time and trouble to *bring up*, so as to escape his censure. I learnt from him, that Poetry, even that of the loftiest, and, seemingly, that of the wildest odes, had a logic of its own, as severe as that of science; and more difficult, because more subtle, more complex, and dependent on more, and more fugitive causes. In the truly great poets, he would say, there is a reason assignable, not only for every word, but for the position of every word; and I well remember, that, availing himself of the synonimes to the Homer of Didymus, he made us attempt to show, with regard to each, *why* it would not have answered the same purpose; and *wherein* consisted the peculiar fitness of the word in the original text.

I had just entered on my seventeenth year, when the Sonnets of Mr. Bowles, twenty in number, and just then published in a quarto pamphlet, were first made known and presented to me, by a school-fellow who had quitted us for the University, and who, during the whole time that he was in our first form (or, in our school language, a GRECIAN), had been my patron and protector. I refer to Dr. Middleton, the truly learned, and every way excellent Bishop of Calcutta—

> 'Qui laudibus amplis
> Ingenium celebrare meum, calamumque solebat,
> Calcar agens animo validum. Non omnia terræ
> Obruta! Vivit amor, vivit dolor! Ora negatur
> Dulcia conspicere; at flere et meminisse relictum est.'
>
> *Petr. Ep. Lib. 7. Ep. 1.*

It was a double pleasure to me, and still remains a tender recollection, that I should have received from a friend so revered, the first knowledge of a poet, by whose works, year after year, I was so enthusiastically delighted and inspired. My earliest acquaintances will not have forgotten the undisciplined eagerness and impetuous zeal, with which I laboured to make proselytes, not only of my companions, but of all with whom I conversed, of whatever rank, and in whatever place. As my school finances did not permit me to purchase copies, I made, within less than a year and an half, more than forty transcriptions, as the best presents I could offer to those who had in any way won my regard. And, with almost equal delight, did I receive the three or four following publications of the same author.

Though I have seen and known enough of mankind to be well aware that I

shall perhaps stand alone in my creed, and that it will be well, if I subject myself
to no worse charge than that of singularity; I am not therefore deterred from
avowing, that I regard, and ever have regarded the obligations of intellect
among the most sacred of the claims of gratitude. A valuable thought, or a
particular train of thoughts, gives me additional pleasure, when I can safely
refer and attribute it to the conversation or correspondence of another. My
obligations to Mr. Bowles were indeed important, and for radical good. *At a
very premature age, even before my fifteenth year, I had bewildered myself in metaphysicks, and in theological controversy. Nothing else pleased me. History, and
particular facts, lost all interest in my mind.* Poetry (though for a school-boy of that
age, I was above par in English versification, and had already produced two
or three compositions which, I may venture to say, without reference to my
age, were somewhat above mediocrity, and which had gained me more credit,
than the sound, good sense of my old master was at all pleased with)—*poetry
itself, yea novels and romances, became insipid to me.* In my friendless wanderings
on our *leave-days* (for I was an orphan, and had scarcely any connexions in
London), highly was I delighted, if any passenger, especially if he were drest
in black, would enter into conversation with me. For I soon found the means of
directing it to my favourite subjects

> Of providence, fore-knowledge, will, and fate,
> Fix'd fate, free-will, fore-knowledge absolute,
> And found no end in wandering mazes lost.

This preposterous pursuit was, beyond doubt, injurious, both to my natural
powers, and to the progress of my education. It would perhaps have been
destructive, had it been continued; but from this I was auspiciously withdrawn,
partly indeed by an accidental introduction to an amiable family, chiefly
however by the genial influence of a style of poetry, so tender, and yet so manly,
so natural and real, and yet so dignified and harmonious, as the sonnets, &c.
of Mr. Bowles! Well were it for me, perhaps, had I never relapsed into the
same mental disease; if I had continued to pluck the flower, and reap the
harvest from the cultivated surface, instead of delving in the unwholesome
quicksilver mines of metaphysic depths. But if in after-time I have sought a
refuge from bodily pain and mismanaged sensibility, in abstruse researches,
which exercised the strength and subtlety of the understanding, without
awakening the feelings of the heart; still there was a long and blessed interval,
during which my natural faculties were allowed to expand, and my original
tendencies to develop themselves—my fancy, and the love of nature, and the
sense of beauty in forms and sounds.

Mr. Coleridge seems to us, from this early association, to overrate
the merits of Bowles's Sonnets, which he prefers to Warton's, which
last we, in our turn, prefer to Wordsworth's, and indeed to any Sonnets
in the language. He cannot, however, be said to overrate the extent of
the intellectual obligations which he thinks he owes to his favourite

writer. If the study of Mr. Bowles's poems could have effected a permanent cure of that 'preposterous' state of mind which he has above
described, his gratitude, we admit, should be boundless: but the
disease, we fear, was in the mind itself; and the study of poetry, instead
of counteracting, only gave force to the original propensity; and Mr.
Coleridge has ever since, from the combined forces of poetic levity and
metaphysic bathos, been trying to fly, not in the air, but under ground—
playing at hawk and buzzard between sense and nonsense, floating or
sinking in fine Kantean categories, in a state of suspended animation
'twixt dreaming and awake, quitting the plain ground of 'history and
particular facts' for the first butterfly theory, fancy-bred from the mag-
gots of his brain, going up in an air-balloon filled with fetid gas from
the writings of Jacob Behmen and the mystics, and coming down in a
parachute made of the soiled and fashionable leaves of the *Morning
Post*, promising us an account of the Intellectual System of the Universe,
and putting us off with a reference to a promised dissertation on the
Logos, introductory to an intended commentary on the entire Gospel
of St. John. In the above extract, he tells us, with a degree of *naïveté*
not usual with him, that, 'even before his fifteenth year, history and
particular facts had lost all interest in his mind'. Yet, so little is he
himself aware of the influence which this feeling still continues to
exert over his mind, and of the way in which it has mixed itself up in
his philosophical faith, that he afterwards makes it the test and definition of a sound understanding and true genius, that 'the mind is
affected by thoughts, rather than by things; and only then feels the
requisite interest even for the most important events and accidents,
when by means of meditation they have passed into *thoughts*'. . . .
We do not see, after this, what right Mr. C. has to complain of those
who say that he is neither the most literal nor logical of mortals; and
the worst that has ever been said of him is, that he is the least so. If it
is the proper business of the philosopher to dream over theories, and to
neglect or gloss over facts, to fit them to his theories or his conscience;
we confess we know of few writers, ancient or modern, who have come
nearer to the perfection of this character than the author before us.

After a desultory and unsatisfactory attempt (Chap. II.) to account
for and disprove the common notion of the irritability of authors, Mr.
Coleridge proceeds (by what connexion we know not) to a full, true
and particular account of the personal, domestic, and literary habits of
his friend Mr. Southey, to all which we have but one objection, namely,
that it seems quite unnecessary, as we never heard them impugned,

except indeed by the Antijacobin writers, here quoted by Mr. Coleridge, who is no less impartial as a friend, than candid as an enemy. The passage altogether is not a little remarkable.

It is not, however [says our author], from grateful recollections only, that I have been impelled thus to leave these my deliberate sentiments on record; but in some sense as a debt of justice to the man, whose name has been so often connected with mine, for evil to which he is a stranger. As a specimen, I subjoin part of a note from the 'Beauties of the Anti-Jacobin', in which, having previously informed the Public that I had been dishonoured at Cambridge for preaching Deism, at a time when, for my youthful ardour in defence of Christianity, I was decried as a bigot by the proselytes of French philosophy, the writer concludes with these words—'*Since this time he has left his native country, commenced citizen of the world, left his poor children fatherless, and his wife destitute. Ex his disce his friends, Lamb and Southey*'. With severest truth [continues Mr. Coleridge], it may be asserted, that it would not be easy to select two men more exemplary in their domestic affections, than those whose names were thus printed at full length, as in the same rank of morals with a denounced infidel and fugitive, who had left his children fatherless, and his wife destitute! *Is it surprising that many good men remained longer than perhaps they otherwise would have done, adverse to a party which encouraged and openly rewarded the authors of such atrocious calumnies?*

With us, we confess the wonder does not lie there: all that surprises us is, that the objects of these atrocious calumnies were *ever* reconciled to the authors of them; for the calumniators were the party itself. The Cannings, the Giffords, and the Freres,[1] have never made any apology for the abuse which they then heaped upon every nominal friend of freedom; and yet Mr. Coleridge thinks it necessary to apologize in the name of all good men, for having remained so long adverse to a party which recruited upon such a bounty; and seems not obscurely to intimate that they had such effectual means of propagating their slanders against those good men who differed with them, that most of the latter found there was no other way of keeping their good name but by giving up their principles, and joining in the same venal cry against all those who did not become apostates or converts, ministerial Editors, and 'laurel-honouring Laureates' like themselves! What! at the very moment when this writer is complaining of a foul and systematic conspiracy against the characters of himself, and his most intimate friends, he suddenly stops short in his half-finished burst of involuntary indignation, and ends with a lamentable affectation of surprise at the

[1] Tories who had been chiefly responsible for the *Anti-Jacobin* and who had subsequently become major contributors to the *Quarterly Review*.

otherwise unaccountable slowness of good men in yielding implicit confidence to a party, who had such powerful arts of conversion in their hands, who could with impunity, and triumphantly, take away by atrocious calumnies the characters of all who disdained to be their tools, and rewarded with honours, places, and pensions all those who were. This is pitiful enough, we confess; but it is too painful to be dwelt on.

Passing from the Laureate's old Antijacobin, to his present Anti-ministerial persecutors—'*Publicly*', exclaims Mr. Coleridge, 'has Mr. Southey been reviled by men, who (I would fain hope, for the honour of human nature) hurled fire-brands against a figure of their own imagination, *publicly* have his talents been depreciated, his principles denounced'. This is very fine and lofty, no doubt; but we wish Mr. C. would speak a little plainer. Mr. Southey has come voluntarily before the public; and all the world has a right to speak of his publications. It is those only that have been either depretiated or denounced. We are not aware, at least, of any attacks that have been made, publicly or privately, on his private life or morality. The charge is, that he wrote democratical nonsense in his youth; and that he has not only taken to write against democracy in his maturer age, but has abused and reviled those who adhere to his former opinions; and accepted of emoluments from the party which formerly calumniated him, for those good services. Now, what has Mr. Coleridge to oppose to this? Mr. Southey's private character! He evades the only charge brought against him, by repelling one not brought against him, except by his Anti-jacobin patrons—and answers for his friend, as if he was playing at cross-purposes. Some people say, that Mr. Southey has deserted the cause of liberty: Mr. Coleridge tells us, that he has not separated from his wife. They say, that he has changed his opinions: Mr. Coleridge says, that he keeps his appointments; and has even invented a new word, *reliability*, to express his exemplariness in this particular. It is also objected, that the worthy Laureate was as extravagant in his early writings, as he is virulent in his present ones: Mr. Coleridge answers, that he is an early riser, and not a late sitter up. It is further alleged, that he is arrogant and shallow in political discussion, and clamours for vengeance in a cowardly and intemperate tone: Mr. Coleridge assures us, that he eats, drinks, and sleeps moderately. It is said that he must either have been very hasty in taking up his first opinions, or very unjustifiable in abandoning them for their contraries; and Mr. Coleridge observes, that Mr. Southey exhibits, in his own person and family, all the regularity and praiseworthy punctuality of an eight-day clock.

With all this we have nothing to do. Not only have we said nothing against this gentleman's private virtues, but we have regularly borne testimony to his talents and attainments as an author, while we have been compelled to take notice of his defects. Till this panegyric of Mr. Coleridge, indeed, we do not know where there was so much praise of him to be found as in our pages. Does Mr. Coleridge wish to get a monopoly for criticising the works of his friends? If we had a particular grudge against any of them, we might perhaps apply to him for his assistance.

Of Mr. Southey's prose writings we have had little opportunity to speak; but we should speak moderately. He has a clear and easy style, and brings a large share of information to most subjects he handles. But, on practical and political matters, we cannot think him a writer of any weight. He has too little sympathy with the common pursuits, the follies, the vices, and even the virtues of the rest of mankind, to have any tact or depth of insight into the actual characters or manners of men. He is in this respect a mere book-worm, shut up in his study, and too attentive to his literary duty to mind what is passing about him. He has no humour. His wit is at once scholastic and vulgar. As to general principles of any sort, we see no traces of any thing like them in any of his writings. He shows the same contempt for abstract reasoning that Mr. Coleridge has for 'history and particular facts'. Even his intimacy with the metaphysical author of *The Friend*, with whom he has chimed in, both in poetry and politics, in verse and prose, in Jacobinism and Antijacobinism, any time these twenty years, has never inoculated him with the most distant admiration of Hartley, or Berkeley, or Jacob Behmen, of Spinosa, or Kant, or Fichte, or Schelling. His essays are in fact the contents of his commonplace-book, strung together with little thought or judgment, and rendered marketable by their petulant adaptation to party-purposes—'full of wise saws and modern instances', with assertions for proofs, conclusions that savour more of a hasty temper than patient thinking—supported by learned authorities that oppress the slenderness of his materials, and quarrel with one another. But our business is not with him; and we leave him to his studies.

With Chap. IV begins the formidable ascent of that mountainous and barren ridge of clouds piled on precipices and precipices on clouds, from the top of which the author deludes us with a view of the Promised Land that divides the regions of Fancy from those of the Imagination, and extends through 200 pages with various inequalities and declensions to the end of the volume. The object of this long-winding metaphysical march, which resembles a patriarchal journey, is to point out and settle the true grounds of Mr. Wordsworth's claim to originality as a poet; which, if we rightly understand the deduction, turns out to be, that there is nothing peculiar about him; and that his poetry, in so far as it is good for anything at all, is just like any other good poetry. The learned author, indeed, judiciously observes, that Mr. Wordsworth would never have been 'idly and absurdly' considered as 'the founder of a school in poetry', if he had not, by some strange mistake, announced the fact himself in his preface to the *Lyrical Ballads*. This, it must be owned, looks as if Mr. Wordsworth thought more of his *peculiar* pretensions than Mr. Coleridge appears to do, and really furnishes some excuse for those who took the poet at his word; for which idle and hasty conclusion, moreover, his friend acknowledges that *there was* some little foundation in diverse silly and puerile passages of that collection, equally unworthy of the poet's great genius and classical taste.

We shall leave it to Mr. Wordsworth, however, to settle the relative worthlessness of these poems with his critical patron, and also to ascertain whether his commentator has discovered, either his *real* or his *probable* meaning in writing that Preface, and should now proceed with Mr. Coleridge up those intricate and inaccessible steeps to which he invites our steps. 'It has been hinted', says he, with characteristic simplicity, 'that metaphysics and psychology have long been my hobby-horse. But to have a hobby-horse, and to be vain of it, are so commonly found together, that they pass almost for the same'. *We own the soft impeachment*, as Mrs. Malaprop says, and can with difficulty resist the temptation of accepting this invitation—especially as it is accompanied with a sort of challenge. 'Those at least', he adds, 'who have taken so much pains to render me ridiculous for a perversion of taste, and have supported the charge by attributing strange notions to me, on no other authority than their own conjectures, owe it to themselves as well as to me, not to refuse their attention to my own statement of the theory which I *do* acknowledge, or shrink from the trouble of examining the grounds on which I rest it, or the arguments which I offer in its justification'. But, in spite of all this, we must not give way to temptation—and cannot help feeling, that the whole of this discussion is so utterly unreadable in Mr. Coleridge, that it would be most presumptuous to hope that it would become otherwise in our hands. We shall dismiss the whole of this metaphysical investigation, therefore, into the law of association and the nature of fancy, by shortly observing, that we can by no means agree with Mr. C. in refusing to Hobbes the merit of originality in promulgating that law, with its consequences, that we agree with him, generally, in his refutation of Hartley, and that we totally dissent from his encomium on Kant and his followers.

With regard to the claims of the philosopher of Malmesbury as the first discoverer of the principle of association, as it is now understood among metaphysicians, Mr. C. thinks fit to deny it *in toto*, because Descartes's work, *De Methodo*, in which there is an intimation of the same doctrine, preceded Hobbes's *De Natura Humana by a whole year.* What an interval to invent and mature a whole system in! But we conceive that Hobbes has a strict claim to the merit of originality in this respect, because he is the first writer who laid down this principle as *the sole and universal law* of connexion among our ideals: which principle Hartley afterwards illustrated and applied to an infinite number of particular cases, but did not assert the general theorem itself more broadly or explicitly. We deny that the statement of this principle, as *the* connecting band of our ideas, is to be found in any of those writers before Hobbes, whom Mr. Coleridge enumerates; Descartes or Melancthon, or those more 'illustrious obscure', Ammerbach, or Ludovicus Vives, or even Aristotle. It is not the having remarked, that association was one source of connexion among certain ideas, that would anticipate this discovery or the theory of Hartley; but the asserting, that this principle was alone sufficient to account for every operation of the human mind, and that there was no other source of connexion among our ideas, a proposition which Hobbes was undoubtedly the first to assert, and by the assertion of which he did certainly anticipate the system of Hartley; for all that the latter could do, or has attempted to do, after this, was to prove the proposition in detail, or to reduce all the phenomena to this one general law. That Hobbes was in fact the original inventor of the doctrine of Association, and of the modern system of philosophy in general, is matter of fact and history; as to which, we are surprised that Mr. C. should profess any doubt, and which we had gratified ourselves by illustrating by a series of citations from his greater works—which nothing but a sense of the prevailing indifference to such discussions prevents us from laying before our readers.

As for the great German oracle Kant, we must take the liberty to say, that his system appears to us the most wilful and monstrous absurdity that ever was invented. If the French theories of the mind were too chemical, this is too mechanical: if the one referred every thing to nervous sensibility, the other refers every thing to the test of muscular resistance and voluntary prowess. It is an enormous heap of dogmatical and hardened assertions, advanced in contradiction to all former systems, and all unsystematical opinions and impressions. He has but one method of getting over difficulties: when he is at a loss to account for any thing, and cannot give a reason for it, he turns short round upon the inquirer, and says that it is self-evident. If he cannot make good an inference upon acknowledged premises, or known methods of reasoning, he coolly refers the whole to a new class of ideas, and the operation of some unknown faculty, which he has invented for the purpose, and which he assures you *must* exist, because there is no other proof of it. His whole theory is machinery and scaffolding—an elaborate account of what he has undertaken to do, because no one else has been able to do it—and an *assumption* that he has done it, because he has undertaken it. If the will were to go for the deed, and to be confident were to be wise, he would indeed be the prince of philosophers. For example, he sets out with urging the indispensable necessity of answering Hume's argument on the origin of our idea of cause and effect; and because he can find no answer to this argument, in the experimental philosophy, he affirms, that this idea *must be* 'a self-evident truth, contained in the first forms or categories of the understanding'; that is, the thing must be as he would have it, whether it is so or not. Again, he argues that external objects exist because they seem to exist; and yet he denies that we know any thing at all about the matter, further than their appearances. He defines beauty to be perfection, and virtue to consist in a conformity to our duty; with other such deliberate truisms; and then represents necessity as inconsistent with morality, and insists on the existence and certainty of the free-will as a faculty necessary to explain the *moral sense*, which could not exist without it. This transcendental philosopher is also pleased to affirm, in so many words, that we have neither any possible idea, nor any possible proof of the existence of the Soul, God, or Immortality, by means of the ordinary faculties of sense, understanding, or reason; and he therefore (like a man who had been employed to construct a machine for some particular purpose), invents a new faculty, for the admission and demonstration of these important truths, *namely*, the *practical reason*; in other words, the will or determination that these things should be infinitely true because they are infinitely desirable to the human mind, though he says it is impossible for the human mind to have any idea whatever of these objects, either as true or desirable. But we turn gladly from absurdities that have not even the merit of being amusing; and leave Mr. Coleridge to the undisturbed adoration of an idol who will have few other worshippers in this country. His own speculations are, beyond all comparison, more engaging.

In Chap. IX Mr. Coleridge, taking leave of that 'sound booklearned-ness' which he had opposed, in the Lay Sermon, to the upstart preten-sions of modern literature, praises the inspired ignorance, upward flights, and inward yearnings of Jacob Behmen, George Fox and De Thoyras, and proceeds to defend himself against the charge of plagiar-ism, of which he suspects that he may be suspected by the readers of Schlegel and Schelling, when he comes to unfold, in fulness of time, the mysterious laws of the drama and the human mind. And thereafter, the 'extravagant and erring' author takes leave of the Pantheism of Spinoza, of Proclus, and Gemistius Pletho, of the philosopher of Nola, 'whom the idolaters of Rome, the predecessors of that good old man, the present Pope, burnt as an atheist in the year 1660'; of the *Noumenon*, or Thing in itself; of Fichte's ORDO ORDINANS, or exoteric God; of Simon Grynæus, Barclay's *Argenis* and Hooker's *Ecclesiastical Polity*, from whom the author 'cites a cluster of citations, to amuse the reader, as with a voluntary before a sermon'—to plunge into Chap. X, entitled 'A Chapter of Digressions and Anecdotes, as an interlude preceding that on the Nature and Genesis of the Imagination or Plastic Power!'

As this latter chapter, by the advice of a correspondent, has been omitted, we must make the most of what is left, and 'wander down into a lower world obscure and wild', to give the reader an account of Mr. Coleridge's setting up the *Watchman*, which is one of the first things to which he *digresses*, in the tenth chapter of his Literary Biog-raphy. Out of regard to Mr. C. as well as to our readers, we give our longest extract from this narrative part of the work—which is more likely to be popular than any other part—and is, upon the whole, more pleasingly written. We cannot say much, indeed, either for the wit or the soundness of judgment it displays. But it is an easy, gossip-ping, garrulous account of youthful adventures—by a man sufficiently fond of talking of himself, and sufficiently disposed to magnify small matters into ideal importance.

Toward the close of the first year from the time that, in an inauspicious hour, I left the friendly cloysters, and the happy grove of quiet, ever-honoured, Jesus College, Cambridge, I was persuaded, by sundry Philanthropists and Anti-polemists, to set on foot a periodical work, entitled THE WATCHMAN, that (according to the general motto of the work) *all might know the truth, and that the truth might make us free!* In order to exempt it from the stamp-tax, and likewise to contribute as little as possible to the supposed guilt of a war against freedom, it was to be published on every eighth day, thirty-two pages, large octavo, closely printed, and price only Fourpence. Accordingly, with a flaming prospectus, *'Knowledge is power'*, &c. *to try the state of the political atmosphere*, and so forth, I set off on a tour to the North, from Bristol to Sheffield, for the purpose of procuring customers; preaching by the way in most of the great towns, as a hireless volunteer, in a blue coat and white waist-coat, that not a rag of the woman of Babylon might be seen on me. For I was at that time, and long after, though a Trinitarian (*i.e. ad normam Platonis*) in philosophy, yet a zealous Unitarian in religion; more accurately, I was a *psilanthropist*, one of those who believe our Lord to have been the real son of Joseph, and who lay the main stress on the resurrection, rather than on the crucifixion. O! never can I remember those days with either shame or regret. For I was most sincere, most disinterested! My opinions were indeed in many and most important points erroneous; but my heart was single. Wealth, rank, life itself then seemed cheap to me, compared with the interests of (what I believed to be) the truth, and the will of my Maker. I cannot even accuse myself of having been actuated by vanity; for in the expansion of my enthus-iasm, I did not think of *myself* at all.

My campaign commenced at Birmingham; and my first attack was on a rigid Calvinist, a tallow-chandler by trade. He was a tall dingy man, in whom length was so predominant over breadth, that he might almost have been borrowed for a foundery poker. O that face! a face κατέμφασιν! I have it before me at this moment. The lank, black, twine-like hair, *pingui-nitescent*, cut in a straight line along the black stubble of his thin gunpowder eyebrows, that looked like a scorched *after-math* from a last week's shaving. His coat-collar behind in perfect unison, both of colour and lustre, with the coarse, yet glib cordage, that I suppose he called his hair, and which, with a *bend* inward at the nape of the neck, (the only approach to flexure in his whole figure), slunk in behind his waistcoat; while the countenance, lank, dark, very *hard*, and with strong perpendicular furrows, gave me a dim notion of some one looking at me through a *used* gridiron, all soot, grease, and iron! But he was one of the *thorough-bred*, a true lover of liberty; and (I was informed) had proved to the satisfaction of many, that Mr. Pitt was one of the horns of the second beast in the Revelation, *that spoke like a dragon*. A person, to whom one of my letters of recommendation had been addressed, was my introducer. It was a new event in my life, my first *stroke* in the new business I had undertaken, of an author; yea, and of an author trading on his own account. My companion, after some imperfect sentences, and a multitude of *hums* and *haas*, abandoned the cause to his client; and I commenced an harangue of half an hour to Phileleutheros the tallow-chandler, varying my notes through the whole gamut of eloquence, from the ratiocinative to the declamatory, and in the latter, from the pathetic to the indignant. I argued, I described, I promised, I prophesied; and, beginning with the captivity of nations, I ended with the near approach of the millennium; finishing the whole with some of my own verses, describing that glorious state, out of the 'Religious Musings'.

> Such delights,
> As float to earth, permitted visitants!
> When in some hour of solemn jubilee
> The massive gates of Paradise are thrown
> Wide open: and forth come in fragments wild
> Sweet echoes of unearthly melodies,
> And odours snatch'd from beds of amaranth,
> And they that from the chrystal river of life
> Spring up on freshen'd wings, ambrosial gales!

My taper man of lights listened with perseverant and praiseworthy patience, though (as I was afterwards told on complaining of certain gales that were not altogether ambrosial) it was a *melting* day with him. And what, Sir! (he said, after a short pause) might the cost be? *Only four-pence,* (O! how I felt the anti-climax, the abysmal bathos of that *four-pence!*) *only four-pence, Sir, each Number, to be published on every eighth day.* That comes to a deal of money at the end of a year. And how much did you say there was to be for the money? *Thirty-two pages, Sir! large octavo, closely printed.* Thirty and two pages? Bless me; why, except what I does in a family way on the Sabbath, that's more than I ever reads, Sir! all the year round. I am as great a one as any man in Brummagem, Sir! for liberty, and truth, and all them sort of things; but as to this, (no offence, I hope, Sir!) I must beg to be excused.

So ended my first canvass: from causes that I shall presently mention, I made but one other application in person. This took place at Manchester, to a stately and opulent wholesale dealer in cottons. He took my letter of introduc-tion, and having perused it, measured me from head to foot, and again from foot to head, and then asked if I had any bill or invoice of the thing. I presented my prospectus to him; he rapidly skimmed and hummed over the first side, and still more rapidly the second and concluding page; crushed it within his fingers and the palm of his hand; then most deliberately and *significantly* rubbed and smoothed one part against the other; and lastly, putting it into his pocket, turned his back on me with an '*overrun* with these articles!' and so without another syllable retired into his counting-house—and, I can truly say, to my unspeakable amusement.

This, I have said, was my second and last attempt. On returning baffled from the first, in which I had vainly essayed to repeat the miracle of Orpheus with the Brummagem patriot, I dined with the tradesman who had introduced me to him. After dinner, he importuned me to smoke a pipe with him, and two or three other illuminati of the same rank. I objected, both because I was engaged to spend the evening with a minister and his friends, and because I had never smoked except once or twice in my lifetime; and then it was herb tobacco, mixed with Oronooko. On the assurance, however, that the tobacco was equally mild, and seeing too that it was of a yellow colour (not forgetting the lamentable difficulty I have always experienced in saying, No! and in abstaining from what the people about me were doing), I took half a pipe, filling the lower half of the bole with salt. I was soon, however, compelled to resign it, in consequence of a giddiness and distressful feeling in my eyes, which, as I had drank but a single glass of ale, must, I knew, have been the effect of the tobacco. Soon after, deeming myself recovered, I sallied forth to my engagement; but the walk and the fresh air brought on all the symptoms again; and I had scarcely entered the minister's drawing-room, and opened a small packet of letters which he had received from Bristol for me, ere I sunk back on the sofa, in a sort of swoon rather than sleep. Fortunately I had found just time enough to inform him of the confused state of my feelings, and of the occasion. For here and thus I lay, my face like a wall that is white-washing, *deathy* pale, and with the cold drops of perspiration running down it from my forehead, while, one after another, there dropt in the different gentlemen, who had been invited to meet and spend the evening with me, to the number of from fifteen to twenty. As the poison of tobacco acts but for a short time, I at length awoke from insensibility, and looked around on the party; my eyes dazzled by the candles which had been lighted in the interim. By way of relieving my embarrassment, one of the gentlemen began the conversation with '*Have you seen a paper today, Mr. Coleridge?*'—'Sir! (I replied, rubbing my eyes), I am far from convinced, that a Christian is permitted* to read either newspapers or any other works of merely political and temporary interest.' This remark, so ludicrously inapposite to, or rather incongruous with, the purpose for which I was known to have visited Birmingham, and to assist me in which they were all then met, produced an involuntary and general burst of laughter; and seldom, indeed, have I passed so many delightful hours as I enjoyed in that room, from the moment of that laugh to an early hour the next morning. Never, perhaps, in so mixed and numerous a party, have I since heard conversation sustained with such animation, enriched with such variety of information, and enlivened with such a flow of anecdote. Both then and afterwards, they all joined in dissuading me from proceeding with my scheme; assured me, with

* With all proper allowances for the effects of the Mundungus, we must say that this answer appears to us very curiously characteristic of the exaggerated and canting tone of this poet and his associates. A man may or may not think time misemployed in reading newspapers; but we believe no man, out of the Pantisocratic or Lake school, ever dreamed of denouncing it as unchristian and impious— even if he had not himself begun and ended his career as an Editor of newspapers. The same absurd exaggeration is visible in his magnificent eulogium on the conversational talents of his Birmingham Unitarians.

the most friendly, and yet most flattering expressions, that the employment was neither fit for me, nor I fit for the employment. Yet if I had determined on persevering in it, they promised to exert themselves to the utmost to procure subscribers, and insisted that I should make no more applications in person, but carry on the canvass by proxy. The same hospitable reception, the same dissuasion, and (that failing) the same kind exertions in my behalf, I met with at Manchester, Derby, Nottingham, Sheffield, indeed at every place in which I took up my sojourn. I often recall, with affectionate pleasure, the many respectable men who interested themselves for me, a perfect stranger to them, not a few of whom I can still name among my friends. They will bear witness for me, how opposite, even then, my principles were to those of Jacobinism, or even of Democracy, and can attest the strict accuracy of the statement which I have left on record in the 10th and 11th Numbers of *The Friend*.

We shall not stop at present to dispute with Mr. Coleridge, how far the principles of the *Watchman*, and the *Conciones ad Populum* were or were not akin to those of the Jacobins. His style, in general, admits of a convenient latitude of interpretation. But we think we are quite safe in asserting, that they were still more opposite to those of the Anti-Jacobins, and the party to which he admits he has gone over.

Our author next gives a somewhat extraordinary account of his having been set upon with his friend Wordsworth, by a Government spy, in his retreat at Nether-Stowey—the most lively thing in which is, that the said spy, who, it seems had a great red nose, and had over-heard the friends discoursing about *Spinosa*, reported to his employers, that he could make out very little of what they said, only he was sure they were aware of his vicinity, as he heard them very often talking of *Spy-nosy!* If this is not the very highest vein of wit in the world, it must be admitted at least to be very innocent merriment. Another excellent joke of the same character is his remark on an Earl of Cork not paying for his copy of the *Friend*—that he might have been an Earl of *Bottle* for him! We have then some memorandums of his excursion into Germany, and the conditions on which he agreed, on his return home in 1800, to write for the *Morning Post*, which was at that time not a very ministerial paper, if we remember right.

A propos of the *Morning Post*, Mr. C. takes occasion to eulogise the writings of Mr. Burke, and observes, that 'as our very signboards give evidence that there has been a Titian in the world, so the essays and leading paragraphs of our journals are so many remembrancers of Edmund Burke'. This is modest and natural we suppose for a news-paper editor: but our learned author is desirous of carrying the parallel a little further, and assures us, that nobody can doubt of Mr. Burke's consistency. 'Let the scholar', says our biographer, 'who doubts this assertion, refer only to the speeches and writings of Edmund Burke at the commencement of the American war, and compare them with his speeches and writings at the commencement of the French Revolution. He will find the principles exactly the same, and the deductions the same—but the practical inferences almost opposite in the one case from those drawn in the other, yet in both equally legitimate and confirmed by the results.'

It is not without reluctance that we speak of the vices and infirmities of such a mind as Burke's: but the poison of high example has by far the widest range of destruction; and, for the sake of public honour and individual integrity, we think it right to say, that however it may be defended upon other grounds, the political career of that eminent individual has no title to the praise of consistency. Mr. Burke, the opponent of the American war—and Mr. Burke, the opponent of the French Revolution, are not the same person, but opposite persons—not opposite persons only, but deadly enemies. In the latter period, he abandoned not only all his practical conclusions, but all the principles on which they were founded. He proscribed all his former sentiments, denounced all his former friends, rejected and reviled all the maxims to which he had formerly appealed as incontestable. In the American war, he constantly spoke of the rights of the people as inherent, and inalienable: after the French Revolution, he began by treating them with the chicanery of a sophist, and ended by raving at them with the fury of a maniac. In the former case, he held out the duty of resistance to oppression, as the palladium, and only ultimate resource, of natural liberty; in the latter, he scouted, prejudged, vilified and nicknamed, all resistance in the abstract, as a foul and unnatural union of rebellion and sacrilege. In the one case, to answer the purposes of faction, he made it out, that the people are always in the right; in the other, to answer different ends, he made it out that they are always in the wrong—lunatics in the hands of their royal keepers, patients in the sick-wards of an hospital, or felons in the condemned cells of a prison. In the one, he considered that there was a constant tendency on the part of the prerogative to encroach on the rights of the people, which ought always to be the object of the most watchful jealousy, and of resistance, when necessary: in the other, he pretended to regard it as the sole occupation and ruling passion of those in power, to watch over the liberties and happiness of their subjects. The burthen of all his speeches on the American war was conciliation, concession, timely reform, as the only practicable or desirable alternative of rebellion: the object of all his writings on the French Revolution was, to deprecate and explode all concession and all reform, as encouraging rebellion, and an irretrievable step to revolution and anarchy. In the one, he insulted kings personally, as among the lowest and worst of mankind; in the other, he held them up to the imagination of his readers as sacred abstractions. In the one case, he was a partisan of the people, to court popularity; in the other, to gain the favour of the Court, he became the apologist of all courtly abuses. In the one case, he took part with those who were actually rebels against his Sovereign; in the other, he denounced, as rebels and traitors, all those of his own countrymen who did not yield sympathetic allegiance to a foreign Sovereign, whom we had always been in the habit of treating as an arbitrary tyrant.

Judging from plain facts and principles, then, it is difficult to conceive more ample proofs of inconsistency. But try it by the more vulgar and palpable test of comparison. Even Mr. Fox's enemies, we think, allow *him* the praise of consistency. *He* asserted the rights of the people in the American war, and continued to assert them in the French Revolution. He remained visibly in his place; and spoke, throughout, the same principles in the same language. When Mr. Burke abjured these principles, he left this associate; nor did it ever enter into the mind of a human being to impute the defection to any change in Mr. Fox's sentiments—any desertion by him of the maxims by which his public life had been guided. Take another illustration, from an opposite quarter. Nobody will accuse the principles of his present Majesty, or the general measures of his reign, of inconsistency. If they had no other merit, they have at least that of having been all along actuated by one uniform and constant spirit: yet Mr. Burke at one time vehemently opposed, and afterwards most intemperately extolled them; and it was for his recanting his opposition, not for his persevering in it, that he received his pension. He does not himself mention his flaming speeches in the American war, as among the public services which had entitled him to this remuneration.

The truth is, that Burke was a man of fine fancy and subtle reflection; but not of sound and practical judgment, nor of high or rigid principles. As to his understanding, he certainly was not a great philosopher; for his works of mere abstract reasoning are shallow and inefficient: nor a man of sense and business; for, both in counsel and in conduct, he alarmed his friends as much at least as his opponents: but he was a keen and accomplished pamphleteer—an ingenious political essayist. He applied the habit of reflection, which he had borrowed from his meta-physical studies, but which was not competent to the discovery of any elementary truth in that department, with great felicity and success, to the mixed mass of human affairs. He knew more of the political machine than a recluse philosopher; and he speculated more profoundly on its principles and general results than a mere politician. He saw a number of fine distinctions and changeable aspects of things, the good mixed with the ill, the ill mixed with the good; and with a sceptical indifference, in which the exercise of his own ingenuity was always the governing principle, suggested various topics to qualify or assist the judgment of others. But for this very reason he was little calculated to become a leader or a partisan in any important practical measure: for the habit of his mind would lead him to find out a reason for or against any thing: and it is not on speculative refinements (which belong to *every* side of a question) but on a just estimate of the aggregate mass and extended combinations of objections and advantages, that we ought to decide and act. Burke had the power, almost without limit, of throwing true or false weights into the scales of political casuistry, but not firmness of mind—or, shall we say, honesty enough—to hold the balance. When he took a side, his vanity or his spleen more frequently gave the casting vote than his judgment; and the fieriness of his zeal was in exact proportion to the levity of his understanding, and the want of conscious sincerity.

He was fitted by nature and habit for the studies and labours of the closet; and was generally mischievous when he came out; because the very subtlety of his reasoning, which, left to itself, would have counteracted its own activity, or found its level in the common sense of mankind, became a dangerous engine in the hands of power, which is always eager to make use of the most plausible pretexts to cover the most fatal designs. That which, if applied as a general observation on human affairs, is a valuable truth suggested to the mind, may, when forced into the interested defence of a particular measure or system, become the grossest and basest sophistry. Facts or consequences never stood in the way of this speculative politician. He fitted them to his preconceived theories, instead of conforming his theories to them. They were the playthings of his style, the sport of his fancy. They were the straws of which his imagination made a blaze, and were consumed, like straws, in the blaze they had served to kindle. The fine things he said about Liberty and Humanity, in his speech on the Begum's affairs, told equally well, whether Warren Hastings was a tyrant or not: nor did he care one jot who caused the famine he described, so that he described it in a way to attract admiration. On the same principle, he represents the French priests and nobles under the old regime as excellent moral people, very charitable, and very religious, in the teeth of notorious facts, to answer to the handsome things he has to say in favour of priesthood and nobility in general; and, with similar views, he falsifies the records of our English Revolution, and puts an interpretation on the word *abdication*, of which a schoolboy would be ashamed. He constructed his whole theory of government, in short, not on rational, but on picturesque and fanciful principles; as if the King's crown were a painted gewgaw, to be looked at on gala-days; titles an empty sound to please the ear; and the whole order of society a theatrical procession. His lamentation over the age of chivalry, and his projected crusade to restore it, is about as wise as if any one, from reading the *Beggar's Opera*, should take to picking of pockets; or, from admiring the landscapes of Salvator Rosa, should wish to convert the abodes of civilized life into the haunts of wild beasts and banditti. On this principle of false refinement, there is no abuse, nor system of abuses, that does not admit of an easy and triumphant defence; for there is something which a merely speculative inquirer may always find out, good as well as bad, in every possible system, the best or the worst; and if we can once get rid of the restraints of common sense and honesty, we may easily prove, by plausible words, that liberty and slavery, peace and war, plenty and famine, are matters of perfect indifference. This is the school of politics, of which Mr. Burke was at the head; and it is perhaps to his example, in this respect, that we owe the prevailing tone of many of those newspaper paragraphs, which Mr. Coleridge thinks so invaluable an accession to our political philosophy.

Burke's literary talents, were, after all, his chief excellence. His style has all the familiarity of conversation, and all the research of the most elaborate composition. He says what he wants to say, by any means, nearer or more remote, within his reach. He makes use of the most common or scientific terms, of the longest or shortest sentences, of the plainest and most downright, or of the most figurative modes of speech. He gives for the most part loose reins to his imagination, and follows it as far as the language will carry him. As long as the one or the other has any resources in store to make the reader feel and see the thing as he has conceived it, in its nicest shade of difference, in its utmost degree of force and splendour, he never disdains, and never fails to employ them. Yet, in the extremes of his mixed style there is not much affectation, and but little either of pedantry or of coarseness. He everywhere gives the image he wishes to give, in its true and appropriate colouring: and it is the very crowd and variety of these images that have given to his language its peculiar tone of animation, and even of passion. It is his impatience to transfer his conceptions entire, living, in all their rapidity, strength, and glancing variety—to the minds of others, that constantly pushes him to the verge of extravagance, and yet supports him there in dignified security:

> Never so sure our rapture to create,
> As when he treads the brink of all we hate.

He is, with the exception of Jeremy Taylor, the most poetical of prose writers and at the same time his prose never degenerates into the mere glitter or tinkling of poetry; for he always aims at overpowering rather than at pleasing; and consequently sacrifices beauty and grandeur to force and vividness. He has invariably a task to perform, a positive purpose to execute, an effect to produce. His only object is therefore to strike hard, and in the right place; if he misses his mark, he repeats his blow; and does not care how ungraceful the action, or how clumsy the instrument, provided it brings down his antagonist.

Mr. C. enters next into a copious discussion of the merits of his friend Mr. Wordsworth's poetry, which we do not think very remarkable either for clearness or candour; but as a very great part of it is occupied with specific inculpations of our former remarks on that ingenious author, it would savour too much of mere controversy and recrimination, if we were to indulge ourselves with any observations on the subject. Where we are parties to any dispute, and consequently to be regarded as incapable of giving an *impartial* account of our adversary's argument, we shall not pretend to give any account of it at all;*

* If Mr. C. had confined himself to matter of argument, or to statements contained in the Review, we should have added no note to this passage, but left him in quiet possession of the last word on the critical question he has thought fit to resume. But as he has been pleased to make several averments in point of fact, touching the personal conduct and motives of his Reviewer, we must be indulged with a few words to correct the errors into which he has fallen: for, though we have no ambition to maintain public disputations with every one who may chuse to question the justice of our opinions, it might appear as if we acquiesced in averments of a personal and injurious nature, if we were to review a work in which they occur, without taking any notice of their inaccuracy.

In a long note at page 52d of his first volume, Mr. C. has stated that some years ago the principal conductor of this Review paid a visit at Keswick, 'and was, notwithstanding, treated with every hospitable attention by him and Mr. Southey'—that he paid Mr. C. more compliments than he ever received in the same time from any other person—that he was distinctly told that he and Mr. Southey and Mr. Wordsworth had only come together by accident, and that they did not consider themselves as belonging to any school, but that of good sense, confirmed by the study of the best models of Greece, Rome, Italy and England— that, notwithstanding all this, one of the first things this Reviewer did after his return, was to write an article, in which he characterized these gentlemen as 'the school of whining and hypochondriacal poets that haunt the lakes'. Moreover, that after Mr. C. had written a letter to the same gentleman on the comparative merits and defects of our best prose writers before Charles II, he printed an article on this subject, in which he stated, that it was one of his objects to separate a rational admiration of those writers from the indiscriminate enthusiasm of a recent school, who praised what they did not understand, and caricatured what they could not imitate; and added the names of Miss Baillie, Southey, Wordsworth and Coleridge, as the persons to whom he alluded: that Mr. C. has heard 'from authority which demands his belief', that the Reviewer, upon being questioned as to the motive of this apparently wanton attack, answered, that Miss B. had declined being introduced to him when on a visit at Edinburgh—that Mr. Southey had written, and Mr. Wordsworth spoken against him—and that the name of Coleridge always went with the two others! Mr. C. has further stated, at p. 299th of his second volume, apparently with reference to the same gentlemen, that what he there terms the malignant review of 'Christabel', which appeared in this Journal, was generally attributed to a man who, both in his presence and his absence, had repeatedly pronounced it the finest poem of its kind in the language— and, finally, at p. 302 of that volume, Mr. C. is pleased to assert, that his *Lay Sermon*, having been reviewed somewhere by anticipation, with avowed personal malignity, the author of that lampoon was chosen (of course by the conductors of that work), to review it in the *Edinburgh*—the author being a person very fit for the task, if he had been allowed to write what he himself really thought;—and that, therefore, Mr. C. 'confines his indignant contempt to his employer and suborner'.

These are Mr. C.'s charges against the principal conductor of the *Edinburgh Review*; to which, in order to avoid all equivocation, that individual begs leave to answer distinctly, and in the first person as follows.

I do not know that I need say any thing in answer to the *first* imputation; as I suppose I might lawfully visit and even pay compliments to an ingenious gentleman, whose poetry I was, notwithstanding, obliged to characterize as whining and hypochondriacal; and if I found two or three such gentlemen living together —publishing in the same volume, and adopting the same peculiar style and manner, I conceive I was entitled to hold them up as aiming, *de facto*, at the formation of a new school—especially if I gave my reasons and proofs at large for that opinion— although one of them did not agree in that opinion, and had modestly assured me, 'that they belonged to no school but that of good sense, confirmed by the long established models of the best times of Greece, Italy and England'. But as Mr. C.'s statement is so given, as to convey an imputation of great ingratitude or violation of the laws of hospitality on my part, I shall mention, in a few words, as nearly as I can now recollect them, the circumstances of this famous visit.

It was in 1810, I think, that I went with some of my near relations to Cumberland. I had previously been in some correspondence of a literary nature with

Mr. C., though I had never seen him personally. Mr. Southey I had seen in the company of some common friends, both at Edinburgh and Keswick, a year or two before; and though he then knew me to be the reviewer of his *Thalaba* and *Madoc*, he undoubtedly treated me with much courtesy and politeness. I had heard, however, in the *interim*, that he had expressed himself on the subject of the *Edinburgh Review* with so much bitterness, that I certainly should not have thought of intruding myself spontaneously into his company. When I came to Keswick, I had not the least idea that Mr. C. lived in Mr. Southey's house; and sent a note from the inn, saying, I should be glad to wait on him. He returned for answer, that he *and Mr. Southey*, would be glad to see me. I thought it would be pitiful to decline this invitation; and went immediately. Mr. Southey received me with cold civility—and, being engaged with other visiters, I had very little conversation with him. With Mr. C. I had a great deal; and was very much amused and interested. I believe coffee was offered me—and I came away in an hour or two. I did not see Mr. Southey afterwards. Next day, Mr. C. and I spent all the morning together in the fields, he did me the honour to dine with me at the inn, and next morning I left Keswick, and have not seen him since.

At this distance of time I do not pretend to recollect all that passed between us. I perfectly recollect, however, that I was much struck with the eloquence and poetical warmth of his conversation; of which all my friends can testify that I have ever since been in the habit of speaking with admiration. I dare say I may have expressed that sentiment to him. Indeed, I remember, that when dissuading him from publishing on metaphysical subjects, I exhorted him rather to give us more poetry, and, upon his replying that it cost him more labour, I observed, that his whole talk to me that morning was poetry. I think I said also, that the verses entitled 'Love' were the best in the *Lyrical Ballads*, and had always appeared to me extremely beautiful. These are the only compliments I can remember paying him; and they were paid with perfect sincerity. But it rather appeared to me that Mr. C. liked to receive compliments; and I may have been led to gratify him in other instances. I cannot say I recollect of his telling me that he and his friends were of no school but that of good sense, &c.; but I remember perfectly that he complained a good deal of my coupling his name with theirs in the Review, saying, that he had published no verses for a long time, and that his own style was very unlike theirs. I promised that I would take his name out of the firm for the future; and I kept my promise. We spoke too of 'Christabel', and I advised him to publish it; but I did not say it was either the finest poem of the kind, or a fine poem at all; and I am sure of this, for the best of all reasons, that at this time, and indeed till after it was published, I never saw or heard more than four or five lines of it, which my friend Mr. Scott once repeated to me. That eminent person, indeed, spoke favourably of it; and I rather think I told Mr. C. that I had heard him say, that it was to it he was indebted for the first idea of that romantic narrative in irregular verse, which he afterwards exemplified in his *Lay of the Last Minstrel*, and other works. In these circumstances, I felt a natural curiosity to see this great original; and I can sincerely say, that no admirer of Mr. C. could be more disappointed or astonished than I was, when it did make its appearance. I did not review it.

As to Mr. C.'s letter to me, on our older prose writers, I utterly deny that I borrowed any thing from it, or had it at all in my thoughts, in any review I afterwards wrote: and with regard to the reasons which I am alleged to have assigned for specifying Miss Baillie, and Messrs Southey, Wordsworth and Coleridge, as injudicious imitators of these writers, I must say, in direct terms, that the allegation is totally and absolutely false; and that I never either made any such statement, or could have made it, without as great a violation of truth as of common sense and decency. I cannot, indeed, either remember, or find in the Review, any such passage as Mr. C. has here imputed to me—nor indeed can I conjecture what passage he has in view, unless it be one at p. 283 of Vol. XVIII., in which I do not say one word about their praising what they do not understand, or caricaturing what they could not imitate, but merely observe, in the course of a general review of the revolutions in our national taste and poetry, that 'Southey, Wordsworth, Coleridge, and Miss Baillie, have all of them copied the manner of our older poets; and, along with this indication of good taste, have given great proofs of original genius. The misfortune, however, (I add) is, that *their* copies of these great originals are liable to the charge of great affectation'; and after explaining this remark at some length, I conclude, that 'notwithstanding all these faults, there is a fertility and a force, a warmth of feeling and exaltation of fancy about them, which classes them with a much higher order of poets than the followers of Dryden and Addison, and justifies an anxiety for their fame in all the admirers of Milton and Shakespeare'. I cannot think that there was anything in the tone or manner of these remarks that savoured at all of personal pique or hostility: and, that I was most naturally and innocently led to make them in the place where they occur, will be evident, I conceive, to any one who will take the trouble to look back, either to the passage to which I have referred, where they will be found to *constitute* a *necessary* part of the historical deduction in which I was engaged, or to what I had previously said, in other articles, of the style and diction of these several authors, and in particular of their affected imitation or injudicious revival of antiquated forms of expression. In the reviews of their separate works, I had imputed this to them as a fault, and had dwelt upon it, and illustrated it by examples at considerable length. This the reader will find done, with regard to Miss Baillie, at p. 283 of vol. II. and p. 270 of vol. XIX.; with regard to Mr. Southey at p. 16, &c. of vol. VII., and Mr. Wordsworth at p. 217 vol. XI. It is very true, that Mr. Coleridge had not been previously censured in detail for this fault, because he had published nothing with his name, from the commencement of the Review up to the period in question: but the author of the 'Antient Mariner' could not well complain of being thus classed with the other writers of the *Lyrical Ballads*. Now, when, after this, I had been led to say a great deal on the exquisite diction of many of our old writers, was it not natural that I should endeavour to meet the charge of inconsistency that might be suggested to superficial observers, by recurring to the errors and imperfections, as they appeared to me, of the imitations which *they* had attempted, and which had made their unskilful adoption of old words a mere deformity? With regard to the genuine love and knowledge of these antients, which might be shown in Mr. C.'s letter, I am sorry to say, that I have mislaid it, so as not to be able to refer to it. According to my recollection, however, there were not above two sentences on the subject; and, at all events, it is obvious to remark, that the most thorough acquaintance with these authors is not at all inconsistent with an unlucky selection, or injudicious use of words borrowed from their writings. Of the justice of my observations on the archaisms of the authors I have reviewed, the public will ultimately judge. I made them with sincerity—and I adhere to them; nor can I understand how my having received this letter from Mr. C. can bring that sincerity into question.

As to the review of the *Lay Sermon*, I have only to say, in one word, that I never employed or suborned any body to abuse or extol it or any other publication. I do not so much as know or conjecture what Mr. C. alludes to as a malignant lampoon or review by anticipation, which he says had previously appeared somewhere else. I never saw nor heard of any such publication. Nay, I was not even aware of the existence of the *Lay Sermon* itself, when a review of it was offered me by a gentleman in whose judgment and talents I had great confidence, but whom I certainly never suspected, and do not suspect at this moment, of having any personal or partial feelings of any kind towards its author. I therefore accepted his offer, and printed his review, with some retrenchments and verbal alterations, just as I was setting off, in a great hurry, for London, on professional business, in January last.

It is painful, and perhaps ridiculous, to write so much about one's self; but I would rather submit to this ridicule than to the imputations which Mr. C. has permitted himself to make on me—or even to the consciousness of having made these rash and injurious imputations.   F.J.

and therefore, though we shall endeavour to give all due weight to Mr. C.'s reasonings, when we have occasion to consider any new publication from the Lake school, we must for the present decline any notice of the particular objections he has here urged to our former judgments on their productions; and shall pass over all this part of the work before us, by merely remarking, that with regard to Mr. Wordsworth's ingenious project of confining the language of poetry to that which is chiefly in use among the lower orders of society, and that, from horror or contempt for the abuses of what has been called poetic diction, it is really unnecessary to say anything—the truth and common sense of the thing being so obvious, and, we apprehend, so generally acknowledged, that nothing but a pitiful affectation of singularity could have raised a controversy on the subject. There is, no doubt, a simple and familiar language, common to almost all ranks, and intelligible through many ages, which is the best fitted for the direct expression of strong sense and deep passion, and which, consequently, is the language of the best poetry as well as of the best prose. But it is not the exclusive language of poetry. There is another language peculiar to this manner of writing, which has been called *poetic diction*,—those flowers of speech, which, whether natural of artificial, fresh or faded, are strewed over the plainer ground which poetry has in common with prose; a paste of rich and honeyed words, like the candied coat of the auricula; a glittering tissue of quaint conceits and sparkling metaphors, crusting over the rough stalk of homely thoughts. Such is the style of almost all our modern poets; such is the style of Pope and Gray; such, too, very often, is that of Shakespeare and Milton; and, notwithstanding Mr. Coleridge's decision to the contrary, of Spenser's *Faery Queen*. Now this style is the reverse of one made up of *slang* phrases; for, as they are words associated only with mean and vulgar ideas, poetic diction is such as is connected only with the most pleasing and elegant associations; and *both* differ essentially from the middle or natural style, which is a mere transparent medium of the thoughts, neither degrading nor setting them off by any adventitious qualities of its own, but leaving them to make their own impression, by the force of truth and nature. Upon the whole, therefore, we should think this ornamented and coloured style, most proper to descriptive or fanciful poetry, where the writer has to lend a borrowed, and, in some sort, meretricious lustre to outward objects, which he can best do by enshrining them in a language that, by custom and long prescription, reflects the image of a poetical mind, as we think the common or natural style is the truly dramatic style, that in which he can best give the impassioned, unborrowed, unaffected thoughts of others. The pleasure derived from poetic diction is the same as that derived from classical diction. It is in like manner made up of words dipped in 'the dew of Castalio', tinged with colours borrowed from the rainbow, 'sky-tinctured', warmed with the glow of genius, purified by the breath of time, that soften into distance, and expand into magnitude, whatever is seen through their medium, that varnish over the trite and commonplace, and lend a gorgeous robe to the forms of fancy, but are only an incumbrance and a disguise in conveying the true touches of nature, the intense strokes of passion. The beauty of poetic diction is, in short, borrowed and artificial. It is a glittering veil spread over the forms of things and the feelings of the heart; and is best laid aside, when we wish to show either the one or the other in their naked beauty or deformity. As the dialogues in *Othello* and *Lear* furnish the most striking instances of plain, point-blank speaking, or of the real language of nature and passion, so the Choruses in *Samson Agonistes* abound in the fullest and finest adaptations of classic and poetic phrases to express distant and elevated notions, born of fancy, religion and learning.

Mr. Coleridge bewilders himself sadly in endeavouring to determine in what the essence of poetry consists; Milton, we think, has told it in a single line:

Thoughts that voluntary move
Harmonious numbers.

Poetry is the music of language, expressing the music of the mind. Whenever any object takes such a hold on the mind as to make us dwell upon it, and brood over it, melting the heart in love, or kindling it to a sentiment of admiration; whenever a movement of imagination or passion is impressed on the mind, by which it seeks to prolong and repeat the emotion, to bring all other objects into accord with it, and to give the same movement of harmony, sustained and continuous, to the sounds that express it—this is poetry. The musical in sound is the sustained and continuous; the musical in thought and feeling is the sustained and continuous also. Whenever articulation passes naturally into intonation, this is the beginning of poetry. There is no natural harmony in the ordinary combinations of significant sounds: the language of prose is not the language of music, or of *passion*: and it is to supply this inherent defect in the mechanism of language, to make the sound an echo to the sense, when the sense becomes a sort of echo to itself to mingle the tide of verse, 'the golden cadences of poesy', with the tide of feeling, flowing, and murmuring as it flows, or to take the imagination off its feet, and spread its wings where it may indulge its own impulses, without being stopped or perplexed by the ordinary abruptnesses, or discordant flats and sharps of prose—that poetry was invented.

As Mr. C. has suppressed his Disquisition on the Imagination as unintelligible, we do not think it fair to make any remarks on the 200 pages of prefatory matter, which were printed, it seems, in the present work, before a candid friend apprised him of this little objection to the appearance of the Disquisition itself. We may venture, however, on one observation, of a very plain and practical nature, which is forced upon us by the whole tenor of the extraordinary history before us. Reason and imagination are both excellent things; but perhaps their provinces ought to be kept more distinct than they have lately been. 'Poets have such seething brains', that they are disposed to meddle with everything, and mar all. Mr. C., with great talents, has, by an ambition to be everything, become nothing. His metaphysics have been a dead weight on the wings of his imagination, while his imagination has run away with his reason and common sense. He might, we seriously think, have been a very considerable poet, instead of which he has chosen to be a bad philosopher and a worse politician. There is something, we suspect, in these studies that does not easily amalgamate. We would not, with Plato, absolutely banish poets from the commonwealth; but we really think they should meddle as little with its practical administration as may be. They live in an ideal world of their own; and it would be, perhaps, as well if they were confined to it. Their flights and fancies are delightful to themselves and to every body else; but they make strange work with matter of fact; and, if they were allowed to act in public affairs, would soon turn the world upside down. They indulge only their own flattering dreams or superstitious prejudices, and make idols or bugbears of what they please, caring as little for 'history or particular facts', as for general reasoning. They are dangerous leaders and treacherous followers. Their inordinate vanity runs them into all sorts of extravagances; and their habitual effeminacy gets them out of them at any price. Always pampering their own appetite for excitement, and wishing to astonish others, their whole aim is to produce a dramatic effect, one way or other—to shock or delight their observers; and they are as perfectly indifferent to the consequences of what they write, as if the world were merely a stage for them to play their fantastic tricks on. As romantic in their servility as in their independence, and equally importunate candidates for fame or infamy, they require only to be distinguished, and are not scrupulous as to the means of distinction. Jacobins or Antijacobins—outrageous advocates for anarchy and licentiousness, or flaming apostles of persecution—always violent and vulgar in their opinions, they oscillate, with a giddy and sickening motion, from one absurdity to another, and expiate the follies of their youth by the heartless vices of their advancing age. None so ready as they to carry every paradox to its most revolting and nonsensical excess, none so sure to caricature, in their own persons, every feature of an audacious and insane philosophy. In their days of innovation, indeed, the philosophers crept at their heels like hounds, while they darted on their distant quarry like hawks; stooping always to the lowest game; eagerly snuffing up the most tainted and rankest scents; feeding their vanity with the notion of the strength of their digestion of poisons, and most ostentatiously avowing whatever would most effectually startle the prejudices of others. Preposterously seeking for the stimulus of novelty in truth, and the eclat of theatrical exhibition in pure reason, it is no wonder that these persons at last became disgusted with their own pursuits, and that, in consequence of the violence of the change, the most inveterate prejudices and uncharitable sentiments have rushed in to fill up the *vacuum*

genius and madness are very nearly allied, and of the tenuity of the partition the present volumes exhibit, we think, a melancholy illustration. Here and there some amusement and information will be found; but the whole that is valuable is intermingled with such a cloudiness of metaphysical jargon in the mystical language of the Platonists and schoolmen, of Kant and Jacob Behmen, as to lose the good effect which it might have produced had it been presented with more simplicity. One chapter upon the misfortune of making authorship a profession is worth all the rest; but it is too short, and appears to disadvantage amidst disquisitions on poetry and the abstractions of the human intellect; the associations of ideas, and the progress of the doctrine of materialism. We are whirled about in such rapid confusion from Aristotle to Hobbes, from Thomas Aquinas to Hume, then by abrupt transitions to Southey and Cowley, to Wordsworth and Milton, that in the endless maze we forget our company, the subjects on which we have been engaged, and are as glad to escape from the literary life and opinions of Mr. Coleridge, as we would to the light of day from the darkened cell of a religious enthusiast whose visions and prophecies have rendered confinement necessary for himself and society.

77. Unsigned review, *Monthly Magazine*

September 1817, xliv, 154

Our curiosity was raised by the announcement of *Biographia Literaria, or Biographical Sketches of my Literary Life and Opinions*, by S. T. Coleridge, esq. We knew Mr. C. when his zeal in a good cause entitled him to general esteem; we heard with regret that he had enlisted among the mercenaries of abused power; and he now imposes on us the pain of seeing him exhibit the decrepitude of genius! He complains, in the true spirit of misanthropy, of the malignity of enemies, and the force of criticism; but it is clear that he has far more reason to complain of the falsehood of friendship, which flatters him into the publication of volumes of which the following is the CONCLUDING, and by rhetorical rule, the most PERSPICUOUS, passage:

It is within the experience of many medical practitioners, that a patient, with strange and unusual symptoms of disease, has been more distressed in mind, more wretched, from the fact of being unintelligible to himself and others, than from the pain or danger of the disease: nay, that the patient has received the most solid comfort, and resumed a genial and enduring chearfulness, from some new symptom or product, that had at once determined the name and nature of his complaint, and rendered it an intelligible effect of an intelligible cause: even though the discovery did at the same moment preclude all hope of restoration. Hence the mystic theologians, whose delusions we may more confidently hope to separate from their actual intuitions, when we condescend to read their works without the presumption that whatever our fancy (always the ape, and too often the adulterator and counterfeit of our memory) has not made or cannot make a picture of, must be nonsense,—hence, I say, the mystics have joined in representing the state of the reprobate spirits as a dreadful dream in which there is no sense of reality, not even of the pangs they are enduring—an eternity without time, and as it were below it—God present without manifestation of his presence. But these are depths, which we dare not linger over. Let us turn to an instance more on a level with the ordinary sympathies of mankind. Here then, and in this same healing influence of *light* and distinct beholding, we may detect the final cause of that instinct which in the great majority of instances leads and almost compels the afflicted to communicate their sorrows. Hence too flows the alleviation that results from '*opening out* our griefs': which are thus presented in distinguishable forms instead of the mist, through which whatever is shapeless becomes magnified and (literally) *enormous*.

On such an *emphatical* conclusion of two volumes on his *own dear self*—a subject which the author must be supposed to understand better than any other—can a humane critic do otherwise then express his *pity*—or a just one, his *contempt*?

78. 'Christopher North,' *Blackwood's Edinburgh Magazine*

October 1817, ii, 1-18

An unsigned review attributed to John Wilson (A. L. Strout, 'Samuel Taylor Coleridge and John Wilson of *Blackwood's Magazine*', *The Publications of the Modern Language Association*, xlviii, 1933, 102). Wilson (1785-1854), better known as 'Christopher North', was Professor of Moral Philosophy at Edinburgh and a minor poet.

When a man looks back on his past existence, and endeavours to recall the incidents, events, thoughts, feelings, and passions of which it was composed, he sees something like a glimmering land of dreams, peopled with phantasms and realities undistinguishably confused and intermingled—here illuminated with dazzling splendour, there dim with melancholy mists, or it may be, shrouded in impenetrable darkness. To bring, visibly and distinctly before our memory, on the one hand, all our hours of mirth and joy, and hope and exultation, and, on the other, all our perplexities, and fears and sorrows, and despair and agony (and who has been so uniformly wretched as not to have been often blest?—who so uniformly blest as not to have been often wretched?), would be as impossible as to awaken, into separate remembrance, all the changes and varieties which the seasons brought over the material world, every gleam of sunshine that beautified the Spring, every cloud and tempest that deformed the Winter. In truth, were this power and domination over the past given unto us, and were we able to read the history of our lives all faithfully and perspicuously recorded on the tablets of the inner spirit, those beings, whose existence had been most filled with important events and with energetic passions, would be the most averse to such overwhelming survey—would recoil from trains of thought which formerly agitated and disturbed, and led them, as it were, in triumph beneath the yoke of misery or happiness. The soul may be repelled from the contemplation of the past as much by the brightness and magnificence of scenes that shifted across the glorious

325

drama of youth, as by the storms that scattered the fair array into disfigured fragments; and the melancholy that breathes from vanished delight is, perhaps, in its utmost intensity, as unendurable as the wretchedness left by the visitation of calamity. There are spots of sunshine sleeping on the fields of past existence too beautiful, as there are caves among its precipices too darksome, to be looked on by the eyes of memory; and to carry on an image borrowed from the analogy between the moral and physical world, the soul may turn away in sickness from the untroubled silence of a resplendent Lake, no less than from the haunted gloom of the thundering Cataract. It is from such thoughts, and dreams, and reveries, as these, that all men feel how terrible it would be to live over again their agonies and their transports; that the happiest would fear to do so as much as the most miserable; and that to look back to our cradle seems scarcely less awful than to look forward to the grave.

But if this unwillingness to bring before our souls, in distinct array, the more solemn and important events of our lives, be a natural and perhaps a wise feeling, how much more averse must every reflecting man be to the ransacking of his inmost spirit for all its hidden emotions and passions, to the tearing away that shroud which oblivion may have kindly flung over his vices and his follies, or that fine and delicate veil which Christian humility draws over his virtues and acts of benevolence. To scrutinize and dissect the character of others is an idle and unprofitable task; and the most skilful anatomist will often be forced to withhold his hand when he unexpectedly meets with something he does not understand—some conformation of the character of his patient which is not explicable on his theory of human nature. To become operators on our own shrinking spirits is something worse; for by probing the wounds of the soul, what can ensue but callousness or irritability. And it may be remarked, that those persons who have busied themselves most with inquiries into the causes, and motives, and impulses of their actions, have exhibited, in their conduct, the most lamentable contrast to their theory, and have seemed blinder in their knowledge than others in their ignorance.

It will not be supposed that any thing we have now said in any way bears against the most important duty of self-examination. Many causes there are existing, both in the best and the worst parts of our nature, which must render nugatory and deceitful any continued diary of what passes through the human soul; and no such confessions could, we humbly conceive, be of use either to ourselves or to the world.

But there are hours of solemn inquiry in which the soul reposes on itself; the true confessional is not the bar of the public, but it is the altar of religion; there is a Being before whom we may humble ourselves without being debased; and there are feelings for which human language has no expression, and which, in the silence of solitude and of nature, are known only unto the Eternal.

The objections, however, which might thus be urged against the writing and publishing accounts of all our feelings, all the changes of our moral constitution, do not seem to apply with equal force to the narration of our mere speculative opinions. Their rise, progress, changes, and maturity, may be pretty accurately ascertained; and as the advance to truth is generally step by step, there seems to be no great difficulty in recording the leading causes that have formed the body of our opinions, and created, modified, and coloured our intellectual character. Yet this work would be alike useless to ourselves and others, unless pursued with a true magnanimity. It requires, that we should stand aloof from ourselves, and look down, as from an eminence, on our souls toiling up the hill of knowledge; that we should faithfully record all the assistance we received from guides or brother pilgrims; that we should mark the limit of our utmost ascent, and, without exaggeration, state the value of our acquisitions. When we consider how many temptations there are even here to delude ourselves, and by a seeming air of truth and candour to impose upon others, it will be allowed, that, instead of composing memoirs of himself, a man of genius and talent would be far better employed in generalizing the observations and experiences of his life, and giving them to the world in the form of philosophic reflections, applicable not to himself alone, but to the universal mind of Man.

What good to mankind has ever flowed from the confessions of Rousseau, or the autobiographical sketch of Hume? From the first we rise with a confused and miserable sense of weakness and of power, of lofty aspirations and degrading appetencies, of pride swelling into blasphemy, and humiliation pitiably grovelling in the dust, of purity of spirit soaring on the wings of imagination, and grossness of instinct brutally wallowing in 'Epicurus' style', of lofty contempt for the opinion of mankind, yet the most slavish subjection to their most fatal prejudices, of a sublime piety towards God, and a wild violation of his holiest laws. From the other we rise with feelings of sincere compassion for the ignorance of the most enlightened. All the prominent features of Hume's character were invisible to his own eyes; and in that meagre sketch which has been so much admired, what is there to instruct, to rouse, or to elevate, what light thrown over the duties of this life or the hopes of that to come? We wish to speak with tenderness of a man whose moral character was respectable, and whose talents were of the first order. But most deeply injurious to every thing lofty and high-toned in human Virtue, to every thing cheering, and consoling, and sublime in that Faith which sheds over this Earth a reflection of the heavens, is that memoir of a worldly-wise Man, in which he seems to contemplate with indifference the extinction of his own immortal soul, and jibes and jokes on the dim and awful verge of Eternity.

We hope that our readers will forgive these very imperfect reflections on a subject of deep interest, and accompany us now on our examination of Mr. Coleridge's 'Literary Life', the very singular work which caused our ideas to run in that channel. It does not contain an account of his opinions and literary exploits alone, but lays open, not unfrequently, the character of the Man as well as of the Author; and we are compelled to think, that while it strengthens every argument against the composition of such Memoirs, it does, without benefitting the cause either of virtue, knowledge, or religion, exhibit many mournful sacrifices of personal dignity, after which it seems impossible that Mr. Coleridge can be greatly respected either by the Public or himself.

Considered merely in a literary point of view, the work is most execrable. He rambles from one subject to another in the most wayward and capricious manner; either from indolence, or ignorance, or weakness, he has never in one single instance finished a discussion; and while he darkens what was dark before into tenfold obscurity, he so treats the most ordinary common-places as to give them the air of mysteries, till we no longer know the faces of our old acquaintances beneath their cowl and hood, but witness plain flesh and blood matters of fact miraculously converted into a troop of phantoms. That he is a man of genius is certain; but he is not a man of a strong intellect nor of powerful talents. He has a great deal of fancy and imagination, but little or no real feeling, and certainly no judgment. He cannot form to himself any harmonious landscape such as it exists in nature, but beautified by the serene light of the imagination. He cannot conceive simple and majestic groupes of human figures and characters acting on the theatre of real existence. But his pictures of nature are fine only as imaging the dreaminess, and obscurity, and confusion of distempered sleep; while all his agents pass before our eyes like shadows, and only impress and affect us with a phantasmagorial splendour.

It is impossible to read many pages of this work without thinking that Mr. Coleridge conceives himself to be a far greater man than the Public is likely to admit; and we wish to waken him from what seems to us a most ludicrous delusion. He seems to believe that every tongue is wagging in his praise, that every ear is open to imbibe the oracular breathings of his inspiration. Even when he would fain convince us that his soul is wholly occupied with some other illustrious character, he breaks out into laudatory exclamations concerning himself; no sound is so sweet to him as that of his own voice: the ground is hallowed on which his footsteps tread; and there seems to him something more than human in his very shadow. He will read no books that other people read; his scorn is as misplaced and extravagant as his admiration; opinions that seem to tally with his own wild ravings are holy and inspired; and, unless agreeable to his creed, the wisdom of ages is folly; and wits, whom the world worship, dwarfed when they approach his venerable side. His admiration of nature or of man—we had almost said his religious feelings towards his God—are all narrowed, weakened, and corrupted and poisoned by inveterate and diseased egotism; and instead of his mind reflecting the beauty and glory of nature, he seems to consider the mighty universe itself as nothing better than a mirror, in which, with a grinning and idiot self-complacency, he may contemplate the Physiognomy of Samuel Taylor Coleridge. Though he has yet done nothing in any one department of human knowledge, yet he speaks of his theories, and plans, and views, and discoveries, as if he had produced some memorable revolution in Science. He at all times connects his own name in Poetry with Shakespeare, and Spenser, and Milton; in politics with Burke, and Fox, and Pitt; in metaphysics with Locke, and Hartley, and Berkeley, and Kant; feeling himself not only to be the worthy compeer of those illustrious Spirits, but to unite, in his own mighty intellect, all the glorious powers and faculties by which they were separately distinguished, as if his soul were endowed with all human power, and was the depository of the aggregate, or rather the essence, of all human knowledge. So deplorable a delusion as this has only been equalled by that of Joanna Southcote, who mistook a complaint in the bowels for the divine afflatus; and believed herself about to give birth to the regenerator of the world, when sick unto death of an incurable and loathsome disease.

The truth is, that Mr. Coleridge is but an obscure name in English literature. In London he is well known in literary society, and justly admired for his extraordinary loquacity: he has his own little circle of devoted worshippers, and he mistakes their foolish babbling for the voice of the world. His name, too, has been often foisted into Reviews, and accordingly is known to many who never saw any of his works. In Scotland few know or care any thing about him; and perhaps no man who has spoken and written so much, and occasionally with so much genius and ability, ever made so little impression on the public mind. Few people know how to spell or pronounce his name; and were he to drop from the clouds among any given number of well informed and intelligent men north of the Tweed, he would find it impossible to make any intelligible communication respecting himself; for of him and his writings there would prevail only a perplexing dream, or the most untroubled ignorance. We cannot see in what the state of literature would have been different, had he been cut off in childhood, or had he never been born; for, except a few wild and fanciful ballads, he has produced nothing worthy remembrance. Yet, insignificant as he assuredly is, he cannot put pen to paper without a feeling that millions of eyes are fixed upon him; and he scatters his Sibylline Leaves around him, with as majestical an air as if a crowd of enthusiastic admirers were rushing forward to grasp the divine promulgations, instead of their being, as in fact they are, coldly received by the accidental passenger, like a lying lottery puff or a quack advertisement.

This most miserable arrogance seems, in the present age, confined almost exclusively to the original members of the Lake School, and is, we think, worthy of especial notice, as one of the leading features of their character. It would be difficult to defend it either in Southey or Wordsworth; but in Coleridge it is altogether ridiculous, Southey has undoubtedly written four noble Poems—*Thalaba, Madoc, Kehama*, and *Roderick*; and if the Poets of this age are admitted, by the voices of posterity, to take their places by the side of the Mighty of former times in the Temple of Immortality, he will be one of that sacred company. Wordsworth, too, with all his manifold errors and defects, has, we think, won to himself a great name, and, in point of originality, will be considered as second to no man of this age. They are entitled to think highly of themselves, in comparison with their most highly gifted contemporaries; and therefore, though their arrogance may be offensive, as it often is, it is seldom or ever utterly ridiculous. But Mr. Coleridge stands on much lower ground, and will be known to future times only as a man who overrated and abused his talents, who saw glimpses of that glory which he could not grasp, who presumptuously came forward to officiate as High Priest at mysteries beyond his ken, and who carried himself as if he had been familiarly admitted into the Penetralia of Nature, when in truth he kept perpetually stumbling at the very Threshold.

This absurd self-elevation forms a striking contrast with the dignified deportment of all the other great living Poets. Throughout all the works of Scott, the most original-minded man of this generation of Poets, scarcely a single allusion is made to himself; and then it is with a truly delightful simplicity, as if he were not aware of his immeasurable superiority to the ordinary run of mankind. From the rude songs of our forefathers he has created a kind of Poetry, which at once brought over the dull scenes of this our unimaginative life all the pomp, and glory, and magnificence of a chivalrous age. He speaks to us like some ancient Bard awakened from his tomb, and singing of visions not revealed in dreams, but contemplated in all the freshness and splendour of reality. Since he sung his bold, and wild, and romantic lays, a more religious solemnity breathes from our mouldering abbeys, and a sterner grandeur frowns over our time-shattered castles. He has peopled our hills with heroes, even as Ossian peopled them; and, like a presiding spirit, his Image haunts the magnificent cliffs of our Lakes and Seas. And if he be, as every heart feels, the author of those noble Prose Works[1] that continue to flash upon the world, to him exclusively belongs the glory of wedding Fiction and History in delighted union, and of embodying in imperishable records the manners, character, soul, and spirit of Caledonia; so that, if all her annals were lost, her memory would in those Tales be immortal. His truly is a name that comes to the heart of every Briton with a start of exultation, whether it be heard in the hum of cities or in the solitude of nature. What has Campbell ever obtruded on the Public of his private history? Yet his is a name that will be hallowed for ever in the souls of pure, and aspiring, and devout youth; and to those lofty contemplations in which Poetry lends its aid to Religion, his immortal Muse will impart a more enthusiastic glow, while it blends in one majestic hymn all the noblest feelings which can spring from earth, with all the most glorious hopes that come from the silence of eternity. Byron indeed speaks of himself often, but his is like the voice of an angel heard crying in the storm or the whirlwind; and we listen with a kind of mysterious dread to the tones of a Being whom we scarcely believe to be kindred to ourselves, while he sounds the depths of our nature, and illuminates them with the lightnings of his genius. And finally, who more gracefully unostentatious than

[1] The authorship of the Waverley novels was not acknowledged until 1827.

Moore, a Poet who has shed delight, and joy, and rapture, and exultation, through the spirit of an enthusiastic People, and whose name is
associated in his native Land with every thing noble and glorious in the
cause of Patriotism and Liberty. We could easily add to the illustrious
list; but suffice it to say, that our Poets do in general bear their faculties
meekly and manfully, trusting to their conscious powers, and the
susceptibility of generous and enlightened natures, not yet extinct in
Britain, whatever Mr. Coleridge may think; for certain it is, that a host
of worshippers will crowd into the Temple, when the Priest is inspired,
and the flame he kindles is from Heaven.

Such has been the character of great Poets in all countries and in all
times. Fame is dear to them as their vital existence—but they love it not
with the perplexity of fear, but the calmness of certain possession. They
know that the debt which nature owes them must be paid, and they
hold in surety thereof the universal passions of mankind. So Milton
felt and spoke of himself, with an air of grandeur, and the voice as of
an Archangel, distinctly hearing in his soul the music of after generations, and the thunder of his mighty name rolling through the darkness
of futurity. So divine Shakespeare felt and spoke; he cared not for the
mere acclamations of his subjects; in all the gentleness of his heavenly
spirit he felt himself to be their prophet and their king, and knew,

> When all the breathers of this world are dead,
> That he entombed in men's eyes would lie.

Indeed, who that knows any thing of Poetry could for a moment
suppose it otherwise? What ever made a great Poet but the inspiration
of delight and love in himself, and an impassioned desire to communicate them to the wide spirit of kindred existence? Poetry, like Religion,
must be free from all grovelling feelings; and above all, from jealousy,
envy, and uncharitableness. And the true Poet, like the Preacher of the
true religion, will seek to win unto himself and his Faith, a belief
whose foundation is in the depths of love, and whose pillars are the
noblest passions of humanity.

It would seem, that in truly great souls all feeling of self-importance,
in its narrower sense, must be incompatible with the consciousness of a
mighty achievement. The idea of the mere faculty or power is absorbed
as it were in the idea of the work performed. That work stands out in
its glory from the mind of its Creator; and in the contemplation of it,
he forgets that he himself was the cause of its existence, or feels only a
dim but sublime association between himself and the object of his

admiration; and when he does think of himself in conjunction with others, he feels towards the scoffer only a pitying sorrow for his blindness—being assured, that though at all times there will be weakness, and ignorance, and worthlessness, which can hold no communion with him or with his thoughts, so will there be at all times the pure, the noble, and the pious, whose delight it will be to love, to admire, and to imitate; and that never, at any point of time, past, present, or to come, can a true Poet be defrauded of his just fame.

But we need not speak of Poets alone (though we have done so at present to expose the miserable pretensions of Mr. Coleridge), but look through all the bright ranks of men distinguished by mental power, in whatever department of human science. It is our faith, that without moral there can be no intellectual grandeur; and surely the self-conceit and arrogance which we have been exposing, are altogether incompatible with lofty feelings and majestic principles. It is the Dwarf alone who endeavours to strut himself into the height of the surrounding company; but the man of princely stature seems unconscious of the strength in which nevertheless he rejoices, and only sees his superiority in the gaze of admiration which he commands. Look at the most inventive spirits of this country,—those whose intellects have achieved the most memorable triumphs. Take, for example, Leslie in physical science, and what airs of majesty does he ever assume?[1] What is Samuel Coleridge compared to such a man? What is an ingenious and fanciful versifier to him who has, like a magician, gained command over the very elements of nature, who has realized the fictions of Poetry, and to whom Frost and Fire are ministering and obedient spirits? But of this enough. It is a position that doubtless might require some modification, but in the main, it is and must be true, that real Greatness, whether in Intellect, Genius, or Virtue, is dignified and unostentatious; and that no potent spirit ever whimpered over the blindness of the age to his merits, and, like Mr. Coleridge, or a child blubbering for the moon, with clamorous outcries implored and imprecated reputation.

The very first sentence of this 'Literary Biography' shews how incompetent Mr. Coleridge is for the task he has undertaken.

It has been my lot to have had my name introduced both in conversation and in print, more frequently than I find it easy to explain; *whether I consider the*

---

[1] Sir John Leslie (1766-1832), mathematician and scientist, who on a later occasion obtained damages for libel from *Blackwood's*.

ewness, unimportance, and limited circulation of my writings, or the retirement and
distance in which I have lived, both from the literary and political world.

Now, it is obvious, that if his writings be few, and unimportant,
and unknown, Mr. Coleridge can have no reason for composing his
'Literary Biography'. Yet in singular contradiction to himself:

If, . . . *the compositions which I have made public, and that too in a form the most
certain of an extensive circulation, though the least flattering to an author's
self-love, had been published in books, they would have filled a respectable
number of volumes.*

He then adds,

Seldom have I written that in a day, the acquisition or investigation of which
had not cost me *the precious labour of a month!*

He then bursts out into this magnificent exclamation,

Would that the criterion of a scholar's ability were the number and moral
value of the truths which he has been the means of throwing into general
circulation!

And he sums up all by declaring,

By what I *have* effected am I to be judged by my fellow men.

The truth is, that Mr. Coleridge has lived, as much as any man of
his time, in literary and political society, and that he has sought every
opportunity of keeping himself in the eye of the public, as restlessly as
any charlatan who ever exhibited on the stage. To use his own words,
'In 1794, when I had barely passed the verge of manhood, I published
a small volume of juvenile poems'. These poems, by dint of puffing,
reached a third edition; and though Mr. Coleridge pretends now to
think but little of them, it is amusing to see how vehemently he defends
them against criticism, and how pompously he speaks of such paltry
trifles. 'They were marked *by an ease and simplicity* which I have studied,
perhaps with inferior success, to bestow on my later compositions'. But
he afterwards repents of this sneer at his later compositions, and tells us,
that they have nearly reached his standard of perfection! Indeed, his
vanity extends farther back than his juvenile poems; and he says, 'For a
school boy, I was *above par in English versification,* and had already
produced two or three compositions, which I may venture to say,
without reference to my age, were somewhat above mediocrity'. Happily he
has preserved one of those wonderful productions of his precocious

boyhood, and our readers will judge for themselves what a clever child it was.

> Underneath a huge oak-tree,
> There was of swine a huge company;
> That grunted as they crunch'd the mast,
> For that was ripe, and fell full fast.
> Then they trotted away, for the wind grew high,
> One acorn they left, and no more might you spy.

It is a common remark, that wonderful children seldom perform the promises of their youth, and undoubtedly this fine effusion has not been followed in Mr. Coleridge's riper years by works of proportionate merit.

We see, then, that our author came very early into public notice; and from that time to this, he has not allowed one year to pass without endeavouring to extend his notoriety. His poems were soon followed (they may have been preceded) by a tragedy, entitled, the *Fall of Robespierre*, a meagre performance, but one which, from the nature of the subject, attracted considerable attention. He also wrote a whole book, utterly incomprehensible to Mr. Southey, we are sure, in that Poet's *Joan of Arc*; and became as celebrated for his metaphysical absurdities, as his friend had become for the bright promise of genius exhibited by that unequal but spirited poem. He next published a series of political essays, entitled, the *Watchman*, and *Conciones ad Populum*. He next started up, fresh from the schools of Germany, as the principal writer in the *Morning Post*, a *strong opposition paper*. He then published various outrageous political poems, some of them of a gross personal nature. He afterwards assisted Mr. Wordsworth in planning his *Lyrical Ballads*; and contributing several poems to that collection, he shared in the notoriety of the Lake School. He next published a mysterious periodical work, *The Friend*, in which he declared it was his intention to settle at once, and for ever, the principles of morality, religion, taste, manners, and the fine arts, but which died of a galloping consumption in the twenty-eighth week of its age. He then published the tragedy of *Remorse*, which dragged out a miserable existence of twenty nights, on the boards of Drury-Lane, and then expired for ever, like the oil of the orchestral lamps. He then forsook the stage for the pulpit, and, by particular desire of his congregation, published two *Lay-Sermons*. He then walked in broad day-light into the shop of Mr. Murray, Albemarle Street, London, with two ladies hanging on each arm, Geraldine and Christabel—a bold step for a person at all desirous of a good reputation, and most of the trade have looked shy at him since that exhibition. Since that time, however, he has contrived means of giving to the world a collected edition of all his Poems, and advanced to the front of the stage with a thick octavo in each hand, all about himself and other Incomprehensibilities. We had forgot that he was likewise a contributor to Mr. Southey's *Omniana*, where the Editor of the *Edinburgh Review* is politely denominated an 'ass', and then *became himself a writer in the said Review*. And to sum up 'the strange eventful history' of this modest, and obscure, and retired person, we must mention, that in his youth he held forth in a vast number of Unitarian chapels—preached his way through Bristol, and 'Brummagem', and Manchester, in a 'blue coat and white waistcoat'; and in after years, when he was not so much afraid of 'the scarlet woman', did, in a full suit of sables, lecture on Poesy to 'crowded, and, need I add, highly respectable audiences', at the Royal Institution. After this slight and imperfect outline of his poetical, oratorical, metaphysical, political, and theological exploits, our readers will judge, when they hear him talking of 'his retirement and distance from the literary and political world', what are his talents for autobiography, and how far he has penetrated into the mysterious nonentities of his own character.

Mr. Coleridge has written copiously on the Association of Ideas, but his own do not seem to be connected either by time, place, cause and effect, resemblance, or contrast, and accordingly it is no easy matter to follow him through all the vagaries of his 'Literary Life'. We are told,

At school *I enjoyed the inestimable advantage* of a very sensible, though at the same time a very severe master. * * * I learnt from him, that Poetry, even that of the loftiest and wildest odes, had a logic of its own as severe as that of science. * * * * * Lute, harp, and lyre; muse, muses, and inspirations; Pegasus, Parnassus, and Hippocrene; were all an abomination to him. In fancy I can almost hear him now exclaiming, '*Harp? Harp? Lyre? Pen and Ink! Boy you mean! Muse! boy! Muse! your Nurse's daughter you mean! Pierian Spring! O Aye! the cloister Pump!*' * * * * Our classical knowledge was the least of the good gifts which we derived from his zealous and conscientious tutorage.

With the then head-master of the grammar-school, Christ Hospital, we were not personally acquainted; but we cannot help thinking that he has been singularly unfortunate in his Eulogist. He seems to have gone out of his province, and far out of his depth, when he attempted to teach boys the profoundest principles of Poetry. But we must also add, that we cannot credit this account of him; for this doctrine of poetry being at all times logical, is that of which Wordsworth and Coleridge take so much credit to themselves for the discovery; and verily it is one too wilfully absurd and extravagant to have entered into the head of an honest man, whose time must have been wholly occupied with the instruction of children. Indeed Mr. Coleridge's own poetical practices render this story incredible; for, during many years of his authorship, his action was wholly at variance with such a rule, and the strain of his poetry as illogical as can be well imagined. When Mr. Bowyer prohibited his pupils from using, in their themes, the above-mentioned names, he did, we humbly submit, prohibit them from using the best means of purifying their taste and exalting their imagination. Nothing could be so graceful, nothing so natural, as classical allusions, in the exercises of young minds, when first admitted to the fountains of Greek and Latin Poetry; and the Teacher who could seek to dissuade their ingenuous souls from such delightful dreams, by coarse, vulgar, and indecent ribaldry, instead of deserving the name of 'sensible', must have been a low-minded vulgar fellow, fitter for the Porter than the Master of such an Establishment. But the truth probably is, that all this is a fiction of Mr. Coleridge, whose wit is at all times most execrable and disgusting. Whatever the merits of his master were, Mr. Coleridge, even from his own account, seems to have derived little benefit from his instruction, and for the 'inestimable advantage', of which he speaks, we look in vain through this Narrative. In spite of so excellent a teacher, we find Master Coleridge,

Even before my fifteenth year, bewildered *in metaphysicks and in theological controversy.* Nothing else pleased me. *History and particular facts* lost all interest in my mind. Poetry itself, yea novels and romances, became insipid to me. This preposterous pursuit was beyond doubt *injurious, both to my natural powers and to the progress of my education.*

This deplorable condition of mind continued 'even unto my seventeenth year'. And now our readers must prepare themselves for a mighty and wonderful change, wrought, all on a sudden, on the moral and intellectual character of this metaphysical Greenhorn. '*Mr. Bowles'* Sonnets, twenty in number, and just then published in a quarto volume (a most important circumstance!) were put into my hand!' To those Sonnets, next to the Schoolmaster's lectures on Poetry, Mr. Coleridge attributes the strength, vigour, and extension of his own very original Genius.

By those works, year after year, I was enthusiastically delighted and inspired. My earliest acquaintances will not have forgotten the undisciplined eagerness and impetuous zeal with which I labour'd to make proselytes, not only *of my companions, but of all with whom I conversed, of whatever rank, and in whatever place*. As my school finances did not permit me to purchase copies, I made, within less than a year and a half, *more than forty transcriptions, as the best presents I could make to those who had in any way won my regard*. My obligations to Mr. Bowles were indeed important, and for radical good.

There must be some grievous natural defect in that mind which, even at the age of seventeen, could act so insanely; and we cannot but think, that no real and healthy sensibility could have exaggerated to itself so grossly the merits of Bowles' Sonnets. They are undoubtedly most beautiful, and we willingly pay our tribute of admiration to the genius of the amiable writer; but they neither did nor could produce any such effects as are here described, except upon a mind singularly weak and helpless. We must, however, take the fact as we find it; and Mr. Coleridge's first step, after his worship of Bowles, was to see distinctly into the defects and deficiencies of Pope (a writer whom Bowles most especially admires, and has edited), and through all the false diction and borrowed plumage of Gray!* But here Mr. Coleridge drops the subject of Poetry for the present, and proceeds to other important matters.

* There is something very offensive in the high and contemptuous tone which Wordsworth and Coleridge assume, when speaking of this great Poet. They employ his immortal works as a text-book, from which they quote imaginary violations of logic and sound sense, and examples of vicious poetic diction. Mr. Coleridge informs us that Wordsworth 'couched him', and that, from the moment of the operation, his eyes were startled with the deformities of the 'Bard' and the 'Elegy in the Country Church-yard'! Such despicable fooleries are perhaps beneath notice; but we must not allow the feathers of a Bird of Paradise to be pecked at by such a Daw as Coleridge.

> Fair laughs the Morn, and soft the Zephyr blows,
> While proudly riding o'er the azure realm,
> In gallant trim the gilded Vessel goes,
> Youth at the Prow, and Pleasure at the Helm!
> Regardless of the sweeping Whirlwind's sway,
> That, hush'd in grim repose, expects its evening Prey. GRAY's *Bard*.

On this beautiful and sublime passage Mr. Coleridge has not one word of admiration to bestow, but tells us with a sneer (for what reason we know not), that 'realm' and 'sway' are rhymes dearly purchased. He then says, 'that it depended wholly in the compositor's putting or not putting *a small capital*, both in this and in many other passages of the same Poet, whether the words should be personifications or mere abstracts. This vile absurdity is followed by a direct charge of Plagiarism from Shakespeare.

> How like a younker or a prodigal
> the skarfed bark puts from her native bay,
> hugg'd and embraced by the strumpet wind!
> how like a prodigal doth she return,
> With over-weather'd ribs and ragged sails,
> Torn, rent, and beggar'd by the strumpet wind!
>
> SHAKESPEARE.

Now we put it to our readers to decide between us and the Critic. We maintain that here there is no plagiarism nor imitation. Both Poets speak of a Ship, and there all likeness ends. As well might Falconer be accused of imitation in his glorious description of a vessel in full sail leaving harbour—or Scott, in his animated picture of Bruce's galley beating through the Sound of Mull—or Byron, in his magnificent sketch of the Corsair's war-ship—or Wordsworth, in his fine simile of a vessel 'that hath the plain of Ocean for her own domain'—or Wilson, in his vision of the moonlight vessel sailing to the Isle of Palms—or the Ettrick Shepherd, in his wild dream of the Abbot's pinnace buried in the breakers of Staffa[1]—or Mr. Coleridge himself, in his spectre-ship in the 'Ancient Mariner'. For, in the first place, Shakespeare describes his ship by likening it *to something else, namely, a prodigal*; and upon that moral meaning depends the whole beauty of the passage. Of this there is nothing in Gray. Secondly, Shakespeare does not speak of any ship in particular, *but generally*. The beauty of the passage in Gray depends on its being *prophetic of a particular misfortune*, namely, the drowning of young Prince Henry. Thirdly, in Shakespeare, the vessel 'puts from her native bay'; and upon that circumstance the whole description depends. In Gray we only behold her majestically sailing in the open sea. Fourthly, in Shakespeare 'she returns'; but in Gray she is the prey of the evening whirlwind. Fifthly, in Shakespeare she returns 'with over-weather'd ribs and ragged sails'. In Gray she is sunk into the deep, 'with all her bravery on'. Sixthly, in Gray we behold a joyous company on her deck, 'Youth at her prow, and Pleasure at her helm'; but in Shakespeare we never think of her deck at all. Seventhly, in Shakespeare she is a 'skarfed bark'; in Gray, a 'gilded vessel'. Eighthly, Shakespeare has, in the whole description, studiously employed the most plain, homely, familiar, and even unpoetical diction, and thereby produced the desired effect. Gray has laboured his description with all the resources of consummate art, and it is eminently distinguished for pomp, splendour, and magnificence. Lastly, except articles, prepositions, and conjunctions, there is not *a single word common to the two passages*; so that they may indeed with propriety be quoted, to shew how *differently* the same object can appear to different poetical minds; but Mr. Coleridge 'has been couched', and Mr. Wordsworth having performed the operation unskilfully, the patient is blind.

We regret that Mr. Coleridge has passed over without notice all the

---

[1] The passages referred to occur in Canto i of William Falconer's *The Shipwreck*; Canto iv of Scott's *The Lord of the Isles*; Canto i of Byron's *The Corsair*; lines 65–6 of Wordsworth's *The White Doe of Rylstone*; Canto i of John Wilson's *The Isle of Palms*; and 'The Seventeenth Bard's Song' in James Hogg's *The Queen's Wake*.

years which he spent 'in the happy quiet of ever-honoured Jesus College, Cambridge'. That must have been the most important period of his life, and was surely more worthy of record than the metaphysical dreams or the poetical extravagancies of his boyhood. He tells us, that he was sent to the University 'an excellent Greek and Latin scholar, and a tolerable Hebraist'; and there might have been something rousing and elevating to young minds of genius and power, in his picture of himself, pursuits, visions, and attainments, during the bright and glorious morning of life, when he inhabited a dwelling of surpassing magnificence, guarded, and hallowed, and sublimed by the Shadows of the Mighty. We should wish to know what progress he made there in his own favourite studies; what place he occupied, or supposed he occupied, among his numerous contemporaries of talent; how much he was inspired by the genius of the place; how far he 'pierced the caves of old Philosophy', or sounded the depths of the Physical Sciences.* All this unfortunately is omitted, and he hurries on to details often trifling and uninfluential, sometimes low, vile, and vulgar, and, what is worse, occasionally inconsistent with any feeling of personal dignity and self-respect.

After leaving College, instead of betaking himself to some respectable calling, Mr. Coleridge, with his characteristic modesty, determined to set on foot a periodical work called *The Watchman*, that through it *'all might know the truth'*. The price of this very useful article was *'fourpence'*. Off he set on a tour to the north to procure subscribers, 'preaching in most of the great towns as a hireless Volunteer, in a blue coat and white waistcoat, that not a rag of the Woman of Babylon might be seen on me'. In preaching, his object was to shew that our Saviour was the real son of Joseph, and that the Crucifixion was a matter of small importance. Mr. Coleridge is now a most zealous member of the Church of England—devoutly believes every iota in the thirty-nine articles, and

---

* The fact is, that Mr. Coleridge made no figure at the University. He never could master the simplest elements of the mathematics. Yet in all his metaphysical and indeed many of his critical writings, there is an ostentatious display of a familiar and profound knowledge of the principles of that science. This is dishonest quackery; for Mr. Coleridge knows that he could not, if taken by surprise, demonstrate any one proposition in the first book of Euclid. His classical knowledge was found at the University to be equally superficial. He gained a prize there for a Greek Ode, which for ever blasted his character as a scholar; all the rules of that language being therein perpetually violated. We were once present in a literary company, where Porson offered to shew in it, to a gentleman who was praising this Ode, 134 examples of bad Greek.

that the Christian Religion is only to be found in its purity in the homilies and liturgy of that Church. Yet, on looking back to his Unitarian zeal, he exclaims,

O, never can I remember those days *with either shame or regret!* For I was *most sincere, most disinterested! Wealth, rank, life itself,* then seem'd cheap to me, compared with the interests of truth, and the will of my Maker. I cannot even accuse myself of having been actuated by *vanity!* for in the expansion of my enthusiasm *I did not think of myself at all!*

This is delectable. What does he mean by saying that life seemed cheap? What danger could there be in the performance of his exploits, except that of being committed as a Vagrant? What indeed could rank appear to a person thus voluntarily degraded? Or who would expect vanity to be conscious of its own loathsomeness? During this tour he seems to have been constantly exposed to the insults of the vile and the vulgar, and to have associated with persons whose company must have been most odious to a gentleman. Greasy tallow-chandlers, and pursey woollen-drapers, and grim-featured dealers in hard-ware, were his associates at Manchester, Derby, Nottingham, and Sheffield; and among them the light of truth was to be shed from its cloudy tabernacle in Mr. Coleridge's Pericranium. At the house of a 'Brummagem Patriot' he appears to have got dead drunk with strong ale and tobacco, and in that pitiable condition he was exposed to his disciples, lying upon a sofa, 'with my face like a wall that is white-washing, *deathy* pale, and with the cold drops of perspiration running down it from my forehead'. Some one having said 'Have you seen a paper to-day, Mr. Coleridge?' the wretched man replied, with all the staring stupidity of his lamentable condition, 'Sir! I am far from convinced that a Christian is permitted to read either newspapers, or any other works of merely political and temporary interest'. This witticism quite enchanted his enlightened auditors, and they prolonged their festivities to an 'early hour next morning'. Having returned to London with a thousand subscribers on his list, the *Watchman* appeared in all his glory; but, alas! not on the day fixed for the first burst of his effulgence; which foolish delay incensed many of his subscribers. The *Watchman*, on his second appearance, spoke blasphemously, and made indecent applications of Scriptural language; then, instead of abusing Government and Aristocrats, as Mr. Coleridge had pledged himself to his constituents to do, he attacked his own Party; so that in seven weeks, before the shoes were old in which he travelled to Sheffield, the

Watchman went the way of all flesh, and his remains were scattered 'through sundry old iron shops', where for one penny could be purchased each precious relic. To crown all, 'his London Publisher was a——'; and Mr. Coleridge very narrowly escaped being thrown into jail for this his heroic attempt to shed over the manufacturing towns the illumination of knowledge. We refrain from making any comments on this deplorable story.

This Philosopher, and Theologian, and Patriot, now retired to a village in Somersetshire, and, after having sought to enlighten the whole world, discovered that he himself was in utter darkness.

Doubts rushed in, broke upon me from the fountains of the great deep, and fell from the windows of heaven. The fontal truths of natural Religion, and the book of Revelation, alike contributed to the flood; and it was long ere my Ark touched upon Ararat, and rested. My head was with Spinoza, though my heart was with Paul and John.

At this time, 'by a gracious Providence, for which I can never be sufficiently grateful, the generous and munificent patronage of Mr. Josiah and Mr. Thomas Wedgewood enabled me to finish my education in Germany'. All this is very well; but what Mr. Coleridge learnt in Germany we know not, and seek in vain to discover through these volumes. He tells us that the Antijacobin wits accused him of abandoning his wife and children, and implicated in that charge his friends Mr. Robert Southey and Mr. Charles Lamb. This was very unjust; for Mr. Southey is, and always was, a most exemplary Family-man, and Mr. Lamb, we believe, is still a Bachelor. But Mr. Coleridge assumes a higher tone than the nature of the case demands or justifies, and his language is not quite explicit. A man who abandons his wife and children is undoubtedly both a wicked and pernicious member of society; and Mr. Coleridge ought not to deal in general and vague terms of indignation, but boldly affirm, if he dare, that the charge was false then, and would be false now, if repeated against himself. Be this as it may, Mr. Coleridge has never received any apology from those by whom he was insulted and accused of disgraceful crime; and yet has he, with a humility most unmanly, joined their ranks, and become one of their most slavish sycophants.

On his return from Germany, he became the principal writer of the political and literary departments of the *Morning Post*. This, though unquestionably a useful, respectable, and laborious employment, does not appear to us at all sublime; but Mr. Coleridge thinks otherwise—compares himself, the Writer of the leading Article, to Edmund

Burke—and, for the effect which his writings produced on Britain, refers us to the pages of the *Morning Chronicle*. In this situation, he tells us that 'he wasted the prime and manhood of his intellect', but 'added nothing to his reputation or fortune, the industry of the week supplying the necessities of the week'. Yet the effects of his labours were wonderful and glorious. He seems to think that he was the cause of the late War; and that, in consequence of his Essays in the *Morning Post*, he was, during his subsequent residence in Italy, the specified object of Bonaparte's resentment. Of this he was warned by Baron Von Humboldt and Cardinal Fesch; and he was saved from arrest by a Noble Benedictine, and the 'gracious connivance of that good old man the Pope'! We know of no parallel to such insane vanity as this, but the case of the celebrated John Dennis,[1] who, when walking one day on the sea-beach, imagined a large ship sailing by to have been sent by Ministry to capture him; and who, on another occasion, waited on the Duke of Marlborough, when the congress for the peace of Utrecht was in agitation, to intreat his interest with the plenipotentiaries, that they should not consent to his being given up. The Duke replied, that he had not got himself excepted in the articles of peace, yet he could not help thinking that he had done the French almost as much damage as even Mr. Dennis.

We have no room here to expose, as it deserves to be exposed, the multitudinous political inconsistence of Mr. Coleridge, but we beg leave to state one single fact: he abhorred, hated, and despised Mr. Pitt —and he now loves and reveres his memory. By far the most spirited and powerful of his poetical writings, is the War Eclogue, 'Slaughter, Fire, and Famine'; and in that composition he loads the Minister with imprecations and curses, long, loud, and deep. But afterwards, when he has thought it prudent to change his principles, he denies that he ever felt any indignation towards Mr. Pitt; and with the most unblushing falsehood declares, that at the very moment his muse was consigning him to infamy, death, and damnation, he would 'have interposed his body between him and danger'. We believe that all good men, of all parties, regard Mr. Coleridge with pity and contempt.

Of the latter days of his literary life Mr. Coleridge gives us no satisfactory account. The whole of the second volume is interspersed with mysterious inuendos. He complains of the loss of all his friends, not by death, but estrangement. He tries to account for the enmity of the world to him, a harmless and humane man, who wishes well to all created

[1] John Dennis (1657-1734), tragedian and literary critic.

things, and 'of his wondering finds no end'. He upbraids himself with indolence, procrastination, neglect of his worldly concerns, and all other bad habits, and then, with incredible inconsistency, vaunts loudly of his successful efforts in the cause of Literature, Philosophy, Morality, and Religion. Above all, he weeps and wails over the malignity of Reviewers, who have persecuted him almost from his very cradle, and seem resolved to bark him into the grave. He is haunted by the Image of a Reviewer wherever he goes. They 'push him from his stool', and by his bedside they cry, 'Sleep no more'. They may abuse whomsoever they think fit, save himself and Mr. Wordsworth. All others are fair game—and he chuckles to see them brought down. But his sacred person must be inviolate; and rudely to touch it is not high treason, it is impiety. Yet his 'ever-honoured friend, the laurel-honouring-Laureate', is a Reviewer, his friend Mr. Thomas Moore is a Reviewer, his friend Dr. Middleton, Bishop of Calcutta, was the Editor of a Review, almost every friend he ever had is a Reviewer; and to crown all, he himself is a Reviewer. Every person who laughs at his silly Poems, and his incomprehensible metaphysics, is malignant—in which case, there can be little benevolence in this world; and while Mr. Francis Jeffrey is alive and merry, there can be no happiness here below for Mr. Samuel Coleridge.

And here we come to speak of a matter, which, though somewhat of a personal and private nature, is well deserving of mention in a Review of Mr. Coleridge's 'Literary Life'; for sincerity is the first of virtues, and without it no man can be respectable or useful. He has, in this Work, accused Mr. Jeffrey of meanness, hypocrisy, falsehood, and breach of hospitality. That gentleman is able to defend himself, and his defence is no business of ours. But we now tell Mr. Coleridge, that instead of humbling his Adversary, he has heaped upon his own head the ashes of disgrace—and with his own blundering hands, so stained his character as a man of honour and high principles, that the mark can never be effaced. All the most offensive attacks on the writings of Wordsworth and Southey had been made by Mr. Jeffrey before his visit to Keswick. Yet does Coleridge receive him with open arms, according to his own account—listen, well-pleased, to all his compliments, talk to him for hours on his Literary Projects, dine with him as his guest at an inn, tell him that he knew Mr. Wordsworth would be most happy to see him, and in all respects behave to him with a politeness bordering on servility. And after all this, merely because his own vile verses were crumpled up like so much waste paper, by the grasp of a powerful hand in the *Edinburgh Review*, he accuses Mr. Jeffrey of abusing hospitality which he never received, and forgets, that instead of being the Host, he himself was the smiling and obsequious Guest of the man he pretends to have despised. With all this miserable forgetfulness of dignity and self-respect, he mounts the high horse, from which he instantly is tumbled into the dirt; and in his angry ravings collects together all the foul trash of literary gossip to fling at his adversary, but which is blown stifling back upon himself with odium and infamy. But let him call to mind his own conduct, and talk not of Mr. Jeffrey. Many witnesses are yet living of his own egotism and malignity; and often has he heaped upon his 'beloved Friend, the laurel-honouring Laureate', epithets of contempt, and pity, and disgust, though now it may suit his paltry purposes to worship and idolize. Of Mr. Southey we at all times think, and shall speak, with respect and admiration; but his open adversaries are, like Mr. Jeffrey, less formidable than his unprincipled Friends. When Greek and Trojan meet on the plain, there is an interest in the combat; but it is hateful and painful to think, that a hero should be wounded behind his back, and by a poisoned stiletto in the hand of a false Friend.*

The concluding chapter of this Biography is perhaps the most pitiful

---

* In the *Examiner* of April 6th, 1817, there is a letter, signed 'Vindex', from which the following extract is taken:

The author of the *Friend* is troubled at times and seasons with a treacherous memory; but perhaps he *may* remember a visit to Bristol. He *may* remember (I allude to no confidential whisperings—no unguarded private moments—but to facts of open and ostentatious notoriety) he may remember, *publicly*, before several strangers, and in the midst of a public library, turning into the most merciless ridicule 'the dear Friend' whom he now calls Southey the Philologist, 'Southey the Historian', Southey the Poet of *Thalaba*, the *Madoc*, and the *Roderic*. Mr. Coleridge recited an Ode of his dear Friend, in the hearing of these persons, with a tone and manner of the most contemptuous burlesque, and accused him of having stolen from Wordsworth images which he knew not how to use. Does he remember, that he also took down the *Joan of Arc*, and recited, in the same ridiculous tone (I do not mean his *usual* tone, but one which he meant should be ridiculous) more than a page of the poem, with the ironical comment, '*This*, gentlemen, *is Poetry?*' Does he remember that he then recited, by way of contrast, some forty lines of his own contribution to the same poem, in his usual bombastic manner? and that after this disgusting display of egotism and malignity, he observed, 'Poor fellow, he may be a *Reviewer*, but Heaven bless the man if he thinks himself a *Poet*'?

> Absentem qui rodit amicum
> Hic *niger est*: hunc tu Romane caveto.   VINDEX.

of the whole, and contains a most surprising mixture of the pathetic and the ludicrous.

Strange . . . as the delusion may appear, yet it is most true, that three years ago I did not know or believe that I had an enemy in the world; and now even my strongest consolations of gratitude are mingled with fear, and I reproach myself for being too often disposed to ask,—Have I one friend?

We are thus prepared for the narration of some grievous cruelty, or ingratitude, or malice, some violation of his peace, or robbery of his reputation; but our readers will start when they are informed, that this melancholy lament is occasioned solely by the cruel treatment which his poem of 'Christabel' received from the *Edinburgh Review* and other periodical Journals! It was, he tells us, universally admired in manuscript—he recited it many hundred times to men, women, and children, and always with an electrical effect—it was bepraised by most of the great poets of the day—and for twenty years he was urged to give it to the world. But alas! no sooner had the Lady Christabel 'come out', than all the rules of good-breeding and politeness were broken through, and the loud laugh of scorn and ridicule from every quarter assailed the ears of the fantastic Hoyden. But let Mr. Coleridge be consoled. Mr. Scott and Lord Byron are good-natured enough to admire 'Christabel', and the Public have not forgotten that his Lordship handed her Ladyship upon the stage. It is indeed most strange, that Mr. Coleridge is not satisfied with the praise of those he admires, but pines away for the commendation of those he contemns.

Having brought down his literary life to the great epoch of the publication of 'Christabel', he there stops short; and that the world may compare him as he appears at that æra to his former self, when 'he set sail from Yarmouth on the morning of the 10th September 1798, in the Hamburg Packet', he has republished, from his periodical work the *Friend*, seventy pages of 'Satyrane's Letters'. As a specimen of his wit in 1798, our readers may take the following:

We were all on the deck, but in a short time I observed marks of dismay. The Lady retired to the cabin in some confusion; and many of the faces round me assumed a very doleful and frog-coloured appearance; and within an hour the number of those on deck was lessened by one half. I was giddy, but not sick; and the giddiness soon went away, but left a feverishness and want of appetite, which I attributed, in great measure, to the '*sæva mephitis*' of the bilge-water; and it was certainly not decreased by the *exportations from the cabin*. However, I was well enough to join the able-bodied passengers, one of whom observed, not inaptly, that Momus might have discovered an easier *way to see a man's inside* than by placing a window in his breast. He needed only have taken a salt-water trip in a packet-boat. I am inclined to believe, that a packet is far superior to a stage-coach as a means of making men *open out to each other!*

The importance of his observations during the voyage may be estimated by this one:

At four o'clock I observed a wild duck swimming on the waves, *a single solitary wild duck!* It is not easy to conceive how interesting a thing it looked in that round objectless desert of waters!

At the house of Klopstock, brother of the poet, he saw a portrait of Lessing, which he thus describes to the Public. 'His eyes were uncommonly *like mine!* if any thing, rather larger and more prominent! But the lower part of his face! and his nose—O what an exquisite expression of elegance and sensibility!' He then gives a long account of his interview with Klopstock the Poet, in which he makes that great man talk in a very silly, weak, and ignorant manner. Mr. Coleridge not only sets him right in all his opinions on English literature, but also is kind enough to correct, in a very authoritative and dictatorial tone, his erroneous views of the characteristic merits and defects of the most celebrated German Writers. He has indeed the ball in his own hands throughout the whole game; and Klopstock, who, he says, 'was seventy-four years old, with legs enormously swollen', is beaten to a standstill. We are likewise presented with an account of a conversation which his friend W. held with the German Poet, in which the author of the *Messiah* makes a still more paltry figure. We can conceive nothing more odious and brutal, than two young ignorant lads from Cambridge forcing themselves upon the retirement of this illustrious old man, and, instead of listening with love, admiration, and reverence, to his sentiments and opinions, insolently obtruding upon him their own crude and mistaken fancies, contradicting imperiously every thing he advances, taking leave of him with a consciousness of their own superiority, and, finally, talking of him and his genius in terms of indifference bordering on contempt. This Mr. W. had the folly and the insolence to say to Klopstock, who was enthusiastically praising the *Oberon* of Wieland, that he never could see the smallest beauty in any part of that Poem.

We must now conclude our account of this 'unaccountable' production. It has not been in our power to enter into any discussion with Mr. Coleridge on the various subjects of Poetry and Philosophy, which he has, we think, vainly endeavoured to elucidate. But we shall, on a future occasion, meet him on his own favourite ground. No less than 182 pages of the second volume are dedicated to the poetry of Mr. Wordsworth. He has endeavoured to define poetry, to explain the philosophy of metre, to settle the boundaries of poetic diction, and to shew, finally, 'what it is probable Mr. Wordsworth meant to say in his dissertation prefixed to his *Lyrical Ballads*'. As Mr. Coleridge has not only studied the laws of poetical composition, but is a Poet of considerable powers, there are, in this part of his Book, many acute, ingenious, and even sensible observations and remarks; but he never knows when to have done, explains what requires no explanation, often leaves untouched the very difficulty he starts, and when he has poured before us a glimpse of light upon the shapeless form of some dark conception, he seems to take a wilful pleasure in its immediate extinction, and leads 'us floundering on, and quite astray', through the deepening shadows of interminable night.

One instance there is of magnificent promise, and laughable nonperformance, unequalled in the annals of literary History. Mr. Coleridge informs us, that he and Mr. Wordsworth (he is not certain which is entitled to the glory of the first discovery) have found out the difference between Fancy and Imagination. This discovery, it is prophesied, will have an incalculable influence on the progress of all the Fine Arts. He has written a long chapter purposely to prepare our minds for the great discussion. The audience is assembled, the curtain is drawn up, and there, in his gown, cap, and wig, is sitting Professor Coleridge. In comes a servant with a letter; the Professor gets up, and, with a solemn voice, reads it to the audience. It is from an enlightened Friend; and its object is to shew, in no very courteous terms either to the Professor or his Spectators, that he may lecture, but that nobody will understand him. He accordingly makes his bow, and the curtain falls; but the worst of the joke is, that the Professor pockets the admittance-money, for what reason, his outwitted audience are left, the best way they can, to 'fancy or imagine'.

But the greatest piece of Quackery in the Book, is his pretended account of the Metaphysical System of Kant, of which he knows less than nothing. He will not allow that there is a single word of truth in any of the French Expositions of that celebrated System, nor yet in any of our British Reviews. We do not wish to speak of what we do not understand, and therefore say nothing of Mr. Coleridge's Metaphysics. But we beg leave to lay before our readers the following Thesis, for the amusement of a leisure hour.

This principium commune essendi et cognoscendi, as subsisting in a WILL, or primary ACT of self-duplication, is the mediate or indirect principle of every science; but it is the mediate and direct principle of the ultimate science alone, i.e. of transcendental philosophy alone. For it must be remembered, that all these Theses refer solely to one of the two Polar Sciences, namely, to that which commences with and rigidly confines itself within the subjective, leaving the objective (as far as it is exclusively objective) to natural philosophy, which is its opposite pole. In its very idea, therefore, as a systematic knowledge of our collective KNOWING (scientia scientiæ), it involves the necessity of some one highest principle of knowing, as at once the source and the accompanying form in all particular acts of intellect and perception. This, it has been shown, can be found only in the act and evolution of self-consciousness. We are not investigating an absolute principium essendi; for then, I admit, many valid objections might be started against our theory; but an absolute principium cognoscendi. The result of both the sciences, or their equatorial point, would be the principle of a total and undivided philosophy, as, for prudential reasons, I have chosen to anticipate in the Scholium to Thesis VI. and the note subjoined.

We cannot take leave of Mr. Coleridge, without expressing our indignation at the gross injustice, and, we fear, envious persecution, of his Criticism on Mr. Maturin's *Bertram*. He has thought it worth his while to analyse and criticise that Tragedy in a diatribe of fifty pages. He contends evidently against his own conviction, that it is utterly destitute of poetical and dramatic merit, and disgraceful, not to Mr. Maturin alone, but to the audiences who admired it when acted, and the reading Public, who admired it no less when printed. There is more malignity, and envy, and jealousy, and misrepresentation, and bad wit, in this Critical Essay, than in all the Reviews now existing, from the *Edinburgh* down to the *Lady's Magazine*. Mr. Coleridge ought to have behaved otherwise to an ingenious man like Mr. Maturin, struggling into reputation, and against narrow circumstances. He speaks with sufficient feeling of his own pecuniary embarrassments, and of the evil which Reviewers have done to his wordly concerns; but all his feeling is for himself, and he has done all in his power to pluck and blast the laurels of a man of decided Poetical Genius. This is not the behaviour which one Poet ought to show to another; and if Mr. Coleridge saw faults and defects in *Bertram*, he should have exposed them in a dignified manner, giving all due praise, at the same time, to the vigour, and even originality, of that celebrated Drama. Mr. Coleridge knows that *Bertram* has become a stock play at the London Theatres, while his own *Remorse* is for ever withdrawn. Has this stung him? Far be it from us to impute mean motives to any man. But there is a bitterness, an anger, a scorn, we had almost said, a savage and revengeful fierceness, in the tone of Mr. Coleridge, when speaking of Mr. Maturin, which it is, we confess, impossible to explain, and which, we fear, proceeds (perhaps unknown to his metaphysical self) from private pique and hostility, occasioned by superior merit and greater success. As a proof that our opinion is at least plausible, we quote Mr. Coleridge's description of Bertram.

This *superfetation of blasphemy upon nonsense*—this *felo de se* and thief captain—this *loathsome and leprous confluence* of robbery, adultery, murder, and cowardly assassination—this monster, whose best deed is, *the having saved his betters from the degradation of hanging him, by turning Jack Ketch to himself.*

What a wretched contrast does Mr. Coleridge here afford to Mr. Walter Scott. That gentleman, it is known, encouraged Mr. Maturin, before he was known to the public, by his advice and commendation; and, along with Lord Byron, was the principal means of bringing *Bertram* on the stage. Such conduct was worthy of the 'Mighty Minstrel', and consistent with that true nobility of mind by which he is characterized, and which makes him rejoice in the glory of contemporary genius. Mr. Coleridge speaks with delight of the success of his own Tragedy—of his enlightened audience, and the smiling faces of those he recollected to have attended his Lectures on Poetry at the Royal Institution. How does he account for the same audience admiring *Bertram*? Let him either henceforth blush for his own fame, or admit Mr. Maturin's claims to a like distinction.

We have done. We have felt it our duty to speak with severity of this book and its author—and we have given our readers ample opportunities to judge of the justice of our strictures. We have not been speaking in the cause of Literature only, but, we conceive, in the cause of Morality and Religion. For it is not fitting that he should be held up as an example to the rising generation (but, on the contrary, it is most fitting that he should be exposed as a most dangerous model), who has alternately embraced, defended, and thrown aside all systems of Philosophy, and all creeds of Religion; who seems to have no power of retaining an opinion, no trust in the principles which he defends, but who fluctuates from theory to theory, according as he is impelled by vanity, envy, or diseased desire of change, and who, while he would subvert and scatter into dust those structures of knowledge, reared by the wise men of this and other generations, has nothing to erect in their room but the baseless and air-built fabrics of a dreaming imagination.

79. 'J. S.', *Blackwood's Edinburgh Magazine*

December 1817, ii, 285-8

This letter in answer to John Wilson's review of *Biographia Literaria* (No. 78) may have been written by Wilson himself (see A. L. Strout, op. cit., 106n.).

Sir,

To be blind to our failings, and awake to our prejudices, is the fault of almost every one of us. Through all time, and in all ages, it has been the shadow of our life, and the ugly stain upon our conduct. It is the same with me, the same with Mr. Coleridge, and it is, I regret to state it, the same with his reviewer! These simple observations must suffice as the exordium of those I attempt on the review, you, Sir, have put forth in the number of *Blackwood's Edinburgh Magazine* I have just received, and which review (may I prove a false prophet!) will not better the cause, or increase the profit, of that publication. I speak not alone mine own opinion, but the opinion of others who have perused that ungenerous piece of laboured criticism, that coarse exertion of individual opinion.

I pass entirely unnoticed your preliminary observations, as having nothing to do with the review itself; they are probably correct, and certainly well written, but, like a beautiful portico, serve only by the contrast to heighten the deformity of the principal object.

The best reparation we can make for early errors is a candid confession of them, coupled with an earnest warning to others to avoid their concomitant dangers; and as Mr. Coleridge has done this (by your own admission), I cannot see why it should not benefit the cause both of virtue and religion. At all events, a once-deluded mortal, awaking from his dream of insanity to confess his follies and amend his frailties, is not that despicable being you would fain picture, nor is the publication of his delusion to be so harshly treated by one, who, for aught the world knows, before he became, as Mr. Coleridge has become, a reviewer, might have been, as Mr. Coleridge has been, a deluded politician, or a preaching enthusiast. So far in extenuation of our author's publishing

351

this part of his work, and we will speak as shortly respecting the other—
I mean what may be termed the literary. There I am free to allow, in a
great measure, the matter of your observations, but not the manner:
the one may be generally correct, the other certainly is every thing but
liberal criticism. Mr. Coleridge may be vain, nay, sometimes arrogant;
he may judge lightly of his superiors, and foolishly of the world; but
for these mistakes of mind, these errors of judgment, why should all
men view him with contempt, and why should he deserve it? With
equal justice may I dogmatically affirm, that because Mr. C. in judgment and in wisdom is but in his first age, you, from your querulous-
ness and illiberality, are verging into your last. How, indeed, do we
know, but that you may be one of those who have fallen under the bad
opinion of Mr. C., and have taken this secure, because anonymous,
means of paying off old scores upon him. Pardon the supposition, but
it is possible, and I use it.

You charge Mr. C. with arrogance, and then add, 'In Scotland few
know or care anything about him', first, however, admitting, that in
London 'he is well known in literary society, &c.', thus contrasting
the judgments of the two countries, and, of course, insinuating the
superior intelligence of your own. With this I have nothing to do;
national love, and national prejudice too, are to a degree pleasing: but
when you talk of arrogance again, weigh well the accusation, lest it
recoil on the person that discharges it. Again, if you really mean what
you say, in stating that *few* know and *none* care about Mr. C., what in
the name of wonder and common sense could induce *you* to bring his
name, and his works, before your countrymen, unless it was the desire
of turning schoolmaster and teaching them to spell, or the more noble
one of wiping the stigma you have cast on your country away, by at
last making it acquainted with 'so much genius and ability' as Mr.
Coleridge has occasionally displayed! Your countrymen and yourself
must have been at issue on the question; they must have been dunces
and you dilatory, or you would have before (since Mr. C. has written
so much, and sometimes so well) introduced them to a little more
genius and ability than they were possessed of, and Scotland boasted.
You will answer, that the danger of the publication demanded your
attention; but again, I say, in the name of *common sense*, is it probable
that those who had before not given a moment's thought to Mr. C.,
or his writings, should *o' the sudden* conceive him a very notorious
character, or that those who had failed to consult his former publication
should study his last? It has been said, that every writer has his peculiar

admirers; and admitting this as a fact, it might have been as well had you said less of Scott (a man whose style of poetry has gradually been declining, and whose innumerable and glaring faults of rhyme, and ridiculous affectation of gothic terms, satirized by every review, have scarcely been atoned for by the beauties of his landscapes), than your partiality has wrung from you; for I am not sure whether the *poor verses* of Mr. Scott, on our triumph at Waterloo, or the extravagant effusion of Coleridge's 'Christabel', gained the greater *credit* for its author! Nor do we hear much of the *Vision of Don Roderick*; and the *Lord of the Isles* has not half as good a name as the *Lady of the Lake*. Now I am willing to admit all this has nothing to do with Mr. Coleridge's *Biographia Literaria*, and yet you, Sir, for the purpose of exalting your Scotch demigod to the skies, neglect the work for the purpose of vilifying the man.

I avoid saying a word as to the folly of your introducing Campbell and Moore in the review of the works of their brother bard (I dare say they do not thank you for it), though of the modesty of the latter gentleman I have heard strange stories, and the complimentary verses to Kemble of the former well deserve, but for the occasion, some contempt.

What you blame in the conduct of Mr. Coleridge you are yourself particularly guilty of; and it is on this account, as shewing a rancour more than we can understand against Mr. C. (for the man who can write and argue as you, Sir, do against its commission, cannot *involuntarily* be led into the error), that I principally express my indignation; I say, Sir, you are to the full as prone to scatter dirt on Mr. C. as Mr. C. on others, and if he has forgotten the gentleman in his observations on *Bertram*, you have not recollected the liberal-minded man in your observations respecting his *Remorse*, a drama which will at least weigh in the balance with the extravagant, though sometimes nervous play of Mr. Maturin, and not be found wanting. That Coleridge has, in gone by days, vilified Mr. Southey, is no excuse for Mr. Jeffrey's conduct to Mr. C.; and till a better defence has been made for him than you have volunteered, I must think him, what his writings prove him to be, an ungenerous and not one of the best hearted men.

That Mr. Scott and Lord Byron admired 'Christabel', and encouraged its publication, you yourself admit. Now it follows, therefore, that you and Mr. Scott are at issue on your judgments: he says the work is good—you, that it is good for nothing at all. Which shall we believe? *the true poet*, or the man who *only talks about poetry?* Perhaps you will say, partiality induced Mr. Scott to deal kindly by his friend; let this be granted. Might not the praise he has bestowed on Maturin's *Bertram* be *partial too?* Therefore, turn which way we will, consider how we will, I really must believe you had written without due consideration, and penned opinions that you should blush and be sorry for.

I will just say, with reference to the conclusion of your philippic, that the example afforded by a man who has forsworn former errors, and acknowledged former follies, will be more likely to make a deeper impression on the mind than the contemplation of a character, which has been *uniformly* equal in its habits, conduct, and feelings: many will slight the warnings of the good, and yet be awed by the conversion of the frail.

I trust I need scarcely add, that it is not from a knowledge of Mr. C., or any of his friends, that I have been induced thus to address you; I have never seen him or them; but is from a love I have for generous and fair criticism, and a hate to every thing which appears personal, and levelled against the man and not his subject—and your writing is glaringly so—that I venture to draw daggers with a reviewer. You have indeed imitated, with not a little of its power and ability, the worst manner of the *Edinburgh Review* critics. Forgetting the axiom of Plutarch, that freedom of remark does not exclude the kind and courteous style, you have, with them, entirely sunk the courteousness in the virulency of it. But recollect also, with the same author, that 'He who temperately and modestly attends to what is advanced, receives and retains what is useful, *yet appears* a friend to truth, not censorious, or prone to strife and contention'.

I have added my name, which you are, if you please, at liberty to insert; but as I am not ambitious of appearing so publicly, perhaps it will satisfy you if I request your permission to sign myself, your obedient servant, J.S.

80. Unsigned review, *British Critic*

November 1817, viii, 460-81

The review also deals very briefly with *Sibylline Leaves*.

When a writer sets down to record the history of his own life and opinions, it certainly affords a presumption that he conceives himself to be an object of greater curiosity with the public, than it is quite modest in any man to suppose; but for a writer, the whole of whose works would probably not form a fair sized octavo volume, to compose an account of how he was educated, in what manner he formed his taste, what he has been in the habit of thinking upon this or that subject, and so forth, sounds even somewhat ridiculous. It is, however, but just to say, with respect to the excellent author of the 'Biographical Sketches', before us, that it would be unfair to estimate the interest which his readers may be supposed to take in his history and opinions, by the number or importance of the writings which he has published; for some reason or other his name is familiar to numbers who are altogether unacquainted with his compositions; and connected as it has been with the names of his two celebrated friends, Mr. Southey and Mr. Wordsworth, it has certainly been mentioned both in conversation and in print, more frequently than it is perhaps quite easy to account for. In Mr. Coleridge's poetical compositions we own that we see but little on which it would be prudent to bestow unqualified commendation. They exhibit few traces of deep or fine feeling, and still fewer of correct and polished taste; wildness of imagination is the predominant quality of his genius, but it is so apt to degenerate into extravagance, that if we except his 'Ancient Mariner', the verses called 'Love', and perhaps a few, and but a few others, which might be mentioned, we think the character of his poetry is far from being pleasing. To follow his flights requires very commonly a painful effort of attention, and when we have gained the heights to which he carries us, instead of any objects opening upon our view to repay us for our labour, we

355

commonly find ourselves enveloped in mistiness and clouds. But still his writings bear the impression of a mind of considerable powers; in whatever he composes, the workings of thought are almost always perceptible; and his failures are rather the result of an understanding that has been misguided than of any deficiency in respect to the requisite quantity of talent.

Mr. Coleridge tells us that the question 'What is poetry?' is so nearly the same thing as to ask 'What is a poet?' that in order to define the former he will give a description of the latter.

The poet (says he), described in *ideal* perfection, brings the whole soul of man into activity, with the subordination of its faculties to each other, according to their relative worth and dignity. He diffuses a tone, and spirit of unity, that blends, and (as it were) *fuses*, each into each, by that synthetic and magical power, to which we have exclusively appropriated the name of imagination. This power, first put in action by the will and understanding, and retained under their irremissive, though gentle and unnoticed, controul (*laxis effertur habenis*) reveals itself in the balance or reconciliation of opposite or discordant qualities; of sameness, with difference; of the general, with the concrete; the idea, with the image; the individual, with the representative; the sense of novelty and freshness, with old and familiar objects; a more than usual state of emotion, with more than usual order; judgment ever awake and steady self-possession, with enthusiasm and feeling profound or vehement; and while it blends and harmonizes the natural and the artificial, still subordinates art to nature; the manner to the matter; and our admiration of the poet to our sympathy with the poetry.

With such very intelligible ideas of the office of a poet, our readers need not be surprised if our author's conception of poetry is not always such as people, who think and feel in a common way, will easily enter into; but however his practice is not quite what his theory would lead us to anticipate; his verses are, indeed, often not intelligible, but they are not always so; in poetry as in prose, he is ever aiming at something that is transcendental, and in both cases his error (and an inexpiable error it is) is deliberate, and of fore-thought; but still he is not always in the clouds; he sometimes walks upon the earth like other men; and when he does, both his prose and his poetry evince an amiable, cultivated, and original mind.

We have said thus much respecting the character of our author's poetical genius, principally because it is with his poetry chiefly, that the public are acquainted; but partly because it appears to be his wish, that the two publications prefixed to this article, should be considered as belonging to each other; nevertheless, as all the poems (with two inconsiderable exceptions) included in the former, have been long before the public in an authentic shape, we do not think it necessary to enter into any detailed criticism of their separate merits. In fact, it is not our wish to review Mr. Coleridge's literary Life itself; our intention is to confine our attention to these 'Sketches' of it, which Mr. Coleridge has presented us with; and this with a view to give our readers some idea of the book itself, considered simply as a literary performance, rather than as a record of facts connected with the life of its author.

In naming the volumes, to which we propose confining our remarks, 'Biographical Sketches of his literary Life and Opinions', Mr. Coleridge has signified very accurately the real nature of his publication; for it is with circumstances that have a relation to his literary life only, that he makes his reader acquainted; with respect to his birth, parentage, and personal history, he says almost nothing; these he tells us may afford materials for a separate work which he seems to contemplate; in the present he tells us little more of himself, than that he was educated at Christ's Hospital, was a member of Jesus College, Cambridge, was, at the beginning of the French revolution, editor of a paper called the *Watchman*; and subsequently, at the time of the peace of Amiens, conducted the *Morning Post*. These circumstances are only mentioned incidentally; the volumes are exclusively filled with abstracts of the literary opinions which he entertains; some of them upon subjects interesting enough, but a very large proportion upon subjects, which we fear our author will find some difficulty, in persuading his readers to feel quite so much respect for, as he seems to think them entitled to. The three prominent topics, upon which it would appear that our author has chiefly reflected, are, in the first place, philosophy; by which our readers must not suppose us to mean the writings of Locke or Newton, or Bacon or Aristotle, but of Jacob Behmen, Gemisthiu. Pletho, de Thoyras, Plotinus, and above all, the inscrutable Kants The subject which seems to hold the second place in our author's esteem, is poetry; and to which (in subordination to a critical review of Mr. Wordsworth's productions) a very considerable portion of the two volumes is devoted. The third object of his attention, are anonymous critics in general, but more particularly the *Edinburgh Review*. This last topic, indeed, forms a sort of *running accompaniment* to the second; for they seem so intimately connected in his thoughts, that he is seldom able to speak of poetry, or poets, or poetical criticism, but what we perceive (to use a very favourite expression of our author) an *under-current* to all his observations of hatred and contempt against our fellow-labourers (though we trust not in the same vineyard) of the north.

With respect to the general character of the work, it is certainly an able, and, notwithstanding our author's endless and bottomless discussions on metaphysical matters, upon the whole, an entertaining performance. Our author's incidental remarks upon criticism, politics, religion, and such other subjects as fall within the reach of an ordinary man's comprehension, are often just and striking, and invariably display a tone of mind that is both scholar-like and amiable. As to his style, we hardly know what to say of it; it is certainly expressive, but it does not seem to be constructed upon any settled principles of composition, farther than are implied in an apparent preference of our early writers, not only over those upon whose style the taste of the present day seems to be chiefly modelled, but over Addison and Dryden, and the writers of what we cannot but think the Augustan age of our prose literature.

Now, if our author is resolved to see no medium between the involved constructions and cumbrous phraseology of Milton and Jeremy Taylor, and the cheap finery of the *stylum pene cantiam* of our fashionable historians and philosophers, we undoubtedly approve of the taste by which his preference has been guided. The faults of Clarendon and Hooker proceeded merely from a want of skill in composition, whereas the faults of those writers whom Mr. Coleridge seems so studious of not imitating, proceed from affectation and pretension. To say that our author has succeeded in reminding us of the models whom he appears desirous of emulating, is not saying much in his praise. It is just as easy to put into one sentence what ought properly to form three, as to put into three, what ought properly to form only one; nor is it a matter of much greater difficulty to sprinkle our manner of speaking with learned phrases and obsolete forms of expression. For example, when our author tells us that he 'had undertaken the new business of an author, *yea*, of an author trading on his own account'. This, in fact, is only a peculiar species of coxcombry, and is better than the coxcombry of one of our modern *beau* writers, only as the gravity of a broad-brimmed hat, may be preferred to the levity of the *chapeau-bras*.[1] It would, however, be unjust to our author, were we to describe the merits of his style, as consisting in a mere clumsy imitation of our early prose writers; on the contrary, he writes in general with an air of

[1] A flattenable hat which could be carried under the arm.

truth and simplicity, which is plainly natural to him; and his language, though sometimes pedantic, and often by no means free from that philosophical jargon which is almost the characteristical affectation of the present race of writers, is nevertheless, that of a scholar; to which we may add, that although a little innocent vanity is every now and then making its appearance, yet in general it merely gives an air of naiveté and quaintness to his expressions, and never assumes the form of arrogance and self-conceit. But we have said enough respecting the style of the volumes before us; it is time to let our readers know something of their contents.

Of course, a work, which professes to give an account of opinions, that are linked to each other by no other connection, than that which arises from their having belonged to the same individual, cannot be supposed to be arranged upon any method founded on the nature of things; and consequently to give a systematic criticism of them, would be altogether impracticable. We shall, therefore, not trouble ourselves by attempting to give our author's thoughts any better arrangement than he has himself thought necessary; but content ourselves with following his steps, merely stopping now and then to intersperse our abstracts and citations with such incidental remarks, as may happen at the moment to suggest themselves.

Our author's first chapter contains rather an interesting account of the discipline which his poetical taste received, while at Christ's Hospital, under the direction of the Rev. J. Bowyer, at that time the head master. In this age of systematic education, perhaps a plan of instruction which has the sanction of Mr. Coleridge's approbation, and of the benefits of which he considers his own taste a practical exemplification, may not be unacceptable to our readers.

At school I enjoyed the inestimable advantage of a very sensible, though at the same time a very severe master.* He early moulded my taste to the preference of Demosthenes to Cicero, of Homer and Theocritus to Virgil, and again of Virgil to Ovid. He habituated me to compare Lucretius, (in such extracts as I then read) Terence, and above all the chaster poems of Catullus, not only with the Roman poets of the, so called, silver and brazen ages; but with even those of the Augustan era: and on grounds of plain sense and universal logic to see and assert the superiority of the former, in the truth and nativeness, both of their thoughts and diction. At the same time that we were studying the Greek Tragic Poets, he made us read Shakespeare and Milton as lessons: and they were the lessons too, which required most time and trouble to *bring up*, so as to escape

* The Rev. James Bowyer, many years Head Master of the Grammar-School, Christ Hospital.

his censure. I learnt from him, that Poetry, even that of the loftiest, and, seemingly, that of the wildest odes, had a logic of its own, as severe as that of science; and more difficult, because more subtle, more complex, and dependent on more, and more fugitive causes. In the truly great poets, he would say, there is a reason assignable, not only for every word, but for the position of every word; and I well remember, that availing himself of the synonimes to the Homer of Didymus, he made us attempt to show, with regard to each, *why* it would not have answered the same purpose; and *wherein* consisted the peculiar fitness of the word in the original text.

In our own English compositions (at least for the last three years of our school education) he showed no mercy to phrase, metaphor, or image, unsupported by a sound sense, or where the same sense might have been conveyed with equal force and dignity in plainer words. Lute, harp, and lyre, muse, muses, and inspirations, Pegasus, Parnassus, and Hipocrene, were all an abomination to him. In fancy I can almost hear him now, exclaiming '*Harp? Harp? Lyre? Pen and ink, boy, you mean! Muse, boy, Muse? your Nurse's daughter, you mean! Pierian spring? Oh, aye! the cloister-pump, I suppose!*' Nay certain introductions, similies, and examples, were placed by name on a list of interdiction. Among the similies, there was, I remember, that of the Manchineel fruit, as suiting equally well with too many subjects; in which however it yielded the palm at once to the example of Alexander and Clytus, which was equally good and apt, whatever might be the theme. Was it ambition? Alexander and Clytus!—Flattery? Alexander and Clytus!—Anger? Drunkenness? Pride? Friendship? Ingratitude? Late repentance? Still, still Alexander and Clytus! At length, the praises of agriculture having been exemplified in the sagacious observation, that had Alexander been holding the plough, he would not have run his friend Clytus through with a spear, this tried, and serviceable old friend was banished by public edict in secula seculorum.

We cannot say that we see any thing to object against, in any of the particulars related in this account of Mr. Bowyer's plan; yet we are very doubtful how far we should be desirous of seeing it generally practised; as it appears to us it may have answered very well with respect to particular boys, and perhaps under the superintendance of a particular schoolmaster; but we own, that in general, we would rather entrust the education of a boy's *taste* to nature and his own turn of mind, working upon the models that must in the regular course of instruction be placed before him, than subject it to the censorship of any ordinary schoolmaster: many reasons might be given for this; but it is sufficient to say, that the proper business of the master (of a large school, more especially) is to put into the hands of his scholars, the means and instruments of taste and learning; but taste and learning themselves are the growth of age and after-reflection.

The subject of his early education leads our author to notice the effect made upon his mind, when at the age of seventeen, by a perusal of Bowles's Sonnets: we shall not stop to examine the grounds of the very warm admiration, which Mr. Coleridge seems still to entertain, for what gave him so much pleasure, and inspired him with so much emulation when young; only we may be permitted to remark, that he seems to attach much more importance to the history of his poetical taste, than his readers will probably be made to feel. At whatever age Mr. Coleridge may have become first sensible of the inferiority of Pope's system of poetical diction to that of Milton, and of one or two of our early Poets, we confess we see nothing so remarkable in the discovery, as to require a detailed account of the grounds and process of it; we shall therefore not follow him through all the discussions into which this part of his subject leads him, but passing over the remainder of this first chapter, and all the second (in which he attempts to disprove the imputation of peculiar irritability, under which men of poetical genius are supposed to labour) we shall proceed to chapter the third. The subject of this is very high matter, being no less than that of a discussion concerning the usefulness, rights, and prerogatives of us, 'synodical individuals', who call ourselves reviewers; nor does our author think it necessary to treat us hypothetically, and with reference to the principles of Plato's republic; but he denounces us by name, as nuisances to the republic of letters. Now we are not sure whether it quite comports with our dignity, to sanction any thing like an argument as to the competency of our tribunal; nevertheless, as we cannot but allow that our author has no particular reason to congratulate himself upon having been born in this age of critical illumination, we shall overlook the indiscreetness with which he speaks of reviews generally, in consideration of his particular case, and permit him to utter, what we should be very sorry our readers should believe. Our author tells us,

It might correct the moral feelings of a numerous class of readers, to suppose a Review set on foot, the object of which was to criticise all the chief works presented to the public by our ribbon-weavers, calico-printers, cabinet-makers, and china-manufacturers; a Review conducted in the same spirit, and which should take the same freedom with personal character, as our literary journals. They would scarcely, I think, deny their belief, not only that the 'genus irritabile' would be found to include many other *species* besides that of bards; but that the irritability of *trade* would soon reduce the resentments of *poets* into mere shadow-fights (σκιομαχιας) in the comparison. Or is wealth the only rational object of human interest? Or even if this were admitted, has the poet no property in his works? Or is it a rare, or culpable case, that he who serves at the altar of the muses, should be compelled to derive his maintenance from the altar, when too he has perhaps deliberately abandoned the fairest prospects of rank and opulence in order to devote himself, an entire and un-distracted man, to the instruction or refinement of his fellow-citizens? Or should we pass by all higher objects and motives, all disinterested benevolence, and even that ambition of lasting praise which is at once the crutch and ornament, which at once supports and betrays the infirmity of human virtue; is the charac-ter and property of the individual, who labours for our intellectual pleasures, less entitled to a share of our fellow feeling, than that of the wine-merchant or milliner.

There is in the work before us, a good deal of reasoning like this, which we apprehend to be not very original, however plausible it may appear; and to say that it is even plausible, is perhaps saying quite as much as it deserves. For even taking our author's own illustration; if individuals retail adulterated wines or any other commodity of in-ferior quality, the public surely are benefited by being made acquainted with the fact, nor is it reasonable to accuse those of injustice, from whom the information is obtained. But the truth is, the illustration is by no means in point, except it be with reference merely to the com-paratively harmless quality of an author's dullness; a writer, however, without being dull, may display bad taste or mischievous principles; he may distort facts from ignorance, or pervert them from prejudice; in short, his writings may in innumerable ways do a much more lasting injury to his readers, than merely sending them to sleep. To expose faults like these, has no doubt a tendency to diminish the sale of the work, in which they are contained; but an author has no better right to complain in such a case of the injury done to his private interests, by anonymous criticism, than a statesman to complain of being turned out of office, in consequence of his measures being proved to be prejudicial to the public. Authors are just as much public char-acters as secretaries of state are; if they voluntarily come forward upon the stage of public life, under pretence of being able to enlighten, or in any other way to benefit the community at large, of course they must expect that their pretensions will be canvassed; that their opinions and principles will become a subject of discussion; misrepresentation and misconception, unreasonable censure and blind admiration—these are matters of course—the penalty paid in all cases for publicity; but it would be about as wise to complain of the daily papers, on account of the abuse, which they mutually pour forth against the opponents of their respective parties, as to complain of anonymous critics, for the bitterness, with which they sometimes review the works of those, who profess principles and opinions, of which the former disapprove; and about as much for the interests of the community, to repress or discountenance them.

If the writers in either case, not content with combating principles and opinions, and public acts, trespass upon the sanctity of private life, and endeavour to prepossess the minds of their readers, by slander and calumny and personal invective; this no doubt is highly disgraceful to the individual, who so misuses his privilege of discussion; but his virulence is of little importance to the public, and nine times in ten, of not much more to him, who is the object of it. If one party condemn in excess, another will generally be found to praise in an equal excess; and after the first fermentation of contending opinions has a little subsided, the real truth gradually separates itself from the errors, with which it had been mixed, and becomes perhaps better and more certainly distinguishable, than by almost any other process, to which it could have been subjected. As in our courts of justice, one advocate is paid, to say all that can be said in favour of one side of the question; another, to urge in like manner all that can be said against it, the decision in the meanwhile resting with the jury; so it is with us critics; one review is set up by men strongly biassed in favour of one system of principles; another starts in opposition to it by men as warmly favourable to the opposite; both of them, indeed, affect to speak with the authority, that belongs to the judicial office; but they are listened to as judges, only by those of their own party; the public knows well, that they are mere advocates, hired by their prejudices to plead the cause of a particular sect; and by listening to both sides, is much more likely to be put in possession of all the arguments in favour of each, than if it implicitly trusted to the impartiality, with which any single review could state them. So far then, with respect to our author's sentiments concerning the merits of reviews generally; but the fact is, that his indictment, though worded somewhat sweepingly, is really intended to be preferred against one particular journal, which both in taste, morals, politics, religion, and even in manners, happens to have embraced a set of opinions directly counter to those which Mr. Coleridge approves of. Now, in bringing forward what our author has to urge, in reprobation of the abusive spirit, in which the above-mentioned critics have reviewed his writings and the writings of his friends, we shall not enter into the critical merits of the case. Our opinions upon most of the subjects, upon which our author and his anonymous, though well known reviewer have split, are already before the public. That much childishness is mixed up with Mr. Wordsworth's poetry, and some extravagance in the poetry, and some want of moderation in the prose, of Mr. Southey, are, we apprehend, truths not to be denied; and if there are some, professing to be judges in these points, who are able to see in the writings of neither, any qualities besides, we really know not how the matter is to be mended by mere discussion. On this subject our author tells us a story, which will illustrate the real nature of the case before us, as well as the grounds of a great many other differences of opinion upon questions of taste.

When I was at Rome, among many other visits to the tomb of Julius II, I went thither once with a Prussian artist, a man of genius and great vivacity of feeling. As we were gazing on Michael Angelo's MOSES, our conversation turned on the horns and beard of that stupendous statue; of the necessity of each to support the other; of the super-human effect of the former, and the necessity of the existence of both to give a harmony and *integrity* both to the image and the feeling excited by it. Conceive them removed, and the statue would become *un*-natural, without being *super*-natural. We called to mind the horns of the rising sun, and I repeated the noble passage from Taylor's *Holy Dying*. That horns were the emblem of power and sovereignty among the Eastern nations, and are still retained as such in Abyssinia; the Achelous of the ancient Greeks; and the probable ideas and feelings, that originally suggested the mixture of the human and the brute form in the figure, by which they realized the idea of their mysterious Pan, as representing intelligence blended with a darker power, deeper, mightier, and more universal than the conscious intellect of man; than intelligence; all these thoughts and recollections passed in procession before our minds. My companion who possessed more than his share of the hatred, which his countrymen bore to the French, had just observed to me, 'a Frenchman, Sir! is the only animal in the human shape, that by no possibility can lift itself up to religion or poetry': When, lo! two French officers of distinction and rank entered the church! *Mark you*, whispered the Prussian, '*the first thing, which those scoundrels—will notice (for they will begin by instantly noticing the statue in parts, without one moment's pause of admiration impressed by the whole) will be the horns and the beard. And the associations, which they will immediately connect with them will be those of a* HE-GOAT *and a* CUCKOLD.' Never did man guess more luckily. Had he inherited a portion of the great legislator's prophetic powers, whose statue we had been contemplating, he could scarcely have uttered words more coincident with the result: for even as he had said, so it came to pass.

In the *Excursion* the poet has introduced an old man, born in humble but not abject circumstances, who had enjoyed more than usual advantages of education, both from books and from the more awful discipline of nature. This person he represents, as having been driven by the restlessness of fervid feelings, and from a craving intellect, to an itinerant life; and as having in consequence passed the larger portion of his time, from earliest manhood, in villages and hamlets from door to door.

> A vagrant merchant bent beneath his load.

Now whether this be a character appropriate to a lofty didactick poem, is perhaps questionable. It presents a fair subject for controversy; and the question is to be determined by the congruity or incongruity of such a character with what shall be proved to be the essential constituents of poetry. But surely the critic who, passing by all the opportunities which such a mode of life would present to such a man; all the advantages of the liberty of nature, of solitude and of solitary thought; all the varieties of places and seasons, through which his track had lain, with all the varying imagery they bring with them; and lastly, all the observations of men,

> Their manners, their enjoyment and pursuits,
> Their passions and their feelings

which the memory of these yearly journies must have given and recalled to such a mind—the critic, I say, who from the multitude of possible associations should pass by all these in order to fix his attention exclusively on *the pin-papers*, and *stay-tapes*, which *might* have been among the wares of his pack; this critic in my opinion cannot be thought to possess a much higher or much healthier state of moral feeling, than the FRENCHMEN above recorded.

This is a pleasant apologue and significantly applied; it is however plain, that if our author had no other grounds of complaint against his critics, than the above passage affords, he certainly would not be justified in using the epithets, made use of in the last sentence; for a critic cannot with any more propriety be called a 'quack' (because he happens to be wanting in taste (even assuming the fact), than a poet could be, who should happen to be wanting in imagination. To speak passionately about questions of opinion, or contemptuously of whatever else we have not ourselves a taste for, are not to be sure the most unequivocal marks of a superior understanding; but men cannot obtain sense by merely wishing for it; and critics, like others, can only speak as they feel; all that authors or the public, can reasonably expect, is, that critics should *really* speak as they think, and not give decisions which they know to be partial, merely for the purpose of gratifying feelings of a personal nature. Now this is the charge which Mr. Coleridge explicitly and formally presses against the reviewer of himself and friends; and supposing, that the facts, which he asserts, are correctly stated, we think, that the public (supposing them to interest themselves about the matter) will not feel disposed to blame our author, for the strong language in which he sometimes expresses his sense of the unjustifiable persecution of which he, but in a more particular manner Mr. Southey and Mr. Wordsworth, have been for many years the constant objects. We shall not quote the passages (that are scattered through almost every part of his work) in which our author gives vent to the feelings, excited in his mind by the conduct of which he complains; but state the facts by which he conceives the resentment expressed by him to be warranted; and this we shall do, partly from regard to justice, and partly because reviews and reviewers seem to have been uppermost in our author's mind, when he projected the work before us, as they are scarcely ever lost sight of by him in the progress of it. There are few of our readers, probably, but are aware of the unmeasured contempt and unmitigated ridicule, with which the writings of Mr. Wordsworth have been treated in the journal, of which our author complains; few persons would, we think, imagine that the writer of the article, in which the offensive criticism was conveyed, could ever have expressed himself in private conversation in the manner in which Mr. Coleridge in the following passage states himself to have heard.

Let not Mr. Wordsworth be charged with having expressed himself too indignantly, till the wantonness and the systematic and malignant perseverance of the aggressions have been taken into fair consideration. I myself heard the commander in chief of this unmanly warfare make a boast of his private admiration of Wordsworth's genius. I have heard him declare, that whoever came into his room would probably find the *Lyrical Ballads* lying open on his table, and that (speaking exclusively of those written by Mr. Wordsworth himself), he could nearly repeat the whole of them by heart.

In another part of the work Mr. Coleridge informs us that some years ago, upon occasion of the reviewer in question paying a visit to Cumberland, he was at his own request introduced to Mr. Southey, drank tea at his house, and was in all respects hospitably treated; but so far was he from permitting the recollection of the courtesies which he had received, to soften the asperity of his criticism, that his very first employment upon returning to Edinburgh, was to write a lampoon upon his host, in language still more offensive than upon any former occasion; designating him and the friends whom he met at his house, as 'whining and hypochondriacal poets', and saying many other things, which a critic perhaps had a right to say, but which it was just as easy to have said in civil as in disrespectful language. The note, in which the charge is made, contains many other particulars, and is somewhat long; but as the contents of it have been thought so weighty, as to induce the reviewer to come forward in his own person and under his own name, in order to rebut it, perhaps it may gratify our readers to have the whole passage before them.

Some years ago, a gentleman, the chief writer and conductor of a celebrated review, distinguished by its hostility to Mr. Southey, spent a day or two at Keswick. That he was, without diminution on this account, treated with every hospitable attention by Mr. Southey and myself, I trust I need not say. But one thing I may venture to notice; that at no period of my life do I remember to have received so many, and such high coloured compliments in so short a space of time. He was likewise circumstantially informed by what series of accidents it had happened, that Mr. Wordsworth, Mr. Southey, and I had become neighbours; and how utterly unfounded was the supposition, that we considered ourselves, as belonging to any common school, but that of good sense confirmed by the long-established models of the best times of Greece, Rome, Italy, and England; and still more groundless the notion, that Mr. Southey (for as to myself I have published so little, and that little, of so little importance, as to make it almost ludicrous to mention my name at all) could have been con- cerned in the formation of a poetic sect with Mr. Wordsworth, when so many of his works had been published not only previously to any acquaintance between them; but before Mr. Wordsworth himself had written any thing but in a diction ornate, and uniformly sustained; when too the slightest exam- ination will make it evident, that between those and the after writings of Mr. Southey, there exists no other difference than that of a progressive degree of excellence from progressive developement of power, and progressive facility from habit and increase of experience. Yet among the first articles which this man wrote after his return from Keswick, we were characterized as 'the School of whining and hypochondriacal poets that haunt the Lakes'. In reply to a letter from the same gentleman, in which he had asked me, whether I was in earnest in preferring the style of Hooker to that of Dr. Johnson; and Jeremy Taylor to Burke; I stated, somewhat at large, the comparative excellences and defects which characterized our best prose writers, from the reformation, to the first half of Charles 2nd; and that of those who had flourished during the present reign, and the preceding one. About twelve months afterwards, a review appeared on the same subject, in the concluding paragraph of which the reviewer asserts, that his chief motive for entering into the discussion was to separate a rational and unqualified admiration of our elder writers, from the indiscriminate enthusiasm of a recent school, who praised what they did not understand, and caricatured what they were unable to imitate. And, that no doubt might be left concerning the persons alluded to, the writer annexes the names of Miss BAILLIE, W. SOUTHEY, WORDSWORTH and COLERIDGE. For that which follows, I have only hear-say evidence; but yet such as demands my belief; viz. that on being questioned concerning this apparently wanton attack more especially with reference to Miss Baillie, the writer had stated as his motives, that this lady when at Edinburgh had declined a proposal of intro- ducing him to her; that Mr. Southey had written against him; and Mr. Words- worth had talked contemptuously of him; but that as to *Coleridge* he had noticed him merely because the names of Southey and Wordsworth and Coleridge always went together. But if it were worth while to mix together, as ingredients, half the anecdotes which I either myself know to be true, or which I have received from men incapable of intentional falsehood, concerning the characters, qualifications, and motives of our anonymous critics, whose decisions are oracles for our reading public; I might safely borrow the words of the apocryphal Daniel; '*Give me leave* O SOVEREIGN PUBLIC, *and I shall slay this dragon without sword or staff*'. For the compound would be as the '*Pitch, and fat, and hair, which Daniel took, and did seethe them together, and made lumps thereof, and put into the dragon's mouth, and so the dragon burst in sunder; and Daniel said* LO; THESE ARE THE GODS YE WORSHIP.'

Now, in the answer which our reviewer has put forth to the above charges, he takes no notice of the warm admiration, which he is said to have expressed for the poetry of Mr. Wordsworth; we have there- fore a right to conclude, that the article in which that gentleman's writings have been reviewed, were intended to convey into the mind of the reader, a different opinion from that which the reviewer himself conscientiously entertained. As to the high-flown compliments with which he gratified Mr. Coleridge's vanity, we are told, that the reviewer paid them, because he thought he could perceive that they were as agreeable to our author, as they are to most people; by which we are left to infer, that what our honest reviewer *says*, is no better criterion of his real sentiments, than what he *writes*; and since he certainly cannot be accused of having flattered our author in the *latter* way, we suppose it is his opinion, that any injury done to truth by praising a man more than he deserves by word of mouth, and before his face, is wiped away, by abusing him in an equal degree beyond what truth will warrant, in writing, and behind his back. With respect to the other charge, which he pleads guilty to, it is to be sure rather of a ridiculous nature; he admits that he was received at Mr. Southey's house, and 'believes that coffee was handed to him'; but as he was not given to understand that this was offered to him, under any implied condition of praising on all future occasions, the poetry of his host, and that of his friends, he contends that he had a right to speak of them and their writings on his return to Edinburgh, in the same discourteous and abusive language as before. This is not to be disputed; the circumstance of having been received into his house, and treated with respect and civility, by a person to whom we were personally strangers, would weigh with some minds, to a certain extent at least; it might not, and perhaps ought not, to disarm justice, but it would, at all events, be an additional argument against passing sentence in the language of contempt and insult; it might not call forth any strong expressions of civility, nor make us express a degree of admiration, which we did not feel; but still one should suppose, that it would not produce an opposite effect; it would not excite an unfavourable prejudice, nor induce us to keep down our real feelings, and give utterance to none except such as were harsh and disrespectful. A man is not called upon to flatter another, merely because he has been in his house and received no unfriendly treatment; yet it would surely be still more strange to give this as a reason for abusing him.

It is true, indeed, if Mr. Southey and Mr. Wordsworth and Mr. Coleridge, whom he distinguishes as 'anti-jacobin poets', are really and truly the sort of persons whom he describes them to be, our astonishment will cease; and we shall be forced to admire the moderation, with which he has expressed himself, when speaking of them and their works.

Their inordinate vanity runs them into all sorts of extravagances, and their habitual effeminacy gets them out of them at any price. Always pampering their own appetite for excitement and wishing to astonish others, their whole aim is to produce a dramatic effect one way or other, to shock or delight their observers; and they are as perfectly indifferent as to the consequence of what they write, as if the world were merely a stage for them to play their fantastic tricks on. As romantic in their servility as in their independance, and equally importunate candidates for fame or infamy, they require only to be distinguished and are not scrupulous as to the means of distinction. Jacobins or anti-jacobins—outrageous advocates for anarchy and licentiousness, or flaming apostles of persecution—always violent and vulgar in their opinions, they oscillate with a giddy and sickening motion from one absurdity to another, and expiate the follies of their youth, by the heartless vices of their declining age. None so ready as they to carry every paradox to its most revolting and nonsensical excess, none so sure to caricature in their own persons every feature of an audacious and insane philosophy. In their days of innovation, indeed, the philosophers crept at their heels like hounds, while they darted on their distant quarry like hawks; stooping always to the lowest game; eagerly snuffing up the most tainted and rankest scents—

But we really can proceed no further with this delicately touched, nicely discriminated and altogether striking portrait; we have informed our readers, that the original from which it is drawn, are the author of *Don Roderic*, and his friends Mr. Wordsworth and Mr. Coleridge. Upon what feature of their characters or writings, the resemblance is founded, is not stated; but assuredly, if there be any truth whatever in the picture, we need not be surprized, if a reviewer should think it a matter of conscience, to allow no feelings either of admiration or of common courtesy, to interfere with the duty of discountenancing altogether writers of such a portentous, though somewhat non-descript kind of poetry. We shall not offend the pride of Mr. Southey, against whom the above sober piece of criticism was more particularly discharged, by taking up his defence against an adversary, whose weapons consist, in the use of such language as that which we have just quoted; for a critic to apply the epithets of 'audacious', and 'insane', and 'nonsensical', to a writer; to talk of his being 'an apostle of perse-cution', and a 'snuffer up of the rankest scents'; and then ingeniously to add, with an affected air of superior gentility, that he is, moreover, '*vulgar and violent*', is a stroke of character worth recording. But enough of reviews and reviewers; we have been led to say much more upon the subject than its importance deserved; to go on speaking of Mr. Southey may perhaps be considered as a sort of continuation of the discussion; but as his name has been introduced so often, we cannot resist a temptation to gratify our own feelings by presenting our readers with a character of this terrible 'anti-jacobin poet', drawn indeed by a friend who has known him intimately for years, but who is not on that account the less able to speak of him as he really is. We are not sorry for an opportunity of contributing, by any means in our power, to the weight and reputation of a writer, who has written almost upon every subject, and exercised his talents in almost every species of composition, and in each displayed powers which would have ensured his name an honourable place in the annals of literature, even had he never attempted any other. The clearness, purity, and eloquent simplicity of his style, the richness of his fancy, and facility of his versification, form only one of his titles to our esteem; voluminous as his works are, we are not aware that he has ever published a line, at which the chastest delicacy, or the most severe morality could justly take offence. What-ever fame Mr. Southey possesses, is of that sort which will continue to increase; he has addressed himself, on no occasion, to the base and malignant feelings of mankind; and if his zeal, and the natural warmth of an ardent imagination, have sometimes carried him beyond the bounds of moderation, his indiscretion has arisen from the overflow of good feelings, and such as are only blameable in their excess.

Publicly has Mr. Southey been reviled by men, who (I would feign hope for the honor of human nature) hurled fire-brands against a figure of their own imagination, publicly have his talents been depreciated, his principles denounced; as publicly do I therefore, who have known him intimately, deem it my duty to leave recorded, that it is SOUTHEY's almost unexampled felicity, to possess the best gifts of talent and genius free from all their characteristic defects. To those who remember the state of our public schools and universities some twenty years past, it will appear no ordinary praise in any man to have passed from innocence into virtue, not only free from all vicious habit, but unstained by one act of intemperance, or the degradations akin to intemperance. That scheme of head, heart, and habitual demeanour, which in his early manhood, and first controversial writings, Milton, claiming the privilege of self-defence, asserts of himself, and challenges his calumniators to disprove; this will his school mates, his fellow-collegians, and his maturer friends, with a confidence proportioned to the intimacy of their knowledge, bear witness to, as again realized in the life of Robert Southey. But still more striking to those, who by biography or by their own experience are familiar with the general habits of genius, will appear the poet's matchless industry and perseverance in his pursuits; the worthiness and dignity of those pursuits; his generous submission to tasks of transitory interest, or such as *his* genius alone could make otherwise; and that having thus more than satisfied the claims of affection or prudence, he should yet have made for himself time and power, to achieve more, and in more various departments than almost any other writer has done, though employed wholly on subjects of his own choice and ambition. But as Southey possesses, and is not possessed by, his genius, even so is he the master even of his virtues. The regular and methodical tenor of his daily labours, which would be deemed rare in the most mechanical pursuits, and might be envied by the mere man of business, loses all semblance of formality in the dignified simplicity of his manners, in the spring and healthful chearfulness of his spirits. Always employed, his friends find him always at leisure. No less punctual in trifles, than stedfast in the performance of highest duties, he inflicts none of those small pains and discomforts which irregular men scatter about them, and which in the aggregate so often become formidable obstacles both to happiness and utility; while on the contrary he bestows all the pleasures, and inspires all that ease of mind on those around him or connected with him, which perfect consistency, and (if such a word might be framed) absolute *reliability*, equally in small as in great concerns, cannot but inspire and bestow: when this too is softened without being weakened by kindness and gentleness.

I know few men who so well deserve the character which an antient attributes to Marcus Cato, namely, that he was likest virtue, in as much as he seemed to act aright, not in obedience to any law or outward motive, but by the necessity of a happy nature, which could not act otherwise. As son, brother, husband, father, master, friend, he moves with firm yet light steps, alike unostentatious, and alike exemplary. As a writer, he has uniformly made his talents subservient to the best interests of humanity, of public virtue, and domestic piety; his cause has ever been the cause of pure religion and of liberty, of national independence and of national illumination. When future critics shall weigh out his guerdon of praise and censure, it will be Southey the poet only, that will supply them with the scanty materials for the latter. They will likewise not fail to record, that as no man was ever a more constant friend, never had poet more friends and honorers among the good of all parties; and that quacks in education, quacks in politics, and quacks in criticism were his only enemies.

From the eloquent and well-deserved panegyric upon Mr. Southey, of which the above forms only an extract, our author proceeds, without any apparent plan in the selection, to discuss a variety of topics; Mr. Burke, the Spanish Revolution, the principles upon which our author conducted the *Morning Post*, during the time in which he was the editor of it, a vindication of himself from the charge of indolence which has so frequently been brought against him; these and similar discussions, alternately engage his attention, until we arrive within about one hundred pages from the end of the first volume: at this place our author takes a sudden plunge into a bottomless discussion respecting the esemplastic (from εις ἑν πλαττω) power of man and the phenomena of mind, that 'lie on the other side of the natural consciousness'; he continues out of sight of every human eye, groping in darkness for imaginary wealth, until the opening of the second volume, when he again rises upon our view, preparing to enter into a discussion of the merits and defects of Mr. Wordsworth's writings. This is a subject which our author discusses at so much length, that it is altogether out of our power to follow him through the progressive steps of his criticism: as we coincide with our author for the most part, in the substance of the opinions which he expresses upon his controverted subject, we shall merely extract a specimen of this critical judgment, and content ourselves with recommending this part of the volume to the attention of our readers, as containing one of the fairest and most able reviews of the peculiarities of Mr. Wordsworth's poetry, that we have met with. Mr. Coleridge's observations upon the diction of Mr. Wordsworth, contain many just and striking thoughts; and the analytical criticisms which occur in various parts of the discussion, upon one or two of the poems contained in the *Lyrical Ballads*, impressed us with a very favourable opinion of his good taste and discrimination. As a specimen of his impartiality, and of the reasonable conditions under which he approves of the critical opinions of Mr. Wordsworth, concerning the proper objects and philosophical language of poetry, we shall select what our author says respecting the propriety of putting sentiments of a high and elevated tone into the mouths of persons taken from the lower ranks of life.

But be this as it may, the feelings with which,

> I think of CHATTERTON, the marvellous boy,
> The sleepless soul, that perish'd in his pride:
> Of BURNS, that walk'd in glory and in joy
> Behind his plough upon the mountain-side—

are widely different from those with which I should read a *poem*, where the author, having occasion for the character of a poet and a philosopher in the fable of his narration, had chosen to make him a *chimney-sweeper;* and then, in order to remove all doubts on the subject, had *invented* an account of his birth, parentage and education, with all the strange and fortunate accidents which had occurred in making him at once poet, philosopher, and sweep! Nothing, but biography, can justify this. If it be admissible even in a *Novel*, it must be one in the manner of De Foe's, that were meant to pass for histories, not in the manner of Fielding's: in the life of Moll Flanders, or Colonel Jack, not in a Tom Jones or even a Joseph Andrews. Much less then can it be legitimately introduced in a *poem*, the characters of which, amid the strongest individualization, must still remain representative. The precepts of Horace, on this point, are grounded on the nature both of poetry and of the human mind. They are not more peremptory, than wise and prudent. For in the first place a deviation from them perplexes the reader's feelings, and all the circumstances which are feigned in order to make such accidents less improbable, divide and disquiet his faith, rather than aid and support it. Spite of all attempts, the fiction *will* appear, and unfortunately not as *fictitious* but as *false*. The reader not only *knows*, that the sentiments and language are the poet's own, and his own too in his *artificial* character, *as poet*; but by the fruitless endeavours to make him think the contrary, he is not even suffered to *forget* it. The effect is similar to that produced by an epic poet, when the fable and the characters are *derived* from Scripture history, as in the *Messiah* of *Klopstock*, or in *Cumberland's Calvary:* and not merely *suggested* by it as in the *Paradise Lost* of Milton. That *illusion*, contradistinguished from *delusion*, that *negative* faith, which simply permits the images presented to work by their own force, without either denial or affirmation of their real existence by the judgment, is rendered impossible by their immediate neighbourhood to words and facts of known and absolute truth. A faith, which transcends even historic belief, must absolutely *put out* this mere poetic Analogon of faith, as the summer sun is said to extinguish our household fires, when it shines full upon them. What would otherwise have been yielded to as pleasing fiction, is repelled as revolting falsehood. The effect produced in this latter case by the solemn belief of the reader, is in a less degree brought about in the instances, to which I have been objecting, by the baffled attempts of the author to *make* him believe.

Add to all the foregoing the seeming uselessness both of the project and of the anecdotes from which it is to derive support. Is there one word for instance, attributed to the pedlar in the *Excursion*, characteristic of a *pedlar*? One sentiment, that might not more plausibly, even without the aid of any previous explanation, have proceeded from any wise and beneficent old man, of a rank or profession in which the language of learning and refinement are natural and to be expected? Need the rank have been at all particularized, where nothing follows which the knowledge of that rank is to explain or illustrate? When on the contrary this information renders the man's language, feelings, sentiments, and information a riddle, which must itself be solved by episodes of anecdote? Finally when this, and this alone, could have induced a genuine *poet* to inweave in a poem of the loftiest style, and on subjects the loftiest and of most universal interest, such minute matters of fact, (not unlike those furnished for the obituary of a magazine by the friends of some obscure *ornament of society lately deceased* in some obscure town, as

> Among the hills of Athol he was born.
> There on a small hereditary farm,
> An unproductive slip of rugged ground,
> His Father dwelt; and died in poverty:
> While he, whose lowly fortune I retrace,
> The youngest of three sons, was yet a babe,
> A little one—unconscious of their loss.
> But 'ere he had outgrown his infant days
> His widowed mother, for a second mate,
> Espoused the teacher of the Village School;
> Who on her offspring zealously bestowed
> Needful instruction.
>
> From his sixth year, the Boy of whom I speak,
> In summer, tended cattle on the hills;
> But through the inclement and the perilous days
> Of long-continuing winter, he repaired
> To his step-father's school.— &c.

For all the admirable passages interposed in this narration, might, with trifling alterations, have been far more appropriately, and with far greater verisimilitude, told of a poet in the character of a poet.

The above observations, and indeed the whole tenor of our author's criticisms upon poets and poetry, are for the most part so reasonable, that we own we have frequently found it difficult to understand, how the same author should have written them, and the 'Ode to the Rain', and one or two other of the poems contained in the *Sibylline Leaves*; poems which might perhaps have been *written* by a man of sense, but how a man like Mr. Coleridge should have thought them of so much value as to be worth *publishing*, is above our power to explain.

We should not be sorry, were we here to take leave of our author: for we are apprehensive that what we may add farther, will rather injure than improve the favorable impression which the greater part of what we have hither to said, is calculated to convey of his talents. But in justice to our readers it is necessary to state, that a very large proportion of the two volumes which we have recommended to their perusal, is filled up with matter, which our author calls Philosophy; but it is philosophy of so very heteroclite a description, that we really hardly know how to allude to the subject, without using words that would convey an impression of our thinking much more slightingly of Mr. Coleridge's understanding, than the good sense displayed in other parts of the work would justify. Had we met with the metaphysical disquisitions, to which we now allude, in an anonymous publication, we should unquestionably have laid them aside, as the production of a very ordinary writer indeed, with respect to talents; and supposing we had given ourselves the trouble of thinking farther about them, should probably have concluded that some doubts might be entertained respecting the perfect sanity of the mind in which they were engendered. 'The foolishness of fools, is folly'; but 'the foolishness' of a man like Mr. Coleridge, must, we take for granted, be impregnated with some portion of sense and reason. Impressed with a conviction of this, we were at the pains of reading faithfully, and as far as we were able, impartially, all our author's ten theses; his refutation of materialism; his discussions relative to the priority of 'subject' and 'object', 'mind' and 'nature'; together with his other incidental criticisms upon Behmen, and Schilling, and Fichti, and Kant, and other inscrutable thinkers. What we think on all these subjects, and what we think of Mr. Coleridge's remarks upon them, we shall not venture to express; but we know so much of the present state of feeling in this country, upon the subjects into which, Mr. Coleridge wishes to embark philosophy, as emboldens us to prophesy, that if he persists in his present resolution of imparting to the world his intended commentary upon the Gospel of St. John, in the form of a dissertation upon the 'Productive Logos', he will draw down upon his head such a tempest of ridicule and derision, as he may probably live long enough to repent of.

tively brief analysis of the work before us; and, following the writer's own divisions, animadvert on the defects or lay open the fairer parts of the performance.

The most interesting portion of the first chapter is that in which the author narrates his early school-instruction, and offers a tribute of (we doubt not) deserved respect to the memory of his master, the Reverend James Bowyer, of Christ's Hospital. From this account of the first formation of Mr. Coleridge's taste, we shall make a selection:

[quotes *BL*, i, 4, l. 9 to 6, l. 3]

We should like to see those '*grounds of plain sense and universal logic*' on which 'the superiority of Lucretius and Catallus' in the extracts read by Mr. Coleridge at Christ's Hospital, and of Terence throughout, is to be established, in their comparison with the writers of the Augustan æra! The art of extracting sun-beams from cucumbers, as recorded in the Voyage to Laputa, we should conceive to be *nothing*, compared to the above-mentioned most wonderful process. Waiving, however, the positive nonsense of the opinion here so cavalierly asserted by Mr. Coleridge, we detect in it the germ of that false taste which, as we observed in our report of his *Sibylline Leaves*, has obstructed his own progress towards a sound and permanent reputation; while, we fear, it has largely contributed, in his lectures and other temporary endeavours, to confirm the false estimate entertained by many of our countrymen respecting our own older writers. Here is the origin of that spirit which has been so idly at work for many years, and especially among the scribblers of the Lake-school, to depreciate the writings of the æras of William, Anne, and the Georges; and to extol far beyond their due degree (with all their faults and all their follies included in the gross panegyric) the productions of the reigns of Elizabeth and the Stuarts. No opportunity is lost, in the pursuit of this unwise and invidious object. The 'stale, flat, and unprofitable' objections to the celebrated passage at the conclusion of the eighth book of Pope's version of the *Iliad* are here repeated; and they form indeed the sort of *single text* of the critical preachers of the day. It is all that they can discover as the basis of their censure of the great bard of Twickenham: it is a revival of the monotonous, confined, and obstinate *Zoilism* of the dunces of his own period. Why will no modern admirer of this great English genius attempt to *tack on* a fifth book to the *Dunciad?*— prophetic, if he pleases; and therefore, of course, inoffensive to his contemporaries.

Ye unborn heroes, crowd not on my soul!

would rush into the mind of such a writer.

The couplet which Mr. Coleridge has selected for reprobation, from the passage in Pope's version, is this:

> Around her throne the vivid planets roll,
> And stars unnumber'd gild the glowing pole:

of which he says that it is difficult to determine 'whether the sense or the diction be more absurd'. He has given *no* reasons for this opinion—and we must wait till the publication of his celebrated lectures, recently delivered (with which he positively threatens us) for an opportunity to canvass his arguments, here so pompously and triumphantly announced. Meanwhile, when it is considered that the whole of this passage, in Pope's Homer, is obviously a paraphrase and not a translation of the original, it surely will follow that the proper subject for discussion is this; whether the English author has presented a great and glowing picture to the reader, sufficiently similar to the Greek for the purposes of general resemblance? With regard to his judgment, in chusing to paraphrase instead of translating Homer on this occasion, the unsuccessful attempts of Mr. Cowper, and of some others, to make a closer copy, will perhaps be deemed sufficient to decide the question.

In the same objectionable note in which the above heterodoxical paragraph occurs, is also an attack on Gray's Elegy; which Mr. Wordsworth (forsooth) has manifested to Mr. Coleridge, by the aid of his microscopic spectacles, to contain sundry blemishes!

> ''Twas *I*', says the Fly,
> 'With my LITTLE eye!'

These two *illuminati* have therefore been holding their conjoint 'farthing candle to the sun': but the only spots, which Mr. Coleridge has told us they have detected in his bright countenance, are the subjoined. In the stanza in 'the Bard' (for in the 'Elegy' they are not kind enough to communicate their notable discoveries) which begins, 'Fair laughs the morn', &c. Mr. Coleridge objects to the words 'realm' and 'sway'; which, he says, 'are rhymes dearly purchased'. What he means by this, we are at a loss to imagine. 'The azure realm' and 'the whirlwind's sway' appear to us as unobjectionable combinations as could be put together; and we plainly defy Mr. Coleridge to point out any intelligible or tenable objections to them. Does he deem it right to cast these reflections even *on the epithets* of the most fastidious of poets, without specifying their faults? He can venerate, even to idolatry, the loosest and most careless phrases of Shakespeare; and when he talks of the *imitation* in 'the Bard', and then *contrasts* the noted simile in Shakespeare with the foregoing passage in Gray, he should have the candour to acknowledge that the *'sweeping whirlwind'* is at least as good and as poetical an image as the *'strumpet wind'*; although the said 'strumpet' is twice introduced, and, no doubt, with appropriate effect in a dramatic and sarcastic passage; as unlike, by the way, in the character of the feelings which it wishes to impress on the hearer, as it is in its tone of expression, to the calm, dignified, and more soothingly pathetic description in Gray. We are not fond of *pitting* such great poets against each other; particularly where the points of similarity are so general and so faint as in the present passages: but Mr. Coleridge must answer for this offence; and he has been guilty, we fear, of many offences, indeed, of a like nature, for which he owes a severe atonement to insulted taste and discrimination. We must add that Mr. C.'s preference of the *original*, as he calls it, to the *imitation* in the preceding instances, rests 'on the ground, that in the imitation it depended wholly, in (on) the compositor's putting or not putting a *small capital* both in this, and *in many other passages* of the same poet,★ whether the words should be personifications or mere abstracts'. May not this be said of almost any personification?—and

Youth at the Prow, and Pleasure at the helm,

are to be degraded by this contemptible species of *hyper*, or, rather, *hypo-criticism*. We cannot follow Mr. C. at present into his assertions as to the supposed corruption of English poetry, either by an imitation of the *Iliad* of Pope or by the practice of composing in Latin verse. With respect to the last of these intimations, we would ask him one question;—does he think that the exercise of writing Latin hexameters and pentameters impeded the poetic genius of Milton? We will also venture to subjoin a positive refutation, from our own knowledge and experience, of his opinion that 'it is not to be supposed in the present day that a youth can *think* in Latin'. Every upper form in our public schools could afford many examples to the contrary; and when we compared this opinion with the previous *assurance* that the master of Christ's Hospital 'sent *us* to the University *excellent* Latin and Greek scholars, and tolerable Hebraists', we could not help considering it as

---

★ *This* is the manner in which we have brought ourselves to talk of Gray!—*Exoriare aliquis*, &c., &c.

an *assurance* indeed; nor could we, with our best endeavours, refrain from something very like a smile. It is modestly added; '*our* classical knowledge was the *least* of the good gifts which *we* derived from his zealous and conscientious tutorage'.

It is not allowable for us, however, to dwell longer on this portion of the biography; though, with the exception, perhaps, of that to which we shall next call the attention of our readers, we regard it as the most amusing in the whole publication. With the metaphysics, indeed, and the rest of the *omne scibile* of the work, saving the extraordinary criticisms on Mr. Wordsworth, we shall not interfere; and our readers are now about to contemplate Mr. Coleridge in his early and most striking designation of an itinerant philosopher. Attend, then,

> Thelwall, and ye that lecture *as ye go;*

stationary as ye may now have become, the reminiscences of one of your most distinguished erratic brethren, of the very prince of the British Peripatetics, may be serviceable to you, and must be interesting, even in your most dignified retirements.

After having related an admirable story or two of unsuccessful authorship, whether in his own case or that of others (stories which we seriously recommend to the careful perusal of those who are concerned), Mr. Coleridge thus opens the narrative of his political and theological pilgrimage:

[quotes the story of the fate of *The Watchman* (*BL*, i, 114, l. 11 to 117, l. 2)]

Much more occurs, of the same amusing cast: but our limits forbid us to extract it, and we must proceed to another class of anecdotes; namely, the instances of most ludicrous as well as detestable *espionage* which Mr. C. has mentioned as having been exercised over him and a philosophical friend, during the reign of terror in England. Some of these incidents, indeed, wear *a little* the appearance of having been *heightened* for the purposes of entertaining narration; that, for example, in which a spy with a large nose, sent down to *watch* the author at his residence in the country, overhears him talking of *Spy Nosy* (Spinoza) and considers it as a personal allusion to himself! ! In any case, however, the present division of the 'Literary Life' is very lively and laughable; and we offer our thanks to Mr. Coleridge for much good-humoured and rational exposure of his own follies, and those of the government (if *they* can be designated by so lenient a name) which descended to such unmeaning persecution.

Mr. Coleridge concludes the chapter in which these matters are detailed, with a brief retrospect of time mis-spent and talents mis-employed; with a simple and touching appeal to the sympathies of his readers, both in English and Latin verse: but the section which follows presents a peculiar claim to the attention of that numerous race of well-educated young men in England, who are, or are aspiring to become, authors. The end of this chapter, we think, deserves quotation; and then (passing over the metaphysics) we must advance to the second volume, or rather to that division of it which relates to Mr. Wordsworth.

It would be a sort of irreligion, and scarcely less than a libel on human nature to believe, that there is any established and reputable profession or employment, in which a man may not continue to act with honesty and honor; and doubtless there is likewise none, which may not at times present temptations to the contrary. But woefully will that man find himself mistaken, who imagines that the profession of literature, or (to speak more plainly) the *trade* of authorship, besets its members with fewer or with less insidious temptations, than the church, the law, or the different branches of commerce. But I have treated sufficiently on this unpleasant subject in an early chapter of this volume. I will conclude the present therefore with a short extract from HERDER, whose name I might have added to the illustrious list of those, who have combined the successful pursuit of the muses, not only with the faithful discharge, but with the highest honors and honorable emoluments of an established profession. 'With the greatest possible solicitude avoid authorship. Too early or immoderately employed, it makes the head *waste* and the heart empty; even were there no other worse consequences. A person, who reads only to print, in all probability reads amiss; and he, who sends away through the pen and the press every thought, the moment it occurs to him, will in a short time have sent all away, and will become a mere journeyman of the printing-office, a *compositor*'. To which I may add from myself, that what medical physiologists affirm of certain secretions, applies equally to our thoughts; they too must be taken up again into the circulation, and be again and again re-secreted in order to ensure a healthful vigor, both to the mind and to its intellectual offspring.

The criticisms on Mr. Wordsworth, with which Mr. Coleridge commences his second volume, we have justly denominated *extraordinary*; for, though we may have perfect faith in his professed admiration of his friend, Mr. C. has nevertheless pointed out so many errors of design and execution in this very moderate writer (as we must ever consider him), and has furnished a clue to the exposure of so many more

absurdities, that we cannot but here rank Mr. C. among the uninten-
tional defenders of good taste and good sense in poetry. He *confines his
opposition* to Mr. Wordsworth's *system* (if we must so call it) to the
following points: first, to what Mr. W. intitles 'a selection of the *real*
language of men'; secondly, to his 'imitation', and his 'adoption, *as far
as possible*, of the very language of men in low and rustic life'; and,
thirdly, to his assertion that 'between the language of prose and that of
metrical composition, there neither is, nor can be, any essential difference'. When it is recollected that these points form the very ground-
work, and much of the superstructure, of Mr. Wordsworth's plan for
vulgarizing poetry, it seems strange that Mr. Coleridge should talk of
confining his opposition to them alone; and, by a few extracts from the
second volume of this 'Literary Life', we think that we shall be able
to expose the manifest flaws in Mr. W.'s title to *any* estate or heritage
in the manors of Parnassus, Helicon, and the lands lying thereabout.
Mr. Coleridge saves his consistency, indeed, by an asseveration that
the faults of Mr. W.'s theory are *rarely* exemplified in his practice: but,
as the force of this remark lies entirely in the adverb *rarely*, an arithmetical process, instituted on the cases in question in the *Lyrical
Ballads*, will be the only method of settling the dispute between our
brother-critic and ourselves. The result of our sum is very different
from his: but we are perfectly agreed in our principles of calculation.

Mr. C. thus marshals his objections to his friend's absurd fancies on
the foregoing topics:

I object, in the very first instance, to an equivocation in the use of the word
'real'. Every man's language varies, according to the extent of his knowledge,
the activity of his faculties, and the depth or quickness of his feelings. Every
man's language has, first, its *individualities*; secondly, the common properties
of the *class* to which he belongs; and thirdly, words and phrases of *universal*
use. The language of Hooker, Bacon, Bishop Taylor, and Burke, differ from
the common language of the learned class only by the superior number and
novelty of the thoughts and relations which they had to convey. The language
of Algernon Sidney differs not at all from that, which every well-educated
gentleman would wish to write, and (with due allowances for the undeliberate-
ness, and less connected train, of thinking natural and proper to conversation)
such as he would wish to talk. Neither one or the other differ half as much from
the general language of cultivated society, as the language of Mr. Wordsworth's
homeliest composition differs from that of a common peasant. For 'real',
therefore, we must substitute *ordinary*, or *lingua communis*. And this, we have
proved, is no more to be found in the phraseology of low and rustic life, than
in that of any other class. Omit the peculiarities of each, and the result of

course must be common to all. And assuredly the omissions and changes to be made in the language of rustics, before it could be transferred to any species of poem, except the drama or other professed imitation, are at least as numerous and weighty, as would be required in adapting to the same purpose the ordinary language of tradesmen and manufacturers. Not to mention, that the language so highly extolled by Mr. Wordsworth varies in every county, nay in every village, according to the accidental character of the clergyman, the existence or non-existence of schools; or even, perhaps, as the exciseman, publican, or barber happen to be, or not to be, zealous politicians, and readers of the weekly newspaper *pro bono publico*. Anterior to cultivation, the *lingua communis* of every country, as Dante has well observed, exists every where in parts, and no where as a whole.

These remarks we regard as very sensible, and urged with much conciseness and force of reasoning. Combined with what follows, they are obviously and utterly destructive of the very foundations of Mr. Wordsworth's *system*. We subjoin another extract, with a quotation from the *Lyrical Ballads*; to which we shall add several others, and then close this brief but we trust convincing exposure of the greatest piece of folly and arrogance (the pretensions, we mean, of Mr. W.'s poetry to any thing either meritorious or original*), which has disgraced the present *prodigious* æra of our poetical literature.

I conclude, therefore, that the attempt is impracticable; and that, were it not impracticable, it would still be useless. For the very power of making the selection implies the previous possession of the language selected. Or where can the poet have lived? And by what rules could he direct his choice, which would not have enabled him to select and arrange his words by the light of his own judgement? We do not adopt the language of a class by the mere adoption of such words exclusively, as that class would use, or at least understand; but likewise by following the *order*, in which the words of such men are wont to succeed each other. Now this order, in the intercourse of uneducated men, is distinguished from the diction of their superiors in knowledge and power, by the greater *disjunction* and *separation* in the component parts of that, whatever it be, which they wish to communicate. There is a want of that prospectiveness of mind, that *surview*, which enables a man to foresee the whole of what he is to convey, appertaining to any one point; and by this means so to subordinate and arrange the different parts according to their relative importance, as to convey it at once, and as an organized whole.

Now I will take the first stanza, on which I have chanced to open, in the *Lyrical Ballads*. It is one the most simple and the least peculiar in its language.

* We deny the originality of this author, on the ground of those numerous nursery-poems which existed before his own weak attempt to palm such productions on mature understandings.

> In distant countries I have been,
> And yet I have not often seen
> A healthy man, a man full grown,
> Weep in the public road alone.
> But such a one, on English ground,
> And in the broad highway I met;
> Along the broad highway he came,
> His cheeks with tears were wet.
> Sturdy he seem'd, though he was sad,
> And in his arms a lamb he had.

The words here are doubtless such as are current in all ranks of life; and of course not less so, in the hamlet and cottage, than in the shop, manufactory, college, or palace. But is this the *order*, in which the rustic would have placed the words? I am grievously deceived, if the following less *compact* mode of commencing the same tale be not a far more faithful copy. 'I have been in a many parts far and near, and I don't know that I ever saw before a man crying by himself in the public road; a grown man I mean, that was neither sick nor hurt', &c. &c.

We shall merely, *en passant*, observe on a criticism by Mr. Wordsworth, applied to Gray's 'Sonnet on the Death of West', and here quoted by Mr. Coleridge, that, when Mr. W. asserts that the only lines good in the Sonnet are those which he has marked with italics, he has betrayed his usual caprice. For example; one of his *italic* lines is the following:

> A different object *do* these eyes require;

and one of his *roman* lines (not supposed to have the same merit) is this:

> These ears, alas! for other notes repine.

If such capricious nonsense were allowed to pass for *criticism*, we should be inclined to resign our office in shame and confusion. We find ourselves unable to abridge, with any clearness, Mr. Coleridge's train of argument which establishes, in opposition to his whimsical friend, the *essential* difference between the language of prose and that of poetry. We must therefore be satisfied with quoting his final appeal to an undeniable fact; leaving the inference with our readers, who perhaps may consider so *self-evident* a matter as scarcely worth a dispute in the 19th century.

Lastly, I appeal to the practice of the best poets of all countries and in all ages, as *authorizing* the opinion, (*deduced* from all the foregoing) that in every import of the word ESSENTIAL, which would not here involve a mere truism, there may be, is, and ought to be, an *essential* difference between the language of prose and of metrical composition.

Let us now quote the promised examples of the happy results of Mr. W.'s theory. Will that mistaken gentleman ever be persuaded that, if thought be the soul of poetry, expression is its body; and that both body and soul are of a peculiar and plainly distinguished cast and character? With the *Lyrical Ballads* before us, we could add, *usque ad nauseam*, to the subjoined list of childish trifles: but, in a review of Mr. Coleridge's life, we are bound to confine ourselves to *his* criticisms on passages in Mr. Wordsworth.

> *The last three Stanzas of the Sailor's Mother.*
>
> And thus continuing, she said
> I had a son, who many a day
> Sailed on the seas; but he is dead;
> In Denmark he was cast away:
> And I have travelled far as Hull, to see
> What clothes he might have left, or other property.
>
> The bird and cage, they both were his;
> 'Twas my son's bird; and neat and trim
> He kept it; many voyages
> This singing bird hath gone with him;
> When last he sailed he left the bird behind;
> As it might be, perhaps, from bodings of his mind.
>
> He to a fellow-lodger's care
> Had left it, to be watched and fed,
> Till he came back again; and there
> I found it when my son was dead;
> And now, God help me for my little wit!
> I trail it with me, Sir! he took so much delight in it.

How are we sure what a book-maker will vend next for poetry, who has already offered for sale such inconceivable trash as this?

We owe it to Mr. Coleridge to state that he labours very assiduously, by selections from his friend's few successful attempts, to counter-balance, nay to overwhelm, the effect of his own vituperative criticisms, on the remaining and (as we contend) much the larger portion of his poems. We are quite ready to allow that, when Mr. Wordsworth steps out of himself, when he no longer appears in the character of the *rustic egotistical metaphysician*, he writes very passably, and just like other poets on similar topics: but, as we are of opinion that a great part of the bad taste of the day has arisen from that foolish good-nature which, for the sake of a few unobjectionable or even excellent passages, praises and gives popularity to whole poems, we hold it to be the duty of every classical scholar, or lover of genuine poetry, to discountenance either by a judicious silence, or by a well chosen opportunity of vigorous censure, the vain assumptions of our numerous poetical *charlatans.*

From the Blind Highland Boy.

And one, the rarest, was a shell,
Which he, poor child, had studied well:
The shell of a green turtle, thin
And hollow;—you might sit therein,
    It was so wide and deep.

Our Highland Boy oft visited
The house which held this prize, and led
By choice or chance did thither come
One day, when no one was at home,
    And found the door unbarred.

In a succeeding extract, Mr. Coleridge applauds a couplet in which a lark is described (a 'drunken lark'! by the way),

With a soul as strong as a mountain river
Pouring out praise to th' Almighty giver!

De gustibus, &c.

Again;—Mr. C. quotes, but not with applause,

Close by a pond, upon the further side
He stood alone; a minute's space I guess,
I watch'd him, he continuing motionless;
To the pool's further margin then I drew;
He being all the while before me full in view.

Which of the numerous happy parodists of Mr. Wordsworth has attributed to him a heaviness and an absurdity greater than the preceding?—Again;—extracted from a general panegyric, by Mr. Coleridge himself:

He with a smile did then his tale repeat;
And said, that, gathering leeches far and wide
He travelled; stirring thus about his feet
The waters of the ponds where they abide.
'Once I could meet with them on every side,
But they have dwindled long by slow decay;
Yet still I persevere, and find them where I may'.

We beg our readers to pardon us for so long detaining them on such perfectly ludicrous matters: but we hope that we may be spared, in future, the necessity of troubling them or ourselves with any exposure of the hollowness of Mr. W.'s poetical reputation. If it be thought that we have already dwelt too much on his follies, be it remembered that he is the very founder and father of that modern school, which we have always wished to see held up to the general ridicule that it deserves; and if it be not thus overpowered, woe to the taste, judgment, and whole understanding of the rising generation!—It must also be considered that the space, which we have allotted to Mr. Coleridge's just but evidently reluctant criticisms on his friend, has enabled us to give our readers so much the less of Mr. C. himself as a biographer and metaphysician; and that we have had the charity to abstain altogether from any mention of Mr. Southey, who claims his portion in this volume of triple admiration: dedicated to that trio, whose mutual puffs have so often linked them in harmonies of applause, but at whose frequent union in literary censure Mr. Coleridge expresses the most innocent surprize!

We are sorry to be obliged to omit a large remaining portion of the *Biographia Literaria;** and especially the chapter of it in which Mr. Coleridge presents us with a masterly, spirited, and moral critique on that reproach to the tragic muse of England, the *tragedy* of *Bertram. O si sic omnia!*

* Among our omissions, we must reckon the discovery of a plagiarism in David Hume from Thomas Aquinas.

SIBYLLINE LEAVES

1817

---

83. Unsigned review, *Literary Gazette*

26 July 1817, 49-50

Announcing that he must henceforward devote himself to far different studies:

> Ite hinc, Camœnæ! Vos quoque ite suaves,
> Dulces Camœnæ! Nam (fatebimur verum)
> Dulces fuistis!—Et tamen meas chartas
> Revisitote: sed pudenter et raro!—[1]

Mr. Coleridge has this week* bequeathed to the public not only the above strangely christened work, but also another in two volumes, called *Biographia Literaria or Biographical Sketches of my Literary Life and Opinions*. From the late period of the week at which these publications issued from the press, we have only had time to dip so cursorily into the latter as to discover, that it is, where not metaphysical, an entertaining production, whether with reference to what is to be laughed with or to be laughed at in its contents, and shall therefore dismiss its analysis till our next Number. The *Sibylline Leaves* we think we may do justice to in our present.

'Sibylline', says our Dictionary, 'of or belonging to a Sibyl or *Prophetess*': the word cannot therefore, we hope, be appropriated by Mr. Coleridge, who is not so humble a poet as to assume, voluntarily, the character of an old woman. But on refreshing our classic memory we grasp the very essence and soul of this mysterious title. The Sibyl wrote her prophecies on leaves; so does Mr. Coleridge his verses—the prophecies of the Sibyl became incomprehensible, if not instantly gathered; so does the sense of Mr. Coleridge's poetry; the Sibyl asked

---

[1] 'Get ye hence, ye Muses...' (Virgil, *Catalepton*, v, 11-14).

* Written for last Saturday's *Gazette*, but omitted in consequence of the press of other matter.

the same price from Tarquin for her books when in 9, 6, and 3 volumes; so does Mr. Coleridge for his, when scattered over sundry publications, and now as collected into one—as soon as the Sibyl had concluded her bargain she vanished, and was seen no more in the regions of Cumæ so does Mr. Coleridge assure us he will be seen no more on Parnassus— the Sibylline books were preserved by Kings, had a College of Priests to take care of them, and were so esteemed by the people, that they were very seldom consulted; even so does Mr. Coleridge look to delight Monarchs, his book will be treasured by the Eleven Universities, and we venture to suppose that it will be treated by the public, quoad frequent perusal, pretty much in the same way with the ravings of his Archetypes.

We put it to the reader, if we have not cleanly unriddled the title-page of *Sibylline Leaves*, though we do not thank the author for allotting us time-pressed Critics the trouble of turning over Varro, Ælian, Diodorus, Pliny, Lucan, Ovid, Sallust, Cicero, and even Pausanias and Plato, for the manifestation of his recondite enigmas.

Having fortunately surmounted the stumbling-block on the threshold of this volume, we come to the Preface, whence we learn that it contains the whole of the author's poetical compositions from 1793 to the present date, except a few works not yet finished (Heaven defend us from more of 'Christabel' ! ! !), and some juvenile poems, over which he has no controul. Preface furthermore requests us to divide these Poems into three classes, viz. 1st. those originally published in Wordsworth's *Lyrical Ballads*; 2d. those originally published in various obscure or (alas!) perishable Journals; and 3d. and last, those really original from MSS. With this request we would gladly comply (as it seems to be of much importance to the writer); but as no clue is furnished whereby we can unravel the complexity of the labyrinth, we are compelled to take the Poems, unclassed, in the way they are divided and subdivided on the *Sibylline Leaves*, price ten and sixpence.

From the manner in which we speak of this publication, it will scarcely be anticipated that we intend to enter at all into the question which every production of the school to which it belongs invariably raises, i.e. whether it is poetry or drivelling, the true and genuine effusion of unsophisticated nature, or the very babbling of imbecility, mistaking meanness for simplicity, and the most ludicrous grotesque for the best, because the nearest resembling, portrait of Reality. We will leave the determination of this case to those who consider it of more interest than we do; and proceed very briefly to give an account of the volume before us. The Preface goes on fidgeting and fighting with the world or somebody in it, ascribing malevolence and worthlessness, and all uncharitableness to a person or persons unknown, and decidedly disproving an assertion in the *Biographia*, wherein Mr. C. affirms, that authors (particularly Poets), are neither irritable nor revengeful! In the body of the work we have two school-boy poems, and as one of them is really about the most amusing of the whole, we shall annex it as a favourable specimen. Then comes 'The Ancient Mariner', in seven parts, whimsically indexed on the margin, like a history. The next division consists of Poems on Political Events, of which we do not remember to have seen before a pretty long one, with a much longer circumstantial 'apologetical' detail in prose of the how, when, and wherefore it was written, entitled (horrible to read) 'Fire, Famine, and Slaughter'! Melting down from the terrible, the ensuing division is 'Love Poems', but oh! such love! One of them is to an *'unfortunate woman at the Theatre'*, and begins—*'Maiden* that with sullen brow'; and *be-maidening* the miserable prostitute all through the piece. From love we come to Meditative Poems, in blank verse (such *loves* often produce cause for reflection!) and wind up with Odes and Miscellanies. Among these varieties there seems to us to be very little of novelty, though we cannot charge ourselves with having perused all Mr. Coleridge's productions formerly published. There is a fragment of a Sexton's Tale, 'The Three Graves', remarkable for illustrating the style in language and the style of thought which distinguish the Bards of the Lakes. We gather that it is tragical from there being three graves, but are not informed whose graves they are, except we can guess as shrewdly as Lord Stanley. A widow conceives a violent passion for her daughter's received lover, who rejects her, and she pours down a horrible maternal curse, not only on her rival child, but on another daughter with whom she lives on terms of sisterly affection. This curse makes a dreadful impression on the minds of the children, and ultimately consigns them to superstition and misery. In the telling of this story, we have all the characteristics of the author. There is the close alliance of beauty and deformity; the union of fine poetical thought with the most trivial commonplace; feeling bound to vulgarity; dignity of language to the vilest doggrel—in fine, it resembles the horrid punishment of barbarism which linked dead and living bodies together, and gave the vital spark to perish with the rotting carcase. An example will suffice—Mary complains with much native sweetness, though by no comparison the finest passage:

> My sister may not visit us,
>   My Mother says her nay:
> O Edward! you are all to me,
> I wish for your sake I could be
>   More lifesome and more gay.

> I'm dull and sad! indeed, indeed
>   I know I have no reason!
> Perhaps I am not well in health,
>   And 'tis a gloomy season.

Ellen, the sister, however, does visit them, and thus meanly does the poet tell us so:

> Oh! Ellen was a faithful friend,
>   More dear than any sister!
> As cheerful too as singing lark;
> And she ne'er left them till 'twas dark,
>   And then—(why then)—they always miss'd her!

Again,

> Well! it passed off! the gentle Ellen
>   Did well nigh dote on Mary;
> And she went oftener than before,
> And Mary loved her more and more—*(fine alliteration.)*
> *(Grand Climax)* She managed all the Dairy!!!

Eheu jam satis! Trifles are swelled into importance, and important things shorn into trifles, the sublime and the ridiculous have not even a step between them; and the pathetic and the silly, the sensible and the absurd, are so disgustingly dovetailed together, that we have not patience with the artizan. We have, however, promised one of the school-boy poems, and we add it.

[quotes 'The Raven' (*PW*, i, 169–71)]

84. Unsigned notice, *Monthly Magazine*

September 1817, xliv, 156

Mr. Coleridge's *Sybilline Leaves* prove that, though in days of *error*, he was a man of sterling genius, yet that the light of *truth*, which now blazes upon him, has blighted his fancy. This is as it should be, fable and poetry; fact and dullness. 'Fire, famine, and slaughter', the poet's master-piece, written in 1794, fills six pages of the volume; but in 1817 he judges it necessary to preface it by twenty-four pages of apology, in which PITT, his fiend, is, by the same pen, in 1817, converted into 'a good man and great statesman'. Alas, poor Yorick!

85. Unsigned review, *Edinburgh Magazine*

October 1817, i, 245-50

Every reader of modern poetry is acquainted of course with 'The Ancient Mariner' of this author. It is one of those compositions, indeed, which cannot be perused without a more than ordinary excitation of fancy at the time; and which, when once read, can never afterwards be entirely forgotten. What we mean, however, more particularly to say at present, is, that this production has always appeared to us in the light of a very good caricature of the genius of its author. It displays, in fact, all the strength and all the weakness, all the extravagancies and eccentricities, all the bold features, and peculiar grimace, if we may so express ourselves, of his intellectual physiognomy, and in forming an opinion respecting the talents which he possesses, this composition may serve the very same purpose which an overcharged drawing of a countenance could answer to one who would form to himself some general idea of the kind of features by which an individual was distinguished. In order to adapt such a representation to the reality of the case, we must of course soften its prominences and correct its extravagancies; we must raise some parts and depress others; and while we retain the general likeness and grouping of the individual features which compose the countenance, we must reduce the whole to that medium character, from which, amidst the infinite varieties that occur, it is the rarest of all things to meet with any great deviation.

Mr. Coleridge, we understand, has sometimes expressed an un-willingness, in so far as the character of his poetry is concerned, to be classed with the other members of what has been called the Lake School; and it is impossible, we think, for any candid mind not to perceive, that, as in some respects the individuals of that association differ essentially from each other, there are also respects in which the compositions of this author are strikingly and most advantageously distinguished from those of all the rest. He displays, it is true, on many occasions, the same sickly sentimentality, the same perverted disposition to invest trifling subjects with an air and expression of great importance and interest, to treat subjects of real grandeur in a manner unsuited to their native majesty of character, and to employ, occasionally, expres-sions which are merely vulgar or ridiculous, instead of that direct and simple diction which is the most natural language of intense feeling. Along with these peculiarities, however, it cannot be denied, that there are other qualities of Mr. Coleridge's poetry which entitle it to a place among the finest productions of modern times. There is, in particular, a wildness of narrative, and a picturesque grouping of qualities and objects, which are in fine contrast to the tameness and placidity of ordinary poetry; a freshness of colouring and a delicacy of shading, which mark the hand of a great master. Amidst some obscurity and occasional failures, there are also every where to be discovered those incidental touches of true grace which indicate the native riches and power of the artist; and along with all these qualities, there is a fine adaptation, frequently, of the style and manner of our older masters to the improved design of modern times, which sheds a venerable air over the whole composition, and seems to embalm it with all the flowers and odours of the 'olden time'. These better qualities, it ought also to be recollected, are the more prevailing characteristics of our author's manner, and though there are occasional passages, and even entire pieces, in this collection, which none but a poet of the Lake school could have written, and which, without any intimation of the name of the author, would at once, in the opinion of any ordinary judge, determine his place of residence and habits of fellowship, there is no doubt that there is a still greater number of passages which remind us of an era of far better things.

Nothing, we apprehend, is more difficult than to characterize correctly the genius of an author whose productions possess so many opposite qualities, and whose excellencies and extravagancies are so curiously blended; especially as the work in which these combinations occur is not one uniform picture of any landscape in nature, or one unbroken narrative of some moral tale; not a regular and didactic poem, nor even a series of poems, marked by one prevailing character, and intended for the production of one common effect; but a great assemblage of unconnected pieces, which differ in subject, in character, and in style, sibylline leaves, which have long been tossed by all the winds of heaven, and are now collected into one precious fasciculus, some inscribed with interesting lessons of domestic love and family affection, some dedicated to enthusiastic celebration of the grand or the beautiful in natural scenery, not a few devoted to inspired wailings over the fates and hopes of national enterprise, and a very considerable number merely employed by the poet, for the purpose of being inscribed, as might suit his humour, with the incoherent ravings of his indolence or gaiety. Taking them altogether, however, we shall endeavour, though with a very general and rapid glance, to mark the prevailing qualities of the group, and to enable our readers also, by the specimens we shall select, to form for themselves an estimate of the merits of our author, independent of any judgment we may happen to express.

We have already hinted, that the prevailing characteristic of the compositions of this author is a certain air of wildness and irregularity, which equally belongs to his narrations of events, and to the pictures he has offered of the aspects of Nature. It would require, we believe, a greater expenditure, both of time and of space, than we can at present afford, to say exactly wherein this quality consists. We think, indeed, that an examination of its nature presents a subject of very interesting study to those who delight to speculate on the wonderful varieties of human character, or to mark, with the eye of philosophical discernment, the predilections which determine the excursions of fancy throughout the unbounded range of ideal combinations. Every person, however, may form to himself some analogical representation of this attribute of mind, who can contrast, in the imagination of external nature, the scenery of a rugged and finely wooded landscape, with the drowsy stillness of a champaign country, of which riches and uniformity are the prevailing characteristics, or the progress of a torrent amidst rocks and forests, with the course of a stream which flows full and unbroken through the placid abundance of a cultivated region, or the music of the winds as it is modulated and aided in its progress through a landscape of woods and of mountains, with those harmonious adaptations of kindred sounds which science and taste are capable of forming. We cannot pretend, however, to give instances of this quality, which is, indeed, the characteristic attribute of our author's genius, and which, of course, displays itself in some degree in all his productions; we must, therefore, content ourselves at present with referring such of our readers as think they should, above all things, be delighted with a genius of this order, to the actual productions of the author before us, as the greatest master in this style with whom we are acquainted; and, in the meantime, we shall proceed to notice some other qualities of his works which can more readily be illustrated by quotations and references.

Mr. Coleridge, like Mr. Southey, possesses, in no ordinary perfection, the power of presenting to the imagination of his readers a correct idea of natural scenery. There is a remarkable difference, however, as it appears to us, in the character assumed by this faculty in the case of these two writers. The delineations of Mr. Southey are true to the reality, as if his single object in description had been to represent every hue and variation of the object before him; his descriptions, accordingly, are admirably adapted for affording subjects to a painter; and, indeed, we know not any author by whose writings so many admirable facilities of this nature are afforded. His descriptions, at the same time, are frequently destitute of that far higher character which they might have assumed, if employed only as the ground-work for the production of emotion. We do not see wandering round his tablet those countless forms of moral excellence which almost bedim, by the brilliancy of their superior nature, whatever of beautiful belongs to mere form or colours; nor do we so often feel, as in the writings of Mr. Coleridge, that his chief object in presenting to us a picture of woods, or waters, or lofty mountains, was to aid him in communicating, with more perfect success, the vivid emotion which was present to his mind; and which, while it adds prodigiously to the effect of his scenes, throws often around them an aërial dimness, that seems to take something away from their merely material nature. This, we apprehend, is one of the chief excellencies of the author before us, and though we might refer in proof of it to almost any page of the present volume, we shall select as a specimen the opening of the 'Hymn, before sun-rise, in the vale of Chamouny', in which this peculiarity is at once exemplified and explained:

[quotes ll. 1-38 (*PW*, i, 376-8)]

And so on, in a strain of most exquisite poetry, of which we regret that we cannot continue our extract.

A second characteristic of our author's power of description, and one which is intimately connected with that we have already noticed, is the delightful freshness which nature seems to assume whenever the light and sunshine of his genius fall on it. It is never nature merely as invested with form and colour which he paints, but nature breathing all pleasant odours, and glittering with all brilliant lights, nature as she appears when moistened and sparkling with the rain of heaven, and when all her finest contrasts are exhibited beneath the cloudless radiance of a summer sky. As an instance, we may quote the following lines from the beginning of the poem entitled 'Fears in Solitude':

[quotes ll. 1-21 (*PW*, i, 256-7)]

The conclusion of this poem will awaken, we are persuaded, many kindly feelings in the bosoms of those who, like ourselves, have often gained, after a day of solitary wandering among the hills, the summit of the highest mountain in the group, and have felt the sight of the open landscape operate like a sudden restoration to life itself, upon the mind wearied and depressed with intense meditation.

[quotes ll. 203-32 (*PW*, i, 263)]

With respect to Mr. Coleridge's powers of description, we have still further to remark, that we do not know any author who possesses a finer talent for relieving his pictures by judicious contrast. As an evidence of which, the reader may take the following passage, the admirable picture in which is merely produced by way of contrast to the dark and barren character of the desart stream that is intended to be described:

[quotes ll. 72-101 of 'The Picture' (*PW*, i, 371-2)]

And so on, with some more beautiful painting; after which the author thus proceeds:

> Not to thee,
> O wild and desart Stream! belongs this tale:
> Gloomy and dark art thou—the crowded firs
> Tower from thy shores and stretch across thy bed,
> Making thee doleful as a cavern well.

The pages of Mr. Coleridge are not characterized by those fine touches of genuine pathos, which, amidst all the ravings of his mystical poetry, give often so inexpressible a charm to the compositions of Mr. Wordsworth. Yet is there a pathos of another kind which is very frequent with our author; a gentle and subdued tone of sympathy with human happiness or human suffering; an exquisite feeling of the charities and joys of domestic life; and a just appreciation of the necessity and value of religious consolations to the agitated and wayward heart of man—which communicate to his poetry not the least delightful of its attractions, and which never fail to make us love, while we respect, the author. We may assert, indeed, that the whole tone of our author's poetry is favourable to virtue and to all the charities of life, and we could quote several beautiful passages of this nature, did not the very copious extracts we have already given preclude us from this pleasure.

We must confess, at the same time, that, along with these excellencies, there are several great and very obvious defects in the poetry of Mr. Coleridge. His manner of describing natural objects is too apt to degenerate, as we have already hinted, into that morbid sentimentality which of late has become so general a characteristic of the poetry of this country—he is fond of expressing and illustrating the notion, that

> Outward forms, the loftiest, still receive
> Their finer influence from the life within.

And that mystical interpretation of the expressions of Nature, which has become the favourite occupation of Mr. Wordsworth's muse, and which has infected the taste of Lord Byron himself, has frequently exerted a seductive power over the fancy and feelings of this still more congenial spirit. We might mention also among the faults of his poetry, a degree of obscurity which sometimes occurs, not to such a pitch, perhaps, as in any instance to render his writings absolutely unintelligible, but sufficiently often to make the reader uneasy lest he should at every step encounter some such mystical passage—and to lead him onward, not with the gaiety and confidence which the song of the poet ought always to inspire, but with that sort of watchful jealousy which is natural to a person who is in the company of one that is disposed to puzzle him. We may mention, in the last place, that there is a good deal of affectation occasionally in the style of our author; he sometimes uses expressions which are altogether unsuitable to the dignity of poetry; and curious inversions of phrase are every now and then occurring, which, to our ears at least, give neither grace nor vivacity to his works. There is one form of expression, in particular, of which our author is so fond, as to have rendered his frequent use of it quite ridiculous, it occurs in such lines as the following:

> *Nor* such thoughts
> Dim and unhallowed dost thou *not* reject.

> *Nor* dost *not* thou sometimes recal those hours.

To this enumeration of faults we may add, that there are some pieces in this collection which to us appear to be quite silly and vapid. The following 'Verses', for instance, 'to a Young Lady on her recovery from a Fever':

> Why need I say, Louisa, dear!
> How glad I am to see you here,
>   A lovely convalescent;
> Risen from the bed of pain and fear,
>   And feverish heat incessant.

> The sunny Showers, the dappled Sky,
> The little Birds that warble high
>   Their vernal loves commencing,
> Will better welcome you than I,
>   With their sweet *influencing*.

> Believe me, while in bed you lay,
> Your danger taught us all to pray:
>   You made us grow devouter!
> Each eye looked up, and seemed to say,
>   How can we do without her?

> Besides, what vexed us worse, we knew
> They have no need of such as you
>   In the place where you were going:
> This World has angels all too few,
>   And Heaven is overflowing!

We shall not, however, quote any thing more of this kind. From what we have said, the reader will perceive, that we entertain a very high idea of Mr. Coleridge's poetical merits. He has intimated, however, in his preface, that he intends for the future to devote himself chiefly to studies of a different nature. We do not, it is true, give much credit to such a promise—because we have something of the same idea respecting the writing of poems, which Goldsmith had respecting slander, that it is like the propensity of a tyger which has once tasted of human blood, not easily divested of the appetite it has indulged. Taking the promise of the poet, however, as seriously given, we should be disposed to say, that if he is conscious of no desire to produce poems more free from faults than most of those in the volume before us, we do not think that the reputation of the artist would be much injured by his relinquishing the study; because, what is now attributed to mere negligence and apathy, would soon come to be considered as an inherent defect in his genius. We cannot help adding, however, that if Mr. Coleridge would give his mind more exclusively to what appears to us to be his true vocation, and would carefully avoid those extravagancies of sentiment and singularities of expression to which we have slightly alluded, we have no doubt that he might yet produce a work which would place him in the first rank of British poets, which would entirely justify the high opinion very generally entertained of the capabilities of his genius, and be fully adequate to all the compliments, whether sincere or adulatory, he has ever received.

86. Unsigned review, *Monthly Review*

January 1819, lxxxviii, 24-38

Gifted as, in our judgment, Mr. Coleridge is with much the strongest and most original powers of all the WATER-POETS[1] of the day, why has he fallen short even of the confined praise, and comparative popularity, which have attended his brethren of the Lakes? Is the answer to this question to be found in any caprice or corruption of national taste, or in the abuse of those gifts of nature and (we may add) of those acquirements of art, which this author so eminently possesses? The solution of the problem depends on a reference to both these causes. With a more

[1] An ironical coupling of the term usually applied to the naïve verse of John Taylor (1580-1653) with the name given to the new school.

vigorous and distinguishing imagination, with a more condensed and vivid phraseology, and lastly with deeper learning, than most of his poetical rivals and contemporaries, why, we say, is Mr. C. surpassed by almost all of them in literary reputation? Perhaps the exertion of thought which it requires to enter into all his higher qualities as a poet, or perhaps the purely moral and (as we think) often soundly political cast of his sentiments, may have obstructed his favour with a light and frivolous generation of readers. On the other hand, he has frequently dealt in those wonders and horrors, and in that mysterious delineation of bad passions, which seem to characterize the exclusively favourite style of the present moment in Great Britain. How, then, has he missed the aim of all, that golden celebrity which several inferior writers of the same kind have attained? In the first place, it must be allowed, and here perhaps is the principal cause of the phænomenon, that Mr. Coleridge, in these Germanized productions of the hyperbolically tremendous school, has even out-horrorized the usual *quantum suff.* of the horrible; and he has, with equal injudiciousness, contrived to blend even with such matters as would have pleased the unhealthy palate of the public, certain Platonic reveries or metaphysic mysticisms of his favourite modern philosopher Kant; which even the love for the unintelligible, now so prevalent among us, cannot entirely pretend to relish.

Again: we have to allege against Mr. Coleridge, considered as a candidate for contemporary popularity, the extraordinary fault of being too varied and too short in his productions. Had the 'Ancient Mariner', or the 'Christabel', been dilated into metrical romances, first published in quarto (some two or three hundred copies, *at the most*), and then rapidly succeeded by several editions, of four or five hundred each, in octavo; or had one *well-seasoned* edition re-appeared, like an old friend with a new face, with sundry fresh title-pages, even before the town was again empty; wonders might have been worked in this way for Mr. Coleridge's popularity. In the first instance, however, he compresses matter enough for *a handsome volume* into a two-penny pamphlet; then he lets a friend bury his jewels in a heap of sand of his own; then he scatters his 'Sibylline Leaves' over half a hundred perishable news-papers and magazines; then he suffers a manuscript-poem to be handed about among his friends till all its bloom is brushed off; and how can such a poet, so managing his own concerns, hope to be popular? It is a hope, we should think, that Mr. C. must have long renounced; and, if he *amuses* himself by composition, he must be satisfied with *profiting* others. The charges of brevity and of mismanagement, which we have brought against Mr. C., neither he nor his friends will be disposed to consider as very serious accusations: but, at all events, they must allow them their due weight in the question of popularity.

We fancy that we hear it asked, 'How has Mr. Coleridge been guilty of *variety*? Surely, there is a sameness, and a monotony too, in his Cumæan murmurs, which should guard him against any such imputation'. Granted: but we mean that Mr. C. has not endeavoured to impress on incongruous poems, poems that agree neither in subject nor in character, *one general* and pompous appellation. He has never given us a series of trifles, under the imposing and *uniform* superscription of 'Poems of Fancy', 'Poems of Imagination', &c., &c., &c.; and, by avoiding these common-place arts of book-making, or these presuming displays of vanity, he has proportionably suffered in fame with the larger and less discriminating mass of *professing* readers of poetry. It is surprizing, indeed, to a person newly initiated in these mysteries, to observe how much of modern literary distinction depends on *form*, and how little on *substance*! Mr. Coleridge has, doubtless, deserted the high post which appears to have been assigned to him among his countrymen; and he has, in two respects, rendered his conspicuous talents of little comparative utility to himself or others: he has never endeavoured to produce one great, sustained work, on a generally interesting subject; he has never concentrated his scattered rays of intellect into one luminous body, round which the minor efforts of his genius might have revolved in calm and obedient brilliancy. Possessed as he is of several languages, versed in the best authors of many ages and countries, and necessarily improved by the varied observations of a life passed neither in one scene nor in one species of occupation,* Mr. C. might surely have *commanded* his poetical powers into a more noble and useful channel than that in which they have hitherto run on, in a noiseless sort of obscurity. The stream has wound among rocks, varied indeed with lichens and mosses, overhung by the weeping birch and the dwarfish oak, and occasionally betraying some venerable ivy-mantled tower on its banks: but we wish to see it emerging from these lovely solitudes, and, increased by kindred fountains from the neighbouring hills, flow over the open plains in rich and majestic beauty, wash the walls of many a noble city, and

* We learn these facts from Mr. Coleridge's literary life and opinions; a recent work, to which we hope soon to direct the attention of our readers.[1]

[1] See No. 82.

issue, crowned with honours and wealth and blessings, into the unbounded ocean. We must not pursue the metaphor and contemplate
the stream in question as buried in that said ocean of posterity; for we
really believe that such a fate, as this last, would not attend any worthy
and patient exertion of the genius and learning of Mr. Coleridge.

Of the second great deficiency of this author, viz. of his *taste*, we
have hitherto said nothing: but many and great are his offences when
weighed in the balance, if measured by the standard of classical
antiquity. By his lectures on poetical subjects, we believe that he contributed, very materially, to prepare the public mind first for an endurance, then for an approbation, of those various and anomalous compositions which of late years have wholly altered, and to our fancies
wholly debased, the popular character of English poetry. By an overcharged fondness for our more early writers; by an unjust depreciation
of the genius and style of their successors; by dwelling with ardent love
on the gigantic prodigies of Elizabeth, and James, and the first Charles,
and marking with comparatively cold applause the happiest efforts of
the subsequent periods; by making our *Augustan* age, in a word, a
Lucretian instead of a *Virgilian* æra; Mr. Coleridge (and we have no
doubt that he will rejoice in the accusation) has, we are persuaded by
many testimonies and by many indications, succeeded in Gothicizing,
as largely as any one of his contemporaries, the literary taste of his
countrymen of the passing century.* We shall not any farther anticipate what we have to say of this gentleman's perverse critical labours,
ut nigra in candida vertat, to turn Cowper and Wordsworth into poets;
reserving any requisite observations of this kind to our examination
of his *Biographia Literaria*, and at present confining ourselves to the
topics more exclusively suggested by his *Sibylline Leaves*.

The following collection has been entitled SIBYLLINE LEAVES; in allusion to the
fragmentary and widely scattered state in which they have been long suffered
to remain. It contains the whole of the author's poetical compositions, from
1793 to the present date, with the exception of a few works not yet finished,
and those published in the first edition of his juvenile poems, over which he
has no controul. They may be divided into three classes: first, A Selection from
the Poems added to the second and third editions, together with those originally
published in the LYRICAL BALLADS, which, after having remained many years out

---

* It may be asked, how this opinion is consistent with the comparative unpopularity of Mr. C.? We answer that we distinguish the critic and the lecturer from
the poet; and, moreover, that the unpopularity in question arises rather from
accidental than from essential causes.

of print, have been omitted by Mr. Wordsworth in the recent collection of all his minor poems, and of course revert to the author. Second, Poems published at very different periods, in various obscure or perishable journals, &c., some with, some without, the writer's consent; many imperfect, all incorrect. The third and last class is formed of Poems which have hitherto remained in manuscript. The whole is now presented to the reader collectively; with considerable additions and alterations, and as perfect as the author's judgment and powers could render them.

We could not give a shorter account of this volume, and have therefore extracted the preceding passage. At the risk of some repetitions,* we shall take a cursory view of the whole publication; since, as the author informs us, he is to be henceforth employed in very different studies; and he now bids adieu to the Muses, not as Judge Blackstone did, but in the words of Virgil, or pseudo-Virgil:

> Ite hinc, Camœnæ! Vos quoque ite, suaves,
> Dulces Camœnæ! Nam (*fatebimur verum*)
> Dulces fuistis! Et tamen meas chartas
> Revisitote: sed pudentèr, et rarò.

> Go hence, ye Muses! charming to my youth,
> And cherished Muses! for (I'll own the truth)
> Cherished ye were:—yet go! If e'er again
> Ye come, come rarely to my modest strain. REV.

Since, then, Mr. Coleridge, according to his own most suspicious intimation, is not likely again to appear before us as a poet, we think that we are required in this place to give some general estimate of the only complete collection of his productions which he has presented to the public.

We will not, however, *begin with the beginning* in this case; for the childish poems, which some kind friends have persuaded Mr. C. to prefix to his real exordium, are wholly unworthy of his maturer abilities.

'The Rime of the Ancient Mariner' appeared at a time when, to use a bold but just expression, with reference to our literary taste, 'Hell made holiday', and 'Raw heads and bloody-bones' were the only fashionable entertainment for man or woman. Then Germany was poured forth into England, in all her flood of sculls and numsculls: then the romancing novelist ran raving about with midnight torches, to shew death's heads on horseback, and to frighten full-grown children with

* The reader will find accounts of Mr. Coleridge's various publications by consulting the *General Index* to our New Series, which has just appeared.

mysterious band-boxes, hidden behind curtains in bed-rooms: then was Ossian revived as a seer of ghosts, and a lurker in caverns of banditti: then rocks were vocal, amid all their snows, with the moans of passing spirits; and then sang the Ancient Mariner:

Lord bless us, *how* he sang!

It would be labour wasted, and time miscounted, if at the present moment we were to busy ourselves 'in thrice slaying the slain', and in chasing hobgoblins from the field who have already vanished into their native darkness. We shall therefore occupy our precious moments in a better task; in selecting from the said 'Ancient Mariner' a few bright and inspired lines,

(*Apparent rari nantes in gurgite vasto,*

as Fielding's critic has it)[1] which will live long and merrily, when their numerous surrounding brethren are buried in congenial forgetfulness.

A Ship becalmed.

Day after day, day after day,
  *We stuck,** nor breath nor motion;
As idle as a painted ship
  Upon a painted ocean.

Sleep.

Oh Sleep! it is a gentle thing,
  Beloved from pole to pole;—
To Mary Queen the praise be given!
She sent the gentle sleep from heaven,
  That slid into my soul.

Awaking, after Illness.

I moved, and could not feel my limbs:
  I was so light—almost
I thought that I had died in sleep,
  And was a blessed ghost.

---

[1] 'Here and there swimmers appear in the vast abyss' (Virgil, *Aeneid*, i, 118).

* How vexatious it is not to be able to quote even four lines, without some drawback from their merit! When a sailor even is made to speak in *verse*, he should not be vulgar.

The first Sight of our Country, after long and dangerous Absence.

Oh! dream of joy! is this indeed
The light-house top I see?
Is this the hill? Is this the kirk?
Is this my own countree?

A Calm Night at Sea.

The harbour-bay was clear as glass,
So smoothly it was strewn!
And on the bay the moonlight lay,
And the shadow of the moon.

We have purposely avoided any of the horrors of this poem; and, as far as we could, any passage which required the aid of the context to give it due effect: but these little selections will surely prove what Mr. Coleridge *could do* in this humbler ballad style, if he would but

fling away the worser part of him,
And live the purer with the better half.

We shall devote our undivided attention to that 'better half', as long as we can; and, when we *must* change the key, we can assure him that it will sound almost as discordantly in our ears as in his own.

In the author's youthful zeal for freedom, he felt, 'like thousands equally on fire', the joy, and the glory, and the exultation, of the first dawn of liberty in France. Like the same thousands, he wept over the dream of mistaken honour; found revolutionary despotism, where he sought for rational freedom; and awoke to painful conviction at the moment when Swisserland was invaded, and patriotic defence was turned into tyrannical aggression. His spirited 'Ode to France', on this occasion, was mentioned in our xxixth vol.[1]

The calmer and more domestic reflections which follow, intitled 'Fears in Solitude', written in 1798, strike us as very pleasing in thought, and as very powerful in realizing those visions of retirement which all ardent imaginations, at some period of life, delight to embrace. They were noticed by us at the same time and in the same volume of the M.R. with the 'Ode to France'.

The next object of our panegyrical selection is the poem well intitled 'Love'. We scarcely know, any where, a more touching and delicate description of the first interchange of affection, than he has given in this little piece: but our readers are, doubtless, acquainted with the simple charms of 'Genevieve'. The picture, taken from this subject, and placed some years since in the exhibition of the Royal Academy,

[1] See No. 22.

appeared to us very inadequate to the expression of the original.[1]

> The moonshine, stealing o'er the scene,
> Had blended with the lights of eve;
> And she was there, my hope, my joy,
> My own dear Genevieve. . . .
>
> I told her how he pined; and ah!
> The deep, the low, the pleading tone,
> With which I sang another's love,
> Interpreted my own. . . .
>
> All impulses of soul and sense
> Had thrill'd my guileless Genevieve;
> The music, and the doleful tale,
> The rich and balmy eve;
>
> And hopes, and fears that kindle hope,
> An undistinguishable throng,
> And gentle wishes long subdued,
> Subdued and cherish'd long!
>
> She wept with pity and delight,
> She blush'd with love and virgin-shame;
> And like the murmur of a dream
> I heard her breathe my name.

How is it possible for a poet, who possesses such an art as this, to deviate from the style in which he is sure to give delight, the old, the established classical style of English poetry, and to run after meteors which he himself, and Mr. Southey, and Mr. Wordsworth, have kindled: meteors of prosaic expression, meteors of vulgar and most familiar talk, meteors of dim and obstinate dullness?

We meet with some pretty lines (indeed, two sets of pretty lines) to an 'Unfortunate Woman'. Mr. Coleridge's early object of admiration, Mr. Bowles, taught him this title, and perhaps turned his mind to the subject: but Mr. Bowles writes like a person who has seen and has had a sympathy in the actual misery which he describes; while Mr. Coleridge, from beginning to end, calls the poor being a '*myrtle-leaf*'! This reminds us, strongly enough, of some mock stanzas which we once saw, addressed to Messrs. Wordsworth, Southey, and Co., on their fellow-feeling, their Hindu compassion, for all the tribes of vegetables. The author is supposed to have found a handsome *oak-apple*, rolled in the dust, in a vale in Devonshire; and, as King Charles's day was near, he thus expressed himself:

[1] The painting, by George Dawe (1781-1829), was exhibited in 1812.

Ill-fated fruit! thou should'st have been enroll'd
In a broad covering of resplendent gold!...
God help thee, oak-apple!—thy fate is hard.

The stanzas which follow, on the same wretched subject of female prostitution, are more feeling: but they, too, end with 'sky-larks', and we know not what. The pathos of Mr. Coleridge is rather general than particular; it is the tenderness of a benevolent and reflecting mind, rather than the sudden impulse of an afflicted heart.

We are much amused by the verses composed in a *Concert Room*; for they certainly convey no unjust description of the sham admiration of music, and the stupid pretence of being 'moved with concord of sweet sounds', which are so evident to any real musician, or real lover of music, on all such occasions. These verses, by the way, clearly prove the satirical powers of their author; in which, we are inclined to think, his main strength lies; and which he would do well to cultivate by every auxiliary study, and to direct against their proper objects of condemnation, with all virtuous exercise of reflection.

The lines sent with Falconer's 'Shipwreck' to a lady are commonplace, but pleasing; while all that follow, of this mood or measure, must be remanded to our vituperative division.

We are almost inclined to revoke our *censure* of Mr. Coleridge for not classing his compositions better, when we see him affixing the designation of 'Meditative Poems' to a large portion of his work. This proves him not to be so wholly ignorant of the arts of *puffing* as we had imagined; and we give him our praise accordingly. However we may settle this point, we cannot but agree with him in his feelings of rapture and of devotion, when he sees the sun rise on Mont Blanc:

[quotes ll. 24-85 of 'Hymn before Sun-rise, in the Vale of Chamouni' (*PW*, i, 378-80)]

We do not think that we have much descriptive or devotional blank verse, in our language, which is better than this.

Several of the 'Copies of Verses' that follow are, in our opinion, more adapted to the silence and the privacy of domestic enjoyment, than to glaring and repulsive publication. The author's sympathies with his family are surely too sacred for general notice. These things should be shewn 'through a glass darkly'; and they should be known to be real, only by the vivid image which they present through the interposed medium of fiction.

The Verses to the Rev. George Coleridge are delightful, and are truly a brother's tribute. If they must yield, as all things must, to the enchanting 'Traveller' of Goldsmith, even in the just expression of fraternal affection, still they are very beautiful; and, did not our limits forbid their entire insertion here, as absolutely as our feeling of their great merit precludes the idea of mutilating them by partial quotation, we would enable our readers to share the pleasure which we have received from the perusal of them.

'This Lime-tree Bower my Prison', or a poem in which the author records his feelings when left at home from illness, while his friends were wandering about the beautiful country in his neighbourhood, is very pretty and pleasing; especially in the following passage:

> Yes! they wander on
> In gladness all; but thou, methinks, most glad,
> My gentle-hearted Charles! for thou hast pin'd
> And hunger'd after Nature, many a year,
> In the great city pent, winning thy way
> With sad yet patient soul, through evil and pain
> And strange calamity! Ah! slowly sink
> Behind the western ridge, thou glorious Sun!
> Shine in the slant beams of the sinking orb,
> Ye purple heath-flowers! richlier burn, ye clouds!
> Live in the yellow light, ye distant groves!
> And kindle, thou blue ocean! So, my friend,
> Struck with deep joy may stand, as I have stood,
> Silent with swimming sense, &c.

The cold metaphysical abstractions which ensue, clothed as they are in mock energy and in pretended rage, contribute much towards the destruction of all effect from the beautiful and feeling extract above.

We must here pause in our praises, although above a hundred pages of the work are yet unexamined: but these we shall leave untouched, either by the sweet or the bitter end of our wand of criticism; save, indeed, a few drops from the latter. We must now retrace our steps; and, with painful but necessary severity, hold up the mirror to the deformities of this ingenious author's theory of poetical expression. He is not a poet who sins by chance: his is the guilt of erroneous literary principle, and it should be pursued with proportionate awards of reprobation. Having waived our right to criticise his preliminary childish effusions, come we then to particular passages in the remaining portion of his work which are necessarily submitted to our censure.

We speak not of the *general nonsense* of the 'Ancient Mariner', but of its specific offences:

> Nor dim, nor red, LIKE GOD'S OWN HEAD,
> The glorious sun uprist.

How came the author to *re-publish this*? Pious as he undoubtedly is, we think that we discover a *methodistical* sort of freedom about him,

> A freedom with the Unutterable Name.

> And every tongue, through utter drought,
> Was wither'd at the root;
> We could not speak, *no more than if*
> *We had been chok'd with soot.*

Will not a due reflection at length teach Mr. Coleridge, that such passages as the above, whether they are to be found in Mr. Wordsworth's poems or in his own, belong to the *Comic Familiar*, and not to the *Simple Narrative*?

> The lightning fell *with never a jag.*

This is merely vulgar.

> But in a minute she 'gan stir
> *With a short uneasy motion,*
> Backwards and forwards half her length,
> *With a short uneasy motion.*

Repetition, they say, is the '*soul* of ballad-writing': but surely it should not be the *body* too; and there is something too *substantial* in this sort of frequent re-appearance of the same solid creature, '*with a short uneasy motion*'.

> His rosy face besoiled with unwiped tears.

This is a nasty infant: not an infant adapted to poetic admiration.

> *My God!* it is a melancholy thing ...
> *Oh my God!*
> It is indeed a melancholy thing.

That a thousand verses like this might be spun in a morning, by any one gifted with sufficient *dullness and irreverence* for the task, is most manifest.

The rhapsody which follows, about the universal unredeemed wickedness of the world, is 'most musical, most melancholy'; and these words bring us to a curious note of the author, declaring that no charge could be more painful to him than that 'of having alluded with levity *to a line* in Milton'; 'except, *perhaps*, that of having *ridiculed his Bible*'. We have seldom seen a more grotesque instance of hyperbolical exaggeration, than that which is contained in this assertion.

On certain occasions, Mr. C. has displayed considerable humour: but it fails him in the poem of the 'Mad Ox'; and in that of 'Parliamentary Oscillators', a laborious and unhappy title, for the *jeu d'esprit* to which it is prefixed.

'Fire, Famine, and Slaughter', most of our political readers will remember. The severity of the satire is one thing; the merit of the poetry is another; and undoubtedly many will dispute the justice of the first, but none, we think, can with candour deny the energy of the last. The 'Apologetic Preface', as it is quaintly called, which the author has placed before the poem, was surely unnecessary: since nothing but the rankest bigotry, or the most stupid perversion, could misinterpret the feelings of the writer of a political lampoon on that obnoxious minister, who so long wielded and exhausted the strength and the resources of Great Britain, in enterprises which made her friends alternately shiver with alarm and with poverty, and which elated the hopes and aggrandized the dominion of her enemies.

Never was writer more digressive than the present. He leaps from Mr. Pitt upon Jeremy Taylor; and the French Revolution fixes him in admiration of Milton. The last transition, indeed, is by much the most natural of the two. We admire, however, his comparison and contrast of the royalist and the republican of the age of Charles the First.

> *Slush!* my heedless feet from under, &c. &c.

There is no end to these imitative sounds. We could startle Mr. Coleridge with a volley of them, sanctioned by his own example. Does he remember the chorus of *Hisses* which followed Gil Blas' friend poor Melchior Zapator, as he walked from the spring where he had been soaking his crusts?[1] Does he remember *all* the catcalls of Madrid?

> A curious picture, with a master's haste
> *Sketch'd on a strip of pinky-silver skin,*
> *Peel'd from the birchen bark!*

This is what we would call the *Natural Affectation*:—by which we do

---

[1] The incident occurs in Le Sage's *Gil Blas*, Book ii, chapter 8.

not mean the *affectation of a natural*, but the affectation of describing natural objects *as they are, exactly*; and without any addition of the *beau idéal* of art. Perhaps many happier instances than the above, of this radical defect in the poetry of Mr. Coleridge and of all his school, might be selected. They all abound in this affectation, this sort of minute Dutch painting; and again in another species of the same variety, the hearty, honest, homespun, 'hail fellow-well-met', style:

> Quæ mera libertas dici vult, veraque virtus.[1]

Speaking of the reasons which made him regret the illness of a beautiful and amiable woman, the author says:

> Besides what vexed us worse, we knew,
> They have no need of such as you
> In the place where you were going:
> This world has angels all too few,
> And Heaven is overflowing.

This is in Little's[2] youngest style of levity.

> I love my love, and my love loves me.

> I slit the sheet, &c. &c.:

but the only *idea* in this song is as old as the Pastor Fido; and, no doubt, older still.

The '*Happy* Husband', instead of being *happy*, is mystical and un-impressive. So also are the verses on a most interesting occasion, the author's *approach* to his home, when he has heard of a child being born to him. Even here he is *Platonic, Pythagoric*, we had almost said, *Paregoric*. He administers, indeed, a very strong and very repulsive dose to our natural feelings: but he redeems his fault in the simple and beautiful lines which follow, on the first sight of his child.

The lines to *a Gentleman*, who had recited a poem about the '*growth of an individual mind*', we conclude are verses addressed to Mr. Wordsworth, on some nonsensical piece of mysticism, spouted forth by that solemn but flimsy author. Why will these three lake-poets, Messrs. Southey, Wordsworth, and Coleridge, and their admirers, so often remind us of the story of the men who were acquainted with the three clever sisters, and each thought that the other knew the one who was really so famous for her cleverness?

[1] A variant on Horace, *Epistles*, i, 18, 8, 'while wishing to pass for simple candour and pure virtue'.

[2] See p. 87, n 1

The notion of taking a child out into an orchard at night, to look at the moon, when it was frightened by that 'strange thing, an infant's dream', is original enough; unless, indeed, it was suggested by the practice of some medical men in fevers, who expose the patient to a cold air-bath.

> She smil'd, and smil'd, and pass'd it off,
>   *E'er* from the door she stept;
> But all agree *it would have been*
>   *Much better had she wept.*

Again the farcical, meant to be pathetic.

> 'Twas such a foggy time, as makes
>   Old sextons, Sir! like me,
> *Rest on their spades to cough; the spring*
>   *Was late uncommonly.*

We must here leave this *rural author* for the present: but not without bestowing praise on him which we are sure will be very welcome. He speaks, then, like a sexton, most naturally; and, had he stripped his sexton of as many waistcoats as his brother grave-digger, when represented by poor Suett,[1] was wont to pull off in Hamlet, he might have deserved the full praise of the Roman critic,

> *Quinetiam agrestes satyros nudavit; et asper*
> *Incolumi gravitate* jocum *tentavit.*[2]

We shall shortly revisit Mr. C. in his biography of himself.

---

[1] Suett (1755-1805) specialised in Shakespearean clowns in the latter part of his acting career.

[2] Variant on Horace, *The Art of Poetry*, 221-2; 'he soon brought on unclad woodland satyrs and with no loss of dignity attempted humour'.

ZAPOLYA

1817

87. Unsigned review, *Edinburgh Magazine*

December 1817, i, 455-9

There seems to be a great barrenness of invention and dearth of conception among our modern dramatists. We have had nothing either very touching or bold in the shape of native English tragedy for fifty years. The pathos of Otway, the deep and heart-rending distress of Southerne,[1] are not likely to be soon imitated, and, at all events, the reproduction of them has been so long suspended, as to mark a sensible variation of capacity, though, even under a more depraved state of morals, it does not strike us that this would mark a change of national taste. To enjoy the strong sensation which flows from a sympathy with theatrical woe, or tenderness, or passion, it is not necessary that we should be most virtuous. It is not unusual for men to spare a tear for fictitious distress, or illustrious misery, at the very moment, perhaps, when they are wilfully and knowingly in the habitual neglect of some essential and obvious duty. Be that as it may, the pathos and the deep distress are, now, hardly ever seen on our stage. Thomson tried something which was a mixture of both these;[2] but it was a great deal too pure, too raised from active human nature, and had too much to do with the passive excellencies which shine like a winter-moon, cold, powerless, and only bright. He took not pains enough to catch hold on any lurking traits of prejudice in favour of peculiar privileges, or admiration of vigorous villany. Home tried the same track;[3] and, as men of mediocrity and of chastised tastes never fail to do, fairly ran it down. Since that time we have been diluting the highly flavoured

[1] Thomas Southerne (1659-1746), author of *Oroonoko*.

[2] James Thomson's *Sophonisba* (1730).

[3] John Home's *Douglas* (1756).

413

strong drink of the Germans—or giving servile and spiritless *versions* from the romantic and poetical among our old English playwrights. We have gone on this way, one man writing his six epics of chivalry, and another his six epics of pure romance, while, in lyric and impassioned poetry, chords which had not been touched before, have not only been struck, but sounded in all their pitch and compass. The tragic and poetical drama alone is left as it were in despair. That author who must be strictly said to have by far the happiest genius—not of his country merely, but of his age—and who possesses greater fecundity of invention, and versatility of exertion, than any human being that ever wrote to please a fashion, or to gratify an appetite which he himself had created; even Scott has hitherto abstained from that species of composition, in which to excel, would be the summit of his fame. All the world knows the merits of Miss Baillie. But none of her plays could ever bear long to be represented on the stage; and her compositions are too philosophically constructed and connected ever to please as dramas. Mr. Coleridge himself has tried the bold, vigorous, and sinewy style of tragedy which prevailed from the Elizabethan age down to Dryden's time, when it was corrupted by the Gallicisms, and, to use his own phrase, 'dashed and brewed' by the spurious transplantations with which he deformed his inventions, and wasted down the vigour of his 'mighty line'. But *Remorse*, though it had many beauties, both of thought and expression, and though its interest rested on nothing strained in incident, or monstrous in the conception of character—nothing in the style of Lewis's *Castle Spectre*,[1] nor like some late tragedies, yet it possessed too little *adaptation*, and only a very scanty interest in its plot or scene. It was a classical composition of its kind, however. Its first run was considerable, it procured for its author a greater honour than has been bestowed on any dramatic poet by an audience since the time of Voltaire;[*] and though it seems now to be laid by, *not* to remain as a *stock acting play*, yet it will always please in the closet. It has several passages which attest the powerful bard that struck the chord of the lyric ode with a wilder tone, and a more prevailing sway, with a more raised, enthusiastic, and commanding

---

[1] M. G. Lewis's *The Castle Spectre* (1797).

[*] On one of the nights in which *Remorse* was performed at DRURY LANE, Mr. Coleridge appeared in a stage-box, when the audience in the Pit rose simultaneously, as soon as he was observed, and testified their respect to the author of the tragedy by cheers, and clapping hands!

spirit, than any English poet, with the exceptions only of Dryden and of Gray.*

The story of this drama of Zapolya is soon told: Andreas, king of Illyria, is at the point of death, while his queen, Zapolya, is about to be delivered of a child. Andreas dies, leaving as regents of his kingdom, and guardians of his child, the Queen, Prince Emerick, and Raab Kiuprili, Emerick usurps the sovereign power, Zapolya is obliged to fly with her infant to the woods, and Raab Kiuprili, who had openly resisted the tyrant, and dared him to his face, is taken prisoner. Chef Ragozzi, who had chosen to act a part of feigned submission, the more surely to subvert the design of Emerick, furnishes the royal mother with the means of flight for herself and her infant; and, having been enjoined by Emerick to send intimation to the chiefs of the army in different places, of his usurped accession, releases Raab Kiuprili, and sends *him* on one of these errands. Thus ends 'THE PRELUDE, *entitled,* "*The Usurper's Fortune*"'. A civil war ensues, in which Emerick has the best of it for twenty years, at which period the drama itself begins. This Mr. Coleridge has called 'THE SEQUEL, *entitled,* "*The Usurper's Fate*"'. Young Andreas, the royal infant, had now become a fine spirited youth, with high aspirations of his destiny, a tormenting wish to know his origin, and a restless yearning to learn the fate of his mother, who was supposed to have expired at the time he was found wrapt up in the mantle of a lady who was discovered hard by in a dying state. Andreas was sheltered as an orphan by Bathory, a rude and simple-minded mountaineer, and a dependent on Lady Sarolta, wife to Cassimer, the Lord High Steward of Illyria, under Emerick the usurper, with whom he had taken part against his noble father Raab Kiuprili. The second act introduces Zapolya and Kiuprili in a horrid cave, whither they had fled, and in which they had passed a precarious existence. They are discovered by Glycine, a young girl who had fallen in love with Bethlen, and whose affection is, it strikes us, very beautifully and strikingly pourtrayed. Bethlen Bathory (Andreas's foster name) had gone to the savage wood in which this cavern was situated, on a hint that it was there his mother had breathed her last; and Glycine, prompted by her love, followed him to ascertain his safety. All this passes at the country residence of Cassimer, where his lady, Sarolta, spends her time, in compliance with some early vows, and pious resolutions. Glycine reaches the cave first. Bethlen comes just

* See the 'Ode to the Departing Year', p. 51, of Mr. Coleridge's recent volume of poetry.

after she had divulged the object of her visit to its unhappy inmates, and after some maternal forebodings had been excited in the breast of Zapolya by the simple narrative of the love-sick girl. She discovers her son. The scene is one of undoubted beauty, though unfortunately so constructed, as to make impossible that requisite and immediate impression which, on a second reading, a careful reader thinks he *might* have felt from a certain pastoral pathos and picturesque horror which it must be allowed to possess. The plot now, at the third act, runs quickly forward in its unravelment. Emerick, who had come on a hunting expedition to Casimir's seat, is struck with the beauty of Lady Sarolta. Introduced into her chamber by the treachery of a babbling, weak, and villanous servant, Laska, he attempts to violate the chaste Sarolta. She resists him, till Bethlen comes in fully armed—we are at a loss to know how. In the fight which ensues, and after Emerick has been disarmed, Casimir comes in, and, though he had been warned of the tyrant's designs on his wife, makes rather absurdly no instant attempt to avenge the insult, but defers his vengeance. In the fourth act, Casimir and Rudolph concert means for avenging themselves on Emerick. Rudolph is to lead the hunt, in which Emerick joins, to a part of the forest where Casimir, with a chosen band, is to set on him. Laska, the villanous servant, is, with Pestalutz, an hired murderer, on an errand of assassination against Casimir, when they are encountered singly by Bethlen. Laska is about to stab him in the back with a javelin, when the villain is killed by the faithful Glycine, who had been at the cave with Zapolya and Raab Kiuprili, near which the encounter takes place. The heroic girl saves her lover's life with a bow and poisoned arrow, which the half wild Laska had but the moment before laid down there in reserve for Pestalutz, the assassin, to whom he is acting as guide, and who falls, almost at the same moment with himself, under the sword of Bethlen. Casimir, who had been threading this part of the forest, watching to execute his vengeance on Emerick, meets at the cave his injured father, Raab Kiuprili, and is reconciled to him. Emerick at length arrives and stumbles on the dead body of Pestalutz, over which, as Casimir's mantle had been thrown on it, he exults; till, lifting up the mantle, he has just time to vent an exclamation of astonishment, when Casimir rushes in, and, after a momentary struggle, kills the tyrant with the very sword of Raab Kiuprili, which he had picked up on his entrance to the cave. The confederates against Emerick proclaim Andreas, the quondam Bethlen, King of Illyria. Glycine is found to be the daughter of Chef Ragozzi, who had saved the lives of Zapolya and her son. To this affectionate girl Zapolya gives the hand of her son the king.

Such is this drama, which has glimpses of poetry, and a polish, and a sort of high-toned and picturesque beauty, which, it is likely, no other poet now living could have given to it in an equal degree with Mr. Coleridge, without also giving it more force and effect, without bringing home a tangible interest, and making it tell on obvious and general feelings. In its present shape, we conceive it has about it that indescribable something, which, if not the dead weight of mediocrity to sink it, will ensure a speedy neglect from the bulk of readers, and check for ever the hopes of Mr. Coleridge's admirers in him as a dramatic writer. There is not a tittle of interest in this story as he manages it. To understand the plot, and keep in view its progress, the reader must take some pains; and this is what no reader will ever do, except in a case where his attention may have been called off for a while by some excellent *bye-play*. Our author's idea of passion is by far too *elementary*. He wants *adaptation*. Much of the most striking parts of his story is related, and not acted. He has always before him, as it were, a good map of the chief lines and figures of passion, but then he does not enforce these with the exact sentiment which is to body them forth to the reader or hearer, and to serve also, in pushing on the story, that purpose of dramatic action for which they were copied or sketched out, both at once, and in the quickest possible manner. But this is what a dramatic writer must do.

Zapolya, then, as a drama, will never succeed. Nor, as a tale, is there any thing in it to captivate. It must exist as a poem; and, even in that case, we decidedly think it is too long. We shall, as fair critics, however, point out a few of the beauties which have occurred to us.

> O most lov'd, most honour'd;
> The mystery that struggles in my looks,
> Betrayed my whole tale to thee, if it told thee
> That I am ignorant; but fear the worst.
> And mystery is contagious. *All things here*
> *Are full of motion: and yet all is silent:*
> *And bad men's hopes infect the good with fears.*

This, we think, is a true, and what constitutes great merit, a succinct and striking picture of the uncertainty, the doubt, and feverish excitement which prevail when contending parties are secretly at work with the great machine of human affairs.

Emerick the usurper tries, in the subsequent passage, we think very forcibly, to stagger the strong representations of honest Raab Kiuprili in favour of the direct line of succession.

[quotes ll. 302-14 of the Prelude, scene i (*PW*, ii, 893)]

Zapolya is thus finely and impressively introduced with her infant in her arms, when she had fled, after the death of her husband, from the usurper of his throne:

[quotes ll. 433-50 of the Prelude, scene i (*PW*, ii, 897)]

Bethlen's agony of uncertainty respecting his parents is finely shewn:

[quotes ll. 314-18, Part II, Act I, scene i (*PW*, ii, 911-12)]

He speaks now of his mother.

[quotes ll. 379-83 and 430-45, Part II, Act I, scene i (*PW*, ii, 913-15)]

The poetical turn of those four passages, which we are now to give, is so sweet and touching, as to be, with us, a relief from the hurry and vehemence of the impassioned parts.

[quotes ll. 72-81, Part II, Act IV, scene i (*PW*, ii, 939); ll. 32-6, 46-50, and 150-4, Part II, Act I, scene i (*PW*, ii, 902, 905-6); and ll. 118-24 of the Prelude, scene i (*PW*, ii, 887-8)]

Zapolya, just before she leaves the capital of her dead husband, utters this animated and powerful exclamation, as she looks back on the palace.

[quotes ll. 516-40 of the Prelude, scene i (*PW*, ii, 899-900)]

It is surely to be regretted that any thing should prevent a man so highly gifted with poetical language, and knowledge, and fancies, as the author of these passages, from following out his poetical vein to its fullest extent. We could now enter into much speculation about Mr. Coleridge's literary character, in which we take a real interest on many accounts, and have more to say of his poetical genius than a Magazine-Review will allow us to give out at once. We have watched him through his career as an author pretty closely; and, though the fruit of his fair promise has been unfortunately so small—still we think a few hints on the nature of the models which he seems to have studied (which all men of aspiring genius and a peculiar taste are likely to study, if they take to any models at all) and on the particular direction of his fancy, might be neither unuseful nor uninstructive as discussion, nor unfair to a man of unquestionable learning and ingenuity, who has suffered much from the injudicious panegyrics of friends, and the exaggerated and malevolent misrepresentations of enemies, as much almost as from the awkward bent of a restive imagination, and powers of judgment rather imperfectly developed. At another time we mean to take up this important and delicate literary question.

88. Unsigned notice, *Monthly Magazine*

January 1818, xliv, 541

Mr. Coleridge, in his *Zapolya, a Christmas Tale*, has kept pretty near to the letter of his title: but we observe few strong delineations of character, or poetical combinations, which we should wish to remember. He is, however, less obscure than in some other of his works, which we have had occasion to notice, although the *sel poignant d'esprit* seems, in a great measure, to have evaporated: this is, we suppose, as it should be, for, as we grow older, we ought to grow wiser. We are sorry to observe that this poem cannot add much to Mr. Coleridge's fame.

89. Unsigned notice, *New Monthly Magazine*

January 1818, viii, 544

This dramatic poem is avowedly constructed in imitation of Shakespeare's *Winter's Tale*, and, like that, so far violates the doctrine of the unities as to bring the events of twenty years together between the ordinary acts. Bold as this may be, and still bolder to take up the bow of Shakespeare, truth compels us to say, that Mr. Coleridge has drawn it with a powerful arm, and produced a piece of no ordinary merit. The scene is laid in Illyria, and the story is that of a usurper, who succeeds for a long time; but after a series of crimes falls by the hand of the very noble that assisted him in gaining the throne, but towards whom the tyrant subsequently behaves with the wonted treachery of men who have betrayed their country. The queen dowager Zapolya and her son, which last has attained maturity, are restored, and the whole ends happily. There is a considerable beauty in the language, and the characters are all delineated in a manner that would, we are inclined to think, render the play attractive upon the stage.

90. Unsigned review, *Theatrical Inquisitor*

February 1818, xii, 107-11

In the Advertisement prefixed, Mr. Coleridge tells us that '*the form of the following dramatic poem is in humble imitation of the* Winter's Tale *of Shakespeare, except that the first part is called a Prelude, instead of a first act, as a somewhat nearer resemblance to the plan of the ancients, of which one specimen is left us in the Æschylian Trilogy of the* Agamemnon, *the* Orestes, *and the* Eumenides. *Though a matter of form merely, yet two plays, on different periods of the same tale, seem less bold than an interval of twenty years between a first and second act'*. There is, as may be concluded from the foregoing extract, a considerable lapse of time between the two parts of this Christmas tale, a licence which is sanctioned by the model he has chosen, and the evils of which are somewhat lessened by the more complete division adopted by Mr. Coleridge. That which would, in exact imitation of Shakespeare, be called the first act is in this instance called the prelude; and the drama itself contains four acts only. The scene is in Illyria; the play opens as the king of that province, *Andreas*, is at the point of death, an event which is announced in the first scene. A faction exists for depriving his queen and her infant of their regal possessions; at the head of which is *Emerick*, an ambitious courtier, who alledges that the queen's representations of her having become a mother are fallacious; and, by the aid of the soldiery, invests himself with the vacant functions of royalty. *Raab Kiuprili*, an honest, loyal warrior, at this juncture, returns from the camp, and is informed of their traitorous intentions. He bears a paper sent to him by *Andreas*, appointing him, in conjunction with the *Queen* and *Emerick*, guardians of the state and of the royal infant, which the latter treats as the act of a madman, and refuses to obey. The usurper has succeeded in seducing from his allegiance *Casimir*, the son of *Kiuprili*. The parent, however, severely reprehends the conduct of his son, and remains inflexible in his loyal and honest attachment to the family of his late sovereign; this so provokes *Emerick*, that the first act of his lawless authority is the seizure of *Kiuprili*, and his confinement in a dungeon. *Casimir* in vain pleads for his father, whom the tyrant dooms to die. The queen, *Zapolya*, in the mean time, escapes with her infant boy from assassination purposed by *Emerick*. *Ragozzi*, a faithful friend of the virtuous persons in the drama, effects the escape of *Kiuprili* from prison, and accidentally meeting *Zapolya*, undertakes to conduct her and her infant to a place of safety. At this period of the story the prelude ceases.

The sequel introduces several new personages; and those who remain are so altered by the lapse of twenty years, that they are equally strange to the reader. The Queen and *Ragozzi*, it appears, were pursued by the usurper's troops; and *Zapolya*, wounded and apparently dying, is forced to abandon her son to the protection of a peasant, *Old Bathory*, who adopts the royal infant, and rears it as his own, calling him *Bethlen*. *Casimir*, who has married the *Lady Sarolta*, inhabits a domain, adjacent to the abode of this peasant. A dispute occasioned by the servants of *Casimir*, brings *Bathory* and *Andreas* (his supposed son) before *Sarolta*. She learns from the former the circumstances under which his adopted son was discovered in the wood; and she, interested by the recital, undertakes to become the protectress of both. In the mean time the tyrant *Emerick*, who has sinister designs upon the wife of *Casimir*, visits the neighbourhood, under pretence of enjoying the diversions of the chase, but, in reality, to effect by force his criminal purposes with regard to the *Lady Sarolta*. *Andreas*, eager to know his parentage, wanders into a forest, the reputed residence of supernatural beings, near which he learns his mother first entrusted him to *Bathory*; and by a series of concurring causes, discovers that she is alive, habited like a savage, and protected by the faithful and loyal *Kiuprili*. He returns to the mansion of *Casimir* (whom the king has taken care to employ afar off, in order that he may the better succeed with his wife), just in time to protect his patroness, who screams out for assistance, and whom he saves from the designs of *Emerick*. The injured husband and other confederates, disgusted with the tyranny of the usurper, agree to subvert his power. An attempt of his to assassinate *Casimir* is detected, the assassin is slain; and *Casimir* avenges the outrage offered his wife's honour, by himself slaying *Emerick*. The claims of *Andreas* are acknowledged, he inherits the throne of his ancestors, and all ends as it should do. Some inferior personages are also interwoven in the progress of the drama.

It will be seen by this slight sketch of the poem, that there is room for some very fine declamation; and in this we apprehend its chief merit to consist. The language, disfigured as it often is by the author's quaintness and childishness, is nevertheless nervous and original; it abounds with images which are just and expressive. We cannot avoid mentioning one which is natural and elegant. *Sarolta* is detailing to *Andreas* (then called *Bethlen*) the story of his discovery in the wood; he intreats her to disclose who and what he is: she says,

> I know not who thou art;

and he exclaims,

> Blest spirits of my parents,
> Ye hover o'er me now—ye shine upon me!
> And, *like a flower that coils forth from a ruin,*
> *I feel and seek the light I cannot see!*
>
> Act i. sc. i.

He has also forcible images derived from common life; for instance, when the same person is in the forest conversing with the unknown *Kiuprili*, in answer to a question of his name, he replies,

Ask rather the poor roaming savage,
Whose infancy no holy rite had blest.
To him, perchance, rude spoil or ghastly trophy,
In chase or battle won,* have given a name.
I have none—but like a dog have answered
To the chance sound which he that fed me called me!

Act ii. sc. 1.

It is greatly to be lamented, that so clever a man as the writer of this dramatic poem should indulge in such quaint and unintelligible expressions as these:

The *bald accident* of a midwife's handling
The unclosed sutures of an infant's skull.
Hush Glycine!
It is the ground swell of a teeming instinct.

Act 1, sc. 1.

Nor is it quite in character for a usurping tyrant, in threatening the man who has frustrated his iniquitous designs to quibble and introduce so coloquial a phrase as the following. *Sarolta*, after the fortunate arrival of *Andreas*, when rescued, says:

This is the hour, that fiends and damned spirits
Do walk the earth, and take what form they list!
Yon devil hath assumed a king's!
Beth. (Andreas)   Usurped it!
Emerick. The King will play the devil with thee indeed!

Act 3, sc. 2.

As a specimen of this poem, we subjoin the concluding part of the last scene of the prologue. *Zapolya* is just on the point of flight with *Ragozzi*, a faithful soldier and attendant—before she departs, she exclaims:

[quotes ll. 494-540 of the Prelude, scene i (*PW*, ii, 899-900)]

In conclusion, although we cannot extend to this poem our entire approbation, we readily allow that there are abundant beauties, and those of no common order to be found in *Zapolya*. Mr. Coleridge's mind is highly gifted, and were he to get rid of his peculiarities and affectation, he would become one of the most pathetic and original writers of the age.

* Hath.

423

91. Private opinions

Henry Crabb Robinson on 'Christabel', which had been read to him—extract from his diary, 9 October 1811: 'It has great beauties and interests more than any so small a fragment I ever met with, and that purely by the force of poetic painting. . . . The mystic sentimentality of Coleridge, however, adorned by original imagery, can never interest the gay or frivolous, who are to be attracted by the quick succession of commonplace and amusing objects; and for the same reason the deep glances into the innermost nature of man and the original views of the relations of things which Coleridge's works are fraught with are a stumbling-block and an offence to the million, not a charm' (*On Books and Their Writers*, i, 47-8).

Sara Coleridge—extract from a letter of 24 May 1816: 'You will be sorry for another thing respecting him—Oh! when will he ever give his friends anything but pain? he has been so unwise as to publish his fragments of "Christabel" & "Koula-Khan". Murray is the publisher, & the price 4s. 6d.—we were all sadly vexed when we read the advertisement of these things' (*Minnow among Tritons*, 48).

Sara Hutchinson (1775-1844), Coleridge's 'Asra' and sister-in-law of Wordsworth—extract of a letter of 17 February 1817: 'Have you seen Mr. Coleridge's "Lay Sermons"? The first they say addressed to the higher classes is of all obscures the most obscure—we have not seen either and hear very little that is satisfactory of his goings-on . . .' (*The Letters of Sara Hutchinson from 1800 to 1835*, ed. Kathleen Coburn, London 1954, 105).

Dorothy Wordsworth (1771-1855), sister of the poet—extract from a letter of 2 March 1817: 'Have you seen Coleridge's "Bible, the Statesman's best Manual". I think it is ten times more obscure than the darkest parts of the Friend' (*Letters of William and Dorothy Wordsworth: The Middle Years*, ed. Ernest de Selincourt, Oxford 1937, ii, 780).

Charles Lamb—extract from a letter of 23 September 1816: 'God bless him, but certain that rogue-Examiner has beset him in most unmannerly strains. Yet there is a kind of respect shines thro' the disrespect that to those who know the rare compound (that is the subject of it) almost balances the reproof, but then those who know him but partially or at a distance are extremely apt to drop the qualifying part thro' their fingers' (*The Letters of Charles and Mary Lamb*, ii, 196).

THE FRIEND

1818

92. Unsigned review, *European Magazine*

February 1819, lxxv, 141-2

We know not whether we shall impair the high estimation in which our Literary Review is held, when we honestly confess, that had it not been for the republication of the present work, we should still have remained in the most profound ignorance of its pre-existence. But such is the naked truth; and indeed this confession the author has himself anticipated, and almost prevented our avowal that we were not among the 'scanty number' of its former circulation. We are, however, indebted for the confession, as it will serve as a protecting armour of defence from the 'arrowy flight' which would otherwise have been directed against us. But surely this seeming neglect and indifference which attended its former introduction into the world, cannot be attributed to any want of interest in the work itself, as it affords abundant matter for the deep and intelligent reader. Neither was its author an upstart in literature, or one who was about to flesh his sword in the field of letters. On the contrary, rather, his shield was emblazoned with the heraldry of his prowess, and his name associated with the captains of the day, while his former achievements ranked high in public estimation. Or, to speak without metaphor, his poetical, as well as prose, works, had been universally read, and as universally admired; and were destined to form, in after ages, a bold specimen of the literature of the nineteenth century. We are still at a loss, therefore, to assign the real cause for the former limited circulation of *The Friend*, which no surmises of our own can satisfactorily account for. But, according to the old adage, 'Better late than never'; and we are confident our readers will join in hearty concurrence with our exclamation, when they shall have perused the work itself. There is much matter dispersed throughout these volumes, which will not bear a transient view, or a rapid perusal. A close and accurate attention, joined with calm and dispassionate feelings, wholly divested of prejudice, will rather oftentimes be required in the examination of many propositions advanced by the author. Much abstract reasoning and nice deductions might be produced from some of his data, and furnish prolific subjects for the display of argumentative subtlety. We question, indeed, whether we have always thoroughly comprehended his meaning, or whether, in reducing his theories to *anticipated practice*, we have not frequently (to ourselves at least) rendered intricacy more intricate. We had not intended making any extracts, but we have been induced from our purpose by the beautiful simplicity of the idea, and striking force conveyed in the following passage:

There never perhaps existed a school-boy who, having, when he retired to rest, carelessly blown out his candle, and having chanced to notice, as he lay upon his bed in the ensuing darkness, the sullen light which had survived the extinguished flame, did not, at some time or other, watch that light as if his mind were bound to it by a spell. It fades and revives—gathers to a point— seems as if it would go out in a moment—again recovers its strength, nay becomes brighter than before: it continues to shine with an endurance, which in its apparent weakness is a mystery—it protracts its existence so long, clinging to the power which supports it, that the observer, who had laid down in his bed so easy-minded, becomes sad and melancholy: his sympathies are touched— it is to him an intimation and an image of departing human life,—the thought comes nearer to him—it is the life of a venerated parent, of a beloved brother or sister, or of an aged domestic; who are gone to the grave, or whose destiny it soon may be thus to linger, thus to hang upon the last point of mortal exis- tence, thus finally to depart and be seen no more. This is nature teaching seriously and sweetly through the affections—melting the heart, and, through that instinct of tenderness, developing the understanding.

Of all the virtues which influence the human breast, friendship is the most pure and exalted. We worship, venerate, and adore, the proud distinctions of so generous a passion. It is, therefore, with no common feelings, that we point out the amiable candour and steady friendship which guides the pen of Mr. Coleridge in the biography of Sir A. Ball, and whose language does as much honour to his mind as his heart. But we think his remonstrances against the silence of that officer's services are ill-timed, and uncalled-for. Was a baronetcy, we believe gratuitously conferred, nothing? Was the approbation of his sovereign, expressly conveyed in a letter to that gallant officer, from the Secretary Dundas (we quote from Mr. Coleridge), of no consideration? Was no value to be attached to the free gift of 1000*l*? Surely these form altogether a most convincing proof of the high estimation in which Sir A. Ball's meritorious conduct was held, and how much his many services were appreciated and acknowledged. The indifferent silence of newspaper reporters cannot be viewed as affecting any officer's services, nor the confined article of an Encyclopædia tend to lower and abase his character. If the ministry neglect to propose the name of such a man to the sovereign, or the sovereign refuse to listen to their proposition, such conduct would well call down reproach and disapprobation. But when, as in Sir A. Ball's case, the reverse is the indisputable fact, we think such censure unauthorized, wanton, and unprovoked. Abating this single circumstance, *The Friend* has proved a most sociable companion in our library, and afforded us unfeigned pleasure. We have derived much information from its contents; we have been led to investigate many subjects, and in tracing the rivulet's course have approached the well-head of useful knowledge; and we even anticipate much entertainment, when we shall return to a second perusal at no very distant period.

93. 'R.', *Edinburgh Magazine*

January 1821, viii, 51-4

Mr. Editor,
I happened some time ago, by the merest accident, to fall in with a copy of Mr. Coleridge's *Friend*, which, though I had often heard it spoken of, at one time with the highest encomiums, and at another with ridicule and almost with contempt, I never had the good fortune to be able to peruse before. I have now done so, and the only return I can make for the pleasure and instruction which I have received is to use my feeble endeavour to call the attention of others to this eloquent and admirable book. In attempting to do so, I shall not be so bold as to venture on any abstract of the profound metaphysical speculations

which form the greater proportion of the work; but, after offering a very few remarks on the objects which Mr. Coleridge has had in view, I shall endeavour to win the attention of your readers to the *Friend*, by bringing under their notice some of the less abstruse, and, at present, more generally interesting discussions, with which Mr. C. has relieved, and rendered more palatable, the weightier matter which it has been his principal purpose to bring forward for the benefit of mankind. If, Mr. Editor, in what I shall offer, I may seem to you to speak of Mr. Coleridge's book in hyperbolical terms, I trust that you will not, on that account, deem my remarks unworthy of a place in your Miscellany. I give my fair and candid sentiments, and these, of course, are open to the animadversion of all those who may differ in opinion with me.

The *Friend*, Sir, appears to me to be the only work published in modern times which breathes the same lofty and profound spirit of philosophy, and is distinguished by the same originality and depth of speculation on the powers and destinies of the soul of man, as were ushered to the world in the brightest days of our literature. In addition to this, it is written with all the majesty and power of expression—with all the free and fearless vigour of language—and with all the copiousness of illustration, and beauty of imagery, which characterize the genuine old English style of our Taylors, and Miltons, and Hookers, and which were so lamentably frittered away into the cautious and nerveless neatness and timid simplicity of the Popes and Addisons of an after generation. It is not little to the credit of Mr. Coleridge, that, with so many temptations in his way, he has scorned to court mere popularity, which he might with the greatest ease have obtained, if he could so far have done violence to his natural propensities, as to have confined himself more to the surfaces of things, and endeavoured only to awaken our sensibilities and kindle our sympathies, by doling forth to us some eloquent pictures of passion, or some sparkling declamations upon themes of transitory interest. He has, happily for himself and for us, taken a higher stand, and pursued a prouder aim. He deals with severe but lofty themes. His object is to arouse the sleeping energies of the heart and soul to the contemplation of great and eternal truths, to lead us to ponder on the scope and destinies of our being, and to find our own scale in the universe, to seek out, by communing with our inner selves, those fixed and immutable laws of thought and action which Heaven has permitted our minds to perceive and know, to bring these to bear upon the different branches of knowledge, and thus lead to the 'formation of fixed principles in politics, morals, and religion'. These are great and difficult themes, possessing few attractions, for those who are contented to live and move in this world with the least possible trouble to themselves, and who are very little disposed to pester themselves with matters requiring the deepest thought and the severest self-examination. The consequence has been (as Mr. Coleridge himself must clearly have anticipated), that his book has been read by few, and has produced but little effect upon most of those who have given themselves the trouble of perusing it. It is not to this age, nor to such men, that Mr. Coleridge must look for his reward, yet he must even now feel a proud consciousness, that there *are* individuals capable of appreciating and of profiting by his labours, and that by these his name will never be pronounced without a feeling of reverence and admiration.

These brief and imperfect remarks cannot be better illustrated than by the following eloquent passage from Mr. Coleridge's first volume, where he notices that class of readers who hunger after the excitement of mere novelty, and who must have something quite new, and 'quite out of themselves, for whatever is deep within them must be old as the first dawn of human reason'.

To find no contradiction in the union of old and new, to contemplate the ANCIENT OF DAYS with feelings as fresh, as if they then sprang forth at his own fiat, this characterizes the minds that feel the riddle of the world, and may help to unravel it! To carry on the *feelings* of childhood into the *powers* of manhood, to combine the child's sense of wonder and novelty, with the appearances which every day, for perhaps forty years, had rendered familiar,

> With sun, and moon, and stars, throughout the year,
> And man and woman.——

This is the character and privilege of genius, and one of the marks which distinguish genius from talents. And so to represent familiar objects as to awaken the minds of others to a like freshness of sensation concerning them, (that constant accompaniment of mental, no less than of bodily convalescence,)—to the same modest self-questioning of a self-discovered and intelligent ignorance, which, like the deep and massy foundations of a Roman bridge, forms half of the whole structure, (*prudens interrogatio, dimidium scientiœ,* says Lord Bacon,)—this is the prime merit of genius, and its most unequivocal mode of manifestation. Who has not a thousand times seen it snow upon water? Who has not seen it with a new feeling since he has read Burns's comparison of Sensual Pleasure,

> To snow that falls upon a river,
> A moment white—then gone forever!

In philosophy, equally as in poetry, genius produces the strongest impressions of novelty, while it rescues the stalest and most admitted truths from the impotence caused by the very circumstance of their universal admission. Extremes meet—a proverb, by the bye, to collect and explain all the instances and exemplifications of which, would constitute and exhaust all philosophy. Truths, of all others, the most awful and mysterious, yet being, at the same time, of universal interest, are too often considered as so true, that they lose all the powers of truth, and lie bedridden in the dormitory of the soul, side by side with the most despised and exploded errors.

I have, perhaps, already dwelt long enough on these matters, yet I cannot help making a single observation in some degree connected with the labours of Mr. Coleridge, and one which seems to me to be of considerable importance. I allude to the incalculable benefit which would accrue to literature alone by the general adoption of one system of fixed principles, which should encompass and bind together, as links of one chain, all its different parts. The greatest and most important defect of our literature, in the present time, is its want of connection throughout its different branches. It resembles rather a number of separate sketches or portraits, than a complete picture, where every single component part goes to make up one grand impression, and where the impression conveyed by the whole reflects light upon all the different parts. We have theories here, and hypotheses there; we have essays, lectures, and periodical criticisms; some written under one supposed system, some under another, and many under none; and the consequence is, that any one who is disposed to examine the literature of the times with a view to its peculiar character and value, finds himself perplexed and confounded amongst opposite and conflicting opinions, and after giving up his mind successively to a hundred different impressions, sits down perfectly bewildered, and can give no reasonable account of the nature or tendency of what he has been endeavouring to understand.

The truth of this remark will, I think, be admitted (to a certain extent at least) by all who have paid any degree of attention to the *criticism* of the present day. Among all the multifarious periodical works and reviews which are so plentifully showered forth upon us, where shall we find one, in which any general principles or canons of criticism have been even attempted to be laid down, by which judgment was to be pronounced upon the different works to be criticised, and by which the merits or defects of every work were to be measured, in order to discover wherein, and to what degree, they existed? Is there ever any attempt to refer to any principle of our mental constitution, the causes of our admiration or dislike of the beauties or faults of any work? It may do very well for a mere reader to be 'pleased he knows not why, and cares not wherefore'; but this will hardly do for a critic, whose very office it is to 'tell us the *manner* of our being pleased'. Were it not that it would trespass far too long on your time, and on that of your readers, I have no doubt that I should easily be able to shew, that this total carelessness about principles is the besetting sin not merely of modern criticism, but of modern literature generally, and that it has introduced a 'dangerous influx of paltry and superficial compositions, alike hostile to soundness of judgment and purity of taste, a sea of frothy conceits and noisy dullness, upon which the spirit of the age is tossed hither and thither, not without great and frequent danger of entirely losing sight of the compass of meditation, and the polar star of truth'. (F. Schlegel.)

In some future paper I may make an attempt to trace the various causes which have contributed to bring about this state of things. I shall merely say at present, that I conceive the only adequate remedy would be, the general adoption of one great set of fixed principles, which should shape into form, and amalgamate together these confused and complicated materials—which should create symmetry and beauty out of this *rudis indigestaque moles*, this chaos of conflicting atoms, and present to us, in all its concentrated power and grandeur, the true spirit of British genius.

It is to the accomplishment of this, among other great ends, that the labours of Mr. Coleridge are directed, and in which he deserves the cordial co-operation of every true lover of the literature of his country. He himself has afforded an admirable and eloquent specimen of philosophical criticism in the examination of Mr. Wordsworth's poetry, which is contained in his 'Literary Life', and a few more of such treatises would go a great way in eradicating the prevailing vices of the criticism of the times.*

I have said so much more on this subject than I had intended, that it

* Mr. Hume justly remarks, in speaking of 'polite letters', that 'an artist must be better qualified to succeed in this undertaking; who, besides a delicate taste and quick apprehension, possesses an accurate knowledge of the internal fabric— the operations of the understanding—the workings of the passions, and the various species of sentiment which discriminate vice and virtue', &c. 'The anatomist presents to the eye the most hideous and disagreeable objects; but his science is highly useful to the painter in delineating even a Venus or an Helen', &c. *Inquiry into the Human Understanding*.

will be impossible for me, in this communication, to direct the attention of your readers to the delightful essays which Mr. Coleridge has interposed between his more profound speculations. I must, therefore, defer this till another period; though I cannot resist filling up the rest of my paper with the following beautiful and affecting tribute which he pays to the memory of a nameless friend.

A lady once asked me if I believed in ghosts and apparitions. I answered, with truth and simplicity, *No, Madam! I have seen far too many myself:* I have, indeed, a whole memorandum book filled with records of these phenomena, many of them interesting as facts and data for psychology, and affording some valuable materials for a theory of perception and its dependance on the memory and imagination. 'In omnem actum perceptionis imaginatio influit efficienter'. Wolfe. But HE is no more, who would have realized this idea,—who had already established the foundations and the law of the theory,—and for whom I had so often found a pleasure and a comfort, even during the wretched and restless nights of sickness, in watching and instantly recording these experiences of the world within us, of the 'gemina natura, quæ fit et facit, et creat, et creatur!' He is gone, my friend! my munificent co-patron, and not less the benefactor of my intellect! He who, beyond all other men known to me, added a fine and ever-wakeful sense of beauty to the most patient accuracy in experimental philosophy, and the profounder researches of metaphysical science; he who united all the play and spring of fancy with the subtlest discrimination and an inexorable judgment; and who controlled an almost painful exquisiteness of taste by a warmth of heart, which, in the practical relations of life, made allowances for faults as quick as the moral taste detected them; a warmth of heart, which was indeed noble and pre-eminent, for, alas! the genial feelings of health contributed no spark, toward it! Of these qualities I may speak, for they belonged to all mankind. The higher virtues, that were blessings to his friends, and the still higher that resided in and for his own soul, are themes for the energies of solitude—for the awfulness of prayer!—virtues exercised in the barrenness and desolation of his animal being; while he thirsted with the full stream at his lips, and yet with unwearied goodness poured out to all around him, like the master of a feast among his kindred in the day of his own gladness! Were it but for the remembrance of him alone, and of his lot here below, the disbelief of a future state would sadden the earth around me, and blight the very grass in the field.   R.

94. Unsigned article, 'An Estimate of the Literary Character and Works of Mr. Coleridge'

Monthly Magazine

December 1818, xlvi, 407-9

The man of genius, struggling with adverse circumstances, is one of the most affecting subjects which can be presented to the imagination. We see him first in remote and humble life, a delicate and ingenuous child, moved to sorrow by the slightest chiding, and pining over the recollection of the most trivial neglect; beloved, however, by his parents with a degree of solicitude beyond the common affection which they feel for their other children, persons of virtuous dispositions, their best efforts are employed to give him an education that may fit him for some department of business where hard labour is not required; and he is sent to a school among his superiors in fortune, where his diffidence is regarded as sullenness, and his thoughtfulness as stupidity. His progress is slow; and he retires from this scene without leaving any favourable impression. His next appearance is either in the office of a lawyer, or the shop of an apothecary, or perhaps in the counting-house of a merchant. The bent of his mind lies not to his business; and his parents, unable to discriminate the stirrings of awakening genius from discontent, become anxious respecting him; and, ascribing the change in his character to the profitless course of his reading, embitter the little leisure that he can devote to study, by reproaching him with misspending his time. By and by he acquires confidence in himself, and, in defiance of the anger of his friends, ventures before the public as an author. He has no literary associate to point out the indications of talent scattered through his first imperfect essays, and his publication consequently incurs contempt. Conscious, however, of possessing within himself the springs of a force not yet excited, and instructed by his first failure, he perseveres on towards the goal in view, and appears, at length, a second time with a little more success. Thus, step by step, unknown, uncheered, unpatronised, he gradually establishes a name; but his privations, his mortifications, his anxieties, and his sufferings, unparticipated and concealed, have, in the mean time, undermined his constitution, and he dies. He is then missed by the public, his works become sought after, *the trade* take up the question of his merits, and, about a century after his decease, the public assign to him a place among the ornaments of his country.

Mr. Coleridge is professedly a man of genius, but we do not know in what respects his career resembles that of the solitary whom we have thus described. It is however well known, that, if he has not been duly applauded in his own time, it has neither been owing to any lack of endeavour on his part, nor to want of assistance from his friends. We know not, indeed, a literary name oftener before the public than that of Coleridge, and we have never ceased to wonder how it should happen to be so. He has, it is true, occasionally sent forth lambent and luminous indications of talent; and we have contemplated them, from time to time, as the aurora of some glorious day, far out of the usual course of things. But, instead of a reddening morn, brightening more and more, the ineffectual phantom has as often been succeeded by a drizzle of nebulous sensibility, or a storm of sound and fury signifying nothing.

It has been prettily observed, that the genius of Mr. Coleridge has wings, but is without hands. It is not, however, in this respect only that it resembles the cherub of a tomb-stone, for it has a marvellous affection towards all the varieties of cadaveries, ghosts, and other church-yard denizens and luminaries. But, to drop the metaphor, it seems to us that this learned Theban possesses the faculty of rousing but one class of intellectual associations, namely, those which are connected with such superstitious sentiments as have a tendency to excite the passion of insane fear. For, whenever he has tried to do any thing else, his failures are among the most laughable extravagancies in literature. While, therefore, we do admit that he is possessed of one peculiar talent, and that one also in some degree 'wildly original', we at the same time take leave to question whether such a faculty is not more akin to genuine frenzy than to that sound and vigorous intellectual power which transmits a portion of its own energy in the impulse that it gives to the public mind.

'The Antient Mariner' of this poet is, in our opinion, the only one of his productions which justifies his pretensions to the title of a man of genius. It is full of vivid description, touches of an affecting simplicity, and, above all, it exhibits in the best manner that peculiar talent which may be considered as characteristic of his powers. It is, without doubt, the finest superstitious ballad in literature, the 'Lenora' of Burger[1] not excepted; and as far superior to the 'Thalabas' and 'Kehamahs' of his friend and reciprocal trumpeter, Southey, the poet-laureate, as the incidents in those stories are remote from probability and common sense. Indeed, common sense and probability have very little to do with any of their poems; but, admitting the principles on which they have constructed them, the fiction in the 'Antient Mariner' is far better sustained. His poem of 'Christabel' is only fit for the inmates of Bedlam. We are not acquainted in the history of literature with so great an insult offered to the public understanding as the publication of that rapsody of delirium, or with any thing so amusing as the sly roguery of those who, with such matchless command of countenance, ventured to recommend it to attention. It has, no doubt, here and there flashes of poetical expression, as every thing from the pen of Mr. Coleridge cannot but possess. But of coherency, and all that shows the superintendence of judgment or reason in composition, it is void and destitute. The indited ravings of a genuine madness would excite pity for the author, but the author of such a work is beyond compassion.

Mr. Coleridge is justly celebrated for his translations of Schiller, and it is much to be lamented that he has not been induced to favor the public with a complete version of that great poet's works. There is no other writer of the present day qualified to perform the task half so well. But, alas! he has taken to preaching *Lay Sermons*, demonstrating that he is an apostate in politics, and that in his reasoning he can be as absurd and unintelligible as in his rhyming. He has also delivered lectures on Shakespeare, whose works he does not at all understand; and he has published two anomalous volumes respecting himself, which contain a few passages of good writing, but so interlarded with idealess nonsense, that they only serve to show that the author has estimated his stature by the length of his shadow in a sun-set of his understanding. Some years ago he obtained a representation of a tragedy, called *Remorse*, which was received with a respectable degree of attention; but, as it contained no idea, either of incident or reflection, that showed the author to be possessed of any knowledge of human nature, it has sunk into oblivion, notwithstanding the beautiful fancies and elegant frenzy with which it abounds. In a word, if Mr. Coleridge is really a man of true genius, it is high time that he should give the world some proof less equivocal than any thing he has yet done.

[1] This poem had been adapted by Walter Scott as *The Chase of William and Helen* (1796).

95. J. G. Lockhart, *Blackwood's Edinburgh Magazine*

October 1819, vi, 3-12

This unsigned article in the series 'Essays on the Lake School' is attributed to J. G. Lockhart (A. L. Strout, op. cit., 112-13). Lockhart (1794-1854), a member of the editorial staff of *Blackwood's*, is now best known for his biography of Sir Walter Scott.

There is no question many of our readers will think we are doing a very useless, if not a very absurd thing, in writing, at this time of day, any thing like a review of the poetry of Mr. Coleridge. Several years have elapsed since any poetical production, entitled to much attention, has been published by him, and of those pieces in which the true strength and originality of his genius have been expressed, by far the greater part were presented to the world before any of the extensively popular poetry of the present day existed. In the midst, however, of the many new claimants which have arisen on every hand to solicit the ear and the favour of the readers of poetry, we are not sure that any one has had so much reason to complain of the slowness and inadequacy of the attention bestowed upon him as this gentleman, who is, comparatively speaking, a veteran of no inconsiderable standing. It is not easy to determine in what proportions the blame of his misfortunes should be divided between himself and his countrymen. That both have conducted themselves very culpably—at least very unwisely—begins at length, we believe, to be acknowledged by most of those whose opinion is of any consequence. As for us, we can never suppose ourselves to be ill employed when we are doing any thing that may serve in any measure to correct the errors of the public judgment on the one hand, or to stimulate the efforts of ill-requited, and thence, perhaps, desponding or slumbering genius on the other. To our Scottish readers we owe no apology whatever; on the contrary, we have no hesitation in saying, that in regard to this and a very great number of subjects besides, they stand quite in a different situation from our English readers. The reading-public of England (speaking largely) have not understood Mr. Coleridge's poems as they should have done. The reading-public of Scotland are in general ignorant that any such poems exist, and of those who are aware of their existence, the great majority owe the whole of their information concerning them to a few reviews, which, being written by men of talent and understanding, could not possibly have been written from any motives but those of malice, or with any purposes but those of misrepresentation.

The exercise of those unfair, and indeed wicked arts, by which the superficial mass of readers are so easily swayed in all their judgments, was, in this instance, more than commonly easy, by reason of the many singular eccentricities observable in almost all the productions of Mr. Coleridge's muse. What was already fantastic, it could not be no difficult matter for those practised wits, to represent, as utterly unmeaning, senseless, and absurd. But perhaps those who are accustomed to chuckle over the ludicrous analysis of serious poems, so common in our most popular reviews, might not be the worse for turning to the *Dictionnaire Philosophique*, and seeing with what success the same weapons have been employed there (by much greater wits, it is true), to transform and degrade into subjects of vulgar merriment all the beautiful narratives of the sacred books—their sublime simplicity and most deep tenderness. It is one of the most melancholy things in human nature, to see how often the grandest mysteries of the meditative soul lie at the mercy of surface-skimming ridicule, and self-satisfied rejoicing ignorance. It is like seeing the most solemn gestures of human dignity mimicked into grotesque absurdity by monkeys. Now, to our mind, the impropriety of the treatment which has been bestowed upon Mr. Coleridge, is mightily increased by the very facilities which the peculiarities of the poet himself afforded for its infliction. It is a thing not to be denied, that, even under the most favourable of circumstances, the greater part of the readers of English poetry could never have been expected thoroughly and intimately to understand the scope of those extraordinary productions, but this ought only to have acted as an additional motive with those who profess to be the guides of public opinion, to make them endeavour, as far as might in them lie, to render the true merits of those productions more visible to the eye of the less penetrating or less reflective. Unless such be the duty of professional critics on such occasions—and one, too, of the very noblest duties they can ever be called upon to discharge—we have erred very widely in all our ideas concerning such matters.

However well he might have been treated by the critics—nay, however largely he might have shared in the sweets of popularity—

there is no doubt Mr. Coleridge must still have continued to be a most eccentric author. But the true subject for regret is, that the unfavourable reception he has met with, seems to have led him to throw aside almost all regard for the associations of the multitude, and to think, that nothing could be so worthy of a great genius, so unworthily despised, as to reject in his subsequent compositions every standard save that of his own private whims. Now it was a very great pity that this remarkable man should have come so hastily to such a resolution as this, and by exaggerating his own original peculiarities, thus widened the breach every day between himself and the public. A poet, although he may have no great confidence in the public taste, as a guide to excellence, should always, at least, retain the wish to please it by the effect of his pieces, even while he may differ very widely from common opinions, with regard to the means to be employed. This is a truth which has unfortunately been very inadequately attended to by several of the most powerful geniuses of our time; but we know of none upon whose reputation its neglect has been so severely visited as on that of Mr. Coleridge. It is well, that in spite of every obstacle, the native power of his genius has still been able to scatter something of its image upon all his performances; it is well, above all things, that in moods of more genial enthusiasm he has created a few poems, which are, though short, in conception so original, and in execution so exquisite, that they cannot fail to render the name of Coleridge co-extensive with the language in which he has written, and to associate it for ever in the minds of all feeling and intelligent men, with those of the few chosen spirits that have touched in so many ages of the world the purest and most delicious chords of lyrical enchantment.

Those who think the most highly of the inborn power of this man's genius, must now, perhaps, be contented, if they would speak of him to the public with any effect, to suppress their enthusiasm in some measure, and take that power alone for granted which has been actually shown to exist. Were we to speak of him without regard to this prudential rule—and hazard the full expression of our own belief in his capacities—there is no question we should meet with many to acknowledge the propriety, to use the slightest phrase, of all that we might say, but these, we apprehend, would rather be found among those who have been in the society of Mr. Coleridge himself, and witnessed the astonishing effects which, according to every report, his eloquence never fails to produce upon those to whom it is addressed, than among men who have (like ourselves) been constrained to gather their only ideas of him from the printed productions of his genius. We are very willing to acknowledge, that our own excess of admiration may have been in some measure the result of peculiar circumstances—that it may have arisen out of things too minute to be explained—and which, if explained, would be regarded by many as merely fantastic and evanescent. What, according to our belief, Mr. Coleridge might have been—what, according to the same belief, he may yet be—these are matters in regard to which it may be wise to keep silence. We have no desire, had we the power, to trouble our readers with any very full exposition of our opinions, even concerning what he has done in poetry. Our only wish for the present, is to offer a few remarks in regard to one or two of his individual productions, which may perhaps excite the attention of such of our readers as have never yet paid any considerable attention to any of them, and this, more particularly, as we have already hinted, with a view to our own countrymen in Scotland.

The longest poem in the collection of the *Sibylline Leaves*, is the 'Rime of the Ancient Mariner', and to our feeling, it is by far the most wonderful also, the most original, and the most touching of all the productions of its author. From it alone, we are inclined to think an idea of the whole poetical genius of Mr. Coleridge might be gathered, such as could scarcely receive any very important addition either of extent or of distinctness, from a perusal of the whole of his other works. To speak of it at all is extremely difficult; above all the poems with which we are acquainted in any language, it is a poem to be felt, cherished, mused upon, not to be talked about, not capable of being described, analyzed, or criticised. It is the wildest of all the creations of genius, it is not like a thing of the living, listening, moving world, the very music of its words is like the melancholy mysterious breath of something sung to the sleeping ear, its images have the beauty, the grandeur, the incoherence of some mighty vision. The loveliness and the terror glide before us in turns—with, at one moment, the awful shadowy dimness—at another, the yet more awful distinctness of a majestic dream.

Dim and shadowy, and incoherent, however, though it be, how blind, how wilfully, or how foolishly blind must they have been who refused to see any meaning or purpose in the Tale of the Mariner! The imagery, indeed, may be said to be heaped up to superfluity—and so it is—the language to be redundant, and the narrative confused.

But surely those who cavilled at these things, did not consider into whose mouth the poet has put this ghastly story. A guest is proceeding to a bridal—the sound of the merry music is already in his ears—and the light shines clearly from the threshold to guide him to the festival. He is arrested on his way by an old man, who constrains him to listen— he seizes him by the hand—that he shakes free—but the old man has a more inevitable spell, and he holds him, and will not be silent.

> He holds him with his glittering eye,
> The wedding-guest stood still,
> And listens like a three-years child:
> The mariner hath his will.
>
> The wedding guest sat on a stone,
> He cannot chuse but hear—
> And thus spake on that ancient man,
> The bright-eyed mariner.

*   *   *   *   *

> The bride hath paced into the hall,
> Red as a rose is she:
> Nodding their heads before her goes
> The merry minstrelsy.
>
> The wedding-guest he beat his breast,
> Yet he cannot chuse but hear—
> And thus spake on that ancient man,
> The bright-eyed mariner.

In the beginning of the mariner's narrative, the language has all the impetus of a storm, and when the ship is suddenly locked among the polar ice, the change is as instantaneous as it is awful.

> The ice was here, the ice was there,
> The ice was all around:
> It cracked and growled, and roared and howl'd,
> Like noises in a swound!
>
> At length did cross an Albatross:
> Thorough the fog it came;
> As if it had been a Christian soul,
> We hailed it in God's name.
>
> It ate the food it ne'er had eat,
> And round and round it flew.
> The ice did split with a thunder-fit;
> The helmsman steer'd us through!

And a good south wind sprung up behind;
The Albatross did follow,
And every day, for food or play,
Came to the Mariner's hollo!

In mist or cloud, or mast or shroud,
It perch'd for vespers nine;
Whiles all the night, through fog-smoke white,
Glimmered the white Moon-shine.

'God save thee, ancient Mariner!
From the fiends that plague thee thus!—
Why look'st thou so?'—With my cross-bow
I shot the ALBATROSS!

All the subsequent miseries of the crew are represented by the poet as having been the consequences of this violation of the charities of sentiment; and these are the same miseries which the critics have spoken of, as being causeless and unmerited! We have no difficulty in confessing, that the ideas on which the intent of this poem hinges, and which to us seem to possess all beauty and pathos, may, after all, have been selected by the poet with a too great neglect of the ordinary sympathies. But if any one will submit himself to the magic that is around him, and suffer his senses and his imagination to be blended together, and exalted by the melody of the charmed words, and the splendour of the unnatural apparitions with which the mysterious scene is opened, surely he will experience no revulsion towards the centre and spirit of this lovely dream. There is the very essence of tenderness in the remorseful delight with which the Mariner dwells upon the image of the 'pious bird of omen good', as it

Every day, for food or play,
Came to the Mariner's hollo!

And the convulsive shudder with which he narrates the treacherous issue, bespeaks to us no pangs more than seem to have followed justly on that inhospitable crime. It seems as if the very spirit of the universe had been stunned by the wanton cruelty of the Mariner—as if earth, sea, and sky, had all become dead and stagnant in the extinction of the moving breath of love and gentleness.

All in a hot and copper sky,
The bloody Sun, at noon,
Right up above the mast did stand,
No bigger than the moon.

> Day after day, after day,
> We stuck, nor breath nor motion,
> As idle as a painted ship
> Upon a painted ocean.
>
> Water, water, every where,
> And all the boards did shrink;
> Water, water, every where,
> Nor any drop to drink.
>
> The very deep did rot: O Christ!
> That ever this should be!
> Yea, slimy things did crawl with legs
> Upon the slimy sea.
>
> About, about, in reel and rout
> The death-fires danced at night;
> The water, like a witch's oils,
> Burnt green, and blue, and white.
>
> Ah! well a-day! what evil looks
> Had I from old and young!
> Instead of the cross, the Albatross
> About my neck was hung.

In the 'weary time' which follows, a spectre-ship sails between them and the 'broad bright sun' in the west. This part of the poem is much improved in this last edition of it. The male and the female skeleton in the spectre-ship, or, as they are now called, 'DEATH and LIFE-IN-DEATH', have diced for the ship's crew—and she, the latter, has won the ancient Mariner. These verses are, we think, quite new. The second of them is, perhaps, the most exquisite in the whole poem.

> The naked hulk alongside came,
> And the twain were casting dice;
> 'The game is done! I've won, I've won!'
> Quoth she, and whistles thrice.
>
> *The Sun's rim dips; the stars rush out:*
> *At one stride comes the dark;*
> *With far-heard whisper, o'er the sea,*
> *Off shot the spectre-bark.*
>
> We listen'd and look'd sideways up!
> Fear at my heart, as at a cup,
> My life-blood seem'd to sip!
> The stars were dim, and thick the night,
> The steersman's face by his lamp gleam'd white;

> From the sails the dews did drip—
> Till clombe above the eastern bar
> The horned Moon, with one bright star
> Within the nether tip.

The crew, who had approved in calmness the sin that had been committed in wantonness and madness, die, and the Mariner alone is preserved by the rise of an expiatory feeling in his mind. Pain, sorrow, remorse, there are not enough; the wound must be healed by a heartfelt sacrifice to the same spirit of universal love which had been bruised in its infliction.

> The moving Moon went up the sky,
> And no where did abide:
> Softly she was going up,
> And a star or two beside—
>
> Her beams bemock'd the sultry main,
> Like April hoar-frost spread;
> But where the ship's huge shadow lay,
> The charmed water burnt alway
> A still and awful red.
>
> Beyond the shadow of the ship,
> I watch'd the water-snakes:
> They moved in tracts of shining white,
> And when they reared, the elfish light
> Fell off in hoary flakes.
>
> Within the shadow of the ship
> I watch'd their rich attire:
> Blue, glossy green, and velvet black,
> They coiled and swam; and every track
> Was a flash of golden fire.
>
> O happy living things! no tongue
> Their beauty might declare:
> A spring of love gusht from my heart,
> And I blessed them unaware!
> Sure my kind saint took pity on me,
> And I blessed them unaware.
>
> The self same moment I could pray;
> And from my neck so free
> The Albatross fell off, and sank
> Like lead into the sea.

It is needless to proceed any longer in this, for the principle of the poem is all contained in the last of these extracts. Had the ballad been more interwoven with sources of prolonged emotion extending throughout —and had the relation of the imagery to the purport and essence of the piece been a little more close—it does not seem to us that any thing more could have been desired in a poem such as this. As it is, the effect of the wild wandering magnificence of imagination in the details of the dream-like story is a thing that cannot be forgotten. It is as if we had seen real spectres, and were for ever to be haunted. The unconnected and fantastic variety of the images that have been piled up before us works upon the fancy, as an evening sky made up of half lurid castellated clouds—half of clear unpolluted azure—would upon the eye. It is like the fitful concert of fine sounds which the Mariner himself hears after his spirit has been melted, and the ship has begun to sail homewards.

> Around, around, flew each sweet sound,
> Then darted to the Sun;
> Slowly the sounds came back again,
> Now mixed, now one by one.
>
> Sometimes a-dropping from the sky
> I heard the sky-lark sing;
> Sometimes all little birds that are,
> How they seem'd to fill the sea and air
> With their sweet jargoning!
>
> And now 'twas like all instruments,
> Now like a lonely flute;
> And now it is an angel's song,
> That makes the Heavens be mute.
>
> It ceased; yet still the sails made on
> A pleasant noise till noon,
> A noise like of a hidden brook
> In the leafy month of June,
> That to the sleeping woods all night
> Singeth a quiet tune.

The conclusion has always appeared to us to be happy and graceful in the utmost degree. The actual surface-life of the world is brought close into contact with the life of sentiment—the soul that is as much alive, and enjoys, and suffers as much in dreams and visions of the night as by daylight. One feels with what a heavy eye the Ancient Mariner must look and listen to the pomps and merry-makings—even to the innocent enjoyments—of those whose experience has only been of things tangible. One feels that to him another world—we do not mean a supernatural, but a more exquisitely and deeply natural world—has been revealed, and that the repose of his spirit can only be in the contemplation of things that are not to pass away. The sad and solemn indifference of his mood is communicated to his hearer, and we feel that even after reading what he had heard, it were better to 'turn from the bridegroom's door'.

> O Wedding-Guest! this soul hath been
> Alone on a wide wide sea:
> So lonely 'twas, that God himself
> Scarce seemed there to be.
>
> O sweeter than the marriage-feast,
> 'Tis sweeter far to me,
> To walk together to the kirk
> With a goodly company!—
>
> To walk together to the kirk,
> And all together pray,
> While each to his great Father bends,
> Old men, and babes, and loving friends,
> And youths and maidens gay!
>
> Farewell, farewell! but this I tell
> To thee, thou Wedding-Guest!
> He prayeth well, who loveth well
> Both man, and bird, and beast.
>
> He prayeth best, who loveth best
> All things both great and small;
> For the dear God who loveth us,
> He made and loveth all.
>
> The Mariner, whose eye is bright,
> Whose beard with age is hoar,
> Is gone; and now the Wedding-guest
> Turned from the bridegroom's door.
>
> He went like one that hath been stunned,
> And is of sense forlorn:
> A SADDER AND A WISER MAN,
> HE ROSE THE MORROW MORN.—

Of all the author's productions, the one which seems most akin to the 'Ancient Mariner', is 'Christabel', a wonderful piece of poetry, which has been far less understood, and is as yet far less known than the other. This performance does not make its appearance in the *Sibylline*

Leaves—but we hope Mr. Coleridge will never omit it in any future collection. The reception it met with was no doubt a very discouraging one, more particularly when contrasted with the vehement admiration which seems to have been expressed by all who saw it while yet in MS. Mr. Coleridge, however, should remember that the opinions of the few who saw and admired 'Christabel' then, may very well, without any over-weening partiality on his part, be put into competition with the many who have derided it since. Those who know the secret history of the poem, and compare it with the productions of the most popular poets of our time, will have no difficulty in perceiving how deep an impression his remarkable creation had made on the minds of those of his contemporaries, whose approbation was most deserving to be an object of ambition with such a man as Mr. Coleridge.

'Christabel', as our readers are aware, is only a fragment, and had been in existence for many years antecedent to the time of its publication. Neither has the author assigned any reason either for the long delay of its appearance, or for the imperfect state in which he has at last suffered it to appear. In all probability he had waited long in the hope of being able to finish it to his satisfaction; but finding that he was never revisited by a mood sufficiently genial, he determined to let the piece be printed as it was. It is not in the history of 'Christabel' alone that we have seen reason to suspect Mr. Coleridge of being by far too passive in his notions concerning the mode in which a poet ought to deal with his muse. It is very true, that the best conceptions and designs are frequently those which occur to a man of fine talents, without having been painfully sought after: but the exertion of the Will is always necessary in the worthy execution of them. It behoves a poet, like any other artist, after he has fairly conceived the idea of his piece, to set about realising it in good earnest, and to use his most persevering attention in considering how all its parts are to be adapted and conjoined. It does not appear that even the language of a poem can arise spontaneously throughout like a strain of music, any more than the colours of the painter will go and arrange themselves on his canvass, while he is musing on the subject in another room. Language is a material which it requires no little labour to reduce into beautiful forms, a truth of which the ancients were, above all others, well and continually aware. For although vivid ideas naturally suggest happy expressions, yet the latter are, as it were, only insulated traits or features, which require much management in the joining, and the art of the composer is seen in the symmetry of the whole structure. Now, in many respects Mr. Coleridge seems too anxious to enjoy the advantages of an inspired writer, and to produce his poetry at once in its perfect form, like the palaces which spring out of the desert in complete splendour at a single rubbing of the lamp in the Arabian Tale. But carefulness above all is necessary to a poet in these latter days, when the ordinary medium through which things are viewed is so very far from being poetical, and when the natural strain of scarcely any man's associations can be expected to be of that sort which is most akin to high and poetical feeling. There is no question there are many, very many passages in the poetry of this writer, which shew what excellent things may be done under the impulse of a happy moment, passages in which the language, above all things, has such aërial graces as would have been utterly beyond the reach of any person who might have attempted to produce the like, without being able to lift his spirit into the same ecstatic mood. It is not to be denied, however, that among the whole of his poems there are only a few in the composition of which he seems to have been blessed all throughout with the same sustaining energy of afflatus. The 'Mariner'—we need not say—is one of these. The poem 'Love' is another, and were 'Christabel' completed as it has been begun, we doubt not it would be allowed by all who are capable of tasting the merits of such poetry, to be a third, and, perhaps, the most splendid of the three.

It is impossible to gather from the part which has been published any conception of what is the meditated conclusion of the story of 'Christabel'. Incidents can never be fairly judged of till we know what they lead to. Of those which occur in the first and second cantos of this poem, there is no doubt many appear at present very strange and disagreeable, and the sooner the remainder comes forth to explain them, the better. One thing is evident, that no man need sit down to read 'Christabel' with any prospect of gratification, whose mind has not rejoiced habitually in the luxury of visionary and superstitious reveries. He that is determined to try every thing by the standard of what is called common sense, and who has an aversion to admit, even in poetry, of the existence of things more than are dreamt of in philosophy, had better not open this production, which is only proper for a solitary couch and a midnight taper. Mr. Coleridge is the prince of superstitious poets; and he that does not read 'Christabel' with a strange and harrowing feeling of mysterious dread, may be assured that his soul is made of impenetrable stuff.

The circumstances with which the poem opens are admirably

conceived. There is in all the images introduced a certain fearful stillness and ominous meaning, the effect of which can never be forgotten. The language, also, is so much in harmony with the rude era of the tale, that it seems scarcely to have been written in the present age, and is indeed a wonderful proof of what genius can effect, in defiance of unfavourable associations. Whoever has had his mind penetrated with the true expression of a Gothic building, will find a similar impression conveyed by the vein of language employed in this legend. The manners, also, and forms of courtesy ascribed to the personages, are full of solemn grace.

> —He kissed her forehead as he spake;
> And Geraldine, in maiden wise,
> Casting down her large bright eyes,
> With blushing cheek and courtesy fine,
> Turned her from Sir Leoline;
> Softly gathering up her train,
> That o'er her right arm fell again,
> And folded her arms across her chest,
> And couched her head upon her breast.

This is only one little example of the antique stateliness that breathes over the whole of their demeanour. But if these things are not perceived by the reader, it is altogether in vain to point them out to him.

The general import of the poem cannot yet be guessed at; but it is evident that the mysterious lady whom Christabel meets in the forest—whom she introduces by stealth into the castle of her father—and in whom her father recognizes the daughter of the long-estranged friend of his youth, Sir Roland De Vaux of Triermaine, is some evil being; whether demon or only demon-visited, we have no means to ascertain. Nothing can be finer than the description of the manner in which this strange visitant is first introduced.

[quotes ll. 43-189 (PW, i, 217-22)]

With what exquisite delicacy are all these hints of the true character of this stranger imagined. The difficulty of passing the threshold—the dread and incapacity of prayer—the moaning of the old mastiff in his sleep—the rekindling of the lying embers as she passes—the influence of the lamp 'fastened to the angel's feet'. All these are conceived in the most perfect beauty.

The next intimation is of a far more fearful and lofty kind. The stranger is invited by Christabel to drink of wine made by [her] departed mother; and listens to the tale of that mother's fate who died it seems, 'in the hour that Christabel was born'. Christabel expresses a wish of natural and innocent simplicity:

> O mother dear that thou wert here—
> —I would, said Geraldine she were.—

Mark the result.

> But soon with alter'd voice, said she—
> 'Off, wandering mother! Peak and pine!
> 'I have power to bid thee flee'.
> Alas! What ails poor Geraldine?
> Why stares she with unsettled eye?
> Can she the bodiless dead espy?
> And why with hollow voice cries she,
> 'Off, woman, off! this hour is mine—
> 'Though thou her guardian spirit be,
> 'Off, woman, off! 'tis given to me'.
>
> Then Christabel knelt by the lady's side,
> And rais'd to heaven her eyes so blue—
> Alas! said she, this ghastly ride—
> Dear lady! it hath wilder'd you!
> The lady wip'd her moist cold brow,
> And faintly said, ''Tis over now!'
>
> Again the wild-flower wine she drank:
> Her fair large eyes 'gan glitter bright,
> And from the floor whereon she sank,
> The lofty lady stood upright:
> She was most beautiful to see,
> Like a lady of a far countrèe.

After the notion of evil has once been suggested to the reader, the external beauty and great mildness of demeanour ascribed to the Stranger produce only the deeper feeling of terror: and they contrast, in a manner singularly impressive, with the small revelations which every now and then take place of what is concealed beneath them. It is upon this happy contrast that the interest of the whole piece chiefly hinges, and would Mr. Coleridge only take heart, and complete what he has so nobly begun, he would probably make 'Christabel' the finest exemplification to be found in the English, or perhaps in any language since Homer's, of an idea which may be traced in most popular superstitions.

In these two poems—we might even say in the extracts we have made from them—the poetical faculties of Coleridge are abundantly exhibited in the whole power and charm of their native beauty. That such exercise of these faculties may have been so far injudicious as not calculated to awaken much of the ordinary sympathies of mankind, but rather addressing every thing to feelings of which in their full strength and sway only a few are capable, all this is a reproach easy to be made, and in a great measure perhaps it may be a well-founded reproach. But nothing surely can be more unfair, than to overlook or deny the existence of such beauty and such strength on any grounds of real or pretended misapplication. That the author of these productions is a poet of a most noble class, a poet most original in his conceptions, most masterly in his execution, above all things a most inimitable master of the language of poetry, it is impossible to deny. His powers indeed, to judge from what of them that has been put forth and exhibited, may not be of the widest, or even of the very highest kind. So far as they go, surely, they are the most exquisite of powers. In his mixture of all the awful and all the gentle graces of conception, in his sway of wild, solitary, dreamy phantasies, in his music of words, and magic of numbers, we think he stands absolutely alone among all the poets of the most poetical age.

In one of the great John Müller's early letters (compositions, by the way, which it is a thousand pities the English reader should have no access to admire)[1] there is a fine passionate disquisition on *the power of words*—and on the unrivalled use of that power exemplified in the writings of Rousseau. 'He sways mankind with that delicious might', says the youthful historian, 'as Jupiter does with his lightnings'. We know not that there is any English poet who owes so much to this single element of power as Coleridge. It appears to us that there is not one of them, at least not one that has written since the age of Elizabeth, in whose use of *words* the most delicate sense of beauty concurs with so much exquisite subtlety of metaphysical perception. To illustrate this by individual examples is out of the question, but we think a little examination would satisfy any person who is accustomed to the study of language of the justice of what we have said. In the kind of poetry in which he has chiefly dealt, there can be no doubt the effect of his peculiar mastery over this instrument has been singularly happy, more so than, perhaps, it could have been in any other. The whole essence of his poetry is more akin to music than that of any other poetry

[1] Johannes von Müller (1752-1809), historian.

we have ever met with. Speaking generally, his poetry is not the poetry of high imagination, nor of teeming fancy, nor of overflowing sentiment, least of all, is it the poetry of intense or overmastering passion. If there be such a thing as poetry of the senses *strung* to imagination, such is his. It lies in the senses, but they are senses breathed upon by imagination, having reference to the imagination though they do not reach to it, having a sympathy, not an union, with the imagination, like the beauty of flowers. In Milton there is between sense and imagination a strict union, their actions are blended into one. In Coleridge what is borrowed from imagination or affection is brought to sense—sense is his sphere. In him the pulses of sense seem to die away in sense. The emotions in which he deals, even the love in which he deals, can scarcely be said to belong to the class of what are properly called passions. The love he describes the best is a romantic and spiritual movement of wonder, blended and exalted with an ineffable suffusion of the powers of sense. There is more of aerial romance, than of genuine tenderness, even in the peerless love of his Genevieve. Her silent emotions are an unknown world which her minstrel watches with fear and hope, and yet there is exquisite propriety in calling that poem 'Love', for it truly represents the essence of that passion, where the power acquired over the human soul depends so much upon the awakening, for a time, of the idea of infinitude, and the bathing of the universal spirit in one interminable sea of thoughts undefineable. We are aware that this inimitable poem is better known than any of its author's productions, and doubt not that many hundreds of our readers have got it by heart long ago, without knowing by whom it was written, but there can be no harm in quoting it, for they that have read it the most frequently will be the most willing to read it again.

[quotes 'Love' (*PW*, i, 330-5)]

We shall take an early opportunity of offering a few remarks on Mr. Coleridge's efforts in tragedy, and in particular on his wonderful translation, or rather improvement of the *Wallenstein*. We shall then, perhaps, be able still more effectually to carry our readers along with us, when we presume to address a few words of expostulation to this remarkable man on the strange and unworthy indolence which has, for so many years, condemned so many of his high gifts to slumber in comparative uselessness and inaction.

> A cheerful soul is what the muses love—
> A soaring spirit is their prime delight.

96. Excerpts from unsigned articles on the state of the contemporary theatre, *London Magazine*

April 1820, i, 436
December 1820, ii, 687

... But what shall we say of Mr. Coleridge, who is the author not only of a successful but a meritorious tragedy? We may say of him what he has said of Mr. Maturin, that he is of the transcendental German school. He is a florid poet, and an ingenious metaphysician, who mistakes scholastic speculations for the intricate windings of the passions, and assigns possible reasons instead of actual motives for the excesses of his characters. He gives us studied special-pleadings for the involuntary bursts of feeling, and the needless strain of tinkling sentiments, for the point-blank language of nature. His *Remorse* is a spurious tragedy. Take the following passage, and then ask, whether the charge of sophistry and paradox, and dangerous morality, to startle the audience, in lieu of more legitimate methods of exciting their sympathy, which he brings against the author of *Bertram*, may not be retorted on his own head. Ordonio is made to defend the project of murdering his brother by such arguments as the following:

> What? if one reptile sting another reptile?
> Where is the crime? The goodly face of nature
> Hath one disfeaturing stain the less upon it.
> Are we not all predestined Transiency,
> And cold Dishonor? Grant it, that this hand
> *Had* given a morsel to the hungry worms
> Somewhat too early—where's the crime of this?
> That this must needs bring on the idiotcy
> Of moist-eyed Penitence—'tis like a dream!
> Say, I had lay'd a body in the sun!
> Well! in a month there swarm forth from the corse
> A thousand, nay, ten thousand sentient beings
> In place of that one man.—Say, I had *killed* him!

> Yet who shall tell me that each one and all
> Of these ten thousand lives is not as happy,
> As that one life, which being push'd aside
> Made room for these unnumber'd!

This is a way in which no one ever justified a murder to his own mind. . . . the duller the stage grows, the gayer and more edifying must we become in ourselves: the less we have to say about that, the more room we have to talk about other things. Now would be the time for Mr. Coleridge to turn his talents to account, and write for the stage, when there is no topic to confine his pen, or 'constrain his genius by mastery'. 'With mighty wings outspread, his imagination might brood over the void and make it pregnant'. Under the assumed head of the Drama, he might unfold the whole mysteries of Swedenborg, or ascend the third heaven of invention with Jacob Behmen: he might write a treatise on all the unknown sciences, and finish the *Encylopedia Metropolitana* in a pocket form: nay, he might bring to a satisfactory close his own dissertation on the difference between the Imagination and the Fancy, before, in all probability, another great actor appears, or another tragedy or comedy is written. He is the man of all others to swim on empty bladders in a sea, without shore or soundings: to drive an empty-coach without passengers or lading, and arrive behind his time; to write marginal notes without a text: to look into a millstone to foster the rising genius of the age; to 'see merit in the chaos of its elements, and discern perfection in the great obscurity of nothing', as his most favourite author, Sir Thomas Brown, has it on another occasion. Alas! we have no such creative talents: we cannot amplify, expand, raise our flimsy discourse, as the gaseous matter fills and lifts the round, glittering, slow-sailing balloon, to 'the up-turned eyes of wondering mortals'.

97. Excerpts from an unsigned article, 'The Mohock Magazine', *London Magazine*

December 1820, ii, 668-77

Attributed to the editor of the *London Magazine*, John Scott (1783-1821) (Walter Graham, *English Literary Periodicals*, New York 1930, 281).

Blackwood's Magazine, therefore, may fairly be complimented with the title of THE INFAMOUS SCOTCH HOAX;[1] and it will be admitted infinitely to outshine the *Stock Exchange Hoax* of pillory fame.[1] These are assertions, however, that ought not to be made in language at all akin to that of levity; for they must heap indelible disgrace, either on the persons against whom they are directed, or on us by whom they are hazarded. We accept and acknowledge the responsibility thus conveyed; and challenge attention to the facts we are about to bring forward, as not only sufficient to prove the substantial truth of our allegations, but adequate to warrant the favourable presumption we claim for our motives in undertaking this task of exposure. We do most seriously and sincerely declare, that we have been induced to write these articles solely by the indignation rising and swelling in our minds at the still-renewed spectacle of outrage, hypocrisy, and fraud, which the succeeding Numbers of Mr. Blackwood's Publication present. Long impunity, or, at least, insufficient exposure, from whatever cause proceeding, has at length converted what was at first but a system of provocation, into a downright *system of terror*. We know for a fact, and dare contradiction, that Blackwood has openly vaunted of holding to grateful behaviour an individual who had been first *abused*, and then *defended* by the *same writer* in his Magazine: '*if he is not duly respectful, we have more for him from the same hand!*' Such is the triumph of Scotch toryism over Scotch whiggism in Blackwood! A few more such victories will be sufficient to disgrace it for ever. It is impossible, almost, to conceive any one species of deceit, of unfair aggression, of the violation

[1] For a discussion of this attempt to defraud the public, which was made on 21 February 1814, see Alex. McRae, *A Disclosure of the Hoax* (1815).

454

of all the rules of proper criticism, of individual persecution, of false pretension, and audacious boasting, falling within the range of literary profligacy, which the writers in this publication do not habitually practice. It has been their aim, from its very commencement, as we observed in our last paper under this head, to excite the public expectation and attention, by the perpetration of gross wrongs, affecting the honour of literature, and the peace of individuals. In their endeavours to do this, they have not restricted themselves to the malignancy of satire, and the bitterness of personal invective; but, with these, they have coupled a duplicity and treachery, as mean and grovelling as their scurrility has been foul and venomous—*Three times within the space of very little more than two years, have they been compelled to pay, to injured individuals, heavy forfeitures, for calumnies uttered against private character, and to the detriment of private interests;* AND IN NO ONE OF THESE THREE HAVE THEY ATTEMPTED DEFENCE OR JUSTIFICATION OF ANY KIND! No attempt has been made by them, in any of these cases, to show mistake or misconception; nor have they once dared to stand boldly on the honesty of their strictures, and vindicate manfully what they had uttered rancorously. No, in each of these instances, the offence has been flagrant and scandalous, and the penalty has been paid, quietly and unresistingly. In two of them, wilful malice was apparent beyond contradiction, and the means taken to gratify it were still more disgraceful than the intention. In the first, bodily infirmity was alluded to, amidst a heap of slanders and indecencies, which were afterwards apologised for in the lump, and have been since repeated in detail. In the second, wilful falsehood, as well as wilful malice, stood barefacedly exposed: the writer of the queries addressed to Mr. Hazlitt, affirmed, under the guise of an interrogation, what he could not but know was untrue, nay totally without foundation of any kind, and, when called to account for this, he acknowledged the lie by silently paying its forfeit! This writer, who assumed *the mask of a correspondent*, is now *known to be Mr. Blackwood's principal Editor*, not the gentleman who has been recently withdrawn from the Magazine to Moral Philosophy, but *Doctor Morris,** the individual who has been obliged, the other day, to pay (being the third penalty) four hundred pounds to a wantonly injured tradesman, and whose hand, it is now well understood, has thrown most of the envenomed darts, launched against character and

---

* His *alias* is well known.[1]

[1] The pseudonym was used by J. G. Lockhart.

feeling from the quarter in question. Nothing in the annals of disgraceful publication can be quoted to equal the course of conduct pursued by this man, in his capacity of Editor. While he has been uttering these calumnies, and paying these penalties, he has *forged testimonials from living and celebrated men to the merits of his Magazine,* which he has published with their names at full, trusting to the very audacity of the measure to escape detection, or, at least, exposure. We have lately seen him giving, as from a private letter from Goethe, *a sentence of clumsy German!* After writing, as the first fruits of his Editorship, a most virulent and offensive libel against Mr. Coleridge, in which the 'grinning and idiot self-complacency' of that gentleman is talked of; in which he is described as having exposed himself 'dead drunk in the house of a Brummagem Patriot'—after all this, he has found means to draw, for once, a private and civil letter from the object of these indecent aspersions; and this letter, contrary to the usage of gentlemen, he has published in his Magazine, without the writer's consent, and, as we have reason to know, *very much to the writer's displeasure.* It appears, then, that either way is indifferent to this person: if the letters are written, confidence is violated in their publication; if they are not written, they are fabricated for that purpose. . . .

On the head of equal insincerity in praise and abuse, let us turn to the pseudo Doctor—the malignant Emperor of the Mohocks. *Morris* is understood to be the author of the extremely scurrilous article on Mr. Coleridge, which appeared in No. 7, of *Blackwood.*[1] Of Mr. C. it is there said, 'it seems impossible that he can be greatly respected, either by the public or himself': 'he seems to consider the mighty universe itself as nothing better than a mirror, in which, with a grinning and idiot self-complacency, he may contemplate the physiognomy of Samuel Taylor Coleridge': 'so deplorable a delusion as his, has only been equalled by that of Joanna Southcote, who mistook a complaint in the bowels for the divine afflatus': the article proceeds to allude to 'drunkenness', and 'desertion of wife and children', but we are by no means inclined to prolong unnecessarily our quotations; nor have we any thing further to say of them than that Mr. Coleridge has been since *hoaxed* into believing the author of the above well-inclined towards him! Under the influence of this idea, with all the simplicity of a metaphysical philosopher, he lately addressed a private letter to the present Editor of *Blackwood's Magazine,* which private letter was no sooner received, *than it was sent off to Blackwood's printing office;* and in

[1] See No. 78.

No. 42, there, sure enough, it appears,[1] with the signature of S. T. Coleridge (not Samuel Taylor in full) and an accompanying note from Dr. *Morris*, calling attention to it as 'a very *characteristic* letter of one, whom', says the Doctor, 'I well know that *you*', Christopher North—alias Doctor Morris himself, 'agree with *me* in honouring among the highest!' It happens that we can put the infamous treachery of this treatment of Mr. Coleridge beyond all doubt. Christopher North is the *nomme de guerre* for the Editor of Blackwood; and Morris, the same individual, under another mask, adopted for the purpose of puffing the Magazine, says he is sure of the Editor's sympathy with himself *in honouring S. T. C. amongst the highest*. So far so good: this is in No. 42. Turn we now then to No. 7, where we find S. T. C. described as 'lying dead drunk in the house of a Brummagem patriot', 'exposing himself to the insults of the vile and vulgar': *who*, may we venture to ask, wrote this piece of abuse? It stands the *first article* of the Number; and the number too is the *first of the Mohock's management;* and the paper *is* not *signed, with initials, or any assumed name, as from a Correspondent*, but is conveyed as from the Editor in the usual editorial style. *More than all this*, in a notice, given in the name of the Editor, which we find on the very page facing this piece of abuse, it is thus announced: 'Our OWN OPINIONS, *and those of our* REGULAR CORRESPONDENTS *will be found* UNIFORMLY CONSISTENT—*but we invite all intelligent persons who choose it, to lay their ideas before the world in our publication; and we only reserve to ourselves* THE RIGHT OF COMMENTING UPON WHAT WE DO NOT APPROVE'. What are the palpable deductions here? If the article accusing Mr. Coleridge of *'dishonest quackery'* be not written by the *Editor himself*, it must be written by one of his *regular Correspondents*, for it is the first article of the new management, and is not signed, as it would have been if written by a casual correspondent. *'Our own opinions, and those of our regular Correspondents will be found uniformly consistent!'* The Editor is thus incontestably bound to the numerous traducing assertions made in the article; among others, to this, *'that all good men, of all parties, regard Mr. Coleridge with pity and contempt!'* We say, he is, in every way, and without the possibility of escape, bound to them, for, supposing he were to affirm that the article in question was written neither by the Editor of the Magazine, nor by a regular Correspondent, we might ask, where then is *the comment upon what he did not approve*, which he expressly reserved to himself the right of making in such cases? He now declares himself to be one of those who *honour Mr. Coleridge amongst the*

[1] *Blackwood's Edinburgh Magazine*, September 1820, vii, 629-31.

highest: could he, then, as an honest man have permitted a chance contributor to traduce the object of his veneration in the most insulting language, without a word of caution, without an expression of dissent —immediately too after telling the reader that with all the matter which should appear in the Magazine, running in the usual editorial style, the Editor was to be considered as agreeing in opinion? Careless oversight cannot be thought of with reference to the first Number of the new management: this was to afford a specimen of the spirit, and execution of the work; and would the commencing article be slightly regarded under such circumstances? Would it be selected strongly hostile to the Editor's own sentiments: calumnious in the last degree towards one whom the Editor *honoured amongst the highest?* It would be trifling with the understandings of our readers to endeavour to strengthen the argument. The present Editor of *Blackwood's Magazine*, whether challenged in his own name, or under his *aliases* of Doctor Morris and Christopher North, stands deprived of all benefit from his numerous disguisements, and counterfeited, and falsified titles, and is clearly convicted of foul treachery towards 'Samuel Taylor Coleridge', 'the illustrious and excellent friend', whom he, Peter Morris, declares to himself, Christopher North, he holds *in honour amongst the highest!*

We have gone into this examination of evidence tediously, perhaps, and we believe unnecessarily: the present Editor of *Blackwood's Magazine* stands on the face of the publication chargeable with the remarks on the *Biographia Literaria* of Mr. Coleridge: they bear their own evidence of being his, and we might have spared ourselves the trouble of going through the process of proving what he will not, we should think, dare to deny. There is now a perfect understanding in Edinburgh, that the same man wrote the *first* article, at least, signed Z. in which Mr. Coleridge is styled 'a still greater quack than Leigh Hunt'. The most infamous part, however, of the treatment, which Mr. Coleridge has received at this person's hands, clearly is the recent *unauthorized publication of his private letter.* No man who reads that letter can avoid perceiving that it is as unfit to be given to the public eye as any letter can be; and the dirty design of exposing the writer to the sneers and ridicule of the sarcastic; the insolent advantage taken of the injudicious confidence of a strangely constituted, though eminently gifted mind; the laughing in his face, and winking at the bye-standers, worthy of a Mohock, plainly to be discerned in the insulting introduction, couple infamously with the abusive article in No. 7 of this Magazine, and add consummate treachery as the last aggravation of an outrage, which is as unmanly as it is gross. Its perpetrator deprives himself of all pretension to the character of a gentleman, or rather, we should say, shows himself to be '*a fellow by the hand of nature marked, quoted, and signed, to do a deed of shame*'. Personal communication with such a man is deadly: one would suspect his palm to be poisoned, if he extended his hand in apparent friendship. If there be one point of honour more settled and recognized than another in society, it is the sanctity of a private letter: the individual who receives it has even a less right to make it public without the permission of its writer, than the individual who might happen to find it, were it accidentally lost. Innumerable are the dissensions, the disgusts, the irreparable mischiefs that would desolate private life if this rule were once questioned. In this very letter of Mr. Coleridge we can see a cause of alienation and pain, which ought, at least, to give great regret to its over-confiding writer, now it is in print, and which we have no doubt has done so. We can take upon ourselves to state that he disclaims having ever authorised or contemplated its publication; and that he considers such publication as a most unfair advantage taken of him. The forgery of a signature, as a hoax, even when malevolently and treacherously done, is not so absolutely irreconcileable with the existence of some degree of honour and honesty, as this infidelity in regard to private correspondence. We could be much more easily brought to overlook the former than the latter.

Not, however, that such forgeries are to be lightly regarded. As jokes they are miserably easy, and unmeaning; while they are calculated to give the greatest pain to the abused individuals, and even to inflict serious injury on their interests. *Blackwood's Magazine* stands alone in taking this unwarrantable liberty with private respectability. A cunning sordidness is the motive, when it is not black malignity. The appearance of a real name in print sets scandalous curiosity agog, and produces an interest of a coarse and vulgar, but very general nature; an interest altogether independent of literary ability, or any of those qualities of sentiment and style, that render a written composition valuable, but which are not always within the reach of authors, or the comprehension of readers. Nothing can be more ruinous to the literary taste of a people than the feeding of this natural appetite for impertinent and indecent interference. The example being once set amongst the competitors for popular encouragement, the offenders are seen to profit by their crime, and thus they tempt the better disposed to follow their bad example. All seriousness of principle is out of the question when the flippancies of personal allusion become fashionable. Insensibility, insincerity, and spite, are necessarily engendered by them; and when the poisonous stimulus exercises its full strength, treachery and malignity darken the aspect, and corrupt the influence of what may be termed the literary pleasures of general society. The infamous distinction of industriously and selfishly pandering to these unlawful desires, and systematically contriving seductions addressed to them, belongs to *Blackwood's Magazine*. Its present management set out with offering gross captivations to the coarsest appetites in this way; and Iscariot treachery, and Iago malice, took for auxiliaries the levity and folly of a tea-table gossip, and the saucy freedoms of an intermeddling buffoon. England, Ireland, and Scotland, have been traversed to introduce the names of towns, and of individuals residing in them, in order to gratify the stupid or the ill-natured craving for localities and personalities. Directed by the vulgarity of their own minds, the principal writers in this infamous publication have calculated on *names* as the surest means of getting off their numbers. It is not necessary for this purpose to put any real meaning into the allusion: the relations, friends, and acquaintance of the party named, find interest enough in the simple notice. Mr. Peterkin hears that Mr. Crawfurd is in *Blackwood*, and he needs no other inducement to order the work.

The mere impertinence and frivolity of this system are enough to render it odiously contemptible: but it also involves serious fraud and mortal malice, entitling it to hatred and indignation. . . .

minds, who, by the Philosopher's own system, are to be the *media*ʼ through which the original rays of light, springing from that system, may be transmitted and scattered over the nations. The substance of this objection has, I am aware, been often urged before; and Mr. Coleridge has, in his *Friend* and elsewhere, repeatedly put in his answer; —that his subject is the most profound and abtruse to which we can apply ourselves; that to make an actual advance in it requires new modes of thinking, new modes of expression in the author, and a corresponding effort in the reader, to follow him; that the present age especially is overrun with the plague of superficial education; and that, abstractedly considered, the attempts to popularize learning and philosophy must end in the plebeification of knowledge! Be it so:—I am as far from being gratified at the notion of a 'Reading Public' as Mr. Coleridge can be; and I perfectly detest the whole system so much in fashion now of making easy what ought not to be learnt without some difficulty; for examples of which precious practice take, *The History of England made perfectly easy to Children, in a series of Maps; The System of Linnæus rendered intelligible to Young Ladies, in a series of Questions and Answers;* nay, very lately, *The Whole Duty of a Christian Exemplified— by a Pack of Cards;* which last I suppose is meant, amongst other Christian duties, to inculcate the use and practice of Gambling! But then assuredly there is another extreme; and, if Mr. Coleridge has fallen into it, perhaps it was the natural effect of the re-action of his mind occasioned by these convictions;—but that there is such an extreme who will deny?—and that the first volume of the *Biographia Literaria* can show some specimens of it, perhaps not many will be found hardy enough to dispute. Lord Bacon and Sir Isaac Newton both made as great advances in the knowledge of Mind and Nature as any two men that ever lived; yet both have, I apprehend, been understood, and both *acted* upon;—but where are we to find in Mr. Coleridge's philosophy that solid, sensible ground, upon which we may venture to build up an abiding-place for our doubts and our desires? I do not affirm that this whole system of commingled Platonism, Kantism, and Christianism *may* not be true; but I do affirm, and I fear not contradiction, that it will never be useful. Perhaps if *The Friend* live so long—and I do not fear its dying—in the transcendent illumination of the Earthly Millennium its doctrines will be recognized, and its conjectures realized; but till that happy period in the Latter Days, while we are still perplexed with doubts and fears, and our minds bedimmed with passion and prejudice; whilst we persist in demanding plain reason for what we are to believe from men, and will not place that *Faith* in mortal ingenuity which we rest alone in Omnipotent Wisdom; so long, methinks, will *The Friend* be the dark seer of an unknown land; so long will he sit enshrouded in his cloudy tabernacle, possessed, Cassandra-like, by a Spirit, which may denounce or may teach, but whose denunciations or whose teachings will be disregarded, be pitied, or be unnoticed by all.

But it is high time to turn to the particular subject of this Letter; from which, indeed, I should not have so long abstained, had I not thought a cursory mention of Mr. Coleridge's philosophical pretensions interesting, if not necessary, in a complete view of the productions of his Genius. And, for my own part, I confess I have never felt my regret at his present exclusive pursuit of undefinable mysticism so vivid, as when I have been charmed, tranquillized, and thrown into delicious musings, by the perusal of his exquisite Poems. These last have fared, with a few very splendid exceptions, much in the same manner as those of Wordsworth; and, to solicit for them a candid examination, is, I am conscious, to ask what will hardly be granted by the obdurate and almost malicious prejudices of many people. And yet, notwithstanding this general neglect or contempt, I declare it as my settled opinion, which has not been formed hastily, or without previous acquaintance with his all-praised contemporaries, that in many very most important respects, in a transparency of genius, a purity of conception, a matchless ear, and splendor of diction, Mr. Coleridge is not only equal, but once and again superior to all of them put together. With the same continual working of the soul upon its own energies, which is so conspicuous in Wordsworth, he is less abstracted and ideal; not so philosophically sublime, he is more humanly passionate; not so anatomizing, if I may so speak, in the operations of the heart and the mind, he is more diffused, more comprehensive. From the natural bent of his genius there is a tendency to the strange, the wild, and mysterious; which, though intolerable in the cool pursuit of Truth, is yet oftentimes the fruitful parent of the very highest Poetry. To this he adds a power of language truly wonderful, more romantically splendid than Wordsworth's, and more flexible and melodious than that of Southey. Indeed his excellence is so great in this particular, that in my judgment many finished specimens of perfect harmony of thought, passion, measure, and rhyme, may be selected from his Poems, which will hardly yield the palm to the most celebrated passages in Spenser, Shakespeare, or Milton. I shall quote an instance or two of this, when I come to speak more particularly of his Love Poetry. In the mean time, to give those who may be strangers to Mr. Coleridge's powers an idea of what he once could perform, and at the same moment to display that high and bright mysteriousness so peculiar to him, couched in what appears to me very beautiful numbers, I will present you with a view of his 'Ode on the Departing Year'.

> Spirit who sweepest the wild Harp of Time!
> It is most hard, with an untroubled ear
> Thy dark inwoven harmonies to hear!
> Yet, mine eye fixt on Heaven's unchanging clime,
> Long had I listened, free from mortal fear,
> With inward stillness, and submitted mind;
> When lo! its folds far waving on the wind,
> I saw the train of the Departing Year!
> Starting from my silent sadness,
> Then with no unholy madness,
> Ere yet the enter'd cloud foreclos'd my sight,
> I rais'd the impetuous song, and solemnized his flight.

Then follows a very fine invocation to all Nature to suspend its woes and joys for a season—then a vivid description of the war incidents of the Year; after which comes the Vision:

> Departing Year! 'twas on no earthly shore
> My soul beheld thy vision! Where alone,
> Voiceless and stern, before the cloudy throne,
> Aye Memory sits: thy robe inscrib'd with gore,
> With many an imaginable groan
> Thou storied'st thy sad hours! Silence ensued,
> Deep silence o'er the etherial multitude,
> Whose locks with wreaths, whose wreaths with glories shone.
> Then, his eye wild ardours glancing,
> From the choired gods advancing,
> The Spirit of the Earth made reverence meet,
> And stood up, beautiful, before the cloudy seat.

> V
> Throughout the blissful throng,
> Hush'd were harp and song:
> Till wheeling round the throne the Lampads Seven,
> (The mystic Words of Heaven)
> Permissive signal make;
> The fervent Spirit bow'd, then spread his wings and spake!
> 'Thou in stormy blackness throning

> Love and uncreated Light,
> By the Earth's unsolaced groaning,
> Seize thy terrors, Arm of might!'

And so on for many lines; imprecating, in an impassioned style, the
vengeance of God upon the tyrannies and bloodthirsty persecutions of
the Great Ones of this Earth. The Vision is ended:

VI

> The voice had ceased, the vision fled;
> Yet still I gasp'd and reel'd with dread.
> And ever, when the dream of night
> Renews the phantom to my sight,
> Cold sweat-drops gather on my limbs;
> My ears throb hot; my eye-balls start;
> My brain with horrid tumult swims;
> Wild is the tempest of my heart;
> And my thick and struggling breath
> Imitates the toil of death!

After this a burst of affectionate enthusiasm for his country prevails
over his settled conviction of her guilt and impending punishment:

VII

> Not yet enslav'd, not wholly vile,
> O Albion? O my mother Isle!
> Thy valleys, fair as Eden's bowers,
> Glitter green with sunny showers;
> Thy grassy uplands' gentle swells
> Echo to the bleat of flocks;
> (Those grassy hills, those glitt'ring dells
> Proudly ramparted with rocks)
> And Ocean 'mid his uproar wild
> Speaks safety to his Island-Child!
> Hence, for many a fearless age,
> Has social Quiet lov'd thy shore;
> Nor ever proud Invader's rage,
> Or sack'd thy towers, or stain'd thy fields with gore.

Then the prophecy of the Destruction that is to ensue; and the Ode
concludes with his own feelings and prayers.

VIII

> Abandon'd of Heaven! mad Avarice thy guide,
> At cowardly distance, yet kindling with pride—
> 'Mid thy herds and thy corn-fields secure thou hast stood,

And join'd the wild yelling of Famine and Blood!
The nations curse thee, and with eager wond'ring
Shall hear Destruction, like a vulture, scream!
Strange-eyed Destruction! who with many a dream
Of central fires through nether seas up-thund'ring
Soothes her fierce solitude; yet as she lies
By livid fount, or red volcanic stream,
If ever to her lidless dragon-eyes,
O Albion! thy predestin'd ruins rise,
The fiend-hag on her perilous couch doth leap,
Muttering distemper'd triumph in her charmed sleep.

IX

Away, my soul, away!
In vain, in vain the Birds of warning sing—
And hark! I hear the famish'd brood of prey
Flap their lank pennons on the groaning wind!
Away, my soul, away!
I, unpartaking of the evil thing,
With daily prayer and daily toil
Soliciting for food my scanty soil,
Have wailed my country with a loud Lament.
Now I recentre my immortal mind
In the deep sabbath of meek self-content;
Cleans'd from the vaporous passions that bedim
God's Image, sister of the Seraphim.

The disposition to the mysterious and preternatural, which I remarked above as constituting a very principal moving spring in almost all Mr. Coleridge's writings, is nowhere more absolutely developed, or more splendidly arrayed, than in the 'Rime of the Ancient Mariner'. This is one of the best known and most admired of his poems; and certainly, in whatever light it is viewed, in whatever temper it is read, it must be allowed to be a most singular and astonishing work, both in conception and execution. I have quoted largely already, yet I cannot refrain from giving a stanza or two of this wonder of Poetry:

[quotes ll. 263-87 and 354-72 (*PW*, i, 197-8 and 200-1)]

But notwithstanding the striking success and perfect originality of his compositions in the manner of the poem quoted above (for the whole pervading spirit of the 'Christabel', that unjustly-vilified fragment, is intensely the same with that of the 'Ancient Mariner'), and

not forgetting either the energy, the dramatic excellence, and splendor
of the *Remorse*, or the softer and more fanciful elegance of *Zapolya*,
yet it is in his Love Poems that the genius of Coleridge is poured forth
in a more peculiar and undivided stream. As a Love Poet he is strictly
and exclusively original, or if that be not possible for any one in these
latter days, yet indisputably the most genuine and original writer that
has existed since the times of *Romeo and Juliet*. It is to his amatory
Poetry that I would particularly call the attention of a young or old
lover of the Muse; to the one it will seem bright and prospective, to the
other gentle and contemplative; and, indeed, this portion of his works
has been acknowledged to be excellent, even by those who have
affected to despise his other productions. Assuredly no one who had
any regard for his own reputation as a critic would forbear praising
such Poems as those called 'Love' and the 'Circassian Love-Chaunt';
but I cannot think that they have been sufficiently admired, nor their
essential distinctive principles thoroughly examined. None of the Love
Poetry of the present day can, to my mind, be for an instant compared
to them in any one particular. The love of Lord Byron is the love, if
we may so degrade that term, of a Turkish Sultan, revelling in the
indiscriminate obedience of a haram of slaves; perilously, indeed, alive
to the violent excesses of the passion, but despotic, troubled, desperate,
short-lived. The love of Moore (ever excepting what ought to be
forgotten) is something more refined and natural; but still it is so
bedecked and beplastered with cumbrous Orientalisms, that we are
but rarely or never in perfect unison with it. There is positively nothing
to be called love in Wordsworth: he has indeed an intellectual devotion,
a deep communion of sentiment; but no love, as that word was understood by Shakespeare and Fletcher. But in Coleridge there is a clear
unclouded passion, an exquisite respect, a gentleness, a Knightly
tenderness and courtesy, which recals us in a moment to our old
dramatists; not too sensual, as in Byron, nor too intellectual, as in
Wordsworth. The purity of his feelings is unequalled; yet, with seeming contradiction, they are ardent, impatient, and contemplative. It is
Petrarch and Shakespeare transfused into each other. It is, if I may be
allowed so fanciful an illustration, the Midsummer Moonlight of Love
Poetry. Take for example, and mark the complete harmony of expression, flow, and rhyme, with the feelings conveyed in these stanzas:

[quotes ll. 21-36, 41-4, 53-6, 61-80, and 85-92 of 'Love' (*PW*, i,
333-4)]

Yet a few words more upon the character of the very extraordinary Author of these Poems, and I have done. Mr. Coleridge has now for many years been what is called before the public, in the shapes of Poet, Politician, and Metaphysician. In the commencement of his life he shared in the general spirit resulting from the auspicious exordium of the French Revolution, and declared and advocated his sentiments with a brilliant enthusiasm which unfortunately lost him many friends, and procured him hundreds of foes; but let it be remembered that his enthusiasm was directed solely to political objects; from the irreligious, atheistic, impure systems of miscalled philosophy attendant upon the Revolution no man was ever more alien, more estranged. Indeed, he has ever been an eminently devout and fervent Christian, and it is one among many other proofs and indications of the genuine greatness of his mind, that he was able to resist with firmness the seductions of infidelity, at a time when it came recommended to his feelings by its alliance with what he deemed true in other respects; whilst many of the younger men of genius of the present day have degenerated into a contemptible scepticism, the very dregs and lees of the basest of French principles, discountenanced, as it should be to a mind with any spark of purity in it, by its intimate congeniality with the worthless and pernicious spirit of Radicalism. I know it would be to incur the ridicule of nine out of ten, who may read these pages, if I were to assert my opinion, that Mr. Coleridge is the greatest Genius, in every respect, of the present day; we have all been so accustomed to hear him and Wordsworth abused, laughed at, and cut up, by critics of every dimension, that we cannot emancipate ourselves from the habitual delusion. We have seen a weak poem cited as a *chef d'œuvre*, an obscure disquisition as a sample of his poetry and philosophy; and it but rarely occurs to us that this may be all trick, nay, and a trick so contemptibly easy of execution, that it is notorious that the shallowest scribblers have, under the character of the Anonymous 'We', *written down* with success the writings, and broken the hearts of men of the most exquisite and hence susceptible genius. Kirke White cannot and ought not to be forgotten.[1]
Well! but you forget Lord Byron! think of *Childe Harold, The Corsair, Don Juan*, and *The Bride of Abydos'*, says one;—'and Moore', says another;—'or Southey—or at least your idol Wordsworth!'—True, I hear you all and know your own convictions, and know also that the first, second, and third of you have the world on your side. Howbeit, I am a Mede or Persian in this my opinion, and will not

[1] Henry Kirk White (1785-1806), a minor poet.

retract or soften it even at the name of Wordsworth himself. To enter into a critical examination of *meum* and *tuum* between Wordsworth and Coleridge; to show or rather hint that much of the very essence of the former's poetical being is a transfusion of the life-blood of the latter; to demonstrate this fact by remarking upon the gradual decrease of intellectual vigour, observable in the recent poems of Mr. Wordsworth, occasioned, as I would have it, by his less intimate communion of late with the friend of his youth; all this would require, though it might justify, more time, labour, and delicacy of touch, than at present I can possibly afford it.

That to Coleridge and Wordsworth the poetry, the philosophy, and the criticism of the present day does actually owe its peculiar character, and its distinguishing excellence over that of the last century, those who would trace the origin of the present opinions back for thirty years would find no difficulty in believing. These two men, essentially different as they are in many respects, have been copied, imitated, and parodied by every poet who now lives. Lord Byron has owned his obligations to Mr. Coleridge, and the third Canto of *Childe Harold* could not have been written unless Wordsworth had lived before it. The author of *The Lay of the Last Minstrel* can best tell what poem was the *motive* of his own work, and the *Lady of the Lake* is indebted almost for the very words of many of its most admired passages to Wordsworth's Poems. I do not deny that there are many assignable causes of the neglect which the writings of Mr. Coleridge have met with; I have myself hinted above at the uncouth dress of his metaphysical meditations, and the general difficulty and hardness of his reasoning; but this censure does not apply to an immense portion even of *The Friend*, or the first *Lay Sermon*; to the second Sermon not all; and surely it is a little unreasonable to excommunicate the works of a man of such acknowledged excellence in most respects because of his obliquities in a few particulars.

It is not much to the purpose, but yet I cannot help adverting to his personal manners and qualities; for they are such as when once seen and felt have never been forgotten, or not reverenced and loved even by his enemies themselves. Gentle and patient to every one; communicative and sympathizing, you perceive at the very first glance that you are near an extraordinary and self-subdued being; his powers of conversation have, I suppose, never been equalled; there is a fervid continuousness of discourse, a brilliancy and justness of images and similes which charm and convince every hearer; and a learning so deep, so various, so perfectly under command, that you may come away from an evening's conversation with him, with more curious facts, well-conceived explications, and ingenious reasonings upon them, than you could possibly gain from a week's reading. Those who have attended his Lectures on Shakespeare may form some idea of what I would express; but they cannot know all his winning fascination, all his almost infantine simplicity of manners, all his exquisite humour. I do not indulge myself in wilful flattery of this great man by these expressions; for it is little probable that a Number of *The Etonian* should ever creep in between his Plato and his Bible; but I use them because they are justly his due; because they have been long and maliciously withheld or denied; and because, besides his universal claim for respect from his Genius and Eloquence, he has ties of another kind which assure him the love and esteem of

GERARD MONTGOMERY

99. Leigh Hunt, *Examiner*

21 October 1821, 664-7

This unsigned article in the series 'Sketches of the Living Poets', has been attributed to Leigh Hunt (Edmund Blunden, *Leigh Hunt's 'Examiner' Examined*, London 1928, 109). Hunt (1784-1859), essayist and poet, edited the *Examiner* and other journals and had a considerable influence on younger poets such as Keats and Shelley.

Samuel Taylor Coleridge was born in the year 1773 at St. Mary Ottery, in Devonshire, where his father, the Rev. John Coleridge, an eminent scholar, was vicar of the parish. He was grounded in classical learning at Christ-Hospital under the Rev. Mr. Bowyer, who with a daringness of expression to which that learned person and pains-taking schoolmaster was not often excited, used to call him to mind as 'that sensible fool, Cŏlĕrĭdge'.[1] Mr. Coleridge, in his Literary Life, as well as Mr. Lamb in his Recollections of the School, has given a sufficiently grateful account of his old master; yet he informs us that he is apt to have dreams of him at night, to this hour, not very soothing: and his account did not hinder it from being said after Mr. Bowyer's death, that it was lucky for the cherubim who bore the old gentleman to heaven, that they had only heads and wings, or he would infallibly have flogged them by the way. At nineteen, Mr. Coleridge went to Jesus College, Cambridge, where he exhibited, we believe, equal indifference to university honour; and power to obtain them. On his leaving college, his speculative susceptibility led him through a singular variety of adventures, some of which he has touched upon in his *Biographia Literaria*. He became a journalist, a preacher, a dragoon. In the second character he bewitched, among others, William Hazlitt, then on the look out for a 'guide and philosopher'. In the last, he astonished a party of ladies and gentlemen who were at an exhibition, by explaining a huge compound word from the Greek, by which the

[1] Hunt had also been one of Mr. Bowyer's pupils.

471

nature of it was made 'dark with excessive bright' over the door. He had become in the mean time the head of a literary and speculative circle of young men, consisting chiefly of Messrs. Lamb, Lloyd, Southey, and Lovell, of the two latter of whom he became the brother-in-law by their marrying three sisters at Bath. A project was formed to go with these ladies to America, and found a Pantisocracy, or system of equal government, in which every thing but the best was to be in common; but it did not take place. In 1798, the late public-spirited 'Etrurians', Josiah and Thomas Wedgewood, enabled Mr. Coleridge to finish his studies of men and books in Germany, where he met Mr. Wordsworth, with whom he had lately become acquainted. At Hamburgh they paid a visit to Klopstock. Klopstock complained of the English translation of his *Messiah*, and wished Mr. Coleridge 'to revenge him' by versions of select passages. The thought was ingenious; but his visitor seems to have reckoned it not equally fair; for he concludes his interesting account of this interview, in the *Friend*, by saying, that when the Pastor of the town called his countryman 'the German Milton', he could not help muttering to himself 'a very *German* Milton indeed!'—Mr. Coleridge was afterwards secretary, for about a year and a half, to Sir Alexander Ball, Governor of Malta, of whom he gives so exalted, and, we dare say, so just a character in the work above mentioned. He then returned to England, and after living some time in the Lakes and other places, and publishing various pieces of prose and poetry, took up his abode at Highgate, where he seems to live like the scholar in Chaucer, who would rather have

> At his bed's head
> A twenty bokes, clothid in black and red,
> Of Aristotle and his philosophie,
> Than robes rich, or fiddle, or psaultrie.

Mr. Coleridge was reckoned handsome when young. He is now 'more fat than bard beseems', and his face does not strike at first sight; but the expression is kind, the forehead remarkably fine, and the eye, as you approach it, extremely keen and searching. It has been compared to Bacon's, who was said to have 'an eye like a viper'. At first, it seems reposing under the bland weight of his forehead.

The principal works of Mr. Coleridge are the *Friend*, a series of essays; *Remorse*, a tragedy; *Biographia Literaria*, or his *Literary Life*; *Lay Sermons*, Theologico-Political; the poem of 'Christabel'; and *Sybilline Leaves*, a collection of the greater part of his other poetical pieces, including the 'Ancient Mariner'. We are acquainted with Mr. Coleridge's prose writings, but we have not a sufficient knowledge of them, nor perhaps sufficient knowledge of any other kind, to pronounce upon their merits. Our general impression is, that they are very eloquent, imaginative, and subtle, more masterly in words than in the sum total of style, and more powerful in thoughts than in conclusions. In many passages, indeed (we allude to his essays entitled the *Friend*), it is impossible not to recognize that weakness of the will, or liability to the same amount of impression from all views of a question, which has been observed by a critic better able to speak of him, with this exception, which perhaps only proves the rule, that he is very fond of bringing whatever he likes in the speculations of other men, from the Father of the Church to the Pantheist, to assimilate with his notions of the Christian religion; while on the other hand he has a good handsome quantity of dislike for modern innovators, and refuses to make a harmony out of their 'differences', which he thinks by no means 'discreet'. In other words, he is a deep thinker, and good natured indolent man, who, entrenched in his old books and habits, and grateful to them, all round, for the occupation they have afforded his thoughts, is as glad to make them all agree at this dispassionate distance of time, as he is anxious not to have them disturbed by men who have not the same hold on his prejudices. This may account for his being numbered among those who have altered their opinions on the necessity of political change. Mr. Coleridge is prepared to argue, that he has *not* altered his opinions, nor even suppressed them; and though his arguments might appear strange to those who recollect such productions as the *Watchman*, he would go nigh to persuade thirty persons out of forty that he really had not:—all which amounts perhaps to thus much, that he can fetch out of things, apparently the most discordant, their hidden principles of agreement; but not having been able to persuade people of the agreement when he was advocating political change, he turns upon them for their disobedience, and would shew them, with equal subtlety, that what he advocated was none of the change which they wanted, whatever they might have flattered themselves it was. In other words, his turn of mind was *too* contemplative for action; and seeing that all the world would not become what he wished it, on the pure strength of ratiocination, he becomes, out of indolence, what Mr. Wordsworth became out of pride, and Mr. Southey out of vanity. But indolence, such as his, is a more disinterested and conscientious thing than pride and vanity; and accordingly he became neither a distributor of stamps, nor a poet-laureate. That those more active and consistent politicians, who were in some measure taught by himself, should be very angry with him, is extremely natural; but so were those consequences of his turn of mind, that produced their anger. He is all for thought and imagination, and nothing else. It might have been better had he been more active, just as it might have been better for Lord Bacon had his being all for experiment not tempted him to take leave of sentiment and imagination in trying to raise his paltry worldly greatness. But let Mr. Coleridge have his due; which is seldom given to such abstract personages. He is a kind of unascetic Bramin among us, one who is always looking inwardly, and making experiments upon the nature and powers of his soul. Lord Bacon refused to license inquisitions of that nature, and said some hard things about cobwebs and dark keeping;but surely they are not only allowable to the few who are likely to indulge in them, but are also experiments after their kind, and may open worlds to us by and by, of which the philosopher no more dreams at present, than the politician did of Columbus's.

Mr. Coleridge speaks very modestly of his poetry—not affectedly so, but out of a high notion of the art in his predecessors. He delighted the late Mr. Keats, in the course of conversation, with adding, after he had alluded to it—'if there is any thing I have written which may be *called poetry*': and the writer of the present article heard him speak of verses, as the common tribute which a young mind on its entrance into the world of letters pays to the love of intellectual beauty. His poetry however has an 'image and superscription' very different from this current coin. We do not, it is true, think that it evinces the poetical habit of mind—or that tendency to regard every thing in its connexion with the imaginative world, which in a minor sense was justly attributed to the author of the *Seasons*, and in its greater belonged to Spenser and Milton. But it is full of imagination and of a sense of the beautiful, as suggested by a great acquaintance with books and thoughts, acting upon a benevolent mind. It is to the scholar of old books and metaphysics, what Milton's was to the Greek and Italian scholar. It is the essence of the impression made upon him by that habit of thinking and reading, which is his second nature. Mr. Coleridge began with metaphysics when at school; and what the boy begins with, the man will end with, come what will between. He does not turn metaphysical upon the strength of his poetry, like Spenser and Tasso; but poet upon the strength of his metaphysics. Thus in the greater part of his minor poems he only touches upon the popular creeds, or wilful creations of their own, which would occupy other poets, and then falls musing upon the nature of things, and analysing his feelings. In his voyage to Germany, he sees a solitary wildfowl upon 'the objectless desert of waters', and says how interesting it was. It was most probably from a train of reflection on the value of this link between land and the ship, that he produced his beautiful wild poem of the 'Ancient Mariner', which he precedes with a critico-philosophical extract from Burnet's *Archaeologia*. We do not object to this as belonging to his genius. We only instance it, as shewing the nature of it. In the same spirit, he interrupts his 'Christabel' with an explanation of the wish sometimes felt to give pain to the innocent; and instead of being content to have written finely under the influence of laudanum, recommends 'Kubla-Khan' to his readers, not as a poem, but as 'a psychological curiosity'. All this however is extremely interesting of its kind, and peculiar. It is another striking instance of what we have often remarked, the tendency of all great knowledge and deep delight in it, of whatever kind, to extend itself into poetry, which lies like a heaven in the centre of the intellectual world for those to go to and be refreshed with, more or less, who are not bound to the physical world like slaves to the soil. Every lover of books, scholar or not, who knows what it is to have his quarto open against a loaf at his tea, to carry his duo-decimo about in his pocket, to read along country roads or even streets, and to scrawl his favourite authors with notes (as 'S.T.C.' is liberally sanctioned to do those of others by a writer in the *London Magazine*)[1] ought to be in possession of Mr. Coleridge's poems, if it is only for 'Christabel', 'Kubla Khan', and the 'Ancient Mariner'. The first comprises all that is ancient and courteous in old rhythm, and will also make any studious gentleman, who is not sufficiently imaginative, turn himself round divers times in his chair, as he ought to do, to see if there is not 'something in the room'. 'Kubla Khan' is a voice and a vision, an everlasting tune in our mouths, a dream fit for Cambuscan and all his poets, a dance of pictures such as Giotto or Cimabue, revived and re-inspired, would have made for a Storie of Old Tartarie, a piece of the invisible world made visible by a sun at midnight and sliding before our eyes.

> Beware, beware,
> His flashing eyes, his floating hair!

[1] Charles Lamb in 'The Two Races of Men', *London Magazine*, December 1820, ii, 625.

Weave a circle round him thrice,
And close your lips with holy dread,
For he on honey dew hath fed,
And drank of the milk of Paradise.

Justly is it thought that to be able to present such images as these to the mind, is to realise the world they speak of. We could repeat such verses as the following down a green glade, a whole summer's morning:

A damsel with a dulcimer
In a vision once I saw,
A lovely Abyssinian maid;
And on her dulcimer she played,
Singing of Mount Aborah.

As to the 'Ancient Mariner', we have just this minute read it again, and all that we have been saying about the origin of the author's poetry, appears to be nonsense. Perhaps it is, and we are not sorry that it should be. All that we are certain of is, that the 'Ancient Mariner' is very fine poetry, and that we are not the 'one of three' to whom the sea-faring old greybeard is fated to tell his story, for we are aware of the existence of other worlds beside the one about us, and we would not have shot the solitary bird of good omen, nor one out of a dozen of them.

It is an Ancient Mariner,
And he stoppeth one of three:
'By thy long grey beard and thy glittering eye,
Now wherefore stopp'st thou me?

The Bridegroom's doors are open'd wide,
And I am next of kin;
The guests are met, the feast is set;
Mayst hear the merry din'.

He holds him with his skinny hand,
'There was a ship,' quoth he,
'Hold off! unhand me, grey-beard loon!'
Eftsoons his hand dropt he.

He holds him with his glittering eye—
The wedding guest stood still,
And listens like a three year's child:
The Mariner hath his will.

The Ancient Mariner was one of a crew, who were driven by a storm to the south pole. An albatross appeared, who became familiar with the sailors, and a good wind sprang up. The Mariner not having the

476

fear of a violation of kindness and gentleness before his eyes, killed the albatross, for which the others said he would be pursued with a misfortune; but the good breeze still continues, and carries them as far back as the line, for which they laugh at his offence, and say it was a good thing. But now 'the ship has been suddenly becalmed'. (We proceed to quote the marginal summary which the author has added in imitation of old books.)

The ship hath been suddenly becalmed, and the albatross begins to be avenged. A spirit had followed them; one of the invisible inhabitants of this planet, neither departed souls nor angels; concerning whom the learned Jew, Josephus, and the Platonic Constantinopolitan, Michael Psellus, may be consulted. They are very numerous, and there is no climate or element without one or more. The shipmates, in their sore distress, would fain throw the whole guilt on the ancient mariner, in sign whereof they hang the dead sea-bird about his neck. The Ancient Mariner beholdeth a sign in the element afar off. At its nearer approach it seemeth him to be a ship; and at a dear ransom he freeth his speech from the bonds of thirst. A flash of joy. And horror follows. For can it be a ship that comes onward without wind or tide? It seemeth him but the skeleton of a ship. And its ribs are seen as bars on the face of the setting sun. The spectre-woman and her death-mate, and no other on board the skeleton ship. Like vessel, like crew. DEATH, and LIFE-IN-DEATH, have diced for the ship's crew, and she (the latter) winneth the Ancient Mariner. At the rising of the moon, one after another, his shipmates drop down dead; but LIFE-IN-DEATH begins her work on the Ancient Mariner. The wedding-guest feareth that a spirit is talking to him; but the Ancient Mariner assureth him of his bodily life, and proceedeth to relate his horrible penance. He despiseth the creatures of the calm, and envieth that *they* should live, and so many lie dead. But the curse lieth for him in the eye of the dead men. In his loneliness and fixedness he yearneth toward the journeying moon, and the stars that still sojourn, yet still move onward; and every where the blue sky belongs to them, and is their appointed rest, and their native country, and their own natural homes, which they enter unannounced, as lords that are certainly expected, and yet there is a silent joy at their arrival. By the light of the moon he beholdeth God's creatures of the great calm. Their beauty and their happiness. He blesseth them in his heart. The spell begins to break. By grace of the holy Mother, the Mariner is refreshed with rain. He heareth sounds and seeth strange sights and commotions in the sky and the element. The bodies of the ship's crew are inspirited, and the ship moves on—

> 'I fear thee, ancient Mariner!'
> Be calm, thou Wedding-Guest!
> 'Twas not those souls that fled in pain,
> Which to their corses came again,
> But a troop of spirits blest.

For when it dawned—they dropped their arms,
And clustered round the mast;
Sweet sounds rose slowly through their mouths,
And from their bodies passed.

Around, around, flew each sweet sound,
Then darted to the sun;
Slowly the sounds came back again,
Now mixed, now one by one.

Sometimes a-dropping from the sky
I heard the sky-lark sing;
Sometimes all little birds that are,
How they seemed to fill the sea and air
With their sweet jargoning!

And now 'twas like all instruments,
Now like a lonely flute;
And now it is an angel's song,
That makes the Heavens be mute.

It ceased; yet still the sails made on
A pleasant noise till noon,
A noise like of a hidden brook
In the leafy month of June,
That to the sleeping woods all night
Singeth a quiet tune.

Till noon we quietly sailed on,
Yet never a breeze did breathe:
Slowly and smoothly went the ship,
Moved onward from beneath.

The lonesome spirit from the South-pole carries on the ship as far as the line, in obedience to the angelic troop, but still requireth vengeance.

The Polar Spirit's fellow-dæmons, the invisible inhabitants of the element, take part in his wrong; and two of them relate, one to the other, that penance long and heavy for the *Ancient Mariner* hath been accorded to the Polar spirit, who returneth southward. The Mariner hath been cast into a trance; for the angelic power causeth the vessel to drive northward, faster than human life could endure. The supernatural motion is retarded; the Mariner awakes, and his penance begins anew. The curse is fully expiated. And the Ancient Mariner beholdeth his native country. The angelic spirits leave the dead bodies, and appear in their own forms of light. The Hermit of the wood approacheth the ship with wonder. The ship suddenly sinketh. The Ancient Mariner is saved in the Pilot's boat. The Ancient Mariner earnestly entreateth the Hermit to shrieve him; and the penance of life falls on him. And ever and anon throughout his future life an agony constraineth him to travel from land to land. And to teach by his own example, love and reverence to all things that God made and loveth.

This is a lesson to those who see nothing in the world but their own unfeeling common-places, and are afterwards visited with a dreary sense of their insufficiency. Not to have sympathy for all, is not to have the instinct that suffices instead of imagination. Not to have imagination, to supply the want of the instinct, is to be left destitute and forlorn when brute pleasure is gone, and to be *dead-in-life*. This poem would bear out a long marginal illustration in the style of the old Italian critics, who squeeze a sonnet of Petrarch's into the middle of the page with a crowd of fond annotations. Be the source of its inspiration what it may, it is a poem that may serve as a test to any one who wishes to know whether he has a real taste for poetry or not. And be Mr. Coleridge what he may, whether an author inspired by authors or from himself, whether a metaphysical poet or a poetical metaphysician, whether a politician baulked and rendered despairing like many others by the French Revolution, or lastly, and totally, a subtle and good-natured casuist fitted for nothing but contemplation, and rewarded by it with a sense of the beautiful and wonderful *above* his casuistry, we can only be grateful for the knowledge and delight he affords us by his genius, and recognise in him an instance of that departure from ordinary talent, which we are far from being bound to condemn, because it does not fall in with our own humours. If it is well for the more active that his prose does not talk quite well or vivaciously enough to turn them from their stream of action, and so unfit them for *their* purposes, they ought to be glad that they have such men to talk to them when they are at rest, and to maintain in them that willingness to be impartial, and that power of 'looking abroad into universality', without which action itself would never be any thing but a mischievous system of re-action and disappointment, fretting and to fret.

They also serve, who only stand and wait.

100. 'R.', *Literary Speculum*

July 1822, ii, 145-51

Excerpts from an article entitled 'On the Poetry of Coleridge'.

Cold must be the temperature of that man's mind, who can rise from the perusal of the poems of Coleridge, without feeling that intense interest, and those vivid emotions of delight, which are ever excited by the wondrous operations of the magic wand of genius. To those whom constitution and cultivation have initiated into the sacred mysteries of song, whose mental optics have often been enraptured with the delights of extatic vision, and whose ear is tremulous to the touch of those harmonious undulations which Fancy pours from her soul-subduing shell; to such, the genius of Coleridge, even in its wildest aberrations, can never be listened to with indifference. Warm admirers of his powers, we have often, however, painfully regretted the irregularity of their application. We regret that he, who is so capable of raising a chastely beautiful Grecian temple, should endeavour, seemingly for the sake of being the founder of a new order of poetic architecture, to erect a grotesque pagoda, where good taste may be sacrificed on the shrine of novelty. We regret this, because we are convinced that many of his admirers, mistaking the cause of his powerful influence on their minds, seize upon the grosser and reprehensible parts, as objects of their applause and imitation; and indeed it requires no little exercise of reflection and nice discrimination to convince them, that it may not be that very unsubdued irregularity of thought, and the illegitimacy of expression connected with it, which form the spell of that enchantment which binds us within the verge of its circle, benumbing the faculty of reason by delivering us up to the empire of feeling; and while we listen to the charm, depriving us of the power of perceiving the incongruity of its parts. We must confess it is only when the strain has ceased, that we feel ourselves best qualified to perceive its want of conformity to the laws of well regulated harmony. It is when we are freed from the immediate influence of its celestial inspiration, that we can observe and lament its accompanying terraqueous grossness: we must add, that in proportion as we admire and honour the genius of Mr. Coleridge, so we lament that while possessed of strength sufficient to march forward with dignity in the path of legitimate excellence, unassisted and triumphant, he should thus wilfully stray aside to its more rugged borders, merely, it should seem, to form a track of his own; that he who could attune the muse's lyre with heavenly concord, should descend to the trickery of *panto-mime* poetry, if such a term can be made use of to express our ideas of any verbal description; a term, the fitness of which we shall refer to the judgment of the reader of the following lines:

[quotes 'Christabel', ll. 1-14, 309-10, 81-2, 123-6 (*PW*, i, 215-26); 'An Ode to the Rain', ll. 49-54 (*PW*, i, 384); and 'Answer to a Child's Question', ll. 9-10 (*PW*, i, 386)]

Revolting as this is to our pre-conceived notions of excellence, could it be proved that the pleasure we have felt and the improvement we have received from the poetry of Mr. Coleridge arose in any degree from what we consider the inordinate peculiarities of his manner, we should not fastidiously reject the emotions arising from recalled ideas of delight, because of the vehicle by which they were conveyed to us. We do not avert our eyes from the animated picture, because of the coarseness of the canvass. It is so often our lot to meet with dulness and insipidity, that while we thirst for a refreshing draught from the springs of genius, we may say to each other, with Horace:

Num, tibi cum fauces urit sitis, aurea quaeris
Pocula?[1]

We are far, very far, also from wishing to bind for ever any opera-tion of the soul, and least of all heaven-born poesy in the trammels which art has thought it expedient to coil around her. But while we are desirous that the space assigned for the flight of fancy be intermin-able, we only rejoice when she directs her course in the track of the sunbeams. We are also so far from being fastidiously enemies to novelty, that where it carries the recommendation of utility in the refinement of our feelings, or the cultivation of our judgment, we are always eager to be among the first to hail the aurora of its approach. We remember reading of a prince who offered a premium for the invention of a new pleasure; in like manner we should feel ourselves greatly indebted to the man who could charm us with a new species of

[1] 'Surely you do not ask for golden cups when thirst parches your jaws?' (Horace, *Satires*, i, 2, 114).

poetry, and we should be little disposed to depreciate the source of that fountain from which we had quaffed so grateful a beverage. Our pleasure, however, would be greatly alloyed by the fear which would naturally arise in our minds on reflecting that when once an enterprising genius, confident of his own strength, ventures to pass the boundaries of human cultivation and launch out into the untrodden wilderness, he may draw many to follow his footsteps who cannot boast of possessing either his vigour or his resources. This is the more to be feared, as the present is an age, in which, as all are readers, many are naturally prompted to become writers. The literary arena is like a theatre, where the spectators have been so agitated by the cunning of the scene, that many of them have been irresistably impelled to become partakers of the action.

We have thus far given way to the supposition that the genius of Coleridge has discovered, and is triumphantly moving in a radiant atmosphere of its own; but we strongly suspect this is not the case. We suspect that it is only when he moves in a less eccentric orbit that his corruscations illuminate any but himself, and that all which really interests the feelings will be found likewise to satisfy the judgment. We suspect that all else rather tends to destroy the effect it is meant to produce, and that like the builders of Babel, he is, by the introduction of strange and uncouth terms, only preventing the completion of that edifice which it has been the dearest wish of his heart to erect. This is a position, which if we could once establish, we should perhaps be the humble instruments of rescuing a genius whom we admire from the temptation of winging his flight amidst a chaos of disjointed elements, or vainly endeavouring to strengthen the boldness of descriptions by verbal trickery. Such talents as those of Mr. Coleridge can never need to seek for notoriety in the paths of singularity. He who can speak well has no occasion to make use of violent and distorted gesticulation. . . . We are far from inferring that the muse of Mr. Coleridge can only appear lovely when she is arrayed in that garb and in those colours which are generally worn. We are of opinion that there is no one who is better qualified to seek for laurels in the fair field of originality. We, however, assert, that within the boundaries we should prescribe for her excursions, there are many beauties yet undiscovered, many a delightful isle yet untrodden, and many a blooming flower, which, though it lays in the regular path, would surprise as much by its novelty as charm by its beauty. We are thankful we have no occasion yet to invest poetry with a new form; she has not exhausted all those bewitching attitudes in which may be placed all that we have so long and so ardently admired. As a proof that Mr. Coleridge can delight the imagination while he satisfies the judgment; that he can bring to the mind's eye all the treasures of his rich and elegant fancy, without having recourse to the trifling earnestness of reiteration, or the ludicrous imitation of sounds foreign to the human organ, we subjoin the following beautifully wrought effusions:

[quotes ll. 418-26 of 'Christabel' (*PW*, i, 229)]

We should add also the beautiful 'conclusion' to part the second of the above Poem, did we not imagine that many of our readers have had the pleasure of perusing it so often as to have it ever mingled with their most delightful poetical recollections.

Very few passages in ancient or modern poetry, are equal to the following:

[quotes ll. 73-88 of 'Songs of the Pixies' (*PW*, i, 43-4)]

Does not the following bring to the mind's eye many a spot of bliss in lovely England?

[quotes ll. 1-9 of 'Reflections on having left a place of retirement' (*PW*, i, 106)]

The following panoramic view is in the most beautiful style of poetic painting:

[quotes ll. 29-40 of the same poem]

We regret that our limits will not allow us to give insertion to the full tide of ideas, which flow upon us, at the recollection of that wildly beautiful, we had almost said superhuman piece of poetic painting, the 'Ancient Mariner'; this and the drama of *Remorse* well deserve becoming the subject of a separate essay. The passages in Mr. Coleridge's other poems, which we have now quoted, may not perhaps be the best he has written, but they occur to our memory, as being sufficient to convince us, that his song breathes the air of heaven, and to cause us to admire him as the elegant poet of truth, of nature, and of virtue.

101. John Wilson, *Blackwood's Edinburgh Magazine*

October 1823, xiv, 500

An excerpt from 'Noctes Ambrosianae', attributed to John Wilson (John Wilson *et al.*, *Noctes Ambrosianae*, ed. Shelton Mackenzie, New York 1866, i, xvi).

NORTH

Who, think ye, Tickler, is to be the new editor of the *Quarterly*? Coleridge?

TICKLER

Not so fast. The contest lies, I understand, between him and O'Doherty.[1] That is the reason the Adjutant has not been with us to-night. He is up canvassing.

THE OPIUM-EATER

Mr. Coleridge is the last man in Europe to conduct a periodical work. His genius none will dispute; but I have traced him through German literature, poetry, and philosophy; and he is, sir, not only a plagiary, but, sir, a thief, a *bonâ fide* most unconscientious thief. I mean no disrespect to a man of surpassing talents. Strip him of his stolen goods, and you will find good clothes of his own below. Yet, except as a poet, he is not original; and if he ever become Editor of the *Quarterly* (which I repeat is impossible) then will I examine his pretensions, and shew him up as impostor. Of Shakespeare it has been said, in a very good song, that 'the thief of all thiefs was a Warwickshire thief'; but Shakespeare stole from Nature, and she forbore to prosecute. Coleridge has stolen from a whole host of his fellow-creatures, most of them poorer than himself; and I pledge myself I am bound over to appear against him. If he plead to the indictment, he is a dead man—if he stand mute, I will press him to death, under three hundred and fifty pound weight of German metaphysics.

NORTH

Perhaps it is a young Coleridge—a son or a nephew.[2]

[1] Adjutant O'Doherty was an alias of William Maginn.

[2] Probably a reference to J. T. Coleridge.

AIDS TO REFLECTION

1825

---

102. Unsigned notice, *British Review*

August 1825, xxiii, 486

We can recollect no instance, in modern times, of literary talent so entirely wasted, and great mental power so absolutely unproductive, as in the case of this eminent author. Whether it be for want of due regulation, of proper self-government, or of studied fixedness of purpose, it is certain, that few works are now produced, even from the pens of notoriously feeble writers, so deplorably *unreadable* as those of Mr. Coleridge. Will our readers feel much attracted towards the present volume, by the following extract? which we assure them is far from an unfavourable specimen.

And now for the answer to the question, What is an IDEA, if it mean neither an impression on the senses, nor a definite conception, nor an abstract notion? (And if it does mean either of these, the word is superfluous: and while it remains undetermined which of these is meant by the word, or whether it is not *which you please*, it is worse than superfluous. See the STATEMAN'S MANUAL, Appendix *ad finem*.) But supposing the word to have a meaning of its own, what does it mean? What is an IDEA? In answer to this I commence with the *absolutely* Real, as the PROTHESIS; the *subjectively* REAL, as the THESIS; the *objectively* REAL, as the ANTITHESIS: and I affirm, that Idea is the *Indifference* of the two—so namely, that if it be conceived as in the subject, the Idea is an Object, and possesses Objective Truth; but if in an Object, it is then a Subject, and is necessarily thought of as exercising the powers of a Subject. Thus an IDEA conceived as subsisting in an object becomes a LAW; and a law contemplated *subjectively* (in a mind) is an idea.

103. From an unsigned review, *British Critic*

October 1826, iii, 239-80

The review also discusses Archbishop Leighton's *Whole Works*.

Before we proceed to analyze the contents and to discuss the merits of the work before us (a task, we confess, of no mean difficulty), we are anxious, as members of the Christian community, and in especial duty bound as conductors of this Review, to express our obligation to Mr. Coleridge, for the various lights thrown by his writings upon the excellence and the beauty of the Christian scheme. He is, indeed, only one of a distinguished phalanx of lay-writers who have voluntarily stood forward in our times in support of that religion which recommends itself to the understandings of mankind in proportion as knowledge and civilization are diffused; but it is not every one who has had the same range of inquiry and contemplation as Mr. Coleridge; and when a man of his undoubted genius and learning, after all his excursive wanderings into the regions of fancy, all his minute researches through the subtleties of metaphysics and the refinements of philosophy, rests at last, at a mature age, in the conviction that the *Christian faith is the perfection of human intelligence*, the result, however he may arrive at it, cannot but be a source of the truest satisfaction to all who have the honour of the Gospel and the happiness of their fellow-creatures at heart. Nor will it be a small addition to this pleasure in the minds of churchmen, that the authors who have engrossed the greatest share of his attention and his praise, and from whom his strongest convictions have been derived (for he was not always what he is), are the chief founders and ornaments of our Episcopal establishment; and further, that the doctrines he has adopted, as including the true sense of scripture, are mainly, if not entirely, those which are set forth in the articles and embodied in the liturgy of our church. But while we offer this sincere and ready homage of our gratitude to Mr. Coleridge, we cannot refrain from an observation, which the present work, above every other, has forced upon us, how infinitely more valuable and useful his labours would have been, had they been more simple and more popular;

popular, we mean, not as 'giving back to the people their own weaknesses and prejudices', but as rendering plain and accessible to the average intellect of mankind, those involved or retiring truths which his
learned leisure and superior sagacity have enabled him to work out. But
this quality, so essential to the value and permanency of mental labours,
Mr. Coleridge has rarely shewn; and the consequence has been, that
his prose-writings have never possessed that influence with any class
of readers to which, in other respects, they would be justly entitled.
Men of ordinary minds turn away at once from his speculations, as
leading them out of the common track of their thoughts, and, indeed,
of their language; while those of more refinement are rarely tempted
to persevere in a path pursued through so many intricacies, and beset
with so much obscurity. The present work, however, must be judged
of by itself, and without adverting to other causes elsewhere connected
with this fault. There is one very prominent and striking fault in the
part sustained by Mr. Coleridge, which we are compelled to notice,
because the mischief by no means terminates with the obscurity it
creates, and that is, his ambition of intruding, upon the Christian doctrines, the innovating language, and the mystical notions of the critical
philosophy.[1] It is quite impossible for an intelligent man to contemplate
the infinite importance of the Christian faith to every human being,
and the authority on which it rests, without coming immediately to
the conclusion, that no alleged fact or principle, moral or physical,
ought to be applied to it as a ground of reasoning, until it has been
confirmed by the fullest experience, and approved by the understandings and consciences of the wise and good. But this philosophy,
however explained, has not been sanctioned by any of these tests: it
has not stood its ground even in the place which gave it birth; and Mr.
Coleridge, in the transgression of this rule, has ventured upon an experiment as dangerous as it is incautious and rash. We give him credit for
his intentions, and we believe, that wrapped up as he seems to be in the
importance of his own speculations, he is not aware of all the consequences to which they lead. It requires, however, no great stretch of
intellect to predict the effect of them upon others, and we venture to
affirm that they will neither contribute to his own reputation, nor, what
is of much more importance, to the benefit of his readers. They may
amuse some and perplex others—some again they may mislead, and a
few they may puff up with conceited notions of their own sagacity,
but we fear they will edify none.

[1] I.e. Kantian philosophy.

We mean no offence to Mr. Coleridge, for many of whose qualities we entertain a high respect; but in a cause so vital we dare not shrink from the free expression of our opinion; and as we learn, upon his own authority, that he is on the eve of publishing a great work upon the Christian Religion, the labour of his whole life, in which the same principles are to be further developed, we do earnestly entreat him to learn fairly from his friends the results of the present trial, before he proceeds further in the same career.

It is time that we should turn, however, to the work in question, of which we shall give a short history, partly derived from the preface, and partly from its own internal evidence.

This volume, then, was at first intended as a selection of such passages from the writings of Archbishop Leighton as appeared most striking for their beauty, or valuable for their piety, with a few notes and a biographical preface from the selector. As the work advanced, however, new prospects opened to his view, and new objects engaged his pursuit. The lofty and spiritual tone which characterises the writings of Leighton, was calculated to excite the prolific energies of Mr. Coleridge in no ordinary degree, while his conversations with his friends and his own private studies were perpetually suggesting fresh matter, more or less applicable to the subject. Thus by degrees the character and the objects of the work were changed. The archbishop, who had entered as a principal, soon became only an auxiliary. Other authors were permitted to dispute the place with him; and above all, the reflections of the editor himself, fermented by the spirit of the critical philosophy, swelled to such a magnitude as to become the dominant feature of the whole; and at last, instead of the beauties of Leighton, there came out a motley collection, consisting of aphorisms, introductions, and sequels to, and commentaries upon aphorisms, with notes indifferently upon them all; which after being arranged in order, as prudential, moral, and spiritual, have been ushered into the world under the imposing title of *Aids to Reflection*. How far the work is entitled, generally speaking, to this distinction will be shown hereafter from the extracts which will be produced: our first business is with Archbishop Leighton, for whose name and writings we have long entertained a high respect: his simple and beautiful sayings, though labouring under the disadvantage of being presented in small specimens, and apart from their native beds, still shine with singular lustre amidst the various productions around him; and though we should have been much more indebted to Mr. Coleridge if he had adhered to his original plan, we still think that if the éclat of his name, and the approbation he has stamped upon the author, should be the means of bringing his works into more general influence and circulation, he will have conferred a greater service upon Christianity, than by all that he has done before. Under this impression we have placed a new edition of Leighton's works at the head of this article, and as Mr. Coleridge has neglected to furnish the biographical notice he had promised, we shall endeavour to supply its place by a few particulars of his life and writings, principally extracted from a spirited and eloquent memoir prefixed to the new edition, by the Rev. Norman Pearson.

[after a lengthy discussion of Pearson's edition of Leighton, the review begins to discuss samples of *Aids to Reflection*]

The next extract we shall make exhibits a striking specimen of that bad taste in which Mr. Coleridge sometimes permits himself to indulge.

APHORISM XXXVI   LEIGHTON

Your blessedness is not—no, believe it, it is not where most of you seek it, in things below you. How can that be? It must be a higher good to make you happy.

Nothing can be more simple, or more just, than this aphorism; but now attend to the following reflection of Mr. Coleridge.

Every rank of creatures, as it ascends in the scale of creation, leaves death behind it or under it. The metal at its height of being seems a mute prophecy of the coming vegetation, into a mimic semblance of which it crystallizes. The blossom and flower, the acmé of vegetable life, divides into correspondent organs with reciprocal functions, and by instinctive motions and approximations seems impatient of that fixture, by which it is differenced in kind from the flower-shaped Psyche, that flutters with free wing above it. And wonderfully in the insect realm doth the irritability, the proper seat of instinct, while yet the nascent sensibility is subordinated thereto—most wonderfully, I say, doth the muscular life in the insect, and the musculo-arterial in the bird, imitate and typically rehearse the adaptive understanding, yea, and the moral affections and charities, of man. Let us carry ourselves back, in spirit, to the mysterious week, the teeming work-days of the Creator: as they rose in vision before the eye of the inspired historian of 'the generations of the heaven and the earth, in the days that the Lord God made the earth and the heavens'. And who that hath watched their ways with an understanding heart, could contemplate the filial and loyal bee; the home-building, wedded, and divorceless swallow; and, above all, the manifoldly intelligent ant tribes, with their commonwealths and confederacies, their warriors and miners, the husbandfolk, that fold in their tiny flocks on the honeyed leaf, and the virgin sisters, with the holy instincts of maternal love, detached and in selfless purity; and not to say to himself, behold

the shadow of approaching humanity, the sun rising from behind, in the kindling morn of creation! Thus all lower natures find their highest good in semblances and seekings of that which is higher and better. All things strive to
ascend, and ascend in their striving. And shall man alone stoop?

Our first inquiry when we are perplexed by an author of reputation,
as Mr. Coleridge observes with regard to Jeremy Taylor, is, 'what
can the author mean?' And this, we confess, we had at first some
difficulty in answering. At last, however, having rejected from the
passage much that is totally irrelevant, stripped it of many fine words,
and construed many hard ones, we came to the argument, the sum of
which seems to be this, that throughout the whole extent of being,
from the dust we tread upon, to man, the lord of the creation, there
exists in every class, a perpetual seeking and striving to rise to that
above, that the mineral crystallizes into a resemblance of the flower,
that the flower blossoms into structure and organization, resembling
those of the insect, that the instinct of the insect, and of the bird,
aspires to the adaptive understanding of the man; and to sum up all in
his own words, 'all lower natures find their highest good in semblances
and seekings of that which is higher and better'. Therefore men, from
their example, ought to rise too.

This may be very poetical and sublime in Mr. Coleridge's view,
but it is neither fact nor argument, and, therefore, not adapted for
students in Theology. There may be some resemblances to the minds
of the spectator; but what seekings and strivings are there in the things
themselves? They know no more about them, than the man in the
moon knows of his resemblance to the man on earth who is gazing at
him. In truth, the very reverse of this seeking is the case. These beings
remain precisely where they are placed by Almighty God, and neither
find nor seek for change. Nay, we have better ground for this statement
than our own, nothing less than the joint authority of Leighton and
Coleridge, for if our readers will only turn to Aphorism xlvii, they
will find the same inference drawn from an hypothesis directly contradicting this.

APHORISM XLVII L. & ED.

God hath suited every creature he hath made with a convenient good to which
it tends, and in the obtainment of which it rests, and is satisfied. Natural bodies
have all their own natural place, whither, if not hindered, they move incessantly
till they be in it; and they declare, by resting there, that they are (as I may say)
where they would be. Sensitive creatures are carried to seek a sensitive good,

as agreeable to their rank in being, and, attaining that, aim no further. Now, in this is the excellency of man, that he is made capable of a communion with his maker, and, because capable of it, is unsatisfied without it; the soul, being cut out (so to speak) to that largeness, cannot be filled with less.

But there are others more worthy of Mr. Coleridge, and we are happy to present them.

APHORISM X   L. & ED.
WORLDLY MIRTH

As he that taketh away a garment in cold weather, and as vinegar upon nitre, so is he that singeth songs to a heavy heart. Prov. xxv, 20. Worldly mirth is so far from curing spiritual grief, that even worldly grief, where it is great and takes deep root, is not allayed but increased by it. A man who is full of inward heaviness, the more he is encompassed about with mirth, it exasperates and enrages his grief the more; like ineffectual weak physic, which removes not the humour, but stirs it and makes it more unquiet. But spiritual joy is seasonable for all estates; in prosperity, it is pertinent to crown and sanctify all other enjoyments, with this which so far surpasses them; and in distress, it is the only *Nepenthe*, the cordial of fainting spirits: so, Psal. iv. 7, *He hath put joy into my heart.* This mirth makes way for itself, which other mirth cannot do. These songs are sweetest in the night of distress.

There is something exquisitely beautiful and touching in the first of these similies; and the second, though less pleasing to the imagination, has the charm of propriety, and expresses the transition with equal force and liveliness. A grief of recent birth is a sick infant, that must have its medicine administered in its milk, and sad thoughts are the sorrowful heart's natural food. This is a complaint that is not to be cured by opposites, which for the most part only reverse the symptoms while they exasperate the disease; or like a rock in the mid channel of a river swoln by a sudden rain-flush from the mountain, which only detains the excess of waters from their proper outlet, and make them foam, roar, and eddy. The soul in her desolation hugs the sorrow close to her, as her sole remaining garment: and this must be drawn off so gradually, and the garment to be put in its stead so gradually slipt on, and feel so like the former, that the sufferer shall be sensible of the change only by the refreshment. The true spirit of consolation is well-content to detain the tear in the eye, and finds a surer pledge of its success in the smile of resignation that dawns through that, than in the liveliest shows of a forced and alien exhilaration.

APHORISM XV   L. & ED.
THE CHRISTIAN NO STOIC

Seek not altogether to dry up the stream of sorrow, but to bound it, and keep it within its banks. Religion doth not destroy the life of nature, but adds to it a life more excellent; yea, it doth not only permit, but requires some feeling of afflictions. Instead of patience, there is in some men an affected pride of spirit suitable only to the doctrine of the *Stoics*, as it is usually taken. They strive not to feel at all the afflictions that are on them; but where there is no feeling at all, there can be no patience.

Of the sects of ancient philosophy the Stoic is, doubtless, the nearest to Christianity. Yet even to this, Christianity is fundamentally opposite. For the Stoic attaches the highest honour (or rather, attaches honour *solely*) to the person that acts virtuously in spite of his feelings, or who has raised himself above the conflict by their extinction; while Christianity instructs us to place small reliance on a virtue that does not *begin* by bringing the feelings to a conformity with the commands of the conscience. Its especial aim, its characteristic operation, is to moralize the affections. The feelings that oppose a right act must be wrong feelings. The *act*, indeed, whatever the agent's *feelings* might be, Christianity would command: and under certain circumstances would both command and commend it—commend it, as a healthful symptom in a sick patient; and command it, as one of the ways and means of changing the feelings, or displacing them by calling up the opposite.

We now enter upon the most difficult, but by no means the most pleasing, or the most edifying, portion of the work; the Aphorisms on spiritual religion. It is here that Mr. Coleridge, feeling himself particularly in his own element, expatiates with unbounded license, and leaves his coadjutors at a distance; but in proportion as he becomes more elevated and more isolated, he is less and less intelligible; and we are compelled to confess, with some degree of shame, that if our duty had not imperiously urged us on, we should have stopped at the very threshold of these mysteries. Fortunately, however, he does not plunge us into them at once. He detains us agreeably enough with a few aphorisms on spiritual influence, by Henry More, Leighton, &c., which, like fertile spots upon the borders of a great desert, serve to refresh the traveller at the commencement of his journey, but afford neither guide nor criterion of that which lies beyond.

APHORISM II   H. MORE

There are two very bad things in this resolving of men's faith and practice into *the immediate suggestion* of a spirit not acting on our understandings, or rather into the illumination of such a spirit as they can give no account of, such as does not enlighten their reason, or enable them to render their doctrine intelligible to others. First, it defaces and makes useless that part of the image of God in us which we call REASON: and, secondly, it takes away that advantage which raises Christianity above all other religions, that she dare appeal to so solid a faculty.

APHORISM IV

ON AN UNLEARNED MINISTRY, UNDER PRETENCE OF A CALL OF THE
SPIRIT AND INWARD GRACES SUPERSEDING OUTWARD HELPS

Tell me, ye high-flown *Perfectionists*, ye boasters of the *light within* you, could the highest perfection of your inward light ever show to you the history of past ages, the state of the world at present, the knowledge of arts and tongues, without books or teachers? How then can you understand the Providence of God, or the age, the purpose, the fulfilment of prophecies, or distinguish such as have been fulfilled from those to the fulfilment of which we are to look forward? How can you judge concerning the authenticity and uncorruptedness of the Gospels, and the other sacred Scriptures? And how without this knowledge can you support the truth of Christianity? How can you either have, or give a reason for the faith which you profess? This *light within*, that loves darkness, and would exclude those excellent gifts of God to mankind, knowledge and understanding, what is it but a sullen self-sufficiency within you, engendering contempt of superiors, pride, and a spirit of division, and inducing you to reject for yourselves, and to undervalue in others, the *helps without*, which the grace of God has provided and appointed for his Church—nay, to make them grounds or pretexts of your dislike or suspicion of Christ's ministers who have fruitfully availed themselves of the helps afforded them—HENRY MORE.

APHORISM V

There are wanderers, whom neither pride nor a perverse humour have led astray; and whose condition is such, that I think few more worthy of a man's best directions. For the more imperious sects having put such unhandsome vizards on Christianity, and the sincere milk of the *word* having been everywhere so sophisticated by the humours and inventions of men, it has driven these anxious melancholists to seek for *a teacher* that cannot deceive, the voice of the *eternal* word within them; to which if they be faithful, they assure themselves it will be faithful to them in return. Nor would this be a groundless presumption, if they had sought this voice in the reason and the conscience, with the Scripture articulating the same, instead of giving heed to their fancy and mistaking bodily disturbances, and the vapors resulting therefrom, for inspiration and the teaching of the Spirit—HENRY MORE.

After these we are introduced to the main object of the author; 1. to exhibit the true and scriptural meaning and intent of several articles of faith, that are rightly classed among the mysteries and peculiar doctrines of Christianity.

2. To show the rationality of these doctrines when examined by their proper organ, the reason and conscience of man.

3. To exhibit from the works of Leighton an affecting picture, &c. &c.

Being well convinced that few of our readers will have the courage to follow Mr. Coleridge through the whole of his views, we have endeavoured to extract from the mass of intricate and excursive matter in which they are involved, some of the most important positions he maintains, and the results to which they tend; confessing fairly, that in this attempt, upon the success of which we do not pique ourselves, we have passed through a variety of feelings, being often interested and amused, sometimes perplexed and bewildered, occasionally instructed, and now and then grievously mortified and disappointed. The first great object of Mr. C., in the prosecution of his design, is to impress upon his readers a distinction between the reason and the understanding. For this distinction he has been labouring, as he affirms, more than twenty years, casting his bread upon the waters; and if it should occur to our readers, as it did at first to ourselves, that he would have found it ready-made to his hands in almost every book in metaphysics he could have recourse to, they must be early taught that this is not the distinction at which Mr. Coleridge aims. He means to contend, that the understanding and the reason are different in source and quality, and not in degree; and that they have in truth nothing in common by which they can be justly ranged under the same genus. Accordingly, he defines the understanding to be (in the language of Kant) the faculty, judging according to sense, by which we reflect, &c.; and he states its operations to be only these:—1. Attention—2. Abstraction—3. Generalization (including the construction of names). Under this view, he concludes, that the understanding of man is the same in kind as the instinct or adaptive intelligence in brutes, and that it differs only from the best and highest specimens of this adaptive intelligence, in consequence of its co-existence with far higher powers of a diverse kind in one and the same subject, viz.; reason, free-will, and self-consciousness. For proofs of this fact, he sends us to the dog, the bee, and the ant, and more especially to the substance of some lectures on anatomy lately delivered in London, whose conclusions, coinciding in some measure with his own views, he hails with great triumph, and expatiates upon with sincere delight. Having made this step, which, by the by, puts him directly at issue with his great master Bacon, who declares that the faculties of the human mind differ not only in degree but in kind from the instincts of animals, he proceeds to the reason; and here, if he should be thought to have degraded the understanding by confining it to objects of sense, and associating it with the instinct of brutes, he makes ample compensation, by the lofty views and sublime origin he assigns to the reason; defining it, in the language of the critical philosophy, as the power of necessary convictions, the source and substance of truths above sense, and having their evidence in themselves. According to its application, it is distinguished into two kinds, the speculative and the practical. In reference to *formal* or *abstract* truth, it is speculative; in reference to *actual or moral* truth, as the fountain of ideas, or the light of the conscience, it is practical.

Again, to give a fuller notion to our readers, who may not at once comprehend the force of this definition: the reason is considered by him as synonymous with spirit—as pre-eminently spiritual—even our spirit through an effluence of the same grace by which we are privileged to say 'Our Father'. Further, according to this principle, though the understanding may be termed human, the reason *cannot*; there is but *one reason*, one and the same, the light that lighteth every man's individual understanding, and thus makes it a reasonable understanding, one only, yet manifold; it goeth through all understanding, and remaining in itself, regenerateth 'all other powers' ('Wisdom of Solomon', cviii). In short, it is an influence from the glory of the Almighty—the Divine Word. Hence an important deduction, which properly belongs to a more advanced stage of the argument: 'Whenever, by self-subjection to this universal light, the will of the individual—the particular will—has become a will of reason, the man is regenerate, and reason is then the spirit of the regenerated man, whereby the person is capable of a quickening inter-communion with the divine spirit'. To give a further insight into the distinct operations of these two faculties, 'Take', he says, 'a familiar illustration':

My sight and touch convey to me a certain impression, to which my understanding applies its pre-conceptions (*conceptus antecedentes et generalissimi*) of quantity and relation, and thus refers it to the class and name of three-cornered bodies—We will suppose it the iron of a turf-spade. It compares the sides, and finds that any two measured as one are greater than the third; and, according to a law of the imagination, there arises a presumption, that in all other bodies of the same figure (*i.e.*, three-cornered and equilateral) the same proportion exists. After this, the senses have been directed successively to a number of three-cornered bodies of *unequal* sides—and in these, too, the same proportion has been found without exception, till at length it becomes a fact of *experience*, that in *all* triangles hitherto seen the two sides are greater than the third: and there will exist no ground or analogy for anticipating an exception to a rule, generalized from so vast a number of particular instances. So far and no farther could the understanding carry us: and as far as this 'the faculty, judging according to sense', conducts many of the *inferior* animals, if not in the same, yet in instances analogous and fully equivalent.

The reason supersedes the whole process; and on the first conception presented by the understanding, in consequence of the first sight of a triangular figure, of whatever sort it might chance to be, it affirms with an assurance incapable of future increase, with a perfect *certainty*, that in all possible triangles any two of the enclosing lines *will* and *must* be greater than the third. In short, understanding in its highest form of experience remains commensurate with the experimental notices of the senses, from which it is generalized. Reason, on the other hand, either pre-determines experience, or avails itself of a past experience to supersede its necessity in all future time; and affirms truths which no sense could perceive, nor experiment verify, nor experience confirm.

So far he is at least intelligible; but try the next:

Yea, this is the test and character of a truth so affirmed, that in its own proper form it is *inconceivable*. For *to conceive* is a function of the understanding, which can be exercised only on subjects subordinate thereto. And yet to the forms of the understanding all truth must be reduced, that is to be fixed as an object of reflection, and to be rendered *expressible*. And here we have a second test and sign of a truth so affirmed, that it can come forth out of the moulds of the understanding only in the disguise of two contradictory conceptions, each of which is partially true, and the conjunction of both conceptions becomes the representative or *expression* (=the *exponent*) of a truth *beyond* conception and inexpressible. Examples. Before Abraham *was*, I *am*.—God is a circle whose centre is everywhere and circumference nowhere.—The soul is all in every part.

Having settled this point, he next proceeds to show the difference betwixt nature and spirit, the one being the antithesis of the other, that is, whatever is not nature is spirit, and *vice versà*. But nature (*natura*, about to be born) is the term in which we comprehend all things representable in the forms of time and space, and subjected to the relations of cause and effect, and the cause of whose existence is therefore something antecedent. Whatever, therefore, originates its own acts is spiritual; but the will originates its own acts, therefore it is spiritual, supernatural, but not miraculous.

These views, Mr. Coleridge says, form the ground-work of his scheme; but it may be proper to inquire, how far we are advanced at present, and though there is a deplorable want of method in the work, we may venture to state, that the conclusion is simply this—as the reason and the will of man are spiritual, they are therefore capable of communion with the Divine Spirit; in the words of the author thus, the reasonableness of the real influence of a divine spirit—the compatibility and possible communion of such a spirit in principle individuals —and an answer to the question, whether there is any faculty in man by which a knowledge of spiritual truths, or of any truths not abstracted from nature, is *rendered possible*. See Aphor. viii. And here we would pause for a moment to inquire, what practical good, supposing the theory to be correct, a sensible Christian would derive from this conclusion? What difficulty does it remove? What bulwark does it strengthen? What Christian hope or feeling does it create or animate? It proves only the possibility of a fact of which he has already the strongest and the plainest testimony. Every intelligent Christian, whether he has read Descartes and Locke or not, must possess in his own consciousness, a stronger testimony of the existence of spiritual faculty within him, the source of thought, &c., than of the existence of the material world around him, and a better knowledge of its operations too. Further, he has a plain and explicit promise from one who cannot lie, the Father of light and truth, that his Holy Spirit shall co-operate with his spirit for the renewal in his mind of the divine image which had been defaced in him, and for the support of faith and holiness. What further proof can we desire? Shall we question whether God can govern the mind which he himself has made? Shall he bring to the birth and not bring forth? Really we cannot help recommending to Mr. Coleridge an aphorism of Leighton, which he will do well to study upon this very topic. 'And the most profitable way of considering this regeneration and sonship, is certainly to follow the light of those holy writings, and not to jangle in disputes about the order and manner of it, of which, though somewhat may be profitably said, and safely, namely, so much as the scripture speaks, yet much that is spoken of it, and debated by many, is but an useless expense of time and pains'. Nay, they are worse than useless in the present case. Their lightest mischief is, that they draw the mind of the Christian from the true and solid ground of his faith, to that which is delusive and unsatisfactory. Their worst, that, by the admission of new principles into theology, they lead to vain and rash speculations in other doctrines, of which neither the bearings nor the consequences can be seen. We may fancy what the scholars would effect, when we see more clearly what confusion the master himself would produce.

The next step is the application of his principles to the mysteries of our faith; of which the Trinity, and the origin of evil, would naturally be the first. In mercy, however, to those who require aids to reflection, he reserves these mysteries for the masters in Israel, men of greater abstraction and reach of thought; and we applaud his consideration. It puts us in mind of saying of Fontenelle, 'That a wise man with his hand full of truths should content himself with opening his little finger', and we only regret that Mr. Coleridge has not felt somewhat more of this self-restraint. But we shall now proceed with him to the two heads of necessary faith which he has undertaken, namely, original sin, and the redemption. Upon the first topic he is unusually obscure, but we will endeavour to state his meaning; desiring our readers to keep in mind the positions already laid down, *viz.*, that the reason and the will are spiritual, and that the will originates its own acts.

We shall pass over a long discussion upon the several schemes of Jeremy Taylor and our first Reformers, respecting the doctrine of original sin, because we think our readers will be less anxious to know how he proposes to refute the opinions of others, than what he means to substitute in their stead. It may suffice to say, however, that his doctrine is avowedly opposed both to Calvinism and Arminianism; and, if we mistake not, no less at variance with our own article and with the scriptures. Let us hear, however, what he says: having proved, much at length, that original sin (sin having an origin) is a doctrine not peculiar to Christianity, but acknowledged as the basis of every religion, and of all philosophy, throughout the civilized world; he adds, that it was and is a mystery, arising from the very admission of a responsible will:

For this is the essential attribute of a will, and contained in the very *idea*, that whatever determines the will acquires this power from a previous determination of the will itself. The will is ultimately self-determined, or it is no longer a *will* under the law of perfect freedom, but a *nature* under the mechanism of cause and effect. And if by an act, to which it had determined itself, it has subjected itself to the determination of nature (in the language of St. Paul, to the law of the flesh), it receives a nature into itself, and so far it becomes a nature; and this is a corruption of the will and a corrupt nature. It is also a *fall* of man, inasmuch as his will is the condition of his personality; the ground and condition of the attribute which constitutes him *man*. And the ground-work of *personal* being is a capacity of acknowledging the moral law (the law of the spirit, the law of freedom, the divine will) as that which should, of itself, suffice to determine the will to a free obedience of the law, the law working thereon *by its own exceeding lawfulness*. This, and this alone, is *positive* good: good in itself, and independent of all relations. Whatever resists and, as a positive force, opposes *this* in the will is therefore evil. But an evil in the will is an evil will; and as all moral evil (*i.e.* all evil that is evil without reference to its contingent physical consequences) is *of* the will, this evil will must have its source in the will. And thus we might go back from act to act, from evil to evil, *ad infinitum*, without advancing a step.

Now let the grounds, on which the fact of an evil inherent in the will is affirmable in the instance of any one man, be supposed equally applicable in *every* instance, and concerning all men: so that the fact is asserted of the individual, *not* because he has committed this or that crime, or because he has shown himself to be *this* or *that* man, but simply because he is *a* man. Let the evil be supposed such as to imply the impossibility of an individual's referring to any particular time at which it might be conceived to have commenced, or to any period of his existence at which it was not existing. Let it be supposed, in short, that the subject stands in no relation whatever to time, can neither be called *in* or *out of* time; but that all relations of time are as alien and heterogeneous in this question, as the relations and attributes of space (north or south, round or square, thick or thin) are to our affections and moral feelings. Let the reader suppose this, and he will have before him the precise import of the scriptural *doctrine* of original sin: or rather of the fact acknowledged in all ages, and recognised, but not originating, in the Christian scriptures.

A moral evil is an evil that has its origin in a will. An evil common to all must have a ground common to all. But the actual existence of moral evil we are bound in conscience to admit; and that there is an evil common to all is a fact; and this evil must therefore have a common ground. Now this evil ground cannot originate in the divine will: it must therefore be referred to the will of man. And this evil ground we call original sin. It is *mystery*, that is, a fact, which we see but cannot explain; and the doctrine a truth which we apprehend, but can neither comprehend nor communicate. And such, by the quality of the subject (*viz.* a responsible *will*) it must be, if it be truth at all.

Should a professed believer ask you whether that, which is the ground of responsible action in *your* will, could in any way be responsibly present in the will of Adam? Answer him in these words: *You*, Sir! can no more demonstrate the negative, than I can conceive the affirmative. The corruption of my will may very warrantably be spoken of as a *consequence* of Adam's fall, even as my birth of Adam's existence; as a consequence, a link in the historic chain of instances, whereof Adam is the first. But that it is *on account* of Adam; or that this evil principle was, *a priori*, inserted or infused into my will by the will of another—which is indeed a contradiction in terms, my will in such case being no *will*—this is nowhere asserted in Scripture, explicitly or by implication. It belongs to the very essence of the doctrine, that in respect of original sin *every* man is the adequate representative of *all* men. What wonder, then, that where no inward ground of preference existed, the choice should be determined by outward relations, and that the first *in time* should be taken as the diagram? Even in Genesis the word Adam is distinguished from a proper name by an article before it. It is *the* Adam, so as to express the *genus*, not the individual—or rather, perhaps, I should say, *as well as* the individual. But that the word with its equivalent, *the old man*, is used symbolically and universally by St. Paul, (1 Cor. xv. 22. 45. Eph. iv. 22. Col. iii. 9. Rom. vi. 6.) is too evident to need any proof.

These, we think, . . . are the principal passages in which his doctrine is laid down; and something, he says, might be added to the clearness of the preceding views (we defy him to add to their obscurity), if the limits of the work had allowed him to clear away the several delusive and fanciful assertions respecting the state of our first parents, their wisdom, &c. That is, in our view of the matter, if he had professedly borne away at one fell swoop every particle of the Mosaic history respecting our first parents; if he had denied to them any meaning, either allegorical or literal, as these principles effectually do, his own doctrine would have been just as obscure as it is now, but not so decidedly at variance with history and established opinions. For to what does it amount? Let us bring some of his positions closer together. The will is ultimately self-determined; the act of the will determining itself to nature (the law of the flesh), instead of the moral law, is the corruption or fall of man. It is impossible to refer this evil to any particular time; it has no relation to time; it can neither be called in time, nor out of time; it was not derived from Adam, nor is it on account of Adam; it does not originate in God; is not eternal. It is in man, because he is a man, not because he commits this or that crime; and in this respect there is no difference between Adam and his posterity. Adam is the representative of every man, and every man a representative of Adam; but Adam being the first in time (mark this, reader), may be taken as the diagram. In Genesis, the word Adam is distinguished from a proper name by an article before it—the Adam—so that it seems doubtful, in this scheme, whether there was any such person as Adam at all.

It requires, we think, but a moderate degree of intelligence to observe that these positions are inconsistent and incoherent with each other; and very little reading to be convinced, that they are totally irreconcileable with the Scriptures, and with every sound commentary upon them, from the Gospel times down to the present day. The history of our first parents in Genesis, by whatever rule it may be construed, and the reasoning of that apostle who declared that he had his revelation, not from man, but from his divine Master himself, evidently affirm or imply these things—a law given by God to man; a temptation to which he was submitted; his disobedience, and a curse entailed on his posterity in consequence of his apostasy (*depravatio naturæ cujuslibet hominis ex Adamo naturaliter propagati*, as our article expresses it);[1] and although many different opinions have been entertained and promulgated respecting the degree and extent of the corruption thus incurred, and the decrees of God connected with it, yet these positions lie at the common root of all their arguments; and, excepting by the Pelagians and Socinians, are held by all the Christians of Europe at the present day. But Mr. C.'s doctrine would sweep them all away, letter and spirit. Try only one or two instances at the fountain head. He affirms, that original sin is not on account of Adam, is not derived from Adam! But what says St. Paul?—'By one man's disobedience many were made sinners'; 'Many are dead through the offence of one'; 'As in Adam all die, so in Christ shall all be made alive'; 'As, by the offence of one, judgment came upon all men to condemnation: even so, by the righteousness of one, the free gift came upon all men unto justification of life'.

Again, Mr. C. sets out with the position, that 'the will, being *spiritual* and transcendental, originates its own acts, and cannot be determined by *nature* or *circumstances*'. What says St. Paul, in his most memorable piece of reasoning?—'I know that in me (*i.e.* in *my flesh*) dwelleth no good thing'; '*To will* is present with me, but how to perform that which is good I know not; for the good that *I would* I do not, but the evil *I would not* that I do; for I delight in the law of God after the *inward man*: but I have another law in my members warring against the law of my mind'. Consider the *will*, and its operations, as explained by Locke and Burnet, and accepted by our best divines, and all this struggle is perfectly intelligible. Try it by your own conscience, and it will be felt as well as understood—submit it to the hypothesis of Mr. Coleridge, and it is all confusion and contradiction.

One more trial, and we have done. The Scriptures not only point out the person by whom the taint of original sins was introduced, but they mark distinctly the time at which it took place too—tracing, step by step, the descendants of Adam through their several generations, which correspond to the interval, down to the birth of our Lord; and, again, in the Gospel, retracing the genealogy of Christ, through David and Abraham, up to Adam. But Mr. Coleridge instructs us,

[1] '... the corruption of the nature of the way of man that naturally is engendered of the offspring of Adam' (the ninth of the Thirty-nine Articles, 'On Original Sin').

that it is impossible to refer this evil to any particular time—that it is neither in time, nor out of time—not eternal—not generated by God—not inserted by another's will.

To what purpose, then, shall we ask, has all this violence been done to history, to revelation, and to experience? What compensation does Mr. Coleridge promise to us? A will originating its own acts, and, in consequence of a *corruption* or *disease*, departing from its communion with God, and determining to nature, or the flesh, and therefore *responsible*—for he argues, that when a man is induced by circumstances to evil for want of a power to resist, such evil is not sin—it may be a subject of *regret*, but not of *remorse*. But this is shifting the difficulty, not removing it. For why should a man be more responsible for the effects of a disease in the will, not planted there by himself, than for the effects of a weakness in the will which he inherited? Mr. C. will tell us, that since our will is spiritual, it is possible that the divine will may hold communion with it, and restore it to the guidance of right reason; but we have better authority than his philosophy to assure us—that it is God that worketh *in us to will and to do*.

But Mr. Coleridge is shocked, it seems, at the old stumbling block of hereditary sin, which he calls 'a monstrous fiction'. And yet, mysterious as this doctrine is, and revolting as it may be to our natural reason, there is no tenet delivered to us in which revealed and natural religion harmonize more strongly than in this. To cavil at it, is to cavil against the Creator and Governor of the world, 'whose wisdom reacheth from one end to another, and sweetly doth order all things'. The evidence of the fact is on every side of him; he cannot cast his eyes around for a moment without perceiving innumerable instances of children suffering for the profligacy and crimes of their parents or progenitors. The offspring of the intemperate and licentious is still smitten by the same hand which struck the child that Uriah's wife bare unto David; nor can a more awful, or a more awakening lesson be conveyed to the mind of man, than the thought, that upon his own conduct may depend the welfare or misery of numbers yet unborn, who must be near and dear to him. Alas! Mr. Coleridge, if God should turn to us in the language of Ezekiel, 'Yet say we the way of the Lord is not equal; the fathers have eaten sour grapes, and the children's teeth are set on edge; therefore will I judge you, O, house of Israel! every one according to his ways'. Surely we should then find how much better we might have been employed in attending to our own duties and leaving God, 'who giveth not account of any of his matters', to do what he thinks fit, and what we shall one day know to be the best for us too: he does not 'exact the tale of bricks where he has not furnished the straw'; he will not suffer us to be tempted above what we are able. St. Paul was surely as zealous for the honour of God as Mr. Coleridge—but how does he shew it? Not in accounting for the evil mysteriously permitted by God, but by bringing forward his goodness exerted in our behalf. He never speaks of the curse of Adam but he reminds us at the same time of the redemption by Christ; thus interweaving the mercy and justice of God together, and quelling every rebellious thought before it could rise to inquire. After the first offence, says Taylor, God could not stay from redeeming, nor could Paul stay from preaching that we are redeemed. *Beware of arguments, says Mr. C. against Christianity, which cannot stop here, and consequently ought not to have commenced there.*

Our author next proceeds to the doctrine of the Redemption, to which we would gladly follow him, if our time and our attention did not at once warn us to forbear; but lest a forward student of theology should indulge in a smile at our weakness or want of spirit, we shall leave him to digest one sentence from this description, and then let him continue it if he can.

He wishes to shew, that the abolition of guilt, the redemption, &c., cannot properly be represented by the payment of a debt for another: and that the expressions of St. Paul upon this subject are metaphorical.

Now it would be difficult if not impossible to select points better suited to this purpose, as being equally familiar to all, and yet having a special interest for the Jewish converts, than those are from which the learned apostle has drawn the four principal metaphors, by which he illustrates the blessed *consequences* of Christ's redemption of mankind. These are: 1. sin-offerings, sacrificial expiation. 2. Reconciliation, atonement, καταλλαγη. 3. Ransom from slavery, redemption, the buying back again, or being bought back, from *re* and *emo*. 4. Satisfaction of a creditor's claims by a payment of the debt. To one or other of these four heads all the numerous forms and exponents of Christ's mediation in St. Paul's writings may be referred. And the very number and variety of the words or periphrases used by him, to express one and the same thing, furnish the strongest presumptive proof, that all alike were used *metaphorically*. [In the following notation, let the small letters represent the *effects* or *consequences*, and the capitals the efficient *causes* or *antecedents*. Whether by causes we mean acts or agents, is indifferent. Now let X signify a *transcendent*, *i.e.* a cause beyond our comprehension, and not within the sphere of sensible experience; and, on the other hand, let A, B, C, and D represent, each, some one known and familiar cause in reference to some single and characteristic effect: viz. A in reference to k, B to l, C to m, and D to n. Then I say X+k l m n is in different places expressed by (or as =) A+k; B+l; C+m; D+n. And these I should call *metaphorical* exponents of X.]

Now John, the beloved disciple who leant on the Lord's bosom, the evangelist κατα πνευμα, i.e. according to the *Spirit*, the inner and substantial truth of the Christian creed—John, recording the Redeemer's own words, enunciates the fact itself, to the full extent in which it is enunciable for the human mind, simply and *without any metaphor*, by identifying *it in kind* with a fact of hourly occurrence—*expressing* it, I say, by a familiar fact, the same *in kind* with that intended, though of a far lower *dignity*;—by a fact of every man's experience, *known* to all, yet not better *understood* than the fact described by it. In the redeemed, it is a re-*generation*, a *birth*, a spiritual seed impregnated and evolved, the germinal principle of a higher and enduring life, of a *spiritual* life—that is, a life, the actuality of which is not dependent on the material body, or limited by the circumstances and processes indispensable to its organization and subsistence. Briefly, it is the *differential* of immortality, of which the assimilative power of faith and love is the *integrant*, and the life in Christ the *integration*.

With this precious morceau we shall take our leave of the critical philosophy, trusting that our students in theology will learn from it at least one lesson, which is, the utter vanity, hopelessness, and presumption of such experiments. We want reflection, as Mr. Coleridge says, in this inquiring age; but these are not the aids by which it should be formed, nor this the philosophy in which it should be founded. *Non tali auxilio, nec defensoribus istis.*[1] We want men of other qualities, and of another stamp; men of sound judgment and sober views, as well as of extensive learning; with less of the pretensions, and more of the power of *human reason*, modest, cautious, and circumspect, above all, men strongly imbued with a sincere and unaffected reverence for the sanctuary of the Christian doctrines, and thoroughly averse from all tampering experiments with them. Under their guidance, we can never fear the application of any human discovery to those truths which God in his wisdom has revealed to us. In the mean time we want sound practical piety, content to form itself upon the model of the faith once delivered to the Saints, and looking for no other guide. In the christian philosophy there is nothing exoteric; there is not one language for the learned, and another for the vulgar. Its precepts and its lessons find an echo in every good man's breast; and as for its mysteries, they are much better comprehended by those who trace them to their scriptural consequences, and their purifying influences upon

---

[1] 'Not such defenders, not such aids as these . . .' (Virgil, *Aeneid*, ii, 521).

our hearts and lives, than by those who would merely scan and weigh them. Such knowledge is too high for us.

We have now only one act of justice to perform before we take our leave of Mr. C., and that is to notice a part of these spiritual aphorisms, where, descending from his metaphysical abstractions, he has condescended to indulge in personal feeling, which has left a more painful impression upon our minds. We allude to his observations upon Dr. Paley, particularly with regard to the Resurrection.[1]

It was owing, perhaps, to inadvertency in the first instance, that the charge and the subject of it are placed at a great distance from each other, and in a wrong order; the former at p. 336, the latter at 403. This should not have been permitted on any account. Mr. Coleridge must be aware, that to read one without the other, whichever it may be, must always be a disadvantage to the person whose opinion is impugned. We have too much respect for the manly sense and important Christian labours of Paley, to pass over this charge lightly, and that we may do justice to both the parties we shall bring the whole together. In p. 403, at the close of the aphorisms on spiritual religion, will be found Paley's words, inserted at the suggestion of a friend. Why did not Mr. Coleridge think of this act of justice himself?

Had Jesus Christ delivered no other declaration than the following—'The hour is coming, in the which all that are in the grave shall hear his voice, and shall come forth: they that have done good, unto the resurrection of life; and they that have done evil, unto the resurrection of damnation;'—he had pronounced a message of inestimable importance, and well worthy of that splendid apparatus of prophecy and miracles with which his mission was introduced, and attested: a message in which the wisest of mankind would rejoice to find an answer to their doubts, and rest to their inquiries. It is idle to say, that a future state, had been discovered already:—it had been discovered as the Copernican system was; it was one guess among many. He alone discovers, who *proves*; and no man can prove this point, but the teacher who testifies by miracles that his doctrine comes from God.

To do justice to this celebrated passage, which never, surely, would have been the subject of this minute criticism if it had not been unhappily distinguished by exaggerated praise (see Dr. Parr, p. 335),[2]

---

[1] William Paley (1753–1805). Coleridge opposed the arguments in Paley's *Evidences of Christianity* (1794).

[2] Samuel Parr (1747–1825), whose *The End of Religious Controversy* appeared in 1825.

we must premise, that miracles afford no direct proof of doctrine, but only of the divine commission of him who delivers it. To furnish, therefore, that perfect proof which amounts to a discovery, in the sense of Paley, it is necessary that two things should combine. First, a clear, full, and specific promulgation of the doctrine itself; and, secondly, a miraculous power, attesting the divine authority of him who declares it. In the annunciation of a future state by our Lord, these two qualities are found each of them full and perfect, but in no other; and what Dr. Paley means to affirm is, not that there was no evidence of a future state before his coming into the world, but that there was not such a clear and sufficient promulgation of the truth upon divine authority as might entirely satisfy the minds of men, and preclude all further inquiry. To this distinction we beg to draw the attention of our readers, because we think that it affords a key to all the difficulties in which Mr. Coleridge has embroiled the question, and an answer to all his objections. That there existed, generally, in the Gentile world an internal persuasion of a future state, whether planted directly by the hand of God, or springing up from a common sense of the difference between good and evil, and of every man's being accountable at the great tribunal for the things done in the flesh, there is, we think, abundant reason to believe; and that the Jews, in addition to this internal evidence, might have inferred, from the writings of Moses, the reality of a resurrection, we have the testimony of our Lord himself, in his reasoning with the Sadducees (St. Luke, xx. 32), afterwards quoted by Mr. Coleridge.

But the belief with both was comparatively feeble, partial, and unsteady, and their prospects beyond the grave clouded with obscurity, utterly inconceivable in the presence of that light and immortality which was brought by the Gospel. 'The whole creation groaneth and travaileth together until now', says the Apostle, in allusion to these very difficulties; and the evil was, that no human aid or sagacity was able to relieve its throes. In the Gentile world, the poets and philosophers, so far from giving strength and clearness to the persuasion which they found, had, by their speculations and inventions, weakened and obscured it. 'The plain draught of nature was almost hid under the shades and colours with which they endeavoured to beautify and adorn it'. And as for the Jews, the very fact of the existence of a sect among them, powerful and distinguished, if not numerous, who held the authority of Moses and the Prophets, and denied the Resurrection (who can imagine such a class among Christians?)* proves satisfactorily, apart from all other evidence, that the doctrine had not been promulgated by that Divine Lawgiver with the clearness and fulness required. Even those amongst them who believed in the Resurrection held it defectively. Josephus tells us, 'that the Pharisees taught the resurrection of the just, but not of the unjust, who were to remain in torment'. And St. Paul, in his defence at Cesarea, evidently alludes to this opinion, Acts xxiv. 15—'And have hope toward God, which they themselves also allow, that there shall be a resurrection of the dead, both of the just and unjust'.

Such was the uncertainty in which this important matter was surrounded, till Christ came, and all was light—and beautifully and consistently was it ordained by eternal wisdom, that the clear annunciation of this great doctrine should synchronize with the redemption. That man might feel and understand the important value of that salvation which was then brought for them; that they might comprehend at once the odiousness and the danger of sin, and render thanks to God, who has given them the victory through Jesus Christ. And much does it delight us in this discussion to adduce the testimony of Sherlock[1]—*magnum et venerabile nomen*, whose opinions in his sixth sermon, though delivered in different words, convey a sense perfectly conformable to that of Paley. He not only admits the defect and obscurity of the doctrine before our Saviour came, but very ingeniously accounts for it, 'the wise man tells us, that God made not death; for he created all things that they might have their being; and the generations of the world were healthful; and there is no poison of destruction in them: nor the kingdom of death upon earth; for righteousness is immortal—but ungodly men with their works and words called it to them'. 'If immortality was the condition of the creation, if death came in as a surprise upon nature, no wonder if she stands mute and astonished at the fatal change, and seems neither willing to part with her hopes of immortality, nor yet able to maintain them'.

God made man immortal, and gave him consistent hopes and fears: man made himself mortal by sin: must not then those hopes, which were consistent hopes upon the foot of immortality, become very absurd when joined to a state of mortality? and thus the coming in of death obscured the hopes of immortality— lastly, if we consider how our Saviour has enlightened this doctrine, it will appear, that he has removed the difficulty at which nature stumbled. As death

* Hymeneus and Pheleteus, judaizing Christians, argued only that it was past.
[1] William Sherlock (1641-1707).

was no part of the state of nature, so the difficulties arising from it were not provided for in the religion of nature. To remove these was the proper work of Revelation, these our Lord has effectually cleared by his gospel, and shown us, that the body may and shall be united to the spirit in the day of the Lord, so that the complete man shall stand before the great tribunal to receive a just recompence of reward for things done in the body.

This account is given in the words immediately preceding,

Who hath abolished death, and brought life and immortality to light through the Gospel. Now, if the abolishing of death was the bringing to light life and immortality, it is plain, that the coming in of death was that which darkened nature in this great point of religion.

Again,

There is still something farther that nature craves, something which, with unutterable groans, she pants after, even life and happiness for evermore. She sees all her children go down to the grave: all beyond the grave is to her one wide waste, a land of doubt and uncertainty; when she looks into it, she has her hopes and she has her fears; and, agitated by the vicissitudes of these passions, she finds no ground whereon to rest her foot. How different is the scene which the Gospel opens. There we see the heavenly Canaan, the new Jerusalem, in which City of the great God there are mansions, many mansions, for receiving them, who, 'through faith and patient continuance in well-doing, seek for glory and immortality'.

See also Leland, *passim*.[1]

Having thus explained Dr. Paley's opinion, and shown its conformity with right reason and the opinions of our divines, we must now proceed to the charge brought against him by Mr. Coleridge. After expressing, in no measured terms, his cordial admiration of the passage, as a masterpiece of composition, he denies that it is true. He doubts the validity of the assertion as a general rule; and denies it as applied to matters of faith. Now, with respect to the general rule (*viz.* he only discovers who proves), Mr. Coleridge has given no reason whatever for his doubts, and, therefore, we are not bound to say much in refutation of them. We have no hesitation, however, in stating, that in the sense in which the words *discover* and *prove* are here used by Mr. Paley—that is, in their approved and accepted sense, the proposition is, generally speaking, true—there may be many reasons at present for believing in the existence of a north-west passage. Such, for instance, as the direction and the velocity of currents, the trending of the coast, the partial accounts of natives, &c., &c.; but whatever probability

[1] John Leland (1691-1766), non-conformist minister.

may arise from this evidence, it does not amount to a proof—but when Captain Parry, or Captain Franklin, or some other intelligent traveller, shall return to Europe with his crew, after having ascertained, by actual observation, the continuity of the coast from the Atlantic to the Pacific, and shall have clearly and unequivocally announced it, then shall we say with one voice, that the north-west passage has been *discovered*, because it has been *proved*. But let this pass, and proceed we to the application. Mr. Coleridge denies the rule as applied to matters of faith, to the verities of religion, in which he says, there must always be somewhat of moral election, 'an act of the will as well as of the understanding'.

True Christian faith must have in it something of in-evidence, that must be made up by duty and by obedience—Taylor's *Worthy Communicant.*[1]

Without dwelling upon the distinction, that, in this last sentence quoted from Taylor, the faith of a Christian in the great doctrines of Christianity, and not in this awful sanction of them, is intended; we will admit something of this inbred evidence, and allow Mr. C. to make the most of it, and then ask, how a doctrine disbelieved by some of the philosophers, questioned by others, and almost disregarded by the generality, a doctrine, at the very mention of which at Athens, by St. Paul, some mocked, and others declared that they would hear him again about it, could supersede the necessity of the Christian demonstration of it?

Still does Paley's proposition remain firm—still has Christ abolished death, and brought life and immortality to light (enlightened and cleared it up, if you please) by the Gospel.

But to come to those serious objections which constitute the worst feature of the case:

The obvious inference from the passage in question, if not its express import, is: Miracula *experimentum crucis* esse, quo solo probandum erat, Homines non, pecudum instar, omnino perituros esse. Now this doctrine I told to be altogether alien from the *spirit*, and without authority in the *letter*, of Scripture. I can recall nothing in the history of human belief that should induce me, I find nothing in my own moral being that enables me, to understand it. I can, however, perfectly well understand the readiness of *those* divines in hoc PALEII Dictum ore pleno jurare, qui nihil aliud in toto Evangelio invenire posse profitentur. The most unqualified admiration of this superlative passage I find perfectly in

[1] Jeremy Taylor, *The Worthy Communicant* (1660).

character for those, who, while Socinianism and Ultra-Socinianism are spreading like the roots of an elm, on and just below the surface, through the whole land, and *here and there* at least have even dipt under the garden-fence of the church, and blunted the edge of the labourer's spade in the gayest *parterres* of our Baal-hamon, (*Sol. Song*, viii. 11,)—who, while heresies, to which the framers and compilers of our Liturgy, Homilies, and Articles, would have refused the very name of Christianity, meet their eyes on the list of religious denominations for every city and large town throughout the kingdom—can yet congratulate themselves with Dr. Paley (in his Evidences) that *the Rent has not reached the foundation*—i.e. that the corruption of man's will; that the responsibility of man in any sense in which it is not equally predicable of dogs and horses; that the Divinity of our Lord, and even his pre-existence; that sin, and redemption through the merits of Christ; and grace; and the especial aids of the Spirit; and the efficacy of prayer; and the subsistency of the Holy Ghost; may all be extruded without breach or rent in the essentials of Christian faith?— that a man may deny and renounce them all, and remain a *fundamental* Christian, notwithstanding! But there are many that cannot keep up with latitudinarians of such a stride; and I trust, that the majority of serious believers are in this predicament. Now for all these it would seem more in character to be of Bishop's Taylor's opinion, that the belief in question is *presupposed* in a convert to the truth in Christ—but at all events not to circulate in the great whispering-gallery of the religious public suspicions and hard thoughts of those who, like myself, *are* of this opinion! who do not dare decry the religious instincts of humanity as a baseless dream; who hold, that to excavate the ground under the faith of all mankind, is a very questionable method of building up our faith as Christians; who fear, that instead of adding to, they should detract from, the honour of the incarnate word, by disparaging the light of the Word, that was in the beginning, and which lighteth *every* man; and who, under these convictions, can tranquilly leave it to be disputed, in some new 'Dialogues in the Shades', between the fathers of the Unitarian Church on one side, and Maimonides, Moses Mendelsohn, and Lessing on the other, whether the famous passage in Paley does or does not contain the three dialectic flaws, Petitio principii, argumentum in circulo, and argumentum contra rem a premisso rem ipsam includente.

Upon a review of this passage, we are not so much surprised at the boldness of assertion, and absence of all argument observable in it (for we know how often these two qualities are connected) as at the total want of candour and charity towards the memory of a man who has really done more for the Christian cause than all the modern critical philosophers, in their several places and generations combined. We cannot conjecture what evil star could have come across the path of this philosophic divine to lead him from his usual course. Not content with stating Paley's proposition defectively in Latin, after his own fashion, calling it unscriptural and untrue, suddenly, when we are expecting his proofs, he turns round upon the author, and all who approve of this passage, with insinuations of Latitudinarianism and Socinianism, imputing to them indifference to the great doctrines of Christianity, the corruption of man's will, the redemption, the aiding of the spirit, the efficacy of prayer; and this, too, of Dr. Paley above all others! and then, having exhausted this effusion of his hyper-orthodox spirit, he finishes with complaints equally unseasonable and unlooked-for, of suspicions and hard thoughts circulated in the great whispering-gallery of the religious public about himself—complaints, by the by, for which we never heard that there was any foundation, and in which, after this attack, we believe that few will be found to sympathize.

At last, however, after all this trifling, we come to something like argument, which we shall give at full length:

Yes! fervently do I contend, that to satisfy the understanding that there is a future state, was not the *specific* object of the Christian dispensation; and that neither the belief of a future state, nor the *rationality* of this belief, is the *exclusive* attribute of the Christian religion. An *essential*, a *fundamental*, article of *all* religion it is, and therefore of the Christian; but otherwise than as in connexion with the salvation of mankind from the *terrors* of that state, among the essential articles *peculiar* to the Gospel creed (those, for instance, by which it is *contra*-distinguished from the creed of a religious Jew) I do not place it. And before sentence is passed against me, as heterodox, on this ground, let not my judges forget, who it was that assured us, that if man did not believe in a state of retribution after death, previously and on other grounds, 'neither would he believe, though a man should be raised from the dead'.

Again, I am questioned, as to my *proofs* of a future state, by men who are so far, and *only* so far, professed believers, that they admit a God, and the existence of a law from God: I give them; and the questioners turn from me with a scoff or incredulous smile. Now should others of a less scanty creed infer the weakness of the reasons assigned by me from their failure in convincing *these* men; may I not remind them, WHO it was, to whom a similar question was proposed by men of the same class? But at all events it will be enough for my own support to remember it; and to know, that HE held such questioners, who could not find a sufficing proof of this great all-concerning verity in the words, 'The God of Abraham, the God of Isaac, and the God of Jacob', unworthy of any other answer! men not to be satisfied by *any* proof!—by any such proofs, at least, as are compatible with the ends and purposes of all religious conviction! by any proofs that would not destroy the faith they were intended to confirm, and reverse the whole character and quality of its effects and influences! But if, notwithstanding all here offered in defence of my opinion, I must still be adjudged heterodox and in error,—what can I say, but malo cum Platone errare, and take refuge behind the ample shield of BISHOP JEREMY TAYLOR.

It is painful to direct once more the attention of our readers to the injustice done in this statement to Dr. Paley. His proposition neither declares nor implies, 'that a future state was the specific object of the Christian dispensation; or that the belief of a future state, or the rationality of this belief, was the exclusive attribute of the Christian religion'; but simply, that the fact itself is one of the greatest importance, and that the discovery of it was reserved for Jesus Christ. In whatever way, therefore, these sayings of our Lord, which follow, may be supposed to apply to these gratuitous assertions (and God forbid that we should detract from them a single particle, on whatever side they may weigh!) they do not affect the real proposition at issue. At the close of the parable of the rich man and Lazarus, Abraham is made to say, 'If they hear not Moses and the Prophets (instructing them in the will of God, calling them to repentance, and setting before them the consequences of sin), neither will they be convinced, though one rose from the dead'. The words convey an awful lesson against the deceitfulness of riches and the parable admits and presupposes a resurrection, to the Jewish notion of which it is accommodated; but they leave the question of the sufficiency of these notions where they found it, implying only, that a man's rising from the dead was a miracle, affording the highest species of evidence that could apply to the human mind.

Of the answer of our Lord to the Sadducees, Matt. xxii. 31, 32, enough has been already said. Have you not read, 'I am the God of Abraham, the God of Isaac, the God of Jacob: God is not the God of the dead, but of the living'? Unquestionably our Lord intended to shew that the law of Moses afforded evidence of a future life, which is perfectly consistent with Dr. Paley's proposition.

But, setting aside the fact that the Jewish religion was exclusive, addressing itself especially to a particular nation, 'Hear, O Israel, I am the God', &c., still there is a mighty difference between an inference thus casually pointed out to the Sadducees by our Lord, and that full, particular, and awful assurance of a resurrection, with all its consequences, delivered by our Lord himself to all nations, as the rule and guide of their conduct, a difference of the greatest practical importance, giving a new feature to the life of man upon earth, and casting a bright effulgence over his future prospects—inspiring new hopes, new consolations, and a new responsibility; for, 'at the times of this ignorance, God winked', as St. Paul declares, in announcing the resurrection to the Athenians, 'but now commandeth all men, everywhere, to repent. Because he hath appointed a day, in the which he will judge the world in righteousness, by that man whom he hath ordained, whereof he hath given assurance unto all men, in that he hath raised him from the dead'.

Upon the whole, we are compelled to state, that Mr. Coleridge has not improved our opinion of him by these disquisitions. Of learning, genius, fancy, and acuteness, there are many proofs throughout the present work; but he has mistaken his talents, and is deficient in many qualities of the very last importance for such an undertaking. He wants judgment, simplicity of language, and sobriety of views, and, above all, clearness, method, and stability in his reasoning. Nor has he been at all happy in the mode of composition which he has adopted. It cannot be denied, that this species of writing has its advantages: it awakens reflection, gives force to single impressions, and facility to the memory; and, what is more, by avoiding transitions, which are said to be the most difficult part of composition, it saves an infinity of trouble to the author; but to adopt it, as Mr. Coleridge has done in the latter part of his work, as the channel of intricate and expanded reasoning, dispersing the substance of a single argument over several Aphorisms, is to apply it to a purpose to which it is totally repugnant and unsuited. By dislocating the parts which ought to be viewed together, it obscures their mutual connexion and dependence, and perplexes the reader, who never knows when the matter is ended; and at last the Aphorisms are no Aphorisms at all, but only broken and shapeless masses, which the reader himself must examine and put together, before he can make out what they mean.

THE POETICAL WORKS

1828

104. Unsigned review, *London Weekly Review*

June 1828, ii, 369-70

Mr. Coleridge may certainly be ranked among the most fortunate
men of this age. He has acquired the reputation of lofty genius in
poetry, profound metaphysical knowledge, and unrivalled powers of
conversation. Numbers have committed themselves on these points,
and stand pledged to prove their words. He has consequently a party;
and in the eyes of this party, which, if not numerous, is enthusiastic
and indefatigable, he is everything but a god. He knows whatever can
be known—he has weighed all authors in his balance—he has philos-
ophized—he has discoursed—he has written upon every thing—he is
the high-priest of nature. In one thing only is he deficient—the art of
being intelligible. This, in one way or another, is pretty generally
acknowledged: it is differently accounted for. His friends assert that
his meaning escapes us only because, like a river rolling through
Alpine chasms, it lies too deep to be reached by the eye; his adversaries
insinuate that the stream of his thoughts appears deep, because it is
muddy. By friends and foes the fact, that his meaning is frequently not
perceived, is admitted. We have in fact met with one of the initiated,
who assured us that there were not above eight persons in this populous
city (himself included), who could be said to understand Mr. Coleridge.
We were quite of that opinion; but had no claim to be numbered
among the mystical *eight*. We certainly do not always understand him.
We feel that there is some mysterious power at work near us, as we
know in the dark, by the whirring and rustling of its wings, that some
night bird is passing over us, but cannot tell what manner of being it is,
or whither it is tending. His disciples, to whom darkness is visible,
should they stand beside us at these moments, point out to us a strange

514

being, 'aloft, incumbent on the dusky air, that feels *unusual weight*'; but we can distinguish neither 'member, joint, nor limb'. This makes us peevish: we cannot tell whether it be an eagle or an owl.

Let us, however, grant, in spite of his obscurity and imperfections, that Mr. Coleridge is a poet; and that in denying him to be one (as we once did) we were unjust. It still remains to be decided in what rank we are to place him. The most rash of his admirers will scarcely claim for him a station among the first class of poets—among those whose imagination seems to have thrown a new glory and beauty over nature herself, to have made dawn and sunset more lovely, given brilliancy to the flowers and verdure of the field, sublimity to the ocean, solemnity and religion to the stars and the night, and holiness and divinity to love. He has sung no glorious theme, no field where the passions develope themselves in sublime actions, and where man exhibits an energy, both intellectual and physical, which seems to belong to a higher nature. He has imagined no new combination of passions, affections, and opinions, which we denominate character; nor has he thrown out those burning flashes, as from a furnace mouth, which men, who are themselves possessed by powerful passions, throw out upon the world. On the contrary, his fancy, compared with his invention and emotions, appears like the head of a Hydrocephalic child, too cumbrous and weighty for the body. His images have no glow, no fire in them. Like polar clouds, they are sometimes rich and gaudy, but they are cold. If the reader can imagine the difference between a huge army marching unwillingly, and with measured footsteps in a pageant, and the same army, animated by martial music, and the fierce thirst of action, rushing to the field of battle, he may understand in what Mr. Coleridge differs from a great poet. In the former, all is constraint and inertness, in the latter, spontaneous motion, and rapidity, and energy, and fire. Coleridge wearies and sends us to sleep; the great poet seems to awaken in us a principle of life that we knew not of. Mr. Coleridge's is the poetry of study, and meditation, and labour, and appears what it is; genuine poetry is truly the offspring of inspiration: it is the soul itself, melting with its own fire, and running spontaneously into beautiful forms. The former is an artificial beauty, painted, and curled, and ornamented for show; the latter, a lovely woman, glowing with health and beauty, and walking by the light of her own eyes.

Yet Mr. Coleridge is a poet. But of what class? Of that in which, apparently, he is least ambitious of being ranked. He is of the didactic class. In this, had he perceived it early enough, and been content with his lot, he might have rivalled the greatest, Lucretius, perhaps, excepted. His fertile fancy and high-sounding language, are well adapted for casting a pomp and glitter over a string of moral or other truths, and rendering it agreeable. He might have written a good poem on the nature of things, on agriculture, on fishing, on fowling, or on political virtue or consistency.

Many poets, who fail in larger matters, contrive to make fine little revelations of the secrets of their own heart, little pictures of their emotions, feelings, misfortunes, &c. which delight us exceedingly. But Mr. Coleridge's egotism is not agreeable. Whatever else he may have in his bosom, he seems to have no sunshine there; and therefore, when he attempts to lift the veil from his inner nature, his hand appears to falter, his resolution fails him, and he drops the half-lifted curtain, and screens himself from observation. This may be the effect of natural timidity, or it may proceed from pride. But some conjecture that there is another cause. Our opinion is this: Mr. Coleridge, standing in the 'wind and tempest' of political innovation, has been driven hither and thither by the storm, and has picked up new opinions in his new positions, without altogether ridding himself of the old. By this means his mind is a kind of chaos, where moist and dry, cold and hot, square and round, are mingled in confusion, and fight eternally with each other. He finds the weeds and tares of his old creed springing up among the more recently sown grain, and that too thickly to be eradicated, without leaving bald patches of very unseemly appearance. His mind has no unity, none of the property of quicksilver, which, throw it where you please, will gather itself up, like Vathek's Indian,[1] into a ball, and always present the same surface to the eye. He finds himself embarrassed with his irreconcileable opinions, and shrinks from showing himself for the contradiction that he is. This is more honourable to him than the supposition, not without a show of truth, that he is in every respect a cunning sophist, determined at all hazards to exhibit the force and versatility of his mind, and so accustomed, in the display of his mountebank dexterity, to confound truth and falsehood, that he is no longer capable of distinguishing the one from the other.

Be this as it may, there are wonderful contradictions in his works. You may discover in them the roots of every opinion, from pantheism to the most orthodox belief; and all this united with a degree of hypocrisy, unexampled in the history of literature. When in his war-

[1] In William Beckford's *Vathek* (1786).

eclogue he devoted Pitt to the penalty of eternal fire, he was honest, for he damned him with a heartiness and *gusto*, which nothing but honesty could inspire; but he was canting and hypocritical when he afterwards protested, that at the time he was thus dooming the tyrannical minister, he was merely jesting, and would have shielded him from danger at the peril of his life. We are not contending that Mr. Coleridge had no right to change his opinions, and forswear democracy and the rights of man, for high-Tory and high-church principles. We find fault with him for insinuating (what may, however, be very true, though we do not believe it) that when he advocated liberal principles he was in jest, but is now in earnest. In his *Biographia Literaria*, speaking of his preaching days, he says, 'O! never can I remember those days with either shame or regret. For I was most sincere, most disinterested'. We think so too. The young heart is rarely hypocritical. He may be wiser now, but we doubt his being so 'sincere', so 'disinterested'.

They who have heard him converse, think very highly of his talents for discourse. We have not had this advantage; but, making allowance for the usual degree of exaggeration, we can readily believe, from the nature of his works, that he is an accomplished talker. Talking requires rather copiousness and readiness, than depth or continuous exertion. The applause, or the applauding looks of the company, may supply that excitement which his sluggish temperament appears to require to keep it going. We know a literary man whose presence throws light over a whole room, like a sun-beam; who sits or stands before you, while he talks, like an Apollo, and whose very voice is music. We never knew any one grow tired of him. But people complain of Coleridge's being tedious, and little to the purpose. He rambles, they say, over every possible topic, but that on which you are conversing with him, and will not be brought to the point. Besides, like other persons that we could name, he has a trick of usurping your ideas, and of returning them to you as his own, when he has dressed them up in his own fashion. Still, when every allowance is made, his conversation must be very splendid. It must be rich, various, and eloquent. It is, in fact, his works. To return, however, to his poetry.

What great poem has he written? Which of his works deserves to be housed up in that glorious treasury, where the intellectual riches of human nature are hoarded for all eternity? We put these questions to his disciples; for we cannot name one considerable poem of his that is likely to remain upon the threshing-floor of fame, after the dreadful winnowing of time. Fragments of the 'Ancient Mariner' may survive, and two stanzas of 'Christabelle', with 'Love', and a few very short pieces. But will such things justify the reputation he has acquired? Will they seem to the eyes of posterity the fragments of a gigantic statue, shattered by Time, but worthy to have braved him? We fear not. We fear we shall seem, to our children, to have been pigmies, indeed, in intellect, since such a man as Coleridge could appear great to us! The art of writing has preserved much ancient stuff that is never read, and no doubt the art of printing, a far more safe preservative of nonsense, will bequeath vast quantities of contemporary dulness to the spiders of after times. But dulness, though printed by Davison, and bound in Russia, is not read; nor is the mere physical existence of a book immortality. To be immortal, is to have our thoughts imprinted on the minds of a whole people; to be associated with their ideas of pleasure, enjoyment, happiness, augmented by our means. Nothing short of this is immortality. We have sometimes doubted whether, rigidly speaking, any poetry ought to live that would not live engraven on the memory of mankind, though writing and printing were not; such, for example, as the lyrics of Pindar, and Horace, and Campbell, and as Mr. Coleridge's own 'Love'.

To show that, whatever his admirers may suppose, we have not, in the above remarks, been actuated by any prejudice against Mr. Coleridge, we shall here collect a few of his best lines, which, seen separately from the dulness that surrounds them in his works, may seem to contradict our general opinion of him. The following lines on the skylark are beautiful:

> And dreaming hears thee still, O singing lark,
> *That singest like an angel in the clouds.*

The verses we shall next copy from the same short poem, show what a minute and careful observer of nature Mr. Coleridge has been:

> But the dell,
> Bathed by the mist, is fresh and delicate
> As vernal corn-field, or *the unripe flax*,
> When, *through its half-transparent stalks*, at even,
> The *level sunshine glimmers* with *green light*.

The following passage rather exhibits delicacy of touch, as the painters would say, and felicitous expression, than originality:

> But now the gentle dew-fall sends abroad
> The fruit-like perfume of the golden furze:

The light has left the summit of the hill,
Though still a sunny gleam lies beautiful
Aslant the invied beacon.

There is considerable depth and tenderness, though little of the warmth or energy of passion, in his love-poems. But it is in striking similes, and picturesque ideas and expressions, that he chiefly excels. The following passage is an example of his characteristic excellencies:

My *gentle* feet from under
Slip the crumbling banks for ever;
Like echoes to a distant thunder,
They plunge into the gentle river.
The river swans have heard my tread,
And *started* from their *reedy* bed.

The repetition of the word *gentle* in so small a number of lines, otherwise so fine, shows, either that he dismisses his poems from his mind with slovenly haste, or that he is still more deeply infected with affectation than with the love of fame. It is not difficult to discover, from the favourite images and comparisons of poets, the character of their genius: the strong and fiery mind naturally throws thunder and lightning, and storms and rushing cataracts, and the roar of wild beasts into his verses, and renders them rough and animating; the more placid genius, which we would term the didactic or elegiac, dwells with more pleasure upon moonlight, the twinkling stars, the vernal winds, peaceful birds, bowers, and shades. Mr. Coleridge is decidedly of the latter class. Almost all his images incline to the tranquil. The swan affords him many similes, and is generally introduced in comparison with the fair bosom of a lovely woman. For example:

I then might view her bosom white
Heaving lovely to my sight,
As these two swans together heave,
On the gently swelling wave.

In the very first page of the present collection the same comparison occurs:

Fair, as the bosom of the swan,
That rises graceful o'er the wave,
I've seen your breast with pity heave.

Smitten with the beautiful appearance of the same birds, when gliding over peaceful moonlight waters, he exclaims:

> O beauteous birds! 'tis such a pleasure
> To see you move beneath the moon,
> I would it were your true delight
> To sleep by day and wake all night.

In a poem, entitled 'The Picture', there is the following fine picture of poetical solitude:

> Here will I couch my limbs,
> Close by this river, in this silent shade,
> *As safe and sacred from the step of man,*
> *As an invisible world*—unheard, unseen,
> And listening only to the pebbly brook
> That murmurs with a dead, yet bell-like sound
> Tinkling, *or bees that in the neighbouring trunk*
> *Make honey hoards.*

Bees have always been in great favour with rural poets. Virgil evidently loved them. Mr. Coleridge is particularly partial to them, and introduces them frequently, and with good effect, into his poems. In another place, he says:

> This sycamore, oft *musical with bees.*

And again:

> Now the bat
> Wheels silent by, and not a swallow twitters,
> Yet still the solitary humble *bee*
> Sings in the bean-flower.

In the hymn written in the valley of Chamouni, are these fine lines:

> O struggling with the darkness all the night,
> And visited all night by troops of stars.

It is upon the verses we shall next quote, that the accusation of pantheism has been framed against Mr. Coleridge.

> And what if all of animated nature
> Be but organic harps diversely framed
> That tremble into thought, as o'er them sweeps,
> Plastic and vast, one intellectual breeze,
> At once the soul of each, and god of all!

The poem on the nightingale has been often quoted entire; but these lines deserve to be repeated:

On moonlight bushes,
Whose dewy leafits are but half disclosed,
You may perchance behold them on the twigs,
Their bright, bright eyes—their eyes both bright and full,
Glistening, *while many a glow-worm in the shade*
Lights up her lone torch.

The fourth line is here deformed by useless repetition.

But no thought in all Mr. Coleridge's works has pleased us more than the following, which is in his peculiar manner: it occurs in a description of midnight.

Sea, and hill, and wood,
With all the numberless goings on of life,
INAUDIBLE AS DREAMS!

The verses we have quoted prove Mr. Coleridge to be a poet, and a very original and sweet one too; but, though beautiful in themselves, they would not lift him above that calm, didactic class, who delight us greatly in our tranquil moments, but never interest profoundly or agitate us with sublime emotions.

105. Unsigned review, *Literary Gazette*

23 August 1828, 535-6

We are rejoiced to see these volumes, the collected fruits of one of the most original minds in our time. Scattered, unappropriated, neglected, and out of print, as many of these poems have been, yet what an influence have they exercised! How many veins of fine gold has Coleridge, with all the profusion of genius, laid open for others to work! In these pages how many lines start up old familiar friends, met with in quotations we knew not whence! and how completely do they bear the impress of the true poet!—thoughts whose truth is written in our own hearts; feelings that make us lay down the book to exclaim, 'How often have I felt this myself!'—touches of description so exquisite, that henceforth we never see a green leaf or sunny spot, like to what they picture, without their springing to our lips; tenderness which, both in poet and reader, gushes forth in tears; and imagination whose world is built of the honey extracted even from the weeds of this. Out on those who would melt down the golden strings of the poet's harp to be coined at the mint, and would cut up the ivory frame into tooth-brushes! Out on those who would banish Homer from their republic, declaiming against poetry as a vain and useless art! Is it nothing, in this harsh and jarring sphere of ours, to have our noblest impulses and kindliest feelings called forth like fountains by the prophet? Is it nothing to have our selfishness counteracted by sympathy with others? We appeal to these compositions; and if the reader does not rise from them, like their own marriage-guest, 'a wiser and a sadder man', he is, indeed, what such theories would make him—a machine, whose thoughts go by clock-work, and his actions by steam; and Coleridge is not so sure of his immortality as we had believed.

Yet even volumes like these are matters of regret: how much more might not, ought not, Coleridge to have done! His fine imagination has rioted in its own idleness; he has been content to think, or rather dream, so much of his life away: too fanciful an architect, he has carved the marble, and planned the princely halls, but wandered continually away and left the palace in fragments, from which other artists may copy more finished works; and of which, like those from the Elgin Marbles, how few will equal the grace and beauty of the original! The first to break through the trammels of artificial versification, to deem nature in its simplicity meet study for the poet, Coleridge is the founder of our present noble and impassioned school of poetry: his spirit, like the fire which fertilises the soil it pervades, has impregnated the mind of most of our modern bards, 'giving a truth and beauty of its own'.

We are now going to quote just a few fragments, just lines, stanzas, or but a single image, yet all of them bearing the stamp of everlasting fame, each and all of the finest poetry. Speaking of change produced in him by happy love:

[quotes ll. 43-72 of 'Lines written at Shurton Bars' (*PW*, i, 98-9); ll. 1-28 of 'Fears in Solitude' (*PW*, i, 256-7); and ll. 1-28 of 'Lines written in the album at Elbingerode' (*PW*, i, 315-16)]

Never in any fiction has nature so finely blended with the supernatural as in the 'Ancient Mariner'; what a picture of desolation, relieved by a gleam of hope, is in this verse!:

[quotes ll. 63-6 (*PW*, i, 189)]

How vivid the following!:

quotes ll. 103-18 (*PW*, i, 190-1)]

Then how exquisite the way in which the charm begins to break!

[quotes ll. 272-91 (*PW*, i, 198)]

Then this description of music:

[quotes ll. 363-72 (*PW*, i, 200-1)]

Perhaps the supernatural was never so depicted by a single touch as in the ensuing:

[quotes ll. 452-9 (*PW*, i, 204)]

And his return!:

[quotes ll. 464-71 (*PW*, i, 204)]

Never did poet compress into single lines more of strength and beauty:

> the silence sank
> Like music on my heart.
>
> Large tears that leave the lashes bright!
>
> Hope draws toward itself
> The flame with which it kindles.
>
> And tears take sunshine from thine eyes!

But the following exquisite ballad we must quote entire.

[quotes 'Love' (*PW*, i, 330-5)]

We shall insert but one other little piece, as a variety among our specimens; a piece which well suits its playful title.

[quotes 'Something childish, but very natural' (*PW*, i, 313)]

From the mode in which the foregoing is introduced, it is evident that whenever Coleridge condescends to trifle he is aware of the fact, which is not always the case with poets, many of whom esteem their poorest productions more than their most successful efforts. It is curious, however, to remark, that with this just sense of the pure ore and the dross, even Coleridge frequently falls into the errors of puerility and doggrel. But this is not a review of censure: it is of well-earned admiration.

And we may boldly ask, what can be added to a mosaic of poetical gems like these? We have only one other observation to make, which is, how much the force of his description is increased by the reiteration of images: for instance, how the repeated allusion to the lark in our second quotation impresses it on the imagination. This is a part of his art in which he is eminently happy.

We shall not at present attempt to analyse the magnificent translation of *Wallenstein*: we have done enough for our readers in the specimens we have given of three of the most exquisite poetical volumes in the English language; and have only to add, that they are printed in a style which does credit even to the taste of Mr. Pickering.[1]

half an hour, have created half a dozen senators, lawyers, or cardinals, and given them life and logic enough of themselves to silence all the oracles of all the schools that then were flourishing in their Aristotelian pride. Not Jeremy Taylor; for he was a poet too, no mean one either; a poet whose name indeed may be transplanted among the logicians, and it will take root and flourish there, like one of his own metaphors so rich and redolent of beauty, and twining gracefully about the intellect which could cut so finely in casuistry as to be a qualified *Ductor Dubitantium*, and lay down principles so broad as those which yet sustain unshaken the liberty of prophesying. Not Wordsworth; for he makes syllogisms of odes and odes of syllogisms, and his 'song is but the eloquence of truth'—the truth of our inmost souls—the truth of humanity's essence, brought up from those abysses which exist in every bosom, and just moulded into metre without being concealed or disfigured by the workmanship. No, it is not among great poets that we are to look for men who cannot handle the foils of logical fence, well enough to disarm in a trice the dullest dog that ever tumbled over the dry bones of Aristotle. They are all of them at home in the business. They have keen swords beneath their myrtle garlands. They can despatch an opponent and then chant his dirge. They can win a fight and then sing the song of victory. Pity that they are not always on the right side. But that misfortune befalls the philosophers as well as the poets. And that reminds us, that we have to summon from among them, too, witnesses to the position, that the higher degrees of the ratiocinative and imaginative powers are usually found together. And here it is fit to begin with the first and highest name upon the roll, even with the founder of the reformed philosophy, Lord Bacon. Let any man read his Essays, and say if they be not abundant in the materials of the richest and purest poetry. How beautifully he often bodies forth a principle in an image; and what an eye he had for nature's paintings, what an ear for nature's melodies. There is nothing in Thomson's *Seasons* half so good as Bacon's essay *Of Gardens*. How true his perception that 'the breath of flowers is far sweeter in the air than in the hand', because there 'it comes and goes like the warbling of music'; and what a 'royal ordering' does he make of 'gardens for all the months of the year', 'that you may have *ver perpetuum*, as the place affords'. Hobbes's great work, tough as it is, is but the amplification of a poetical conception. The *Leviathan* is only a personification filling a folio. He could versify too; and that seldom without vigour—sometimes with a good deal of beauty. The eloquence both of South and Barrow often rises into poetry.[1] The one strikes off a beautiful thought at a heat; the other elaborates it into perfection, by the faithful and complete accumulation of particulars. It is enough to name Burke, the most splendid example of an intellect alike surpassing by the facility with which it generalized the most multifarious political details into principles, and by the vivacity, variety, and power of its pictorial delineations. And pursuing the topic into which the *Edinburgh Review* provoked us, in our twentieth Number, it would be easy to shew that the most acute and vigorous mind of the present age—that mind which has perhaps never been rivalled in any age for its powers of logical deduction and comprehensive analysis; we speak of Mr. Bentham—is far more free from failure, when directed to the purpose of conveying the truth he would teach by means of material illustration, than the most fanciful of the carping critics, who look up alike despondingly and enviously to his intellectual elevation. A philosopher must always have something of poetry in him, and a poet of philosophy, for in the nature of things, which is the source of both, they are inextricably intertwined; there is no dissociating the true and the beautiful; and however exclusively the mind may be devoted to the pursuit of the one, its perceptions must be quickened to the apprehension of the other, by finding it in constant contact therewith.

Thus Mr. Coleridge is a Benthamite in his poetry; a Utilitarian; a 'greatest happiness' man; for, as a poet, he writes under the controlling and dictating power of truth and nature, under the inspiration of his own profound convictions and emotions. It is different, indeed, in his prose. There he is not his own man. There he has something else in view besides telling out what he thinks and feels in the melodious words which it spontaneously assumes. But with that, thank heaven, we have not now to do. Our present business is solely with his poetical character, which is brought under our notice by this edition of his works, in which he may be considered as packing up his pretensions to the laurel for posterity. There is little doubt that the consignment will reach its destination, and the award be decidedly favourable. And the anticipation is grounded not only on the appreciation of the truth, reason, sound philosophy, which are to be found enshrined in his verses, but also in the application of those tests with which we are furnished by the very principle whose adoption is often stupidly represented as inconsistent with even the capacity for perceiving poetry and feeling its influences. So far from its being proscribed by Utilitarian

[1] Robert South (1634-1766) and Isaac Barrow (1630-77), divines.

notions, they demand its existence, as amongst the most effective agencies of human enjoyment; they suggest the laws to which, for that end, it must be subjected, and by which, therefore, criticism must make trial of its worth; and as they inspire a high idea of the art itself, so have they also impelled us to assign to Mr. Coleridge a distinguished place among its professors.

That verse is not poetry we have abundant evidence daily; and that poetry of a very high order may be written in prose is a proposition which it is scarcely needful to back by the authority of Wordsworth, or the example of Jeremy Taylor. The metrical arrangement of words, however, is so pleasurable in itself, and has so close an affinity with the other elements of poetical enjoyment, that it may fairly be required of the professed poet; and we place it first because it is the most mechanical, and stands at the bottom of an ascending scale of qualities. Whether in prose or verse, a sentence should be grammatically constructed and convey a distinct meaning to the understanding, but when it is also rendered harmonious to the ear, when it gratifies the musical sense, there is a clear gain of so much pleasure. The man who makes a flowing verse benefits the world by the aggregate of all the enjoyment which the organs of speech and hearing receive in repeating it, and in listening to its repetition. The poet must not stop here. He is but at the very threshold of the temple. The eye is a far nobler inlet of pleasure than the ear. He must be a painter as well as a musician. He must give us pictures. The actual sight of lovely forms and colouring is beyond his art; but he must stimulate us to their mental reproduction, and that in new and becoming combinations. His words should be such as are associated with the most common and most vivid recollections of those external objects whose presence most gratifies the senses. This end is not best gained by laboured and minute description. It rather requires a felicitous selection of expressions; such as we shall presently have occasion to exemplify. There is a yet higher source of pleasure in sympathy, emotion, passion. The poet's melody, like the musician's, should express, recall, or excite a sentiment. The poet's sketch, as well as the painter's, should touch the heart; penetrating thither through the imagination as that does through the sight. A great master of the art can play upon the nervous system, and produce and control its vibrations as easily as the well-practised performer can try the compass and power of a musical instrument, and with a produce of enjoyment, which seems a combination of animal and intellectual, not easily calculated. Then a poem, however short, should be a narrative, or a drama, and have something of that sort of interest, and consequently of pleasure, which we experience in being conducted through a train of events to a catastrophe, in which, whether joyous or mournful, the mind rests as in the close of that portion of Nature's annals. By dramatic we do not mean that the poet should have recourse to personæ and dialogue; but he should at least employ those defined and contrasted feelings which will, in very narrow space, shadow forth the strivings of the external and literal drama; and his narrative will be not the less efficient for not being the current of outward circumstances, but that of the phantoms which are ever passing in long procession through the brain. And over the whole, to crown the work, there should be the charm of 'divine philosophy'; truth should be there in the wildest fictions, and wisdom in the gayest sportings: the whole should be based upon a profound knowledge of human nature, its constitution and history, its strength and weaknesses, its capabilities and its destiny; and where there is this science of man in the poet's mind, its existence will be ever felt; it will breathe a pervading spirit of power into his compositions; of power which is yielded to with a sort of solemn gladness; which almost identifies poetical with religious inspiration, raises the pleasure of fanciful reveries into the delight of holy musings, and makes us worshippers in that 'metropolitan temple' which God hath built and sanctified to himself 'in the hearts of mighty poets'.

Our standard of excellence in poetry is, then, a very high one, and we have a corresponding estimate of its worth as a means of enjoyment. It is an essence distilled from the fine arts and liberal sciences; nectar for the gods. It tasks the senses, the fancy, the feelings, and the intellect, and employs the best powers of all in one rich ministry of pleasure. It must be by a rare felicity, that the requisite qualities for its production are found in a man; and when they are, we should make much of him—he is a treasure to the world. He does that immediately which other benefactors of mankind only expect to accomplish in the remote consequences of their exertions. The legislator proposes to increase men's happiness, by his enactments, in the course of years. The philosopher will advance it by his speculations in the lapse of generations. The divine promises it in the world to come. But the poet seizes upon the soul at once and 'laps it in Elysium'.

High as our standard is, Mr. Coleridge comes up to it; and we rejoice in the facilities afforded for substantiating his claims, by the collection of his compositions now before us. Such a collection was needful to make the full extent of his powers felt, and render us aware of the amount of enjoyment for which we are his debtors. How could he be rightly judged of, by the public generally, when they had only now and then a stray scrap, one forgotten before another came, 'like angel visits, few and far between', too short and too distant to leave any distinct and permanent impression of the splendid visitant? But now it is incumbent on us to do him justice. We shall proceed to indicate in his works, following the order of their arrangement in these volumes, the several qualities of genuine and excellent poetry which have been just enumerated, as they may present themselves to notice.

The first division consists of poems, which are only distinguished from the rest as *Juvenile*. The term very accurately characterizes them. They are the effusions of a mind yet unformed and immature; and shew that the author's powers were of slow development. Most of them might as well have been suppressed. At least we perceive but one good reason for their retention. The number of fragments in the collection, gives an impression of the author's indolence, which is greatly counteracted by a comparison of these poems with his subsequent productions. The mind which made such advances as that comparison indicates, could not be an indolent mind, to whatever infirmity of purpose it might sometimes be liable. The happier choice and greater command of words; the superior sweetness and richness of the melody of the versification; reflections more profound, and illustrations more vivid; combinations more striking and original; and a more continuous flow of true, and affecting, and picturesque, and powerful thought, are conclusive evidence that the mental faculties had been actively, and laboriously, and successfully exercised. Of whatever other purposes they might have failed, the important one of their own improvement had been achieved. This improvement is particularly apparent in the pictorial faculty. The imagery in the Juvenile poems is comparatively common-place. With some beautiful exceptions, of which we know not exactly how many, some we are aware, are the additions of a later period, it chiefly consists of those cold personifications of qualities which never live in the mind, nor become any more objects of interest, admiration, or affection, than so many wax-work figures. Thus;

> TOIL shall call the charmer HEALTH his bride,
> And LAUGHTER tickle PLENTY's ribless side;

And he shews 'Remorse' with 'the poisoned arrow in his side', and 'bids Vanity her filmy network spread', and the like. This automaton manufactory was fashionable when Mr. Coleridge was a reading boy, and these lay figures were thought bold creations by the generation of versifiers who preceded him. Happily he soon ascended into a purer region of fancy; and that not without leaving the print of his steps in the clay from which he sprung. The personifications in his Sonnet on the expatriation of Dr. Priestley, are as good as such things can be. The concluding reference to Priestley's philosophical discoveries, might suggest a noble group for the sculptor.

> Though rous'd by that dark Vizir RIOT rude
> Have driven our PRIESTLEY o'er the ocean swell;
> Though SUPERSTITION and her wolfish brood
> Bay his mild radiance, impotent and fell;
> Calm in his halls of brightness he shall dwell!
> For lo! RELIGION, at his strong behest,
> Starts with mild anger from the papal spell,
> And flings to earth her tinsel-glittering vest,
> Her mitred state and cumbrous pomp unholy;
> And JUSTICE wakes to bid the oppressor wail
> Insulting aye the wrongs of patient Folly:
> And from her dark retreat by Wisdom won
> Meek NATURE slowly lifts her matron veil
> To smile with fondness on her gazing son!

There are other instances in these Juvenile Poems, of the felicity with which our author could employ a kind of imagery which he had soon the sound judgment to discard:

> And the stern FATE transpierc'd with viewless dart
> The last pale Hope that shiver'd at my heart!

Before dismissing the Juvenile Poems, it should be observed, that they contain both the principle and the practice of that truer poetical faith which is the great charm of the maturer productions. The old personifiers were quite mistaken in supposing they could make a living soul, by merely misusing a pronoun. When the poet would incorporate his thoughts so as to render them visible and tangible to the mind, he must make them assume and animate the forms of natural objects. Genius must breathe its breath of life into some one of the innumerable shapes of loveliness which are scattered around us in the material universe. It can give a soul better than it can mould a body. It can animate the human frame with fire from heaven, like Prometheus; but if, with Frankenstein, it pretends to create, it only produces a monster. It must identify itself with nature; and then it will behold there its own thoughts and emotions already embodied:

> For all that meets the bodily sense, I deem
> Symbolical, one mighty alphabet
> For infant minds——

And he who uses that alphabet in a poetical spirit, need no more be afraid of the imputation of common-place in the employment of the simplest objects, than in that of the letters by which every blockhead expresses his truisms or his blunders. How beautiful is the everlasting simile of the flower in the well-known 'Epitaph on an Infant', 'Ere sin could blight or sorrow fade'; and yet more the as common streamlet in the last line of the religious musings:

> Till then
> I discipline my young noviciate thought
> In ministeries of heart-stirring song,
> And aye on Meditation's heaven-ward wing
> Soaring aloft I breathe the empyreal air
> Of Love, omnific, omnipresent Love,
> Whose day-spring rises glorious in my soul
> As the great sun, when he his influence
> Sheds on the frost-bound waters—The glad stream
> Flows to the ray and warbles as it flows.

The *Sibylline Leaves* constitute the next portion of this publication, consisting of political, amatory, and meditative poems.

Of the 'Poems occasioned by political events or feelings connected with them', there are two which particularly deserve notice, the 'Fears in Solitude', written in April 1798, and the celebrated 'War Eclogue'.

The first of these is the most perfect specimen of Mr. Coleridge's manner and powers, at which we have yet arrived. It is a narrative of thought and emotion, as complete in its construction as ever epic was; the chain of association is unbroken, and every link is bright; the ideas follow in that natural succession in which they would present themselves to the mind of a man of genius, in a solitude at once profound and beautiful, with the love of his country and his kind strong at his heart, and intensely interested in the important movements of the busy world, yet who seeks not to guide the current of his feelings, but gives himself up to the influence of the scene around, and the spontaneous workings of the principle within. Accordingly it begins with mere description.

> A green and silent spot, amid the hills,
> A small and silent dell! O'er stiller place
> No singing sky-lark ever poised himself.

A few touches, few but graphic, conjure up before us the complete localities of this 'quiet spirit-healing nook'; and we are then introduced to one

> Who, in his youthful years
> Knew just so much of folly as had made
> His early manhood more securely wise,

and who here 'might lie on fern or withered heath', resigning his mind to his senses, and his senses to the 'sweet influences' around and above, till they lull him into a waking dream of better worlds, which it is sad to think must be alloyed and dashed by the thought of what storms of strife are stirring in the earth, and perchance even now 'in his native isle'; for the alarm of an invasion was then abroad in the country. The poet has thus brought us to the very heart of his subject. National dangers obviously suggest national offences, which he proceeds to arraign in a strain of solemn, indignant, and yet mournful vituperation, which rolls along most majestically, till the vividness of the delineations of guilt brings home so powerfully the prospect of retributory infliction, that he bursts forth in supplication to Providence, to 'spare us yet awhile', and from supplication rises into an animated call upon all true hearts to stand forth and repel the foe.

> And oh! may we return
> Not with a drunken triumph, but with fear:
> Repenting of the wrongs with which we stung
> So fierce a foe to frenzy!

This again suggests the 'bitter truths' which he has told, 'but without bitterness', although aware that this may not secure him from being vilified by the idolaters of power as an enemy of his country:

> Such have I been deemed—
> But O, dear Britain! O, my mother isle!
> Needs must thou prove a name most dear and holy
> To me, a son, a brother, and a friend,
> A husband and a father! who revere
> All bonds of natural love, and find them all
> Within the limits of thy rocky shores.
> O, native Britain! O, my mother isle!
> How shouldst thou prove aught else but dear and holy

To me, who from thy lakes and mountain-hills,
Thy clouds, thy quiet dales, thy rocks and seas,
Have drunk in all my intellectual life,
All sweet sensations, all ennobling thoughts,
All adoration of the God in nature,
All lovely and all honourable things,
Whatever makes this mortal spirit feel
The joy and greatness of its future being.
There lives nor form nor feeling in my soul
Unborrowed from my country. O divine
And beauteous island! thou hast been my sole
And most magnificent temple, in the which
I walk with awe, and sing my stately songs,
Loving the God that made me!

The violence of his emotions has now exhausted itself. Passion has subsided into calmness. The train of thoughts which external objects had originally suggested, and which grew so absorbing and powerful, that those external objects were altogether unheeded, gradually becomes less vivid, and as it wanes, they resume their ascendancy, make their presence and their influence again felt, and the poem concludes, as it began, with description. This transition is beautifully managed:

> May my fears,
> My filial fears, be vain! and may the vaunts
> And menace of the vengeful enemy
> Pass like the gust, that roared and died away
> In the distant tree: which heard, and only heard
> In this low dell, bowed not the delicate grass.

But the final description has more of variety, extent, and associated feeling, than that at the commencement. Evening has come on; the changed appearances of things rapidly recall him from his bodings; he pursues his path from the dell 'up the heathy hill', and is startled at the burst of prospect, 'the shadowy main', and the 'rich and elmy fields', which seem like society

> Conversing with the mind, and giving it
> A livelier impulse——

And the village church, and his friend's house, and the trees which hide his own lowly cottage, draw him on with 'quickened footsteps', grateful, as he says,

That by Nature's quietness
And solitary musings, all my heart
Is softened, and made worthy to indulge
Love, and the thoughts that yearn for human kind.

It is difficult to imagine stronger contrasts or more varied emotions than are presented or excited by different parts of this poem. The scene shifts from a most 'soft and silent spot' shut in by hills, to 'college and wharf, council and justice-court'; thence to the field of battle; and thence again to a wide and peaceful but not unanimated prospect, closing in the social seclusion of a cottage home. The feeling varies from passive, dreamy reverie, to painful sympathy, burning indignation, trembling apprehension, solemn supplication, animated appeal, tempered triumph, calm expostulation, devout confidence, till it ends in the contemplative enjoyment of benevolent affection. And yet we are never startled by any abrupt transition; all is unforced, natural, and continuous; and we are carried on without any consciousness of the extent of the circle through which the mind is borne until the revolution is completed, and the same external objects present themselves as at the outset; but present themselves as does the scenery of his native land to the traveller who has voyaged round the globe, and who brings to its contemplation the change, the extension, the elevation of thought produced by an intermediate acquaintance with the most remote and dissimilar regions. This history of the feelings of a solitary hour is as diversified, and as interesting, as the narrative of an eventful life. It is a tale alike powerful in its progress and satisfactory in its conclusion. What is the value of a succession of events but the corresponding succession of emotions? To produce these in the mind of the reader or spectator, is the triumph of the novelist's, or the dramatist's, art. The poet has here accomplished the same result by the simpler means of throwing open to us the train of his own thoughts and feelings. Here is the essence of all narrative, adventure, plot, and catastrophe. It has been said, that all the beings and events in the world are but the thoughts of the Deity: in this instance, the thoughts of the poet are beings and events; they affect us in the same way; we are complacent in their quiet; agitated in their crimes and conflicts; exultant in their triumph; and close the poem in glad and satisfied sympathy as they subside into calm and enlightened enjoyment.

The 'War Eclogue' is a splendid composition; the scene a desolated tract in La Vendée (it was written in 1796); the speakers, Fire, Famine, and Slaughter; the dialogue consisting of an exulting recapitulation of the horrors they had perpetrated since they were let loose by one whose name they will not utter, because 'twould 'make an holiday in Hell', but whom they describe enigmatically, and consult how to 'yield him honour due'. Famine proposes to excite the starving multitude against him; Slaughter promises that 'they shall tear him limb from limb'; Fire rebukes them:

> O thankless beldames and untrue!
> And is this all that you can do
> For him who did so much for you?
> Ninety months he, by my troth!
> Hath richly cater'd for you both;
> And in an hour would you repay
> An eight years' work?—Away! away!
> I alone am faithful! *I*
> *Cling to him everlastingly.*

Mr. Coleridge has deemed an 'Apologetic Preface' to this poem needful; in which he assures us that he meant no harm towards Mr. Pitt. It is a pitiful compound of cant and sophistry. That he would not, had he been standing by the door of the infernal regions when Pitt arrived there, have pushed him in and turned upon him the key of that lock, whose bolt would not be shot back to all eternity, we very readily believe; and we suppose nobody ever doubted. But that he wrote in right earnest; that he regarded that atrocious minister as the scourge of his country and the human race; that he felt towards him as became a man, whose brethren had been insulted, plundered, oppressed, demoralized, starved, slaughtered by wholesale; that in his conscience he pronounced him guilty of immolating the prospects of France, the liberties of Britain, and the peace of Europe, at the shrine of aristocratical prejudice or interest; that he held him worthy of whatever penalty might be the appropriate result of such foul misdeeds; that, though he might have deprecated the multitudes acting as Famine and Slaughter prompted them, yet he would have deemed their doing so only another instance, in addition to many which history records and palliates, of the vengeance which outraged humanity takes; and that, though he would not have been accessary to the eternal burning of William Pitt, or of any one else, yet that he saw no better prospect for the Premier's soul, according to the common version of the religion whose prelates chose him as their altar's champion: this we do believe, and of this we hold the poem itself, even without the corroboration afforded by other indications of the author's opinions and feelings at that period, to be conclusive evidence. We will apply to it the very tests, by the use of which Mr. Coleridge would conduct us to an opposite conclusion. We will prove him an honest man, or at least an honest poet, in spite of himself. He says, and very justly, that 'prospects of pain and evil to others, and in general, all deep feelings of revenge, are commonly expressed in a few words, ironically tame and mild'. Exactly so; can there be an apter instance than the conclusion of our last quotation? Is not Fire quite affectionate? Not loquaciously, nor boisterously so; not with the agitated and agitating fervours of a passionate lady-love, but with the calm confidence of a betrothed, who feels herself already a wedded wife, and talks composedly of a long and lasting intercourse of every-day endearment? If the 'Eclogue' were got up as a theatrical interlude, and Mr. Kean played the 'hot wench in flame-coloured taffeta', what an effect he would produce by that last line. The low, equable voice, almost a whisper, with an affectation of tenderness in the tone; the arms slowly and softly folding on the breast, so as to suggest the pressure of a gentle but long embrace; the smile, the beautiful smile, with the curl of the lip, scarcely perceptible at first, becoming more distinct, with every slowly-enunciated word, till the character of the expression was transformed into the grin and the sneer of ferocity; the eye alone, all the time, with its fixed and intense glare, indicating the real feeling within; these would be the actor's commentary on the poet's language; its true and genuine exposition. Mr. Coleridge has, with singular infelicity, introduced for the purpose of contrast, what serves for an excellent parallel, namely 'Shylock's tranquil "*I stand here for law*"'. Nobody but himself, we may venture to predict, will ever recognize in this the moral antipodes of the conclusion of the 'War Eclogue', or find any resemblance to it in the 'infinite deal of nothing', poured forth by that 'skipping spirit', the 'good-natured Gratiano'.

Again, it is truly observed, in the 'Apologetic preface', that 'the images that a vindictive man places before his imagination will most often be taken from the realities of life; they will be images of pain and suffering which he has himself seen inflicted on other men, and which he can fancy himself as inflicting on the object of his hatred'. But the poet does not come forward personally in the 'War Eclogue', as the agent of retribution. He assigns that work to the creatures of his imagination. And Famine, Slaughter, and Fire, in their amiable propositions, follow the very course here marked out. They simply contemplate the exaction of payment in kind from the great debtor of the human race.

Like the worthy Stephen Steinenherz von Blutsacker,[1] they would ennoble themselves by doing their office upon their employer. And although Fire may possess the singular advantage of prolonging her operations into another world, yet that world, so far as its torments are particularized, is of necessity only an accumulation of the evils which we behold inflicted here. The case comes therefore within the author's own rule, and is established by both the tests which he has set up to explain it away.

It is with strong emotions of disgust that we arrive at the climax of this apology in which the author gravely makes the following affirmations:

Were I now to have read by myself for the first time the Poem in question, my conclusion, I fully believe, would be, that the writer must have been some man of warm feelings and active fancy; that he had painted to himself the circumstances that accompany war in so many vivid and yet fantastic forms, as proved that neither the images nor the feelings were the result of observation, or in any way derived from realities. I should judge, that they were the product of his own seething imagination, and therefore impregnated with that pleasurable exultation which is experienced in all energetic exertion of intellectual power; that in the same mood he had generalized the causes of the war, and then personified the abstract, and christened it by the name which he had been accustomed to hear most often associated with its management and measures. I should guess that the minister was in the author's mind at the moment of composition, as completely $\alpha\pi\alpha\theta\dot{\eta}s$, $\alpha\nu\alpha\iota\mu\dot{o}\sigma\alpha\rho\kappa os$ as Anacreon's grasshopper, and that he had as little notion of a real person of flesh and blood,
Distinguishable in member, joint, or limb,
as Milton had in the grim and terrible phantoms (half person, half allegory) which he has placed at the gates of Hell.

'Give me breath', as Timon says. 'Heaven and earth, but this is wondrous strange'. Perhaps then there actually never was such an event as the French Revolution, nor such a man as William Pitt; they were both inventions of Mr. Coleridge in his 'energetic exertion of intellectual power'. What is there in the 'War Eclogue' that he can dare to particularize as not being 'in any way derived from realities'? Was there no 'desolated tract in La Vendée'? Did Slaughter *not* drink the blood of 'thrice three hundred thousand men'? Were there really no mothers and infants perishing with starvation? Was there never a cottage burned, nor a 'naked rebel shot' in Ireland? We thought something of the sort had been matter of history. We thought moreover

---

[1] The executioner in Scott's *Anne of Geierstein* (1829).

that Mr. Coleridge had left tolerably strong proofs on record of his having been, at that period, if an erring, yet an acute, observant, zealous, and deeply interested politician; of his knowing something of Mr. Pitt in some other character than that of a 'personified abstract'; and of rather more clear, correct, and philosophical views of his connexion with the anti-revolutionary war than those exhibited in the old story of Tenterden Steeple and Goodwin Sands.[1] It seems we were mistaken. But our mistake was nothing in comparison with that which Mr. Coleridge makes if he thinks that this 'Apologetic Preface' can do him any credit with any body, or give a particle of pleasure to any being in existence—except the Devil.

The next division of the *Sibylline Leaves* consists of the Love Poems. This title is a complete misnomer. Two or three of the pieces classed under it are Poems *on* Love; two or three others are pretty expressions of infantile affection; and the rest are still less 'germane to the matter'. Mr. Coleridge evidently knows nothing of the passion of love, but by observation and reflection; so far as these enable him, he philosophizes upon it excellently well, and there his excellence ends. We look in vain for the peculiar and genuine language of that mightiest of the passions. In the search, however, we find many very beautiful passages. There is, in the 'Circassian love-chant', a most exquisitely-touched sketch of cloud-scenery, heightened by the gentle tint of sentiment spread over it.

> I saw a cloud of palest hue,
> Onward to the moon it pass'd:
> Still brighter and more bright it grew,
> With floating colours not a few,
> Till it reach'd the moon at last;
> Then the cloud was wholly bright,
> With a rich and amber light!
> And so with many a hope I seek,
> And with such joy I find my Lewti;
> And even so my pale wan cheek
> Drinks in as deep a flush of beauty!
> Nay, treacherous image! leave my mind
> If Lewti never will be kind.
> The little cloud—it floats away,
> Away it goes; away so soon?
> Alas! it has no power to stay:

[1] An allusion to the quaint tradition that Tenterden Steeple was the cause of Goodwin Sands. See Brewer's *Dictionary of Phrase and Fable*.

> Its hues are dim, its hues are grey—
> Away it passes from the moon!
> How mournfully it seems to fly,
> Ever fading more and more,
> To joyless regions of the sky—
> And now 'tis whiter than before!
> As white as my poor cheek will be,
> When, Lewti! on my couch I lie,
> A dying man for love of thee.

The poem entitled 'Love', the tale of Genevieve, which was originally published with Wordsworth's *Lyrical Ballads*,[1] in an example of
that analysis or exposition of this passion which our author succeeds
so well in. It is one of his finest compositions. It is a minstrel's tale of
how he won his bride; and the time, the scene, all the accompanying
circumstances, and the 'old and moving story' in which he pleaded for
her heart, are so harmonized in their influences that many a father might
exclaim:

> I think this tale would win my daughter too.

It would not be easy to find another such combination as is here
produced, of metaphysical analysis with pictorial delineation; and of
both with the sweetest melody of verse. The author has generalised
Dryden's assertion (Dryden was no contemptible metaphysician), that
'Pity melts the soul to love'. He maintains that:

> All thoughts, all passions, all delights,
> Whatever stirs this mortal frame,
> All are but ministers of Love,
> And feed his sacred flame.

This is the prelude of his song, giving us the theme, tone, sentiment,
before he paints the scene, tells the tale, and describes the result, which
is to furnish the illustration. Almost every stanza bears upon the subject
with logical accuracy and force. The enumeration, arrangement, and
combination, of the 'impulses of soul and sense' by which the minstrel
'won his Genevieve', are as correct and complete as if made in a chapter
of Hartley or Brown.[2] Yet the scenery and narrative, by which these
objects are accomplished, are such that painters' imaginations may catch
inspiration from the one, and young eyes glisten and overflow at the
pathos of the other. How graphic, how true and luxuriant, not only

[1] In the second edition of 1800.

[2] David Hartley (1705-57) and John Brown (1778-1820), associationist philosophers.

to the eye but to the very principle of sensation, is the description of that 'rich and balmy eve'.

Oft in my waking dreams do I
Live o'er again that happy hour,
When midway on the mount I lay,
Beside the ruin'd tower.

The moonshine, stealing o'er the scene,
Had blended with the lights of eve;
And she was there, my hope, my joy,
My own dear Genevieve!

She lean'd against the armed man,
The statue of the armed knight:
She stood and listen'd to my lay,
Amid the lingering light.

Few sorrows hath she of her own,
My hope! my joy! my Genevieve!
She loves me best, whene'er I sing
The songs that make her grieve.

I play'd a soft and doleful air,
I sang an old and moving story—
An old rude song, that suited well
That ruin wild and hoary.

She listen'd with a flitting blush,
With downcast eyes and modest grace;
For well she knew, I could not chuse
But gaze upon her face.

Time would fail to enter upon the story, or to discuss the limitations to the author's position that all excitement, physical and mental, has an amatory tendency; a position to which, though generally true, there are large exceptions.

The 'Meditative Poems in Blank Verse', which follow, afford a good opportunity to speak of our author's philosophy; his poetical philosophy, which he has preserved pure, unchanged, and unstained, from first to last, notwithstanding all his political tergiversation. His jacobinism, and his antijacobinism, his nonconformity, and his church-of-Englandism, his declamations in favour of pantisocracy and of legitimacy, have happily scarcely touched his poetry (with the exception of two or three minor pieces on the one side, and the trumpery drama of *Zapolya* on the other); and of the Muse, in his mind, more truly than was said, and beautifully said, by the *Edinburgh Review* of a certain patriot in the cabinet, may it be affirmed that she has 'sojourned undefiled in the tabernacles of corruption'. The *poet* Coleridge is a metaphysical and ethical teacher after our own hearts. He understands humanity; he loves humanity; he would improve, dignify, and bless humanity, in the persons of all its possessors. In his theology the Deity is no tyrant of the universe, whose glory blazes in the conflagration of worlds, and kindles up a quenchless bonfire of immortal beings. With him, God is Benevolence personified, and invested with omnipotence and omniscience. His piety is not that of bodily gesticulation, or verbal repetition, or spiritual cajolery, or importunity, but a communion of spirit and will with Infinite Goodness. His morality is neither lax nor ascetic, nor selfish, but consists in the attainment of one's own happiness by the promotion of other's happiness, and ministering to the pleasurable sensation of every thing that lives and feels. He reverences man and nature. By intense reflection on the faculties, passions, and tendencies, of our constitution, he has traced the influences to which they are subject, and those which they exercise. In his poetry, love, that is to say, benevolence, the disposition to create and multiply enjoyment, the adoption in heart and soul of the Greatest Happiness Principle, is the dictate of Nature and of God, the summary of virtue, the agency of reformation and improvement, the condition of well-being, the germ of perfect felicity. He is a prophet in the religion of which Mr. Bentham is the high-priest: he sings what we say. Proof of almost all these assertions might be adduced from the subdivision of his poems more immediately before use. Its conclusiveness will be increased by taking a wider range, and the complete consistency of his (poetical) philosophy thereby shewn. The materials are uniform and abundant throughout these volumes, from those compositions which bear the earliest to those of latest date.

It is the more needful to adduce this proof, as Mr. Coleridge would be very likely vehemently to disclaim any affinity between his own system and that of the great master-spirit of moral and political science. The secret of the discrepancies between Mr. Coleridge's poetry and his prose has been already hinted at. On that there is no occasion to enlarge. His poetry is what has been described, because it *is* poetry, and because he is a poet. Happy would it have been for himself and mankind if he had never been any thing else. But all else will be forgotten. Future generations will know him only in that character, and the fame which he will then enjoy is a sufficiently glorious destiny.

O framed for calmer times and nobler hearts!
O studious poet, eloquent for truth!
Philosopher! contemning wealth and death,
Yet docile, child-like, full of life and love.

If there has ever been a pure and true theology upon earth—a
theology which can abide the strictest application of the rules of
ratiocination to its evidences, and of the principle of utility to its
influences, it is that inculcated in the 'Religious Musings':

There is one Mind, one omnipresent Mind,
Omnific. His most holy name is Love.
Truth of subliming import! with the which
Who feeds and saturates his constant soul,
He from his small particular orbit flies
With blessed outstarting! From HIMSELF he flies,
Stands in the sun, and with no partial gaze
Views all creation; and he loves it all,
And blesses it and calls it very good!
This is indeed to dwell with the Most High!
Cherubs and rapture-trembling Seraphim
Can press no nearer to the Almighty's throne.

The same truth, but in a different style, and with a different bearing,
appears in the moral of the 'Ancient Mariner':

O sweeter than the marriage feast,
'Tis sweeter far to me,
To walk together to the kirk
With a goodly company!

To walk together to the kirk,
And all together pray,
While each to his great Father bends,
Old men, and babes, and loving friends,
And youths and maidens gay.

Farewell, farewell! but this I tell
To thee, thou wedding-guest!
He prayeth well, who loveth well,
Both man and bird and beast.

He prayeth best, who loveth best
All things both great and small;
For the dear God who loveth us,
He made and loveth all.

The character of the ritual usually corresponds with that of the Deity. Our notions of worship must be coloured in conformity with our picture of its object. No ceremonial would be an appropriate pendant to the theology of these poems:

> Ere on my bed my limbs I lay,
> It hath not been my use to pray
> With moving lips or bended knees;
> But silently, by slow degrees,
> My spirit I to love compose,
> In humble trust mine eyelids close,
> With reverential resignation
> No wish conceived, no thought express'd!
> Only a sense of supplication,
> A sense o'er all my soul imprest
> That I am weak, yet not unblest,
> Since in me, round me, every where
> Eternal strength and wisdom are.

Was there ever a better commentary on that passage in the Bible which enjoins us to 'worship the Father in spirit and in truth'?

The principle of our author's morality, the pursuit of happiness by its diffusion, the expansion of the idea of self by the agency of sympathy, the realizing of the sufferings or enjoyments of our fellow beings in the imagination until they come to constitute our own, assume the regulation of our feelings, give the prevailing impulse to our actions, and form the end and aim of our being, is also clearly stated in the 'Religious Musings':

> A sordid, solitary thing
> Mid countless brethren with a lonely heart
> Through courts and cities the smooth savage roams
> Feeling himself, his own low self the whole;
> When he by sacred sympathy might make
> The whole ONE SELF! SELF, that no alien knows!
> SELF, far diffused as Fancy's wing can travel!
> SELF, spreading still! oblivious of its own,
> Yet all of all possessing! This is FAITH!
> This the MESSIAH's destined victory.

A mind imbued with this principle looks abroad on universal Nature with affectionate complacency. It will pour forth such moral music as we have in the lines 'On an Eolian Harp'. We give it with the delicious prelude which precedes:

Such a soft floating witchery of sound
As twilight elfins make when they at eve
Voyage on gentle gales from Fairy-land,
Where melodies round honey-dropping flowers
Footless and wild, like birds of Paradise,
Nor pause, nor perch, hovering on untam'd wing!
O the one life within us and abroad,
Which meets all motion and becomes its soul,
A light in sound, a sound-like power in light,
Rhythm in all thought, and joyance every where—
Methinks it should have been impossible
Not to love all things in a world so fill'd;
Where the breeze warbles, and the mute still air
Is music slumbering on her instrument.

The most interesting poetical development of a moral system consists in pourtraying the various states of mind, the different modifications of thought and feeling which flow from it, as observation is directed to different characters. Amongst very much of this sort of illustration we may refer particularly to the self-reproaches of one who has lived, but not enough lived, for his species; the admiration of those who, by making 'audible' some 'lay of truth profound', have placed themselves 'in the choir of ever-enduring men', the 'sacred roll' of the world's benefactors; the pity and love, the respect and gratitude, which repel harsh censures on the frailty of those who have yet been good and great; the self-administered spirit-stirring exhortation to useful activity; its enforcement upon others who neglect the exercise of their power of beneficence; and the devotedness of soul to the welfare of humanity, which in age, and amid desertion and depression, remains unchanged and unshaken. These are displayed, the two first-mentioned in the lines occasioned by 'the Recitation of a poem on the Growth of an Individual Mind'; and the rest, respectively, in those on 'the Last words of Berengarius'; 'on having left a place of retirement'; to a 'young man of fortune who abandoned himself to an indolent and causeless melancholy'; and 'Duty surviving self-love the only sure friend of declining life'. And there is a touching expression of the mood which some of these pieces were designed to rebuke in the deep and rich melody of those mournful lines entitled 'Work without Hope'. There would be pleasure in quoting all these, but that may not be. There is another passage which belongs to them; a contrast between the dealings of man and those of nature with criminality. It is the speech of

Alvar at the commencement of the fifth act of *Remorse*. The scene, a dungeon:

> And this place my forefathers made for man!
> This is the process of our love and wisdom
> To each poor brother who offends against us;

and then, for room cannot be afforded for the whole, after describing the hardening process by which, in what is commonly deemed the administration of criminal justice, and criminal justice it is, the wretch is

> Circled with evil till his very soul
> Unmoulds its essence, hopelessly deform'd
> By sights of evermore deformity;

He presents the other picture:

> With other ministrations thou, O Nature!
> Healest thy wandering and distemper'd child:
> Thou pourest on him thy soft influences,
> Thy sunny hues, fair forms, and breathing sweets;
> Thy melodies of woods, and winds, and waters!
> Till he relent, and can no more endure
> To be a jarring and a dissonant thing
> Amid thy general dance and minstrelsy;
> But, bursting into tears, wins back his way,
> His angry spirit heal'd and harmoniz'd
> By the benignant touch of love and beauty.

These verses contain the true moral of the tragedy of *Remorse*, which is a representation of the superiority of the benignant over the vindictive principle in their influences upon the guilty. Ordonio is twice a murderer in intention, though only once in act. Alvar, his supposed victim in the one case; and Alhadra, the widow of his real victim in the other, are alike bent upon making him feel the consequences of his crime; but the one would waken remorse within him only as the agency for recovering his heart to the pure and generous sentiments of humanity, and thus enabling him to enjoy and bestow happiness; while the other desires it merely as an aggravation of his payment of 'the rigid retribution, blood for blood'. Both are, to a certain extent, successful; but how different their triumph. Alhadra sheds his blood, and Alvar saves his soul.

Principles such as these consecrate the poetry in which they are worthily enshrined. Nor is it to be lamented that they are not taught

systematically, or more elaborately illustrated. That is the business of
the philosopher and the moralist. It is enough for the poet if he
inculcate them, as the Bible, so much of which consists in the compositions of the bards of Judea, inculcates our duty—'Here a little and
there a little', as *his* inspiration may move him to take up his parable.
We have no right to expect more. Nor perhaps would an ethical
system, in the guise of poetry, be more. Only portions of it would be
poetry; and it is better to have them by themselves. Give us the
Sibylline leaves. They may be only fragments, but they are fragments
of

An Orphic song indeed,
A song divine of high and passionate thoughts,
To their own music chaunted!

Mr. Coleridge's addictedness to metaphysical theories, which are
said to succeed one another in his mind like travellers at an inn, each
making itself quite at home there during its temporary abode, has no
more spoiled his poetry than has his political partizanship. The metaphysics of these volumes are of the most useful and least disputable
description. There is the delineation and solution of some interesting
mental phenomenon to be constantly met with. The solution is usually
as satisfactory as the delineation is beautiful, and both, by an exertion
of art pre-eminently happy and admirable, are made productive of
emotion in the reader. This is indeed the most extraordinary quality,
the most absolute peculiarity of his poetry. It combines to an unparalleled extent the investigation or exposition of the workings of the
human mind with the expression or excitation of whatever affects
the heart or delights the imagination. It propounds abstract truth in
'thoughts that breathe, and words that burn'. His selection of terms is
often such as that we become at once conscious of their peculiar appropriateness and their resistless power. They convey the truth precisely
and completely; and they convey it with all those melancholy, tender,
or joyous associations which it is the poet's especial business to call up.
They are like sunbeams; and their light and heat are inseparable. It is
as if he announced a philosophical fact in hieroglyphics; but they are
perfectly distinct and intelligible hieroglyphics; and their forms are
lovely to the eye; and they combine harmoniously into a picturesque
group; and their grouping tells a story, a story which makes the nerves
thrill and the bosom throb, and leaves us morally better for its agitating
interest.

Many of these compositions, including some which belong to the purest, the highest, and the most powerful kind of poetry, are, in their construction and object, as instanced in the beautiful ballad of Gene-vieve, specimens of metaphysical analysis. Such is also the 'Ode to the Duchess of Devonshire', 'Constancy to an Ideal Object', 'the Blossom-ing of the Solitary Date Tree', the 'Sonnet on his Child being first presented to him', and the verses which he calls, we know not why, the conclusion to the second part of 'Christabel'. All these are portions of the most splendid work on the philosophy of the human mind that was ever conceived. They are glimpses of that clear profundity of truth, of which we trace emanations in almost every one of his com-positions, 'The blue sky bends over all'. Passages are continually occurring which shew the deep reflection of the author, his intense self-inspection, a knowledge of our nature acquired in the best school, the study of himself. There is one of these in the 'Hymn before Sun-rise, in the Vale of Chamouny'.

> O dread and silent Mount! I gaz'd upon thee,
> Till thou, still present to the bodily sense,
> Didst vanish from my thought: entranc'd in prayer
> I worshipp'd the Invisible alone.

> Yet like some sweet beguiling melody,
> So sweet, we know not we are listening to it,
> Thou, the meanwhile, was't blending with my Thought,
> Yea, with my Life, and Life's own secret Joy:
> Till the dilating soul, enrapt, transfus'd,
> Into the mighty vision passing—there,
> As in her natural form, swell'd vast to Heaven!

Equally true is the following sketch, in the 'Night Scene', of the ministry of one passion to another, but mightier, which seems its opposite:

> The inquietudes of fear, like lesser streams,
> Still flowing, still were lost in those of love;
> So love grew mightier from the fear, and Nature,
> Fleeing from Pain, sheltered herself in Joy.

And what a picture is that in 'Christabel', of the strange fascination by which we are impelled, involuntarily, to the corporeal imitation of an object or action on which the mind is dwelling with abhorrence and dread: the innocent girl assumes the look of her serpent-eyed tormentor:

The maid, alas! her thoughts are gone,
She nothing sees—no sight but one!
The maid, devoid of guile and sin,
I know not how, in fearful wise
So deeply had she drunken in
That look, those shrunken serpent eyes,
That all her features were resign'd
To this sole image in her mind:
And passively did imitate
That look of dull and treacherous hate,
And thus she stood, in dizzy trance,
Still picturing that look askance,
With forc'd unconscious sympathy
Full before her father's view—
As far as such a look could be,
In eyes so innocent and blue.

Mr. Coleridge writes more, and more felicitously, from the unforced, and seemingly unguided association of ideas in his own mind, than any man we know of. We do not refer now to such mere reverie pieces, most delicious in their way, as 'Fancy in Nubibus', the 'Day Dream', and 'Kubla Khan', proofs as they are how truly he says

My eyes make pictures when they are shut—
I see a Fountain, large and fair,
A Willow and a ruin'd Hut,

but to the Meditative Poems, and others which resemble them in this particular, that there seems to have been no previously designed aim or plan in their composition, except simply to delineate the flow of thoughts originated by some scene or occurrence. They are exhibitions of the writer's mind under certain circumstances or influences. They shew what at least appear to be its involuntary trains of thought and feeling. Few minds could be so exposed with any very pleasurable results to writer or reader. The process is a test of the strength or weakness, the wealth or poverty of the intellect, and of its poetical and moral qualities. It is a sort of Algebraic equation (this article is an attempt to work it), in which the circumstances and the result, are known or given quantities, and the author's intellectual rank, the unknown quantity, to be discovered by their means. The solution scarcely leaves Mr. Coleridge an equal amongst the philosophical poets of our country. It is, moreover, by *extracting*, that we, as well as the algebraist, have arrived at the demonstration of the problem. And we are sorely tempted to extract yet more largely, to illustrate the justice of our estimate. We must content ourselves with a reference, which may be made to every poem in this department, with the exception of two or three, which do not come properly under the description just given— such as the Hymn which stands first, the 'Tombless Epitaph', and the 'Inscription for a Fountain on a Heath', which commences with those two well-known lines, of such matchless beauty and richness,

> This Sycamore, oft musical with bees,—
> Such Tents the Patriarchs loved!

Of the 'Odes and Miscellaneous Poems', which conclude the *Sibylline Leaves*, it is only needful for us to notice the 'Psychological Curiosity', 'Kubla Khan'. The author informs us that this is such a portion as he could recollect of a much longer poem, which was composed during 'a profound sleep, at least of the external senses', 'if that, indeed, can be called composition, in which all the images rose up before him as *things*, with a parallel production of the correspondent expressions, without any sensation or consciousness of effort'. The tale is extraordinary, but 'Kubla Khan' is much more valuable on another account, which is, that of its melodious versification. It is perfect music. The effect could scarcely have been more satisfactory to the ear had every syllable been selected merely for the sake of its sound. And yet there is throughout a close correspondence between the metre, the march of the verse, and the imagery which the words describe. How appropriate are the full tone and slow movement of the commencing lines:

> In Xanadu did KUBLA KHAN,
> A stately pleasure-dome decree:
> Where ALPH, the sacred river, ran
> Through caverns measureless to man,
> Down to a sunless sea.

The 'sunny greenery', the 'romantic chasm', and the 'mighty fountain', are equally *well set*, and beautifully varied; and he who has ever heard read, by a voice of any tolerable degree of sweetness, guided by any tolerable degree of sense, the 'damsel with a dulcimer', &c. without exquisite enjoyment at the time, and a haunting recollection at intervals ever after, certainly hath no music in his soul, and deserves never again to have any in his ears. And what, except the river itself, can equal the gentle liquidity of the following lines, heightened as the effect is by the startling contrast at their conclusion:

> Five miles meandering with a mazy motion,
> Through wood and dale the sacred river ran,
> Then reach'd the caverns measureless to man,
> And sank in tumult to a lifeless ocean:
> And 'mid this tumult Kubla heard from far
> Ancestral voices prophesying war.

The elements of this melody are only the common and well-known ones of English versification; our author is always felicitous in their management, but no where has he blended them in so perfect a combination as in this instance.

It might well be imagined that what Mr. Coleridge has mentioned as a peculiarity of this composition had almost always happened to him in the production of his poems, viz., that 'the images rose up before him as *things*, with a parallel production of the correspondent expressions'. We cannot but believe that usually his 'visions flit very palpably before him', from the effect of his descriptions or allusions on the reader. His expressions have peculiar power in calling up the correspondent images. They often do this merely by suggestion. There is a song in *Remorse*, of the last two verses of which every line is a picture, and the whole gradually, but most distinctly, rises upon the mind as perfect a scene as ever was painted.

> And at evening evermore,
> In a chapel, on the shore,
> Shall the chaunters, sad and saintly,
> Yellow tapers burning faintly,
> Doleful masses chaunt for thee,
> Miserere Domine!

> Hark! the cadence dies away,
> On the yellow, moonlit sea:
> The Boatmen rest their oars and say,
> Miserere Domine!

The second volume contains, besides some short miscellaneous pieces, several of which have been already noticed, the 'Ancient Mariner', 'Christabel', and the Dramas of *Remorse* and *Zapolya*. The last of these belongs, both in spirit and execution, to his prose works. We therefore pass that over. Nor will *Remorse*, although the conception is good, and there are many passages which few men living could have written, do any thing for his fame. His talent is not dramatic. Cleverness is worth much more than genius in the production of a good acting play. Morton and O'Keefe[1] are better men for the boards than Scott and Byron. And Mr. Coleridge has not much cleverness. He wants also the versatility which is essential to a good reading play. He does not throw his own mind into those of his characters, but absorbs theirs into his. They are, each and all, only Coleridge slightly modified. Nor can we linger now on 'Christabel', although we should not despair of making good its claim to the well-known panegyric of Byron. The third volume consists wholly of the translations of the *Piccolomini* and the *Death of Wallenstein*. A word or two on the 'Ancient Mariner', and we have done.

The hope of a poet's immortality might be safely built, and would securely rest, on 'The Rime of the Ancient Mariner' alone. The hero is a most poetical personage, with his tall gaunt form, his embrowned visage, his skinny hand, long white beard, and glittering eye, passing 'like night, from land to land', and doing penance for the wanton cruelty of shooting a harmless sea-bird, by the agony which ever and anon constraineth him to tell his story, 'and to teach, by his own example, love and reverence to all things that God made and loveth'. The voyage on which this adventure happened, involves a succession of scenes which are described with a rapidity demanded by the interest of the story, but with that graphic power which shews every thing by a few bold strokes. The storm and the calm are two specimens out of many:

And now the STORM-BLAST came, and he
Was tyrannous and strong:
He struck with his o'ertaking wings,
And chas'd us south along.

With sloping masts and dipping prow,
As who pursued with yell and blow,
Still treads the shadow of his foe,
And forward bends his head;
The ship drove fast, loud roar'd the blast,
The southward aye we fled. . . .

Down dropt the breeze, the sails dropt down,
'Twas sad as sad could be;
And we did speak only to break
The silence of the sea!

[1] Thomas Morton (1764-1838) and J. O'Keefe (1747-1833) were minor playwrights.

All in a hot and copper sky,
The bloody sun, at noon,
Right up above the mast did stand,
No bigger than the moon.

Day after day, day after day,
We stuck, nor breath nor motion,
As idle as a painted ship
Upon a painted ocean.

The supernatural Agents are finely-imagined and delineated. The first introduced is the author of all the mischief which befel the Ancient Mariner and his shipmates, out of revenge for the death of the Albatross, probably almost the only living thing in the dreary region about the south pole, which this spirit inhabited, and therefore proportionably dear to him.

The Spirit who bideth by himself
In the land of mist and snow,
He lov'd the bird that lov'd the man
Who shot him with his bow.

While this vindictive spirit is pursuing his plans of retribution, 'the Ancient Mariner beholdeth a sign in the element afar off', prefiguring the destiny of himself and his comrades. It is a spectre ship, in which Death and Life-in-death dice for the crew, and she (we must introduce her) wins the Ancient Mariner.

Her lips were red, her looks were free,
Her locks were yellow as gold:
Her skin was white as leprosy,
The night-mare LIFE-IN-DEATH was she,
Who thicks man's blood with cold.

Milton's Death, with all his regality, might have been proud to woo and win such a mate as this.

After the death of the crew, their bodies are animated by 'a troop of spirits blest', who leave them every morning, not visibly, but in music.

For when it dawn'd—they dropp'd their arms,
And cluster'd round the mast;
Sweet sounds rose slowly through their mouths,
And from their bodies pass'd.

Around, around, flew each sweet sound,
Then darted to the sun;
Slowly the sounds came back again,
Now mix'd, now one by one.

Sometimes a dropping from the sky,
I heard the sky-lark sing,
Sometimes all little birds that are,
How they seem'd to fill the sea and air
With their sweet jargoning!

And now 'twas like all instruments,
Now like a lonely flute;
And now it is an angel's song,
That makes the heavens be mute.

It ceas'd; yet still the sails made on
A pleasant noise till noon;
A noise, like of a hidden brook
In the leafy month of June,
That to the sleeping woods all night,
Singeth a quiet tune!

These angels, sent down by the Virgin Mary, to whom the Mariner had prayed in his penitence, preserve him from the vengeance of the angry spirit, and bring him back to his own country, where the curse is finally expiated. Then they appear for a moment, each one 'a man of light, a seraph man', casting his 'crimson shadow' on the calm waters of the bay in the pale moonlight. But the great power of the poem is in the truth of the emotions which it ascribes to the Ancient Mariner, who is himself the narrator. There is an indescribable charm in this preservation of what is natural amid the supernatural; nay, in making the supernatural only serve to unfold and illustrate what is natural, and the wildest and boldest creations of imagination develop the essential principles of humanity. This it is which distinguishes the masters of the magic art from the mere miracle-monger; and makes us believe in Shakespeare's witches, while we only laugh at Monk Lewis's goblins. Our author excels here; or rather his excellence is made more apparent by the extraordinary character of the supposed events; it exists as really, and is as admirable, where the events are such as actually occur. For instance, in the conclusion of the first part, the old man shrinks from that avowal of his offence which he yet knows he must make. He lingers and lingers on his description of the Albatross, and of its growing familiarity with the sailors, and goes on adding circumstance to circumstance, each of which is an aggravation of the deed, but which serves to postpone his acknowledgement of it, till at last it is elicited by a demand of the cause of his obvious agony, and then it bursts from him in the fewest words that could express the fact:

> God save thee, Ancient Mariner!
> From the fiends that plague thee thus!—
> Why look'st thou so?—With my cross-bow
> I shot the ALBATROSS!

And when his ship-mates perish, it is his conscience, and not the external organ of sense, which hears the sound of their departing souls:

> One after one, by the star-dogg'd moon,
> Too quick for groan or sigh,
> Each turned his face with a ghastly pang,
> And curs'd me with his eye.

> Four times fifty living men,
> (And I heard nor sigh nor groan)
> With heavy thump, a lifeless lump,
> They dropp'd down one by one.

> The souls did from their bodies fly,—
> They fled to bliss or woe!
> And every soul it pass'd me by,
> Like the whizz of my CROSS-BOW!

The description of his solitude, after his desolation, commencing with:

> Alone, alone, all, all alone,
> Alone on a wide, wide sea,

And of his sensations in its endurance, is a study both for the painter and the philosopher. And then how touchingly is his penitence told; how beautifully produced by the contemplation of the gay creatures of the element which sported around the vessel. The Albatross, it should be mentioned, had been fastened round his neck, in token of his crime.

> Beyond the shadow of the ship,
> I watch'd the water-snakes:
> They mov'd in tracks of shining white,
> And when they rear'd, the elfish light,
> Fell off in hoary flakes.

> Within the shadow of the ship
> I watch'd their rich attire;
> Blue, glossy green, and velvet black,
> They coiled and swam; and every track
> Was a flash of golden fire.

O happy living things! no tongue
Their beauty might declare:
A spring of love gush'd from my heart,
And I bless'd them unaware!
Saw my kind saint took pity on me,
And I bless'd them unaware.

The self-same moment I could pray;
And from my neck so free
The Albatross fell off, and sank
Like lead into the sea.

Much more remains, which it would be pleasant to tell, both on this particular, and as to the general merit of Mr. Coleridge's poems. But enough has surely been adduced, both of pleading and of evidence, to make out our case, and justify our admiration. Here then we stop, and resign our pages to what many may deem more appropriate and more important topics. Thus much the occasion called for; and we have gladly availed ourselves of it to discharge a debt of justice and of gratitude—of individual gratitude even; for the writer of this article would apply to Mr. Coleridge's poems what he says, in the conclusion of his Preface, of poetry itself. The study of his 'poetry has been to me its own "exceeding great reward": it has soothed my afflictions; it has multiplied and refined my enjoyments; it has endeared solitude; and it has given me (or at least strengthened in me) the habit of wishing to discover the good and the beautiful in all that meets and surrounds me'.

107. Unsigned article, *Athenaeum*

16 January 1830, 17-18

The 'Utilitarians', (a word which is not English, and a name disclaimed we believe by some of those who once gloried in bearing it, and who did it the greatest honour) are a set who only exist as separated from the rest of mankind by virtue of a blunder. If many of them had not employed the word utility in two senses, and hopped from one to the other as best suited their momentary convenience, they never would have appeared as either so singular or so important as some people for a year or two were inclined to hold them. Utility in its popular, and as we believe, its legitimate sense, means nothing more than applicability to the practical and ordinary affairs of life, as distinguished from its enjoyments and its higher duties. As the foundation of a moral theory, it signifies that the only standard of right and wrong, is the view taken by the agent, of the consequences of his actions in the production of pleasure and pain. The few persons who maintain that utility in the former of these senses, is alone or chiefly worthy of attention, assume a ground so narrow and repulsive, that they have little chance of converting the world. The others announce as the basis of a system of morals, a notion, which, in truth, excludes all real morality, arising from the operation of the conscience. It is, however, in this larger signification, that utility has been employed as a watchword by the ablest of those who have shouted it among the astonished vulgar. We have of course a very firm conviction, that they profess a grievous and most pernicious error; but we are far from thinking that all those who do so are consciously unprincipled; and the very article before us, the first in the XXIIIrd number of the *Westminster Review*, is an evidence of more than average honesty in the writer.

He does not appear to be a person of remarkable intellects; his critical opinions have all been taught among us for several years, by men very superior to him. But they have been taught by persons against whom the 'Utilitarians' are strongly prejudiced, and they necessarily include a high admiration for the poetry of Coleridge, the man whom those among them that can at all comprehend him, are bound the most vehemently to condemn. The Reviewer, however, though with rather too much ostentation of candour, is honest enough to proclaim the truth, which we question whether he could have discovered for himself, and really admires the poetry which he criticises with a heartiness that does him exceeding honour. But he has fallen by the way into some mistakes, which, as they are the errors and follies of one desirous to be right, we think it worth while to notice.

The opening periods are for the most part distinguished by a noisy and boyish conceit, which gives an unfavourable impression of the writer. He sets about proving what no one but a 'Utilitarian' ever doubted, with a degree of importance and grandiloquence much more accurately proportioned to the dignity of the subject than to his capacity for treating it. In the beginning of this loud loquacity, he speaks of persons who have 'had woeful experience that Utilitarians are somewhat logical'; but in fact, all the experience on this point proves, that while the present 'Utilitarians' talk a great deal about logic, they reason *worse* than all other men, from premises which *no* other men admit. In the recent controversy with the *Edinburgh Review*, there can we think be no question, that although their opponent is far enough from a scientific view of 'Government', he has completely demonstrated how inconsistent and hollow is that of Mr. Mill. ,

But the subject which has moved us at all to speak of the *Westminster Review*, is the character of Mr. Coleridge's mind and writings, which is very oddly dealt with by this critic. The second paragraph of the article begins as follows:

Thus Mr. Coleridge is a Benthamite in his poetry; a Utilitarian; a 'greatest happiness' man: for, as a poet, he writes under the controlling and dictating power of truth and nature, under the inspiration of his own profound convictions and emotions. It is different, indeed, in his prose; there he is not his own man, there he has something else in view besides telling out what he thinks and feels in the melodious words which it spontaneously assumes. But with that, thank heaven, we have not now to do.

So say we; thank heaven that this author has nothing to do with the prose writings of Coleridge; for to be worthily mastered, they require the study of a subtle and reflecting mind. Now we would ask, supposing we were to judge the writer from nothing but the sentences above quoted, what order of mind should we assign to him? First, we are told, as something very marvellous, that in his poetry, Mr. Coleridge is a 'Utilitarian', meaning thereby, not we presume that he maintains a speculative doctrine (which by-the-bye was taught much more than two thousand years before the birth of Mr. Bentham) but that in his poetry he wishes to give pleasure, and succeeds in it. And this is stated as something very new and surprising, in a sentence, which is immediately followed by an expression of the utmost contempt for the prose works of Mr. Coleridge. Can this person ever have read the books he speaks of? or has he written thus without knowing that the *Biographia Literaria* contains the most elaborate and satisfactory analysis of poetry in the language, and that Mr. Coleridge there maintains the giving pleasure to be the one direct purpose of all poetry? Now let us look at the exquisite reasoning of this logician: Mr. Coleridge, quoth he, is a

Benthamite, a greatest happiness man; Indeed! And why do you say that he is so, how do you prove it? 'Because he writes under the controlling and dictating power of truth and nature, under the inspiration of his own profound convictions and emotions'. He writes with a view to outward consequences, because he writes without any view to consequences at all! He is a Benthamite, because he writes from his convictions and emotions! A compendious method truly, for demonstrating that Æschylus and Plato, Dante, Luther, Shakespeare, Milton, all were *'Benthamites'*! This is indeed a flight beyond the audacity of Vidocq, Cagliostro, or the Bottle-Conjuror.[1]

The doctrine of the remainder of our extract is inculcated, incidentally, in various other parts of the article. The writer evidently thinks, that to write the truest, deepest, and loveliest poetry, is one knack—and to write honest and powerful prose, another knack; and finds nothing at all startling in the opinion, that a first-rate poet may write nothing but drivelling and fallacious nonsense in all his prose compositions. Can such a critic have any idea of a human being as a complex, but homogeneous whole? Is it possible to conceive all the poetry-making part of a mind as sound, and the prose-making part as corrupt, through the whole of life; and to fancy that the health shall not heal the disease, nor the malady infect the health? Is there nothing at first sight astounding in such a notion? Is it not certain, that the very same faculties are employed in both these mental occupations? And that the love of truth and of mankind, which cannot but exist in every poet of the highest order, will necessarily guide his application of his powers to all other subjects as well as the poetical? These would seem to be strong presumptions against the theory of the Reviewer; and what have we, in the first place, to set against them? Nothing, absolutely nothing, except the assertion of one man, whose criticism gives evidence of no remarkable fitness for his task, except the will to say what he believes, and the susceptibility of impressions from the outward world, which has made him an admirer of the vivid poetry of Mr. Coleridge. Those, therefore, who have not read *The Friend*, the *Biographia Literaria*, and the *Aids to Reflection*; those who, from want of habit of reflection, are incompetent to judge of them, and those who will not bestow the requisite labour, have to choose, whether they will believe, on the one hand, that an honest but conceited man, who writes in the

---

[1] Vidocq, a contemporary French criminal who had turned detective; Cagliostro (1743-95), an alchemist and impostor; the Bottle-Conjurer, for whose performance a gullible public turned up at the New Theatre in the Haymarket in 1749.

Westminster Review, is idle, rash, and presumptuous; or, on the other, that a poet of the noblest rank, and distinguished among poets for intense and comprehensive thought, has published several laborious volumes, on subjects to which he has devoted his life, written in the purest style, and with a tone of the most profound earnestness; and that these are uniformly and utterly trivial, false, and 'disgusting'. Surely, when this alternative is presented to the Reviewer himself, he can hardly fail to see cause for recommencing his examination. To understand, and embrace, the whole meaning of the books in question, undoubtedly requires much industry and thought, more than any but a few among us are inclined to bestow. But, without having paid the price for knowledge, who is entitled to claim its privileges?

We own that we have other grounds for our opinion, besides the calculation of chances which we have just suggested. In the first place, we have known several students of Mr. Coleridge's writings; and with regard to the 'Apologetic Preface' to the 'War Eclogue', which the Reviewer calls 'a pitiful compound of cant and sophistry', and which gave him, he says, an 'emotion of disgust', we will assure him, not as an advocate speaking to an advocate, but as one lover of letters and of truth to another, that we have heard it mentioned with higher delight and approbation, by more superior men of the most opposite opinions, than any modern English essay. At all events, his reasoning will not hold good as to the analogy between *Shylock's* 'I stand here for law', and the boast of the poetical personage in the 'Eclogue',

I
Cling to him everlastingly.

The Reviewer says, that in each phrase there is the same ferocious concentration of hatred. Perhaps so: but does he mean to say, that the passage in the *Merchant of Venice* proves Shakespeare to have hated *Antonio*? Unless he maintains this, he does nothing towards showing that Mr. Coleridge hated Pitt. Mr. Coleridge asserts, and we think justly, that the vigorous exercise of a creative imagination, is incompatible with a state of malignant passion. The more appropriate, therefore, the thought in question is to the unreal being in the poem, the less can it be taken as an evidence of the poet's individual feeling.

Independently of the authority of others, we rely boldly on our own judgment, as sufficient to convince ourselves, that the philosophical, critical, moral, and religious works of the author of 'Christabel', are, to those who will rightly employ them, the richest possession of our age.

We are the more persuaded that our opinion is accurate, because we have felt, we believe, in their utmost force, all the objections commonly urged against these writings. We know, for we have experienced, that they are difficult and vast; that their strong outbreakings of moral earnestness are shocking to a passive conscience; that they demand rigid attention, active thought, humble self-distrust, and untiring love of Truth. We have found that they lead us into a maze; that, during the first moments, it is hard to discover with how unerring a clue they will furnish us: but that labyrinth must needs be explored by him who would arrive at philosophical certainty. Those who do not think at all, and those who think only that they may defy and suppress their moral convictions, will indeed alike be disappointed by the works of a writer who, more successfully than all other Englishmen, has laboured to reconcile the speculative understanding with the instinctive consciousness.

ON THE CONSTITUTION OF CHURCH AND STATE

1830

---

108. From an unsigned review, *Eclectic Review*

July 1831, vi, 1-28

The review also discusses R. M. Beverley's *A Letter to his Grace the Archbishop of York*, and *Church Reform*. By a Churchman.

Few writers of the present day are so capable of furnishing 'aids to reflection' as Mr. Coleridge; but, 'aids toward a right judgement' of any question, his mode of treating things is not the best adapted to supply. What the late Mr. Hall once remarked of Dr. Owen, may with still greater propriety be applied to the Author of *The Friend*, that he 'dives deep and comes up muddy'.[1] He is, perhaps, the most comprehensive thinker of the age, but it is a comprehensiveness fatal to distinctness; and the vague, generalized survey of a subject, which he loves to take, reminds us of a bird's eye view of a tract of country, or of the appearance of the earth from a balloon. And, if we may pursue the simile, from the elevation to which he transports us, the misty exhalations of thought which come rolling one over another, apparently the sport of accident or impulse, but governed by unknown laws of association, often assume forms of grandeur and beauty which delight the fancy, although they obscure or conceal the field of intellectual vision. Mr. Coleridge's habits of thought are strikingly desultory, and yet, they must be characterized as truly philosophical; and from the combination of these almost incompatible qualities results the peculiar character of his writings. He proceeds in a way the very opposite to that of some eloquent writers, who, having selected a proposition for illustration, concentrate their whole attention upon that point, lavish on it all the

[1] Robert Hall (1764-1831) and John Owen (1766-1822), dissenting clergymen.

strength of argument, and never leave it till the theme is fairly exhausted. Mr. Coleridge, on the contrary, never closes with a subject, never comes to close quarters, but brings the artillery of his learning and eloquence to bear upon large masses. We can hardly conceive of a more striking contrast than that which his writings present, in this respect, to those of Dr. Chalmers.[1] The one is fond of exhibiting a simple idea in every variety of aspect, and of decorating it with multiplied illustrations, making it the central point of the shifting figures, in a manner that has been aptly compared to the effect of the objects in a kaleidoscope. The other surrounds us with a gallery of abstractions, theories, axioms, unfinished sketches, and antique fragments, in which his own conceptions are indiscriminately blended with those of other men; where nothing is well arranged, and scarcely any thing is finished, but here, ideas present themselves roughly blocked out, and waiting for the chisel, there, a rude sketch suggests hints for a study, here is seen a foot of Hercules, there, a head of Juno, here, the *torso* of a Church, and there, the fragments of a Constitution. Now all this is very pleasant as an exhibition, but extremely difficult to deal with. The disorderly opulence of the Author's stores of thought, by which he is himself bewildered, baffles all analysis. We are charmed with the grouping and succession of objects, but they will not fall into perspective; and when we arrive at the end, we seem as far as ever from any definite conclusion. In vain would any but the most attentive reader attempt to disentangle the complex knot of ideas laid before him in the present volume. The style of the composition itself answers to the involution of the thoughts. Digression upon digression, parenthesis within parenthesis, distinctions the most refined, transitions the most abrupt, positions the most paradoxical, keep continually the mind of the reader upon the stretch, wondering whither the erudite and accomplished Writer intends to lead him. A single sentence, taken from the volume before us, will serve to illustrate this peculiarity of the Author's mode of developing his ideas.

The principle itself, which as not contained within the rule and compass of law, its practical manifestations being indeterminable and inappreciable *à priori*, and then only to be recorded as having manifested itself, when the predisposing causes and the enduring effects prove the unific mind and energy of the nation to have been in travail; when they have made audible to the historian that Voice of the People which is the Voice of God;—this Principle, I say, (or the Power, that is the subject of it,) which by its very essence existing and working

[1] Thomas Chalmers (1780-1847), theologian.

as an *Idea* only, except in the rare and predestined epochs of Growth and Reparation, might seem to many fitter matter for verse than for sober argument, I will, by way of compromise, and for the amusement of the reader, sum up in the rhyming prose of an old Puritan poet, consigned to contempt by Mr. Pope, but whose writings, with all their barren flats and dribbling common-place, contain nobler principles, profounder truths, and more that is properly and peculiarly *poetic* than are to be found in his own works.

It would be a somewhat puzzling exercise to a tyro in grammar, to parse this leviathan sentence. The ground-work of the lofty pile of words, is the simple and intelligible announcement: 'The Principle itself . . . I will . . . sum up in the rhyming prose of an old Puritan poet'. This is all that Mr. Coleridge meant originally to say. But, upon this primary thought he has grafted, first, the parenthesis beginning with the word 'which', then suddenly dropped for a series of annotations upon the word 'principle', and not taken up again till the words 'might seem to many fitter matter for verse than for sober argument'; a hundred and six words being interposed between the verb 'might seem' and its nominative 'which'. The intermediate clauses consist of two distinct sub-parentheses, each requiring to be made a separate sentence. Lastly, we have appended to the whole a criticism upon the poetry of Wither, and to this is subjoined a distinct note. This mode of packing words reminds us of the ingenious toy composed of a series of wooden apples one within another, which a child continues to open with increased admiration till he gets to the minute kernel. Disentangled from each other, the several sentences comprised in the above extract, would read as follows.

The principle itself ([that is, a due proportion of the *potential* to the *actual* power [in the body politic]) is not contained within the rule and compass of law, its practical manifestations being indeterminable and inappreciable *à priori*, and then only to be recorded as having manifested itself, when the predisposing causes and the enduring effects prove the unific mind and energy of the nation to have been in travail,—when they have made audible to the historian that voice of the people which is the voice of God.

This principle, or the power that is the subject of it, by its very essence, exists and works as an idea only, except in the rare and predestined epochs of Growth and Reparation.

It might [as such] seem to many fitter matter for verse than for sober argument.

I will [therefore] by way of compromise, and for the amusement of the reader, sum it up in the rhyming prose of an old Puritan poet, George Withers —a Poet consigned to contempt by Mr. Pope, but whose writings, with all their barren flats and dribbling common-place, contain nobler principles, profounder truths, and more that is properly and peculiarly *poetic*, than are to be found in his own works.

But the reader has not yet arrived at the lines in question. In the note above mentioned, Mr. Coleridge guards us against inferring that 'he holds George Withers as great a writer as Alexander Pope'. He moreover calls upon us to mark that, in the stanza about to be cited, the word State is used as synonymous with the entire body politic. On returning to the text, we find him stating whence he copied the passage, from 'a flying sheet of four leaves', printed in 1745 (1645?). At last, after an introductory extract, we come to the kernel.

> Let not your King and Parliament in *One*,
> Much less apart, mistake themselves for that
> Which is most worthy to be thought upon:
> Nor think they are, essentially, the STATE.
> Let them not fancy, that th' Authority
> And Priviledges upon them bestown,
> Conferr'd are to set up a Majesty,
> A Power, or a Glory of their own!
> But let them know, 'twas for a deeper life,
> Which they but *represent*——
> That there's on earth a yet auguster Thing,
> Veil'd tho' it be, than Parliament and King.

With the sentiment conveyed in these rude but forceful lines, our readers will not be displeased; but we doubt whether they will serve as a key to the mysterious 'principle' which they are cited to illustrate. In justice, therefore, to Mr. Coleridge, we have still to supply an explanatory comment upon the sentence we have dissected, and which appears, of course, to the greater disadvantage as being detached from its connexion with the preceding matter.

Of the conditions requisite to the health and constitutional vigour of a body politic, two are selected by the Author as being, in his judgement, the most important, so as to deserve the name of political principles or maxims. The first is, 'a due proportion of the free and permeative life and energy of the Nation to the organized powers brought within containing channels'. In plain English, if we understand the meaning wrapped up in this physiological metaphor, a due balance of the legitimate powers of government on the one hand, with the antagonist rights, privileges, and power of resistance in the people on the other. 'What the exact proportion of the two kinds of force should be', Mr. Coleridge remarks, 'it is impossible to predetermine; but the existence of a disproportion is sure to be detected sooner or later by the effects'. The ancient Greek democracies fell into dissolution, from 'the excess of the permeative energy of the nation', and the relative feebleness of the political organization. The Republic of Venice fell, because all political power was determined to the Government, and the people were nothing: the State, therefore, 'lost all power of resistance *ad extra*'. We agree with Mr. Coleridge, that to find the due proportion of the two kinds of force, the controlling and the resisting, is the most delicate and recondite problem in political science—one that will, perhaps, ever defy precise solution. To preserve the due equilibrium under the existing circumstances of the State, is the true business and highest duty of the Administrative Government. And in order to this, it is of the first importance, that the principle propounded by our Author should be understood and recognised on all sides; that the opposing forces of the Crown and the People should not be supposed to be hostile, when, in fact, they support each other by the equipoise, or to involve contrary interests because they are opposite powers.

The second condition of political health is that which is described in the passage already cited, and the terms of which we are now to explain; namely, 'a due proportion of the *potential* (latent, dormant) to the actual power'. This 'potential power', we have seen, 'exists and works as an *Idea* only'. But we must first explain what Mr. Coleridge understands by an Idea.

By an idea, I mean that conception of a thing, which is not abstracted from any particular state, form, or mode in which the thing may happen to exist at this or that time, nor yet generalized from any number or succession of such forms or modes, but which is given by the knowledge of *its ultimate aim*★. . . . That

★ Mr. Coleridge distinguishes an idea from a conception, defining the latter as a *conscious* act of the understanding, by which it *comprehends* the object or impression; whereas an *idea* may influence a man without his being competent to express it in definite words. Thus, an *obscure* or indistinct conception would seem to be an idea! In a subsequent part of the volume, adverting to the expression, 'abstract conceptions', as occurring in the 'Natural History of Enthusiasm', Mr. Coleridge says: 'By abstract conceptions, the Author means what I should call ideas, and, as such, contradistinguish from conceptions, whether abstracted or generalized'. This distinction, however, is too arbitrary and technical to be generally adopted; nor can we agree with Mr. Coleridge, that a 'peculiar nomenclature' is indispensable or desirable in ethical writing. Upon this point, he avows himself to be at issue with the philosophical writer above mentioned, who asserts, that 'whatever is practically important on religion or morals, may at all times be advanced and argued in the simplest terms of colloquial expression'. 'I do not believe this', which, contemplated *objectively*, (*i.e.* as existing *externally* to the mind,) we call a LAW; the same, contemplated *subjectively*, (*i.e.* as existing in a subject or mind,) is an Idea. Hence Plato often names ideas laws; and Lord Bacon, the British Plato, describes the laws of the material universe as the Ideas in Nature. 'Quod in naturâ *naturatâ* LEX, in naturâ *naturante* IDEA dicitur'.

A remarkable contrast may be discerned, our Author thinks, 'between the acceptation of the word Idea, *before* the Restoration, and the *present* use of the same word'; indicating nothing less than a revolution in philosophy. We admit that the word is not so frequently used now as formerly in the philosophical acceptation of an archetype or model; as when Milton, speaking of the creation, exclaims,

> How good, how fair,
> Answering his great *Idea!*

But the word was never used exclusively in this acceptation, or in any other technical sense. Shakespeare uses it in the simple sense of a mental image; and so Fairfax has it:

> Her sweet idea wandered thro' his thoughts.

On the other hand, it is far from being true, that the word, hackneyed and vulgarised as it has become, is now exclusively used in reference to sensations; or that the ideas of Will, God, Freedom, the Beautiful, are no longer the matter of high discourse, as in the days of Sidney and Spenser, Harrington and Milton, Politian and Mirandula. There can be no propriety, however, in attempting to restrict the use of a familiar word to a technical acceptation; and we should imagine it to be quite easy, by a qualifying epithet, to prevent the possibility of misconception. When we speak, for instance, of the right idea of an abstract quality or principle—as freedom, or happiness— every one understands that we do not mean the idea of a specific state of freedom, or of any definite circumstances of enjoyment, but of that in which freedom or happiness

---

remarks Mr. Coleridge; and he proceeds to represent the maxim as tending to 'deprive Christianity of one of its peculiar attributes, that of enriching and enlarging the mind'—that is, with new terms and phrases, which become 'new organs of thought'. But when it is considered, that the Bible, the only fountain of religious knowledge, is the most *untechnical* of books, and that from nothing Christianity has suffered more prejudice than from the metaphysical jargon of the theological schools, most persons will think that the maxim impugned by Mr. Coleridge is a reasonable and useful one. The vices of his own style are attributable, in great measure, to his fondness for verbal refinements and a technical nomenclature.

essentially consists. Some ideas may be justly considered as primary laws of thought, e.g. the idea of life or of time; and without entering into the dispute respecting innate ideas, others, which have never been made definite objects of consideration with the generality, possess and unconsciously govern the minds of all; as the idea of free-agency and accountability, or the idea of personal right, which is a sense, rather than a notion, a principle of thought, rather than a theory or opinion. Such ideas as these, Mr. Coleridge justly represents as 'the most real of all realities, and of all operative powers the most actual'; for, by their influence, the characters of men are greatly shaped, and their actions determined. Now the Constitution itself, our Author maintains, is an Idea of this description—not generalised from any existing institutions or laws, not a concrete idea made up of historical elements, not the image of any thing actual, but an antecedent principle, a model of thought, or rather a final idea, to which the actual form or mode of things is only an approximation.

A Constitution is an idea arising out of the idea of a State; and because our whole history, from Alfred onward, demonstrates the continued influence of such an idea, or ultimate aim, on the minds of our forefathers, in their characters and functions as public men, alike in what they resisted and in what they claimed; in the institutions and forms of polity which they established, and with regard to those against which they more or less successfully contended; and because the result has been a progressive, though not always a direct or equable advance in the gradual realization of the idea; and that it is actually represented (although, as an idea, it cannot be *adequately* represented) in a corresponding scheme of means really existing; we speak, and have a right to speak, of the Idea itself as actually existing, i.e. as a *principle*, existing in the only way in which a principle can exist—in the minds and consciences of the persons whose duties it prescribes, and whose rights it determines. In the same sense that the sciences of arithmetic and geometry, that Mind, that Life itself, have reality, the Constitution has real existence, and does not the less exist in reality because it both *is*, and *exists as*, an Idea. . . . As the fundamental idea, it is at the same time, the final criterion by which all particular frames of government must be tried.

Instead of terming this Idea, the Constitution, most writers would have preferred to designate it as the spirit of the Constitution, its pervading principle, or the characteristic genius of our institutions and laws. It would be absurd to deny that the British Constitution does in fact exist in the palpable form of Institutional law; that it is not a mere *ens rationale*, but an historical entity—the Constitution as a concrete, and therefore actual idea. But yet, to this actual Constitution belong what are regarded as things unconstitutional, that is, foreign from the true genius and aim of the Constitutional Law—that sublime abstraction which exclusively occupies Mr. Coleridge's mind, and which he regards as the True and Archetypal Idea, or, as the French would say, the *beau Ideal*, that it is sought to realize. Not that this ultimate aim has been the conscious motive of our legislators, or has originated the existing laws; for 'our social institutions have formed themselves out of our proper needs and interests'. But, to this ideal criterion there is a constant, involuntary reference, so that it forms a governing principle, a law of action, although never defined in the terms of a distinct proposition. Whatever may be thought of the propriety of the Author's phraseology, we readily concede to him the importance of keeping clearly in view the distinction on which he insists, between the Constitution as a mere congeries of laws, precedents, and privileges, and the plastic spirit, the 'deeper life which they but represent'.

To return to the position of which we may seem to have lost sight; that, in the body politic there exists, as an Idea or principle, a latent, 'potential power', on the due proportion of which to the actual power, the healthful working of the system very much depends. We must confess that we have undertaken a difficult task, in attempting to render this part of our Author's doctrine into plain English; but, so far as we are able to guess at his meaning, by this potential power, he intends that which resides in the Nation, as distinguished alike from the State, or ruling power, and from the People, but comprehending both; the latent energy of the Nation, or the public mind, which, under extraordinary circumstances, becomes as it were the *constituent power*; of which we have had recently a striking instance in the very 'potential' manifestation of 'the unific mind and energy of the nation' in favour of a parliamentary reform. Under ordinary circumstances, this reserved power, inherent in the Nation, is dormant; but it is never alienated or delegated under a free constitution.

A democratic republic and an absolute monarchy agree in this; that, in both alike, the Nation, or People, delegates its whole power. Nothing is left obscure, nothing suffered to remain in the idea, unevolved and only acknowledged as an existing, yet indeterminable right. A Constitution such states can scarcely be said to possess. The whole will of the Body Politic is in act at every moment. But, in the Constitution of England, (according to the Idea), the Nation has delegated its power not without measure and circumscription, whether in respect of the duration of the Trust, or of the particular interests entrusted.

The limitation imposed on the duration of parliaments, and the necessity of having recourse, originally once in three years, and now at least once in seven years, to a renewal of the legislative trust, by calling into operation the constituent power of the people,—is one obvious and important land-mark of the national liberties; defining the boundary as it were between what Mr. Coleridge would denominate the delegated and the reserved power. The circumscription of the trust in regard to the particular interests entrusted, is not quite so manifest, and has, indeed, our Author thinks, been too much lost sight of. The omnipotence of the Parliament itself, 'that is, the King, the Lords, and the Commons', he regards as a mischievous hyperbole; and he cites with approbation the following passage from *The Royalists' Defence*, a small tract printed in the year 1648.

All Englishmen grant, that Arbitrary power is destructive of the best purposes for which power is conferred: and . . . to give an unlimited authority over the fundamental Laws and Rights of the Nation, even to the King and two Houses of Parliament jointly, though nothing so bad as to have this boundless power in the King alone, or in the Parliament alone, were nevertheless to deprive Englishmen of the security from arbitrary power which is their birthright.

In point of fact, the right of petitioning, as exercised by the people of England, may be considered as a virtual assertion of the principle which imposes limits on the power of Parliament, and as an efficient check upon the delegated power. To the unanimous or preponderant feeling of the nation thus expressed, no wise Government would hesitate to defer. But the concession might be made on the mere ground of expediency; whereas Mr. Coleridge would attribute to the national voice, a paramount *authority*. His doctrine is (and, coming from him, it will hardly be ascribed to radical notions) that that political freedom which is the birthright of Englishmen, is incompatible with arbitrary and irresponsible power, whether it be that of an autocrat, or exercised by King and Parliament; that there are interests—such as involve yet higher relations than those of the citizen to the State—which the Nation has never entrusted to its rulers; that the Mind of the Nation, though simply an Idea, is a real power, working as such on the reason and conscience; and that this is a yet auguster thing than the idea of the State, taken in the narrower sense of the term, or than the Majesty of either King or Parliament. Further, our Author maintains it to be a necessary condition of the health of the body politic, that the energy of the Public Mind should bear due proportion to the actual political

REVIEW IN *Eclectic Review* 1831

powers, so as not to be over-active on the one hand, or wholly torpid on the other.

With the Author's application of this doctrine to 'the late Catholic Bill', we do not concern ourselves. We undertook only to expound a single sentence, but, in so doing, we have endeavoured to give a general idea of the political principles which the work is designed to establish; principles which we think sound in the main, and well worthy of being studied by all who can afford time for thinking. Having seen, however, what is our Author's Idea of a Constitution, and of a State, our readers may be curious to see what is his Idea of a Church. The following description of the Christian Church, as contra-distinguished from any National Church, contains much that is at once profoundly just and forcible.

The Christian Church is not a kingdom, realm, or state of the world; ... nor is it an estate of any such realm, kingdom, or state; but it is the appointed *opposite* to them all collectively;—the sustaining, correcting, befriending opposite of the World! the compensating counterforce to the inherent and inevitable evils and defects of the State, *as* a State, and without reference to its better or worse construction as a particular State; while whatever is beneficent and humanizing in the aims, tendencies, and proper objects of the State, it collects in itself as in a focus, to radiate them back in a higher quality. Or, to change the metaphor, it completes and strengthens the edifice of the State, without interference or commixture, in the mere act of laying and securing its own foundations. *And for these services, the Church of Christ asks of the State neither wages nor dignities.* She asks only *protection, and to be let alone.* These, indeed, she demands; but even these only on the ground that there is nothing in her constitution, nor in her discipline, inconsistent with the interests of the State, nothing resistant or impedimental to the State in the exercise of its rightful powers, in the fulfilment of its appropriate duties, or in the effectuation of its legitimate objects. It is a fundamental principle of all legislation, *that the State shall leave the largest portion of personal free-agency to each of its citizens, that is compatible with the free-agency of all,* and not subversive of the ends of its own existence as a State. And, though a negative, it is a most important distinctive character of the Church of Christ, that she asks nothing for her members as Christians, which they are not already entitled to demand as citizens and subjects.

In the primitive times, and as long as the churches retained the form given them by the Apostles and Apostolic men, every community, or, in the words of a father of the second century, (for the pernicious fashion of assimilating the Ohristian to the Jewish, as afterwards to the Pagan ritual, by false analogies, was almost coëval with the Church itself,) every altar had its own bishop, every flock its own pastor, who derived his authority immediately from Christ, the universal Shepherd, and acknowledged no other superior than the same Christ——* Hence, the unitive relation of the churches to each other, and of each to all, being equally *actual* indeed, but likewise equally *Ideal*, i.e. mystic and supersensual, as the relation of the whole church to its one Invisible Head, the Church with and under Christ, as a one kingdom or state, is hidden: while, from all its several component monads, the particular visible churches, Cæsar, receiving the things that are Cæsar's, and confronted by no rival Cæsar,—by no authority which, existing locally, temporally, and in the person of a fellow-mortal, must be essentially of the same *kind* with his own, notwithstanding any attempt to belie its true nature under the perverted and contradictory name of *spiritual*,†—sees only so many loyal groupes who, claiming no peculiar rights, make themselves known to him as Christians, only by the more scrupulous and exemplary performance of their duties as citizens and subjects.

Another distinguishing and essential character of the Church of Christ, Mr. Coleridge proceeds to remark, is its Catholicity.

It is neither Anglican, Gallican, nor Roman; neither Latin nor Greek. Even the Catholic and Apostolic Church *of* England, is a less safe expression than, the Churches of Christ in England: though the Catholic Church *in* England, or (what would be still better) the Catholic Church under Christ throughout Great Britain and Ireland, is justifiable and appropriate. For, through the

* Mr. Coleridge finishes the sentence by adding—'the same Christ, speaking by his spirit in the unanimous decision of any number of bishops or elders, according to his promise, 'Where two or three are gathered together in my name, there am I in the midst of them'. And in a note, he endeavours to justify this application of the promise (Matt. xviii. 20.), by interpreting it as of 'a spiritual *immanence*', comparing it with 1 John iii. 24. The words, ἐν μέσῳ αὐτῶν, hardly support this gloss. Against the Author's comment, however, we have little to object; but his extension of the application of the words to ecclesiastical councils, is not a little startling, and required to be better defined and guarded. The abuse which the Papists make of this passage, he well knows. '*In quo*', remarks Calvin, '*se prodit crassa Papistarum inscitia. Clamant non potuisse errare concilia, ideoque standum omnibus eorum decretis*'. Our Lord, however, is promising his special presence as an encouragement to social prayer (ver. 19), not as a sanction of ecclesiastical decrees and councils. Even Calvin seems to have mistaken the true import: '*Dominus se adfuturum declarat . . . . . ut dirigat eos consilio.*' But can this be what is meant by γενήσεται αὐτοῖς—'it shall be done for them by my Father'?

† 'In the only appropriate sense of the words', Mr. Coleridge remarks, '*spiritual* power is a power that acts on the *spirits* of men'. 'Our great church dignitaries sit in the Upper House of the Convocation as *prelates* of the National Church; and, as prelates, may exercise *ecclesiastical* power. In the House of Lords, they sit as barons, and by virtue of the baronies which, much against the will of these haughty prelates, our kings forced upon them: and as such, they exercise a *parliamentary* power. As bishops of the Church of Christ only, can they possess, or exercise, a *spiritual* power, which neither King can give, nor King and Parliament take away'.

presence of its only head and sovereign, entire in each, and one in all, the Church universal is spiritually perfect in every true Church, and of course in any number of such churches, which, from circumstance of place, or the community of country or of language, we have occasion to speak of collectively. It is at least an inconvenience in our language, that the term *Church*, instead of being confined to its proper sense, Kirk, *Ædes Kyriacæ*, or the Lord's House, should likewise be the word by which our forefathers rendered the *ecclesia*, or the *eccleti* (ἐκκλῆτοι), i.e. *evocati*, the called out of the world, named collectively; and likewise our term for the clerical Establishment. To the Called at Rome —to the Church of Christ at Corinth—or in Philippi—such was the language of the Apostolic age; and the change since then, has been no improvement.

What then is the relation which the Church *of* England, that is, the National Church improperly so called, or 'Clerisy', bears to the Church of Christ *in* England, or to Christianity itself? Mr. Coleridge's answer to this inquiry is, that the National Church is 'a great venerable estate of the realm'—an integral part of the body politic; having no necessary connexion with Christianity, because it 'might exist, and has existed, *without*, because *before* the institution of the Christian Church; as the Levitical Church in the Hebrew Constitution, the Druidical in the Celtic, would suffice to prove'.

In relation to the National Church, Christianity, or the Church of Christ, is a *blessed accident*, a providential boon, a grace of God, a mighty and faithful friend, the envoy, indeed, and liege subject of another State, but which can neither administer the laws, nor promote the ends of this State, which is *not of the world*, without advantage, direct and indirect, to the true interests of the States, the aggregate of which is what we mean by the World.

Paley has remarked, that 'a religious Establishment is no part of Christianity: it is only the means of inculcating it'. He regards it as simply 'a scheme of instruction', the only legitimate end of which is, 'the preservation and communication of religious knowledge'. 'Every other idea, and every other end that has been mixed with this', he adds, 'as the making of the Church an engine, or even an ally of the State; converting it into the means of strengthening or diffusing influence, or regarding it as a support of regal, in opposition to popular forms of government; have served only to debase the institution, and to introduce into it numerous corruptions and abuses'. Mr. Coleridge's idea of a religious Establishment differs very widely from the hypothesis of the learned Dean; and though, at first sight, it appears the less plausible of the two, and even somewhat paradoxical, it not only approaches more nearly to fact, but presents, we are inclined to think, the only ground upon which an advocate of the National Church can safely take his stand. Both writers agree in this; that a religious Establishment is no part of Christianity; that it is simply a political institute, having only an accidental relation to Christianity, since what is, in this country, a means of inculcating Christian knowledge, becomes, under other circumstances, a means of inculcating the religion of the Koran or of the Vedas. But Mr. Coleridge, more consistently, as we think, maintains, that the Established Church of this country not only is a political order, an estate of the realm, a thing 'of this world', but has for its primary and legitimate object and end, the promotion of civil and temporal interests; that it is a part of the State, intended to promote the well-being of the State, by advancing the 'national civilization'; in other words, that its legitimate end is to make good citizens, rather than good Christians—to civilize men, not to save them.

The final cause of the whole, by the office and purpose of the greater part, is, to form and train up the people of the country to obedient, free, useful, organizable subjects, citizens, and patriots, living to the benefit of the State, and prepared to die for its defence. The proper *object* and end of the National Church, is, civilization with freedom; and the duty of its ministers, could they be contemplated merely and exclusively as officiaries of the *National* Church, would be fulfilled in the communication of that degree and kind of knowledge to all, the possession of which is necessary for all, in order to their CIVILITY. By civility, I mean all the qualities essential to a citizen.

'Whatever of higher origin, and nobler and wider aim, the ministers of the National Church, in some other capacity, and in the performance of other duties, might labour to implant and cultivate in the minds and hearts of their congregations and seminaries', all that the State requires of the National Church, is, that its instructions should make the people good subjects. Again, our Author thus recapitulates his Idea of a National Church.

Among the primary ends of a State (in that highest sense of the word in which it is equivalent to the Nation, considered as one body politic, and therefore includes the National Church) there are two, of which the National Church (according to its Idea) is the especial and constitutional organ and means. The one is, to secure to the subjects of the realm generally, the hope, the chance of bettering their own or their children's condition. And though, during the last three or four centuries, the National Church has found a most powerful surrogate and ally for the effectuation of this great purpose in her former wards and foster-children, i.e. in trade, commerce, free industry, and the arts,—yet still, the *nationalty*, [by which we are to understand, the reserved property of the Nation], under all defalcations, continues to feed the higher ranks, by drawing up whatever is worthiest from below; and thus maintains the principle of Hope in the humblest families, while it secures the possessions of the rich and noble.... [Among the instances of the blindness, or, at best, of the shortsightedness which it is the nature of cupidity to inflict, I know few more striking than the clamours of the farmers against Church property. Whatever was not paid to the clergyman, would inevitably, at the next lease, be paid to the landholder; while, as the case at present stands, the revenues of the Church are in some sort the reversionary property of every family that may have a member educated for the Church, or a daughter that may marry a clergyman: instead of being *fore-closed* and immoveable, it is, in fact, the only species of landed property that is essentially moving and circulative.]

This is one of the two ends. The other is, to develop, in every native of the country, those faculties, and to provide for every native that knowledge and those attainments which are necessary to qualify him for a member of the State, the free subject of a civilized realm. We do not mean those degrees of moral and intellectual cultivation which distinguish man from man in the same civilized society, much less those that separate the Christian from the *thisworldian*; but those only that constitute the civilized man in contradistinction from the barbarian, the savage, and the animal.

Now, whether this be the right idea of the National Church, or not, it must be allowed to correspond to the views which are actually taken of the Church, as a profession, by the majority of the clergy and of those who are in any way interested in Church property. It has the advantage, too, of harmonizing with the Author's ideas of that limitation of the trust vested in the Constituted Powers of the realm, which is the only security against arbitrary power. The interests of the Church of Christ, the personal religious interests of every individual, interests involving higher relations than those of the citizen to the State, cannot be included among those which are entrusted to King, Lords, and Commons. The power which the Nation has delegated, is not so boundless as to extend to these. No *spiritual* power can belong to any civil rulers, or to any estate of the realm, civil or ecclesiastical; and the claim to any such power, in the ecclesiastical magistrate, whether Popish or Protestant, is, therefore, an anti-Christian usurpation. Such are, if we understand Mr. Coleridge aright, *his* views, as they are our own. It is true, that powers have been assumed by English Parliaments, which the Nation never delegated, and which neither reason nor religion has sanctioned. Witness, says the Author of *The Royalists' Defence*,[1] 'the several statutes in the times of King Henry VIII, Edward

[1] Charles Dallison. The work appeared in 1648.

VI, Queen Mary, and Queen Elizabeth, setting up and pulling down each other's religion, every one of them condemning even to death the profession of the one before established'. 'With this experience', adds Mr. Coleridge, 'and it would not be difficult to increase the catalogue, can we wonder that the nation grew sick of Parliamentary Religions? or that the Idea should at last awake and become operative, that what virtually involved their humanity, was not a matter to be voted up and down by fluctuating majorities?'

To represent the National Church as a Christian Institution, or a part of Christianity, is at once to place the Church in a false position, and to misrepresent the religion of Christ. Those who, in their zeal for the honour of the Establishment, take this ground, and stake the cause of the 'National Clerisy' on its being designed, primarily and mainly, to subserve the interests of religion, interests not of this world, are but pronouncing the condemnation of a system which so ill corresponds to its pretended object. They must overlook the notorious fact, that, of the cumbrous machinery, a very small portion only is even professedly brought to bear upon what is (on this hypothesis) its only legitimate end; the property of the Church would therefore seem to be so far held on a false pretence, which might almost vitiate the tenure. . . .

But we must revert to what Mr. Coleridge regards as the primary ends of a National Church. One of these, which, though seldom put forward by the clergy themselves, or by their advocates, has the greatest influence as an *Idea*, is, that the Church holds out to the subjects of the realm generally, 'a chance of bettering their own or their children's condition'—an avenue to honourable advancement. Now, putting religion out of consideration, we are not disposed to deny, that society has been greatly benefited, especially in the early stages of national civilization, by the existence of such a link between the aristocrasy and the people, as was supplied by the clerical order. Before the mercantile and commercial classes had risen into importance, so as to form an influential body 'in antithesis' (as Mr. Coleridge would say) to the Landed Interest, the National Church was, to a certain extent, a substitute for the 'burgess order'—a check, on some occasions, upon the Prerogative, on others, upon the power of the Nobles. During this period, says our Author,

The National Church presented the only breathing-hole of hope. The Church alone relaxed the iron fate by which feudal dependency, primogeniture, and

entail would otherwise have predestinated every native of the realm to be lord
or vassal. To the Church alone could the nation look for the benefits of existing
knowledge, and for the means of future civilization. Under the fostering wings
of the Church, the class of free citizens and burghers were reared. To the feudal
system we owe the forms, to the church the *substance* of our liberty. We
mention only two of many facts that would form the proof and comment of
the above; first, the origin of towns and cities, in the privilege attached to the
vicinity of churches and monasteries, and which, preparing an asylum for the
fugitive vassal and oppressed franklin, thus laid the first foundation of a class of
freemen detached from the land. Secondly, the holy war which the national
clergy, in this instance faithful to their national duties, waged against slavery
and villenage; and with such success, that, in the reign of Charles II, the law
which declared every native of the realm free by birth, had merely to sanction
an *opus jam consummatum.*

One of the original purposes of the *National Reserve*, Mr. Coleridge
contends, was, 'the alleviation of those evils which, in the best forms
of worldly States, must arise from the institution of individual properties
and primogeniture'. 'All advances in civilization, and the rights and
privileges of citizens, are especially connected with, and derived from,
the four classes of the mercantile, the manufacturing, the distributive,
and the professional'. Now, there was a time when the last of these
was almost entirely identified with the Church. Professors and practitioners of law, of medicine, of the arts and sciences, and schoolmasters
of all descriptions were, for the most part, *clerks.* But for the church
property, in the infancy or minority of commerce and manufactures,
all professional men must have been absolutely dependent upon the
patronage of the Aristocrasy. This reserve of national property,
therefore, by which an interest was created, distinct from that of the
landed order—a property not heritable, but reversionary—must have
been no small benefit to the community. Now that the National
Church, instead of being a distinct estate, has become little more than
an *appanage* to the landed Interest, its political character has become so
entirely changed, that we are apt to forget that it was not always in
abject bondage to the Aristocrasy and the Crown. A similar revolution,
Mr. Coleridge remarks, 'has transferred to the Magnates of the
Landed Interest so large a portion of that Borough Representation
which was to have been its *counterbalance*'. In order to have a distinct
idea of the encroachment of that leviathan Interest, thus swelled by
the spoils of the Church, as well by a large share of its patronage, on
the one hand, and by that foul source of corruption, borough-dealing

on the other, we must conceive of it as having converted to its own purpose, and assimilated as it were to its own structure, institutions that were originally designed to protect the nation against the domination of the feudal Proprietorship.

'Wherever Agriculture is the principal pursuit, there, it may certainly be reckoned, that the people will be living under an absolute government'. This remark is cited by Mr. Coleridge, with deserved approbation, from Mr. Crawfurd's *History of the Indian Archipelago*; and the history of all countries would supply ample illustrations of the truth of the axiom. So long as Italy was commercial, it was free; or (which comes nearly to the same thing) so long as the Republics preserved their freedom, commerce flourished. But, when they relapsed into principalities, manufactures, commerce, and public liberty declined and became extinct together; and as M. Sismondi expresses it, 'all Italy fell to ruin'.[1] The progress of desolation was, in great measure, arrested by the efforts of the Medicean princes. Agriculture revived under their patronage; but it was at the expense of commerce, for all the great capitalists became transformed into nobles and territorial proprietors. The consequence was, that amid the specious magnificence of the patrician order, public spirit and national wealth were being dried up at their sources. 'It was the profound policy of the Austrian and the Spanish courts', remarks Mr. Coleridge, 'by every possible means to degrade the profession of trade; and even in Pisa and Florence themselves, to introduce the feudal pride and prejudice of less happy, less enlightened countries. Agriculture, meanwhile, with its attendant population and plenty, was cultivated with increasing success; but, from the Alps to the Straits of Messina, the Italians are slaves'.

Such might have been, in our own country, the result of the enormous aggrandizement of the Agricultural Aristocrasy, connected as it has been with the appropriation of parliamentary and ecclesiastical patronage, by which 'the very weights intended for the effectual counterpoise of the great landholders, have been shifted into the opposite scale'—such might have been the catastrophe of our civil liberties, but for the increasing importance of the monied Interest (i.e. the manufacturing and the commercial) which is, however, closely allied to the landed Interest, and is perpetually passing into it; and still more, for the creation of 'new forces', which have preserved in some degree the equilibrium. Among these, our Author enumerates, 'roads,

[1] J. C. L. de Sismondi (1773–1842), author of *L'histoire des républiques italiennes du moyen âge* (1817).

canals, machinery, the press, the periodical and daily press, the might of public opinion, the consequent increasing desire of popularity among public men and functionaries of every description, and the increasing necessity of public character, as a means and condition of political influence'. It is strange, that he should altogether overlook the rise and consolidation of one most influential professional body, who might seem, more than any other, to have replaced the 'National Clerisy', as a check upon the Landed Interest, and to have supplied the defalcation of the Church, as providing the humblest families with the means of education and a path to intellectual and social advancement. We of course refer to the Dissenting Ministry of this country, to which we find no other reference or allusion than is obscurely conveyed in the following paragraph, unworthy alike of the good sense and the liberality of the philosophical Author.

But neither shall the fear of scorn prevent me from declaring aloud, and as a truth which I hold it the disgrace and calamity of a professed statesman not to know and acknowledge, that a permanent, nationalized, learned order, a national clerisy or church, is an essential element of a rightly constituted nation, without which it wants the best security alike for its permanence and its progression; and for which neither tract-societies, nor *conventicles*, nor Lancastrian schools, nor mechanics' institutions, nor lecture-bazaars under the absurd name of universities, nor all these collectively, can be a substitute. For they are all marked with the same asterisk of spuriousness, shew the same distemper-spot on the front, that they are empirical specifics for morbid *symptoms* that help to feed and continue the disease.

Mr. Coleridge needs not fear provoking either our scorn or our anger; but we regret to observe the *tone* betrayed by this effusion of splenetic prejudice. As regards what our Author himself tells us are the 'primary ends' of a National Clerisy, these institutions which he decries as spurious, are an actual succedaneum for the Church; and these new 'forces', or 'organs', or 'means', have been called into operation, because the Church has not kept pace with the progress of society, or adequately discharged its engagements. The cardinal and essential defect of the Church as a political apparatus, is, that it is wholly incapable of self-adjustment, or of being accommodated to the varying scale and circumstances of the population. In its fiscal system only, it has kept pace with the improvement and expansion of society. The revenues of the Church have increased far beyond their due proportion to the rent of the soil; but every thing else has remained immutably fixed. The means of liberal education, of religious instruction, of parochial oversight, which the Establishment provided for three or four millions of people, it has satisfied itself with furnishing for twelve or fourteen millions. The only additions have, at least, been recent, forced, and scanty. A parish which, two hundred years ago, contained two thousand persons, may have decupled its population, but it is a parish still; and though the tithe has risen in value a hundredfold, the service rendered for it shall be, as regards the tithe-holder, the same. Every difficulty is thrown in the way of increasing the provision for parochial instruction; and whenever a new church is to be built, the chief matter of solicitude, is, that the revenues of the old incumbent should not be taxed or infringed upon. The Church, as 'an estate of the realm', has, out of that national fund, the tithe, contributed literally nothing towards meeting the wants of an ever-growing population. The National Schools, the Lincoln's Inn fields 'tract-society', the King's College 'lecture-bazaar', which Mr. Coleridge would probably exempt from the sarcasms bestowed upon Lancastrian schools and 'saint and sinner societies', are supported by the voluntary contributions of church-men, but not by 'the Church', not by the Establishment as such, nor out of the church-revenues. They must therefore be set aside, equally with the more 'spurious' substitutes for a National Clerisy, in estimating the efficiency of the Establishment as a scheme of instruction—in examining the wisdom of its constitution, or its practical results. So far as regards a very great part of the means of education and civilization now provided for the lower classes within the pale of the Established Church, the Tithe, the national reserve, as Mr. Coleridge styles it, is of no avail whatever. Scarcely any part of the money raised, consists of a charge upon this national fund, notwithstanding its immense augmentation.

But, in addition to the means of education provided by the voluntary subscriptions of individual churchmen, all the 'spurious' substitutes for the labours of 'a permanent, nationalized, learned Clerisy', must be taken into account as so much done towards effectuating the 'primary end' of the Establishment, and so much *left to be done*, by other means: whether it is better or worse done, is not the question. The provision made and supported by the Church for communicating moral and religious instruction, for teaching even 'the morality which the State requires in its citizens for its own well-being', confessedly falls very far short of the demand; and the people supply the deficiency by what Mr. Coleridge calls the substitute, but which is the substitute for what has never existed. To the full extent of what is thus substituted for the tithe-paid service, the people are the gratuitous surrogates for the National Church. . . .

Within the last forty years, it has been supposed, that the wealth of this country has increased one half; our annual taxation has increased by about thirty-five millions sterling; the national consumption has increased not less wonderfully; besides which, the amount of British income spent abroad by voluntary absentees, has been estimated at not less than five millions.* To the people of this country, then, a million or two more or less would be no such great burden, if, for the cost, they could ensure an equivalent in value received. It cannot be said with any truth, that the inferior clergy of the Establishment are overpaid. The National Church does not, out of its ample revenues, decently provide for those of her own household; and 'the hope, the chance of bettering their own or their children's condition', which she once held out to the subjects of the realm generally, is almost confined at present to the holders of advowsons or to the higher classes. Not only trade, commerce, free industry, and the arts, now compete with the Church in this respect, but even the Dissenting ministry, or the function of a school-master, affords a more certain compensation. Besides which, the professions of law and medicine, long since detached from the Church, and no longer dependent in any degree on the national reserve, better answer this 'primary end' of the Church, than the close monopoly of the tithe-paid Clerisy. These are the grounds, and not the simple amount of the Church revenues, on which the political expediency of the Establishment may most reasonably be questioned.

We say, the political expediency, because we have all along waived the consideration of the religious question. 'The authority of a Church establishment', Dr. Paley says, 'is founded on its utility'; and he would limit this utility to 'the preservation and communication of religious knowledge'. This is taking a very narrow view of the subject for a philosopher; and we have been anxious, on the contrary, to consider its utility in all its bearings, not simply as a scheme of instruction, but as an element of the constitution, and a National Trust. 'The Church of Christ', we say in the words of Mr. Coleridge, 'asks of the State neither wages nor dignities: she asks only protection and to be let alone'.

The Christian Church, as such, has no nationalty entrusted to its charge. It forms no counterbalance to the collective *heritage* of the realm. The phrase,

* *Quarterly Review*, No. lxxxii. pp. 515, 520.

Church and State, has a sense and a propriety in reference to the *National* Church alone. The Church of Christ cannot be placed in this conjunction and antithesis without forfeiting the very name of Christian. The true and only contra-position of the Christian Church is to the World.

The Church of Christ consists, not of an order of clergy, but of 'visible and public communities', connected together by their common relation to their One Invisible Head—'congregations of faithful men, in which the pure word of God is preached, and the sacraments be duly ministered'. These, whether within or without the pale of the Establishment, compose what Mr. Coleridge correctly designates as a Catholic and Apostolic Church *in* England. But the 'Constitutional and Ancestral Church *of* England', is essentially a Property in Trust, vested in a privileged order, for the purpose of national benefits. That this is the case, is manifest from the common expression, 'the Church is in danger'; which always means, and can but mean, the Church property. It is not that the National Church is *maintained* by this property, but it *is* this property; as truly so as the Bank of England means the capital of the Bank. Were the whole of the Church property alienated, the clergy would still retain their system of polity, their formularies and ritual, and would, like the other professions once identified with the clerisy, be supported by the people; but the National Church would be destroyed. Now it is with regard to this Property in Trust, that a fair inquiry may be instituted, how far it is faithfully applied to its proper and national purposes; how far what was designed to be a benefit to the whole nation, has come to be a source of advantage only to a part; to what extent this property, secluded and exempted from the conditions of heritable property, and intended to be, in a sense, circulative and reversionary, instead of lineal, has been, by gross abuse, converted into hereditary estates; how far a Trust, originally adapted for the encouragement and reward of learning, liberal science, and piety among all classes of the community, and serving as a check and counterpoise to the overbearing influence of the Landed Interest, has become, on the contrary, the chief antagonist of the popular Interest, the subservient ally of the Aristocrasy or the Crown. These are points not to be flippantly disposed of: each might be made the head of extended argument. It might, for instance, be urged, that, allowing the Church to have become thus adverse to popular freedom, the increase of the democratic force requires that this weight should be transferred to the opposite scale, in order to maintain the equilibrium. But then, it would require consideration, whether, on the one hand, the Church, when set in array against the weight of public opinion, might not become an odious, and therefore dangerous auxiliary. On the other hand, there can be no doubt that the Church suffers very extensively in popularity, and that disaffection is fast spreading among the 'working clergy' themselves, greatly on account of the corrupt system of ecclesiastical patronage. Now, whatever service an Establishment, as a scheme of Instruction, may be capable of rendering to religion, an unpopular Church must exert an influence hostile to the interests of the faith they are employed to disseminate, and favourable to the growth of infidelity.

Mr. Coleridge announces, as among his 'filial bodings', the spoliation of the Church, or, as he terms it, the Nationalty—'half thereof to be distributed among the land-owners, and the other half among the stock-brokers and stock-owners, in lieu of the interest formerly due to them'. We can hardly believe that such a project is seriously entertained by any party of reformers; and we must confess that we should regard the absorption of any further portion of the national reserve by a bloated aristocrasy, as a serious political evil. The Tithe is not less a burden, when it is in the hands of a farmer or landed proprietor; nor would the nation be relieved by a second alienation of church property, similar to that which took place on the dissolution of monasteries, if no other change ensued than the converting of public into private property. Mr. Rennell[1] contends, indeed, that 'Tithes are not public, but private property; nor are they the less so', he adds, 'because, *in some cases*, a public duty is entailed on their possessors'. This sounds very much like an impudent apology for non-residence, sinecures, and clerical abuses of all descriptions; but we presume that the learned and paradoxical writer did not mean to push his principle to its full extent. Tithes, in the hands of a land-owner, are private property; and so would any other tax become, the right to levy and enjoy the proceeds of which, the Government should confer upon any number of individuals. The Assessed taxes might, in this way, be rendered private property, as well as a land-tax. The tithe, in the hands of a clerical rector, is also private property *for the time being*; but, notwithstanding the licensed sale of advowsons, the tithe, on the death of the incumbent, ceases to be private property, the freehold being determined, and reverts, not to the patron, but to the public, to whom this reservation belongs; and it is granted afresh by the trustee, to a new tenant, on the conditions of public duty. If this statement be denied, there can be no such thing as national property.

[1] Thomas Rennell (1787–1824), author of *Remarks on Scepticism* (1819).

AIDS TO REFLECTION

second edition, 1832

---

109. J. H. Heraud, *Fraser's Magazine*

June 1832, v, 585-97

An unsigned review, 'Some Account of Coleridge's Philosophy', attributed to J. H. Heraud (Miriam H. Thrall, *Rebellious Fraser's*, New York 1934, 270). Heraud (1799-1887), assistant editor of *Fraser's Magazine* from 1830 to 1833, was one of Coleridge's disciples.

We have so frequently quoted S. T. Coleridge, and made so many allusions to his system, in REGINA, that it is high time we should do that profound thinker, writer, and speaker, the justice of devoting a separate paper to his merits. This we may the more readily render, as the public, it would appear, are at length awakened to the importance of his speculations, and have so far rewarded the sage as to demand a second edition of the singularly valuable work with which we have embellished the title of this paper. The venerable author, to this second edition, has prefixed the following address:

TO THE READER

FELLOW-CHRISTIAN!—The wish to be admired, as a fine writer, held a very subordinate place in the author's thoughts and feelings in the composition of this volume. Let, then, its comparative merits and demerits, in respect of style and stimulancy, possess a proportional weight and no more, in determining your judgment for or against 'its contents'. Read it through: then compare the state of your mind, with the state in which your mind was, when you first opened the book. Has it led you to reflect? Has it supplied or suggested fresh subjects for reflection? Has it given you any new information? Has it removed any obstacle to a lively conviction of your responsibility as a moral agent? Has it solved any difficulties which had impeded your faith as a Christian? Lastly, has it increased your power of thinking connectedly? especially on the scheme and purpose of the redemption by Christ? If it have done none of these things, condemn it aloud as worthless; and strive to compensate for your own loss of time, by preventing others from wasting theirs. But if your conscience dictates an affirmative answer to all or any of the preceding questions, declare this too aloud, and endeavour to extend my utility.

Yes, old man! with right gladness of heart will we make this endeavour, and a strenuous one shall it be—for we love thee well— we owe thee much! O how much is owing to thee by the greatest and brightest minds which now shine down upon the republic of letters— kings and priests over a people of kings and priests, or a people who should consist of such. Thou, however, hast done thy part to make them such, and to excite them to a sense of their high calling; and for this, accept the small tribute of gratitude which we are now about to offer at the shrine of philosophic genius—that best of all gifts, which the Divine Benefactor of humankind has bestowed on the chief of its creatures—man! immortal and responsible man!

In the divine Plato we find the characters of poet and philosopher existing in the most intimate union and interdependence, and the highest and most opposite faculties of the mind copresent in every exertion of his mighty intellect. The severest exercise of reason is not irreconcilable with the most elevated imaginings. Though distinguished into its different modes, the mind is incapable of division, and all the faculties are consistent. Judgment is not the only power of the intellect requisite to ascertain truth; and ideas, which are the growth of reason, must, by the intervention of the imagination or fancy, be symbolised before they can be understood. If the great Locke might have made but an indifferent poet, it was not from any essential contrariety be- tween poetry and philosophy. It rather resulted from a mistaken bias of his will, which induced him to prefer the sensible to the intelligible—a bias equally fatal to philosophy as to poetry. Believing the mind to be the passive recipient of ideas externally derived, the white paper on which active nature impressed her notices, it were not to be expected that he would think of rousing his mind to so daring an attempt as to *create* from the 'airy nothing' the 'thing unknown', which is the peculiar occupation of the poet. For neither philosophy nor poetry is reflective, but originative—neither is exclu- sively conversant with the external world, both only employ the verbal images of sensible phenomena as the media of communication— media demanded by the necessities of language, which is a material instrument. Of all philosophers, the metaphysician has the most occasion for the assistance of imagination. Discoursing of objects purely spiritual, and inaccessible to the organs of sense, and transcending natural experience, such as the ideas of God, of the soul, of free-will, of a future state, and of the moral law, how are these objects or ideas to be embodied but by the assistance of the imagination to 'turn them to shape', and the fancy to aggregate and associate the reflex perceptions to which they are to be assimilated, in order that they may be apprehended by the average understanding of mankind? But if whatever is present to the human understanding and reason be but a reflection from the world of the senses, the great act of the imagination is precluded, the presentments of the fancy are already shaped, and there remains only for the philosophic faculty, whatever it be, to analyse, compare, and decide. It is no good reason why a man should not be an excellent poet that he is a philosopher, nor why he should not be a sage that he is a bard. In the earliest ages the characters were united, and of the ancient philosophers many were poets; as Solon, Bias, Epimenides, Anacharsis, Empedocles. If Aristotle be not numbered among them, it must be remembered he wrote on poetry; and that he was not a poet arose, probably, from similar circumstances to those which precluded the mind of Locke from manifesting its energies in the required mode. In support of which notion we may observe, that the principles of their respective philosophic systems are in many important points essentially the same.

Mr. Coleridge is equally eminent as a poet and metaphysician. As a poet, he has transferred to the supernatural and romantic world the interests and affections of humanity, and ascribed reality and truth to unseen and mysterious agency. As a philosopher, he has referred to the things which do not appear for the solution of the things that are seen, and assumed the invisible as the supporter of the apparent. Having elevated his mind to the contemplation of the omnipresent, the absolute, and the indemonstrable, for the ground, the cause, and fountain of all demonstration, he has traced the real in the ideal, and discovered the evidence of reason and religion in themselves. He has emancipated us from the superstition of the senses, and rendered the senses and their objects subservient to higher interests, as the organs and exponents of reason and religion. '*By celestial observations alone can even terrestrial charts be constructed scientifically*'.*

Pyrrho, who, considering all knowledge to be relative, required in every thing a relation to some other thing previously existing, consistently acknowledged no certain truth, and asserting nothing, believing

* *Friend*, vol. iii. p. 121.

nothing—except perhaps that he believed nothing—banished from the dreary region of sceptical sophistry every kind of demonstration. Demonstration ought to be derived from something clear and evident, and requiring no proof. Nothing, he said, in this world can be of this nature, since should things appear evident to us, we should be obliged to prove the truth of the reasoning which makes us converts to this belief.

But man was not constituted to remain in the vale of ignorance and doubt with a satisfied spirit. He looked beyond the horizon of the hills, and, impelled by a mysterious instinct, endeavoured to account for nature by a knowledge transcending nature. He strove from time to time to discover, and remained dissatisfied because in his lapsed condition he could not discover, without the aid of revelation, that great, absolute truth, self-grounded, unconditional, and known by its own light, which *is* because it *is*—self-affirmed, and existing before and independent of all things. Continually failing in this attempt, not because its object was unattainable, but on account of the weakness and corrupt nature of the human will, he was fain at every interval to return to the world of the senses, and repose on empirical evidence. But man cannot long rest content with the testimonies of 'flesh and blood'. Pyrrho and his successors have done good service to philosophy, by disturbing the stagnant waters of material dogmatism, and setting men again on a voyage of discovery after truths which are eternal, immutable, and universal. In our own country, the dogmatism of Locke laid the ground for the scepticism of Hume, and rendered it necessary for philosophy to assume a more elevated position, and to look into the mind of man for higher laws than were to be discovered in external experience, and to refer even the laws of nature herself to the constitution of the human intellect.

In this sublimest department of the philosophy of mind has the genius of Mr. Coleridge manifested itself with astonishing power. Firmly established on the fulcrum of pure reason, he holds in his hands the engine by which the universe of knowledge may be lifted from its foundation, and the indemonstrable positions which constitute the bases of all the sciences discovered and ascertained. To investigate and determine the nature and essence of these fundamental truths, and to announce the while a magnificent system grounded upon them, has been the principal end and aim of all the preceding productions of this author. He now proceeds to develop the theory which he has so frequently propounded, and apply it to the highest interests equally of human being as of human science. The *Aids to Reflection* is the commencement of this great undertaking, and contains premises of works (would that they might be fulfilled!) that will complete the erection of the edifice, of which the substantial elements have been so well understood and defined.

That some of this gentleman's speculations, in prosecuting these important inquiries, should have appeared obscure to ordinary readers, is no matter of surprise. The subject of metaphysics has always been abstruse; and to the majority of readers even Locke's *Essay*, which, having peculiar reference to objects of sense, is of comparatively easy conception by ordinary minds, will not altogether appear the clearest and liveliest of disquisitions; while its want of distinctness subjects it to the censure of the philosopher, and makes its authority of doubtful advantage in speculative discussion. The philosophic writings of Coleridge, on the other hand, have more depth than clearness; but, we venture to say, are infinitely superior, in point of distinctness, to those of any other writer on mind of which this country can boast. It is important to the well-being of men that they should be informed, that the science of metaphysics is a severe study; and that there is no more reason they should be instantly understood and appreciated, than that the mathematics should be of easy and instantaneous acquirement. The intelligibility of both will be in proportion to the intelligence of the student. And if to become a perfect master of one requires the abstraction of a life from ordinary pursuits, can it be expected that the complete systems of logic, metaphysics, morality, and religion, should be comprehended in an hour, if at all? Surely the popular character of a work, on either of these subjects, would furnish strong presumption that it contained very little, if any, original research, and at best could only lead us to expect an adaptation of the result of severe inquiry and abstract reasoning to the average understanding; or, what is yet more likely, a reflection of popular prejudice, and the shallow and diversely-coloured notions of the half-thinking many.

The writings of Coleridge, however, are intended to be of general utility, but meant for that class of persons who possess the peculiar advantages of a good education; and the means adopted by him to render intelligible the truths he taught has been, not by reducing them to the level of the common sense, but by disciplining and exalting the mind, as far as possible, into a correspondence with the excellence of the theme on which he 'discoursed most eloquent music'. This, a difficult task, was rendered more difficult by the peculiar nature of the author's style, which is perhaps more owing to his peculiar genius than to the circumstance of its having been moulded upon the works of the ancients, and of the elder writers in modern languages, to which himself ascribes it. This author's genius as a poet is especially under the dominion of fancy, a fancy, indeed, of lofty daring and aspiring aspect, yet capricious as fancy ever is, even in her noblest efforts, determined by every accident, and taking the colour of every impression. Even when rapt in the fiery chariot of imagination to the faery land of supernatural agency, or supported by reason in the region of the ideal, the fantastic hues of his individual genius redeem his creations within the pale of humanity, and tint them with the light and the shadow of earthly forms and appearances—the loveliest and the loftiest, yet of earth and earthly things. She is to him as a mother; and in his farthest flights he thinks of her. Now this fantastic faculty has more to do with the verbal expression than with any other part of composition—for words are precisely derived from the same source from which she derives her own stores of thought and imagery. Hence the philosophical arguments of Mr. Coleridge gleam and glow with a fulgor not their own, but which is reflected from the accidents of nature; or, rather, the substance from within which shineth through them gives life and expression to every form and feature. This, requiring a fancy of corresponding activity and liveliness in the perusal, makes it difficult for the more phlegmatic reader to follow the reasoning and preserve the connexion. But to minds of a higher order it superinduces a charm on reperusal, which prevents repetition from palling, and becomes a greater beauty the better the book is understood.

As an example of the style to which we allude, we select the following remarkably fine passage from the *Aids to Reflection*, and which might also furnish a good motto or epigraph for the examination on which we are about to enter.

Every rank of creatures, as it ascends in the scale of creation, leaves death behind or under it. The metal at its height of being seems a mute prophecy of the coming vegetation, into a mimic semblance of which it crystallises. The blossom and flower, the acme of vegetable life, divides into correspondent organs, with reciprocal functions, and by instinctive motions and approximations seems impatient of that fixture, by which it is differenced in kind from the flower-shaped Psyche, that flutters with free wing above it. And wonderfully in the insect realm doth the irritability, the proper seat of instinct, while yet the nascent sensibility is subordinated thereto—most wonderfully, I say, doth the muscular life in the insect, and the musculo-arterial in the bird, imitate and typically rehearse the adaptive understanding, yea, and the moral affections and charities, of man. Let us carry ourselves back, in spirit, to the mysterious week, the teeming work-days of the Creator, as they rose in vision before the eye of the inspired historian of 'the generations of the heaven and the earth, in the days that the Lord God made the earth and the heavens'. And who that hath watched their ways with an understanding heart, would contemplate the filial and loyal bee; the house-building, wedded and divorceless swallow; and, above all, the manifoldly intelligent ant tribes, with their commonwealths and confederacies, their warriors and miners, the husbandfolk that fold in their tiny flocks on the honeyed leaf, and the virgin sisters with the holy instincts of maternal love, detached and in selfless purity—and not say to himself, Behold the shadow of approaching humanity, the sun rising from behind, in the kindling morn of creation! Thus all lower natures find their highest good in semblances and seekings of that which is higher and better. All things strive to ascend, and ascend in their striving. And shall man alone stoop? Shall his pursuits and desires, the *reflections* of his inward life, be like the reflected image of a tree on the edge of a pool, that grows downwards, and seeks a mock heaven in the unstable element beneath it, in neighbourhood with the slim water-weeds and oozy bottom-grass, that are yet better than itself and more noble, in as far as substances that appear as shadows are preferable to shadows mistaken for substance! No! it must be a higher good to make you happy. While you labour for any thing below your proper humanity, you seek a happy life in the region of death. Well saith the moral poet—

Unless above himself he can
Erect himself, how mean a thing is man!

But more than all, the great difficulty with which our author has had to contend, is the state of metaphysical science in this country. The strict meaning which he attaches to terms, and the different significations he appropriates to apparent synonymes, coincide not well with the vague and insufficient nomenclature of the metaphysical schools of our own and a neighbouring country; and the immethodical selections from metaphysical systems, of which our popular philosophy is composed, are at war with that close and logical connexion and unity which it has been his endeavour to introduce into metaphysical research. Besides, it is also necessary that the mind of the student should be prepared with considerable historical knowledge of the science, should have thought deeply, and questioned frequently, and advanced through the avenues of doubt into the presence-chamber of certainty, by a way which has been hitherto but little explored, and into which Mr. Coleridge was one of the earliest to adventure.

One of the principal objects of the *Aids to Reflection* is, 'to direct the attention of the reader to the value of the science of words, their use and abuse, and the incalculable advantages attached to the habit of using them appropriately, and with a distinct knowledge of their primary, derivative, and metaphorical sources'.

To expose a sophism [says our author] and to detect the equivocal or double meaning of a word, is, in the great majority of cases, one and the same thing. For if words are not *things*, they are *living* powers, by which the things of most importance to mankind are actuated, combined, and humanised. In a language like ours, where so many words are derived from other languages, there are few modes of instruction more useful or more amusing than that of accustoming young people to seek for the etymology, or primary meaning, of the words they use. There are cases in which more knowledge of more value may be conveyed by the history of a *word*, than by the history of a campaign.

It is not the intention of our author, we apprehend, to send his readers upon the laborious and effectless expedition recommended by the counsel and example of Horne Tooke;[1] but to impress on their attention the importance of rightly using, of selecting with discretion, and determining with precision, the meaning of words; and more particularly to enforce the duty, upon the philosophical student, of ascertaining, as far as possible, the original philosophical signification of terms, under the conviction (to use his own expressions) 'that language (as the embodied and articulated spirit of the race, as the growth and emanation of a people, and not the work of any individual wit or will) is often inadequate, sometimes deficient, but never false or delusive. We have only to master the true origin and original import of any native and abiding word, to find in it, if not the *solution* of the facts expressed by it, yet a finger-mark pointing to the road on which this solution is to be sought for'. 'The very terms', says he, in another work, 'of ancient wisdom are worn out, or (far worse) stamped on baser metal; and whoever shall have the hardihood to re-proclaim its solemn truths, must commence with a glossary'.

We think, however, that the author has departed a little from the rule laid down by himself, in expressing his dislike to the word 'virtue' in the pulpit, as sounding too much of Pagan philosophy. 'The passage in St. Peter's Epistle is the only scriptural authority that can be pretended for its use, which rests either on an oversight of the translators, or on a change in the meaning of the word since their time'. 'Ἀρέτην he contends, should have been translated 'manly energy', entirely

[1] John Horne Tooke (1736-1812); a reference to his Ἔπεα πτερόεντα, *or the Diversions of Purley* (1786, 1798).

neglecting the etymon of the word virtue—virtus, *manhood*, given by himself in another place, which produces the very meaning contended for. Would it not also have furnished an important exception to the rule implied by Horne Tooke, that all our knowledge was of sensible origin—even as words, which are the signs of ideas, have intimate relation to the objects of sense? Is not the word virtue, if bearing a different and less intense meaning now, a term of ancient wisdom stamped on baser metal? A term originally importing, that what we esteem good and great in humanity is not merely a sublimation of the knowledge derived from surrounding nature and 'unspiritual' circumstance, but a vivific energy emanating from what is peculiarly necessary in man—reason, fortitude, and free-will, supervened upon and quickening the knowledge and the faith recommended by the apostle, with the life within—the living, self-subsisting soul which man emphatically *became*—'his proper *being*—his truest *self*—*the* man *in* the man?' If this be so, would it not intimate that our moral declension was and is a falling off from our proper humanity—a resignation of reason, of fortitude, and of will? And if these things be yet part and parcel of our humanity, may there not remain in man an inherent and essential power to return to that divine image in which he was originally created, always supposing his aid and permission by whom he was created? What a basis for Hope to build her goodly expectations upon, relative to the ultimate perfection and final destination of human society and the human soul! To build up this manly character, on the several grounds of prudence, morality, and religion—to furnish it with this fortitude of virtue, this strength of reason, and energy of will, is the intention of our author's present publication.

No one was more aware, in theory, than the immortal Locke, of the great hinderance to knowledge occasioned by the ill use of words. The slightest acquaintance, however, with Reid's *Essays on the Powers of the Human Mind*,[1] which were purposely adapted to common sense, and are levelled to its capacity, will convince every one how improperly Locke used the term of most frequent occurrence in his work, and of the mischievous effects which his misuse had on philosophical disquisition. The conceptions which he exclusively admitted as ideas, were, in fact, no ideas at all. The *sensible species* and *phantasms* of the ancients were certainly never called ideas by them. So far from conceiving ideas to be derivable from experience, or the objects of sense, they were the models uncreated and immutable, either distinct from the Deity, or

[1] Thomas Reid (1710-96), common sense philosopher.

identified with the forms of the Divine understanding, according to which all things were fashioned. The use which he made of the term was entirely an innovation, and led to that want of distinctness observable in his Essay. Those conceptions which he called ideas of reflection, would have a better claim to the title than those which he denominated ideas of sensation, had it not been clearly and ably shewn by Dugald Stewart, and demonstrated before in the speculations of Berkeley, Hume, Hartley, Priestly, and Darwin,[1] as also in the systems of the French philosophers, that his ideas of sensation also were resolvable into consciousness, and those of reflection might be confounded with the ideas of sensation. In the mean time, however, the word idea has been always opposed to an external object, whether present or absent. Add to this, that the ideas of sensation are fictitious and hypothetical, and, as they are founded on the material idealism of Descartes, lead to the immaterial idealism of Berkeley, and to the unqualified idealism of Hume; until, at last, both the material and immaterial world were annihilated, and ideas had neither objects of which they were representative, nor subjects by which they were perceived; yet they existed, were representative, and were perceived.

It must be allowed to be an important question, whether the term idea has any meaning?—whether there be ideas at all? And if they be not what Locke thus denominated, what they really are?

An idea [according to our author] is neither a notion, a sensation, a perception, nor a conception, but an educt of the imagination, actuated by the pure reason, to which there neither is, nor can be, an adequate correspondent in the world of the senses. It is living, productive, partakes of infinity, and, as Bacon has sublimely observed, contains an endless power of semination. Hence it is that science, which consists wholly in ideas and principles, is power; hence the sublime ideas spoken out every where in the Old and New Testament awaken and start up the soul of man, as an exile in a far distant land at the unexpected sounds of his native language, when, after long years of absence and almost of oblivion, he is suddenly addressed in his own mother-tongue. He weeps for joy, and embraces the speaker as his brother.

An idea, as corresponding to a reality out of the mind, becomes a law; and a law, contemplated as a reality in the mind, is an idea. The first man (our author elsewhere observes) on whom the light of an *idea* dawned, did in that same moment receive the spirit and the

---

[1] Dugald Stewart (1753–1828), a disciple of Reid's; Joseph Priestley (1733–1804), a Hartleyan materialist; Erasmus Darwin (1731–1802), physician and versifying botanist.

credentials of a lawgiver; and as long as man shall exist, so long will the possession of that antecedent knowledge (the maker and master of all possible experience), which exists only in the power of an idea, be the one lawful qualification of all dominion in the world of the senses.

The ideas of Mr. Coleridge, therefore, are not the media by the intervention of which we perceive objects; but he uses the word constantly 'in the highest and primitive sense, and as nearly synonymous with the modern word *ideal*; as archetypal, co-essential with the reason, and the consciousness of which is the sign and necessary product of its full development'.

If the word idea mean only either an impression on the senses, or a definite conception, or an abstract notion, it is, he tells us, 'superfluous, and, while it remains undetermined which of these is meant, or whether it is not *which you please*, is worse than superfluous'.

We may safely leave Reid and Stewart to settle with the sceptics the substantial existence of mind and matter. Our author's system requires that the reality of both should be assumed at the outset. So far from possessing any thing in common, he proceeds in a course directly opposite to that of the sceptics: they sought the ideal in the real; he endeavours to find the real in the ideal. In this he ventures farther than Kant, in whose school he studied, and upon whose philosophy, we believe, it has been his great object to improve. 'Whether there be a correspondent reality—whether the knowledge of the mind has its correlative in being, Kant left undecided. According to him, our reason was given to us, indeed, to emancipate our conceptions from the limits of experience and of nature, that by suggesting the probable existence of objects transcending sense, morality might be enabled to extend its practical principles to absoluteness and universality'. But it is the end and aim of our author to conquer all doubts that we may entertain respecting the objective reality of the ideas which not only constitute reason, but, as he contends, are reason itself. We, however, anticipate: let us enter more minutely into our author's system.

That there exist things without us, is an original and innate prejudice implanted by nature in every man, and a position admitted as readily as the existence of his own personal being. This is the oldest realism, and common to all mankind. It believes and requires neither more nor less than that the object which it beholds or presents to itself is the real and very object. Kant, whom we must be allowed to esteem, however unfashionable, as the Euclid of metaphysical science, held our perception of external objects to be intuitive—that is, without the intervention of any medium, hypothetical or theoretical. He confines the term intuition to the effect produced on us by the phenomena of sense. We only judge of things as they appear *to* us and are understood *by* us. What they are in themselves, we know not, for sense presents every thing to us in a mode of its own. Mr. Coleridge apprehends that the founder of the critical philosophy had a different and a deeper meaning in his *Noumenon*, or *thing in itself*, than what his mere words express. We are not inclined to seek after this occult signification of the term, but more willingly turn to another question—whether 'he confined the whole *plastic* power to the forms of the intellect, leaving for the external cause, for the *matériel* of our sensations, a matter without form, which is doubtless inconceivable'? This question of Mr. Coleridge must set him in a fair light in the opinion of those who are disposed to feel their common sense outraged by the doctrine of the German sage, that time and space have rather a subjective than an objective reality— *i.e.* that they merely exist in and for a mind alone, and are, in fact, only the two forms of the faculty of sense: though, after all, he asserted very little more than has been asserted of space by Dugald Stewart, when, speaking of the mathematical affections of matter, he says, 'that our conviction of the necessary existence of extension or space, is neither the result of reasoning nor of experience, but it is inseparable from the very conception of it, and must, therefore, be considered as an ultimate and essential law of human thought'. But to this opinion of Stewart we must add his persuasion, expressed on another occasion, when he considered the subject wholly unfit for argument, and felt that, 'while the frame of his understanding continued unaltered', he must have the clear conviction experienced by Dr. Clarke[1] when a child, and questioned by his parents whether God could do every thing?—that 'there was one thing which God could not do—that he could not annihilate that space which was in the room where they were'. We enter not on this debatable ground out of a principle of opposition to Dugald Stewart, for whose philosophical genius we entertain a high respect, but because of the importance, nature, and tendency of the investigation. The scepticism regarding the power of Deity to annihilate space, either involves the heresy which identifies space with Deity, or includes Deity within the bounds of space. Space must either have been before, co-eternal with, or created by, Deity. Of these three alternatives we take the last. He alone is infinite, and space is included in him, and, like every created thing, presupposes a

[1] Samuel Clarke (1675-1729), philosopher and theologian.

creative and sustaining mind. Cannot he who created annihilate? Its existence, therefore, is inconceivable independent of a mind.

But a distinction very properly arises between the Supreme Mind and the minds of created percipient beings. Berkeley, however, thought it not unphilosophical, in support of his system of perception, that phenomena had no existence independent of a percipient mind; to enforce the position, that supposing all created percipient beings were annihilated, still we could not conceive objects as existing without and independent of the Divine Mind. In this we see nothing more than that instinctive striving of human thought to find itself in the region beyond the world of sense, where only that source of demonstration can be found required by Pyrrho; and which necessity of the mind in thinking is at the same time an earnest of the lawfulness of the endeavour, and of the truth of the ideas which it involves. Their reality not being to be ascertained in the field of experience, is, we take it, the best reason that can be given for the necessity of revelation, that man may be assured of the substantial existence of the objects implied by such ideas. Revelation directly supplies the very fountain of demonstration required by the philosopher, and places it within the reach of the humblest intellect. It would be well were philosophers not to overlook this source, and prefer to commence the series of their inductions there, rather than from crude guesses of the essence and nature of objects, the least iota of which it is impossible for them to know. They would then find, perhaps, in the two first axioms revealed from heaven, principles, in the guiding light of which they might arrive more surely at ultimate satisfaction. These two first axioms are—'in the beginning God created the heavens and the earth', and, 'in the image of God made he man'. The first axiom will demonstrate the impossibility, independent of a mind or spirit, of the existence of any thing having a beginning; and the second would lead us to consider in what way space, and the matter contained therein, exist with respect to man, as a spiritual intelligence and the image of his Creator.

This dogma of the sage of Königsberg[1] may be considerably modified by another principle of his philosophy, which, to be brief, we shall express technically: the test of an objective reality is, that it is subjectively general; which would restore to the external cause form as well as matter, since the conception that objects have arrangement as well as parts is not peculiar to any individual mind, but is common to all minds. This, we think, approximates to what Mr. Coleridge implied

[1] Kant.

by the question which we have considered it expedient to cite, and preserves also the distinction between the supreme and the human intellect; for although upon the one hand we may concede, that objects corresponding with our conceptions are only met with in experience, as products of our understanding from the materials of sense, we, on the other, must guard against the absurdity of being mistaken, to contend that they are actually placed there by human perception. They rather constitute the universal exponents of the external and omnipresent mind, which are thus perceived by man as the exponents of his own conceptions, in virtue of his spiritual similitude to his Almighty Maker. Thus we have, however indistinctly, indicated how the two axioms of inspired wisdom may, in this particular instance, be applied, and for whom it may be reconciled. This is the only way in which we can conceive the assertion to be true, that the phenomena in time and space have no existence—and the only reason that we can give why it is impossible to prove how they exist—independently of a mind. That these phenomena may exist independent of my mind, is certain; that they may exist independent of all minds, is inconceivable; that they can exist independent of the Eternal and Supreme, dare never be asserted.

Space swells out to immensity; time stretches into eternity. So our conception of the human mind enlarges to universality; and we are induced, in our philosophical investigations, to consider it invested with attributes which are superhuman, and more properly belonging to original and uncreated intellect. Even in this, as in all things, we transcend experience. Philosophy has always found it necessary to commence with the idea of the absolute and universal, of which all that we behold, all that we are, is but a symbolic portion—a 'living part, indeed, in the unity of which it is the representative'—yet but a symbol, which (to use the words of our author, whom we only *seem* to have forgotten) 'is characterised by a translucence of the special in the individual, or of the general in the especial, or of the universal in the general; above all, by the translucence of the eternal through and in the temporal'.*

Such is the sublime view which philosophy takes of the soul of man. She considers him as an intelligence enfranchised from the limits of time and space, superior to nature, and independent of her laws. His soul does not reside among the changeable phenomena of nature, and his liberty is secured to him by his independence of them; for he is in

* First *Lay Sermon*.

himself an efficient cause, and is subject only to the law of his own reason and free-will.

But philosophy can never arrive at this conclusion, while she refers all human knowledge to sensible experience, and insists upon compounding our ideas of sensations. Locke no sooner limited the philosophy of mind to a consideration of the human understanding, than his successors reduced the understanding itself to the level of the sensuous faculty, and denominated therefrom every attribute of the intellect—*e.g.* the moral sense, &c. It is easy to shew, says Dugald Stewart, that our notions of right and wrong are to be referred to reason, and not to sense, the provinces of sense and reason being essentially distinct. This opinion of Dugald Stewart would be correct, he had not identified reason with understanding, and, consequently, intended by the word employed other than it properly expresses. This made it necessary for him to explain how the decisions with respect to moral truth differ from those which relate to a mathematical theorem, or the result of a chemical experiment: an explanation which the genuine meaning of the word would have superseded. To substantiate and set forth at large the momentous distinction between understanding and reason, and to restore to each of the words the proper meaning in which it was used by Milton, Archbishop Leighton, Jeremy Taylor, and our elder writers, is another of the most conspicuous objects of the *Aids to Reflection*. A distinction which is not verbal, but essential; the confusion in the words having been consequent upon the confusion in the things.

We perceive many things we do not understand; to understand is therefore more than to perceive. We reason upon things as they are understood. We also attempt to reason of many things which we find it impossible to understand. In these positions the three faculties are clearly distinguished, and the full development of the doctrines they contain would furnish out a complete system of philosophy. They have, besides, the advantage of being immediately intelligible, and from which no man would think of withholding his assent. Yet strange it is, that philosophers for a considerable period consented to overlook two of these three positions, contending, that to understand was no more than to perceive; and now that they are inclined to admit the understanding into active participation, they would exclude reason from any concern, and attribute its proper offices to the inferior faculty. But the science of mind must remain incomplete, till all its provinces are properly explored.

The three faculties of the mind, sense, understanding, and reason, are properly discriminated and differenced in the following passage of Sir Walter Raleigh, extracted from his *History of the World:*

And though nature, according to common understandings, have made us capable, by the power of reason, and apt enough to receive this image of God's goodness, which the sensual souls of beasts cannot perceive; yet were that aptitude natural more inclinable to follow and embrace the false and dureless pleasures of this stage-play world, than to become the shadow of God by walking after him, had not the excelling workmanship of God's wisdom, and the liberality of his mercy, formed eyes to our souls as to our bodies, which, piercing through the impurity of our flesh, behold the highest heavens, and thence bring knowledge and object to the mind and soul, to contemplate the ever-during glory and termless joy prepared for those which retain the image and similitude of their Creator, preserving undefiled and unrent the garment of the new man, which, after the image of God, is created in righteousness and holiness, as saith St. Paul.

Those who identify understanding with reason, would find it difficult, if not impossible, to draw the line of demarcation between the 'sensual souls of beasts' and the 'power of reason', of which Raleigh speaks. They find it hard to establish the position, that reason is the distinctive characteristic of the human intellect. Such a reason as they give to man he must partake with the brute creation, and the divine image becomes a thing of degrees, possessed also by the inferior creatures, only less intensely; which, however monstrous to think of, has not wanted able advocates. From those who by the term reason mean understanding only, we dissent not in opinion. We concede to brutes a portion of understanding, the same in kind with that possessed by man, but differing in degree. Understanding we define with our author, in the words of Archbishop Leighton, 'the faculty that judges according to sense'. Reason is two-fold, sciential and practical: *practical* reason 'is the power of proposing an *ultimate* end, the determinability of the will by IDEAS'; *sciential* reason 'is the faculty of concluding universal and necessary truths from particular and contingent appearances'. Instinct is a power of selecting and adapting means to proximate ends, *according to circumstances*. There is an instinctive intelligence also, or a power of selecting and adapting means to proximate ends, according to *varying* circumstances. But one character is common to both—the purposes are all manifestly predetermined by the organisation of the animals. Suppose this instinctive intelligence (which our author calls the highest species or form of adaptive power) 'to co-exist with reason, *free*-will, and self-consciousness, it instantly becomes UNDERSTANDING; in other words, understanding differs indeed from the noblest form of instinct, but not in itself, or in its own essential properties, but in consequence of its co-existence with far higher powers of a diverse kind in one and the same subject. Instinct in a rational, responsible, and self-conscious animal, is understanding'.

In the numerous well-authenticated instances of the extraordinary actions of dogs for the preservation of their masters' lives, and even for the avenging of their deaths, our author observes: 'Instinctive intelligence is witnessed in connexion with an apparently *moral* end, and co-existent with a purpose apparently *voluntary*; and the action seems neither predetermined by the organisation of the animal, nor in any direct reference to his own preservation, or to the continuance of his race. This dawning of a moral nature, however, is unaccompanied by any the least evidence of *reason*, either practical or sciential'. It is, however, by no means equally clear to Mr. Coleridge that the dog may not possess an *analogon of words*, which are the proper objects of the 'faculty judging according to sense'.

Our author has completely established his position that the understanding and reason differ in kind. 'The understanding is the faculty by which we reflect and generalise. It may be reduced to three acts, all depending on and supposing a previous impression on the senses: first, the appropriation of our attention; second (and in order to the continuance of the first), abstraction, or the voluntary withholding of attention; and, third, generalisation. But the function of generalisation includes the act of comparing one object with another. The act of comparing supposes, in the comparing faculty, certain inherent forms— that is, modes of reflecting not referable to the objects reflected on, but predetermined by the constitution, and, as it were, mechanism of the understanding itself. The senses do not compare, but merely furnish the materials for comparison'. 'We learn all things by *occasion* of experience; but the very facts so learnt force us inward (says our author in another work)* on the *antecedents* that must be supposed, in order to render experience itself possible'. These antecedents are the constituent laws of the human understanding; the ultimate facts in human thought, which cannot be included in any other still more general, and to which all human knowledge must be reduced.

Of these ultimate facts of human thought, our belief in the constancy of nature, and the connexion between cause and effect, is generally

* *Biographia Literaria.*

allowed to be one of the most undoubted and observable. But it is an extraordinary fact, that not only the law of cause and effect (resolvable into the necessity of the mind to interpret a constant precedence into positive causation), but all the laws of nature, are resolvable into ultimate facts of human thought. It is demonstrable that experience is not possible until the phenomena which are its objects are generalised under one or other of the constituent forms of the human understanding, and compared with the standard of these ultimate facts. They are the conditions of experience—they are the laws of nature.

In nature, as in the shadows and reflections of a clear river, man apparently discovers the originals of the forms presented to him in his own intellect. Over these shadows, as if they were the substantial powers and presiding spirits of the stream, Narcissus-like, he hangs delighted: till, finding no where a representative of that free agency which yet is a *fact* of immediate consciousness, sanctioned and made fearfully significant by his prophetic *conscience*; under the tutorage of scientific analysis, he separates the *relations* that are wholly the creatures of his own abstracting and comparing intellect, and at once discovers, and recoils from the discovery, that the *reality* of the *objects* he has been adoring derives its whole and sole evidence from an obscure sensation, which he is alike unable to resist or to comprehend, which compels him to contemplate as without and independent of himself what yet he could not contemplate at all, were it not a modification of his own being.*

It was an indistinct presentiment of this important truth that urged Aristotle to divide and arrange all the subjects of human knowledge under the ten categories. He appears, however, to have had no further end in this than the convenience and elegance of division and arrangement. It was an instinct for method, rather than the discovery of method itself. It has been left for metaphysicians of our times incontrovertibly to demonstrate that a division is possible that shall be adequate to the subject divided, and capable of so exhausting it that nothing thereunto belonging shall be omitted: and this demonstration is derivable from the fact, that 'the evolutions and ordonnance of knowledge are prescribed by the constitution of the human intellect', under the forms of which the objects of our sense, to whose authority the understanding ultimately refers all its judgments, are reflected. Herein consists the chief excellence and utility of the science of mind—that, 'in order to the recognition of himself in nature, man must first learn to comprehend nature in himself, and its laws in the ground of his own existence'.

* *The Friend,* vol. iii, p. 241, 2.

But 'the source of the necessary and universal principles according to which the notices of the senses are either affirmed or denied', is to be sought for in the speculative or scientific reason, considered merely as a faculty of the mind, which subordinates our notions and the rules of experience to absolute principles or necessary laws, and 'is the intellection of the *possibility* or *essential* properties of the things by means of the laws that constitute them'. The peculiar objects of this faculty are the laws of the understanding, those ultimate facts in the human mind, which are the bases of all science, and of every kind and degree of knowledge.

Understanding, says our author, in its highest form of experience, remains commensurate with the experimental notices of the senses, from which it is generalised. Reason, on the other hand, either predetermines experience, or avails itself of a past experience to supersede its necessity in all future time; and affirms truths which no sense could perceive, nor experiment verify, nor experience confirm.

But we have to consider reason as something more than an intellectual power and the ground of formal principles, whose affirmations are only conditionally necessary as applicable to facts of experience, or to the rules and maxims of the understanding. We have to consider it as the practical reason, as the origin of ideas, and of principles absolutely necessary, and as a faculty that in all its decisions appeals to itself as the ground and substance of their truth. It is the organ of the spirit of man, having a similar relation to the intelligible or spiritual world, as the organs of sense have to the material or phenomenal; and its objects, even as those of sense, are intuitive and immediate. The intuition is an evidence of the reality of the ideas which it immediately beholds, even as the intuition of the sensitive faculty is an evidence of the reality of the object which it perceives. All the organs of sense are framed for a corresponding world of sense, and we have it. All the organs of spirit are framed for a correspondent world of spirit; though the latter organs are not developed in all alike. But they exist in all, and their first appearance discloses itself in the *moral* being. Reason, in this higher sense of the word, refers to *actual* or moral truth as the fountain of ideas, and the light of conscience, and is named the *practical* reason. It is not discursive, but fixed—it does not reflect, but contemplate. It is 'an intuition or immediate beholding, accompanied by a conviction of the necessity and universality of the truth so beheld, not derived from the senses; which intuition, when *construed* by *pure* sense, gives birth to the science of mathematics, and when applied to objects supersensuous or spiritual, is the organ of theology and philosophy. For it is an organ identical with its appropriate objects. Thus, God, the soul, eternal truth, are the objects of reason; but they are themselves *reason*. We name God the Supreme Reason; and Milton says, "Whence the soul *reason* receives, and reason is her being". Whatever is conscious self-knowledge is reason'.

We would willingly follow our author through his remaining interesting investigations, and in which the originality of his philosophy is more apparent than in the speculations in which we have endeavoured to go along with him; but to do this effectually would occupy a volume of itself. A meagre abstract of his theological opinions could not but fail of doing justice both to them and him. He moreover expresses an intention of developing this branch of the subject in works of greater compass and magnitude; when, perhaps, we shall have an opportunity of considering it more at large, and by itself. What we have attempted has been principally with a purpose of indicating the peculiar ground on which he stands, and of interesting the reader in the present work. This we have very imperfectly accomplished; and we feel that our wing would indeed be altogether too feeble to soar into the heights of theology, and our critical faculty too gross to breathe the empyreal air of the pure spiritual region in which it is the delight of Mr. Coleridge to expatiate and reason high

> Of providence, foreknowledge, will, and fate,
> Of good and evil,
> Of happiness and final misery.

We are also instinctively reminded that the subject of this article, by our own confession, is abstruse, and therefore likely to exhaust the reader if dwelt upon at too great a length, and the more so from being in itself inexhaustible. For although it be a fact that all men occasionally think on metaphysics, and a demonstrable truth that every man is born a metaphysician, yet it is equally a fact that the greater portion of mankind seldom think at all, and an irrefragable truth that, of those who do, the most part are engaged in the business of providing rather for their temporal than their permanent being—in the gratification of sense, than in the cultivation of the nobler faculties.

> The world is too much with us, late and soon—
> Getting and spending, we lay waste our powers.

The works of the present author are admirably calculated to counter-

act these propensities of our animal nature, and exalt us to the contemplation of ideas and principles; and, above all, to impress us with the
sense of our personal amenability, as involved in the gift of conscience.

At a time when men find it difficult to philosophise on the human
mind without referring every operation to material organisation, and
think that they have explained every phenomenon of the intellect by
the fancied discovery of cerebral convolutions, the labours of Mr.
Coleridge cannot be too highly estimated, which tend to impress them
with the importance of the truth, 'That there is more in man than can
be rationally referred to the life of nature and the mechanism of
organisation; that he has a will not included in this mechanism; and
that the will is in an especial and pre-eminent sense the spiritual part of
our humanity'.

But there are many to whom the science of metaphysics is an interesting subject of research. They will be peculiarly capable of appreciating
the merits of our author; and to them we would say, If for so long a
period, theories, constituted of notions 'the depthless abstractions of
fleeting phenomena, the shadows of sailing vapours, the colourless
repetitions of rainbows', and hypotheses pretending to prove that the
glorious sun in the distant firmament, the moon 'walking in her brightness', and that the stars, 'which are the poesy of heaven', are unreal and
unsubstantial—that matter and spirit, and the great truths of revelation,
and all that we behold and are, have no existence—if these theories and
hypotheses have been able to engross your most patient attention, and
employ your intensest thought, do not refuse all audience to the
enunciation of a science of mind and morals, which, deduced from no
hypothesis or theory, but founded upon the ultimate facts of human
thought, professes to demonstrate that all the phenomena we perceive,
together with the matter in which they inhere, substantially exist—that
there is indeed a spirit in man, a God in heaven, and that our ideas of
Deity, of the soul, of conscience, of free-will, of a future state, and the
moral law, are co-essential with the rational spirit of man, and corre-
lated to absolute realities, which actually exist in regions beyond the
bounds of experience and the limits of sense. To such as have already
felt that 'all the products of the reflective faculty partake of death, and
are as the rattling twigs and sprays in winter, into which a sap is yet to
be propelled, from some root to which they have not yet penetrated,
if they are to afford their souls either food or shelter', the *Aids to
Reflection* will be the lantern and the staff to enlighten and support them
in the difficult and arduous 'investigation of the indwelling and living

ground of all things', to which every man is mysteriously impelled by instinctive and 'unstilled yearning'. But let none delude himself that he will be able to master the subject of the work at once; he will find in it many things hard to be understood, many that he will find it impossible to conceive, and for the reception of most he must discipline his mind to a submissive ductility, and wait for their gradual development in his own consciousness, being, and conduct. Genius is requisite equally in philosophy as in poetry; and the merits of either can only be appreciated by readers of kindred tastes and feelings. To all but the initiate, 'divine philosophy' is 'harsh and crabbed', but to him it is

> musical as is Apollo's lute,
> And a perpetual feast of nectar'd sweets,
> Where no crude surfeit reigns.

GENERAL ESTIMATE

1833

110. William Maginn, *Fraser's Magazine*

July 1833, viii, 64

Unsigned article number xxxviii of the 'Gallery of Literary Characters', attributed to William Maginn (Thrall, *Rebellious Fraser's*, 26). Maginn (1793-1842) was one of the founders of *Fraser's Magazine*.

Sorry are we to present

> The noticeable man with large grey eyes—

the worthy old Platonist—the founder of the romantic school of poetry —the pourer-forth of wisdom multifarious, in language as mellifluous as that of Nestor himself—the good honest old thoroughgoing Tory— even Samuel Taylor Coleridge himself—in an attitude of suffering. But so it is. He is at this present writing under the sheltering roof of worthy Mr. Gillman, on the summit of Highgate hill, labouring under sciatica, jaundice, and other of those ills that afflict mankind. He has come to the third step of the animal who formed the subject of the Sphinx's riddle, and walks hobblingly upon three legs; and more the pity.

Coleridge has himself told us all the more material parts of his life in that queer and pleasant book his *Biographia Literaria*, and it is needless for us now to tell how he was an Unitarian preacher, but soon abandoned that pestilent and cold-hearted heresy—how he was a newspaper editor—how he wrote the *Friend*—how he stirred up wars against Napoleon Buonaparte, late of the island of St. Helena, deceased—how the Emperor wished very particularly to take him under his kind protection, and patronise the editor of the *Morning Post* as he patronised Palm[1]—how he wrote all manner of fine verses, and generally forgot to publish them—how 'Christabel' having been recited to Sir Walter Scott, and a thousand others, was the acknowledged parent of the *Lay of the Last Minstrel*—how Lord Byron, having made free with a passage of it in his *Siege of Corinth*, it was at length produced—how Jeffery, or some of his scrubs, foully abused it in the *Edinburgh Review*—how he valiantly brought Jeffery to the scratch, and made the little fellow apologise—how, in short, he has lectured, talked, preached, written, dogmatised, philosophised, dreamed, promised, begun, neverended, and so forth, are all written by himself, and of course well known to the reader.

What he has done is exquisite, but it is nothing to what he could have done. Σαμερον αδιον ασω,[2] has been unluckily his motto, and the morrow never has come. Procrastination, that thief of time—the quotation is old, though the author is Young—has beguiled him onward in comparative idleness; and his best ideas have been suffered so often to lie unused, that they have at last appeared as the property of others. His graceful 'Christabel' is a flagrant instance of this. It remained twenty years unpublished, but not unknown; and when its example had reared the ballad epic, or poetical novel, to its highest and most magnificent state, it made its appearance, in the eyes of the general reading public an imitation of its own progeny. We do not remember any worse luck in all literary history.

But Coleridge cared for none of these things. On he went, holding

---

[1] Johann Palm, a German bookseller who was executed in 1806 for distributing a seditious pamphlet.

[2] Probably a variant on 'ὕστερον ἄδιον ᾆσω'—'I shall sing later' (Theocritus, *Idylls*, i, 145).

the even tenour of his way, *conversing* with all and sundry. Many a critic deemed original has lived exclusively by sucking Coleridge's brains. The late William Hazlitt was one of the most conspicuous thieves. There was not an observation—not a line—in all Hazlitt's critical works, which was worth reading, or remembering, that did not emanate directly from our old friend the Platonist; other spoliators, more or less known, were as barefaced. It was always worse done than if Coleridge had done it, and sometimes vilely perverted in spirit; but still the seed was good, and he has thus strongly acted upon the public mind of his day. We fear that his *Lay Sermons*, abounding as they do in brilliant and eloquent passages, have not found a very enlarged audience; but what he has spoken and suggested is now diffused throughout the literature of England, and forms part and parcel of every mind worth containing it in the country.

Would that we could see him drinking everlasting glasses of brandy and water in coffee-houses various—or carousing potations pottle-deep, as of old, in the western world of Bristol—or making orations to barmaids and landladies, and holding them by his glittering eye and suasive tongue; and, above all, we most ardently hope to witness the publication of the conclusion of

> The lovely Lady Christabel,
> Finished by Coleridge hale and well!

THE POETICAL WORKS

third edition, 1834

111. Unsigned review, *Literary Gazette*

17 May 1834, 339

The review discusses the first two volumes only.

We have wondered for some time past, that while the *Sybilline Leaves* of other great poets have been collected and published in the most popular forms, those of the Nestor of song should remain unhonoured. Unhonoured at least by that present attention, befitting homage of the present day. We are great friends to the periodical appearance of single volumes; they afford opportunities of purchase to many who would not on the moment be able to meet the outlay for the purchase of the whole. They give time—and one book may be carefully studied ere its companion follows. They also add the pleasure of anticipation to that of possession. A reader, taking in a favourite author, has something to look forward to; he is happier on the first day of every month than the generality of the 'unexpecting crowd'. How many evenings of enjoyment are treasured up in these pages, for those who have perhaps read the 'Ancient Mariner'—the most perfect of Coleridge's poems— only once, or who best know its companions by gleanings amid the 'fitful fancies' of periodicals, whose extracts may or may not have accorded with his own taste. Coleridge is the most unequal of writers. The art of knowing when to 'discreetly blot', is not among his acquirements. He appears to write whatever comes into his head, and to publish with as little remorse. We own that we take a pleasure in these puerile vagaries (we can call them by no other name) of his mind, as curious indications of its peculiar structure. But how much is there that is perfect in beauty of thought, and in melody of expression! and we know no one from whom we could select so many perfect lines, so many touches that are of 'pure gold kindled by fire'. There is a child-like sweetness in his sympathy with nature, that brings forth truths whose depths are forgotten in their simplicity. He luxuriates in the summer sunshine, and the delight is warm upon his page, 'checkering with golden light'. The 'Ancient Mariner' is the finest instance of the supernatural sustained in narrative that we have in our language; and is nobly humanised by the moral of that deep and universal love which it inculcates. Again, how fine is the mystic terror which is the power of 'Christabel'! and where has what may be called the metaphysics of the heart—that subtle music of 'all impulses of soul and sense'—been so charmingly developed, or set to such exquisite music, as in 'Genevieve'? How many lines at every page, however casually opened, tempt us to quotation! How simply—yet connected by what a glorious image—does the following passage express the general care of Heaven!

> But this she knows, in joys and woes,
> That saints will aid if men will call,
> For the blue sky bends over all!

Again, that peculiar feeling which is the very soul of poetry is delightfully expressed in 'Constancy to an Ideal Object'.

[quotes the poem (*PW*, i, 455-6)]

Such, too, is the key-note to Teresa, clinging to grief,

> Sole bond between her and her absent love.

[quotes *Remorse*, Act I, Scene ii, ll. 18-45 (*PW*, ii, 824-5)]

Then, the fine truth of that happy expression:

> Conscience, good my lord,
> Is but the pulse of reason.

Or that of the ensuing extract:

[quotes *Zapolya*, Part II, Act IV, Scene i, ll. 69-81 (*PW*, ii, 939)]

The splendid translation of *Wallenstein* will appear in the coming volume. We have only to add, that the present neat and cheap edition deserves all that we have so often had occasion to say of Mr. Pickering's former publications.

'Why is the harp of Quantock[1] so long silent?' was the affectionate
expostulation of one who remembered its early melodies, and who
lamented that they were so prematurely suffered to expire. But why,
being a poet, it may be asked, did not Mr. Coleridge delight continually
in his high calling? Did he feel no pleasure in the exercise of his art?
how quenched he the fire of inspiration? how sealed his prophetic lips?
In short, why, being a son of Apollo, did he cease to sing? We do not
know that we are authorised even to suppose the cause; but in our days
at least, we think it as much as even men highly gifted can expect, if
they are enabled to rise to eminence in any one accomplishment or art;
and though the mind is enriched and supported by fullness and variety
of attainment, yet undoubtedly there are some studies that exercise
apparently no favourable influence on the cultivation of others. We
suppose no great mathematician was ever a great poet. Now, it is
perhaps possible, that Mr. Coleridge's profound investigations, various
and splendid acquirements, remote speculations, recondite reasonings
and disquisitions, may have carried his mind away from those trains of
thoughts which poetry calls her own, and have given it other associations less favourable and native to it. Perhaps the reason is to be
referred to other causes. To the engrossing nature of the important
questions connected with the constitutional and religious welfare of the
country. Something to the demands of society and distractions of
conversation: something to the reluctance which all occasionally feel
to write, when they can indulge in the luxury of spreading the thoughts
of others before them, and feeding at will on the fruits of *their* rich
imaginations, and gazing on the magnificent creations of *their* genius:
or lastly, perhaps, the *public* mind has been slow in appreciating the
value of Mr. Coleridge's poems, has visited them with neglect, has met
them with ridicule, and has found itself incapable of duly estimating
their merit. We presume that this latter cause may not be without
reason advanced by us. Mr. C. has profoundly studied the principles of

[1] Coleridge had been living in the Quantock Hills in Somerset during his
annus mirabilis.

poetry; he has rigidly adhered to those principles in the execution of his art, and he has left to the public the free choice of approbation or neglect. He has not, as other poets have done, supplicated their favour, followed their direction, bowed to their caprices, and pandered to their desires. Mr. Coleridge has studied, till study has led to well-grounded love and highest admiration, the elder poets of his country: he has recognized the justness of their views, the excellence of their execution; and he has been aware upon what deep and extensive basis they erected the imperishable edifice of their art. But in the meanwhile the public taste had followed far behind him; it had gradually been vitiated and impaired; it had lost its healthy desires and appetites; and became insatiably craving after a different kind of food. There was no lack of supply, when such was the demand; and its pampered gluttony was for ever seeking after new provocations. This has been the case with the poetic taste of the country for many years; and this at once accounts for the long neglect of those who were patiently working on the solid and assured principles of nature and truth, while others, more highly favoured, were throwing off their glittering corruscations before admiring crowds, and supplying with eager rapidity every vicious demand as it arose. Now the effect of all this has been to bring the public mind to a poetical taste and feeling which is decidedly incorrect, and opposed to the best models, ancient or modern, and to the most established rules and precedents. All the different and distinct provinces of poetry have been confounded, which had been so carefully, jealously, and properly guarded and separated. The deepest tragic passions, the most violent emotions, the most terrific inflictions, the most awful catastrophes, peculiar to that domain over which Melpomene presided, have been transplanted into those provinces which had been previously held sacred to feelings of a softer nature, more flexible, more various, more closely associated with the ordinary habits of life, with our habitual trains of thought, and with the associations and impressions which are moderated and subdued, and mingled, when the mind is in a state of health natural to it. Inordinate passion, fierce, uncontrollable resolves, inexorable destinies, and heart-rending catastrophes, have swept away before them every gentler feeling, every diversified incident, every mingled motive, every calmer desire; and all that constitutes the general character, that forms the common nature, and that makes the mingled yarn of which the life of man is woven. From this class of poets, from their erroneous views, and strange creations, and perishable theories, we turn with pleasure to the productions of

Mr. Coleridge's muse. There we meet with natural thoughts clothed in becoming and appropriate language, with fine picturesque imagery, rich fancies, and delicate modulation of language. While we candidly and unreservedly assert, that we do not think Mr. Coleridge successful in the delineation of the higher passions of tragedy; and that there is in his dramatic productions too much pomp of language, and a want of clear, distinct, and forcible character in his persons; while even in some other of his Poems, we still think that the gracefulness of his step is encumbered by the stately magnificence of his drapery; in many, or most of his lyrical productions, we acknowledge with delight their great and various excellence. 'The Ancient Mariner', 'Christabel', and 'Genevieve', are the productions of a truly poetical mind, combining original genius, with a knowledge of the Muse's art, and with a command over the collected treasures of the realms of Parnassus. The thoughts which are conceived are expressed in the truest and most appropriate language, while the imagery that surrounds them is never wanting in harmony, and in fulness of effect. These Poems, however, are well known to the general reader, and safely inshrined in the hearts and heads of all the lovers of song. We will give therefore a fragment of one previously unknown to us, which seems to possess many of Mr. Coleridge's peculiar excellencies—elegant in its design, and chaste in its execution.

[quotes 'The Ballad of the Dark Ladie' (*PW*, i, 293-5)]

The leading quality of Mr. Coleridge's poetry is not to be sought in the moral sublimity, the deep emotion of his great contemporary, the poet of Rydal Mount[1]; nor is it in the pensive tenderness, the thoughtful affection of the Laureate's song; but it consists in a high imaginative power, in a fancy throwing its brilliant and grotesque lights even over the shaded abodes of sorrow, in a feeling of the picturesque, the romantic, the supernatural, in a playful seriousness, dallying with its griefs; sometimes delighting to dwell among the fables of enchantment— amid the pageants of chivalry, in masque and tournament—sometimes in the wild and savage solitudes of nature—anon in gilded palaces, among the breathing forms of art—then is it to be seen fetching from the colder and far off dwellings of philosophy, subtle speculations, and fine analogies; and then again all these are intermingled and fused by the Genius of Poetry, and one of our bard's beautiful and singular

---

[1] Wordsworth.

creations starts up before us. We have only room for one more specimen, which we shall make, of a little poem that has we think a very
pretty and pensive kind of beauty of its own, encased in a tuneful and
elegant versification.

[quotes 'Youth and Age' (*PW*, i, 439–41)]

113. Unsigned review, *Literary Gazette*

9 August 1834, 537–8

The review discusses volume three (*Wallenstein*) only.

The human mind carries on a perpetual and glorious commerce. The
mighty waters of thought are never still—'deep calleth unto deep, and
one sea answereth to another'. Genius, a starry traveller, goes from
world to world, and alike from each 'in its urn draws golden light'.
The past pays tribute to the present; that which is being not only
wondrous and beautiful in itself, but still more wondrous and beautiful
as originating that which is to be. Every great work is the promise of
another; and that not in the cold, faint sense of imitation, but in the
diviner one of inspiration. The sacred writers of Syria and Palestine
were indeed 'the sons of the morning'; but they were followed by the
only less mighty masters of Greece. Next Italy, both in the Latin
tongue, and its softer child, the silken Italian,

> Upreared
> Those verbal monuments which will outlast
> The granite and the marble.

Thence England received the sacred fire at which Shakespeare and
Milton kindled their altars. Germany came next; and her poets were
the worthy foster-children of ours. We would liken this chain of
thought, which one high and holy hand has thrown on to another,

to the knotted rope which, flung from the ship to the shore, carries safe over the stormy waters the precious burden of life. From this progress of the imagination—the imagination which is 'the vision and the faculty divine', the true creative power—we have intentionally excepted France. French literature possesses every variety of talent—but no poetry. This, however, only refers to what has been; we believe at the present day there is more fervour and more originality than was ever before to be found in the literature of that great country. Its actual condition is like that of a land just emerging from some vast inundation. All the elements of confusion have been at work; the storm overhead—the land-flood below. But at length the dark waters have subsided, and the green earth has re-appeared again. Much has been destroyed—but the very destruction was full of the seeds of life. The soil is richer than ever. The very excess of abundance may have generated the monster and the reptile, but they are for cultivation to destroy; and in the meanwhile there is a luxuriance of fertility. But at the time of which we speak, the Nile had not overflowed its set and narrow banks; and all was barren as regarded the warmth and the ideal, which are the world of the poet. But to return to our own country. A more meagre period cannot well be imagined than that from the close of Queen Ann's reign to about the end of the last century. We can only liken it to the celebrated thirty years' drought in Cyprus: ours, alas, was of longer duration. During that dreary era no rain ever fell: the brooks forgot their music, and the flowers their sweetness. One after another the green fields dried up; and, to use the forcible expression of an old historian, 'the very heavens seemed made of brass'. Such was the state of our intellectual atmosphere: Coleridge's own words give its exact picture:

> Day after day—day after day
> We stuck, nor breath nor motion—
> As idle as a painted ship
> Upon a painted ocean.

And Coleridge has the merit that

> He was the first that ever burst
> Into that silent sea.

It is obvious that Germany was the country which gave the impetus, awakening the current, and revealing the hidden treasures of our frozen deep. To our present taste it seems wonderful that such a production as the *Wallenstein* could have been so neglected. It does not explain it to refer to the previous stagnation of taste, and the utter indifference of a public lulled to sleep by small sounds and 'tinkling cymbals'. Both Scott and Byron were received with enthusiasm on their first original appearance. We say original, because the early boyish poems of both were only echoes. *Wallenstein*, too, had none of those drawbacks which, for awhile, delayed the popularity of Wordsworth and of Shelley. They had to create the taste for themselves. Even at this present day, many of their now warm admirers have had their perception of the true and the beautiful taught them. They now appreciate and admire; but their mind has been for some time undergoing a species of mental culture which has enabled them so to do. But *Wallenstein* had a stirring and attractive plot, and a most interesting love-story. The language was bold and simple, and the events suited the spirit of the time when it appeared. Whence, then, its complete failure in drawing attention? We are tempted to believe in luck, and to say, that it was Coleridge's fate to be first known by snatches and quotations, and to build up his temple by golden fragments. The temple is now built, and *Wallenstein* has the merit of being its cornerstone.

Of all branches of literature, translation is that which the most rarely puts forth good fruit. Nothing can be more absurd than the usual method of translation—'done into English by the grace of the dictionary'. A great poet can only do justice to a great poet; and such justice has Coleridge done to Schiller. It matters not to cavil at small faults—we have the great whole visible before us, as it was in the original. There is the spirit which is the life of the body—not a mask of the features taken after death. The more we read this noble drama, the more deeply are we impressed with 'the power, the beauty, and the majesty' of Schiller's magnificent creation. The character of Wallenstein is a master-piece. Nothing can be finer than his own self-consciousness:

> Nothing is common in my destiny,
> Nor in the furrows of my hand. Who dares
> Interpret then my life for me as 'twere
> One of the undistinguishable many?

His great mind has been his destiny: it gave his youth the authority and the experience of age; it led him on from victory to victory, and sheds round his downfall the lustre of the setting sun. And yet

> One touch of nature makes the whole world kin.

We feel, we bow down before his infinite superiority; and yet how keenly are our gentler sympathies enlisted on his side! We know nothing more deeply touching than his speech on hearing of Max.'s death.

> I shall grieve down this blow, of that I'm conscious:
> What does not man grieve down? From the highest,
> As from the vilest thing of every day
> He learns to wean himself: for the strong hours
> Conquer him. Yet I feel what I have lost
> In him. The bloom is vanished from my life.
> For O! he stood beside me, like my youth,
> Transformed for me the real to a dream,
> Clothing the palpable and familiar
> With golden exhalations of the dawn.
> Whatever fortunes wait my future toils,
> The beautiful is vanished—and returns not.

The strong resolve, conscious of its strength; the long experience which has taught the transitory nature of all human things, even of feelings—how exquisitely are they blended with that melancholy craving for affection which is the latest of our illusions! The superstition, too, of Wallenstein is not only perfect as poetry, but also as a profound truth. Most great men whose greatness has had an active career have been superstitious. They must, from their very contact with the common herd, be so fully aware of their immeasurable superiority, that they need to account for it even to themselves. Their career is at once idealised in their own eyes by a reference to fate. Napoleon, like Mahomet, believed in a mission to accomplish. The starry symbols on which Wallenstein waited were but the outward symbols of the ethereal spirit within, which needed a hope and a language not of the ordinary and actual world. All the subordinate characters, too, are so distinctly marked, so real, so apart. There is a degree of truth especially in that of Butler, which is absolutely painful. It makes us feel the justice of Wallenstein's fate. A great fault we could have pardoned, but the small fault is an injustice to himself—we cannot forgive it; and it is the small fault—his deceit towards Butler—which is, as it were, the little hinge on which his fate revolves. Max. Piccolomini is as much the perfect poetry of the heart as Wallenstein is the perfect poetry of the mind. He is the *beau ideal* of youth—frank, generous, confiding, affectionate, brave, and romantic in his devotedness. His had been an incomplete existence had he lived: 'The world was not for him, or the world's art'. But one expression of Wallenstein paints all that would have passed away of transparent candour and noble eagerness—all, too, of the glorious promise of his morning. He says,

> He stood beside me like my youth.

Fancy only what Wallenstein's youth must have been! Again,

> How like a rainbow on the tempest's edge

is the introduction of Thekla!—all there is contrast. The cloistered maiden leaves her convent; love meets her on the threshold, and comprises the whole history of her brief existence. She knows nothing of the vanities, hopes, fears, jealousies—'an indistinguishable throng', which, in after days, must have found entrance in that now pure and guileless mind. She is a child in every thing but the quick beatings of a loving heart. Her's is among the few graves over which we would strew flowers—fragile, sweet, and short-lived, like herself. We have now only space to choose a few favourite passages; but choice here is indeed a difficulty. How beautiful are these two opposed war-pictures!

[quotes *The Piccolomini*, Act I, Scene iv, ll. 90-100 and 139-57 (*PW*, ii, 613-15)]

We cannot but note the many profound truths that are strewn through these pages; every second line is instinct with some deep thought. All history confirms the following passages—the ingratitude rendered to a great man, when the appeal to his genius has answered the necessity:

[quotes Act I, Scene iv, ll. 46-54 (*PW*, ii, 612-13); and Act IV, Scene iv, ll. 54-62 (*PW*, ii, 691)]

The influence of custom:

[quotes Act IV, Scene iv, ll. 81-92 (*PW*, ii, 692)]

Omens:

[quotes *The Death of Wallenstein*, Act V, Scene i, ll. 93-114 (*PW*, ii, 797)]

We conclude with Wallenstein's account of his own tender care of the boy-soldier, Max.:

[quotes Act II, Scene vi, ll. 81-102 (*PW*, ii, 755)]

Need we call attention to the worthy English in which these splendid strangers are arrayed—how musical the verse, and how happy the choice of words. But we have scarcely the heart for praise. We have just announced that he who brought us this music from a far country is numbered with the dead. That eloquent lip is mute for ever; and our aged poet will yield instruction and delight no more. Such losses are too lightly felt: we do not think enough of the departed, nor of the debt due unto them. Let us recall the many hours of entranced enjoyment we have passed amid his creation—the fairy wonders of the 'Ancient Mariner'; the Gothic pictures—half beauty, half terror—which rose upon us after reading 'Christabel'. How many new thoughts has he suggested! How often has he aided us to express our own feelings but more exquisitely; even our dearest—above all things in poetry do we bid

> Another's love
> Interpret for our own.

How much that which was the manation of his mind has passed into ours. We have felt his feelings—thought his thoughts—till they are part of ourselves: and is this a debt to be lightly effaced from memory? Neither is it. Too much do we hurry on, along a worldly and selfish path; but the highway has its resting-place, where we receive those finer influences which abide with us even to the last. At such a time do we dwell upon those memories which it is the poet's fame to leave: then do we thank him for expressing what had else been voiceless music—then are we grateful to the illustrious dead. Coleridge himself said, 'Poetry has been to me its own exceeding great reward. It has soothed my afflictions; it has multiplied and refined my enjoyments; it has endeared solitude; and it has given me the habit of wishing to discover the good and beautiful in all that meets and surrounds me'. What poetry did for himself, Coleridge has done for others. He has refined and widened the sphere of enjoyment; and the three delightful volumes we now mournfully close are his best epitaph and his noblest legacy.

114. H. N. Coleridge, *Quarterly Review*

August 1834, iii, 1–38

Unsigned review, attributed to Henry Nelson Coleridge (*Wellesley Index*, 715).

We lately reviewed the life, and mean hereafter to review the works, of our departed Crabbe.[1] Let us be indulged, in the mean time, in this opportunity of making a few remarks on the genius of the extraordinary man whose poems, now for the first time completely collected, are named at the head of this article. The larger part of this publication is, of course, of old date, and the author still lives; yet, besides the considerable amount of new matter in this edition, which might of itself, in the present dearth of anything eminently original in verse, justify our notice, we think the great, and yet somewhat hazy, celebrity of Coleridge, and the ill-understood character of his poetry, will be, in the opinion of a majority of our readers, more than an excuse for a few elucidatory remarks upon the subject. Idolized by many, and used without scruple by more, the poet of 'Christabel' and the 'Ancient Mariner' is but little truly known in that common literary world, which, without the prerogative of conferring fame hereafter, can most surely give or prevent popularity for the present. In that circle he commonly passes for a man of genius, who has written some very beautiful verses, but whose original powers, whatever they were, have been long since lost or confounded in the pursuit of metaphysic dreams. We ourselves venture to think very differently of Mr. Coleridge, both as a poet and a philosopher, although we are well enough aware that nothing which we can say will, as matters now stand, much advance his chance of becoming a fashionable author. Indeed, as we rather believe, we should earn small thanks from him for our happiest exertions in such a cause; for certainly, of all the men of letters whom it has been our fortune to know, we never met any one who was so utterly regardless of the reputation of the mere author as Mr. Coleridge

[1] George Crabbe had died in 1832.

—one so lavish and indiscriminate in the exhibition of his own intellectual wealth before any and every person, no matter who—one so reckless who might reap where he had most prodigally sown and watered. 'God knows', as we once heard him exclaim upon the subject of his unpublished system of philosophy, 'God knows, I have no author's vanity about it. I should be absolutely glad if I could hear that the *thing* had been done before me'. It is somewhere told of Virgil, that he took more pleasure in the good verses of Varius and Horace than in his own. We would not answer for that; but the story has always occurred to us, when we have seen Mr. Coleridge criticising and amending the work of a contemporary author with much more zeal and hilarity than we ever perceived him to display about anything of his own.

Perhaps our readers may have heard repeated a saying of Mr. Wordsworth, that many men of this age had done wonderful *things*, as Davy, Scott, Cuvier, &c.; but that Coleridge was the only wonderful *man* he ever knew. Something, of course, must be allowed in this as in all other such cases for the antithesis; but we believe the fact really to be, that the greater part of those who have occasionally visited Mr. Coleridge have left him with a feeling akin to the judgment indicated in the above remark. They admire the man more than his works, or they forget the works in the absorbing impression made by the living author. And no wonder. Those who remember him in his more vigorous days can bear witness to the peculiarity and transcendant power of his conversational eloquence. It was unlike anything that could be heard elsewhere; the kind was different, the degree was different, the manner was different. The boundless range of scientific knowledge, the brilliancy and exquisite nicety of illustration, the deep and ready reasoning, the strangeness and immensity of bookish lore— were not all; the dramatic story, the joke, the pun, the festivity, must be added—and with these the clerical-looking dress, the thick waving silver hair, the youthful-coloured cheek, the indefinable mouth and lips, the quick yet steady and penetrating greenish grey eye, the slow and continuous enunciation, and the everlasting music of his tones—all went to make up the image and to constitute the living presence of the man. He is now no longer young, and bodily infirmities, we regret to know, have pressed heavily upon him. His natural force is indeed abated; but his eye is not dim, neither is his mind yet enfeebled. 'O youth!' he says in one of the most exquisitely finished of his later poems:

O youth! for years so many and sweet,
'Tis known that thou and I were one,
I'll think it but a fond conceit—
It cannot be that thou art gone!
Thy vesper bell hath not yet tolled:—
And thou wert aye a masker bold!
What strange disguise hast now put on,
To make believe that thou art gone?
I see these locks in silvery slips,
This drooping gait, this altered size;—
But springtide blossoms on thy lips,
And tears take sunshine from thine eyes!
Life is but thought: so think I will
That Youth and I are house-mates still.

Mr. Coleridge's conversation, it is true, has not now all the brilliant versatility of his former years; yet we know not whether the contrast between his bodily weakness and his mental power does not leave a deeper and a more solemnly affecting impression, than his most triumphant displays in youth could ever have done. To see the pain-stricken countenance relax, and the contracted frame dilate under the kindling of intellectual fire alone—to watch the infirmities of the flesh shrinking out of sight, or glorified and transfigured in the brightness of the awakening spirit—is an awful object of contemplation; and in no other person did we ever witness such a distinction, nay, alienation of mind from body, such a mastery of the purely intellectual over the purely corporeal, as in the instance of this remarkable man. Even now his conversation is characterized by all the essentials of its former excellence; there is the same individuality, the same *unexpectedness*, the same universal grasp; nothing is too high, nothing too low for it: it glances from earth to heaven, from heaven to earth, with a speed and a splendour, an ease and a power, which almost seem inspired: yet its universality is not of the same kind with the superficial ranging of the clever talkers whose criticism and whose information are called forth by, and spent upon, the particular topics in hand. No; in this more, perhaps, than in anything else is Mr. Coleridge's discourse distinguished: that it springs from an inner centre, and illustrates by light from the soul. His thoughts are, if we may so say, as the radii of a circle, the centre of which may be in the petals of a rose, and the circumference as wide as the boundary of things visible and invisible. In this it was that we always thought another eminent light of our time, recently lost to us, an exact contrast to Mr. Coleridge as to quality and style of conversation. You could not in all London or England hear a more fluent, a more brilliant, a more exquisitely elegant converser than Sir James Mackintosh;[1] nor could you ever find him unprovided. But, somehow or other, it always seemed as if all the sharp and brilliant things he said were poured out of so many vials filled and labelled for the particular occasion; it struck us, to use a figure, as if his mind were an ample and well-arranged *hortus siccus*, from which you might have specimens of every kind of plant, but all of them cut and dried for store. You rarely saw nature working at the very moment in him. With Coleridge it was and still is otherwise. He may be slower, more rambling, less pertinent; he may not strike at the instant as so eloquent; but then, what he brings forth is fresh coined; his flowers are newly gathered, they are wet with dew, and, if you please, you may almost see them growing in the rich garden of his mind. The projection is visible; the enchantment is done before your eyes. To listen to Mackintosh was to inhale perfume; it pleased, but did not satisfy. The effect of an hour with Coleridge is to set you thinking; his words haunt you for a week afterwards; they are spells, brightenings, revelations. In short, it is, if we may venture to draw so bold a line, the whole difference between talent and genius.

A very experienced short-hand writer was employed to take down Mr. Coleridge's lectures on Shakespeare, but the manuscript was almost entirely unintelligible. Yet the lecturer was, as he always is, slow and measured. The writer—we have some notion it was no worse an artist than Mr. Gurney himself[2]—gave this account of the difficulty: that with regard to every other speaker whom he had ever heard, however rapid or involved, he could almost always, by long experience in his art, guess the form of the latter part, or apodosis, of the sentence by the form of the beginning; but that the conclusion of every one of Coleridge's sentences was a *surprise* upon him. He was obliged to listen to the last word. Yet this unexpectedness, as we termed it before, is not the effect of quaintness or confusion of construction; so far from it, that we believe foreigners of different nations, especially Germans and Italians, have often borne very remarkable testimony to the grammatical purity and simplicity of his language, and have declared that they generally understood what he said much better than the sustained conversation of any other Englishman whom they had

---

[1] Sir James Mackintosh (1795-1832), philosopher.

[2] Joseph Gurney (1744-1815).

met. It is the uncommonness of the thoughts or the image which prevents your anticipating the end.

We owe, perhaps, an apology to our readers for the length of the preceding remarks; but the fact is, so very much of the intellectual life and influence of Mr. Coleridge has consisted in the oral communication of his opinions, that no sketch could be reasonably complete without a distinct notice of the peculiar character of his powers in this particular. We believe it has not been the lot of any other literary man in England, since Dr. Johnson, to command the devoted admiration and steady zeal of so many and such widely-differing disciples—some of them having become, and others being likely to become, fresh and independent sources of light and moral action in themselves upon the principles of their common master. One half of these affectionate disciples have learned their lessons of philosophy from the teacher's mouth. He has been to them as an old oracle of the Academy or Lyceum. The fulness, the inwardness, the ultimate scope of his doctrines has never yet been published in print, and if disclosed, it has been from time to time in the higher moments of conversation, when occasion, and mood, and person begot an exalted crisis. More than once has Mr. Coleridge said, that with pen in hand he felt a thousand checks and difficulties in the expression of his meaning; but that—authorship aside—he never found the smallest hitch or impediment in the fullest utterance of his most subtle fancies by word of mouth. His abstrusest thoughts became rhythmical and clear when chaunted to their own music. But let us proceed now to the publication before us.

This is the first complete collection of the poems of Samuel Taylor Coleridge. The addition to the last edition is not less than a fourth of the whole, and the greatest part of this matter has never been printed before. It consists of many juvenile pieces, a few of the productions of the poet's middle life, and more of his later years. With regard to the additions of the first class, we should not be surprised to hear friendly doubts expressed as to the judgment shown in their publication. We ourselves think otherwise; and we are very glad to have had an opportunity of perusing them. There may be nothing in these earlier pieces upon which a poet's reputation could be built; yet they are interesting now as measuring the boyish powers of a great author. We never read any juvenile poems that so distinctly foretokened the character of all that the poet has since done; in particular, the very earliest and loosest of these little pieces indicate that unintermitting thoughtfulness, and that fine ear for verbal harmony in which we must venture to think that not one of our modern poets approaches to Coleridge. Upon these points we shall venture a few remarks by and by; but as an instance of the sort of sweetness of versification which seems to have been inborn in our poet, although elaborately cultivated and improved in his after years, take these six lines on the 'First Advent of Love'. They were written at fifteen.

> O fair is love's first hope to gentle mind,
> As Eve's first star thro' fleecy cloudlet peeping;
> And sweeter than the gentle south-west wind
> O'er willowy meads and shadow'd waters creeping,
> And Ceres' golden fields! the sultry hind
> Meets it with brow uplift, and stays his reaping.

In the following verses, some of which were lately quoted in this Journal for another purpose, and which were written only a year or two later than those preceding, we may distinguish a progress in the art, and yet the *natural melody of words* still obviously cultivated to the postponement of the *harmony resulting from rhythmical construction*—

[quotes ll. 37-70 of 'Lines on an Autumn Evening' (*PW*, i, 52-3)]

We, of course, cite these lines for little besides their luxurious smoothness; and it is very observable, that although the indications of the more strictly intellectual qualities of a great poet are very often extremely faint, as in Byron's case, in early youth, it is universally otherwise with regard to high excellence in *versification* considered apart and by itself. Like the ear for music, the sense of metrical melody is always a natural gift; both indeed are evidently connected with the physical arrangement of the organs, and never to be acquired by any effort of art. When possessed, they by no means necessarily lead on to the achievement of consummate harmony in music or in verse; and yet consummate harmony in either has never been found where the natural gift has not made itself conspicuous long before. Spenser's Hymns, and Shakespeare's *Venus and Adonis*, and *Rape of Lucrece*, are striking instances of the overbalance of mere sweetness of sound. Even *Comus* is what we should, in this sense, call luxurious; and all four gratify the outward ear much more than that inner and severer sense which is associated with the reason, and requires a meaning even in the very music for its full satisfaction. Compare the versification of the youthful pieces mentioned above with that of the maturer works of those great poets, and you will recognize how possible it is for verses to be exquisitely melodious, and yet to fall far short of that exalted excellence of numbers of which language is in itself capable. You will feel the simple truth, that melody is a part only of harmony. Those early flashes were indeed auspicious tokens of the coming glory, and involved some of the conditions and elements of its existence; but the rhythm of the *Faerie Queene* and of *Paradise Lost* was also the fruit of a distinct effort of uncommon care and skill. The endless variety of the pauses in the versification of these poems could not have been the work of chance, and the adaptation of words with reference to their asperity, or smoothness, or strength, is equally refined and scientific. Unless we make a partial exception of the *Castle of Indolence*, we do not remember a single instance of the reproduction of the exact rhythm of the Spenserian stanza, especially of the concluding line. The precise Miltonic movement in blank verse has never, to our knowledge, been caught by any later poet. It is Mr. Coleridge's own strong remark, that you might as well think of pushing a brick out of a wall with your forefinger, as attempt to remove a word out of the finished passages in Shakespeare or Milton. The amotion or transposition will alter the thought, or the feeling, or at least the tone. They are as pieces of Mosaic work, from which you cannot strike the smallest block without making a hole in the picture.

And so it is—in due proportion—with Coleridge's best poems. They are distinguished in a remarkable degree by the perfection of their rhythm and metrical arrangement. The labour bestowed upon this point must have been very great; the tone and quantity of words seem weighed in scales of gold. It will, no doubt, be considered ridiculous by the Fannii and Fanniæ[1] of our day to talk of varying the trochee with the iambus, or of resolving either into the tribrach. Yet it is evident to us that these, and even minuter points of accentual scansion, have been regarded by Mr. Coleridge as worthy of study and observation. We do not, of course, mean that rules of this kind were always in his mind while composing, any more than that an expert disputant is always thinking of the distinctions of mood and figure, whilst arguing; but we certainly believe that Mr. Coleridge has almost from the commencement of his poetic life looked upon versification as constituting in and by itself a much more important branch of the art poetic than most of his eminent contemporaries appear to have done. And this more careful study shows itself in him in no technical peculiarities or fantastic whims, against which the genius of our

[1] An allusion to Demetrius Fannius, a character in Jonson's *The Poetaster*.

language revolts; but in a more exact adaptation of the movement to the feeling, and in a finer selection of particular words with reference to their local fitness for sense and sound. Some of his poems are complete models of versification, exquisitely easy to all appearance, and subservient to the meaning, and yet so subtle in the links and transitions of the parts as to make it impossible to produce the same effect merely by imitating the syllabic metre as it stands on the surface. The secret of the sweetness lies within, and is involved in the feeling. It is this remarkable power of making his verse musical that gives a peculiar character to Mr. Coleridge's lyric poems. In some of the smaller pieces, as the conclusion of the 'Kubla Khan', for example, not only the lines by themselves are musical, but the whole passage sounds all at once as an outburst or crash of harps in the still air of autumn. The verses seem as if *played* to the ear upon some unseen instrument. And the poet's manner of reciting verse is similar. It is not rhetorical, but musical: so very near recitative, that for any one else to attempt it would be ridiculous; and yet it is perfectly miraculous with what exquisite searching he elicits and makes sensible every particle of the meaning, not leaving a shadow of a shade of the feeling, the mood, the degree, untouched. We doubt if a finer rhapsode ever recited at the Panathenaic festival; and the yet unforgotten Doric of his native Devon is not altogether without a mellowing effect on his utterance of Greek. He would repeat the

αὐτὰρ Ἀχιλλεὺς

δακρύσας, ἑτάρων ἄφαρ ἕζετο. κ. τ. λ.[1]

with such an interpreting accompaniment of look, and tone, and gesture, that we believe any commonly-educated person might understand the import of the passage without knowing alpha from omega. A chapter of Isaiah from his mouth involves the listener in an act of exalted devotion. We have mentioned this, to show how the whole man is made up of music; and yet Mr. Coleridge has no *ear* for music, as it is technically called. Master as he is of the intellectual recitative, he could not *sing* an air to save his life. But his delight in music is intense and unweariable, and he can detect good from bad with unerring discrimination. Poor Naldi,[2] whom most of us remember, and all who remember must respect, said to our poet once at a

---

[1] 'But Achilles forthwith burst into tears and withdrew from the company of his comrades' (*Iliad*, i, 348–9).

[2] Giuseppe Naldi (1770–1820), actor.

concert 'That he did not seem much interested with a piece of Rossini's which had just been performed'. Coleridge answered, 'It sounded to me exactly like *nonsense verses*. But this thing of Beethoven's that they have begun—stop, let us listen to this, I beg!'

There are some lines entitled 'Hendecasyllables', published for the first time in the second volume of this collection, which struck us a good deal by the skill with which an equivalent for the well-known Catullian measure has been introduced into our language. We think the metrical construction of these few verses very ingenious, and do not remember at this moment anything in English exactly like it. These lines are, in fact, of twelve syllables; but it is in the rhythm that they are essentially different from our common dramatic line:

> In the deep bosom of the ocean buried.

Our readers will please observe that a dactyl is substituted for the spondee, trochee or iambus of the Latin models at the commencement of the verse:

> Hear, my beloved, an old Milesian story!
> High and embosom'd in congregated laurels,
> Glimmer'd a temple upon a breezy headland;
> In the dim distance, amid the skiey billows,
> Rose a fair island; the god of flocks had placed it.
> From the far shores of the bleak resounding island
> Oft by the moonlight a little boat came floating,
> Came to the sea-cave beneath the breezy headland;
> Where amid myrtles a pathway stole in mazes
> Up to the groves of the high embosom'd temple.
> There, in a thicket of dedicated roses,
> Oft did a priestess, as lovely as a vision,
> Pouring her soul to the son of Cytherea,
> Pray him to hover around the slight canoe-boat,
> And with invisible pilotage to guide it
> Over the dusk wave, until the nightly sailor,
> Shivering with ecstacy, sank upon her bosom.

The minute study of the laws and properties of metre is observable in almost every piece in these volumes. Every kind of lyric measure, rhymed and unrhymed, is attempted with success; and we doubt whether, upon the whole, there are many specimens of the heroic couplet or blank verse superior in construction to what Mr. Coleridge has given us. We mention this the rather, because it was at one time, although that time is past, the fashion to say that the Lake school—as two or three poets, essentially unlike to each other, were foolishly called—had abandoned the old and established measures of the English poetry for new conceits of their own. There was no truth in that charge; but we will say this, that, notwithstanding the prevalent opinion to the contrary, we are not sure, after perusing *some passages* in Mr. Southey's 'Vision of Judgment', and the entire 'Hymn to the Earth', in hexameters, in the second of the volumes now before us, that the question of the total inadmissibility of that measure in English verse can be considered as finally settled; the true point not being whether such lines are as good as, or even like, the Homeric or Virgilian models, but whether they are not in themselves a pleasing variety, and on that account alone, if for nothing else, not to be rejected as wholly barbarous. True it is, that without great skill in the poet, English hexameters will be intolerable; but what shall we say to the following?

Travelling the vale with mine eyes—green meadows and lake with green island,
Dark in its basin of rock, and the pure stream flowing in brightness,
Thrill'd with thy beauty and love in the wooded slope of the mountain,
Here, Great Mother, I lie, thy child, with his head on thy bosom!
Playful the spirits of noon, that rushing soft through thy tresses,
Green-haired goddess! refresh me; and hark! as they hurry or linger,
Fill the pause of my harp, or sustain it with musical murmurs.
Into my being thou murmurest joy, and tenderest sadness
Shedd'st thou, like dew on my heart, till the joy and the heavenly sadness
Pour themselves forth from my heart in tears, and the hymn of thanksgiving.
Earth! thou mother of numberless children, the nurse and the mother,
Sister thou of the stars, and beloved by the sun, the rejoicer!
Guardian and friend of the moon, O Earth! whom the comets forget not,
Yea, in the measureless distance wheel round and again they behold thee!
Fadeless and young (and what if the latest birth of Creation?)
Bride and consort of Heaven, that looks down upon thee enamoured!
Say, mysterious Earth! O say, great mother and goddess,
Was it not well with thee then, when first thy lap was ungirdled,
Thy lap to the genial Heaven, the day that he wooed thee and won thee!
Fair was thy blush, the fairest and first of the blushes of Morning!
Deep was the shudder, O Earth! the throe of thy self-retention:
Inly thou strovest to flee, and didst seek thyself at thy centre!
Mightier far was the joy of thy sudden resilience; and forthwith
Myriad myriads of lives teemed forth from the mighty embracement.
Thousand-fold tribes of dwellers, impelled by thousand-fold instincts,
Filled, as a dream, the wide waters; the rivers sang in their channels;

Laughed on their shores the hoarse seas; the yearning ocean swelled upward;
Young life lowed through the meadows, the woods, and the echoing mountains,
Wandered bleating in valleys, and warbled on blossoming branches.

We may also quote from . . . the same volume the following exquisite couplets:

The Homeric Hexameter described and exemplified.
Strongly it bears us along in swelling and limitless billows,
Nothing before and nothing behind but the sky and the ocean.

The Ovidian Elegiac Metre described and exemplified.
In the hexameter rises the fountain's silvery column:
In the pentameter aye falling in melody back.

The keen lines entitled 'Sancti Dominici Pallium', and the following, suggested by the last words of Berengarius, seem to stand about midway between the rhythm of Pope and Dryden.

'No more 'twixt conscience staggering and the Pope,
　Soon shall I now before my God appear;
By him to be acquitted, as I hope;
　By him to be condemned, as I fear.'

Lynx amid moles! had I stood by thy bed,
Be of good cheer, meek soul! I would have said;
I see a hope spring from that humble fear.
All are not strong alike thro' storms to steer
Right onward. What, though dread of threaten'd death
And dungeon torture made thy hand and breath
Inconstant to the truth within thy heart,—
That truth from which, thro' fear, thou twice didst start,
Fear haply told thee, was a learned strife,
Or not so vital as to claim thy life,
And myriads had reach'd heaven who never knew
Where lay the difference 'twixt the false and true!
　Ye, who secure 'mid trophies not your own,
Judge him who won them when he stood alone,
And proudly talk of recreant Berengare,—
O first the age, and then the man compare!
That age how dark! congenial minds how rare!
No host of friends with kindred zeal did burn,
No throbbing hearts awaited his return;
Prostrate alike when prince and peasant fell,
He only disenchanted from the spell,
Like the weak worm that gems the starless night,
Moved in the scanty circlet of his light:—

> And was it strange if he withdrew the ray,
> That did but guide the night-birds to their prey?
> The ascending day-star, with a bolder eye,
> Hath lit each dewdrop on our trimmer lawn;
> Yet not for this, if wise, shall we decry
> The spots and struggles of the timid dawn;
> Lest so we tempt the approaching noon to scorn
> The mist and painted vapours of our morn!

For his blank verse take the following passage as an average example. It is, as will be instantly seen, altogether unlike the Miltonic movement; yet can anything for the purpose be imagined more exquisitely rich and harmonious?

> And that simplest lute
> Placed lengthways in the clasping casement, hark!
> How by the desultory breeze caress'd,
> Like some coy maid half yielding to her lover,
> It pours such sweet upbraiding, as must needs
> Tempt to repeat the wrong! And now, its strings
> Over delicious surges sink and rise,
> Such a soft floating witchery of sound,
> As twilight elfins make, when they at eve
> Voyage on gentle gales from fairy land,
> Where melodies round honey-dropping flowers,
> Footless and wild, like birds of paradise,
> Nor pause, nor perch, hovering on untamed wing!
> Oh! the one life within us and abroad,
> Which meets all motion and becomes its soul,—
> A light in sound, a sound-like power in light,
> Rhythm in all thought and joyance everywhere;—
> Methinks, it should have been impossible
> Not to love all things in a world so filled;
> Where the breeze warbles, and the mute still air
> Is music slumbering on her instrument!

We should not have dwelt so long upon this point of versification, unless we had conceived it to be one distinguishing excellence of Mr. Coleridge's poetry, and very closely connected with another, namely, fulness and individuality of thought. It seems to be a fact, although we do not pretend to explain it, that condensation of meaning is generally found in poetry of a high import in proportion to perfection in metrical harmony. Petrarch, Spenser, Shakespeare, and Milton are obvious instances. Goethe and Coleridge are almost equally so.

Indeed, whether in verse, or prose, or conversation, Mr. Coleridge's mind may be fitly characterized as an energetic mind—a mind always at work, always in a course of reasoning. He cares little for anything, merely because it was or is; it must be referred, or be capable of being referred, to some law or principle, in order to attract his attention. This is not from ignorance of the facts of natural history or science. His written and published works alone sufficiently show how constantly and accurately he has been in the habit of noting all the phenomena of the material world around us; and the great philosophical system now at length in preparation for the press demonstrates, we are told, his masterly acquaintance with almost all the sciences, and with not a few of the higher and more genial of the arts. Yet his vast acquirements of this sort are never but forward by or for themselves; it is in his apt and novel illustrations, his indications of analogies, his explanation of anomalies, that he enables the hearer or reader to get a glimpse of the extent of his practical knowledge. He is always reasoning out from an inner point, and it is the inner point, the principle, the law which he labours to bring forward into light. If he can convince you or himself of the principle *à priori*, he generally leaves the facts to take care of themselves. He leads us into the laboratories of art or nature as a show-man guides you through a cavern crusted with spar and stalactites, all cold, and dim, and motionless, till he lifts his torch aloft, and on a sudden you gaze in admiration on walls and roof of flaming crystals and stars of eternal diamond.

All this, whether for praise or for blame, is perceptible enough in Mr. Coleridge's verse, but perceptible, of course, in such degree and mode as the law of poetry in general, and the nature of the specific poem in particular, may require. But the main result from this frame and habit of his mind is very distinctly traceable in the uniform subjectivity of almost all his works. He does not belong to that grand division of poetry and poets which corresponds with painting and painters; of which Pindar and Dante are the chief; those masters of the picturesque, who, by a felicity inborn, view and present everything in the completeness of actual objectivity—and who have a class derived from and congenial with them, presenting few pictures indeed, but always full of picturesque matter; of which secondary class Spenser and Southey may be mentioned as eminent instances. To neither of these does Mr. Coleridge belong; in his 'Christabel', there certainly are several *distinct pictures* of great beauty; but he, as a poet, clearly comes within the other division which answers to music and the musician, in which you have a magnificent mirage of words with the subjective associations of the poet curling, and twisting, and creeping round, and through, and above every part of it. This is the class to which Milton belongs, in whose poems we have heard Mr. Coleridge say that he remembered but two proper pictures—Adam bending over the sleeping Eve at the beginning of the fifth book of the *Paradise Lost*, and Dalilah approaching Samson towards the end of the *Agonistes*. But when we point out the intense personal feeling, the self-projection, as it were, which characterizes Mr. Coleridge's poems, we mean that such feeling is the soul and spirit, not the whole body and form, of his poetry. For surely no one has ever more earnestly and constantly borne in mind the maxim of Milton, that poetry ought to be *simple, sensuous, and impassioned*. The poems in these volumes are no authority for that dreamy, half-swooning style of verse which was criticized by Lord Byron (in language too strong for print) as the fatal sin of Mr. John Keats, and which, unless abjured betimes, must prove fatal to several younger aspirants—male and female—who for the moment enjoy some popularity. The poetry before us is distinct and clear, and accurate in its imagery; but the imagery is rarely or never exhibited for description's sake alone; it is rarely or never exclusively objective; that is to say, put forward as a spectacle, a picture on which the mind's eye is to rest and terminate. You may if your sight is short, or your imagination cold, regard the imagery in itself and go no farther; but the poet's intention is that you should feel and imagine a great deal more than you see. His aim is to awaken in the reader the same mood of mind, the same cast of imagination and fancy whence issued the associations which animate and enlighten his pictures. You must think with him, must sympathize with him, must suffer yourself to be lifted out of your own school of opinion or faith, and fall back upon your own consciousness, an unsophisticated man. If you decline this, *non tibi spirat*. From his earliest youth to this day, Mr. Coleridge's poetry has been a faithful mirror reflecting the images of his mind. Hence he is so original, so individual. With a little trouble, the zealous reader of the *Biographia Literaria* may trace in these volumes the whole course of mental struggle and self-evolvement narrated in that odd but interesting work; but he will see the track marked in light; the notions become images, the images glorified, and not unfrequently the abstruse position stamped clearer by the poet than by the psychologist. No student of Coleridge's philosophy can fully understand it without a perusal of the illumining, and if we may so say, *popularizing* commentary of his poetry. It is the Greek put into the vulgar tongue. And we must say, it is somewhat strange to hear any one condemn those philosophical principles as altogether unintelligible, which are inextricably interwoven in every page of a volume of poetry which he professes to admire.

No writer has ever expressed the great truth that man makes his world, or that it is the imagination which shapes and colours all things—more vividly than Coleridge. Indeed, he is the first who, in the age in which we live, brought forward that position into light and action. It is nearly forty years ago that he wrote the following passage in his 'Ode on Dejection', one of the most characteristic and beautiful of his lyric poems:

[quotes ll. 21-75 (*PW*, i, 364-6)]

To this habit of intellectual introversion we are very much inclined to attribute Mr. Coleridge's never having seriously undertaken a great heroic poem. The *Paradise Lost* may be thought to stand in the way of our laying down any general rule on the subject; yet that poem is as peculiar as Milton himself, and does not materially affect our opinion, that the pure epic can hardly be achieved by the poet in whose mind the reflecting turn *greatly* predominates. The extent of the action in such a poem requires a free and fluent stream of narrative verse; description, purely objective, must fill a large space in it, and its permanent success depends on a rapidity, or at least a liveliness, of movement which is scarcely compatible with much of what Bacon calls *inwardness* of meaning. The reader's attention could not be preserved; his journey being long, he expects his road to be smooth and unembarrassed. The condensed passion of the ode is out of place in heroic song. Few persons will dispute that the two great Homeric poems are the most delightful of epics; they may not have the sublimity of the *Paradise Lost*, nor the picturesqueness of the *Divine Comedy*, nor the etherial brilliancy of the *Orlando*; but, dead as they are in language, metre, accent—obsolete in religion, manners, costume, and country—they nevertheless even now *please* all those who can read them beyond all other narrative poems. There is a salt in them which keeps them sweet and incorruptible throughout every change. They are the most popular of all the remains of ancient genius, and translations of them for the twentieth time are amongst the very latest productions of our contemporary literature. From beginning to end, these marvellous poems are exclusively objective; everything is in them, except the poet himself. It is not to Vico or Wolfe that we refer, when we say that *Homer* is *vox et præterea nihil;* as musical as the nightingale, and as invisible.

If any epic subject would have suited Mr. Coleridge's varied powers and peculiar bent of mind, it might, perhaps, have been that which he once contemplated, and for which he made some preparations—*The Fall of Jerusalem.* The splendid drama which has subsequently appeared under that name by a younger poet, has not necessarily precluded an attempt on the epic scale by a master genius.[1] Yet the difficulties of the undertaking are appalling from their number and peculiarity; and not the least overwhelming of them are involved in the treatment of those very circumstances and relations which constitute its singular attraction. We have twice heard Mr. Coleridge express his opinion on this point.

The destruction of Jerusalem [he said upon one occasion] is the only subject now remaining for an epic poem; a subject which, like Milton's Fall of Man, should interest all Christendom, as the Homeric War of Troy interested all Greece. There would be difficulties, as there are in all subjects; and they must be mitigated and thrown into the shade, as Milton has done with the numerous difficulties in the *Paradise Lost*. But there would be a greater assemblage of grandeur and splendour than can now be found in any other theme. As for the old mythology, *incredulus odi;* and yet there must be a mythology, or a *quasi*-mythology, for an epic poem. Here there would be the completion of the prophecies; the termination of the first revealed national religion under the violent assault of Paganism, itself the immediate forerunner and condition of the spread of a revealed mundane religion; and then you would have the character of the Roman and the Jew, and the awfulness, the completeness, the justice. I schemed it at twenty-five, but, alas! *venturum expectat.*

Upon another occasion, Mr. Coleridge spoke more discouragingly.

This subject, with all its great capabilities, has this one grand defect—that, whereas a poem, to be epic, must have a personal interest—in the 'Destruction of Jerusalem' no genius or skill could possibly preserve the interest for the hero from being merged in the interest for the event. The fact is, the event itself is too sublime and overwhelming.

We think this is fine and just criticism; yet we ardently wish the critic had tried the utmost strength of his arm in executing the magnificent idea of his early manhood. Even now—vain as we fear any such appeal is—we cannot keep ourselves back from making a respectful call upon this great poet to consider whether his undiminished powers of verse do not seem to demand from him something beyond the little

[1] Reference to Henry Hart Milman's play (1820).

pieces, sweet as they are, which he has alone produced since his middle manhood. We know and duly value the importance of the essays in which his philosophical views have as yet been imperfectly developed, and we look with anxiety to the publication of the whole, or a part, of that great work in which, we are told, the labour of his life has been expended in founding and completing a truly catholic 'System of philosophy for a Christian man'. We would not, for the chance of an epic fragment, interfere with the consummation of this grand and long-cherished design. But is there any necessary incompatibility between the full action of the poet and the philosopher in Mr. Coleridge's particular case? He, of all men, would deny that the character of his studies alone tended to enfeeble the imagination, or to circumscribe the power of expression; and if that be so, what is there to prevent—what is there not rather to induce—a serious devotion of some portion, at least, of his leisure to the planning and execution of some considerable poem? *Poterit si posse videtur*; and could Mr. Coleridge but seem to himself as capable as he seems to others, we believe he would not leave the world without a legacy of verse even richer than aught that has yet come from him.

In attempting any poem of the magnitude suggested by us, unless it were entirely of a moral or philosophical kind, Mr. Coleridge would undoubtedly have to contend with that meditative or reflective habit of intellect which is predominant in him, and characterizes all his works. It dictated to him as a translator the happy choice of *Wallenstein*, and constitutes at once the source of beauty and of weakness in the *Remorse* and *Zapolya*. Unless this be remembered, and some indulgence be shown to it, justice will not be done to these fine poems. Perhaps there never was a translation, with the exception of Pope's *Iliad* and Dryden's *Eneid*, that has become so intimately connected with the poetic fame of the translator as this English *Wallenstein*. It is clearly, in our opinion, one of the most splendid productions of Mr. Coleridge's pen, and will with almost all readers for ever have the charm of an original work. The truth is, that many beautiful parts of the translation are exclusively the property of the English poet, who used a manuscript copy of the German text before its publication by the author; and it is a curious anecdote in literature, that Schiller, in more instances than one, afterwards adopted the hints and translated in turn the interpolations of his own translator. Hence it is, also, that there are passages in the German editions of the present day which are not found in the English version; they were, in almost every case, the subsequent additions of the German poet. Nevertheless, although Mr. Coleridge has not scrupled in some instances to open out the hint of the original, and even to graft new thoughts upon it, his translation is, in the best and highest sense of that term, a preeminently faithful translation; indeed, it preserves, or compensates, the meaning and spirit of the author so perfectly, that we are inclined to think that, upon a balance struck, Schiller has lost *nothing* in the English of his *Wallenstein*. Has he not gained? As to this, we do not immediately refer to those beautiful passages in which Mr. Coleridge has confessedly ventured upon his own responsibility to expand the germ of thought in the original—passages which are familiar to all who take any interest either in Coleridge or Schiller.* We rather look to the total impression left upon the mind of the reader by the character of Wallenstein himself; and the question is, whether a more thorough perception of the idea of Hamlet, and a much greater sympathy with the Hamlet mood of mind, have not helped the countryman of Shakespeare to a grander presentment of Schiller's hero than Schiller's own picture of him. An Englishman and a German, indeed, can scarcely be expected to view such a question as this from precisely the same point; the associations which the mere words of your native language excite are indestructible and irrepressible; and the Shakespearian cast of feeling and reflection, easily distinguishable by us in the English Wallenstein, cannot be fully recognised or appreciated by a foreigner. It may not be *the* tone of Schiller; but it is the tone, or germane to the tone, which the fortunate predominance of Shakespeare has consecrated in England for dramatic poetry. The Germans do not seem to us to have arrived at any sympathy with it. The study of Shakespeare is said to be fashionable amongst all literary

* Mr. Hayward, in the preface to the second edition of his translation of *Faust*, quotes one of these striking passages:
> The intelligible forms of ancient poets,
> The fair humanities of old religion,
> The power, the beauty, and the majesty
> That had their haunts in dale, or piny mountain,
> Or forest by slow stream, or pebbly spring,
> Or chasms, or watery depths,—all these have vanish'd;
> They live no longer in the faith of reason.

These lines are an expansion of two of Schiller's—
> Die alten Fabelwesen sind nicht mehr;
> Das reizende Geschlecht ist ausgewandert;

literally, as Mr. Hayward translates them—
> The old fable-existences are no more;
> The fascinating race has emigrated (wandered out or away).

men in Germany; and some very clever and eloquent books have been written about him by natives of that country. The best of these critics, however, never seem to us to understand their subject. They do not see the absolute uniqueness in kind of Shakespeare's intellectual action. Of the other great authors of the English drama, they appear to know nothing. Tieck, we suspect, is the first German that ever made much acquaintance with any of Shakespeare's mighty contemporaries, Ben Jonson, Beaumont and Fletcher, and Massinger—those giants everywhere but in Shakespeare's presence; and Tieck's own acquisitions in this department appear to be of very recent date. His friend and fellow-labourer, Augustus W. Schlegel, if we remember right, passes in some dozen frigid pages from Shakespeare to Dryden and Otway. This celebrated critic is so excessively superficial upon those masters of the romantic drama, Beaumont and Fletcher, that we are compelled to say that we do not believe he had read through their works when he wrote his *Dramatic Literature*. To us it seems that, upon the whole, Schiller had something in his genius naturally nearer akin to the universality of Shakespeare than any other of the German poets. In depth of thought, in fertility of fancy, in creativeness of imagination, there is no comparison; but Schiller had, as Shakespeare had, that common human feeling—not too high, nor too low—that common tone of the race to which be belonged, which led and enabled him in the maturity of his abilities to give to his countrymen of every circle an historic drama of highest excellence and enduring national interest. This grand work—*Wallenstein*—which, although not similar, is analogous to the historic plays of Shakespeare, will, as we believe, ultimately constitute the permanent claim of Schiller to fame amongst his own fellow-countrymen; and the extraordinary fortune of an English translation which may be read, if we please, without once suggesting the fact of its not being original poetry, will go a great way in extending his fame amongst a people who, by kindred and by moral sympathy, can best appreciate it as it deserves. We have no room for any extracts from this translation; but we particularly refer our readers to act i. scene 4, act iv. scene 7, of the *Piccolomini*, and act v. scene 1 of the *Death of Wallenstein*. These are not amongst the parts commonly quoted; but they are the most powerful and characteristic; and in the intermediate one of the three there is an interesting, but perhaps unintended, parallel with the scene of Macbeth's conference with his wife previously to the murder of Duncan.

It is pretty generally known that Mr. Coleridge was solicited to undertake a translation of *Faust* before Mr. Shelley, Lord Francis Egerton, or Mr. Hayward, had, in their different manners, made that remarkable poem as familiar as it can possibly be made to the mere English reader: for Goethe being, like Coleridge, a great master of verbal harmony, must of necessity lose very considerably in a translation of any kind. His dress sticks to his body; it is inseparable without laceration of the skin. This, amongst some other considerations of graver moment, induced Mr. Coleridge, after a careful perusal of the work, to decline the proposition. We are not very sure that he would have succeeded in it; at least it would probably have been something very unlike Goethe's *Faust*. Mr. Coleridge thinks—perhaps he is the only man who may without presumption think—that Goethe's *Faust* is a failure; that is to say, that the idea, or what ought to have been the idea, of the work is very insufficiently and inartificially executed. He considers the intended theme to be—the consequences of a misology, or hatred and depreciation of knowledge caused by an originally intense thirst for knowledge baffled. But a love of knowledge for itself, and for pure ends, would never produce such a misology, but only a love of it for base and unworthy purposes. There is neither causation nor progression in Faust: he is a ready-made conjurer from the very beginning;—the *incredulus odi* is felt from the first line. The sensuality, and the thirst after knowledge, are unconnected with each other. Mephistopheles and Margaret are excellent, but Faust himself is dull and meaningless. The scene in Auerbach's cellars is one of the best— perhaps the very best; that on the Brocken is also fine, and all the songs are beautiful. But there is no whole in the poem; the scenes are mere magic-lantern pictures, and a large part of the work very flat. Such, in substance, is the opinion which we have heard Mr. Coleridge express of this famous piece: upon the justice of the criticism, we have neither time nor inclination to say a word upon the present occasion; but we cannot miss this opportunity of mentioning the curious fact that long before Goethe's *Faust* had appeared in a complete state, which we think was in 1807*—indeed before Mr. Coleridge had ever seen any part of it—he had planned a work upon the same, or what he takes to be the

---

* The first edition of *Faust*, in an imperfect state, was in 1790; the next edition was in 1807 or 1808, when the poem first appeared in the form to which we have been accustomed. See Hayward's *Faust*, 2nd edition, p. 215. We make no allusion to the wretched second part of *Faust*, which has recently appeared among Goethe's posthumous pieces. The editor who sanctioned its publication has done his utmost to degrade his author's reputation.

same idea. This plan, like many of its fellows, is now in Ariosto's moon; yet its general shape deserves to be recorded, as a remarkable instance of unconscious coincidence between two great individual minds, having many properties in common. Coleridge's misologist— Faust—was to be Michael Scott.[1] He appeared in the midst of his college of devoted disciples, enthusiastic, ebullient, shedding around him bright surmises of discoveries fully perfected in after times, and inculcating the study of nature and its secrets as the pathway to the acquisition of power. He did not love knowledge for itself—for its own exceeding great reward—but *in order* to be powerful. This poison-speck infected his mind from the beginning. The priests suspect him, circumvent him, accuse him; he is condemned and thrown into solitary confine- ment. This constituted the *prologus* of the drama. A pause of four or five years takes place, at the end of which Michael escapes from prison, a soured, gloomy, miserable man. He will not, cannot study; of what avail had all his study been to him? His knowledge, great as it was, had failed to preserve him from the cruel fangs of the persecutors; he could not command the lightning or the storm to wreak their furies upon the heads of those whom he hated and contemned, and yet feared. Away with learning!—away with study!—to the winds with all pretences to knowledge. We *know* nothing; we are fools, wretches, mere beasts. Anon the poet began to tempt him. He made him dream, gave him wine, and passed the most exquisite of women before him, but out of his reach. Is there, then, no knowledge by which these pleasures can be commanded? *That way* lay witchcraft—and accordingly to witchcraft Michael turns with all his soul. He has many failures and some successes; he learns the chemistry of exciting drugs and exploding powders, and some of the properties of transmitted and reflected light; his appetites and curiosity are both stimulated, and his old craving for power and mental domination over others revives. At last Michael tries to raise the devil, and the devil comes at his call. This devil was to be the universal humorist, who should make all things vain and nothing worth by a perpetual collation of the great with the little in the presence of the infinite. He plays an infinite number of tricks for Michael's gratification. In the meantime, Michael is miserable; he has power, but no peace, and he every day feels the tyranny of hell surrounding him. In vain he seems to himself to assert the most absolute empire over the devil, by imposing the most extravagant tasks;—one thing is as easy as another to the devil. 'What next, Michael?' is repeated every day with more

[1] Mediaeval astrologer (1175?-1234?).

imperious servility. Michael groans in spirit; his power is a curse; he commands women and wine—but the women seem fictitious and devilish, and the wine does not make him drunk. He now begins to hate the devil, and tries to cheat him. He studies again, and explores the darkest depths of sorcery for a recipe to cozen hell; but all in vain. Sometimes the devil's finger turns over the page for him, and points out an experiment, and Michael hears a whisper—'Try *that*, Michael!' The horror increases, and Michael feels that he is a slave and a condemned criminal. Lost to hope, he throws himself into every sensual excess —in the mid career of which he sees Agatha, and immediately endeavours to seduce her. Agatha loves him, and the devil facilitates their meetings; but she resists Michael's attempts to ruin her, and implores him not to act so as to forfeit her esteem. Long struggles of passion ensue, in the result of which Michael's affections are called forth against his appetites, and the idea of redemption of the lost will dawns upon his mind. This is instantaneously perceived by the devil; and for the first time the humorist becomes severe and menacing. A fearful succession of conflicts between Michael and the devil takes place, in which Agatha helps and suffers. In the end, after subjecting his hero to every imaginable or unimaginable horror, the poet *in nubibus* made him triumphant, and poured peace into his soul in the conviction of a salvation for sinners through God's grace. Of this sketch we will only say, what probably the warmest admirers of *Faust* will admit, that Goethe might have taken some valuable hints from it. It is a literary curiosity at least, and so we leave it.

The *Remorse* and *Zapolya* strikingly illustrate the predominance of the meditative, pausing habit of Mr. Coleridge's mind. The first of these beautiful dramas was acted with success, although worse acting was never seen. Indeed, Kelly's sweet music was the only part of the theatrical apparatus in any respect worthy of the play. The late Mr. Kean made some progress in the study of Ordonio, with a view of reproducing the piece; and we think that Mr. Macready,[1] either as Ordonio or Alvar, might, with some attention to music, costume, and scenery, make the representation attractive even in the present day. But in truth, taken absolutely and in itself, the *Remorse* is more fitted for the study than the stage; its character is romantic and pastoral in a high degree, and there is a profusion of poetry in the minor parts, the effect of which could never be preserved in the common routine of representation. What this play wants is dramatic movement; there is

[1] William Charles Macready (1793-1873), actor and manager.

energetic dialogue and a crisis of great interest, but the action does not sufficiently grow on the stage itself. Perhaps, also, the purpose of Alvar to waken remorse in Ordonio's mind is put forward too prominently, and has too much the look of a mere moral experiment to be probable under the circumstances in which the brothers stand to each other. Nevertheless, there is a calmness as well as superiority of intellect in Alvar which seem to justify, in some measure, the sort of attempt on his part, which, in fact, constitutes the theme of the play; and it must be admitted that the whole underplot of Isidore and Alhadra is lively and affecting in the highest degree. We particularly refer to the last scene between Ordonio and Isidore in the cavern, which we think genuine Shakespeare; and Alhadra's narrative of her discovery of her husband's murder is not surpassed in truth and force by anything of the kind that we know. The passage in the dungeon scene, in which Alvar rejects the poisoned cup, always struck us as uncommonly fine, although we think the conclusion weak. The incantation scene is a beautiful piece of imagination, and we are inclined to think a quotation of a part of it will put Mr. Coleridge's poetical power before many of our readers in a new light:

[quotes Act III, Scene i, ll. 1-114 (*PW*, ii, 847-50)]

Zapolya is professedly an imitation of *The Winter's Tale*, and was not composed with any view to scenic representation.[1] Yet it has some situations of dramatic interest in no respect inferior to the most striking in the *Remorse*; the incidents are new and surprising, and the dialogue is throughout distinguished by liveliness and force. The predominant character of the whole is, like that of the *Remorse*, a mixture of the pastoral and the romantic, but much more apparent and exclusive than in the latter; and it has always seemed to us that the poem breathed more of the spirit of the best pieces of Beaumont and Fletcher, such as the *Beggars' Bush* for example, than of anything of Shakespeare's. *Zapolya* has never been appreciated as it deserves. It is, in our opinion, the most *elegant* of Mr. Coleridge's poetical works; there is a softness of tone, and a delicacy of colouring about it, which have a peculiar charm of their own, and amply make amends for some deficiency of strength in the drawing. Although this Christmas tale is, perhaps, as a whole, less known than any other part of Mr. Coleridge's poetry, there is, oddly enough, one passage in it which has been quoted as often as any, and seems to have been honoured by the elaborate

[1] An error. See *CL*, iv, 620.

imitation of Sir Walter Scott in *Peveril of the Peake*, . . . 'The innocent Alice', &.

> The traitor Laska!—
> And yet Sarolta, simple, inexperienced,
> Could see him as he was, and often warn'd me.
> Whence learn'd she this?—Oh! she was innocent;—
> And to be innocent is nature's wisdom!
> The fledge-dove knows the prowlers of the air,
> Fear'd soon as seen, and flutters back to shelter;
> And the young steed recoils upon his haunches,
> The never-yet-seen adder's hiss first heard.
> O surer than suspicion's hundred eyes
> Is that fine sense, which to the pure in heart,
> By mere oppugnancy of their own goodness,
> Reveals the approach of evil.

How fine is Bethlen's image!

> Those piled thoughts, built up in solitude,
> Year following year, that press'd upon my heart
> As on the altar of some unknown God;
> Then, as if touch'd by fire from heaven descending,
> Blazed up within me at a father's name—
> Do they desert me now—at my last trial!

And Glycine's song might, we think, attract the attention of some of our composers. How like some of Goethe's jewels it is!

> A sunny shaft did I behold,
>   From sky to earth it slanted,
> And poised therein a bird so bold—
>   Sweet bird, thou wert enchanted!
> He sank, he rose, he twinkled, he troll'd
>   Within that shaft of sunny mist;—
> His eyes of fire, his beak of gold,
>   All else of amethyst!
> And thus he sang—'Adieu! adieu!
> Love's dreams prove seldom true.
> The blossoms they make no delay;
> The sparkling dew-drops will not stay.
> Sweet month of May,
> We must away,
> Far, far away,
> To-day! to-day!'

Upon the whole, then, referring to the *Wallenstein*, the *Remorse*, and *Zapolya*, we think it impossible not to admit that Mr. Coleridge's dramatic talent is of a very high and original kind. His chief excellence lies in the dialogue itself, his main defect in the conception, or at least in the conduct, of the plot. We can hardly say too much for the one, or too little for the other. In this respect, indeed, as in some others, his two plays remind us more of Beaumont and Fletcher than of Shakespeare. Yet we can conceive even the *Zapolya* capable of being charmingly represented under circumstances which the common London stage excludes in modern days. But little would be gained by such an attempt, however successful; it could not much heighten the effect of the poetry, and perhaps it might injure it, whilst defects in the action would become more apparent. The *Remorse* is, indeed, of stronger texture, and has borne, and might again bear, acting by common performers before the common audience; yet even in this instance we doubt whether the representation would not interfere with the more exquisite pleasure attending on the calm perusal of the poetry itself. There are parts in it, as in most of Shakespeare's plays, which neither sock nor buskin can reach, and which belong to the imagination alone.

We have not yet referred to the 'Ancient Mariner', 'Christabel', the 'Odes on France', and the 'Departing Year', or the 'Love Poems'. All these are well known by those who know no other parts of Coleridge's poetry, and the length of our preceding remarks compels us to be brief in our notice. Mrs. Barbauld, meaning to be complimentary, told our poet, that she thought the 'Ancient Mariner' very beautiful but that it had the fault of containing no moral. 'Nay, madam', replied the poet, 'if I may be permitted to say so, the only fault in the poem is that there is *too much*! In a work of such pure imagination I ought not to have stopped to give reasons for things, or inculcate humanity to beasts. *The Arabian Nights* might have taught me better'. They might—the tale of the merchant's son who puts out the eyes of a geni by flinging his date-shells down a well, and is therefore ordered, to prepare for death—might have taught this law of imagination; but the fault is small indeed; and the 'Ancient Mariner' is, and will ever be one of the most perfect pieces of imaginative poetry, not only in our language, but in the literature of all Europe. We have, certainly, sometimes doubted whether the miraculous destruction of the vessel in the presence of the pilot and hermit, was not an error, in respect of its bringing the purely preternatural into too close contact with the actual framework of the poem. The only link between those scenes of out-of-the-world wonders, and the wedding guest, should, we rather suspect, have been the blasted, unknown being himself who described them. There should have been no other witnesses of the truth of any part of the tale, but the 'Ancient Mariner' himself. This by the way: but take the work altogether, there is nothing else like it; it is a poem by itself; between it and other compositions, in *pari materia*, there is a chasm which you cannot overpass; the sensitive reader feels himself insulated, and a sea of wonder and mystery flows round him as round the spell-stricken ship itself. It was a sad mistake in the able artist—Mr. Scott, we believe—who in his engravings has made the ancient mariner an old decrepit man.[1] That is not the true image; no! he should have been a growthless, decayless being, impassive to time or season, a silent cloud—the wandering Jew. The curse of the dead men's eyes should not have passed away. But this was, perhaps, too much for any pencil, even if the artist had fully entered into the poet's idea. Indeed, it is no subject for painting. The 'Ancient Mariner' displays Mr. Coleridge's peculiar mastery over the wild and preternatural in a brilliant manner; but in his next poem, 'Christabel', the exercise of his power in this line is still more skilful and singular. The thing attempted in 'Christabel' is the most difficult of execution in the whole field of romance—witchery by daylight; and the success is complete. Geraldine, so far as she goes, is perfect. She is *sui generis*. The reader feels the same terror and perplexity that Christabel in vain struggles to express, and the same spell that fascinates her eyes. Who and what is Geraldine—whence come, whither going, and what designing? What did the poet mean to make of her? What could he have made of her? Could he have gone on much farther without having had recourse to some of the ordinary shifts of witch tales? Was she really the daughter of Roland de Vaux, and would the friends have met again and embraced?

[quotes ll. 408-26 (*PW*, i, 229)]

We are not amongst those who wish to have 'Christabel' finished. It cannot be finished. The poet has spun all he could without snapping. The theme is too fine and subtle to bear much extension. It is better as it is, imperfect as a story, but complete as an exquisite production of the imagination, differing in form and colour from the 'Ancient Mariner', yet differing in effect from it only so as the same powerful

[1] David Scott (1806-49). The series was begun in 1831.

faculty is directed to the feudal or the mundane phases of the preternatural.

From these remarkable works we turn to the love poems scattered through the volumes before us. There is something very peculiar in Mr. Coleridge's exhibition of the most lovely of the passions. His love is not gloomy as Byron's, nor gay as Moore's, nor intellectual as Wordsworth's. It is a clear unclouded passion, made up of an exquisite respect and gentleness, a knightly tenderness and courtesy, pure yet ardent, impatient yet contemplative. It is Petrarch and Shakespeare incorporate—it is the midsummer moonlight of all love poetry. The following fragment is now first printed:

[quotes ll. 48-78 of 'The Blossoming of the Solitary Date-Tree' (*PW*, i, 396-7)]

We forbear to quote from the celebrated 'All thoughts, all passions, all delights', or any other pieces previously published, in which '*Amor triumphans*' is sung, not only because they are very generally known, but that we may make room for another poem now printed for the first time, in which a rarer and more difficult thing is attempted—an expression of the poet's anguish at the services of kindness as a substitute for love. This theme—the diversity of love and friendship—is several times most exquisitely touched in the new parts of this publication, particularly in a piece called 'Love's Apparition and Evanishment'; but we must confine ourselves to one in the first volume, entitled 'The Pang more sharp than all'. It runs thus:

[quotes it (*PW*, i, 457-9)]

It would be strange, indeed, if we concluded a notice of Mr. Coleridge's poetry without particularly adverting to his Odes. We learn from Captain Medwin,[1] that Mr. Shelley pronounced the 'France' to be the finest English ode of modern times. We think it the most complete—the most finished as a whole; but we do not agree that it is equal in imagination—in depth—in fancy—to 'The Departing Year', or 'Dejection', although these latter are less perfect in composition. It is rather passionate than imaginative: it has more of eloquence than of fancy. We may be wrong in setting up the imaginative before the passionate in an ode, and especially in an ode on such a subject; but we think the majestic strophe with which it concludes will, when compared with any part of the other two odes, prove the accuracy of the distinction taken as a matter of fact.

[1] Thomas Medwin (1788-1869), whose biography of Shelley appeared in 1847.

[quotes ll. 85-105 (*PW*, i, 247)]

Of the other two odes named above, the first is the more varied and brilliant—the last the most subtle and abstract. If we must express an opinion, we must do so without assigning our reasons; and it is, that the ode on 'Dejection' is the higher effort of the two. It does not, in a single line, slip into declamation, which cannot be said strictly of either of the other odes: it is poetry throughout, as *opposed* to oratory.

It has been impossible to express, in the few pages to which we are necessarily limited, even a brief opinion upon all those pieces which might seem to call for notice in an estimate of this author's poetical genius. We know no writer of modern times whom it would not be easier to characterize in one page than Coleridge in two. The volumes before us contain so many integral efforts of imagination, that a distinct notice of each is indispensable, if we would form a just conclusion upon the total powers of the man. Wordsworth, Scott, Moore, Byron, Southey, are incomparably more uniform in the direction of their poetic mind. But if you look over these volumes for indications of their author's poetic powers, you find him appearing in at least half a dozen shapes, so different from each other, that it is in vain to attempt to mass them together. It cannot indeed be said, that he has ever composed what is popularly termed a *great* poem; but he is great in several lines, and the union of such powers is an essential term in a fair estimate of his genius. The romantic witchery of the 'Christabel', and 'Ancient Mariner', the subtle passion of the love-strains, the lyrical splendour of the three great odes, the affectionate dignity, thoughtfulness, and delicacy of the blank verse poems—especially the 'Lover's Resolution', 'Frost at Midnight', and that most noble and interesting 'Address to Mr. Wordsworth'—the dramas, the satires, the epigrams—these are so distinct and so whole in themselves, that they might seem to proceed from different authors, were it not for that same individualizing power, that 'shaping spirit of imagination' which more or less sensibly runs through them all. It is the *predominance* of this power, which, in our judgment, constitutes the essential difference between Coleridge and any other of his great contemporaries. He is the most imaginative of the English poets since Milton. Whatever he writes, be it on the most trivial subject, be it in the most simple strain, his imagination, *in spite of himself*, affects it. There never was a better illustrator of the dogma of the Schoolmen—*in omnem actum intellectualem imaginatio influit*.[1] We believe we might affirm, that throughout

[1] 'The imagination affects every act of the mind'.

all the mature original poems in these volumes, there is not one image, the *expression* of which does not, in a greater or less degree, individualize it and appropriate it to the poet's feelings. Tear the passage out of its place, and nail it down at the head of a chapter of a modern novel, and it will be like hanging up in a London exhibition-room a picture painted for the dim light of a cathedral. Sometimes a single word—an epithet—has the effect to the reader of a Claude Lorraine glass;[1] it tints without obscuring or disguising the object. The poet has the same power in conversation. We remember him once settling an elaborate discussion carried on in his presence, upon the respective sublimity of Shakespeare and Schiller in *Othello* and *The Robbers*, by saying, 'Both are sublime; only Schiller's is the *material* sublime—that's all!' *All* to be sure; but more than enough to show the whole difference. And upon another occasion, where the doctrine of the Sacramentaries and the Roman Catholics on the subject of the Eucharist was in question, the poet said, 'They are both equally wrong; the first have volatilized the Eucharist into a metaphor—the last have condensed it into an idol'. Such utterance as this flashes light; it supersedes all argument—it abolishes proof by proving itself.

We speak of Coleridge, then, as the poet of imagination; and we add, that he is likewise the poet of thought and verbal harmony. That his thoughts are sometimes hard and sometimes even obscure, we think must be admitted; it is an obscurity of which all very subtle thinkers are occasionally guilty, either by attempting to express evanescent feelings for which human language is an inadequate vehicle, or by expressing, however adequately, thoughts and distinctions to which the common reader is unused. As to the first kind of obscurity, the words serving only as hieroglyphics to denote a once existing state of mind in the poet, but not logically inferring what that state was, the reader can only guess for himself by the context, whether he ever has or not experienced in himself a corresponding feeling; and, therefore, undoubtedly, this is an obscurity which strict criticism cannot but condemn. But, if an author be obscure, merely because this or that reader is unaccustomed to the mode or direction of thinking in which such author's genius makes him take delight—such a writer must indeed bear the consequence as to immediate popularity; but he cannot help the consequence, and if he be worth anything for posterity, he will disregard it. In this sense almost every great writer, whose

[1] Coloured glass which, when looked through, made the view look like one of Claude's landscapes.

648

natural bent has been to turn the mind upon itself, is—must be—obscure; for no writer, with such a direction of intellect, will be great, unless he is individual and original; and if he is individual and original, then he must, in most cases, himself make the readers who shall be competent to sympathize with him.

The English flatter themselves by a pretence that Shakespeare and Milton are popular in England. It is good taste, indeed, to wish to have it believed that those poets are popular. Their names are so; but if it be said that the works of Shakespeare and Milton are popular—that is, liked and studied—among the wide circle whom it is now the fashion to talk of as enlightened, we are obliged to express our doubts whether a grosser delusion was ever promulgated. Not a play of Shakespeare's can be ventured on the London stage without mutilation—and without the most revolting balderdash foisted into the rents made by managers in his divine dramas; nay, it is only some three or four of his pieces that can be borne at all by our all-intelligent public, unless the burthen be lightened by dancing, singing, or processioning. This for the stage. But is it otherwise with 'the *reading* public'? We believe it is worse; we think, verily, that the apprentice or his master who sits out *Othello* or *Richard* at the theatres, does get a sort of glimpse, a touch, an atmosphere of intellectual grandeur; but he could not keep himself awake during the perusal of that which he admires—or fancies he admires—in scenic representation. As to understanding Shakespeare—as to entering into all Shakespeare's thoughts and feelings—as to seeing the idea of *Hamlet*, or *Lear*, or *Othello*, as Shakespeare saw it—this we believe falls, and can only fall, to the lot of the really cultivated few, and of those who may have so much of the temperament of genius in themselves, as to comprehend and sympathize with the criticism of men of genius. Shakespeare is now popular by name, because, in the first place, great men, more on a level with the rest of mankind, have said that he is admirable, and also because, in the absolute universality of his genius, he has presented points to all. Every man, woman, and child, may pick at least one flower from his garden, the name and scent of which are familiar. To all which must of course be added, the effect of theatrical representation, be that representation what it may. There are tens of thousands of persons in this country whose only acquaintance with Shakespeare, such as it is, is through the stage.

We have been talking of the contemporary mass; but this is not all; a great original writer *of a philosophic turn*—especially a poet—will almost always have the fashionable world also against him at first, because he does not give the sort of pleasure expected of him at the time, and because, not contented with that, he is sure, by precept or example, to show a contempt for the taste and judgment of the expectants. He is always, and by the law of his being, an idoloclast. By and by, after years of abuse or neglect, the aggregate of the single minds who think for themselves, and have seen the truth and force of his genius, becomes important; the merits of the poet by degrees constitute a question for discussion; his works are one by one read; men recognize a superiority in the abstract, and learn to be modest where before they had been scornful; the coterie becomes a sect; the sect dilates into a party; and lo! after a season, no one knows how, the poet's fame is universal. All this, to the very life, has taken place in this country within the last twenty years. The noblest philosophical poem since the time of Lucretius was, within time of short memory, declared to be intolerable, by one of the most brilliant writers in one of the most brilliant publications of the day. It always put us in mind of Waller—no mean parallel—who, upon the coming out of the *Paradise Lost*, wrote to the duke of Buckingham, amongst other pretty things, as follows:— 'Milton, the old blind schoolmaster, has lately written a poem on the Fall of Man—*remarkable for nothing but its extreme length!*' Our divine poet asked a fit audience, although it should be but few. His prayer was heard; a fit audience for the *Paradise Lost* has ever been, and at this moment must be, a small one, and we cannot affect to believe that it is destined to be much increased by what is called the march of intellect.

Can we lay down the pen without remembering that Coleridge the poet is but half the name of Coleridge? This, however, is not the place, nor the time, to discuss in detail his qualities or his exertions as a psychologist, moralist, and general philosopher. That time may come, when his system, as a whole, shall be fairly placed before the world, as we have reason to hope it will soon be; and when the preliminary works—the *Friend*, the *Lay Sermons*, the *Aids to Reflection*, and the *Church and State*,—especially the last two—shall be seen in their proper relations as preparatory exercises for the reader. His *Church and State*, *according to the Idea of Each*—a little book—we cannot help recommending as a storehouse of grand and immovable principles, bearing upon some of the most vehemently disputed topics of constitutional interest in these momentous times. Assuredly this period has not produced a profounder and more luminous essay. We have heard it asked, what was the proposed object of Mr. Coleridge's labours as a metaphysical philosopher? He once answered that question himself, in language never to be forgotten by those who heard it, and which, whatever may be conjectured of the probability or even possibility of its being fully realized, must be allowed to express the completest idea of a system of philosophy ever yet made public.

My system [said he], if I may venture to give it so fine a name, is the only attempt that I know, ever made, to reduce all knowledge into harmony. It opposes no other system, but shows what was true in each; and how that which was true in the particular in each of them, became error, *because* it was only half the truth. I have endeavoured to unite the insulated fragments of truth, and therewith to frame a perfect mirror. I show to each system that I fully understand and rightfully appreciate what that system means; but then I lift up that system to a higher point of view, from which I enable it to see its former position, where it was indeed, but under another light and with different relations,—so that the fragment of truth is not only acknowledged, but explained. So the old astronomers discovered and maintained much that was true; but because they were placed on a false ground, and looked from a wrong point of view, they never did—they never could—discover the truth—that is, the whole truth. As soon as they left the earth, their false centre, and took their stand in the sun, immediately they saw the whole system in its true light, and the former station remaining—but remaining *as a part* of the prospect. I wish, in short, to connect by a moral copula, natural history with political history; or, in other words, to make history scientific, and science historical;—to take from history its accidentality, and from science its fatalism.

Whether we shall ever, hereafter, have occasion to advert to any new poetical efforts of Mr. Coleridge, or not, we cannot say. We wish we had a reasonable cause to expect it. If not, then this hail and farewell will have been well made. We conclude with, we believe, the last verses he has written:

[quotes 'My Baptismal Birth-Day' (*PW*, i, 490-1)]

Select Index

The following are listed in the index: names of works by Coleridge, names of reviewers and commentators, names of journals (extracts from them being identified by bold face type), names of authors, scientists, artists and composers mentioned in the course of discussions of Coleridge, and names of authorities cited.

Addison, J., 197, 317, 358, 428
Aelian, 389
Aeschylus, 420, 559
Aikin, J., 36
Akenside, M., 26
Alison, A., 177
Amarasinghe, U., 18
Ammerbach, 303
Amory, T., 252
Anacharsis, 587
Anacreon, 538
Analytical Review, 3, 4, **2, 25–6, 29, 32–3, 44–5, 51–2**
Andrews, M. P., 133–4
Annual Review, **67–8**
Anti-Jacobin, **59, 217–21,** 299
Aquinas, 323, 387
Ariosto, 640
Aristotle, 95, 236, 303, 323, 357, 472, 526, 587, 602
Arnold, S. J., 141
Ashmole, E., 251
Athenaeum, **556–61**

Bacon, F., 97, 106, 191, 357, 382, 429, 462, 472, 474, 526, 567, 594, 634
Baillie, J., 153, 155, 161, 173, 315, 317, 368, 414
Baker, H., 205
Barclay, J., 305
Barnes, T., 122, 189
Barrow, I., 526–7
Beaumont, F., 638, 642, 644

Beckford, W., 516
Beethoven, 628
Behmen, J., 298, 301, 305, 323, 357, 375, 453
Bell, A., 260–1, 275–6, 281
Bentham, J., 15, 527, 542, 558
Berkeley, G., 192, 301, 329, 594, 597
Beverley, R. M., 562
Bias, 587
Blackwood, W., 454–5
Blackwood's Edinburgh Magazine, 9, 12–15, **325–54, 436–51,** 454–60, **484**
Blunden, E., 122, 471
Bowles, W. L., 296–8, 337–8, 361, 406
Bowring, J., 525
Brewer, E. C., 539
Bristol Gazette, **30–1**
British Critic, 3–4, 13, 15, **23, 28–9, 32,** 48–9, **57–9,** 65–6, **355–75, 486–513**
British Review, 8, 15, **165–74, 221–6, 485**
Brown, J., 540
Browne, T., 246, 253
Bruno, G., 97, 250
Bunyan, J., 264
Bürger, G. A., 435
Burke, E., 30, 123, 309–13, 329, 343, 367, 372, 382, 527
Burnet, G., 475, 501
Burney, C., 55
Burns, R., 373, 429
Butler, S., 56

Byron, Lord, 6, 10, 17, 209, 213, 216–17, 221, 224, 226–7, 233, 237, 246, 331, 339, 346, 350, 353, 397, 467–9, 552, 607, 616, 625, 633, 646–7

Calvin, J., 572
Campbell, T., 16–17, 331, 353, 518
Canning, G., 299
Catullus, 296, 359, 377
Cervantes, 253
Chalmers, T., 563
Champion, **189–93**
Chatterton, T., 373
Chaucer, 55, 472
Cheever, G. B., 19
Christian Observer, **145–52**
Cicero, 296, 359, 389
Cimabue, 475
Clarendon, Lord, 274, 358
Clarke, S., 596
Clive, J., 18
Coburn, K., 424
Coleridge, H. N., 15, 461, 620
Coleridge, J. T., 175, 484
Coleridge, S. T., Works:
  'Addressed to a Young Man of Fortune', 40, 545
  Aids to Reflection, 14–15, 17, 485–513, 559, 585–606, 650
  'All thoughts, all passions, all delights', *see* 'Love'
  'The Ancient Mariner', 4–5, 12, 14–17, 51–3, 56–60, 195, 317, 339, 355, 390, 392, 400, 403–5, 409, 434–5, 439–45, 447, 466, 473, 475–9, 483, 517, 522–3, 543, 551–6, 609–10, 613, 619–20, 644–5, 647
  'Answer to a Child's Question', 481
  'The Ballad of the Dark Ladié', 72, 613
  Biographia Literaria, 8, 11–14, 17, 32, 145, 221, 295–388, 390, 431, 458, 462, 471–2, 517, 558–9, 601, 607, 633
  'Blessed are ye that sow beside all waters!', 285–94
  'The Blossoming of the Solitary Date-Tree', 548, 646

'Christabel', 8, 10–12, 14–15, 17, 200–33, 235–46, 315–16, 346, 353, 400, 424, 435, 445–9, 466, 472, 475, 481, 483, 518, 548–9, 551, 560, 607–8, 610, 613, 619–20, 632, 644–5, 647
Christabel, Kubla Khan, a Vision; the Pains of Sleep, 8, 10, 199–247
'Circassian Love-chaunt', *see* 'Lewti'
Conciones ad Populum, 2, 25–9, 32, 249, 273, 309, 335
'Constancy to an Ideal Object', 548, 610
'The Day-dream', 549
The Death of Wallenstein, 62, 552, 618, 638
'Dejection: an Ode', 13, 15, 17, 634, 646–7
'The Dungeon', 4, 51, 53, 57, 60
'Duty Surviving Self-love', 545
'Effusion, to Fayette', 34, 68
'Effusion, on a Kiss', 37
'The Eolian Harp', 544–5
'Epitaph on an Infant', 532
The Fall of Robespierre, 2, 21–3, 335
'Fancy in Nubibus', 549
Fears in Solitude, 4, 44–50
'Fears in Solitude', 396, 405, 532–5
'Fire, Famine, and Slaughter: a War Eclogue', 343, 390, 392, 410, 516–17, 532, 535–9, 560
'First Advent of Love', 625
'The Foster-Mother's Tale', 4, 51, 53, 56, 59–60
'France, an Ode', 4, 44, 46–9, 108, 405, 644, 646
The Friend, 5–7, 14, 73–110, 189, 192, 249, 253, 265, 295, 301, 309, 335, 345–6, 424–32, 461–3, 469, 472–3, 559, 562, 587, 602, 607, 650
'Frost at Midnight', 4, 44, 47, 49, 647
'Genevieve', *see* 'Love'
'The Happy Husband', 411
'Hendecasyllables', 628
'Hymn before Sunrise, in the Vale of Chamouni', 396, 407, 520, 548

Coleridge, S. T., Works (cont'd.)
  'Hymn to the Earth', 629
  'Inscription for a Fountain on a
    Heath', 550
  'Kubla Khan', 8, 10, 12, 17, 205–9,
    212, 215–16, 220, 225, 233–4, 246,
    424, 475–6, 549–50, 627
  Lay Sermons, 8, 11, 335, 424, 435,
    469, 472, 608, 650, see also The
    Statesman's Manual (First Lay
    Sermon) and 'Blessed are ye that
    sow beside all waters!' (Second Lay
    Sermon)
  'Lewti', 467, 539
  'Lines on an Autumnal Evening', 625
  'Lines on the Last Words of Beren-
    garius', 545, 630
  'Lines: To a Beautiful Spring in a
    Village', 37
  'Lines written at Shurton Bars', 37,
    522
  'Lines written in the Album at
    Elbingerode', 522
  'Love', 13–16, 34, 316, 355, 405, 447,
    451, 467, 518, 523, 540, 548, 610,
    613, 646
  'The Lover's Resolution', 647
  'Love's Apparition', 646
  'The Mad Ox', 410
  'Monody on the Death of Chatter-
    ton', 33–6
  A Moral and Political Lecture, 2, 24
  'My Baptismal Birth-Day', 651
  'The Nightingale', 4, 51–2, 57–8, 60,
    520
  'Night Scene', 548
  'Ode on the Departing Year', 3,
    39–42, 464–6, 644, 646
  'Ode to Georgiana, the Duchess of
    Devonshire', 548
  'Ode to the Rain', 375, 481
  'On the Christening of a Friend's
    Child', 43
  On the Constitution of Church and
    State, 15, 562–84, 650
  'The Pang more sharp than all', 646
  'The Pains of Sleep', 8, 10, 12, 205,
    212, 216, 221, 225, 234, 246–7

'Parliamentary Oscillators', 410
The Piccolomini, 62, 552, 618, 638
'The Picture', 396, 520
The Plot Discovered, 2, 27, 29
Poems (1797), 3, 42–3
Poems (1803), 5, 67–9
Poems on Various Subjects, 3, 32–8
The Poetical Works (1828), 15, 33,
  514–24
The Poetical Works (1829), 15, 525–
  61
The Poetical Works (1834), 15, 609–51
'The Raven', 391
'Reflections on having left a Place of
  Retirement', 42, 483, 545
'Religious Musings', 3, 33–4, 37,
  307, 532, 543–4
Remorse, 7–9, 14, 16, 111–88, 192,
  195, 241, 247, 335, 349, 353, 414,
  435, 452, 466, 483, 546, 551, 610,
  636, 641–2, 644
'The Rime of the Ancient Mariner',
  see 'Ancient Mariner'
'Sancti Dominici Pallium', 630
'Satyrane's Letters', 109, 346
Sibylline Leaves, 9, 12–13, 355, 375–
  7, 388–412, 439, 445–6, 472, 532,
  539, 609
'The Sigh', 32–3
'Something childish, but very natur-
  al', 523
'Songs of the Pixies', 33, 37, 483
'Sonnet on his child being first
  presented to him', 548
'Sonnet: To the River Otter', 42
The Statesman's Manual, 8, 11,
  248–84, 424, 485
'This Lime-tree Bower My Prison',
  408
'The Three Graves', 6, 10, 73–92,
  390
'To the Memory of a Deceased
  Friend', 72
'To the Rev. George Coleridge', 42,
  408
'To an Unfortunate Woman at the
  Theatre', 390, 406
'To Wordsworth', 411, 545, 647

Coleridge, S. T., Works (cont'd.)
'A Tombless Epitaph', 550
'Verses Composed in a Concert Room', 407
'Verses to a Young Lady on her Recovery from a Fever', 398
Wallenstein, 5, 62–6, 451, 524, 610, 614–19, 636–8, 644, *see also The Piccolomini*, and *The Death of Wallenstein*
The Watchman, 7, 30–1, 249, 273, 295, 305, 309, 335, 340–2, 357, 380, 473
'Work without Hope', 545
'Youth and Age', 614
Zapolya, 9, 14, 413–23, 467, 533, 551, 610, 636, 641–2, 644
See also Lyrical Ballads
Coleridge, Sara, 34, 61, 424
Collins, W., 210
Colman, G., 84, 89
Conder, J., 209
Corneille, 146
Cottle, J., 4
Courier, 5, 221, 249, 259
Cowley, A., 323
Cowper, W., 58, 378, 402
Crabbe, G., 620
Crawfurd, 578
Cristall, A. B., 35
Critical Review, 3, 4, 10, **22**, **25**, **27**, **34–5**, **41**, **42–3**, **49–50**, **53–4**, 60, **64–5**, **153–5**, **199–205**, **278–84**, **289–94**
Cumberland, R., 134, 322, 373
Curry, K., 60
Cuvier, G., 621

Dallison, C., 575
Dana, R. H., 17
Dante, 383, 559, 631
Darwin, E., 594
Davy, H., 621
Dawe, G., 406
Defoe, D., 373
Demosthenes, 296, 359
Dennis, J., 343
De Quincey, T., 15, 484
Descartes, 303, 594

De Selincourt, E., 424
De Thoyras, 305
Dibdin, T., 140–1
Didymus, 296, 360
Digby, K., 246
Diodorus, 389
'D. M.', 21
'D. M. S.', 44
Donne, J., 293
Dryden, 13, 55, 232–3, 237, 317, 358, 414–15, 540, 636, 638
Dyer, G., 2

Eclectic Review, 6, **92–110**, **209–13**, **562–84**
Edinburgh Annual Register for 1808, 6, 16, **72**
Edinburgh Magazine, 13, 14, **392–9**, **413–19**
Edinburgh Review, 9–10, 12–13, 16, 60, **226–36**, **262–77**, **295–322**, 336, 345–6, 349, 354, 357, **427–32**, 527, 542, 558, 607
Egerton, F., 639
Empedocles, 587
Epimenides, 587
Etonian, **461–70**
Euclid, 340, 595
European Magazine, 10, 18, **134–5**, **425–7**
Examiner, 10, 14, **122–4**, 141, **205–9**, 235, **248–62**, 345, 424, **471–9**

Fairfax, E., 567
Falconer, W., 339, 407
Favel, J., 34
Ferriar, J., 62
Fichte, 301, 305, 375
Fichti, *see* Fichte
Fielding, H., 373, 404
Fletcher, J., 467, 638, 642, 644
Foerster, D. M., 18
Fontenelle, 498
Foster, J., 7, 92
Fox, G., 305, 311, 329
Fraser's Magazine, **585–608**
Freilingrath, F., 16
Frere, J. H., 299

Gentleman's Magazine, **611-14**
Gibbon, 255
Gifford, W., 299
Gillman, J., 9
Giotto, 475
Godwin, W., 31
Goethe, 191, 456, 631, 639, 643
Goldsmith, O., 237, 273, 399, 408
Gracchus, C., 31
Graham, W., 175, 454, 461
Gray, T., 4, 55, 319, 338-9, 378-9, 384, 415
Grynaeus, S., 305
Guido, 56

'H.', 140
Hall, R., 562
Hamilton, A., 39
Harrington, J., 567
Hartley, D., 301, 303, 329, 540, 594
Hawkins, A., 55
Hayden, J. O., 209, 236
Hayward, 637, 639
Hazlitt, W., 9-12, 16, 205, 235, 248, 253, 262, 295, 455, 471, 608
Heraclitus, 261, 273-4
Heraud, J. H., 585
Herder, 381
Hobbes, 192, 277, 303, 323, 526
Hodgson, F., 155
Hogarth, 241
Hogg, J., 244, 339
Holford, M., 244
Home, J., 137, 413
Homer, 31, 191-2, 236, 296, 359, 378, 449, 635
Hook, T., 138
Hooker, R., 106, 188, 305, 358, 367, 382, 428
Hopkins, J., 86
Horace, 55, 65, 73, 261, 273, 373, 411-12, 481, 518, 621
Howe, P. P., 205, 248, 253, 262
Hudson, D., 189
Hume, 255, 272, 304, 323, 327, 387, 431, 588, 594
Hunt, L., 6, 458, 471
Hutchinson, S., 424

Hymeneus, 507

Jacobsen, F. J., 16, 18
Jameson, R. F., 125
Jeffrey, F., 12, 60, 295, 344-5, 353, 607
Johnson, S., 55, 278, 367, 624
Jonson, B., 199, 626, 638
Josephus, 477, 507
'J.S.', 351

Kant, 191-2, 301, 303, 323, 329, 348, 357, 375, 400, 494, 595, 597
Keats, J., 471, 474, 633
Kelly, M., 118, 138
Kepler, 262
Klopstock, 191, 347, 373, 472

La Belle Assemblée, **137**
Lady's Magazine, 349
Lamb, C., 34, 43, 60, 67, 69, 194-5, 299, 342, 424, 472, 475
Lancaster, J., 261, 275
Leighton, Archbishop, 486, 488-90, 492-3, 599
Leland, J., 508
Lepaux, 286
Le Sage, 410
Leslie, J., 333
Lessing, 347, 510
Lewis, M. G., 414, 554
Lily, W., 251
Literary Gazette, **388-91, 521-4, 609-10, 614-19**
Literary Panorama, **135-6, 213-16**
Literary Speculum, **480-3**
Little, T., *see* Moore, T.
Lloyd, C., 43, 67, 69, 472
Locke, 276, 284, 329, 357, 501, 586-9, 593, 599
Lockhart, J. G., 14-15, 436, 455-8
London Magazine, 14, **452-60**, 475
London Weekly Review, **514-21**
Lorraine, C., 648
Lovell, R., 472
Lucan, 389
Lucas, E. V., 60
Lucretius, 296, 359, 377, 402, 516, 650

Luther, 109, 559
Lyrical Ballads, 4, 5, 51–61, 295, 302, 316–17, 335, 348, 366, 373, 382–3, 385, 389, 402, 540

Mackenzie, S., 484
Mackintosh, J., 623
Maginn, W., 484, 606
Maimonides, 510
Mallet, D., 91
Marivaux, 177
Marsh, J., 17
Massinger, 638
Mathew, G. F., 236
Maturin, R. C., 145, 221, 349–50, 353–4, 452
McRae, A., 454
Medwin, T., 646
Mendelssohn, M., 510
Middleton, Dr., 344
Mill, J. S., 15
Milman, H. H., 635
Milton, 56–7, 106, 119, 149–50, 176, 189, 191, 195, 232, 296, 317, 319, 323, 329, 332, 358–9, 361, 371, 373, 379, 410, 428, 451, 463, 472, 474, 525, 538, 553, 559, 567, 599, 604, 614, 626, 631, 633–5, 647, 649–50
Mirandula, 567
Montgomery, G., see Coleridge, H. N.
Monthly Magazine, 13–14, 36, 278, 285, 323–4, 392, 419, 433–5
Monthly Mirror, 6, 38, 40, 73–92
Monthly Repository, 286–9
Monthly Review, 3–5, 8, 13, 27, 36–8, 39–40, 45–7, 55–7, 62–3, 155–65, 244–7, 376–87, 399–412
Moody, C. L., 45
Moore, J., 245
Moore, T., 10, 16, 86–7, 226, 332, 344, 353, 411, 467–8, 646–7
More, H., 492–3
More, T., 274
Morehead, C., 60
Morehead, R., 60
Morgenblatt für gebildete Stände, 16
Morley, E. J., 18, 138, 278
Morning Chronicle, 7, 111–17, 127, 343

Morning Post, 5, 7, 117–18, 309, 342–3' 357, 372, 607
Morris, P., see Lockhart, J. G.
Morton, T., 552
Moses, 507, 512
Müller, J. von, 450
Murray, J., 206, 335, 424

Nangle, B. C., 36, 39, 45, 62, 155
Nesbitt, G. L., 525
New Annual Register, 376
New Monthly Magazine, 322–3, 420
Newton, 192, 250–1, 262, 276, 357, 462
North, C., see Wilson, J.
North American Review, 17–19

O'Doherty, see Maginn, W.
O'Keefe, J., 552
Opium-Eater, see De Quincey, T.
Ossian, 68, 331, 404
Otway, T., 146, 156, 165, 413, 638
Ovid, 296, 359, 389
Owen, J., 562

Paine, T., 254
Paley, W., 107, 192, 505–12, 573, 581
Pamphleteer, 194–8
Parr, S., 506
Partridge, E., 18
Pausanius, 389
Pearson, N., 489
Petrarch, 467, 479, 631, 646
Pheleteus, 507
Pichot, A., 16, 18
Pindar, 518, 632
Plato, 95, 97, 100, 264, 321, 361, 389, 470, 513, 567, 586
Pletho, G., 305, 357
Pliny, 389
Plotinus, 357
Plutarch, 354
Poetical Register, 69
Politian, 567
Poloni, Fratres, 288
Poole, T., 7
Pope, A., 13, 55, 232, 276, 319, 322, 338, 361, 377–9, 428, 564–5, 636
Porson, R., 340

Potter, S., 61
Price, L. M., 18
Priestley, J., 53, 594
Proclus, 305
Psellus, M., 477
Pseudo-Virgil, 403
Pyrrho, 587-8, 597
Pythagoras, 100

Quarterly Review, 8-9, 11, 15-16, **175-88**, 299, 484, 581, **620-51**

'R.', 273, 427, 432, 480
Racine, 146-7, 197
Raleigh, W., 274, 600
Raphael, 56, 253
Raymond, J. G., 141
Reid, T., 593, 595
Rennell, T., 583
Reynolds, F., 133
Reynolds, J., 88
Roberts, A., 221
Roberts, W., 221
Robinson, H. C., 11, 18, 138, 278, 289, 424
Rosa, S., 313
Rossini, 628
Rousseau, 327, 450
Ryland, J. E., 92

Sallust, 389
Satirist, 6-7, **70-1**, **125-30**
Scaliger, J. J., 73
Schelling, 301, 305, 375
Schiller, 5, 16, 62, 64, 123, 150, 191, 435, 616, 636-8, 648
Schilling, *see* Schelling
Schlegel, 305, 431, 638
Schneider, E., 226
Scott, D., 645
Scott, J., 454
Scott, W., 17, 149, 237, 244, 316, 331, 339, 346, 350, 353-4, 414, 435-6, 538, 552, 607, 616, 621, 643, 647
Shakespeare, 7-8, 35, 41, 56, 635, 115-17, 126-8, 133, 140-1, 146, 149, 160, 162, 176, 187-9, 197, 245, 271, 296, 317, 319, 329, 332, 338-9, 359,

379, 420-1, 435, 463, 467, 470, 484, 525, 554, 559-60, 567-8, 614, 623, 625-6, 631, 637, 642, 644, 646, 648-9
Shelley, P. B., 471, 616, 639, 646
Sheridan, R. B., 85, 138, 152
Sherlock, W., 507
Sidney, A., 382
Sidney, P., 567
Sigmann, L., 18
Simmons, J., 53
Sismondi, J. C. L. de, 578
Smith, J., 130
Socrates, 274
Solon, 587
South, R., 526-7
Southerne, T., 413
Southey, C. C., 139
Southey, R., 2, 4-5, 9, 21, 34, 36-8, 53, 60, 138-9, 181, 190, 194-5, 233, 235, 237, 256, 260, 286, 295, 298-301, 314-17, 323, 330, 335-6, 342, 344-5, 353, 355, 364, 366-72, 387, 395, 406, 411, 435, 463, 468, 472-3, 613, 629, 632, 647
Spenser, 207, 232, 264, 319, 329, 463, 474, 568, 625, 631-2, 638
Spinoza, 100, 301, 305, 309, 342, 380
St. John, 298, 342, 504
St. Paul, 342, 500-1, 503, 507, 509, 514, 600
St. Peter, 592
St. Thomas, 157
Stanhope, Lord, 38
Sterne, L., 243
Sternhold, T., 86
Stewart, D., 594-6, 599
Strout, A. L., 325, 351, 436
Swedenborg, I., 453

Tacitus, 248
Tartini, G., 216
Tasso, 474
Taylor, Jeremy, 106, 191, 293, 314, 358, 364, 367, 382, 410, 428, 490, 498, 503, 509-10, 512, 526, 528, 599
Taylor, John, 399
Teniers, D., 56
Terence, 296, 359, 377

Theatrical Inquisitor, **131–4, 140–4, 420–3**
Thelwall, J., 3, 380
Theocritus, 296, 359, 607
Thomson, J., 259, 413, 526
Thrall, M. H., 585, 606
Thuanus, 274
Tieck, L., 638
Times, The, 7, **118–21**, 259
Titian, 309
Tobin, J., 137
Tooke, J. H., 592–3
Twiss, H., 133–4

Universal Magazine, **136**

Varius, 621
Varro, 389
Vico, 634
Virgil, 31, 245, 296, 359, 388, 402–4, 504, 520, 621
Vives, L., 303
Voltaire, 245, 250, 414

Wakefield, G., 322
Waller, E., 650

Walton, I., 293
Ward, W. S., 18
Warton, J., 297
Waterston, R. C., 19
Westminster Review, 15, **525–56**, 557, 560
White, H. K., 468
Wieland, 191, 347
Wilson, J., 12, 16, 179, 325, 339, 351, 457–8, 484
Wissowatius, 288
Wither, G., 564–5
Wolfe, C., 432, 635
Wolff, O. L. B., 16, 18
Wordsworth, D., 424
Wordsworth, W., 4–5, 9, 17, 51, 53, 60, 78, 99, 179, 190, 235, 253, 295, 297, 302, 309, 314–15, 317–18, 323, 330, 335, 337–9, 344–5, 347–8, 355, 357, 364, 366–70, 372–3, 378, 380–6, 389, 397, 402–3, 406, 409, 411, 424, 431, 461, 463, 467–9, 473, 526, 528, 558, 613, 616, 621, 646–7. *See also Lyrical Ballads*

Young, E., 607